GEORGE N. SHUSTER

George N. Shuster

GEORGE N. SHUSTER

On the Side of Truth

Thomas E. Blantz, C.S.C

University of Notre Dame Press
Notre Dame   London

Copyright © 1993 by
University of Notre Dame Press
Notre Dame, Indiana 46556
All Rights Reserved
Manufactured in the United States of America

Library of Congress Cataloging–in–Publication Data

Blantz, Thomas E.
　George N. Shuster : on the side of truth / Thomas E. Blantz.
　　p.　cm.
　Includes bibliographical references and index.
　ISBN 0-268-01028-5
　1. Shuster, George Nauman, 1894–　.　2. Hunter College—
Presidents—Biography.　3. Journalists—United States—Biography.
4. Diplomats—United States—Biography.　I. Shuster, George
Nauman, 1894–　.　II. Title.
LD7251.N288B53　　1993
371.1'11—dc20
[B]
　　　　　　　　　　　　　　　　　　　　　　　　　　　92-56867
　　　　　　　　　　　　　　　　　　　　　　　　　　　CIP

　∞　*The paper used in this publication meets the minimum requirements*
of the American National Standard for Information Sciences—Permanence of Paper
for Printed Library Materials, ANSI Z39.48-1984.

FOR
JIM AND MARY KAY

CONTENTS

PREFACE

I first met George Shuster in the mid-1960s. I was then a graduate student at Columbia University and in several of my classes I had made use of that university's oral history collection, transcribed interviews with persons prominent in various areas of public life. Since I was preparing to join the faculty of the University of Notre Dame after completing my studies, I wrote to Notre Dame's president, Father Theodore Hesburgh, C.S.C., and suggested that Notre Dame might consider undertaking an oral history program also, preserving the reminiscences of persons influential in the development of American Catholicism, in Catholic higher education, and in the history of Notre Dame. Father Hesburgh expressed interest and recommended that the next time I was on campus I should make an appointment to discuss the matter with his special assistant, Dr. George Shuster.

This I did. Shuster invited me to lunch at a near-by hotel dining room, had what I later understood to be his usual dry Manhattan and iced tea and, while he enjoyed several Sano cigarettes through a long filter, I described what I knew of the Columbia project. I doubt that Shuster had much familiarity with oral history programs at the time but he asked specific questions, offered me encouragement, and, most important, gave me one thousand dollars from his university account to purchase a tape recorder, become a member of the Oral History Association, and attend the association's next annual meeting.

After joining the Notre Dame faculty in 1968, I saw Doctor Shuster occasionally at university meetings and informal social gatherings until his death in early 1977. A few years later, I received a call from his widow, Mrs. Doris Shuster, inviting me to lunch in that same dining room where I had first met her husband. She was convinced that her husband merited a scholarly biography and she asked if I would undertake to write it. I readily agreed that her husband deserved a biography, but just as readily insisted that I was not the one to attempt it. Shuster had been involved in so many areas of American public life—journalism, education, religion, international affairs—and I feared that, given several other commitments, researching such a life would be too extensive an undertaking at that time. But we agreed to meet again and, the more I considered it, the more fascinated I became with Shuster's life and work. Mrs. Shuster agreed to give me access to her husband's papers and to assist in any way I wished, and I eventually agreed to her request.

Mrs. Shuster was true to her word. She deposited her husband's papers in the Notre Dame Archives for my use; she consented to several long interviews in her home; and she recommended numerous friends, acquaintances, and colleagues of her husband whom I might interview. She had strong views on almost every important event in her husband's life, but she always reminded me to make my own judgments. I regret that she did not live to see this work completed.

The irrepressible Dr. Dooley has somewhere remarked that "Th' further ye get away fr'm anny perryod th' betther ye can write about it. Ye are not subjict to interruptions be people that were there." His words do not apply to this present undertaking. Numerous friends and colleagues of George Shuster—"people that were there"—generously consented to interviews, and the book has profited greatly from their recollections: from Hunter College and New York, Mrs. Frances Abrams, Dr. Ethel Berl, Msgr. Herman Heide, Dean Marguerite Holmes, Dr. Kathryn Hopwood, Mrs. Antoinette Jehle, Ursula Mahoney, Dr. Mina Rees, Margaret Rendt, Dr. Gustave Rosenberg, Frederick Stewart, Dr. John Theobald, and Dr. Ruth Weintraub; Edward Skillin from *The Commonweal*; Rev. Theodore Hesburgh, C.S.C., and Professor Paul Fenlon from Notre Dame; John J. McCloy and Dr. Oron Hale from missions to Germany; Shuster's sisters Catherine Mannick and Mary Schuster; his foster-daughter Jenny Newman; and especially Doris and Robert Shuster. Archivists and manuscript curators in institutions across the country were invariably generous with their time and assistance: The American Council on Education, Boston College, The Carnegie Corporation of New York, The Catholic University of America, The University of Chicago, The Citadel, Columbia University, The Federal Bureau of Investigation, The Ford Foundation, The Franklin D. Roosevelt Library, Georgetown University, The Hagley Museum and Library, The Harry S. Truman Library, The Hoover Institute for War and Peace, Howard University, The Library of Congress, The National Archives and Records Service, The New York City Board of Higher Education, Princeton University, The Rockefeller Archive Center, St. Joseph's College, Saint Lawrence Seminary, Saint Mary's College, The State Historical Society of Wisconsin, The United States Catholic Conference, and Yale University. Of special help and consideration were Dr. Rose Gilligan and Dr. William Omelchenko of Hunter College Archives and Dr. Wendy Schlereth and her associates in the University of Notre Dame Archives. Dr. Robert Clements provided me with taped interviews with Shuster and Dr. Vincent Lannie with Shuster materials in his possession. Others offering generous assistance were Rev. William Byron, S.J., of the Catholic University of America, Professor Roger Daniels of the University of Cincinnati, Sister Alice Gallin, O.S.U., of the Association of Catholic Colleges and Universities, Rev. Robert Krieg, C.S.C., of the University of Notre Dame, Dr. Hans Peter Mensing of Stiftung Bundeskanzler-Adenauer-Haus, and student-assistants Mary Babbington, Lisa Chickos, Fran Cryan Cullina, Pamela Gilchrist, Beth Imbriaco Hjelm, Jacqueline Klaiss, Anne McInerny Policinski, and Jennifer Schlueter. Mrs. Catherine Box typed these pages with invariable good humor and professional expertise , more times than I like to recall. Dr. Philip Gleason and Rev. Wilson Miscamble, C.S.C., read the entire manuscript, and Rev. Ernest Bartell, C.S.C., Rev. Theodore Hesburgh, C.S.C., and Sister M. Basil Anthony O'Flynn, C.S.C., read parts. To all I am deeply grateful. The errors that remain are my own, and undoubtedly would be fewer had I accepted their recommendations more often. Both the Office of the Provost and the Institute for Scholarship in the Liberal Arts of the College of Arts and Letters of the University of Notre Dame extended much appreciated financial assistance. James Langford and his staff at the University of Notre Dame Press patiently and professionally brought the manuscript to publication.

1

EARLY WISCONSIN YEARS
1894–1919

The completion of the new Hunter College building was a major news event in New York City in the fall of 1940. With more than ten thousand full time students, Hunter, one of four municipal colleges in the city, was the largest college for women in the world. The new building itself was striking—sixteen stories high and covering almost a complete city block from Park Avenue to Lexington on the residential Upper East Side. Built to replace the old college structure, which had burned in 1936, the building's classrooms and auditoriums could accommodate five thousand students at a time.[1]

Although disturbed that so much space had to be given to ten banks of elevators and extra-wide corridors in order to move these thousands of students efficiently between classes, critics agreed that the building was most impressive. Lewis Mumford called it "the handsomest modern structure [Park Avenue] can show."[2] The two basement levels housed multicolored dining rooms, the bookstore, student lockers, and a subway entrance. The first and second floors were devoted to reception areas, administrative offices, a large auditorium, and a smaller playhouse near the older Lexington Avenue building, which had not burned. According to Mumford, "the ground floor, with its polished lavender-gray marble walls and handsome white-metal lighting bowls, is surely one of the best interiors in the city." The third floor held classrooms, student lounges, and the Hunter College Elementary School, an experimental school conducted by the college's Department of Education. The fourth, fifth, and sixth floors housed classrooms, laboratories, a gymnasium, and the college swimming pool. At the seventh floor the building narrowed, providing for a pleasant roof terrace over the gymnasium, and the seventh, eighth, and ninth floors were devoted chiefly to classrooms. The tenth and eleventh floors contained the library and reading rooms, and the twelfth through the sixteenth more classrooms, laboratories, and faculty offices.

The massive, sheer, and at times stark outside walls were broken up by large banks of horizontal windows—"the Bakery of a Thousand Windows" the students irreverently dubbed the structure—and the irregularly recessed floors above the seventh reflected other New York skyscrapers. An appropriate quotation was to be boldly engraved on the lower facade, immediately adjacent to the main student entrance. After suitable consultation the new college president, George N. Shuster, selected the words of Emerson: "We are of different opinions at different hours, but we may always be said to be at heart on the side of truth."[3]

The quotation undoubtedly said as much about the new president as it did about the college. George Shuster lived his many-sided life as journalist, professor, college administrator, and government official amid the clash of differing and even contradictory opinions. He grew up Catholic in an age of anti-Catholic prejudice; he was a staunch defender of German culture in a period of anti-German sentiment surrounding two world wars; he was an outspoken ecumenist when most Catholics shunned interreligious cooperation; he was a lay leader in a church almost universally controlled by clerics; he relished the quiet and solitude of reading and writing but spent most of his years in the swirl of public life; he was a public official charged with defending American interests in international forums often dominated by anti-American sentiment; and he was criticized by conservatives as too close to Communism and by liberals as too close to Fascism.[4] His life seemed enmeshed in diversity and conflict—"different opinions at different hours."

Although Shuster's opinions were refined over the years, there was a fundamental consistency in his beliefs and convictions. He endeavored to remain "on the side of truth" as he saw it, even if expressing it was unpopular and a further source of "different opinions." He was content to walk to the beat of his own drummer, as Emerson's fellow-Transcendentalist Henry David Thoreau had expressed it, "however measured or far away."[5] In

1924 he resigned a teaching position at his alma mater, the University of Notre Dame, in part because he could not agree with the academic priorities of a new administration. In his disgust at Adolf Hitler's totalitarian regime, he urged a boycott of the 1936 Olympic games in Berlin, but the United States chose to participate (and a young Jesse Owens enjoyed his finest hour). Shuster refused to support Francisco Franco in the Spanish Civil War and he resigned from *The Commonweal* in 1937 when that journal repudiated his views. As president of Hunter College he permitted leftist public figures to speak on campus but also cooperated with government authorities in dismissing faculty members refusing to deny affiliation with the Communist Party. He supported the United Nations Educational, Scientific, and Cultural Organization (UNESCO) at a time when many high public officials, including secretaries of state Dean Acheson, John Foster Dulles, and Dean Rusk, were far less enthusiastic. Within his own church he understood Pope Pius XII's silence during Nazi persecutions of the Jews but was critical of Pope Paul VI for his encyclical *Humanae Vitae*, which upheld the ban on artificial contraception. In approximately twenty books, three hundred articles, and countless speeches and public addresses over a span of fifty years, Shuster expressed his views and convictions openly, despite frequent questioning and opposition, confident that, in his own heart at least, he was ever standing "on the side of truth."

Three diverse but not unrelated strains converged in his earliest years to help shape his later views and convictions—his German ancestry, his Catholic religion, and the early twentieth century Progressivism of his native Wisconsin.

Shuster's background was solidly German—the Schusters and Wilhelms on his father's side and the Naumans and Gimbles on his mother's had all immigrated to the United States from Germany in the nineteenth century. (Shortly after graduation from college in 1915, George changed the spelling of his surname from Schuster to Shuster. The rest of the family did not.) Such an immigrant background could only complicate acceptance in late nineteenth- and early twentieth-century America during this era of Bismarck's nationalistic *Kulturkamp* in Germany, the intolerant American Protective Association closer to home, the revival of the Ku Klux Klan, and two tragic world wars.[6] Despite occasional instances of bigotry and discrimination in his youth, however, Shuster remained grateful for his German heritage and its impact on his life.

For Shuster, Germany was primarily a people, a culture, not simply a geographical area; national boundaries had been redrawn after too many wars to focus upon that. But German culture had been distinctive and had achieved so much. The world owed a special debt to German philosophy, according to Shuster, and for sheer intellectual brilliance he saw few to rival Immanuel Kant. As a man of letters, Shuster admired the style and creative inspiration of German authors, and Goethe was undoubtedly his favorite. If German culture did not reach its zenith in the writings of Goethe, it certainly did so in the music of Bach, Beethoven, and Wagner. "It is not casually that the Germans have sought their truest form of self-expression in music," Shuster once wrote. "For this of all the arts is the most proper to men who have not phrased or formed the whole of what they are content to be."[7] He wrote admiringly of German art and architecture, of Germany's castles, cathedrals, and public buildings, even the well-patronized museums of the smallest towns—all indicative of a sense of beauty and appreciation of culture. For Shuster, the culture of Germany was not superficial or elitist since the winding rivers and rolling hills and expansive forests offered an environment of leisure and beauty leading the rich and poor alike to enjoy and appreciate the better and more beautiful things of life.

Shuster was especially impressed by what he saw as the Germans' inherent love of freedom and liberty. This may have been the result of the nation's ethnic and geographical diversity, of centuries of local rule and lack of strong centralized administration, or, as George Bancroft and other historians had suggested, of some native Teutonic quality that had been opposing oppression and outside subjugation since the days of Julius Caesar and the Gallic Wars.[8] There was a yearning in the German people to be untrammeled by government authority, to live and develop freely. Shuster noted frequently and with pride that the family of his paternal grandfather had immigrated to the United States after the revolutions of 1848 had fallen short of restoring freedom and democracy to the German people. In *Look Away!*, a novel Shuster wrote about the American Civil War, a young German-American in Wisconsin expressed this quality well:

"That's why we are here, Miss Treloar," he said, pulling at a blade of timothy and biting off the end. "Father was a leader in the freedom movement in our country, but that movement was crushed and we left. Here we are poor but we are free. . . . It does not matter to Father that even the Germans here do not really understand him, or that he must work hard to make a living. He says that his children will be free, and that it is their destiny to help build the greatest democracy in the world. . . . And I agree with him in that. It is a wonderful thing to look into the future and know that our children, too, will cringe before no man.[9]

When that same speaker, Peter Jaeger, is later killed in the war, rescuing the flag from a fallen comrade, his aging father is broken but proud:

"Ach so!" he muttered proudly. "He go down with the flag of freedom in his arms. I am so happy it was so, Miss Edithy. Thanks be to God it was so. . . .

He put his hands over his face, "Dieser war," he said then. "It goes on, it goes on and on. It will cost life to so many young men. I don't unnerstan' it, Miss Edithy. But freedom is even so great a thing. I too—I gladly die for freedom.[10]

Catholicism was as much a part of Shuster's background and early life as was his German ancestry. "A boy reared in a family like mine would have been singularly dull-witted if he had failed to perceive that religion was all around like a suit of clothes or the things in a room," he wrote years later. "Our Wisconsin town was steeped in doctrine and precept."[11] Most of the town's residents were Protestant, chiefly German Lutheran, but Catholics were not an insignificant minority. Shuster later recalled getting up for early Mass each Sunday, even in temperatures well below zero, serving regularly as an altar boy and mumbling Latin responses he did not understand. He attended the local parochial school for the first eight grades. There were rare instances of anti-Catholic hostility, especially after some visiting preacher or itinerant ex-nun or ex-priest would lecture on the machinations of the Vatican, but young Shuster apparently accepted all this as normal.

For Shuster, Catholicism was not primarily a set of dogmas to be learned but rather a life to be lived. "Religion has persistently been to me an affair of persons," he wrote later. "The chain of logic, which for some is almost the chain of being, weaves no magic spell for me. I respected my teachers not for what they said but for what they were. And therewith such intellectual living as I did in my early youth was largely concerned with impressions of good and evil in action."[12] The deepest influence on Shuster's early religious development was undoubtedly his father, and he paid beautiful tribute to him in his later "Spiritual Autobiography":

> No doubt I was most influenced, quite unconsciously, by my father. He was by no means a learned man, and his principal weakness, which could be exasperating as well as amusing, was the result of one of those Celtic imaginations sometimes found in South Germans. This led him to embellish his narrative of every occurrence with incidents having no foundation in fact. But he was a serene and humble Christian, never clerical or anti-clerical, neither pietistic nor worldly-wise. He possessed an instinct for religious conduct which was as rare as it was beautiful. I remember that our parish once had an unworthy priest. My father refused to accompany the unctuous committee of parishioners which went to report sundry goings-on to the Bishop. Instead, on the day of reckoning, he carried the offender's bags to the station (we had neither cars nor taxis in those days) without saying so much as one word; and I am sure that this gesture of reverence for the office, combined with a silent rebuke to its incumbent, did the distraught young cleric a world of good. My father was not a saint, nor was he, like his favorite uncle, a self-taught scholar, but when he was dead I looked at his weary old face and was sure that I should never meet a better Christian.

Growing up in the Wisconsin of Robert LaFollette in the last decade of the nineteenth century and the first decade of the twentieth also had a profound influence on Shuster's later social and political views. The immediate post–Civil War decades, from 1865 to 1890, had been harsh and difficult for many. As industrial giants John D. Rockefeller, Andrew Carnegie, J. Pierpont Morgan, and railroad barons Cornelius Vanderbilt, James J. Hill, and Collis P. Huntington amassed more and more power, benefits to labor in wages, hours, and working conditions did not keep pace. Farmers seemed particularly discontented, due in part to natural disasters—droughts, dust storms, and plagues of grasshoppers—and even more to ever-increasing transportation and marketing costs. They found only minimal relief in the Grange, Greenback, and Populist movements. Black Americans gradually lost whatever gains they had made during the Civil War, and the Supreme Court, in *Plessy v. Ferguson* in 1896, approved segregation in all public facilities. Native Americans were gradually relegated to less productive reservations, and when they did not retreat peacefully, they were driven before the U. S. Army. Immigrants continued to seek hope and a better way of life in America, but they often found instead low wages, exorbitant prices, and flagrant discrimination. Political life was so corrupt that one contemporary historian suggested that "one might search the whole list of Congress, Judiciary, and Executive during the twenty-five years from 1870 to 1895 and find little but damaged reputations."[13]

Wisconsin was one of the first states seriously to address and even remedy several of these problems. Robert LaFollette, like Shuster from southern Wisconsin, broke with Republican Party officials after three terms in the House of Representatives and returned to his home state in 1890 to campaign for political reform and progressive legislation. He served as governor from 1900 to 1906 and senator from 1906 to 1925. Under his leadership, Wisconsin became a laboratory of progressive reform; laws were enacted to regulate banks and railroads, to revise corporate and inheritance taxes, to establish minimum wages for women and protect workers from outside strikebreakers, to set up a state civil service program, and to subject more state officials to direct primary elections.[14]

Shuster grew up admiring Robert LaFollette and remembered going with his father to hear him speak during one of his campaigns.[15] From LaFollette and other Progressives, Shuster learned that government need not be corrupt or self-serving and, in fact, in the right hands, could be a most effective instrument in solving social and economic problems and in bringing relief to those needing it most. Although he was never active in partisan party politics, he remained, perhaps under the influence of LaFollette, a Republican or Independent all his life.

It was into a devote Catholic family of German ancestry in southwestern Wisconsin that George Nauman S(c)huster was born on August 27, 1894. George's paternal great-grandfather had been a public official in Germany, probably a justice of the peace, and had immigrated to the United States in the wake of the

European upheavals of 1848. His son, Peter Schuster, George's grandfather, eventually purchased a farm just outside Hurricane, Wisconsin, a crossroads and general store in farthest southwest Wisconsin, so named because a hurricane or tornado had gone through there some years before. Hurricane was about seven miles from Lancaster, the Grant County seat, and the Schuster farm was in a beautiful location, with a scenic ridge offering an excellent view of the surrounding hills and a narrow ravine known for a long time as "Schuster's Bottom" from the rich bottomland along the stream. A prominent Catholic, Peter was also instrumental in building the small mission church at Hurricane, a mission served each weekend by a priest from one of the nearby towns.[16]

Shuster's paternal grandmother was Mary Wilhelm. She too had immigrated from Germany and had met and married Peter in Grant County. It was a family story that one of her ancestors, because of his impressive size, had been recruited as a bodyguard for Kaiser Wilhelm and was given the name Wilhelm in recognition. Whatever the story's validity, George and his sisters could speculate that they owed their large raw-boned frames to such an ancestor.[17]

On his mother's side Shuster's grandparents were Lutheran. His grandfather, George Nauman, had emigrated from Germany, settled first in Pennsylvania, and eventually bought a farm in southwestern Wisconsin. Purchasing the farm may have been an early introduction to some of the sharper business practices of the time, as Shuster later suggested:

> My grandfather was lured to Wisconsin from his home in Pennsylvania by the blandishments of one who must have been for those days a clever real-estate salesman. When he arrived to survey his manorial estate, into which he had put all his savings, he found ten acres of cleared land on the edge of which was a log house and a barn, a hundred and sixty acres of virgin forest, and an orchard. For years he supported the family by peddling the orchard fruit, meanwhile working as hard as he could to clear more land.[18]

While developing his new farm, George Nauman also met and married Catherine Gimble. Her parents had died in Germany when she was young, and a cousin's family brought her to the United States when they decided to immigrate. The Naumans were still farming outside Lancaster when George was young; he visited the farm often and spent a year working on it after the death of his grandfather.

Shuster's father, Anton, was one of Peter and Mary Schuster's seven children, born in Hurricane in 1858.[19] He had no more than a grade school education but for a long time wished to be a doctor. Money for such medical training was not available, but he did spend two years of his teens traveling around with the local doctor and assisting with whatever operations the doctor was called on to perform. As a result of this experience, he cared for any of the children when they were sick, and he was frequently called by relatives and neighbors in similar situations. He eventually adopted stonemasonry as his trade, building abutments for bridges and other construction projects. He at times had three or four other masons working with him and listed himself as contractor, and he was proud of the fact that he was once hired to lay the abutments for a bridge to span the nearby Mississippi River.[20]

Anton married Elizabeth Nauman in 1893 in a rite performed by the local priest, but it was not strictly a Catholic marriage since Elizabeth was still Lutheran. Elizabeth had had only a grade school education also but always received outstanding grades and retained an intense interest in education and things of the mind throughout her life. Her school experience undoubtedly helped to shape her attitude of toleration, and it was an attitude she transmitted to her children. Her father's farm was surrounded by several other farms, which a southern planter had earlier purchased for slaves he had freed and, for a time, young Elizabeth was the only white child in her classroom. "She was treated like a princess," Shuster later remarked. She regularly took a shortcut through one of the farmyards on her way to school, and often during the cold Wisconsin winters, the mother of the family would ask one of her sons to go out and tramp a path through the snow for Elizabeth, invite her inside to get warm before continuing, and have one of her sons carry little Elizabeth's books to school if they seemed heavy. Elizabeth was especially friendly and sympathetic to the needs of black neighbors for the rest of her life. Two women in that same black family never married but lived together in Lancaster, and every Christmas Elizabeth would pay to have their coal bin filled with coal for the winter. The two women apparently never knew who their benefactor was.[21]

After their marriage in 1893 Anton and Elizabeth Schuster bought a large home on the corner of Tyler Street and Beetown Road, about five blocks southwest from the center of town. Lancaster at that time was an attractive center with a population of about two thousand, the county seat of Grant County in southwestern Wisconsin, bordering Illinois on the south and the Mississippi River on the west. Shuster himself once wrote that he was born "in what is still one of the most charming small towns in Wisconsin."[22] An attractive courthouse stood on the square or town commons, a well-kept lawn dotted by a few Civil War cannons, and the shopping area was built around this commons. The Schuster home was almost a mini-farm—a ten-room house, a barn for a horse and cow, a few chickens, and a large vegetable garden—but it was still within easy walking distance of the town commons and the Catholic church one block closer.

The Schuster household was a happy one. George was born in 1894, his sister Catherine in 1896, and Mary in 1904. Discipline was clear but never harsh. One of the children recalled their father as "the kindest man I ever knew."[23] They were taught right and wrong and were expected to be good, but they never felt oppressed or feared that they were being watched. Their parents, in fact, taught more by example. They lived modest, respectful lives, accepted their responsibilities willingly, were generous to neighbors in need, lived good lives according to the insights they had, and tried to instill the same qualities in their children.

Religion was a central part of their life. St. Clement's Church was only four blocks from home, and Sunday Mass, occasional vespers, and other religious devotions were part of the regular family schedule. For a time Mr. Schuster was a church trustee. The children recalled that religion was not an inconvenience or a duty but simply a normal part of daily life. They learned their first prayers at their mother's knee, and she accompanied them to Mass every Sunday. It was only when she converted to Catholicism at about the time of Mary's birth that the two older children realized that she had not been Catholic all along. She then became a rather strict and evangelical Catholic, extolling all things Catholic, taking special interest in the church's work in Indian and Black American missions, and urging others to join the church.

Lancaster was small, and there were always plenty of children to play with nearby. George at times recalled some anti-Catholic slurs and incidents when he was small but they probably only left the children more tolerant and more conscious of the pain of discrimination. He recalled also that in the Catholic school they prayed for Protestants since they were all going to hell because they did not have the true religion. "I was distressed about this," George wrote later, "particularly because a very pretty little Methodist girl with long blond hair lived just down the street."[24] The children recalled Christmas as a particularly happy time. On Christmas Eve, one of the front rooms was closed off for gifts and the Christmas tree, and since it was next to the dining room, the family ate dinner that evening in the large kitchen. Their father always had to excuse himself during the meal to run downtown for something he had forgotten, and while he was gone, they heard a loud banging on the front room door, a sign that Santa Claus had been there. As a young girl Catherine always felt sorry that her father was never home to hear it and to be there when Santa Claus arrived. When the snow was deep or the weather particularly cold, their father would often carry one of the younger children on his shoulder to early Mass on Christmas morning, singing as he went.

Young Shuster received a good education, both formal and informal. He attended eight grades of St. Clement's Grade School, taught by the School Sisters of Notre Dame. All eight grades were taught in two rooms, and the sisters lived in the other half of the building. Although most of the sisters were of German background, all classes were taught in English. George did well in his subjects and used to surprise the local doctor with his speed in solving rather complex mathematical problems. He was an avid reader and seemed to know so much more than others his age that his sister at one time feared it would be difficult for him to have close friends. German was customarily spoken around the house when the children were very young, but their parents switched almost exclusively to English when the children began school. Mr. Schuster continued to subscribe to German magazines and a German newspaper, however, and George never felt uncomfortable speaking German in later life.[25]

In September 1907, having recently turned thirteen, young George was sent away for high school to St. Lawrence College at

Mt. Calvary, about fifteen miles northeast of Fond du Lac. The monastery of St. Lawrence of Brundusium had been founded by German Capuchin fathers in the 1850s, and they soon after established a school for the training of prospective candidates for the order.[26] The original building burned to the ground in 1868 but was immediately rebuilt. Over the next four decades additional wings were constructed and new halls were built—St. Joseph's Hall in the 1870s, a new college building in 1881, and St. Thomas Hall and auditorium at the turn of the century. By 1907 the preparatory seminary numbered approximately one hundred students and a faculty of ten.[27] Emphasis was placed on traditional classical courses—English, history, mathematics, Latin, Greek, German, French, rhetoric, religion, and basic science. The classes were small, permitting good teacher-student contact, and the education Shuster received there was excellent.

George may never have known the full reason why he was sent to St. Lawrence. It had an excellent scholastic reputation and George's mother would have certainly wanted a school with high academic standards for her clearly gifted son. The fact that it was operated by priests of German background was also an advantage. George himself always thought that his mother was going through a period of poor health and that he was sent away to reduce the possible burden on her at home, but this is questionable. Elizabeth Schuster's health was not good, but there were still two younger children at home and, had he remained with them, George might have been able to assume some of the responsibility from his mother. Mrs. Schuster, however, was a deeply religious woman and probably hoped that George might eventually become a priest. She may well have felt that if he had a religious vocation, the best place to foster and develop it would be a preparatory school like St. Lawrence College.[28]

Shuster spent four years at St. Lawrence, returning to Lancaster for summer, Christmas, and perhaps Easter vacations each year. Years later he recalled it as a place "which was as like a seminary as could be managed. It turned out to be a Swiss preparatory school transplanted to the United States. The course of study would induce in a modern American lad feelings akin to despair. Bed and board were spartan, indeed, but the atmosphere was warm and human."[29] Young George did extremely well there.

The only grades that remain are from his last two years but they are most impressive: solid 100s in Greek, English literature (and conduct); 99 or 100 in religion, 98 in German literature and German rhetoric, 97 to 99 in English composition, English rhetoric, and physics. Of the seventeen to twenty students in each class, George was apparently at the top of his class in every subject except German composition. He also took part in school debates and acted in holiday plays, interests he would retain throughout his life.[30]

The small size of the classes at St. Lawrence was a special advantage because it enabled Shuster to develop a very close friendship with one of the professors, Father Corbinian Vieracker, professor of Greek and German literature, and this relationship developed into almost private tutoring. Shuster paid tribute to him in later years:

> There I met Father Corbinian, beyond any question the greatest teacher I have known. He taught German and Greek, and as a result I devoted myself to the tasks he assigned and the vistas he opened with all the enthusiasm I could muster. I read immense quantities of German literature, from Goethe at one end of the spectrum to Karl May on the other. But the farthest point I reached in Greek was a couple of Plato's *Dialogues* and one or two of the orations of Demosthenes.[31]

Clearly these were happy years. The college was a hundred miles from home, but George kept good contact with the family he loved through regular correspondence and vacation visits. He had been raised in a deeply religious family, his parish church and school were strongly German, and the four years with the German Capuchins deepened his attachment to Catholicism. The atmosphere at school strengthened his appreciation of German culture also, not only because of the German literature he read in class, but because of the appreciation of German art, music, and culture he noted in the college professors he so much admired. The example of these professors, and especially that of Father Corbinian, confirmed his interest in intellectual pursuits and perhaps first suggested to him the possibility of an academic career. George always retained a deep affection for St. Lawrence College and, in the introduction to *The Hill of Happiness*, a collection of light and fictionalized sketches of Franciscan monks in a monastery called

St. Bonaventure's (St. Lawrence in thin disguise), he wrote with personal feeling in 1926:

> Here, then, is a handful of stories about an American monastery. The place described in them is so real that the author has only to make a brief pilgrimage in order to see once again the spires and trees—and even some of the people—he describes. The tales themselves are quite true. Indeed, it would be a gross blunder to spoil with fiction a reality that is so charming and unusual. Well, there is no need for further talk about the matter. If you read carefully, you will be able to find St. Bonaventure's for yourself, even if the name is inexact; and that would surely be a happy ending.[32]

Before enrolling in the University of Notre Dame for college, George took out a year (1911–12) and worked on his grandfather Nauman's farm a few miles from the city. George later suggested that he was having some back problems and for that reason decided to postpone college. His well-built father may also have felt that his tall but gangly son needed to build himself up physically and that a year of farm work would be beneficial. Most important, the farm needed the assistance. George's grandfather had died a few years before and George's mother, an only child, had inherited it. The family at first had hired someone to farm it but that was not satisfactory; then they rented it, and that was even worse. George continued to live at home and drove Nellie, the family horse, over to the farm each day. His sisters later recalled that one hardly had to guide the horse home at the end of the day since she knew the way herself, was anxious to return to the barn, and always returned with a slightly faster gait than when she departed.[33]

After this year of farm labor, George enrolled at the University of Notre Dame, located in northwestern Indiana about two hundred miles from Lancaster. None of George's relatives had gone to Notre Dame, and the reasons for its selection are not clear. George's mother would certainly have insisted on a Catholic college, and professors at St. Lawrence might have recommended Notre Dame. George at one time suggested that it was the athletic program that first attracted him, but never being particularly athletic, this might have been written tongue in cheek.[34] Notre Dame had a good academic reputation throughout the

Catholic Midwest at that time, and George would have wanted the best. Notre Dame seemed the place.

The University of Notre Dame had been founded by Father Edward Sorin and a small band of brothers of the Congregation of Holy Cross in 1842. The university had grown rapidly over the next several decades and by 1912, when George Shuster enrolled, it comprised a campus of approximately twelve hundred acres, including two small lakes, and seventeen academic and residential buildings.[35] The student population at that time was close to one thousand, although almost half of these were in the preparatory department, and the university faculty numbered fifty. The university was divided into twelve academic departments and also boasted the first Catholic law school in the country.

By the turn of the century Notre Dame had known some truly outstanding faculty members. Charles Warren Stoddard offered courses in "Belles Lettres" in the 1880s. After his departure the university hired Maurice Francis Egan, in the words of one recent scholar "the best-known and most admired Catholic layman of his generation."[36] James Edwards taught history at Notre Dame and amassed an outstanding collection of American Catholic Church records for scholarly research. Luigi Gregori of Italy was artist-in-residence from 1874 to 1891. Father John Zahm, C.S.C., taught physics and chemistry, wrote important works on science and religion, and later wrote of his explorations into early cultures of Latin America in the company of ex-president Theodore Roosevelt. His brother, Dr. Albert Zahm, taught engineering at both Notre Dame and the Catholic University of America, did extensive research into the principles of aerodynamics, and was later director of the Aerodynamical Laboratory of the United States Navy.

The level of the Notre Dame faculty had not greatly changed in the first two decades of the new century. Most were conscientious and dedicated teachers, and a few were superior. Fathers Leonard Carrico, C.S.C., Charles O'Donnell, C.S.C., and John Talbot Smith were all members of the English Department. O'Donnell was to become a widely read Catholic poet and later university president. Fathers Alexander Kirsch, C.S.C., and Julius Nieuwland, C.S.C., were fine scientists, and Nieuwland would later be a major discoverer of synthetic rubber. The university librarian was Rev. Paul Foik, C.S.C., a founder of the Irish National Library Foundation and the Catholic Library Association. The chairman of the Architecture Department was Francis Kervick, a well-known architect in Chicago and throughout the Midwest.

Despite the very respectable college education Notre Dame could offer, there was still much of the traditional French boarding school in the university of 1912. Two halls were set aside for high school students and a third for boys under thirteen. Disciplinary regulations were spelled out in the *General Catalogue:* "No student shall leave the University grounds without permission from the President or the person delegated to represent him. . . . The use of cigarettes is strictly forbidden, a second offense being punished by suspension for one month. . . . All students are required to attend divine service at the University church at stated times."[37] Even off-campus conduct was regulated: "Students are required to report at the University immediately after arriving at South Bend. . . . Unnecessary delay in South Bend is looked upon as a serious violation of rule."

Because George had had such excellent preparatory courses at St. Lawrence College, he was admitted into the sophomore class at Notre Dame. He was also asked by an English professor to assist him in correcting freshman themes, and this he did. George's own curriculum was the traditional classical course, with three years each of English, Latin, Greek, and philosophy. His examination grades were consistently high, almost invariably in the 90s, with an occasional 100 and a rare 80.[38] He seemed to value especially his training in Greek:

> We ranged far, at a rapid rate, doing the whole of the *Odyssey* in one semester and nearly all of Appolonius Rhodius in another, ending later with the corpus of Greek drama, from Aeschylus to Aristophanes. . . .Then I discovered one day that I could read Plato in Greek with no more than a cursory help from the dictionary. To me that seemed a feat as unusual as finding the North Pole.[39]

Shuster had a marvelous vocabulary and command of words for the rest of his life, and he often attributed this to his knowledge of Greek and Latin roots. He also found part-time employment each year at the university and thus was able to pay a large part of his education personally. He lived all three years at Sorin Hall, a residence hall with private rooms for upper-class students; one of his fellow students in Sorin at that time was a young man from Norway by way of Chicago, Knute Rockne.

His major extracurricular interests during his years at Notre Dame were debating and writing for the student publication, *The Scholastic*. Shuster once wrote that much of his course of study at Notre Dame was rather routine, "excepting for the university's debating team, which demanded wide reading about some selected theme of current interest as well as writing and speaking skills."[40] George's previous training in reading, writing, and speaking at St. Lawrence had prepared him well, and in his first year at Notre Dame, he was awarded a medal (and ten dollars in gold) for sophomore oratory. This could not have been any surprise to his sister Catherine, who later recalled that on one of his visits home from St. Lawrence she and George had a discussion over a particular point and George thoroughly demolished all her arguments. The point arose again the next day, George took the opposite side, and thoroughly demolished her again.[41]

George apparently went out for debating seriously in the fall of 1913 and for the next two years was a solid member of the university's varsity team. The topic of debate in his junior year was: "Resolved, that Indiana should adopt the Initiative and Referendum." George was the team's lead speaker on the negative side. One account noted that his style was "convincing rather than oratorical" and that his eloquence "was designed to win decisions rather than the plaudits of his audience."[42] But the account noted that he was not any less effective: "Shuster was the star of the St. Mary's debate, for he combined logic, wit and sarcasm in a manner that even the ladies could not resist." The negative team, with a very limited schedule, went undefeated.

Shuster tried out for the debate team again in his senior year and was again selected as one of the university's six varsity debaters. The subject this year was: "Resolved, that capital and labor shall settle disputes affecting the public welfare through legally constituted boards of arbitration." This year George was lead speaker on the affirmative side, and the team was successful in its only intercollegiate debate, against St. Viator's College of

Illinois. Shuster later recalled that victory with a modest smile since the lead speaker on the defeated St. Viator's team was young Fulton J. Sheen, later an outstanding preacher and archbishop. At the Notre Dame commencement exercises of both 1914 and 1915 Shuster was awarded medals for debate.[43]

Shuster was an unusually prolific writer throughout his life, and he began this avocation in college. He published a short story, "My Greatest Play," in *The Scholastic* during his first year. It was a story written in the first person by a fellow making a movie who, dressed in a cowboy suit, entered a bank to get references for a farmer in order to borrow a few horses for the movie. The teller faints on seeing what she thinks is an armed robber. The cowboy is arrested and is saved from lynching only because the farmer comes to look for him and corroborates his story. The plot is simple and easily handled and the story exhibits some of the lightness of style, understatement, and modest circumlocution of which George would later be such a master: "Just as I bent over the girl a man rushed from the vault, dropped his papers, and threw himself violently upon me. I never relished that sort of proceeding, and so, with considerable speed, I relegated him into a prone position in a corner. . . . I stated my story with the utmost clearness and candor, but convinced the audience of everything but my truthfulness. . . . I did not care to die, but the worth of my opinion was just then considerably below par."[44]

Shuster not only continued writing for *The Scholastic* during his final two years at Notre Dame but also joined its board of editors. He published a second short story in his final year, but he now seemed more drawn to literary criticism and personal essays. He wrote of the meaning and beauty of Easter ("Can the world, then, ever grow old if it has a spring for the body and an Easter for the soul?") and the significance of Christmas in 1914 while Europe was at war. He analyzed the writings of F. Marion Crawford, a prolific novelist at the turn of the century, compared his style, themes, and philosophy with those of Poe, Hawthorne, and Hardy, and generally had praise for Crawford's work. He wrote a biographical sketch of General Lew Wallace, author of *Ben Hur*, and a scholarly analysis of the poetry of Pindar. He demonstrated a good knowledge of Pindar's times, discussed the choice of individual words and expressions, and noted that, having lost the music and the dance, critics were forced to judge Pindar only from his lyrics—and he was still a classic.[45]

Shuster himself was writing poetry seriously by this time, and he published frequently in *The Scholastic*. During his senior year he composed the poem "Washington the Free," which was read at special Washington Day exercises, and he was also selected to write the class poem "The Winged Years" for the commencement ceremonies. He had given much thought to the purpose and nobility of poetry, and he tried to explain its value in an article at the time:

> When this poetic imagination expands so that it absorbs the entire soul of a gifted author we have the greatest poems—the loftiest works of man. The bard looks into human life and interprets it; he expresses man's hostility to evil, and his relation with God; he dreams of God and His eternal beauty. . . .
>
> The essential qualities of the bard, then, are faith and sympathy. He must feel certain that he is more than matter if he would rise above it. His soul must throb with the soul of his nation and of the world; it must be lighted with the spark of celestial fire. Poetical genius such as this is the highest form of earthy being; its passionate hope, its endless longing for ideals, make it more sacred to the world than science of any form.[46]

Considering George's classroom performance and his extracurricular accomplishments, it was no surprise to his classmates that, in addition to the debating medal, he received at commencement the university's Quan Gold Medal for the best academic record in his senior year in the Classical Program, the Dockweiler Gold Medal for the best essay on a philosophical theme, and the Meehan Medal for the best essay in English.[47] Years later he recalled the Notre Dame of those years in a personal letter to Father John W. Cavanaugh, C.S.C., then university president:

> Notre Dame may be a thousand things, I guess. She may wrap herself up in football blankets of a more or less international lustre. She may gather sober students about her and march forward to an imposing academic future. Surely I should like to see her do both. But for those of us who know, Notre Dame has been something better, bigger, dearer—a school that was a big, grumbling, radiant, sturdy family gathered around its head. As the years go on those of us who loved and muttered against your reign will

come to realize that we have known something as close to patriar-
chal chivalry as the modern world has known. And I do most
emphatically declare that for me the school is mostly the "old"
school—a place that calls up recollections like those of Wordsworth's Ode and Peck's Bad Boy well mixed.[48]

Shuster left Notre Dame in 1915 and accepted a job teaching
English in a public high school in Hibbing, Minnesota. He had no
complaints about the teaching, but even for someone used to the
winters of southern Wisconsin and northern Indiana, the weather
was a surprise, as he wrote with perhaps some exaggeration:

I am writing this out at school. Cold! Why, every day we have
twenty or thirty degrees below zero. And snow! There has been
good sleighing for two months, but now the snow is so deep that it
is hard to get around.[49]

After a year in Hibbing, Shuster returned to Chicago and
worked for part of a year at Sears Roebuck and part as a reporter
for a Chicago newspaper. During this period he also continued
his writing, contributing two articles to *The Scholastic* and three to
The Catholic World, a scholarly publication of the Paulist Fathers
in New York. His scholarly interests were clearly leading toward
literature, but literature in its relation to religion, literature as the
expression of a human spirit created by God and tending toward
God as its final goal and destiny. His first article was "The
Tragedy of Mark Twain," a study of Twain's literary works and
also his tragic disillusionment as he faced the problem of evil,
depressed and alone, in *The Mysterious Stranger*. In "Our Poets in
the Streets" Shuster considered poets as representatives of common humanity, rejecting Whitman as too self-centered, and preferring Longfellow, who "understood this ordinary American
admirably. He sang of daily toil, the sweat and the rain; he stood
with the artisan on the bridge at midnight, caressed his memories
and whispered of his children and the dead." He was critical of
American Catholic fiction in "Retreat of the American Novel"
("When one has glanced over the list, our books appear almost
invariably trite, juvenile and uninspired"), but he admitted that
constant concern for earning a livelihood and gaining social
recognition partly explained the lack of depth.[50]

In early 1916, while war was raging in Europe and blizzards were blanketing Minnesota, Shuster wrote facetiously from Hibbing: "I am now a peace advocate. To ponder the terrible possibilities of leading a platoon in such a climate as this is enough to make one side with Bryan."[51] Shuster had been an officer in the student cadet corps at Notre Dame and could almost surely have received a commission in the army had he desired, but a few months after American entrance into World War I, he decided to enlist as a private. He admitted later that he was not at all convinced of the justice of this war or of the legitimacy of America's involvement, but other young men were entering the service and he felt it was his obligation as much as theirs.[52]

Shuster enlisted in the army from Chicago in September 1917, was assigned to the infantry, and was sent to Camp Grant in nearby Rockford. After a few weeks, however, he was transferred to the signal corps. "I am writing to let you know about my transfer to the signal corps," he informed his parents. "Although no wish of mine was expressed on the subject, and the curtain was clamped down very suddenly, I am not at all sorry. The signal corps is much better than the infantry and I will get six dollars more." In early 1918 he was transferred to the East Coast, and he realized that this was the prelude to the trip abroad. "In a little while,—just how little, it is impossible to state,—I shall be leaving," he wrote his former English teacher at Notre Dame, Father Leonard Carrico, C.S.C. "The Signal Corps has claimed me, and a month or two from now I expect to be clasping a telephone receiver to my ear somewhere in No Man's Land." He hinted to his parents also that he might soon be going abroad, and to them he was especially optimistic: "For quite some time after we get over, generally from one to six months, troops remain in training. In our case it may be longer as the business is new and rather technical. During this time we can, I understand, write pretty freely and get such things as parcels. . . . For one reason I am anxious to see France, and that is from the writing standpoint."[53]

In late March he was in fact sent to France where, as he had earlier predicted to Father Carrico, he found himself "at the front [at St. Mihiel and Meuse-Argonne] as a member of a Franco-American group assigned to pick up enemy telephone and telegraph conversation." Because of this intelligence assignment he was later one of the first Allied soldiers to overhear on Morse code the German request for an armistice in late 1918. But he was brought face to face with the brutal side of war also:

> Our troops were very green, blunders were frequent and unavoidable. The Germans staged fairly extensive raids, lasting for hours. The roar of exploding shells, the heavy thuds of belching mortars, the smell of gas—all of this left the four of us on duty in the dugout in a state of superanxiety during a fifty-two hour attack. We were wearing masks, bayonets were on our rifles, and grenades were in our hands. But the storm passed us by, my first real wartime storm; and when we went up next morning to prepare our lines on which our work depended, I came upon my first dead soldier, that is, one not in a casket or on a stretcher. He was a young French lad, not more than eighteen with a love letter to his girl in the Loire country still in his pocket. My companion and I carried him back, cursing so vehemently that if the Lord God was listening He must have been shocked. Later on came Chateau Thierry and St. Mihiel, each with its rivers of blood. I was a veteran now, and like all veterans I do not talk about such things.[54]

This wartime experience left a lasting impression upon him. He had witnessed the stupidities and horrors of war firsthand, and he could never in the future view such conflicts as anything but human tragedies. He admitted later that the experience had had a profound effect upon him religiously also:

> It is true that the Church attracted me because so much of what we saw about us in Europe was ancient and beautiful. I shall never forget coming into Chartres a little before dawn, to see the miraculous spires of the cathedral against the grey sky; or observing Palm Sunday in the old Church of St. Radegonde at Poitiers, with the light coming through the matchless Romanesque window above the high altar; or hearing Mass in what for me is still the most impressive Gothic room I have seen, the Cathedral of Metz. The knowledge that generations of men had cared so deeply for the Catholic faith that they made for it so many shrines of matchless loveliness, was simply comforting. . . .[55]

But once again, it was the horror of war that touched him most deeply. "Before that," he wrote, "I had lived up to all the rules and tried to believe what I was supposed to as a Catholic. Now I was personally religious, deeply so, but no longer a subservient soul. It seemed to me that I had found God across all the suffering I had seen."[56]

Shuster may also have fallen in love with a young German woman during the months of American occupation, and although the relationship never developed, he wrote of the experience with feeling more than fifty years later:

> One of my duties was to help find billets for the relatively few new soldiers who came to our town. The young woman appointed by the Germans to do most of the work was attractive and intelligent, indeed very much so. She was a Lutheran which did not trouble me a great deal, but she had lost a father, two brothers and a possible fiance in the fighting. This proved to be a barrier she could not cross with me or any other American. I realized that she had no intention of doing so for my sake. She was not a soft Rhenish girl who wanted above all to get married and have children. But if she had found a man who would pledge himself, without quite knowing, to the kind of icy and yet overwhelming love which marriage would have involved for her, it would have meant for both satisfaction lighted up by religious commitment and feeling. I am sure that she liked and respected me. By reason of her special assignment she knew that not a few of the American conquerors (whether they were officers or not) were brutes and ignoramuses who were like putty in the hands of German pimps and whores. She also knew quite well that I was not putty, but rather perhaps too stalwart and uncompromising a Christian intellectual. Yet doubtless she could not after all quite segregate me from them. There had been too much slaughter and the bitterness of defeat for this daughter of a long line of Civil Servants whose pride had been wounded almost beyond repair. And so I came to understand how hard it is for good women when so many men of their generation are slain. It is difficult enough to marry beneath one's rank and station, but far, far worse when the companion accepted for life does not really know what life means. When I was pulled out of Germany . . . she had left with her mother for a vacation. The note I sent her was not answered. Beyond any question I have loved the Indiana girl of my youth much more than I could have loved that German girl. But it was wonderful to have known her and felt so deeply an affection for her. I have been grateful ever since, for now I was beyond the realm of infatuation and knew what love meant.[57]

Shuster was also able to spend several months at the University of Poitiers after the Armistice, studying the French language, literature, and history. The army apparently provided this opportunity since lack of shipping facilities was delaying troop demobilization. Shuster wrote his parents from the university in April 1919:

> So far as the language is concerned, I'm convinced that when our time is over, I'll be able to speak it well. Reading is already easy, and seeing that when I came I knew nothing whatever about it, I'm satisfied with the progress made. In all it will amount to better than four years of French at an American university. We have a debating society now and it promises well for the future. Perhaps we'll even have debates with other universities. Of course this is like bringing old times to my door. Besides, I'm finding time for a considerable study of politics and for reflection on American life. In all, I believe that life is doing me a good turn in allowing these four months in France that is not torn by war.[58]

Later he recalled, a little less sanguinely: "I grew very fond of the university and some of its professors, emerging finally with a *Certificat d'Aptitude*, which somewhat rashly announced to the world that I was prepared to teach French culture."[59]

Shuster later confessed to being rather muddled and uncertain when he was finally mustered out of service in late July 1919.[60] It is probably true that there was not one clear career path he wanted to select; he had already had some experience in high school teaching, in sales, and in newspaper reporting before the war, but he seemed in no hurry to return to any of these. Yet his interests were narrowing and certainly beginning to focus. He had had good formal education at St. Lawrence College, Notre Dame, and Poitiers, and an academic environment was becoming more attractive. He had enjoyed writing in college and the acceptance of his articles by *The Catholic World* had increased his confidence that he might have success as a writer. His primary scholarly interest seemed now to be in culture and literature, English and American literature principally but also the literature of Germany and France. It was not surprising, then, that when Notre Dame invited him in the fall of 1919 to join its English faculty, Shuster did not hesitate to accept.

2

TEACHER AND HUMANIST
1919–1924

The Notre Dame to which George Shuster returned in the fall of 1919 was in a period of major transition. The university president for the past fourteen years had been Father John W. Cavanaugh, C.S.C., excellent in public relations and a nationally recognized orator. Cavanaugh's personal prestige and popularity added fame to the school he directed.[1] One writer has said of him:

> He was a man of many gifts: brilliant of mind, witty, a fine writer with exceptionally broad background through wide reading, charming and genteel. He was a big man, and his pose and dignity of bearing can justly be described as majestic. No one who saw him sweep onto a platform or into a room, or who listened to one of his sermons or talks, could ever forget him. Being what he was, Father Cavanaugh attracted to himself the great in all walks of life.[2]

But that same author has described him also as "studious but not scholarly," and the characterization is accurate.[3] The university's prestige continued to expand under his presidency, but its academic growth was not striking. He built an impressive and much-needed library and a new chemistry building, which more than tripled the existing facilities, and he inaugurated a summer session in 1918, a major step toward full graduate education at Notre Dame. But in other ways Notre Dame remained much the same. Until the great influx of college students at the close of World War I, elementary and high school students still numbered close to fifty percent of the enrollment. Although the university was divided into departments and colleges, deans and chairmen were not appointed, and all academic administration remained in the hands of the president and director of studies. Father Cavanaugh attracted numerous distinguished lecturers to the campus—William Jennings Bryan, Vice President Charles Fairbanks, Father John Talbot Smith, Cecil Chesterton, Monsignor Robert Hugh Benson, and James J. Walsh among them— but Father Julius Nieuwland, C.S.C., may have been the only internationally recognized scholar to join the faculty permanently. The Notre Dame of Father Cavanaugh was a good school, its academic reputation was high among Catholic institutions, and its religious training was sound, but it still resembled a preparatory boarding school more than the research university of today. All this was to change, however, with the appointment of Father James Burns, C.S.C., as president in 1919.

Father Burns had been born in nearby Michigan City, Indiana, in 1867 and had enrolled in Notre Dame's Manual Labor School at the age of thirteen. Having learned the trade of printing in four years he entered the regular college program and graduated in 1888. He then entered the Congregation of Holy Cross as a seminarian, completed his studies in theology, and was ordained a priest in 1893. That same year he was assigned to teach chemistry at Notre Dame, and he continued in this assignment until 1900. At that time the Congregation opened a House of Studies in Theology in Washington, just off the campus of the Catholic University of America, and Burns was transferred there as religious superior. He remained in Washington for nineteen years, teaching and serving as chief administrator, earning a doctorate in education in 1907, and publishing several works on the history of Catholic education: *The Catholic School System in the United States* in 1908, *Growth and Development of the Catholic School System in the United States* in 1912, and *Catholic Education: A Study of Conditions* in 1917. He was also very active in the work of the Catholic Educational Association, championing especially the Catholic central high school movement and the separation of preparatory high schools from Catholic colleges.[4]

By 1919 Father Burns was one of the country's best-known Catholic educators, but this was probably not the principal reason for his selection that summer as Notre Dame's president. The Congregation of Holy Cross, of which Father Burns was a member, was composed of two branches or societies: a society of priests engaged in parish work, the preaching of retreats and home missions, foreign missions, and higher education; and a society of religious brothers, engaged in higher education and foreign mission work also, but especially in teaching and administration in secondary education. At that time religious superiors and principal administrators of the Congregation's various institutions were elected by provincial and general chapters, gatherings of superiors and elected delegates every three or six years. There was a movement afoot in the second decade of the century, championed by several priests at Notre Dame, to revise the Congregation's statutes so that only priests could vote in the selection of superiors in houses and institutions of priests, and only brothers in selecting superiors in institutions of brothers. The superior general at that time, and numerous other priests and brothers, saw this as a threat to the unity and cohesion of the community and opposed it strongly. But the opposition had even planned to appeal to Rome if the Congregation would not consider this recommendation, and a recommendation also to bring greater democracy into the selection of chapter delegates.[5] Father Burns was respected by persons on both sides of the controversy because, from his position in Washington, he had been removed from the more extreme displays of partisanship. Consequently, when a new president at Notre Dame was called for in 1919, the chapter delegates selected him as the candidate best qualified not only to lead this institution of higher education into the postwar decade, but also to restore peace and harmony to the university and the Congregation.[6]

The three years of Father Burns's presidency, 1919-22, were George Shuster's first three years on the Notre Dame faculty and a period of major change. One significant change, not surprising for a leader of the Catholic central high school movement, was the almost immediate phasing out of the preparatory department on campus.[7] The first two years of high school were eliminated in 1920, the junior year in 1921, and the senior year in 1922. The motive for this decision was twofold: first, if Notre Dame was to become an institution of higher learning on a par with other American institutions it had to concentrate on collegiate and even graduate programs rather than on high school education; and second, with the increase in college applicants at the close of World War I, some might have to be turned away for lack of facilities and Burns hesitated to restrict the collegiate programs. Although the

Manual Labor School and the elementary school continued for a few more years, Notre Dame from this time on was primarily a college.

There was much opposition to the closing of the prep school, in part because the income from it helped cover the expenses of the collegiate programs, but Father Burns had an answer for that also. Even before he had assumed the presidency, he had been in contact with the Carnegie Foundation and the General Education Board, a Rockefeller institution, and he pursued these contacts more earnestly during the 1919–20 academic year. In early 1921 the General Education Board awarded Notre Dame a grant of $250,000 for endowment, provided the university could raise $750,000 on its own by June 30, 1922. A few months later the Carnegie Foundation awarded the university $75,000 as a first step toward the $750,000. Father Burns spent much of his third year as president on this fund drive, and at the June Commencement of 1922 he was able to announce that the million dollar endowment campaign had been successful. Actually, Father Burns had envisioned a second million dollar campaign for new buildings on campus to follow immediately upon the first, but this campaign was not successful. The failure was not critical, however, because, in part, annual income from the athletic program, thanks to Knute Rockne and nationally famous teams like that of the "Four Horsemen" in 1924, increased from less than $700 in 1919–20 to close to $200,000 five years later. Thus, despite the termination of the preparatory program, the university's finances remained secure.[8]

A third major innovation under Father Burns, this one during his first months as president, was the reorganization and decentralization of the university's academic administration. Throughout Father Cavanaugh's presidency, academic decisions were centralized in the hands of the president and the director of studies. One historian has described the role of Father Cavanaugh's director of studies, Father Matthew Schumacher, C.S.C., thus:

> He assigned the students to their classes and also assigned the teachers. He chose the subjects to be taught and supervised the manner of their being taught. Although the University catalogue spoke of colleges and departments, there were neither deans nor

heads of departments. When the commercial studies were raised to collegiate level in 1914, Father Schumacher made the change. When the Medical School was begun in 1917 and closed the same year, it was Father Schumacher with the President who opened and closed it.[9]

Father Burns immediately combined the six nominal colleges into four: Arts and Letters, Science, Engineering, and Law. Engineering absorbed the College of Architecture and Arts and Letters absorbed the College of Music and the School of Library Science. He appointed a dean over each college and a department head over each academic department, and charged both deans and department heads with responsibility for high academic standards. He established an Academic Senate or University Council, made up of both ex officio and elected members, to decide matters of policy, always subject to the president's approval. During its first year, this council established university policy concerning admission requirements and class absences, revised the course of study in the College of Law, and reestablished the Committee on Graduate Studies to oversee the granting of graduate degrees.[10]

Father Burns inaugurated changes in other areas during his presidency also. He established a Board of Lay Trustees to supervise the university's growing endowment, he increased the number of laymen on the faculty from thirty-four to sixty, he established a Student Activities Committee (of students) to supervise campus social life, he added religion to the list of required courses in the undergraduate curriculum, and he approved the requirement of at least one year of liberal arts training before admission into the College of Law.[11] Father Burns was the oldest president ever appointed at Notre Dame (fifty-one) and his term was the shortest, but it still deserves the title one scholar has given it, "The Burns Revolution," a revolution with which young George Shuster seemed very much in sympathy.[12]

Shuster had been mustered out of the army on the last day of July 1919 with his *Certificat d'Aptitude* from the University of Poitiers. Within two months he had received a letter from Father Charles O'Donnell, C.S.C., of Notre Dame's English department, inviting him to join the faculty.[13] There was a sudden increase in student enrollment after World War I, and perhaps some faculty positions were lost in the reassignment of priests in the 1919 provincial chapter, and the English department needed assistance. As a student, Shuster had known Father O'Donnell only slightly, had spoken with him on occasion about poetry, but the articles he published in *The Catholic World* in 1917 probably brought him more clearly to the priest's attention. In fact, writing to another Catholic author in 1917, Dr. Thomas Walsh of New York, O'Donnell had asked: "Who is this Shuster that's got you looking at the turrets of Catholic poetry, and Tom Daly sitting on the doorstep?"[14] Shuster accepted O'Donnell's invitation and returned to his alma mater immediately. He was given a room on an upper floor of Sorin Hall, his old student residence, with a few other "bachelor dons," men who lived on campus and gave a special character to university life. He also joined a faculty that he knew fairly well from his student days and from his work as a student editor of *The Scholastic* magazine.

Shuster taught the normal undergraduate classes and was remembered as a very successful teacher. He was well read and could clarify his points with illustrations and examples from a variety of sources, even French and German literature when appropriate. He had a gentle and attractive classroom manner that encouraged student participation and the expression of personal opinions. He illustrated his lectures on the blackboard with male and female stick people that students remembered years later. He required serious work of his students and was not a particularly easy grader. He later recalled a session he had with an Olympic-caliber track man, encouraging him to select a theme he was confident he knew very well. "I suggested," Shuster recalled, "that one such topic might be how to win the 100 metre dash." Shuster continued: "He sat thinking and biting a pencil during ten minutes or so and then handed me a sheet of paper on which he had written, 'The way to win the hundred metre dash is to git there before the other feller does.'" The story did not end happily. "The admirable succinctness of that sentence," Shuster noted, "did not suffice even then to keep him in good academic standing."[15]

In addition to basic English courses Shuster also began to specialize. He continued his interest in American authors—he had published articles on Mark Twain and the American novel

earlier—and he offered as a senior-level course "American Literature." During the Summer Sessions he also taught graduate courses
in "Contemporary Literature" and "Foreign Influences on Modern English Literature." But the course he liked best, the course
which became a regular in the university's catalogue, and the
course for which he wrote his first major book, was "The Catholic
Spirit in Modern English Literature," the same title he gave his
book, which was published by Macmillan in 1922.[16]

The course apparently followed the textbook closely and was
based on Shuster's conviction that religion was basic to an appreciation of English culture and achievement.[17] "No other constructive force that has come into English literature during the
nineteenth century," he stated early, "is nearly so important as the
Catholic spirit. . . . What cannot be dispensed with is a sense of
fellowship with the religious force which built up Europe from the
ruins of Rome, which maintained certain principles of human liberty and dependence on God, and which taught the Truth without which Beauty is either a corpse or an evil spirit."[18] The book
(and the course) began with a brief discussion of Kenelm Digby
and his exaltation of the Christian culture of the Middle Ages,
and then proceeded to a detailed study of Cardinal Newman's
theological and literary contributions to nineteenth-century
British culture. Turning to poetry, Shuster noted religious themes
in Coventry Patmore, Gerard Manley Hopkins, Aubrey de Vere,
and especially in Francis Thompson, whom he called "the
Master." He discussed the search for beauty in the works of John
Ruskin and Walter Pater, and he treated historians John Lingard
and Alban Butler under the title "Chroniclers of Christendom."
Approaching contemporary times, he examined popular Catholic
novelists Robert Hugh Benson and Francis Marion Crawford; he
considered the brilliant G. K. Chesterton as both poet and journalist, and Hilaire Belloc as historian, poet, and essayist. The
textbook closed with a survey of Catholic literature in Ireland and
America and with a provocative essay on the relation of religion to
art. Shuster was optimistic over the influence of Catholicism in
the postwar world. Not only was religion the wellspring out of
which great art developed but the principles of a supra-nationalis-
tic Catholicism might also provide the foundation for lasting
world peace.[19]

The theme of the book, and of his class, was the impact of Catholicism on English literature, but Shuster insisted throughout that art and literature were to be judged on their own merits and not to be extolled simply because they were Catholic. He admired Kenelm Digby for his recapturing of the glories of medieval Christendom but he admitted that Digby's prose was often overburdened with illustrations and his verse "impossibly tedious." He acknowledged that Cardinal Manning was no great intellectual and that Cardinal Wiseman's popular *Fabiola* exhibited a "somewhat slipshod construction and the tinge of sentimentalism that spoils its art." Chesterton was a "genius," a master of paradox and figurative language, but his convoluted structures often obscured his meaning, and his adherence to favorite symbols led him to unconvincing conclusions. For Shuster, the critic must above all be honest. "Readers must learn to read with discrimination, not to praise a book merely because it is Catholic and also not to heed the silence of hostile criticism and ignore a book because it believes in the soul."[20] Loyal Catholic though he was, Shuster was never hesitant to criticize his co-religionists when that was required to be "at heart on the side of truth."

The book confirmed also that of all modern English authors, Cardinal Newman was clearly Shuster's favorite. He saw Newman as belonging primarily to religion, and to literature only after that. Newman was wrestling with the basic modern problem of the reasonableness of religious belief, of reconciling faith to the intellect's pursuit of compelling evidence, and Shuster saw his solution as convincing. "John Henry Newman," he stated, "triumphing over modern thought by the victory gained within himself, has seemed to many a symbol of the intellectual development through which religiously unsettled moderns may have to pass. He wished to show," Shuster continued, "that, when all the hypotheses of skeptical science had been granted, there remained ample reason for a complete confidence in the truth of revealed religion."[21]

Newman was not primarily a speculative theologian, wrestling with theological abstractions, but a pastor and minister attempting to make Christian belief more acceptable and attractive. His works were often apologetical, even polemical, and his literary style was adjusted to his particular purpose, and Shuster was fascinated by literary style: "He is now restrained, keeping his natural impetuosity sternly in rein, then vigorous in pressing the attack, and finally exuberant, eloquent, copious in the triumphant din of the victory march."[22] Shuster suggested that Newman's sermons might reveal him best, from the somewhat hesitant, groping style of the Oxford years to the more confident, secure preaching of his later life. There was less of the seer and the apostle in the historical works, and the style of these was consequently more scholarly and less literary and artistic. The *Grammar of Assent* and *Apologia pro Vita Sua* were also self-revealing and the style in them probably his best, his very self poured out and set to print. He could be a master of subtlety when this seemed most effective, as in the description of a gentleman in the *Idea of a University*. "Lead, Kindly Light" contained "very simple expressions of simple moods," but there was mature drama in "The Dream of Gerontius." "Newman's art is, then," Shuster concluded, "a large and varied gift which he lent unstintingly to the demands of an apostolic life." A genuine artist, he adapted his style to his purpose, to Truth, and this gave his work a special harmony, a consummate beauty.[23]

For Shuster, of course, religion was much more than a subject to be investigated by literature—it was a relationship to God to be lived. His letters reveal him turning instinctively to prayer in times of family illness, feeling closer to distant loved ones if they were united in prayer, and relying on God in time of need. "I have absolute faith that the fingers of God lead the ways of every one of us," he wrote in 1922. "I am so sure of the arms of Our Lady and their power," he wrote the following spring, "that if I felt you had given yourself over utterly to them, no harm could come to you, no unhappiness, no misfortune." The following summer he wrote: "Every night. . . I go to benediction. You know how well I love the music of those Latin ballads, and even more the whispers that silently bind two worlds."[24]

As one deeply and personally committed to both scholarship and religion, Shuster was especially admired by the sisters he taught in summer school. They corresponded throughout the year, asked his advice in their own teaching assignments, and were sincerely grateful for the classes he taught. Shuster realized that many were convinced that someday he would enter the priesthood. When one sister read the manuscript draft of a novel on which he was working, a novel which was never published, she urged him to cut several passages: "You naturally do not realize that to practically all your Sister-students you are a sort of cross between Aloysius and Aquinas, a Sir Galahad in a professor's gown. Laugh if you want to—it's true. Your getting married is going to be a fearful shock, because they all think you will eventually be a priest." Shuster could understandably become a little impatient at times. "I'm so sick unto death of admiration," he wrote in 1922, "that I'm thinking of getting drunk and hitting this campus about noon-time. But then, I suppose, the reverend Sisters would call it 'nerves' and attribute it to overwork."[25]

Teaching and writing were not all of Shuster's activities during these five years on the faculty. He continued his own formal education, taking additional classes in 1919–20 and receiving a Master of Arts degree from Notre Dame that summer. The subject of his dissertation was the recent French author and convert, "Joris Carl Huysmans: Egoist and Mystic," showing, after his wartime experiences in France and Germany, his growing interest in comparative literature. A few years later he offered a course on "Foreign Influences on Modern English Literature." He served for a time as editor-in-chief of *The Scholastic*, the campus weekly he contributed to as a student, and he received an additional dollar a day in salary for coaching one of the debate teams. He was also appointed chairman of the English department at a salary of three thousand dollars a year, assisting in faculty hiring and helping to oversee academic discipline. As he recalled in an interview years later:

> There was one priest who didn't show up for classes. So Father Burns called me in and said you had better get ahold of Father So-and-So and tell him he had to go to class. So taking my courage in my hands, I went over to call on him. He told me to mind my own business, that it wasn't any affair of mine whether he went to class or not. "Well," I said, "Father, in that case all I'll have to do is go back to Father Burns and tell him what you said." So he turned purple, red and indigo, and said he would meet the class.[26]

He was appointed to the Faculty Board of Athletics and on one occasion found himself called to Indianapolis. "Today, to my great astonishment," he wrote in late 1923, "I'm down here attending an athletic conference of Indiana Colleges. Rockne had to leave for New York, and so selected the famous athlete, gold champion, and poker shark, G.N.S., to take his place. Of course, I don't know what it's all about at all and so am having a lovely party just 'setting' as folks say."[27] Even the most famous of football coaches was not immune from criticism from junior members of the English faculty. Noting a loss to Nebraska that fall, Shuster wrote: "I think it was just an off-day, because the boys have been traveling a lot and playing too hard; but also I think there was a bit of bad coaching involved. Rockne must have lost track of his head for a while."[28]

Perhaps his most important work outside the classroom during these years was the time he spent assisting Father Daniel Hudson, C.S.C., in editing the *Ave Maria* magazine. The *Ave*, as it was affectionately called, was a weekly news and literary journal founded by Father Sorin in the 1860s, and Shuster joined the staff for a time to replace one of the priests who had fallen ill. He wrote occasional articles, edited manuscripts, evaluated poetry, excerpted news items from European journals, and profited immensely from working in the same room, often day after day, with this remarkable priest. "It is easy to misuse the term, 'great man,'" Shuster wrote later. "But I have met no one who possessed either his keenness of mind or his regal classicism of action. Certainly there have been few in American Catholic life to compare with him." "Thus I could truly feel that I had been fortunate, and be grateful," he wrote elsewhere. "And since gratitude imposes an obligation, I could not well avoid trying to give to others some impression of what riches had come to me. That is the reason why I joined the staff of the *Commonweal*." He paid Hudson a beautiful tribute at the time of his death in 1934: "Nothing I shall ever learn or say or do will be more than a supplement to his teaching. There is a hierarchy of values. His was a life which scaled that ladder to the top, going carefully, wisely, humbly and beautifully."[29]

Through the classes he taught, his research for *The Catholic Spirit in Modern English Literature,* his work for the *Ave Maria,* and his own graduate studies, Shuster was beginning to develop his own brand of Christian Humanism. There was a revival of Humanism in the early twentieth century—the writings of Irving

Babbitt and Dr. Paul Elmer More in America and of Catholics G. K. Chesterton, Martin D'Arcy, S.J., Christopher Dawson, and Jacques Maritain in Europe. Like other Humanists, Shuster saw humankind as clearly the center and measure of the universe; he was interested in the whole range of human experience—art, poetry, politics, science, diplomacy—and he was interested primarily in literature because literature above all attempted to express creative insights into this human condition. Like most Humanists, Shuster also saw something limitless and unfathomable about this human condition, with no clear boundaries to what could be attained through intellectual potential, inventiveness, progress in science, and human creativity. This limitless potential was basic for Shuster because he saw all men and women as created in the image and likeness of God and destined for an eternity in heaven, and he was thus doubly convinced of their unique dignity and central position in the universe and their unbounded potential to grow spiritually toward God.[30]

Shuster had read Babbitt and More and Chesterton and Maritain, but his Christian Humanism was influenced even more by other, generally more classical, authors. Next to the Bible, the first of these was probably Saint Augustine. An even earlier influence may have been Plato, since Shuster had an excellent classical education at both St. Lawrence College and Notre Dame, he read Greek well, and he cited Plato frequently in his writings. Yet Shuster was too deeply Christian to embrace Platonism alone. He admired much in Plato, especially his insights into art, politics, ethics, government, and the goals of human life, and he was attracted to the creative literary style of the *Dialogues*, but much of Shuster's Platonism was also filtered through and Christianized by later writers, especially Saint Augustine.[31] Shuster's attraction for Saint Augustine was understandable: Augustine was steeped in Neo-Platonic and Roman culture, his influence on German philosophy and theology was pronounced, and he was a master literary stylist. Shuster may have been especially influenced by Augustine's view of the human person. He accepted the human person as is, motivated by both reason and grace, and he was interested in the whole person—ancestry, education, environment, companions, culture, religion—all are in his masterpiece, *The Confessions.*[32]

If there was one area of Augustine's thinking before which Shuster may have balked, it was perhaps his pessimistic view of human nature, but a corrective for this pessimism could be found in the writings of Saint Thomas. The early decades of the twentieth century were an era of Thomistic revival. In his encyclical letter of 1879, *Aeterni Patris*, Pope Leo XIII had asked the world's bishops to "restore the golden wisdom of Thomas and to spread it far and wide for the defense and beauty of the Catholic faith," and in 1890 the same pontiff named Saint Thomas patron of all Catholic schools.[33] But Shuster always remained more Augustinian than Thomist, perhaps because the syllogistic intellectualism of Saint Thomas seemed to overlook much of the romance and poetry in humanity, and perhaps also because the certitude of the Thomistic system seemed somewhat out of step with so much mystery in the universe. But Shuster could not help but be influenced by the Thomistic revival. The philosophy of Saint Thomas was permeating Catholic higher education, much of Catholic theology was expressed in Thomistic terms, and Shuster was reading more and more of European Catholic authors deeply influenced by Saint Thomas.

For Saint Thomas and the Thomistic tradition, human nature was not evil but created by God and embraced by Christ in the Incarnation, and thus had to be good. For Saint Thomas, there was no contradiction between reason and faith, between the natural and the supernatural. Nature was good because it came from the hand of God, and grace built upon it, elevating each human person to a supernatural plane.[34] Shuster could certainly accept such an optimistic view of human nature.

It is not surprising that one of the authors that Shuster admired most was Johann Wolfgang Goethe, "the ultimate spokesman of humanism" Shuster later called him.[35] The fact that he was German, classically educated, a truly Renaissance man with interests in poetry, politics, art, and diplomacy, and even skeptical and irreverent, endeared him to Shuster all the more.

Goethe's humanism was best epitomized in *Faust*. Faust was a man of universal interests and, having gone through most legitimate ways of knowing, seemed willing to try illegitimate ones. In fact, his thirst for knowledge is the context of his pact with Mephistopheles. As in the *Book of Job*, Mephistopheles has wagered that

Faust, good and God-fearing man that he is, can be seduced into losing his eternal salvation, in this case by finding absorbing satisfaction and fulfillment here on earth. Faust is ultimately saved because, in fact, he never is satisfied; he remains constantly searching. He is not content with any of the splendors he has seen or experienced, and he thus wins his wager with Mephistopheles. As the angels, bearing Faust's soul to heaven, sing triumphantly:

> The soul that still has strength to strive,
> We have the strength to free.[36]

The American writer who exerted the most influence on Shuster was probably Ralph Waldo Emerson. America was young in the early nineteenth century, and it seemed to have infinite potential—a highly revered Constitution, a democratic government, bountiful natural resources, an expanding population, phenomenal economic growth, and geographical isolation from Old World difficulties. Emerson captured American confidence and optimism well. He urged his fellow citizens to take advantage of these unique opportunities, to be truly self-reliant, to strive and accomplish goals no other nation had yet achieved. Emerson also saw a Transcendent power or Oversoul in touch with every human being, giving each one a special nobility, worth, and potential. Emerson was opposed to religious dogmas because he saw them as restrictions on freedom, but Shuster saw Divine Revelation as clarifying the uniqueness that a human being possessed as a child of God. The confidence, optimism, and patriotism of Emerson were reflected in Shuster also, and it was not surprising that when he was searching for a motto to engrave on the wall of Hunter College, he turned to Emerson's *The Conduct of Life*.[37]

If religion was secondary in the humanism of Goethe and Emerson, it was central for John Henry Newman. "There is no other modern author who speaks so much truth about things that are worthwhile," Shuster wrote in 1925. "There is none more helpful in the big job of living nobly and happily."[38] And few influenced Shuster more. In *The Catholic Spirit in Modern English Literature*, he devoted three chapters to Newman—no other author received more than one—and three years later he edited a collection of Newman's writings. He later called *The Idea of a University* "the finest discussion of college education to be found anywhere in English," and the *Apologia pro Vita Sua* "a classic that ranks with the highest spiritual literature in all languages."[39]

Shuster was strongly influenced by Newman's educational theory.[40] The purpose of education, for Newman, was the training and perfection of the intellect, and the education which aimed precisely at the perfection of the intellect was a liberal or universal education, an education in literature, history, mathematics, the physical sciences, philosophy, and theology. For Newman, and for Shuster, a liberal education was one which made a person truly liberated or free—free *from* ignorance and bias and error, and free *for* the pursuit and attainment of humankind's highest and final goal, eternal happiness with God. Newman had no difficulty reconciling science and human knowledge with faith and revelation since all truth was simply a manifestation of God and God's Providence—and thus could not be self-contradictory. The well-trained intellect could see and appreciate God more clearly in God's Providence, and could see and appreciate more clearly also humankind's eternal destiny and the means to attain it. "Newman's books," Shuster wrote, "are, when you view them as a whole, just one long and detailed account of his voyages into the Kingdom of Heaven."[41] And on this voyage, he was a model and guide for others: "Newman has answered more questions, solved a larger number of difficulties, kindled anew in a greater throng of hearts, the glory and peace of faith, than any other modern man."[42]

The most recent influence on Shuster's Humanism was probably Baron Friedrich von Huegel, an English lay theologian whose writings at times were under suspicion in Rome because of their liberalism. Shuster and von Huegel were kindred spirits in many ways: both were Catholic laymen; neither was a systematic philosopher; both were more Platonist than Thomist; and each preferred to move and write in relative independence of Roman supervision.[43]

Von Huegel wrote widely on mysticism, on the personal and intuitive experience of God. "There is an opening wide and energizing of the whole human being in an aspiration and effort after the Infinite and Abiding," he wrote in "Experience and

Transcendence."[44] Such an experience of the mystical was possible even on the natural level since men and women realized that their aspirations for the infinite have not been fulfilled, and this realization implied at least in some confused way an intuition of what was missing. In *The Mystical Element of Religion*, he wrote penetratingly of the supernatural experience of Saint Catherine of Genoa and her special relationship with God.

There would always be something of the contemplative in Shuster also. He loved to rise early and be alone, enjoyed fine music, and wrote thoughtful, sensitive poetry. He closed one of his favorite books, *The Germans*, with the legend of the angel Desuper:

> Hearing one day that Desuper had never visited earth, God invited Him to make the rounds of it in His company. They went over mountains and through valleys until they came to a village down the street of which little children were running and dancing on their way from school. Then Desuper caught sight of several very old men sitting quietly in front of the houses in the sun. "What are the old men for?" he asked. "Why do they not play and laugh with the children?" Our Lord was puzzled, and bade the angel put his query to the old men. "We are here because people would otherwise forget to sit in the sun."[45]

Simply sitting in the sun, thinking and enjoying, was part of Shuster's Humanism also.

Shuster's five years on the Notre Dame faculty not only enabled him to shape his Christian Humanism but also permitted him to form or renew many deep and lasting friendships. He renewed his great respect for Fathers Carrico and Cavanaugh, came to appreciate Father Burns immensely, and admired the work of several of the Sisters at Saint Mary's College whom he got to know well. Of Notre Dame's lay faculty, Paul Fenlon became his closest friend, and of his students, Vincent Engels and Francis Wallace became well-respected writers and remained in contact with him for long years after. The most pleasant and lasting of his friendships, however, was that of a pert, young summer school student in 1920, Doris Parks Cunningham of Saint Mary's, the woman who would become his wife for fifty-two years.

Doris had been born in Washington, in southern Indiana, in 1900, and despite early tragedy had lived a very happy childhood. Her mother died when Doris was born, and her father a year and a half later, and Doris was raised by aunts and uncles, chiefly on her father's side. Her mother and father had actually been second cousins, many of the relatives on both sides had large families, and Doris grew up surrounded by the love and companionship of numerous cousins her own age. She lived for a time on a farm outside Montgomery, Indiana, and then nearby in Loogootee. The families she lived with were always comfortably well off, she never lacked necessities as she was growing, and years later she recalled the excellent meals of her childhood.[46]

Doris began school in the Montgomery public school system but, because she had already been taught to read and write and count at home, she was immediately placed in the second grade. Toward the end of the fourth grade she was placed with an aunt and uncle in Loogootee again, and she entered Saint John's Catholic School there, taught by the Sisters of Providence. That school, however, did not have a fifth grade, probably for lack of a sufficient number of pupils, and Doris was thus promoted to the sixth, skipping the fifth grade entirely. She admitted that at times she was a difficult child—she had a strong will, a mind of her own, and she did not easily accept authority outside the loving guidance she found at home—but she was also very bright. She had wide interests, loved to spend her free time reading, and did well in her classes, despite the fact that she skipped both the first and fifth grades.

For high school Doris was enrolled at Immaculate Conception Academy at Oldenburg, Indiana, a girls' boarding school taught by the Sisters of Saint Francis, mostly from Germany. The school was situated on a beautiful estate, with rolling hills, large trees, and pleasant expanses for walks. More important, the education was excellent. Some girls would not continue on to college, and thus several courses did prepare the student for marriage, family, and perhaps an immediate job, but there was a solid college preparatory curriculum also. Doris later lamented the fact that she did not learn German at that time since she was to spend much time in Germany in her later life (she chose Spanish instead), but she apparently took good advantage of the other opportunities offered. She enjoyed English and history especially, continued her outside reading—at least a book a week—and also took individual voice lessons during her final two years.

Discipline remained at least a minor problem. Student life was fully regulated at the academy—she recalled later that on formal weekend walks, one sister walked at the front of the line, one toward the center, and another at the rear—and Doris found it all too constricting. She did well in what she liked or thought reasonable, but had little use for what she thought unjustified or simply unpleasant. She enjoyed geometry and trigonometry, but cared little for algebra. She discovered that the sister who taught algebra would send her out of the room if she misbehaved in class, and this is what she wanted—she could then spend the period reading one of her library books in the school parlor! Of course, she learned little algebra and the sister failed her. When the sister wrote Doris's aunt that the young girl seemed incorrigible, her aunt responded: "I told you she was difficult when I brought her to the school and you said you could control her. Now control her!"[47]

On graduation from high school her preference was to enter Radcliffe, but her Uncle Frank insisted on a Catholic college. Her family probably preferred St. Mary's of the Woods in Terre Haute, Indiana, because four of her cousins were already enrolled there, but that is probably the reason the free-spirited Doris decided to go elsewhere. She finally decided on Saint Mary's College, just north of South Bend. She had never visited or seen it, but it was a good school, was close to Notre Dame, and her guardian readily approved.[48]

Saint Mary's College, or Academy as it was then called, had been founded by the Marianite Sisters of the Holy Cross in 1844 and was eventually transferred to a large expanse of property adjacent to the University of Notre Dame. To the west flowed the St. Joseph River, whose shift in course about two miles to the south gave South Bend its name, and on the east the main highway between South Bend and Niles, Michigan, a little to the north, separated the college from Notre Dame. The campus was composed of several buildings for the sisters—the convent, church, a small Chapel of Loretto (where Doris was eventually to be married), and a presbytery for chaplains—and even more for the college—a collegiate hall, the academy building, an infirmary, gymnasium, music building, and others. The college had been chartered to educate women in the arts and sciences and it remained true to its liberal arts goal. By the turn of the century the college was especially proud of its programs in art and in music, and it profited also from the proximity of the library and other resources of the University of Notre Dame. As at Notre Dame, the majority of students were probably pre-college, but the collegiate education was good, and becoming increasingly better.[49]

Doris entered Saint Mary's College in the fall of 1918, while the war was still raging in Europe. She majored in English and history, her two favorite subjects, and since her preparation at Oldenburg was truly superior, she still had much time to pursue her own reading. One of her English teachers, Sister Eleanore Brosnahan, C.S.C., became one of her dearest friends and confidants, but Doris always lamented the fact that Sister Madeleva Wolff, C.S.C., later Saint Mary's outstanding poet and long-time president, was away from campus three of her four years. Doris did very well at Saint Mary's: her grades were consistently high, she continued with her voice lessons at both Saint Mary's and Notre Dame, she contributed occasional articles and poetry to the college publication, *St. Mary's Chimes,* and her work eventually earned her a gold medal.[50]

Doris did so well, in fact, that she decided to accelerate her program and apply to graduate after only three years of class, as George Shuster had done at Notre Dame a few years before. In order to do this, she would need some summer credits, and she thus applied to and was accepted in the summer program at Notre Dame in 1920, the summer after her sophomore year. Since English was her major interest, she enrolled in a course on the English novel taught by young George Shuster. She found him a fascinating teacher, enthusiastic and dynamic, and excellent even in his emphasis on grammar and syntax. Doris remembered that he once asked in class if anyone had ever read any non-English novels. Many in the class were graduate students, but Doris was the only one to raise her hand. When called on, she began by saying she had read some of Dostoyevsky—*The Idiot, The Brothers Karamazov,* and so on. "What did you think of them," Shuster asked. "I thought they were terrific," she answered. "The best things I had ever read." "It was the first time he looked at me seriously," she later recalled. "Up to that time I think he thought I was just a little girl."[51]

Doris took her junior year off, 1920–21, and taught for a year at St. Joseph's Academy, a "high class boarding school for young ladies and girls" in Tipton, Indiana. She had taken some education courses at Saint Mary's, passed the state teachers' exam, and was thus licensed to teach. She taught both American and European history, English, and even a class in physical geography. The school was scheduled for a state visitation and the teacher of physical geography did not have a license, so Doris was transferred to that class also, by her own admission staying only one or two pages ahead of the students. She was also happy to learn that, if the Tipton Public Library did not have a book she was seeking, it would borrow it for her from Indianapolis, a privilege of which she made frequent use.[52]

During this year away, her contacts with Shuster continued, both professionally and socially. At the close of summer school she had written him a note to thank him for the excellent class, and he had acknowledged it in a letter to Tipton. He admitted that he had not at first believed she would carry out her plan to teach and he signed that first letter "Mister Mis-taken."[53] In order to accumulate sufficient credits to graduate early, she also arranged to take a directed readings course by correspondence with Shuster during that year away. She submitted papers to him regularly and his comments were generally positive, although not uncritical. "By the way, that paper wasn't bad at all," he wrote in October, "being a rather correct interpretation of a book which it is said only Irishmen can comprehend." His humor was evident three months later: "Now on the matter of papers, I must confess that yours weren't really so bad excepting that they bore certain signs of haste—they reminded me in fact of Marie Antoinette writing a sonnet on her way to execution." But the letters were not all business. Doris made plans for return visits to Saint Mary's, with visits with George arranged also. In one letter she playfully predicted the kind of woman she thought George would eventually marry, and with mock-seriousness Shuster warned her not to fall in love: "'Tis a dangerous business, they say, and apt to lead to sonnets and other public misdemeanors."[54]

Doris returned to South Bend in the summer of 1921, enrolled in Shuster's summer class once again, and then began her final year at Saint Mary's—but her relationship with Shuster was suddenly broken. The reason for the break-up is not entirely clear. Perhaps Shuster felt that a student-faculty courtship was inappropriate, especially during an academic year, and he may have left the question open whether it could resume after her graduation. Maybe Doris's freedom-loving ways and willingness to try the unusual—"cavortings" and "Bohemian" lifestyle, Shuster had apparently called them—began to seem less compatible with the scholarly and literary career he was beginning to envision for himself.[55] He later admitted also that some at Saint Mary's had raised questions whether she would be a suitable partner for him. But whatever the reasons, it is clear that it was Shuster who broke the relationship, and the break was not pleasant. He apparently described some of her actions as "obvious and bizarre," said she lacked "poise, appreciation of experience, and the finesse of tact," and noted that it "is easy to see at a glance that you have been at boarding-school when you should have been at home." "Why don't you find a balanced, experienced woman of the world to confide in utterly," he added. He admitted that his action was "ruthless" and "cruelly slapping your face." Doris was hurt and fought back. "Your letter was rather amusing than otherwise," she wrote. "Far be it from me to encroach upon your time. I know you are busy. Please forgive my feminine garrulity and the use of the typewriter, but both are handy." Months later she confided, "I shall not forget this past year very soon; I'll forgive but the sting is still there."[56] Indeed it was. The subject came up frequently during the rest of their courtship, always to George's embarrassment.

Then, shortly before Doris's graduation, just as suddenly as George had broken off their relationship a year before, he walked over to Saint Mary's and asked to restore it. He was uncertain what his reception would be and made a novena of prayers beforehand. Doris was taken by surprise and was thoroughly confused, but she also knew she still loved him and took him back, with some hesitation. She began a letter to him that summer "My dear George," but soon admitted her dilemma:

> Do you know that half the time I do not know what you mean?. . . I absolutely refuse to take anything at all concerned with you on my own interpretation, and I take absolutely nothing for granted. I do not understand you anyway, I think. I have told you I do not. And I never can understand your attitude towards me the past year.[57]

Despite her confusion, her love was real: "You say you are changeable, does that mean in your affections? I should think when you get these spells of despondency you would feel the need of me, if you care for me at all. I may not be worth a whole lot but at least I love you." George was more than relieved. "No gift that has come into my life," he confided later, "can ever quite be like the love you gave me the night of our reconciliation. It will always be the most beautiful moment in your life, dear, and the most humble one in mine."[58]

Doris spent that summer with relatives and friends in Indiana and Ohio; Shuster was at home in Wisconsin. By fall Doris's "Bohemian" tendencies had reasserted themselves. She decided to go to California to live, and there she remained for the next two years, working as a stenographer and legal secretary. She and George corresponded regularly and, although George occasionally reverted to his professorial status and lectured her on a few of her activities, they were clearly very much in love. "I'm sure you know that I love you," he wrote a few months after her departure. "I have ever since the night we came from Mishawaka and your tenderness was all abloom. There has never been a day since then when I haven't put my soul into the thought of you; and tonight I should like to take you in my arms and kiss you, kiss you, kiss you." He had hurt her once and feared doing it again. "I love you very dearly, dear, and hope ever so many good things for the sweet, strange girl you are," he wrote. "The only thing I can't bear is the thought of you possibly unhappy. It would be hard to forgive any man for bringing that about, and most of all myself."[59]

Despite this love, however, Shuster remained for a time uncertain of marriage. "I can't answer your questions about the future yet," he admitted, "because I haven't worked the matter out for myself." For one thing, Doris thoroughly enjoyed the freedom and independence of her life in Los Angeles and Shuster wondered whether she could be happy in the lifestyle he was choosing. He pleaded with her to find a steady job, and he questioned the prudence of some of the traveling she hoped to do. This left his heart and head divided. "Just now, I can't think of marriage with you as anything but a beautiful experience," he admitted in early 1923, "but *can* I sensibly leave out of sight the whole of what others bid me beware of, the whole, too, of your previous environment and upbringing?" George was deeply religious also, and Doris was at times more skeptical. "You will, of course, always be a blithe little pagan," he wrote, "but many blithe little pagans have been sturdy Catholics." And, finally, George had fallen in love once before, and the experience had shaken his confidence, as he later confided:

> That girl was a handsome creature—that's all. Why she should have bewitched me, I can't tell, but it happened just about the time I finished school, when I was poetic enough to crown with a halo anything that appealed to me. Besides—this will sound ridiculous, but confessions often are so—I was very conscious of being homely, and the idea of a beautiful girl bowled me over by contrast. She never gave me anything except kisses; and when I was just about ready to buy a ring (which I never did) I discovered to my great disillusionment that she hadn't anything else to give, and that she wasn't particular about where she left *them*. I'm not going to expand on this any further, dear. The woman is married, and probably some one with another temperament than mine could have walked away with a smile. I couldn't, and *that* coming hand in hand with my newspaper and army experience gave me such a skeptical vision of women that my heart moved out in the middle of the stream, where fish-lines were of no avail and where boats seldom wandered.[60]

After a year of uncertainty and of wavering back and forth Shuster finally made up his mind and arranged to visit Doris in California in June 1923. His earlier doubts by this time had been alleviated, his love was clearly growing stronger, and he also knew that Doris was dating in California and he might be in danger of losing her. Doris knew clearly the purpose of his visit. "But you know, my dear," he had written earlier, "that I'm not coming across the continent for the sake of taking you to a movie."[61]

To enjoy a little privacy from the other women Doris was living with, they decided to meet in San Francisco. George arrived first and was waiting in the station for Doris when she arrived from Los Angeles. George stayed at the St. Francis Hotel but put her up at the more expensive Fairmont. On the way to dinner the first evening, George asked the taxi driver to drive through Golden State Park first, and during the drive asked him to stop and let the two of them out for a while. The driver whispered to Doris, "Is it all right, Miss?" Doris whispered back; "It's all right; he's going to ask me to marry him." Of course he did, and Doris immediately said yes.[62]

They spent only a short time in San Francisco and then went down to Los Angeles, stopping for some sightseeing at Carmel on the way. Shuster had earlier felt that they should wait a year before getting married but now changed his mind and wanted to get married earlier. It was Doris, who had earlier been impatient with George's hesitancy, who insisted on waiting the full year. After all she had been through, and after that year's break-up earlier, she wanted to be sure. She also wanted to remain in California for the year, and to this George reluctantly agreed.[63]

The year was not an easy one for George. Although he was resigned to postponing the wedding, he could not understand why she insisted on remaining in California. "Now—is it absolutely necessary for your happiness that you stay in California all this year?" he wrote within two months of his visit. "Or go somewhere in which there isn't the slightest ghost of an opportunity for me to see you?" He worried about her health—she seemed to be having difficulties with her throat during their visit—and he urged her throughout that summer to see a doctor. He was still not in favor of the traveling she had in mind and he worried about a possible accident. "If anything happened to you," he wrote that July, "well, the curtain would drop. There would be only one road for me to walk then, dear, an awfully steep and bitter one." It bothered him also that she and her housemates continued to visit the local dance halls on free evenings, dance halls for whose male clientel Shuster had nothing but scorn.[64]

Difficult and even disagreeable as that year was, Shuster usually retained his good sense of humor. He played an occasional round of golf and reported to Doris on the money he won at either bridge or poker. When she wrote that she was not really feeling well, he responded: "Of course I'm very sorry the world hasn't been treating you properly, and has settled upon your dear self a cold. I'm sure that it could be kissed away; but under the circumstances I hope it will not be." When time was too short for a regular letter, he occasionally penned hurried verse:

> This little note will let you know
> I love you dearest, still—and so;
> It's really late, and well, dear me,
> I'm just about as weak's can be.

> Yet all the same, I send this kiss
> Hoping it brings you joy and bliss.
> You are my lady, and my fate —
> But darling! Gracious it is late!
> Amen.[65]

Or he might try to mimic the style of another:

> Thyss note will shew
> I thinke of you
> My darlynge, my dere mayde:
> Don't fynde amisse
> That this my kisse
> So briefely must bee sayde.
> (A la Spencer, in a hurry)

As the year progressed, Shuster was clearly losing patience over Doris's decision to remain in California, especially because he wondered whether she was simply leaving him alone as he had left her alone during her senior year at Saint Mary's. "Well, I am willing to take my medicine, dear," he wrote that July, "if in the end you will see that during a long delay I mistrusted *myself* rather than you." A month later he wrote: "It doesn't make so much difference that we're not to be married before June, but this being engaged in the dark is h—l, pure and simple." Then he added: "Well, perhaps if I hadn't been such an awful fool and had used the time to see more of you while I had the chance, this medicine wouldn't be so upsetting." With the start of the new school year, his letters became more pleading. "But sometimes it seems that you decided so: 'He made me suffer a year, and this is tit for tat,'" he wrote in September. "That may be justice, honey (if I'm right in thinking this of you), but you are the one person on earth besides my mother from whom I expect something more than justice." His pleading continued: "But darling, think—two weeks out of the two years that should have been our courtship! You've seen other men at least three times as much—don't think now I'm trying to blame you for that. It only shows that something is out of gear." By the following spring, his gentle, even temper had departed:

> I'm sick and tired of this arrangement. It is not only tedious, unsatisfactory, worthless—it is positively out of the question any longer.

Between you and me there is no reason, only unreason—only some stupid form of test, some waiting to see what I will do. And as a matter of fact I think I have been experimented with long enough. . . .Can't you see that you're playing with our happiness? It is after all so fragile, so sweet a gift in so delicate a box. And the box is all in your hands. . . .[66]

Despite his pleading, however, Doris remained in California until early June 1924, and even then took a long way back to the Midwest. She traveled first to Portland and Seattle, visited Puget Sound, Vancouver, and Lake Louise, and then made her way east across southern Canada and northern United States to Minneapolis. The lengthy trip had not pleased her fiance at all. "It is perfectly all right to wait until the twenty-second for the ticket," he had written in early May, "but delaying our marriage for the sake of Aberdeen, South Dakota, seems to me a kind of bum joke." Eventually George and Doris met in Lancaster and Doris was introduced to George's family for the first time. The visit was brief but also successful. "The mother is immensely satisfied with you," he wrote Doris after she left, "which is a pleasure of infinite worth to me." He then added with a light touch: "According to all appearances you were very good—how strange—and very loveable—how commonplace. I'm very grateful for both."[67]

After some early discussions that fall and spring of alternative sites and dates, the wedding was scheduled for June 25 in the small Chapel of Loretto on the Saint Mary's campus. Father Leonard Carrico, C.S.C., Shuster's former teacher and more recently colleague on the English faculty, officiated, and Vincent Engels, a former student, and Alice Cunningham, Doris's cousin, were witnesses. Sister Eleanore, C.S.C., Doris's closest friend from her earlier Saint Mary's days, had made most of the arrangements, had invited Doris to stay at the college before the wedding, and she and several other sisters were in attendance. None of George's family were present, but it was not that they disapproved of the marriage in any way. One of George's sisters was married and living in the West (George had not attended her wedding either), Mrs. Schuster had been struggling with serious blood poisoning for some time and was still not in good health, and the Schuster family was simply not in the habit of leaving home and traveling. George and Doris had visited in Lancaster only a week before, and they had shared their best wishes and blessings at that time. After the ceremony the sisters provided a pleasant wedding breakfast, although some apparently could not help but wish it had been an ordination breakfast instead.[68]

Shortly after the wedding, the couple left for a honeymoon trip through Canada—Quebec, the Thousand Islands, Montreal— and then down to their permanent residence in New York. For several months they had been discussing where they might live. Chicago had been a possibility, and George was even willing to try San Diego if Doris's heart was set on the West Coast, but they eventually decided on New York. Notre Dame was an option, too, but George had returned to Notre Dame under Father Burns as president and he apparently found the administration of his successor after 1922 less attractive. He confided to Doris in late 1923:

> And so I don't mind telling you that as matters are now, I should really very much like to get away from Notre Dame. Even though I love the place and love the purpose to which it has been dedicated, I must admit that it seems impossible to expect of Notre Dame anything like what I had once hoped for from it. We have an administration now without any vision or sense of scholarship— much less poetry. It has deteriorated so far that the candid opinion of all the lay faculty is very pessimistic. And of course I saw the future as it could be seen under Father Burns—a new Louvain, with dreams steadily coming true. I have spent many a bitter hour beside the ashes of a dying dream, honey.[69]

When George finally decided on New York, Doris was not opposed. "So it's going to be New York, for a year," she had written in April. "I'll like that, really. I've never been to New York at all you know, and you are not educated until you have spent at least six months in New York. So education must not be neglected, must it?"[70]

A major attraction in New York at this time was George's desire to write. Soon after his return from California in the summer of 1923 he had written Doris: "Oh, gosh! If I had time to write everything I'd like to this world would be paradise, with thou beside me in the wilderness." A few months later he returned to the same topic. "As you know, my one strong desire is to write, and write well," he wrote. "The only other thing is you, which belongs in a higher sphere. But this writing is awfully hard work, and it may take another five years before I can say that my pen is a bread-winner." Finances remained the hurdle. "Maybe in five years," he wrote in December, "there will be enough literary reputation behind the name of George Shuster to mean substantial things, but there isn't enough now. I can make a thousand dollars a year at present, which isn't much."[71] George thus decided to enroll at Columbia University for a doctor's degree in English. In fact, he had taken only a leave of absence from Notre Dame; if writing did not prove feasible he apparently could return. But the opportunity to write proved more than even he had expected.

3

THE COMMONWEAL CATHOLIC
1925–1937

George and Doris Shuster's married life in New York did not begin auspiciously. They left South Bend by train to begin their honeymoon in Canada—Quebec, Montreal, and the beautiful trip through the Thousand Islands. Unfortunately, Doris was not feeling well their last day in Quebec and could not even eat an excellent steak dinner George had arranged. But she hoped it was something passing and decided to continue on to the Thousand Islands trip. By the end of it, however, she was feeling much worse and George immediately rented a hotel room for a day and called a doctor. (Doris later recalled how George, in those days of stricter morality, was quick to show their marriage license when requesting the hotel room during the day.) Doris had had some difficulties with her health the previous summer in California and George felt certain that this time it was tonsillitis. Doris was convinced it was much more serious, diphtheria at least. To George's satisfaction, and Doris's chagrin, the doctor diagnosed it almost immediately as tonsillitis.[1]

As soon as Doris felt well enough to travel again—but barely so—they set out for New York. They rented a room in a hotel, managed somehow to fit all their luggage and possessions into it, and George began looking for an apartment to rent while Doris remained, slowly recovering, in the hotel. George had hoped to live near Columbia University where he intended to pursue his doctorate in English literature, but he found nothing nearby that he thought they could afford. Someone suggested that apartments were more reasonable in Brooklyn, and thus they transferred themselves and their luggage to the St. George's Hotel there and the search began again. George was somewhat more successful this time and soon had two or three apartments he wanted Doris to see. One had no separate kitchen but only a small nook with a hot plate in it. Doris insisted that it would be impossible to cook meals on that and asked George humorously if he planned to earn enough money to allow them to eat out every day. They eventually took an upstairs apartment in the 1600 block of East 14th Street, right off the King's Highway and very close to public transportation to downtown New York.[2]

Although Shuster had hoped to make writing his primary occupation in New York, he also accepted a number of part-time teaching positions to guarantee a more steady income. One of the first of these was as instructor of English at the Polytechnic Institute of Brooklyn, a convenient subway ride from the Shusters' apartment. Although the Institute had been founded to provide training primarily in science, technology, and commerce, the curriculum had a strong liberal arts component also, and, in fact, both a terminal liberal arts course and a college preparatory course eventually developed.[3] The Institute conducted evening sessions also, both to complement the day courses and to accommodate non-degree students, and Shuster apparently taught primarily in the evening session. But he taught there for only one year, 1924–1925, since his other commitments after 1925 were too demanding.[4]

Shuster also fulfilled his commitment to return to Notre Dame and teach in the summer session of 1925. He had originally requested only a year's leave of absence from the university, leaving himself the option of returning full-time if work in New York proved unfeasible. By the spring of 1925 he had decided to remain in the East, but he did keep his commitment to return for the summer. The classes he offered, both on the graduate level, were two of his favorites: "The Catholic Spirit in Modern English Literature" and "Foreign Influences on Modern English Literature."[5] As always, Shuster found teaching very satisfying and he enjoyed renewing acquaintances with old friends—a few former students who were continuing to work toward their degrees, and especially Sister Eleanore, Paul Fenlon, and Father Hudson. It was clear, however, that his relations with the university administration were strained:

Everybody has been most nice. Of course the powers that be—
which are only one or two people—put a trifle of acid into their
greetings. They can' [*sic*] quite forgive the fact that I'm not obliged
to crawl back to Notre Dame for a job to feed my wife and baby.
But the rest of the gang—ever so many of them—have welcomed
me with their hearts as much as their lips. Father Bolger has
insisted upon giving me a walk all over and saying prayers that I
may gain some weight; Father Carrico has furnished his best
Camels; and old Father Hudson all but kissed me.[6]

His disillusionment with the new university administration
was perhaps shared by Father Burns himself. "I went to see
Father Burns last night," he wrote Doris that summer, "and we
had a chat. The poor man is going back to Washington as superior
of Holy Cross Seminary, and is I think wholly disgusted with
Notre Dame. Incidentally he says that he may come to see us
again in Brooklyn, so that you must be prepared for a great deal in
the way of a surprise."[7]

The most difficult aspect of that summer, however, was the
fact that their son, Robert, was born early that June, and Doris
and Bobby remained at home in Brooklyn. Doris's letters always
contained the latest news of the baby's growth—how many ounces
gained since his last weighing, what success in holding up his
head, the appearance of a smile—and each letter could only make
the young father more homesick. "You have no idea how my interest in that child has increased," he confided. "I ache to pick him
up and cart him about, with my hand against his spine. Because
after all he is ourselves—the flower that we made to bloom—and it
is all very wonderful." His return to Notre Dame reminded him
also of Doris's senior year at Saint Mary's (when he had decided to
break off their relationship) and of her two years in Los Angeles,
and he yearned for her all the more. "Well, kiss me by long distance, my very own darling," he wrote, "and be sure that if I had
you beside the bush where we once or twice conversed—or even
under the dome—I should shock a few people by putting my arm
around you about as hard as a whirlwind winds around a tree."
Then he added, with characteristic humor: "Which doesn't mean
that you resemble a tree or I a whirlwind. It's only a figure of
speech. I wish we had the speech. . . . You have the figure."[8]

It was especially difficult to be separated on their first anniversary, June 25, and the experience caused a minor controversy. Already teaching in Notre Dame's summer session, George decided to send Doris a fairly substantial check (for those times) for an anniversary gift. "[T]hen there are thirty dollars, which sum is yours as an anniversary gift," he wrote. "I hope you will buy whatever you wish with it: and it seemed to me under the circumstances, you might rather have it so than get something you might not especially care for." But George did not yet know his wife well. Doris wrote back that a check was not quite acceptable on this occasion. "I hope you didn't feel hurt at what I said about the anniversary gift," she wrote later. "It is just that I want you to select my first anniversary present. Money would be satisfactory any other time, but not this time." She tried to be as gentle as possible: "You didn't see that, dear, because you aren't a woman. Silly sentimental reason, but it's there. No harm done though is there, for you can get something when you return. Please don't think I'm an old crank, will you?"[9]

Shuster also taught at Marquette University one summer, allowing Doris and Bobby to spend these weeks with her relatives in Indiana and Ohio, and he also offered literature classes one or two days a week in the mid-1930s at the Seminary of the Immaculate Conception near Huntington, Long Island, but his major teaching position during this period was at St. Joseph's College for Women in Brooklyn.[10] St. Joseph's College, the first Catholic day school for women in all of Long Island, was still quite young when Shuster joined the faculty in 1924. It had been founded by the Sisters of St. Joseph in 1916, had a student enrollment of approximately two hundred in the mid-1920s, and did not receive its official charter until 1929. The college occupied one large building on Clinton Avenue in a pleasant, residential area of the city, with an annex constructed along one of the side streets, and a new building was erected on Clinton Avenue in 1929. Of a faculty of under thirty in the 1920s, approximately half were sisters, and of the others perhaps half again were male.[11]

Shuster joined the faculty in the fall of 1924 and continued to teach there, part-time but more or less regularly, for the next twelve years.[12] Shuster taught, at one time or another, the whole gamut of freshman composition, oral English or rhetoric, and

English and American literature, and he was held in high regard. He was a frequent guest speaker at student gatherings, at communion breakfasts, and various other college functions, and the responses were invariably favorable. One student had only the highest of praise:

> In the role of teacher, Mr. Shuster is as interesting as in that of writer. Each lesson is a marvel of construction, an evidently carefully planned unit in a definite plan, and yet it is delivered with a spontaneity, an enthusiasm that makes us only aware of the pleasure of listening. With the knack of compressing the essentials in compact and striking form, he unites a fluency, a beauty of diction, a certain contagious fervidness that makes his class a positive delight.[13]

His impact on students might be seen in the lighthearted comments in the college yearbooks' "Class Will and Testament" sections: "To Mr. Shuster, the privilege of using the Auditorium for his large classes," "To Mr. Shuster, our hope that he will someday convince the entire faculty of the futility of midterm examinations," "To Mr. Shuster, our hopes that we may some day have one-tenth of the culture that he considers a minimum."[14] Years later, a former student paid him tribute:

> Those of us who sat spellbound in your classes at St. Joseph's many years ago, will never forget the warmth of your spirit, the depth of your humanity, the keenness of your sense of humor. Your very name carries inspiration for me as a teacher. The use of your little stick figures on the blackboard taught me the value of true simplicity, even then.

Despite his success as a teacher, writing was still his first love. For several years he had wanted to publish a literary biography of Charles Warren Stoddard, professor of literature at Notre Dame and the Catholic University of America, author of *South Sea Idyles* and *The Pleasure of His Company*, and one-time secretary to Mark Twain. Stoddard had lived for a time in California, and Shuster, on his visit to Doris in the summer of 1923, had hoped to visit some of Stoddard's own surroundings in the San Francisco area. He continued his interest in this project after he moved to New York, corresponded on occasion with Rudyard Kipling and others about Stoddard, but apparently nothing ever came of it.[15] He retained his close friendship with Father Hudson, editor of the *Ave Maria* magazine, and also published poetry and several major articles. One of his contributions, "The Pearl of Paradise Mountain," was a children's novelette, serialized over nineteen issues in the last six months of 1924.[16] But Shuster's major literary venture during this period, the one by which he would be known by many for the rest of his life and the one which would leave him little time eventually for teaching, was his association with the newly founded Catholic journal, *The Commonweal*.

Two important events of 1919 had provided the incentive for the founding of *The Commonweal* five years later. The first was adoption by the American bishops of the so-called Bishops' Program of Social Reconstruction. This statement had been drafted by Father John A. Ryan, a noted theologian at the Catholic University of America, and offered specific recommendations for the betterment of postwar American society: maintenance of high employment, especially among returning servicemen; equal pay for women; an adequate family wage for all workers; stringent enforcement of anti-trust legislation; encouragement of cooperatives; abolition of child labor; and legal guarantees of the right of collective bargaining.[17] It was a progressive program and, in the opinion of Shuster, an invitation for American Catholics to "move into the mainstream of American life." Anti-Catholic bigotry of the nineteenth century was a thing of the past, he insisted, and now American Catholics' "responsibility for the total configuration of the United States was much greater, and much more real." "So perhaps the mainspring of *The Commonweal* was that," he concluded. "We hoped we would have a magazine which would be sufficiently ecumenical to meet that demand." A principal idea of the magazine's founders, Shuster wrote later, "was to provide a lay organ which would to some extent . . . implement the Bishops' Declaration of 1919 on social reconstruction."[18]

The second major event of 1919 profoundly influencing the founding of *The Commonweal* was the establishment of the National Catholic Welfare Conference. Two years earlier Cardinal James Gibbons of Baltimore had given approval to a plan of Father John Burke, C.S.P., to call a meeting of representatives of various Catholic organizations and each American diocese at Catholic

University in Washington to discuss possible ways of coordinating various programs to aid Catholic servicemen at home and abroad during World War I. From this August 1917 meeting, the National Catholic War Council was established. When the bishops and archbishops comprising the Board of Trustees of Catholic University met in Washington that November, they realized the important contributions such a coordinating agency could make but they decided also that it needed more official status in the church. They appointed a committee of four bishops to assume responsibility for the council and, two years later, reorganized it on a peacetime basis as the National Catholic Welfare Council, the name changed to the National Catholic Welfare Conference in 1922. Although each of its various departments was to be presided over by a bishop, the purpose of the organization remained to coordinate the various social programs of the American church and extend the church's influence in American public life, and in this purpose the work of the laity had to be central.[19]

The actual founder of *The Commonweal* was Michael Williams, a former newspaper reporter and assistant with the National Catholic War Council. He and the well-known architect Ralph Adams Cram called a meeting of interested associates in New York for mid-October 1922. Present were Professor Summerfield Baldwin of Harvard and Carlton J.H. Hayes of Columbia; Monsignor Francis Kelley of the Catholic Church Extension Society of Chicago; Rev. T. Lawrason Riggs, the Catholic chaplain at Yale; writer and poet Thomas Walsh of New York; Dr. Thomas D.J. Gallagher of Philadelphia; and five or six others. There seemed to be general agreement on the need for a Catholic intellectual journal, a review of literature, the arts, science, and economic and social questions from the Catholic point of view, and Cram noted that non-Catholics, like himself, were also desirous of guidance from Catholic principles. The participants agreed that sufficient Catholic writers were available and thus the major concern would be finances. A ways and means committee was established, at a later meeting Williams was selected as executive secretary, and a fund-raising goal of $300,000 was set, the amount thought necessary to finance the journal for its first three years.[20]

Williams's fund-raising efforts were only partly successful. After two years, he had less than $100,000 on hand, but he had also organized about two thousand supporters nationwide into "The Calvert Associates," a group pledging continuing financial assistance for a minimum of three years, almost guaranteeing the necessary $300,000. The name "Calvert Associates," derived from George Calvert, Lord Baltimore, the founder of the colony of Maryland, was significant. Calvert was a layman, and this new organization was to be primarily lay. Furthermore, the publication was to be in some ways elitist. The American church of the nineteenth and early twentieth centuries was composed primarily of immigrants, often with little opportunity for advanced education unfortunately, but this new publication would be directed also to the older, wealthier, and better-educated Catholics. The journal was to be sufficiently elitist that when the creative, unkempt, and slightly uncouth emigre French activist and poet Peter Maurin appeared at *The Commonweal* offices a few years later, Shuster realized that he would be out of place and introduced him instead to Dorothy Day of *The Catholic Worker*, thus inaugurating a long and fruitful collaboration there.[21] And third, one of the goals of the journal was to demonstrate, with the return of the Ku Klux Klan and anti-immigrant bigotry after World War I, that one could be, like George Calvert, both a good Catholic and a good citizen. With the encouragement and promised support of these Calvert Associates, it was decided to launch the new journal in November 1924. Williams had hoped to name his new venture *The Criterion*, but when he discovered that name had already been taken, his supporters agreed on his second selection, *The Commonweal*. In the first issue Williams listed himself as editor, with Thomas Walsh and Helen Walker, formerly of *The New Republic* and *The Nation*, as assistant editors.[22]

The basic principles and goals of the magazine had been worked out over the preceding several months. Although priests and religious would be encouraged to contribute and even join the editorial board, the journal would be lay-controlled and independent of official church authority. In fact, Shuster saw this as basic. In his view, perhaps mistaken, the National Catholic War Council had been established by Father Burke in 1917 independent of official church structure, but the American bishops had then assumed control over it. *The Commonweal* wanted to retain that independent status which, in Shuster's opinion, the original War Council had lost. The journal would be ecumenical also, as an early press release noted: "Its pages will be open to writers holding different forms of Christian belief, and in some cases to authors who do not profess any form of Christian faith." But loyalty to the church was never a question. The journal would take strong stands on issues that admitted of two sides or that were still open to debate, but it did not intend to criticize church leaders or official policies since a primary goal was to demonstrate the compatibility between these policies and the American way of life. The editors were seeking to apply fundamental religious principles to the worlds of art, literature, philosophy, science, education, economic and political life. Lamenting the "present, confusing, and conflicting complex of private opinions, and personal impressions, mirrored in so many influential journals," they were confident that "nothing can do so much for the betterment, the happiness, and the peace of the American people as the influence of the enduring and tested principles of Catholic Christianity."[23]

It is uncertain when George Shuster first heard of *The Commonweal* plans. In February 1923 Father Vincent Donovan, O.P., wrote to congratulate him on the publication of *The Catholic Spirit in Modern English Literature* and then added:

> The book assures me that you will be interested in a movement a group of us have had under consideration for some time, but which is only now materializing. We are starting a weekly of high literary order to be not the official nor ecclesiastical but the artistic exponent of Catholic principles in every field of human endeavor. As one of the original "Calvert Associates" I am having sent to you a copy of a letter by Michael Williams exposing our purpose and plans. I trust you will be one of us.[24]

But in 1923, Shuster did not feel sufficiently confident of his finances—or perhaps of the venture's success—to invest. He was understandably interested in plans for a new Catholic publication, he kept himself informed and, after his marriage and move to New York, he gradually committed himself to some involvement. His satisfying work for the *Ave Maria* would now be reduced and perhaps similar work for *The Commonweal* could take its place. Still, he had reservations. "Michael Williams' new magazine, *The Commonweal*, is to make its appearance in November," he wrote Father Hudson in August, 1924. "I may tell you confidentially that I have some chance of being closely connected with it. Nevertheless, I am afraid of the venture. Its plans are quite vague, its policy indefinite, and its atmosphere slightly too much steeped in 'convert' moods. Converts are, of course, the best people on earth, but it seems to me they need a little seasoning and aging before they set out to interpret Catholic thought." Father Hudson agreed: "What you had to say about the *Commonweal* was of great interest. You are right. Don't let them induce you to invest in it. Converts certainly do need seasoning—many of them a great deal of it." But by October Shuster had committed himself to at least literary involvement: "To come back to another subject," he wrote Father Hudson, "Mr. Williams' magazine is finally coming near its birthday, and I am scheduled to turn in a number of critical papers, and besides that to do what I tried to handle for you:— matters in German."[25]

Shuster began writing for *The Commonweal* with its third issue, November 24, and he remained with it for the next twelve years. At first, he simply contributed weekly editorials and commentary, drafting them, he later recalled, at his typewriter every Sunday afternoon. His involvement steadily increased, however, and he was named an assistant editor in 1926 and managing editor two years later. In these positions he gradually took over major responsibility for the literary side of the magazine—soliciting manuscripts, editing, proofreading, commissioning editorials, contacting book reviewers—leaving Williams freer to handle public relations and fund-raising. Actually, the journal's staff was always small, the work was never systematically apportioned, and everyone on the staff was eventually drafted into every area of the magazine's production.[26]

Through all of Shuster's twelve years with *The Commonweal* financial stability—and even survival—remained a major concern. The first crisis came in 1927–28. By that time the original money Williams had collected and the three-year pledges he had obtained were near exhaustion, annual income from subscriptions and advertising was projected at $45,000, but estimated costs were closer to $100,000. Circulation was eighteen thousand but the break-even point was twenty-eight thousand. Williams turned almost instinctively for assistance to John J. Raskob, prominent Catholic, treasurer of E. I. duPont and Company, and a vice-president of General Motors. Raskob agreed to sponsor a promotional dinner in New York in the early spring of 1928, Williams delivered the principal address (later published as *The Present Position of Catholics in the United States*), and a small committee was appointed to solicit $300,000 nationwide, the sum projected to put the journal on a self-supporting basis after three more years. Raskob himself pledged $25,000.[27]

Williams was elated with the support demonstrated at the dinner—a "turning point" he called it—but his elation was short-lived. With the stock market crash of late 1929 and the start of the Great Depression, new subscribers were hard to find, old subscribers canceled, and even those pledging sizable sums in 1928 now found it difficult to pay. Expenses were cut, but still the crisis deepened. In 1931 several early supporters, including Raskob again, were approached to pay off their pledges early in order to tide the journal over a particularly difficult period. Two years later, Father John A. Ryan of Catholic University, now a member of *The Commonweal*'s editorial board, agreed to chair a committee seeking subscriptions and financial contributions from the American clergy. Individual dioceses were asked to contribute also. Bishop James Duffy of Grand Island sent one-hundred dollars but added bluntly: "I state the barest truth when I say this diocese 'out in the sticks' cannot raise $500 unless obliged under pain of mortal sin." Through these various fund-raising efforts and advertising campaigns, the magazine managed to survive the depression years, but often barely, and the editors could never be certain that they would still be publishing in six or twelve months time.[28]

Despite these almost constant financial worries, *The Commonweal* under Williams and Shuster was able to realize one of its earliest and most important goals—to provide a forum for some of the best contemporary thinkers on religious questions in both Europe and America. Noted architect Ralph Adams Cram, historian Carlton J.H. Hayes, Catholic activist Dorothy Day, Father

John A. Ryan of the National Catholic Welfare Conference, author and literary critic Agnes Repplier, and interracial champion Father John LaFarge, S.J., all published in the early years. Younger writers were encouraged to publish: Fathers Paul Hanley Furfey, Joseph Fichter, S.J., Leo R. Ward, C.S.C., John Tracy Ellis, Fulton J. Sheen, and John A. O'Brien. Contributors from Europe were even more impressive: G. K. Chesterton, Hilaire Belloc, C. C. Martindale, S.J., and Frank Sheed from England; Jacques Maritain, Georges Bernanos, and Felix Klein from France; Karl Adam, Hermann Bahr, and Romano Guardini from Germany; Giovanni Papini, Carlo Sforza, and Luigi Sturzo from Italy; Louis Mercier from Belgium; Nicholas Berdiaeff from Russia; and Etienne Gilson, more recently from Canada. *The Commonweal*'s subscribers were chiefly among the college educated and professional classes, and Williams and Shuster made some of the best in Catholic and religious thinking available to them. Because of his scholarly contacts in France, Germany, and England, Shuster received much of the credit for attracting the European contributors to the journal.[29]

But Shuster did much more than edit and encourage others to write for *The Commonweal*; he helped shape journal policy and wrote widely himself, even under assumed names at times to conceal how much of the magazine was his own.[30] One of the first national controversies *The Commonweal* covered closely was the John T. Scopes evolution trial in Dayton, Tennessee, in 1925. The last fifty years had seen tremendous advances in science—in electricity, medicine, transportation, genetics, even implements of war—but questions arose whether the evolutionary theories of Charles Darwin, the psychological opinions of Sigmund Freud, and the principles of relativity of Albert Einstein were wholly compatible with traditional Catholic belief. One of the goals of the founders of *The Commonweal* was to show that religious belief had nothing to fear from the legitimate findings of science, and they saw the Scopes trial as an excellent opportunity to demonstrate this conviction.

As might be expected, the position of *The Commonweal* was one of openness and moderation. It could ridicule a city ordinance in Illinois that stipulated that children there be taught that the earth was flat, and yet it also declared its opinion that "[e]volution is not a proved fact in spite of what some may say." It was a serious and legitimate question, the evidence on neither side was overwhelming, and thus neither side should be suppressed:

> Evolution—for the present at least—should be taught as a theory and not as established truth, and the arguments against as well as those in favor should be stated. It should be taught that it may have been the method of creation; but that even so, it cannot and does not, as men like Darwin and Huxley admitted, in any way exclude the idea of a Creator.[31]

The Commonweal followed the trial closely throughout that summer. It published thoughtful articles by Sir Bertram Windle ("The Case Against Evolution"), Forrest Davis ("Tennessee—State of Brave Men"), Frank R. Kent ("What Dayton Thinks"), and T. Lawrason Riggs ("Fundamentalism and the Faith"), and at least every second issue contained a major editorial. The trial was considered sufficiently newsworthy, in fact, that Michael Williams covered it personally from Dayton, Tennessee, sending back firsthand reports. Significant though the case was, especially in dramatizing the intricacies in church-state relations, the editors realized that such a public spectacle, with William Jennings Bryan championing the conservative cause against Clarence Darrow and the liberals, was not going to bring clarity or calm reason to the dispute. As one editorial noted:

> *The Commonweal* considers that the Dayton case is hardly likely to advance genuine knowledge of this highly complex and technical matter, but is very likely to confuse the real issues involved through the stirring up of a raucous and heated debate between such emotional extremists as Mr. W. J. Bryan and Mr. Clarence Darrow, to the accompaniment of the jazz-band to be installed in Dayton's baseball field among the batteries of radio machines and newspaper cameras.[32]

On the basic question of the relation of science to religion, the editors remained confident:

> Catholics at least should know and act upon the fact that there cannot possibly be any real conflict between any fact and the teachings of the Catholic Faith. Let the flood roar and rage—truth

will at last prevail. Catholicism being true, all facts known to be facts, or which came to be known as such, must necessarily harmonize with the truth.[33]

It was a question that Shuster had considered in some detail in the chapter "Newman the Thinker" in *The Catholic Spirit in Modern English Literature* three years before. The world of the nineteenth century had become more skeptical of religious truths, had relied more comfortably on truths demonstrable by science or logic, and Newman had insisted that logic was only one part of life and that many truths were accepted in daily life without logical demonstration. In an unsigned editorial in *The Commonweal* in January 1925 the author, possibly Shuster, returned to Newman once again and emphasized the cardinal's view of the compatibility between science and religion because the God revealed in scripture was the same God revealed in the physical universe all around.[34]

As the embers of one controversy were beginning to burn down in Tennessee that summer, Shuster managed to ignite another one, this time much closer to home and with himself at the center. He published two articles on the state of Catholic higher education, one in *The Commonweal* and one in the Jesuit weekly, *America*. Both were highly critical of Catholic education and both were interpreted by many of his co-religionists as acts of disloyalty, if not to his church, at least to his church's education system.

The first article appeared in *America* on August 15, 1925, and was entitled provocatively "Have We Any Scholars?"[35] Despite the hundreds of Catholic colleges spread across the continent, staffed by thousands of dedicated priests, religious, and lay men and women, and despite a cost of millions of dollars each year to students and their families, Shuster's answer was a resounding no.

> It appears to me . . . that if we try to view Catholic academic life as a whole, we should find that during the past seventy-five years it has produced not a single great literary man or writer on literary subjects; not a scientist, excepting possibly two or three chemists or seismologists, who has made an original contribution to the vast catalogue of recent discoveries; not an historian whose study of a definite field has resulted in a new orientation of our minds toward the past; and, with one exception, no economist whose leadership

has divined new and better social conditions. If we are honest, we must admit that during seventy-five years of almost feverish intellectual activity we have had no influence on the general culture of America other than what has come from a passably active endeavor to spread to the four winds knowledge accumulated either by our ancestors or by sectarian scholars.[36]

Shuster was especially critical of graduate research. "I can say," he continued, "that a relatively careful examination of some twenty-five doctorate theses prepared in Catholic colleges on subjects relating to English literature forced me to conclude that not a single one would have been accepted, simply as research, at a university of the first rank."[37] The tragedy was compounded, according to Shuster, by the fact that the Catholic graduate rarely continued serious study or research after the degree: "He rides his oars merrily, teaches twice as many classes as any human being ought to teach, and by force of circumstances over which he has no control is borne into a mental desuetude which is sometimes pathetic and sometimes ridiculous."

Shuster admitted that some causes of this condition were unavoidable—the relatively recent origin of Catholic higher education in America, the limited schooling of many immigrant Catholics, and often a lack of finances. But the major fault he thought was the proliferation of Catholic colleges across the country without the human and financial resources to make them worth the effort. "Scarcely has a Catholic college been established anywhere than it begins to dream of building up branch universities . . . on the plains, on the desert, on the mountain tops," he wrote. "There are American Catholic colleges in places where the students, if any, would have to seek out their Alma Mater on a pack-mule." Since there were not enough priests and religious to staff these expanding classrooms, college administrators turned to the laity, but almost never accepted them as full partners in the educational enterprise. "I think it can be said," Shuster continued, "that the Catholic college attitude towards laymen is simply that they are either necessary evils or cheap benefits." Shuster insisted that there was not a sufficient demand by qualified students to justify such proliferation. "As a matter of fact," he suggested, "many of our colleges are barely able to collect enough matriculation fees to start a respectable savings account; and if they were sufficiently audacious to risk imposing the usual entrance standards, the enrollment would approach zero with amazing rapidity."[38]

The article was devastating in several ways. It not only criticized the dearth of Catholic scholars but publicized the inadequacies in Catholic graduate education, the proliferation of Catholic colleges, the poor treatment of the lay faculty, and the low academic rating of many Catholic students. Shuster had singled out no one institution for criticism, and he certainly intended his critique to be general, but it did not go unnoted that the only school he was thoroughly acquainted with was Notre Dame. But if Shuster's criticism of his alma mater was only implicit in the *America* article, it was quite specific in his lead editorial, "Insulated Catholics," in *The Commonweal* that August 19.[39]

One of the glories of Notre Dame at that time was its program of student religious life. The prefect of religion was the popular and charismatic Father John O'Hara, C.S.C., later university president, bishop of Buffalo, and cardinal-archbishop of Philadelphia. Father O'Hara, affectionately called "The Pope" by students, placed great emphasis on traditional Catholic practices— keeping the commandments, regular confession, devotion to the Blessed Mother, voluntary self-denial, and especially frequent reception of holy communion. With a chapel in every residence hall, the university was often called "the city of the Blessed Sacrament." Besides circulating a daily "Religious Bulletin," a one-page news sheet of edifying vignettes, encouragement to virtue, friendly criticism of campus abuses, and special requests for student prayers, Father O'Hara also published an annual survey of student religious practices and attitudes—and this was the context of Shuster's editorial.[40]

He began by noting that this was "an age of measurements and statistics, of filing cabinets and card indexes." He professed no criticism of surveys and the gathering and publishing of statistics, but he warned that they often concealed as much as they revealed, and he turned to Father O'Hara and his religious program at Notre Dame as an example. A Canadian archbishop had pointed out that O'Hara's recent annual survey showed much greater emphasis among Notre Dame students on frequent communion and personal religious practices than on works of charity and concern for the needs of others.[41] In a recent address, Shuster noted, Archbishop Austin Dowling of Saint Paul had criticized the religion of most American Catholics as too individualistic:

> Wherever you go in this country, you find the same conditions— prodigious parochial activity and supine indifference to the general needs of the Church. As a consequence, Catholics, where they are the strongest, are isolated, out of touch with the community, exerting no influence commensurate with their numbers, their enterprise, or their splendid constructive thought.

Shuster went on to praise a recent recommendation of his friend, Father James Burns, C.S.C., that Catholic colleges should accept the responsibility of assuring that their graduates be schooled in the social responsibilities of Catholicism also. "Graduates of Catholic schools are rightly expected to have an interest in the welfare of their fellow men," Father Burns had stated, "for this is the natural and obvious expression of Christian charity." Shuster agreed that this was at least a good first step toward overcoming the religious individualism revealed in Father O'Hara's and other surveys, but he insisted that a further step was also needed. That step was the one emphasized in his earlier article in *America*—a dramatic increase in the academic standards in our Catholic colleges:

> But, on our part, we believe that for the colleges the problem is not going to be settled by merely haranguing about social duties and the obligations of citizenship. What is needed is an awakening of the student's intellectual life—the culture of mind for its own sake, with which will come a sympathetic realization of those broad issues upon which the stability of our human world ultimately depends. So long as Catholic education refuses to concede that its goal is not quantity—not buildings and "splurge," but quality— excellent quality achieved at no matter what cost—it will talk in vain about "Christian brotherhood." Leadership is the by-product of intellectual exercise and fidelity to moral obligations. We have not developed such leadership. Why? Because we have not led in education: apart from a number of good professional schools, we have superimposed upon a splendid system of elementary training little more than excellence—in football! There is the rub.[42]

The closing reference to football in the year Knute Rockne's "Four Horsemen" backfield graduated left little doubt again of one university Shuster had in mind.

Shuster had declined to sign *The Commonweal* editorial, probably for two reasons.[43] Appearing at the same time as his article in *America*, he may not have wanted to emphasize that they came from the same pen but hoped they would be considered more for what they said than for who said it. More significantly, Shuster later admitted that he and Father Burns had met during that summer session at Notre Dame and that Father Burns had suggested much of the criticism. Shuster at times almost implied a joint authorship. Leaving the editorial unsigned was certainly a way of shielding Father Burns's participation. But with the minor storm of opposition his article caused on the Notre Dame campus—opposition lasting even to his return to Notre Dame in 1961—Shuster always felt it ironic that a major influence behind both articles was Father Burns, former Notre Dame president, future provincial superior in the Congregation of Holy Cross, and almost universally respected Notre Dame educator.

But if Shuster noted faults in Catholic education, he was in no way embittered. His friendship with many at Notre Dame—Father Burns, Father Cavanaugh, Father Hudson, Paul Fenlon—remained close, and he was preparing at this time one of his most delightful works, *The Hill of Happiness*. This was an imaginative and fantasized memoir of a school and monastery, patterned after *The Little Flowers of St. Francis* but clearly recalling Shuster's own school days at St. Lawrence College.[44] The short vignettes pay tribute to the monks' understanding, devotion to duty, sense of humor, cheerfulness, piety and deep spirituality, all virtues Shuster had admired in the monks he knew during his high school days. He could be outspokenly critical of Catholic education when that criticism was warranted, but the love and gentle admiration shining through *The Hill of Happiness* show his respect and optimism also.

One of the principal reasons for the founding of the *The Commonweal* had been to demonstrate that one could be both a loyal Catholic and a loyal American, and the 1920s provided several challenges to this belief and several opportunities for the editors to reaffirm it. When John Jay Chapman in 1924 publicly opposed the election of a Catholic as a Fellow of Harvard University because of Catholicism's "outspoken purpose . . . to control American education," Ralph Adams Cram replied through

The Commonweal: "Although I am not a Roman Catholic, I happen to know something about this Church, and something about its system and practice of education. I do formally challenge you to show cause for making your amazing statement. For my own part, I deny it explicitly."[45] A recent brochure of the Ku Klux Klan feared "an America Catholicized, mongrelized and circumcised," and saw Roman Catholics "closely allied" to "every bootlegger, moonshiner, jake-seller, libertine, prostitute and black-leg gambler," and an editorial in *The Commonweal*, probably written by Shuster, took up the challenge. "Just how far this ill-written farrago of special pleading, unsupported assumptions, spread eagleism and bad manners is to be regarded as an official document is not clear," the editorial stated. "Americans are not on the way to the abject surrender of the principles which are the very life of the nation. . . . Simply to expose the swollen dreams of petty tyranny indulged in by the exploiters of the ignorant and prejudiced victims of the K.K.K. is, we believe, to expose as well the ridiculous nature of their ambitions."[46]

Although the subject of prejudice and bigotry was serious, Shuster later recalled at least one humorous incident. In one of his articles, this one under the pen name of Paul Crowley, Shuster severely ridiculed a recent stance of Senator Thomas Heflin of Alabama. About two weeks later a letter arrived from Senator Heflin at *The Commonweal* office addressed to Paul Crowley and challenging him to a duel over the remarks he had made. Shuster answered the senator and informed him that unfortunately Mr. Crowley had just left the United States for a tour of Pakistan. The senator wrote a couple of letters further, inquiring about Crowley's eventual return, and Shuster eventually apologized that he had lost contact with Mr. Crowley altogether, never revealing Crowley's true identity.[47]

For *The Commonweal*, as for most of the rest of the country, the question of prejudice and bigotry became most prominent with the nomination of Governor Alfred Smith of New York for the presidency in 1928. On August 29 of that year the editors stated their conviction that the country would be in good hands under either Governor Smith or Secretary Herbert Hoover, but after considering the major issues, they gave their support to Smith. They admitted that the candidates did not seem to differ that much on farm policy, the tariff issue, public utilities, and labor concerns, but they preferred what they considered Smith's less imperialistic stance in foreign policy and his more open and honest attitude toward Prohibition. On the religious question the editors were clear: "*The Commonweal* does not nor will it give its support to Governor Smith because he is a Catholic, but it does and must stand with those men and women of many religious faiths or opinions who condemn and oppose the efforts now palpable and increasing to make a man's religious belief a black mark against his political career."[48]

Despite *The Commonweal's* protestation, the religious issue had already been heatedly raised. Over a year before, *The New Republic* admitted that Smith would probably be the only progressive in the race but raised the question of possible conflict between his religion and his office in the matter of education and in American relations with the Calles government in Mexico.[49] The following month, April 1927, saw the most serious challenge to the Smith candidacy in the form of "An Open Letter to the Honorable Alfred E. Smith" by Charles C. Marshall in *The Atlantic Monthly*. Marshall praised Smith's personal integrity and his fine record of public trust so far but suggested that, as president, Smith would have to make decisions over equal treatment of all religions, control of education, authority over marriages, and possible intervention in Mexico, and these might involve conflicts between his oath of office and pronouncements from Rome.[50]

The Commonweal was quick to respond. To *The New Republic* editorial it replied that there could be no possible conflict over education because the Supreme Court, in the Oregon school case a few years earlier, had established the right of parochial schools to exist, and that it was absurd to think that any president would declare war on neighboring Mexico and alienate most of Latin America for generations simply out of religious resentment.[51] After much debate and some difference of opinion, the editors decided to reply to Marshall also. They pointed out that Catholics had served very well and without conflict as mayors, congressmen, governors, cabinet officers, and Supreme Court justices, and there was no reason to think that the presidency would involve unresolvable conflicts. To Marshall's question about divided loyalty, the editors responded: "In many instances, individual Catholics might be wholly justified in saying as certain Irish political leaders said—that they take their religion from Rome but not their politics." To Marshall's claim that Catholics recognize a higher authority than the Constitution, *The Commonweal* replied that the moral law is above any manmade law—or we could not have justified rebellion against Great Britain in 1776.[52]

The Commonweal kept up its campaign against bigotry and anti-Catholic prejudice throughout 1927 and 1928. It printed critical reviews of some of the more blatantly discriminatory books the 1928 campaign engendered, and it continued to champion the Smith candidacy in the face of religious opposition.[53] In the late summer of 1928, Michael Williams, Ralph Adams Cram, Carlton J.H. Hayes, and others associated with the Calvert Associates organized an Anti-Bigotry Society to combat prejudice and to further religious tolerance through "radio talks, newspaper and magazine advertising, pamphlet distribution" and similar projects.[54] Fifteen thousand copies of a special issue of *The Commonweal* were also distributed. The Calvert Associates also published the *Calvert Handbook of Catholic Facts,* a compendium of questions most frequently raised about Catholicism and Catholic responses to them. The *Handbook* was given wide distribution and was advertised in national newspapers, but it immediately ran into controversy. Some saw nothing more than a piece of campaign literature in support of Al Smith under the guise of a religious tract. Some newspapers refused to carry the book's ad.[55]

The charge was not entirely spurious. It was precisely at this time that *The Commonweal* was struggling through one of its periodic financial crises, and Michael Williams had turned for assistance to John J. Raskob. Raskob agreed both to chair a promotional dinner in New York and to contribute generously from his own personal funds, and with this assistance *The Commonweal* was able to continue publication and also carry on its anti-bigotry campaign. What made the relationship suspect, however, was the fact that Raskob was soon to be appointed chairman of the Democratic National Committee, overseeing the nomination and election campaign of Governor Smith.[56] There is no question of the sincerity of either Raskob or the editors of *The Commonweal* in their opposition to intolerance, and Raskob's involvement in the Smith campaign may have been coincidental, but this *Commonweal*-Raskob relationship in 1928 was at least open to misinterpretation.

Although Shuster rarely shied from a public controversy, he later admitted that he had originally opposed any reply to Charles Marshall and felt that his worst premonitions were justified. Smith's reply, he recalled, "aroused the wrath and disgust of all kinds of right-wing Catholics, and it didn't do any good at all because then Marshall would go and quote from somebody else and prove that Smith was all wet behind the ears, and was covering up the really dastardly deeds of Rome." In fact, the whole 1928 campaign was a near disaster for what *The Commonweal* had hoped to accomplish:

> Catholic public opinion received a jolt which hurt it for twenty years. It lost what I call the elan of World War I, where so many soldiers came back and Catholic boys had been with Protestant boys in France and all over the place, and they came to know each other and make friends, whereas they wouldn't have done that at home. There was a lot in the air, but the atmosphere of the Al Smith campaign made our position, our work, much harder.[57]

As the anti-Catholic sentiment seemed to increase in 1928, even in several respected secular journals, Shuster presented his own views in two significant articles in *The Outlook*. In the first, in February 1928, he emphasized American Catholics' contributions to their country throughout its history.[58] America was essentially a nation of immigrants, Shuster noted, and many of those immigrants—Irish, German, French, and others—were Catholic. They brought with them a deep respect for religion and for the moral law, and America prided itself on both. The culture of America had benefited from the historical studies of John Gilmary Shea and Thomas D'Arcy Magee, the literary contributions of Maurice Francis Egan, Orestes Brownson, Joel Chandler Harris, and Charles Warren Stoddard, and the German Catholic press might have been the best of its kind in the nation. The American Catholic, Shuster concluded, had every reason to feel pride. Catholics had fought nobly and generously in all the nation's wars; American culture had been shaped in by part Irish, French,

German, and Spanish Catholic immigrants; the poor had been cared for for decades in Catholic institutions of charity; and the first official statute of religious toleration had been adopted in Catholic Maryland. American Catholics were second-class citizens to no one.

In a second article, eight months later, Shuster addressed several misconceptions many Americans harbored about Catholicism.[59] The basic difficulty, Shuster suggested, was that people thought that the church desired today everything she may have desired in the past, and this was no more true than that Great Britain today would like to retake Boston. Addressing several major misconceptions directly, Shuster insisted, first, that the church was very comfortable with the present separation of church and state since the Constitution granted the church full liberty and freedom, and these were all she desired. Second, the hierarchical structure of the church did not put it in conflict with the American democratic way of life since the church's jurisdiction was spiritual, not temporal. Third, in any conflict between religion and civil authority, a Catholic would act no differently than a Baptist or Lutheran might, facing a conflict over slavery, for example. Fourth, the church did not wish to use the civil authority to force its religion on others since a belief in free will was an essential tenet of Catholicism. Finally, there was no evidence that Catholics, voting as a block, constituted a threat to political freedom. Religious toleration, in fact, began in Catholic Maryland, Shuster suggested, and political machines were usually more ethnic than religious (Tammany Hall had Jewish members but few German Catholics). "Really there is only one thing to be said in conclusion," Shuster noted; "we Americans can live tranquilly together, with no just fear of 'Catholic domination.'"[60]

Shuster had elaborated on these themes in a major work published the preceding year, *The Catholic Spirit in America*.[61] He investigated there the relationship between Catholicism and American culture and, although he admitted many areas of divergence, he saw no irreconcilable opposition. Church procedures were clearly less democratic than those provided under the American Constitution, but since the jurisdictions of the church and state were different, there was no direct conflict.[62] American culture, in fact, owed much to Catholic tradition: Medieval culture greatly influenced historian Henry Adams and architect Ralph Adams Cram, and there were clear strains of the Catholic Renaissance in Hawthorne, Emerson, and Longfellow.[63] Catholics themselves had played important roles in shaping America— French and Spanish missionaries working among the Indians, the Maryland Act of toleration, the contributions of Catholic immigrant cultures, Catholics' traditional respect for law and morality, and an expanding educational system on the primary, secondary, and college levels.[64] Catholics had made mistakes, and Shuster admitted these also, but his conclusion was positive:

> All these things having been voiced, one could sum up all that has been said in this book by declaring that though there is room for and even need of an intelligent, discerning normative definition of "American," there is absolutely no justification for excluding from that definition anything that is really Catholic. Indeed both past and present, theory and practice, demonstrate that without the riches of the Church our conception of nationhood would be poorer and meaner, in numberless ways.[65]

Hardly had the controversy surrounding the candidacy of Al Smith and the election of 1928 died down than a new crisis broke, more serious and longer lasting—the stock market crash of 1929 and the Great Depression that followed. *The Commonweal* had been no more perceptive than other journals in foreseeing the crisis. "Some stocks go up as easily as others go down—from which we may say that the patient seems normal!" the editors wrote in September 1927.[66] They admitted also that there might be danger in "speculative building construction" and "overloaded installment buying," but their only serious concern seemed to be with unemployment. "Unemployment is more than a proof that intelligent engineering does not control the labor market," the journal stated in early October 1929; "it is final and convincing evidence of urban industry's powerlessness to absorb successive migrations from rural life, and equally good testimony against the social usefulness of capital unification."[67] With that same issue, *The Commonweal* began a four-part treatment of unemployment in the United States by Father John A. Ryan, concluding ironically the week the stock market crashed.[68]

In the first days after the Wall Street crash and the beginning of the Depression, the reaction of *The Commonweal* was moderate, even hesitant. The editors realized that they had no surer answers than the rest of the nation. They lamented the long debate over new tariff rates and were not at all convinced that the end result would be beneficial. Growing unemployment figures were cause for serious concern, and the editors, still sympathetic to Al Smith and an end to Prohibition, suggested half-seriously that the money the government was spending on Prohibition enforcement might better be utilized putting the unemployed to work digging canals. But in the early weeks and months at least, *The Commonweal* refused to blame the Hoover administration. "Let us make it clear, at once, that we do not consider the health or the malaise of business as in any way traceable to the government," an editorial stated in February 1930. "No administration could have acted more promptly and energetically than Mr. Hoover's to check the despair which threatened the financial world a few months ago." In fact, the editors seemed to champion the very moderate solutions the government favored. "After all," the journal stated, "we may be in for the return to favor of ancient maxims which have received a fair amount of endorsement from history—honest work, care in the making of investments and caution in purchasing, mindfulness of the rainy day and desire for a reputation for honesty."[69]

In the late spring of 1931, twenty months after the Wall Street crash and on the fortieth anniversary of Pope Leo XIII's encyclical *Rerum Novarum*, Pope Pius XI issued his own encyclical *Quadragesimo Anno*, "On the Reconstruction of the Social Order." When the full text reached American shores, *The Commonweal* had nothing but praise. In a lead editorial entitled "Father of the Poor," the editors noted that "over and over again, with a solemn, simple tenderness more moving than the most passionate rhetoric could be, the voice pleads for the humble multitudes of the toilers of the world." Any solution to the economic debacle the world was then facing needed to be based on justice and charity, and on this the pope insisted over and over again. The editors singled out the Holy Father's lament over "the almost complete failure of the Catholic leaders of industry to form associations or groups to study and apply Catholic principles of economy, in collaboration with the Catholic associations of working men." Realizing the special appropriateness of this recommendation for the United States, the journal noted: "What an inspiration it would be if some such group as the Knights of Malta, those eminent industrial leaders honored by the Church for their charity, should give group consideration to the problem of how to apply the Pope's program in practical action."[70] Although the encyclical offered strong support to the working classes and the poor, it was significant that *The Commonweal* chose to address business leaders directly in its first editorial. Shuster later reflected that although *The Commonweal* was sympathetic toward labor, it was also elitist and possessed little direct worker-appeal. The majority of subscribers were business and professional people, and the cost of the magazine, ten dollars at first, was more than many workers could afford.[71]

This encyclical became this basis of *The Commonweal's* analysis of the Depression and recommendations for remedying it throughout the 1930s, and nowhere more clearly than in an editorial entitled "Saving the Social Order" in late August 1931. The editors insisted on the necessity to grasp well the roots of the economic crisis facing the nation, and they then added: "For Catholics, anyhow, this means that the study of the encyclical of Pope Pius on 'Reconstructing the Social Order' must be carried on unremittingly." The editorial noted two principal themes of the encyclical emphasized recently in an article circulated by the Social Action Department of the N.C.W.C. The first theme was that private property was good and that the division of management and labor implied by capitalism was wholly legitimate. "The encyclical holds to the right of ownership," the editors repeated. "It also holds that there is nothing essentially unjust in a person working for wages for another. It furthermore holds that it is not of its nature wrong for equipment, tools and materials on one hand and labor on the other to be supplied by different people." But the encyclical also suggested that the present competitive and free enterprise system needed amending. First, employers' associations and labor unions should cooperate more closely in arriving at decisions governing each industry. Second, wages should be increased and the wage contract altered in such a way that the worker becomes more of a partner and thus receives some share of the profits. And third, the government, as the representative or even embodiment of the people in a democracy, must be an active partner also in industrial decision-making and safeguard the common good of all.[72] These two themes—the validity of private ownership and the need to restructure the capitalistic system—were repeated and re-emphasized throughout the decade, preventing the journal from espousing any Marxist solutions for the economic crisis and yet leaving it open at least to various distributionist movements then championed in European intellectual circles.[73]

As the election of 1932 approached, *The Commonweal* attempted to remain neutral. "Neither now nor during the approaching campaign will *The Commonweal* pledge itself to support either party or any candidate," an editorial stated that May. There was no doubt, however, that if Al Smith could not be nominated, the editors found Franklin Roosevelt's candidacy attractive. "All in all," the editorial concluded, "there could be a vastly less impressive candidate for the Presidency than Franklin D. Roosevelt."[74] The editors admired his political skill and supported his early stands on farming, taxation, public utilities, and probably prohibition, although the governor's stand here was not clear. In early October an editorial noted that some still considered Roosevelt too shallow, but it then continued:

> Governor Roosevelt's three main speeches in the West—the one on agriculture, in Kansas, that on public utilities, in Portland, Oregon, and that before the Commonwealth club of San Francisco—have shattered all such trivial weapons used against him. He definitely, very brilliantly, and with a highly welcome strength, proved that he is himself a real leader.[75]

The editors were particularly impressed with Roosevelt's address that fall in Detroit where he quoted approvingly from the encyclical of Pope Pius XI and from other religious documents. "Whatever may be the outcome of the presidential campaign, and irrespective of the merits or demerits of either of the two chief candidates, or of their parties, Governor Roosevelt's Detroit address will stand out as the most noteworthy and praiseworthy utterance of the 1932 campaign. It has brought fundamental principles of moral teaching, as laid down and promoted by the three great religious influences in America . . . fairly and squarely before the consideration of the nation as part of the great debate now proceeding in the political arena."[76]

By election day it was clear that *The Commonweal* saw greater hope for the implementation of Catholic social principles in the program of Franklin Roosevelt than in that of President Hoover, and this was the basis of its response to Roosevelt's election:

> Quite apart from all partisan political considerations, this journal believes . . . that all Catholics who desire to give practical effect to the principles of Social Justice laid down by Pope Pius XI will see that Governor Roosevelt's opportunity to lead the united forces of traditional Americanism (personal liberty, the family as the true unit of society, widely distributed ownership of property, and agriculture as the foundation of the social system) is likewise the Catholic opportunity to make the teachings of Christ apply to the benefit of all.[77]

The magazine's hopes were not disappointed, and the editors generally found themselves in agreement with Franklin Roosevelt's New Deal policies for the rest of the decade.[78] They supported the president's monetary policies, his efforts to control the stock market, the various governmental loan agencies, and the public housing and resettlement programs. They accepted the crop reduction policy of the Agricultural Adjustment Act but had reservations about the increased authority it lodged with the secretary of agriculture. The editors favored the capital-labor-government cooperation of the National Recovery Administration, but they opened their pages to the agency's opponents also. Their only reservation to the president's Social Security program seemed to be that workers were not required to contribute to unemployment insurance and perhaps would have a greater stake in the program if they did. The editors were sympathetic to the needs of the ten million and more unemployed but felt that Roosevelt's public works programs were less than efficient. But most of the journal's reservations were minor. In *Quadragesimo Anno* Pope Pius XI had championed private ownership, greater input of labor and government in economic decision-making, and increased benefits to the poor, and the editors saw Roosevelt's New Deal as at least a partial implementation of these papal recommendations.

The Commonweal also objected to the Roosevelt administration's championing of the proposed child labor amendment, but Shuster did not agree. In a signed editorial (because it was a minority view) in April 1934 Shuster admitted that Catholics were divided on the amendment, some viewing it as a legitimate exercise by the state of its responsibility for the common good, and others fearing it could lead to unnecessary growth of the federal government and to unwarranted interference into the rights of parents in the raising and education of children. The issue was crucial since, in this decade of depression, industry was tempted to cut costs by hiring younger and less expensive workers. Relying on an earlier theory of Orestes Brownson, Shuster suggested that liberty in America was protected and assured through a system of governmental checks and balances, but that in this system, state governments were the weakest links. "Nine out of ten voters know their mayor, their alderman, their congressman, their Senator, their President, at least by name," Shuster suggested. "But who is even aware of the identity of any member of the legislature in any state?" State governments, he continued, were often ineffective and thus such an important issue as protecting the young from the evils of cutthroat competition should not be entrusted primarily to them. Shuster admitted that he was also concerned about the growth of the federal government, which this amendment would abet; he did not desire government ownership of railroads but only government regulation of them, and he did not want government control of child labor but only government regulation of it. He saw little danger of congress devising any "fantastic schemes for ruining youth," he viewed the amendment only as an effort to give a competent body legitimate authority over a serious social problem, and thus, contrary to most American Catholics, he was willing to give it his support.[79]

Shuster also stood firmly on the side of President Roosevelt's New Deal in its increasing opposition to Father Charles Coughlin of Detroit. At first *The Commonweal*'s stance was open and moderate. As early as December 1933 it had criticized the famed "radio priest" for what it considered a personal attack on Al Smith, long a favorite of the magazine and its editors, but when New Deal official Hugh Johnson questioned Coughlin's patriotism in speaking out against the Roosevelt program, *The Commonweal* hurried to the priest's defense. "Father Coughlin may or may not be wrong in this or that particular utterance, or action, or plan," the journal admitted, "but it seems to us that he is basically right in defending not merely his own prerogatives as a free man and a responsible citizen of a free country, but that also he is defending the cause of religion itself, as well as the cause of democracy, by his stand against General Johnson's attack." The editors always insisted, however, that Coughlin's particular views were his own and were not to be confused with official teachings of the church. "Father Coughlin's proposals may or may not be sound, or desirable, or in consonance with Catholic morals," the editors repeated that May. "They are to be debated on their possible merits or their many flagrant demerits—but that debate should not proceed, whether for or against any particular point in Father Coughlin's program, from the assumption that the point in question is invested with the authoritative support of the Catholic Church."[80]

A month before this latest editorial appeared, Shuster had published a calm, well-constructed, yet critical article on Coughlin in the *Review of Reviews*. In reviewing the young priest's early years as a Basilian Father, Shuster noted that order's emphasis at that time on medieval theology and philosophy. A prominent element in medieval culture was its attitude toward money and wealth: wealth, if one had it, was to be used to maintain one's livelihood but what was left over was to be used in the service of others, either as alms for the poor or as loans to assist some legitimate enterprise. But since this was to be a service, it was forbidden to charge interest or to profit from such a loan.[81] Permeated with this doctrine, Coughlin had little use for bankers or for government assistance for financial institutions, according to Shuster. It was not at all surprising, then, that when Coughlin organized his National Union for Social Justice, several of its goals were reforms in banking and monetary policy—nationalization of banking, currency, and natural resources; consistent value of currency; wartime conscription of wealth; and abolition of tax-free bonds.[82]

Shuster viewed Coughlin's new organization with alarm:

> It [the state] can be satisfactorily controlled by the League for Social Justice, the director of which is, of course, Father Coughlin himself. Groups of paying members are enrolled in all congressional districts. They are prepared to make a rumpus whenever called upon to do so; and the people's delegates to the Capitol are notoriously susceptible to rumpuses. Each Congressman must be made to realize that the bomb of League opinion can burst under his feet at almost any time. . . . The League is even a class-conscious organization. Only by joining can one secure information.[83]

As evidence that this was not a pure fantasy, Shuster noted the amazing outpouring of letters and telegrams to government leaders the day after Coughlin spoke against American participation in the World Court.[84]

Shuster then closed his analysis with a disturbing comparison between the Coughlin movement and the rise of Hitlerism in Germany:

> It has not escaped the notice of observers that the general contour of his [Coughlin's] doctrine is oddly similar to that of National-Socialism. Although the nazi dictator has abandoned virtually the whole of the program which he sold to the German people in 1930, the fact remains that it was excellent political copy. The nazis, too, advocated a central national bank, the abolition of interest, government control of labor, a better return for agricultural effort, and—above all—the superiority of human rights to property rights.[85]

The Commonweal took stands on numerous other important issues throughout the 1930s, but it is difficult to determine Shuster's precise contributions. On the race question, the journal published articles of southern conservatives and northern liberals, some bitterly controversial, but its editorials insisted that the welfare of black Americans was one of the most crucial questions facing American society, and they praised the educational efforts of the Cardinal Gibbons Institute in Maryland and Xavier College in New Orleans and especially the work of Father John LaFarge, S.J., and the Catholic Interracial Council.[86] The editors consistently urged the Catholic laity to take a greater role in church affairs, chiefly through Catholic Action programs and cooperation with the works of the hierarchy.[87] They were firm in their support of Pope Pius's encyclical *Casti Connubii*, "On Christian Marriage," and even in its condemnation of all artificial means of birth control.[88] The editors, especially Shuster, were impressed with the growing liturgical movement in Europe and lent their support to similar efforts here, especially the work of Virgil Michel and *Orate Fratres* and of Maurice Lavanoux and the Liturgical Arts Society.[89] *The Commonweal*'s early attitude toward the Mussolini regime in Italy was ambivalent, praising its concordat, which finally settled the so-called "Roman Question" and granted independence to the Vatican, but questioning also its political methods and the permanence of its economic reforms.[90] The editors also opposed President Roosevelt's recognition of the U.S.S.R. in 1933 because of the added prestige this would bring to that atheistic and totalitarian regime.[91]

But it was the confrontation between atheism and totalitarianism in Spain that proved to be George Shuster's greatest controversy in the 1930s and eventually the reason for his departure from *The Commonweal*. In February 1936 the leftist or Popular Front party won a narrow victory in Spain's national elections, and the more radical elements in that coalition immediately undertook a program of land seizures, strikes, and attacks on the Catholic church and clergy. The conflict grew between the leaders of the Popular Front and the Falangists (Spanish Fascists) until in July open civil war broke out, with General Francisco Franco assuming leadership of the right-wing forces. The Popular Front had the support and assistance of the Communist government in the U.S.S.R. and the Falangists the backing of the Fascist regimes in Germany and Italy.[92]

American opinion was clearly divided. It is difficult to say where the majority sentiment lay since the majority may have had no firm opinion at all. The American press and intellectual community, however, were liberal, favored the apparently duly elected Popular Front, and strongly opposed the militaristic and Fascist ideology represented by General Franco. The American Catholic hierarchy and even a majority of American Catholics disagreed. They feared the atheistic, Communistic, and anti-clerical leanings of the Popular Front and saw victory by General Franco as a means of preserving Spain's traditional Catholic culture. The United States did not have to take an official stand since Congress soon passed legislation prohibiting aid to either side, but the controversy raged hotly in the press and in other public forums.[93]

In response to the growing pro-Franco sentiment among American Catholics—especially in the editorials of the Jesuit weekly, *America*, and in reactions to an earlier article in *The Commonweal*—Shuster presented his own views in an article entitled "Some Reflections on Spain" in early April 1937. He began by summarizing—and oversimplifying—the majority opinion of many American Catholics, an opinion with which he disagreed:

> [A] republican government fell under the sway of Communists who began to perform every kind of injustice; and thereupon some

fine old soldiers rallied all staunch Catholics to safeguard religious and national rights against tyranny. This act of rebellion was legitimate, since the government overthrown was elected through fraud and was later guilty of violating the Constitution. If General Franco had waited another month, all the priests and religious in Spain would have been shot. Proof of this is found in the fact that hundreds have been massacred wherever the Reds have gained control. Catholics everywhere ought, therefore, to support the Insurgent cause and to hope for the speedy destruction of all Marxists.[94]

Shuster found three glaring weaknesses in this argument. First, many dedicated observers closer to the scene—in France, for example—simply did not accept it. Even the pope had recently urged neutrality. There were shocking atrocities committed on both sides, and the Catholic Basques would certainly suffer grievously under a Franco government. Second, it was difficult to speak of Catholicism in Spain since few in the poorer and working classes attended church with any regularity. They had apparently been alienated by the church's close union with the state in the past and there seemed little reason to think they would return to a church united with the state under Franco. To the possibility that the state under Franco might be different, Shuster replied in one of his more frequently quoted sentences: "To those who believe that General Franco will inaugurate a beneficent and progressive social order I shall reply very simply that yesterday was not my natal morn."[95] Third, popular opinion among Catholics was caricaturing both sides in the conflict. Fascists seemed bent on destroying the Catholic church in Germany and thus should not be hailed confidently as its savior in Spain. Loyalists, on the other hand, were not exclusively native or foreign Communists but included large numbers of honest, dedicated, and religious peasants and laborers. Shuster pleaded that the issues were terribly complex and wholehearted support of the Franco movement was not yet justified.[96]

Reaction to the article was immediate and almost unanimously negative. Letters poured into The Commonweal office. The New York Chancery Office asked Shuster's parish priest if he still attended Mass, and Father Francis Talbot, S.J., the editor of America, wrote a particularly strong reply. He questioned several of Shuster's interpretations of recent events in Europe and implied that he had probably been duped by liberal propagandists supporting the Loyalist government. He commended Shuster's opposition to Fascism but feared that it might have blinded him to the even greater danger of Communism. "But why does he assume, and rabidly," Talbot asked, "that General Franco is a Fascist and committed to Fascism? Franco never was a Fascist, and I judge that he never will be."[97]

Never one to flee a controversy, especially one in journalism, Shuster replied immediately. To remove any suspicion that there might be some Communist sympathizing in his anti-Fascist stance, he noted that he had had numerous opportunities to join Communist-sponsored demonstrations against Fascism in recent months and had avoided every one. He described himself as "a Borah Republican and, I hope, a Catholic." To Father Talbot's question whether he would prefer a dictatorship by General Franco or one by the Loyalist Caballero, he insisted that he wanted neither. "One's human affection for embattled priests and religious leads one to side with Franco," he admitted, "but one's love for the timeless mission of the Church leads one to believe that he may, after all, prove to be the greater of two evils."[98] Fascism, for Shuster, was an evil system in itself, and he spelled out clearly the reasons why:

> Inherent in Fascism is the assumption that safety is to be found in a purely nationalistic economy which can subordinate both labor and capital to a martial state purpose while allowing a measure of freedom to both. But since this economy is necessarily costly in itself, primarily by reason of the martial state purpose, a heavy burden is created which must be passed on to the toiling masses. Therefore in times of stress the political and social responsibility of the government becomes enormous. It cannot shift part of the blame to other shoulders, for it alone exists. Consequently the Fascist state must proceed to use more and more violent means. Inside the country, private energies are increasingly liquidated. Outside, acts of violence become more and more necessary.[99]

"This is one reason," Shuster continued, "why any identification of the Church with Fascism, however denominated, is so exceedingly dangerous." Fascism by no means stamps out the evils that bring on Communism and thus it must "eventually absorb Communism or perish." A just society demands that the rights of workers must be recognized and that they be exercised freely and creatively, and this is not possible under Communism or Fascism. The condition of labor is terrible in Spain and "it is assumed that Catholicism . . . is backing the other side." "These things mean," Shuster concluded, "that if the Fascist state wins out, the cleavages will be extraordinarily great, and (automatically) that antipathy to the Church will grow."[100]

This was Shuster's final piece as managing editor of *The Commonweal*. Michael Williams had not been in full agreement with Shuster's views and had stated as much in a gentle disclaimer introducing Shuster's first article. The journal at this time was also experiencing another of its financial crises, subscriptions eight years into the Depression stood at only fifteen thousand, and a new fund-raising drive was under way, this time with the assistance of Joseph P. Kennedy. Shuster's articles, unfortunately, were proving unpopular with the Catholic establishment, especially in New York, and the fund drive would assuredly suffer. In this situation Williams decided to turn the magazine strongly in support of Franco. On May 7 he began a series of "Open Letter[s]" to the leaders of the American press, criticizing them for what he considered their superficial analysis of the Spanish situation and their pro-Loyalist sympathies; he allied *The Commonweal* with the American Committee for Spanish Relief; and he took a major part in a mass rally of Franco supporters in Madison Square Garden. Shuster could interpret these activities only as a repudiation of his own stand, and he thus quietly resigned as managing editor.[101]

But if Shuster's departure from *The Commonweal* was relatively peaceful, the aftermath of the controversy was not. Shuster accepted a major grant from the Carnegie Foundation and the Social Science Research Council of Columbia University and set out for Europe to produce a documented history of the Center Party in Germany, but back in *The Commonweal* offices there was growing opposition to Michael Williams's pro-Franco stands and his bitter criticism of his fellow journalists.[102] In one "Open Letter" he had spoken of "a miscellaneous set of radical fanatics, radical rascals, and congenital ignoramuses, in the shape of incompetent or treacherous 'foreign correspondents,' and a riff-raff of badly educated, underpaid and miserably mistreated 'reporters' and copy-desk editors, many of whom cannot understand or make, a plain statement, in plain English."[103] Historian Carlton J.H. Hayes asked that his name be removed from the Editorial Council. Many became increasingly concerned over Williams's apparently declining health, his not infrequent bouts of alcoholism, and his ability to edit the magazine without Shuster's assistance. In a hurriedly called meeting of the Editorial Council and the leaders of the Calvert Associates in mid-June, it was agreed that Williams's effectiveness as editor had been compromised— either by his stance on the Spanish Civil War, his staunchly pro-Roosevelt sympathies (including support for enlarging the Supreme Court), his declining physical and emotional health, or by one or two recent and embarrassing public appearances—and he was asked to resign. Williams was shocked and thoroughly unconvinced but was eventually pressured to accede.[104]

An era ended with the controversial departures of Shuster and Williams, but it was an era of which both could be proud. They had unquestionably been the backbone of the magazine, with Williams handling most of the fund-raising, public relations, and some editorial work, and Shuster other editorial work and major responsibility for putting the magazine together each week. And an influential magazine it had become. Its articles and editorials were quoted frequently in the secular press, it provided a forum for some of the best American and European Catholic (and non-Catholic) thinkers, and it was an excellent example of the contribution Catholic lay men and women could make to the church. Those Catholics who, like the editors, were most often well educated, who strove to demonstrate the compatibility between Catholicism and American culture, who accepted a generally liberal or progressive interpretation of Catholic teachings, and who sought to apply these teachings and principles in bettering American culture and public life, were often known thereafter simply as "Commonweal Catholics." Shuster often acknowledged that those twelve years at *The Commonweal* were perhaps the most satisfying of his life.

4

UNDERSTANDING GERMANY
1930–1939

In an interview toward the end of her life, Doris Shuster mentioned that one reason why her husband did not receive his Ph.D. degree from Columbia University until 1940 was that he became so concerned about the rise of Adolf Hitler and Nazism in Germany that he postponed most other commitments to study and try to understand that threat as clearly as possible.[1] There is much truth in her assertion. Shuster's ancestry was German, his education at St. Lawrence was German, and he had a deep appreciation of the contributions of German culture to America and to the world. With the growth of Nazism in the 1930s, he realized that something terrible was developing. He despised all forms of tyranny, and much of his speaking and writing throughout the decade was devoted to exposing the tragic changes that were taking place in the Germany he loved.

Although Shuster's interest in German history and German culture stemmed from his early years in Lancaster, he did not write extensively about it until the political and economic crisis of the 1930s. In a few earlier articles he had noted the influence of Nietzsche on Theodore Dreiser, had discussed Max Scheler and Romano Guardini as humanists, and had warmly praised the German Catholic press in America, but these were little more than passing references.[2] In 1929 he published a major article on the Benedictine community at Beuron, praising both the scholarly idealism of its schools and the depth and influence of its liturgical life, and he pleaded for alms and contributions in its time of financial need.[3] But his major attention was elsewhere: he was assuming greater responsibility for editing *The Commonweal* each week; after five years' experience on the Notre Dame faculty, he

had decided and controversial views on Catholic higher education; and the heated election campaign of 1928 led him to give
much thought to the dilemma of being both Catholic and
American. *The Catholic Spirit in America* was an early result of
these deliberations.

But in 1930 his principal interest clearly turned to Germany,
now suffering so tragically from the effects of World War I, the
ravages of the widening Depression, and the slow disintegration of
the Weimar republic.[4] Shuster that year applied for and received a
grant from the *Vereinigung Carl Schurz*, a German foundation supporting and encouraging wider American interest in German life
and culture; he listed his occupation as editor and writer (and for
some reason used his wife's middle name, "Magdeline," on their
passport), and sailed from the United States in early October for
eight months in Europe. Arriving in Hamburg, the Shusters spent
the first several weeks in central Germany, with George attending
classes at the *Hochschule fuer Politik* and sitting in on lectures of
the outstanding Catholic theologian Romano Guardini at the
University of Berlin. Enrolling Bobby in a nursery school in
Berlin, George and Doris traveled throughout Germany to conduct interviews with prominent political and religious leaders,
including Heinrich Bruening, then chancellor of Germany.
George had become acquainted with Max Jordan, a German journalist, author, and later Benedictine monk, through his position at
The Commonweal, and it was Jordan and Margarete Gaertner,
director of the *Vereinigung Carl Schurz*, who made the necessary
introductions. George and Doris spent time in Silesia, traveled
along the eastern border of Germany, visited Switzerland and
Bavaria, crossed into Italy and attended Midnight Mass on
Christmas in Milan, and then returned north to Vienna where
Bobby rejoined them once again. After several weeks in Vienna,
where George wrote most of the day and he and Doris took
advantage of the brilliant cultural life in the evenings, the Shusters
made their way to France in the spring and departed for home
again in mid-April, 1931.[5]

One incident, which George and Doris later delighted in
telling, concerned their visit to Koenigsberg in East Prussia.
George had arranged for a meeting with the local bishop, and

probably because of the nature of some of his writings in *The Commonweal*, he had been described as an American theologian. Presuming that this meant a priest and seminary instructor, the bishop's household was more than a little perplexed when George boldly and without even a hint of embarrassment introduced his attractive young wife. Sensing the tension immediately when there was a hesitancy in notifying the bishop of his arrival, George quickly made the necessary explanations, they all shared a hearty laugh, and the interview then proceeded without further incident.[6]

Shuster sent frequent articles back to *The Commonweal*. Ever the humanist, he neglected little of the centuries-old art and culture he encountered, and he shared his appreciation and enthusiasm with his readers. Visiting Italy in December, he was captivated by the blending of Roman and Byzantine art with Christian ritual in the beautiful mosaics of the churches of Ravenna and the magnificent tomb of Galla Placidia.[7] Munich became on this trip, and remained ever after, one of his favorite cities. "From the mayor on down," he wrote, "the city's citizens are first of all out to maintain its reputation as a home of learning and art." As always, he was impressed with creative expression in the service of religion:

> Nowhere else probably is religious worship surrounded with so much radiant loveliness. Whether it be a communion Mass in the chapel of the Benedictines of St. Ottilie, where black-robed monks sit in the choir and chant the Gregorian texts, or a solemn Mass in the cathedral where gorgeous cadences entwine and unwind themselves, as much art is here as these people can give.[8]

Reflecting on the cultural glories of the past in Vienna, he lamented that "one of the oldest, greatest and most beautiful cities of Christendom is directly in the path of any one of those dozen military onrushes now spoken of in central Europe almost as a matter of course." "What counts," he added, "is not that St. Stephen's may crumble into ruins—which, of course, I should greatly deplore—but that one of the oldest bulwarks of Christian civilization may give way before the tides now seething out of the East."[9]

This discontent in Europe, Shuster insisted, could escalate toward war. One source of discontent was the eastern boundary of Germany as drawn at Versailles, at least in part out of hatred toward the defeated power. Shuster described the boundary light-heartedly:

> Here the line suddenly dips in three or four hundred yards to absorb a railroad bridge (Dirschau), or leaps across the river to embrace five villages and a hill, or even bends elastically to draw in dikes which if pulled down might engulf a whole region. Elsewhere the Polish officials have disregarded industrial assets and have torn up railroads and pulled down bridges where these might prove unsalutary in some hypothetical war. The results are often tragically comic. Here a town has been separated from its railroad station; there a farmer awoke to discover that his house was in one country and his field in another, so that a dozen customs officers were needed to supervise every harvest; and here again a factory is left stranded in Poland while the workers who serve it dwell in Germany. For all the humor, the situation was tragic and regrettable: Any impartial American who examined the scene and weighed the elements which comprise it would in all probability feel that the settlement of Germany's eastern boundary made at Versailles expressed the hates and petty ambitions of a moment, not the permanent rights and needs of European civilization.[10]

If there was one small bright spot on this otherwise dark horizon, according to Shuster, it might be that the United States had refused to sign the treaty of Versailles, and thus the Germans might look on Americans with more hope and confidence.[11]

A second major source of discontent was Germany's financial crisis, and here the United States might be of some assistance with foreign aid. Germany still owed billions of dollars in debts and reparations from World War I but, in the midst of a worldwide depression, the burden was too great. Farmers could make a profit perhaps of four percent, but their mortgages were eight or ten percent. Unemployment was high, and yet taxes could not be increased sufficiently to care for the needy. Foreign exporting was essential if the war debts were ever to be paid, and yet export prices needed to be reduced even further to compete with others in the Depression market, and this meant lower wages and reduced tax revenue, and the ominous cycle began again.[12]

Shuster saw only three possible solutions. One was success of the present government of Centrist Party Chancellor Heinrich Bruening. As a student Bruening had studied history, philosophy, and political science; he had traveled extensively in France and England; and he had taken an advanced degree in economics. In office only since March, he was a conscientious public servant but shunned publicity, glitter, and show. "Dr. Heinrich Bruening has no characteristic that suggests the American politician," wrote Shuster. "He seems rather like one of our finer university presidents, or better still like a physician, reflective and unbending, absorbed in the welfare of his patient and yet devoted to the science which exacts his own confidence." Shuster was deeply impressed. "Yet little by little the truth has become evident to all who cared to realize it," he wrote, "that here is a man of character, faith and absolute integrity, who stands in the midst of turmoil like a solid rock." Bruening's plan was *Notverordnung*, thrift everywhere, in order to return the country to a stable financial basis, but in early 1931 it was not at all certain how successful the chancellor would be.[13]

If the chancellor failed, Communism would certainly be attractive to many, as it generally was in times of economic crisis. But Shuster considered this eventuality slim. For him, the more likely threat was that in the face of an economic collapse, the country might turn to Adolf Hitler and his Nazi Party to stave off a victory for Communism. Shuster clearly underestimated the danger posed by Hitler, as did almost everyone else in 1931, two years before the Nazis assumed power. Writing of his visit to Munich, Shuster stated:

> The great man himself [Hitler] condescendingly appeared there during my stay. . . . The man has something of genius. Utterly fearless, a brilliant speaker, he is equipped with ideas of about the same value as those which form the stock-in-trade of the average United States senator. What Germany needs is a few dozen Hitlers, so that the novelty of one will wear off.[14]

Shuster had no sympathy for National Socialism: "When one looks more closely, however, one sees that the codex of its laws is a series of oppositions . . . antagonism to the rest of the world, to the Jews, the ruminative intellect, diplomacy, banks, other party philosophies." He noted approvingly the stance of the bishop of Mayence that "no practical Catholic could adhere to the National-Socialist movement because this opposed not merely the international Church but also fundamental Christian moral doctrine anent the equality of races in the sight of God." Shuster would soon prove himself an implacable foe of everything Hitler stood for, but in 1931 his greater fear was Communism: "For my part, however, I do not believe that a nationalistic wave such as the one described [National Socialism] would mean more than a temporary setback for Catholicism. On the other hand, the triumph of Communism, to the support of which more than four million voters pledged themselves at the last election, would imply genuine religious disaster."[15]

Shuster had also looked into conditions in the church in Germany, had interviewed prominent prelates, and published two major articles on the subject on his return. The deepening Depression was a major complication but there was hope that the church might emerge from the trial even stronger. German Catholics were critical of Jewish influence in the press and theater and the decline in moral standards exhibited there, but there was a marked friendliness between the two groups also. Shuster found the liturgies generally well performed, preaching of especially high quality in Munich, a genuine concern among the hierarchy for the poor and unemployed, and a laudable appreciation for secondary and higher education. But with the growing threat from both the Communist left and the National Socialist right, the freedom and prosperity of the church might depend upon the political success of the Catholic Center Party, and in the turmoil that was Germany in 1930 and 1931 that success was in no way assured.[16]

Shuster repeated some of these same conclusions in *The Germans: An Inquiry and An Estimate*, an excellent introduction to German life published on his return.[17] Emphasizing German art and culture and religion, he did not neglect history and politics. He pointed out that Germany was composed of various kingdoms and states and that, even in a united Germany, each retained its own characteristics and individuality. Generalizations about Germany were thus not easy. He discussed the characteristics of at least the major geographical sections and the larger urban areas, and also the contributions of the different social levels to the country as a whole. He described this diversification with a touch of humor elsewhere:

> A people split into twenty-seven wrangling political parties, five labor organizations suspicious of one another, three mutually hos-

tile churches. A public which subscribes to 3370 daily newspapers, every one of which knows positively that it is right and that none other is. A nation, above all, which is seemingly unable to approve of its form of government and just as unable to decide upon a different form. . . . Small wonder, then, that even patriotic Germans should think of themselves as belonging to a numerous and astonishingly persistent gathering of kilkenny cats.[18]

Shuster insisted that the main weaknesses of the Treaty of Versailles were its delineation of the eastern border and the imposition of unrealistic reparations—"A deceased cow cannot be milked," Shuster noted.[19] His views of Nazism had not changed; he still found it thoroughly unattractive and believed it had little chance of success. "Personally, of course, I find this NSDAP swashbuckling absurd and despicable," he wrote. "A country as committed to the principle of disparity as Germany is will never assent to the kind of dictatorship which a Fascist movement proposes."[20] For Shuster, the more serious disaster would still be a take-over by Communism.[21]

Shuster viewed Germany primarily as a people and a culture, and the qualities he singled out for special emphasis indicated much about his own personality and values. He returned often to the beauty of German liturgical celebrations, this harmonizing of art and religion. Admiring the justifiable confidence and optimism of the German people, he praised Germany's contributions in industry and technology, in philosophy, literature, and music. He described German Catholicism, and probably his own, as more romantic and mystical than philosophical—more Augustinian than Thomistic. He saw much truth in Luther's notion "that the concordance between man's sinfulness and the mercy of Christ is not the carefully balanced tit-for-tat of many scholastics but something like a babe's hunger and its mother's breast."[22] "Even today," Shuster continued, "the philosophy of Thomism, at least in all forms akin to the version of Jacques Maritain, is hardly known in Germany, where the reigning Catholic thinkers are all, in one way or another, steeped in Augustinian ideas."[23]

Shuster later recalled the book's strange fate. It was given a favorable, front-page review in the *New York Times Book Review* and was soon translated into German. But the American publisher unexpectedly went out of business and sales were halted here, and when the Nazis came to power in Germany in 1933, "one of Goebbels' first deeds was to order the volume reduced to pulp." "But far more important than all this," Shuster sadly recalled, "the Germany about which I had written was no more."[24]

The Shusters made a second trip to Europe in 1933 (actually George's third, counting his stint in World War I), and by this time the tragedy that was to engulf Germany in the 1930s was about to unfold. Adolf Hitler had been named chancellor of Germany that January 30.

The emergence of Hitler was not a coup or revolution but the result in part of strategy and in part of chance. German discontent had been growing throughout the 1920s—in the wake of the Treaty of Versailles, Germany had accepted full responsibility for the war, her boundaries had been redrawn almost arbitrarily, war reparations had been set impossibly high, and the nation's economy staggered under the burden. With the Depression of 1929 whatever bases of stability remained began to crumble. Unemployment rose alarmingly and the economic collapse now seemed total. Since the Treaty of Versailles received most of the blame for the nation's woes, the Weimar government, which had accepted the treaty, lost more and more respect. By 1933 democracy seemed to have failed, and, for many, Adolf Hitler was a viable alternative. He was strongly critical of Versailles, insisting that it had undercut the army's success, giving away at the conference table what the military had won on the battlefield. He was anti-Semitic, laying primary blame for both the rise of Communism and Germany's economic condition at the feet of the Jews. His methods were heavy-handed, but democratic methods had seemed ineffective. And at a time of national questioning and discouragement, Hitler exhibited supreme self-confidence. Many hoped that his actions in office would be more moderate than his words out of office, and this hope was based in part on the support he had won from several highly respected figures in art and education and culture.[25]

Shuster could not have picked a more critical time to visit. Heinrich Bruening had been replaced as chancellor by the conservative Franz von Papen in June 1932, only to be succeeded by Defense Minister Kurt Von Schleicher in November when von Papen seemed incapable of warding off challenges from both the

Communists on the left and Hitler's National Socialists on the right. Von Papen then convinced the aging President Hindenburg in January to form a cabinet with Hitler as nominal chancellor but in reality under the domination of von Papen and his conservative followers. Hitler, of course, remained nominal only for a short time. In the *Reichstag* elections in March, the National Socialists received forty-four percent of the vote and their allies eight percent, giving Hitler a working majority of fifty-two percent. On March 23 the Enabling Act was passed, altering the Constitution and giving the Hitler government almost dictatorial powers. By the end of 1933 all other political parties were banned, and the Nazi Party and the state became one. Although Hitler did not succeed as head of state and commander of the army until President Hindenburg's death the following August, his power at the end of 1933 was near absolute. In the midst of this national turmoil, from June to December 1933, the Shusters were visiting Germany again.

This trip was funded by the Oberlaender Trust of Philadelphia, the major benefactor of the Carl Schurz Foundation, which had supported his 1930 visit, and Shuster's principal purpose seems to have been to gather information on the decline of Heinrich Bruening's Center Party and the rise of Adolf Hitler. He traveled widely in Germany, Austria, and Switzerland, studying political changes and interviewing prominent Center Party and church leaders, leaving Bobby again in a German boarding school.[26] On one occasion he also met the National Socialist mayor of Berlin, who apparently encouraged him to visit Hitler at his Berchtesgaden retreat. Shuster declined, maybe out of disgust for the Nazi program. Shuster had purchased a copy of Hitler's *Mein Kampf* on his earlier trip but had not read it until preparing for this one. He later insisted that he was then convinced that "if the author believed half of what he had written his coming to power might prove to be an irreparable disaster for Germany and mankind."[27] The mayor himself was advocating the killing of hospital patients with incurable diseases. But Shuster still underestimated Hitler's lasting influence. In 1933 he remained confident that President Hindenburg could curb the chancellor's excesses, that the French would check any German invasion of the Rhineland, that Czechoslovakia would resist an encroachment

there, and that Mussolini would not tolerate the annexation
(*Anschluss*) of Austria. In all of these estimates, of course, Shuster
was sadly wrong.[28]

Shuster did meet with Bruening, now out of office and a
dejected man. He explained that the Center Party had cooperated
in the Enabling Act only because of assurances from Hindenburg
that the Social Democratic Party, slightly to the left, would be left
unhindered. Bruening was confident that Germany could yet be
saved through a coalition of the Center and Social Democratic
parties, but that, of course, was not to be. The Nazi party was
gaining adherents daily at the expense of others, if only because
party membership was becoming more necessary for retaining
employment. Gustav Oberlaender, founder of the Oberlaender
Trust, was visiting Germany at that time, and Shuster asked
whether money could be available if Bruening needed to flee
Germany. Oberlaender assured him it could, and the offer would
be hastily accepted in less than a year.[29]

Shuster was interested in both the recent political developments and the state of the Catholic church in Germany, and in
both of these the recent Concordat with the Vatican was crucial.
Signed in early July and supported by Cardinal Eugenio Pacelli,
Vatican secretary of state and former apostolic nuncio in Germany, the Concordat permitted the establishment of Catholic
schools, guaranteed freedom of activity to religious organizations,
granted the Vatican full authority in the appointment of Catholic
theologians to university faculties, and promised cooperation with
the Vatican in the selection of bishops. In return for these conces-
sions, the church agreed to the dissolution of all Catholic political
organizations and the prohibition of political involvement by
Catholic churchmen. Although unpopular with many, the
Concordat seemed to others an acceptable compromise. The
church was suffering persecution under the Bolsheviks in the
Soviet Union, and this agreement apparently guaranteed the
church's rights and freedoms in Germany. Church influence in
politics might decline but, in fact, the National Socialists were
more successful than the Centrists had been in curbing evils like
pornography and prostitution. And Hitler was a bitter opponent
of (atheistic) Communism and was even nominally a Catholic.[30]

Shuster hoped to interview several prominent prelates in an effort to learn what effect the Concordat might have. The See of Osnabrueck was too distant, and he always regretted he had not met with Bishop Wilhelm Berning there. It was Berning who later visited a Nazi labor camp and somehow proclaimed it a humane institution. Archbishop Conrad Groeber of Freiburg, who reportedly joined in the Nazi salute on occasion, was reluctant to meet with Shuster, but eventually did so. He admitted that he was now having doubts about the possibility of a *modus vivendi* with Hitler, but he was still hopeful that the millions who had voted for him would not be proved wrong. The bishop later retracted his pro-Nazi position. But Shuster's favorite was clearly Cardinal Michael von Faulhaber of Munich. Shuster had been familiar with the cardinal at least since his attendance at the Eucharistic Congress in Chicago in 1926, and, during his earlier visit he had praised the Munich periodical *Hochland* in a speech which the Cardinal attended. *Hochland* and the chancery were seldom in agreement at that time but the Cardinal did not let that affect their mutual respect. On this visit Shuster admired the great orator's Advent sermons in which, at a time of spreading anti-Semitic sentiment, he insisted that Christianity could not be separated from Judaism, nor the New Testament from the Old. Faulhaber was courageous in his defense of the church, and he often put himself in personal danger, but he also believed in strict separation of church and state and refused to become involved in political concerns, and this stance Shuster found difficult to understand.[31]

But Germany was not his only interest on this trip. Shuster had enrolled in the doctoral program at Columbia University in 1924. He apparently interrupted his studies in 1926 to devote more time to his work at *The Commonweal* and his teaching at St. Joseph's College, and he did not return to classes at Columbia again until 1932. He soon completed his classwork and passed the required proficiency tests in French, German, and Latin, and his Ph.D. oral examinations in English literature the following May.[32] The trip to Europe, therefore, enabled him to continue his research on the English ode, the subject he had selected for his doctoral dissertation. He and Doris crossed over to England and spent time together in libraries and museums in London and

Oxford. With the research now in English, Doris could be of assistance and they often worked together in reading rooms, reviewing and taking notes side by side.[33] Unfortunately, further distractions arose on their return to America, and Shuster's doctoral degree would be delayed another six years.

On his return to the United States, Shuster published two further books on Germany, *Strong Man Rules* in 1934 and *Like a Mighty Army* in 1935. The first was written, at least in part, to correct some of the observations he had made in *The Germans* two years earlier. "This book ought to begin, no doubt, with an apology," he wrote in *Strong Man Rules*. "During 1932 I wrote a treatise on Germany which seemed at the time to incorporate a certain amount of knowledge of that country. Today it is evident that in several respects I was quite mistaken."[34] Still fascinated by German culture and the German character, he strove to understand how the Nazis adapted the German character to their own philosophy. In theory, the Nazis saw the German state as the continuation of and successor to the Holy Roman Empire begun by Charlemagne, and it thus embodied for the present the religious and political qualities of that great civilization of the past. They also saw in the German character a continuation of the ideal of service and public responsibility epitomized in German knighthood of old, an ideal now personified in the military veterans of World War I and perhaps as the necessary corrective to the abuses of the current fumbling democracy.

Germans might recognize that war was unthinkable, especially in the present state of their economy, but they still idealized the virtues of leadership, obedience, cooperation, strength, and self-denial which military life instilled. As a people, Germans saw themselves as the direct descendents of those primitive peoples of the northern Teutonic forests who held so dear the natural virtues and love of freedom that they opposed Roman subjugation two thousand years ago and every other effort at oppression since then. From this, it was perhaps only one step further to reject all non-Teutonic peoples, especially the Jews, as somehow diluting and corrupting these natural, Teutonic virtues.[35]

Although he could not approve of much of this philosophy, Shuster repeated his sympathy with the feelings of discontent many Germans were then experiencing. The Treaty of Versailles

had left Germany near-prostrate economically, politically subservient, and thoroughly dissatisfied with her eastern borders.
Germany had been forced to accept full blame for World War I,
postwar reparations had been set impossibly high, and once
American credit was cut and trade reduced, Germany was left
alone among hostile (and well-armed) nations.[36] In this situation
the rise of Hitler was not wholly inexplicable. To a country teeter-
ing on demoralization, he brought a sense of national pride; to a
people convinced they had been aggrieved and unjustly treated,
he promised rehabilitation; to a nation convinced that only the
army could preserve it from a Communist take-over, he promised
the revitalization of the military.[37]

Whatever the hopes and grievances of the German people,
Hitler's record so far was disheartening. Prices were rising faster
than wages, farm income was inadequate, social welfare programs
were promised but not enacted, the educational system was stag-
nant, university professors were being silenced, newspapers were
losing their independence, laws were oppressive, political opposition was persecuted, and religion was becoming more subservient
to the state.[38] But the most fearful characteristic of the new
Germany was the rising tide of anti-Semitism.

Germans were finding several reasons for despising the Jews,
in addition to the obvious fact that they were not part of the
Teutonic strain. Many Jews had been members of the Democratic
and Socialist parties in the early 1920s, parties that had favored
acceptance of the Treaty of Versailles, and now they were blamed
for its shortcomings. Jewish involvement in the foundation and
spread of Communism was continually underscored and exagger-
ated as the threat from Bolshevik Russia increased. Several prominent Jewish writers were also pacifists, and this conflicted with
rising respect for the military. Jews were prominent in industry,
banking, and the professions, and some were making comfortable
livelihoods at a time when others were suffering from poverty and
unemployment. At a time of deepening Nordic and Aryan pride,
Jews were easy to single out, to separate, and to scorn.[39] The
result was that, when the opportunity presented itself in the Nazi
political victory, anti-Semitism burst into violence. "Everything
which occurred in those terrible days will doubtless never
be known," Shuster wrote, "but enough information has been

gathered to show that hundreds upon hundreds of S.A. meeting-places witnessed vindictive brutality of the most debased and ghastly kind." And if such occurrences might be explained as incidents of unlicensed mob reaction, other events could not. "The really sinister aspects of Nazi anti-Semitism," Shuster continued, "are revealed only in the corpus of law and enactment which give practical form to the theory of race prejudice. Of this it may be said generally that probably no equally serious a challenge to the moral sentiments of the western world has been laid down since England began the practice of sentencing crowned sovereigns to death in the sixteenth and seventeenth centuries." He summarized both his distaste of Nazism and his respect for the Jews in a final passage:

> Pogroms have often occurred; brutal attacks upon individual Jews are commonplace phenomena in all lands. But never before was it made lawful to stamp out or at best reduce to impotence the race to which European civilization owes, under God, its loftiest and most fruitful aspirations.[40]

Shuster reserved his most complete discussion of the antagonism of Nazism to religion to his next book: *Like a Mighty Army: Hitler versus Established Religion.* The underlying theme of the work was that Europe was a religious continent, a Judeo-Christian continent, and the author raised the question of what might happen if religion were to break down or be destroyed. Thus it was "Hitler's challenge to the historic churches of Judaism, Protestantism and Catholicism" that in this work was of primary concern.[41]

The major religious conflict, of course, was with Judaism. As discontent deepened throughout the country toward the mid-1930s, anti-Jewish bitterness increased also. Jews were given major blame for accepting the Treaty of Versailles, for losing the gains the army had won, and for submitting to such a dishonorable peace. As Communism continued to infiltrate other countries from its base in the Soviet Union, Jews were singled out as its principal emissaries and promoters. As Germany and the world were plunged more deeply into the Depression, Jews were attacked as the major proponents of capitalism and the profit economy.[42] Although anti-Semitism was present throughout Europe, Shuster emphasized its unique characteristics in Germany. It was fashionable for the bourgeois to marry Jewesses "for their beauty or their money," but the social code would not permit acceptance of a Jew as political or social equal. Wilhelm II could rely heavily on an adviser like Albert Ballin, although most monarchists would not accept Jews into the party and thus drove them politically to the left. The German Nationalist Party, which helped gain Hitler the chancellorship, was led by Albert Hugenberg, a Christianized Jew, but it soon became bitterly anti-Semitic also. Jewish doctors were still highly sought after by the German populace but the state continued to restrict their licenses.[43]

Shuster admitted that Jews at times should have acted more tactfully—kept wealth more hidden in time of depression and been less vocal in criticizing social welfare programs—but the anti-Semitic outbreaks of the 1930s were in no way justified.[44] In Hitler's first two years in office, before the harsh Nuremberg laws deprived them of all citizenship rights later that year, Jews were, in Shuster's words, "squeezed rather than strangled."[45] Jewish children attended school, but they had to sit through the teacher's propaganda lectures on how immoral and unprincipled Jewish people were, and on the playground they were forced to stand apart like pariahs. Jewish doctors and lawyers could still practice, but it was becoming more and more difficult to renew one's license and increasing numbers were being harassed out of the country. There was apparently no official oppression of Jewish businesses since their participation was needed for economic well-being, but anti-Jewish boycotts still occurred and Shuster remarked that he had "seen and heard enough in cities like Bamberg and Nuremberg to feel permanently disgusted."[46] Jewish workers were ineligible for membership in the government-controlled labor organization, the *Arbeitsfront*.[47]

Shuster admitted that German anti-Semitism had a religious component as well. Catholic and Protestant leaders criticized the liberal press for its views on church matters, and influential editors were often Jewish. Jews were thought to be particularly prominent in the arts and theater, and thus they were blamed for any excesses and vulgarity. Opponents of the sexual emphasis in psychiatry blamed the trend on the Jewish Sigmund Freud, and religious conservatives were outspoken when several Jewish physicians were discovered performing abortions. Of the Christian religions, Catholics might have been more sympathetic than the

Lutherans only because they were probably less nationalistic, but the religious component was seen also in debates on the superiority of New Testament virtues over those of the Old.[48]

Bleak and ghastly as the picture was, Shuster could not resist pointing out the ironies in Nazi racial theory. Dr. Goebbels had once remarked that he held "a Nordic prostitute . . . of greater worth than a Jewish married woman." Noting that Goebbels was actually not Nordic, although Shuster was, Shuster added wryly: "That Dr. Goebbels should so greatly esteem one of our prostitutes is doubtless natural under the circumstances. It is just another case of inferiority complex."[49]

The Hitler regime's relationship with German Protestantism (Lutheranism) was much less bitter but still far from harmonious. According to Shuster, active church membership was declining and the Lutheran communion was divisible into differing theological movements or confessions, all of them quite traditional and conservative. In early April 1933 several Nazi religious leaders had met in Berlin to discuss the possibility of Lutheran unity, ostensibly as a step to counteract atheistic Communism more successfully and to preserve national autonomy. They could not reach agreement and discussions continued for several weeks. Finally, Hitler himself intervened in July and presented a new constitution for this "German Evangelical Church," a moderate constitution permitting much local church autonomy but providing for an authoritative *Reichsbischof*, a council of three, and an annual National Synod. Nazi storm troopers incongruously oversaw the voting on this constitution and, to the surprise of no one, the constitution was eventually accepted.[50]

Opposition to the new church continued, especially in September when Pastor Ludwig Mueller, special adviser to Hitler on religious matters, was elected *Reichsbischof*. Opponents insisted that the source of Christian doctrine was divine revelation, whether it harmonized with current social and political theory or not, that Christianity could in no way be limited to one particular nation or race, and that God's revelation in the Old Testament could not be denigrated or ignored. As the division continued, *Reichsbischof* Mueller hardened. In early 1934 he had several opposition ministers suspended from their positions and deprived

of their salaries, and in March he abrogated the earlier constitution and centered more authority in his own hands. In August an
oath of loyalty and obedience to both Hitler and to the German
Evangelical Church was prescribed for all clergy, and although
most clergy could accept Hitler as the legitimate ruler of Germany,
many balked at promising to "conduct myself in consonance with
the laws of the Evangelical Church and . . . observe scrupulously
instructions given to me under these laws."[51] Opposition bishops
of Wuerttemberg and Bavaria were deposed that fall and pastors
were silenced, dismissed, and imprisoned throughout Prussia.

As the conflict deepened, Hitler suddenly broke the tension
by inviting the three leading opposition bishops of Hanover,
Wuerttemberg, and Bavaria to a personal meeting in late October.
It seemed an open admission that the use of force and intimida-
tion had been unsuccessful and that the growing opposition of
international Protestantism to the new German Christian movement had to be countered. All restrictive measures against the dissenting bishops were removed, and Hitler repeated that his
government was not attempting to impose national unity by force.
But succeeding conferences could not resolve the differences. As
Shuster closed his study in mid-1935, his view was not sanguine:

> In silence and fortitude, in charity and hope, the Lutheran faithful
> must conserve the recollection of what their Church might have.
> Sooner or later, when there is stillness once again on the battle-
> fields, the individual German soul will look in upon itself. The mis-
> sion of the Church is to wait, sometimes through long penitential
> years, for that moment during which the Gospel can be preached.[52]

Shuster's analysis of Nazism's relations with Catholicism
reinforced his earlier opinions. He still had high regard for
Chancellor Bruening's Center Party, whose four basic principles
he saw as defense of the civil and educational rights of the church,
industrial reform according to the social justice teachings of Pope
Leo XIII, submission to legitimate ecclesiastical authority, and
conscientious service to the state. Shuster agreed fully. He admitted that Bruening had not always been politically shrewd, but he
was convinced that his program of thrift and fiscal responsibility
had been the correct one. "I have never had the slightest doubt,"
Shuster concluded, "that he is one of the truly great men of his

time. . . . [He] was the first German statesman since Bismarck to emerge with a plan for the reconstruction of the Fatherland."[53]

In German-Vatican relations in the 1930s, the Concordat of 1933 was both central and perplexing. The German bishops had met at Fulda in May, had recognized the National Socialist government of Adolf Hitler as legitimate, but had also criticized both the "exclusive emphasis on race or blood in defining national allegiance" and the government's program of sterilization. Negotiations between the government and the Vatican continued that spring and the Concordat was finally initialed later that summer. Since political activity by the clergy and Catholic political organizations were both prohibited, Shuster saw the Concordat as effectively terminating the Center Party. On the other hand, the church's rights were now officially guaranteed in the appointment of bishops and university theologians, in the conducting of confessional schools, and in the autonomy of religious organizations. As a strong supporter of Chancellor Bruening and the Center Party, Shuster admitted that the agreement was controversial, but he saw the logic of it also. Hitler may have seen it as a way of solidifying his own position by eliminating his major rival in Bruening and the Center Party, and the Vatican may have been pleased to have the church's rights in Germany officially guaranteed while recognizing in return only what amounted to a *fait accompli*, the authority of Adolf Hitler and the National Socialist Party.[54]

In fact, anti-Catholic demonstrations erupted and the situation deteriorated rapidly. In Bavaria several university professors were harassed out of their positions, and even religious services were interrupted by Nazi demonstrators. Additional restrictions were placed on Catholic youth groups and, as they lost members, the Hitler Youth Corps increased. Shuster saw this as no gain at all. "I venture to believe that the rising German generation will be physically less fit than its predecessor," he wrote. "And mentally and spiritually—well, God help us all!"[55] Confessional schools were discouraged throughout Bavaria, and religious sisters and brothers were imprisoned for violating laws governing financial transactions with foreign benefactors. Priests were arrested for criticizing public officials, and several prominent Catholics— Center Party official Erich Klausener, editor Fritz Gerlich, and professor Friedrich Beck—were murdered in a purge of June 30, 1934. The future, as Shuster completed his book in mid-1935, seemed bleak indeed:

> The end of all this will be terrible. For one who loves Germany as I do, the outlook for the next few years is heartrending. There will be economic catastrophe. Political and military upheavals of an utterly unpredictable kind may lead to either civil or foreign war. Of much that is hallowed by centuries of association with the great and the wise, there may not be left so much as a stone upon a stone.[56]

Some, of course, were able to escape the tragedy that was to come. Shuster had earlier received assurance from the prominent philanthropist Gustav Oberlaender that he would finance Bruening's flight from Germany if that ever became necessary. Sometime thereafter Bruening had met with Chancellor Hitler, had criticized the Chancellor's anti-Semitic program, and had warned that any resort to arms could only be disastrous. As Nazi atrocities increased, Bruening realized that his own life was in danger. Shortly before "The Night of the Long Knives," in which Klausener, Gerlich, and Beck were assassinated, he decided to flee.[57]

Bruening went first to Great Britain, and then to the United States, arriving in New York under an assumed name—Henry Anderson. Ever sensitive, Bruening feared possible reprisals on associates still in Germany if his escape became public. Still using his alias, a room was found for him at Immaculate Conception Seminary on Long Island, where Shuster was also teaching two days a week. The bishop of Brooklyn, Thomas Molloy, had granted his permission, and the seminary rector, Msgr. Patrick Barry, a church historian, was more than pleased to welcome him. Bruening gave occasional lectures to the students and, although all knew his true identity, none divulged his secret. Shuster recalled dining with Bruening at the Player's Club on one occasion and meeting a drama critic and friend. He introduced his guest as Henry Anderson and the critic remarked: "Has anyone ever told you how much you look like Heinrich Bruening?" "Yes," Anderson replied, "People have sometimes pointed that out."

Bruening also lived for a time with Father George B. Ford at Corpus Christi Rectory near Columbia University (where Shuster was still officially registered as a graduate student) and he kept his identity secret for several months until someone in Canada, perhaps accidentally, revealed who he was.[58]

Since part of the reason for Shuster's two trips to Europe in the early 1930s was to collect information on the Weimar Republic and the decline of the Center Party, the presence of Bruening in the United States was too great an opportunity to miss. Shuster visited Bruening in the seclusion of his seminary retreat and conducted long interviews with him, with Bruening pacing up and down while he spoke and Shuster, the former newspaper reporter, taking notes as rapidly as he could. As soon as he returned home, Shuster wrote out the complete interview from his notes and returned them to Bruening for his approval. "There can be no doubt as to their authenticity," Shuster noted. Because of other interests and commitments in the late 1930s, unfortunately, the book on the Center Party was never written.[59]

The Shusters went to Europe again in 1937. On their return the following year, Bruening had taken up residence at Harvard University, first as lecturer and tutor in government and economics, and then as Lucius N. Littauer Professor of Public Administration. His sojourn there was uneven. He thoroughly enjoyed the intellectual stimulation and companionship of the truly outstanding faculty, but as time went on there was also a growing anti-German feeling coloring the campus. His health was beginning to decline and his contacts with Shuster were not as frequent. He hesitated to travel to New York and, as Hunter College president, Shuster was less free to visit Boston. But their respect for each other remained high. They continued to correspond, and Bruening agreed to lecture at Hunter in December 1940. Their visit apparently was most enjoyable. Five years later, on an official trip to Europe in 1945, Shuster was happy to be able rather illegally to cross into the British zone of German occupation, meeting briefly with Bruening's sister and assuring her of her brother's health and well-being.[60]

By this time, however, Bruening was becoming disillusioned, if not embittered. Although uncompromisingly anti-Nazi, his patriotism and love of Germany remained strong, and he was deeply sensitive to the anti-German feeling sweeping America during the war. A staunch opponent of Communism, he considered President Roosevelt too weak in checking the postwar influence of the Soviet Union throughout Europe. Despite their differences of opinion, however, Shuster's respect for Bruening never wavered. "I shall say of Heinrich Bruening," he wrote in 1967, "that he has been a man whom the world and in particular Germany should cherish by reason of a singular combination of greatness of intellectual endowment, untarnished probity and luminous humaneness of character. . . . He has been a great gentleman . . . and Germany has produced far too few of them."[61]

Because of Shuster's great respect, it was sad that their last meeting ended as it did. It was probably in late 1945, and is best told in Shuster's own words:

> Then we were back at Stamford again, and he was our guest. After dinner Bruening, my wife and I sat down to talk a little while. It was clear that his heart was broken, and that sooner or later he would be unable to conceal that fact. But I was not prepared for what happened. He suddenly began to talk about the United States with such bitter hatred that his words seemed to come out of a well unfathomably deep. I wanted to say to him, "Come my dear friend, let us get together with Bruce Hopper and some other friends who have known you for a long time and talk things over." But my wife who had befriended him so often, and been his doting hostess, could not press down the fact that she was an American, every inch an American, without a drop of German blood in her veins.
>
> She said that his attitude was past understanding. She listed all the things which the United States had done for him, even to giving him a special passport, and said she resented the bitterness. After all, who had started the terrible war but Hitler's Germany? He said nothing in reply, but shrugged his shoulders and looked at me as if to say, "Well, George, I suppose this is the end." I knew it was impossible to effect a reconciliation, and that therefore we would never see him in our house again.
>
> I had never before been a party to such a scene. On the one hand the woman whom I loved dearly had challenged her guest, and I knew that everything she had said was right. And on the other, a great man, so broken, so sick at heart by reason of everything that had happened to his country, that he could not longer be coherent or rational. I wanted to say, well it is time to go to bed

and we will talk some more tomorrow, but all I could manage was the first part of the sentence. It was utterly impossible to apologize for her to him, for the only conceivable apology would have been that she did not realize how desperately ill he was.

Therewith my memoir of Bruening comes to an end. I wrote him several times but received no reply. Then of course we moved to Notre Dame and Vermont was far away. It is impossible to tell whether he would even have wished me to call on him. Even so his spirit was great, courteous, deeply ethical. It was wounded to the core by the tragic time. Still, if I were asked to write his epitaph, it would read: It is not wise for a man to love his country as much as he did his.[62]

As Shuster's growing distaste for Adolf Hitler and Nazi Germany became more publicized, he was called on increasingly for assistance to anti-Nazi and refugee movements. One of his favorite spots in all Germany was the abbey at Beuron, combining as it did the religious, academic, and liturgical tradition of the Benedictine community. He had written an article in *The Commonweal* in 1929 praising the group's religious spirit and truly outstanding cultural contributions and closing with an appeal for financial assistance during that period of economic crisis, and he made a pilgrimage to the monastery on his visit to Germany in 1933.[63] Since he had come to their assistance in 1929, the monks felt confident in turning to him in their greater crisis in 1934. As Shuster wrote to his friend, Father John Burke, C.S.P., of the National Catholic Welfare Conference:

> I have just received a confidential letter from the Archabbey of Beuron, Germany, to the effect that the situation in so far as they are concerned is becoming precarious. The Archabbot did not cast a vote for Hitler at the November election, and this gave rise to considerable antipathy which has been exploited by anti-Catholic politicians. The monks, therefore, secretly requested me to begin a press campaign in their behalf over here, should events become critical. They are to give a pre-arranged signal. I am, therefore, wondering if the [N.C.W.C.] News Service could be instructed to accept and play up such a story if the time came when it was desirable to send it out.[64]

Father Burke was sympathetic but felt that the Conference, the official organization of the American bishops, might decide to coordinate any such efforts with the German hierarchy also.[65] In fact, events proceeded so rapidly that such assistance to a single monastery was apparently judged unfeasible.

In 1935 Shuster also became involved in a controversy over American participation in the 1936 Olympic Games scheduled for Berlin. Against the recommendation of the American Olympic committee, Shuster strongly opposed attendance. He took this stand for two reasons. First, even under world pressure, Germany was apparently inviting only two of its own Jewish athletes to participate, an instance of tokenism deeply insulting to every American of Jewish background. Second, German leadership was publicizing the coming Olympics as a demonstration of the success of the athletic programs of the Hitler Youth Corps, and Shuster saw this as clearly unacceptable. Contrary to the Concordat, Catholic youth organizations were not permitted to sponsor athletic programs, and Catholics in the Hitler Youth Corps were discouraged and even hindered from practicing their religion. Thus Shuster saw any participation in or support of the 1936 Olympics as "aiding and abetting an effort to destroy the Christian faith," and he made his position clear:

> It being true that the coming Olympics are designed to be a glorification of the Nazi doctrine of youth, and therewith necessarily a repudiation of the Catholic faith and the Catholic heritage, little stress need be laid upon the fact that American Catholics ought to oppose participation. I know perfectly well that a young man or woman finds it hard to renounce a chance for fame and fortune. It is certainly not I who will pooh-pooh the laurels won by the modern athlete. Just because the honor and the sacrifice are alike great, the chance to make a choice is of such critical importance.
>
> In a life replete with chance and debate, few things are certain. But on the issue under consideration, no doubt exists. It seems to me quite incredible that the Catholic clergy of these United States will not raise their voices against this new temptation to offer incense at the altar of Baal, provided they realize in time what issues are at stake. Those of us who love Germany will hope that the truth is known before it is too late. And those of us who love the Church will remember the steadfast sons of Caesar's Rome who did not offer sacrifice.[66]

The games, of course, proceeded, and the United States took part. Because of that participation, ironically, racist theory suffered a further setback through the memorable performance of the young black American student from Ohio State, Jesse Owens, clearly the most outstanding athlete at the games.

About that same time Shuster became involved in an effort to address the German refugee problem and, as a result, became closely involved in the life and activities of the controversial German emigre priest Father Hans Ansgar Reinhold. Earlier that spring a small group of priests and laymen in New York had met to consider what steps they might take to assist refugees, chiefly Jewish, suffering oppression in Germany. Since Jewish and Protestant organizations were already at work in this area, they decided to organize a Catholic committee and seek official church approval. In late April 1936 Monsignor Gallus Bruder, Father Joseph Ostermann, Professor Carlton Hayes, and Shuster sent a petition to Cardinal Patrick Hayes of New York describing the need as they saw it, recommending the establishment of such a Catholic committee to work with other organizations, and requesting official approbation. They admitted that the German hierarchy had not directly asked for such assistance, but they noted that the hierarchy was no longer free to speak and that the Vatican itself had been encouraging the establishment of such relief agencies.[67]

The group realized that it needed someone to serve both as a direct contact in Europe and as occasional adviser to the committee here in America, they located a benefactor to finance such a position, and they decided to select Father Reinhold.[68] Reinhold had been ordained a priest for the diocese of Osnabrueck in 1925, had been assigned as chaplain to three communities of nuns on the Baltic Sea for two years, and then was sent on for further studies in Rome. His studies were cut short, however, when in 1929 his bishop recalled him to Germany to organize a Catholic ministry to German seamen. He worked first at Bremerhaven and then at Hamburg. A staunch opponent of Hitler, his work was made increasingly difficult when the National Socialists took control of the government in 1933, and in fact, his life may have been in danger. In the spring of 1935 he was forced to give up his work with the seamen and, on the advice of friends, fled the country. He settled eventually in Switzerland where he continued his work of modernizing Catholic worship as a parish curate and where Shuster and his associates contacted him in 1936.

Unfortunately, after receiving Reinhold's agreement to survey other refugee works in Europe and visit with the committee here, the committee was notified by the Chancery Office in New York that official approbation could not be granted at the time. The reason given was that for a project of this importance, the approval of the official Bishops' Conference should be sought rather than that of an individual diocese.[69] This left the committee with two major problems. First, they still desired official recognition to work with other recognized groups and, second, they needed a diocese's approval of residence for Father Reinhold when he arrived. They contacted Archbishop Michael Curley of Baltimore, and he recommended Reinhold to the staff of the National Catholic Welfare Conference in Washington, a city within his own archdiocese. Eventually the Archdiocese of New York agreed to receive him but, suspicious of his frequent travels and perhaps of his occasionally strained relations with religious superiors in Germany, put serious restrictions on his public speaking.[70]

Considering Shuster's love of Germany, his deep appreciation of the modern liturgical movement, and his concern for refugees from Nazism, it was not surprising that he staunchly befriended Reinhold almost from the day of his arrival in August 1936. When officials of the Archdiocese of New York accused him of violating the restrictions imposed on his public speaking, it was Shuster who helped compose his letter of explanation and defense. When Reinhold's residence in New York became too strained and unpleasant, Shuster intervened with Bishop Thomas Molloy of Brooklyn and won an invitation for him to reside there. And through all these months, Reinhold and Shuster met frequently in *The Commonweal* offices, where Shuster sought as much information as possible about current conditions in Germany.[71]

In 1938 Reinhold transferred to the Diocese of Seattle and continued his work with seamen for three years in that port city. As anti-German sentiment increased in America as World War II approached, Reinhold, still a German citizen, was transferred to Yakima, further inland, and was forbidden to travel outside a five mile radius of the city without special permission. After a brief visit to the East again in 1943–1944, he returned to Sunnyside,

near Yakima, as pastor in 1944, and the Shuster connection surprisingly surfaced again. In 1951 Yakima was erected as an independent diocese, and Reinhold had disagreements with the new
bishop, Joseph Dougherty. After five years of strained relations,
Reinhold decided to withdraw from the diocese and seek a bishop
in the East who might welcome him. The bishop of Yakima
insisted that he had left the diocese without permission, had simply deserted his parish, and thus ordered him to return and make
some kind of amends. Shuster's older sister, Catherine, happened
to be a member of the Sunnyside parish and had the highest
regard for Reinhold, who had assisted her family through a religious difficulty a few years before. Catherine led a group of
parishioners in support of Reinhold and also tried to enlist her
brother's aid. Shuster did write to at least one influential priest-
friend for advice, the Jesuit Father John LaFarge, and explained
to his sister how the situation might be resolved satisfactorily. In
fact, Bishop John Wright of Pittsburgh eventually agreed to
accept him, and it was in that diocese that Reinhold served the
rest of his life.[72]

By late 1936, in addition to his activities with Heinrich
Bruening and Father Reinhold, the editorial work for *The Com-
monweal*, and particularly his growing controversy over support for
General Franco, Shuster was committing himself to a major
longer-term project, a third trip to Europe and the publication,
finally, of the history of the German Center Party since World War
I, which he had been contemplating for several years. Shuster and
Bruening had discussed the possibility of publishing such a book
jointly and had asked the advice of Professor Carlton Hayes of
Columbia University, a friend of Shuster through *The Commonweal*. Hayes thought the idea excellent: Bruening would be a guide
and resource person; Shuster would be more objective as principal
author, and Shuster was already sufficiently respected by former
Center Party leaders that they would be eager to cooperate.[73]

Realizing that Shuster would have to leave his position at *The
Commonweal* for a year to do the research, Hayes sought the assistance of the Carnegie Corporation in New York. The Corporation
initially seemed favorable, but one of the persons to whom it
turned for advice had a major objection and altered the project
slightly. This representative of the Social Science Research

Council was cool to the selection of Shuster (whose name he mis-spelled as "Schuster") since both Shuster and Bruening were Catholics and would be writing about a Catholic party, an all-Catholic enterprise. He could accept the proposal and cooperate with it if Shuster were to be collecting primary sources and mak-ing them available to other scholars also. Thus the project became almost twofold, a history of the Center Party from 1919 to 1933 and the publication of documents pertinent to such an investiga-tion. This was satisfactory to all concerned, a budget of nine thou-sand dollars was approved, and the Columbia University Council for Research in the Social Sciences was selected as sponsor.[74]

Shuster spent late 1936 and early 1937 working approxi-mately half-time on the project, conducting long interviews with Bruening, discussing the work with other German scholars, and reading widely in background material. With opposition increas-ing against his stand on Franco and the Spanish Civil War, he resigned his position at *The Commonweal* that May and sailed shortly thereafter for Europe. He and Doris landed in Poland, spent almost a day waiting for their car to be unloaded, and then drove through Poland and Czechoslovakia into Austria. Since George had been blacklisted in Germany since 1935 and had restricted travel there, he decided to make his center of operations Vienna, traveling from there throughout Austria, Switzerland, France, and Holland as needed.[75] This was actually not a major handicap since many of the former Center Party leaders he hoped to interview had already fled Germany and were now living in sur-rounding countries.

Shuster was quite pleased with the interviews he conducted and the material he collected. Extensive notes remain of his inter-views with at least a dozen party leaders, and he undoubtedly spoke with many others.[76] Some of these persons he had known from his earlier visits and others were introduced through Bruening. He spoke with the brilliant scientist Friedrich Dessauer, former Center Party leaders Joseph Joos and Bernhard Letterhaus, former Finance Minister Rudolf Hilferding, and one of Bruening's predecessors as chancellor, Joseph Wirth. Through these inter-views Shuster tried to grasp more clearly the precise condition of the church and the Center Party in the various parts of Germany, the reasons for several of the controversial decisions made by

party leaders, especially cooperation with Hitler in passing the
Enabling Act in 1933 and the support for the Concordat among
party members, and an evaluation of party leadership during this
1919–1933 period. As the terms of his grant stipulated, Shuster
also collected as much documentation as possible, both to support the history he was hoping to write and to be of use to other
historians as well.[77]

Shuster later summarized what he learned of the decline of
the Center Party from these interviews. Center Party leaders had
been willing to cooperate with Hitler in 1933 because they were
confident that President Hindenburg would not tolerate any violation of the Constitution, they felt that Hitler's popular following
was so great that he probably deserved a "chance" to rule, and
they were impressed by warm references to the Holy See in
Hitler's early speeches. The final dissolution of the Center Party
Shuster laid at the feet, not of Rome and the Concordat, but of
the party leaders themselves, especially Msgr. Ludwig Kaas. The
party began to splinter as members feared for their jobs and their
livelihoods, and Kaas was not strong enough to hold them
together. Shuster's verdict was harsh:

> It may therefore seem as if Rome wished to disband the
> Party. But this was by no means true. The largest measure of
> responsibility may be attributed to Kaas. He was doubtless a man
> of intelligence, vitality and oratorical ability. He loved philosophi-
> cal discussion but was essentially a clerical Hamlet. He fought shy
> of responsibility and was therefore unable to lead. Often he could
> interpret the trend of events brilliantly but came to no decision. In
> moments of crisis he invariably became ill. Yet he was deemed
> indispensable because there were so few men in the Party whose
> influence extended beyond its ranks. In all probability it was pri-
> marily he who was responsible for the Party's downfall. Inwardly
> he was no democrat at all but was enamored of the authoritarian
> State.[78]

On one of his trips to Holland, Shuster had a particularly
narrow escape. Several Germans had been invited to meet with
him in Nijmegen, where he had registered at the hotel as "Dr.
Sutorius," the Latin form of his name, so his visitors would not
later be accused of meeting with this blacklisted American. During the meeting his visitors begged him to come to Cologne to talk
with others, but George explained that he had been explicitly

denied a visa in both New York and Vienna. Eventually a plan was devised. Many Dutch workers still commuted regularly to their jobs in Germany, and Shuster decided to dress as a local worker and board the train with them since customs officials rarely patrolled that area. He was told that someone would be waiting for him at a local station, with a pre-arranged sign, and everything went as planned. From the small station they drove to Cologne, and for three days Shuster spoke with numerous persons about a possible resistance movement. "Today at horrible moments my blood still freezes," he wrote later, "when I recall that only a few of those who came to that house escaped the executioner after the attempt on Hitler's life failed in 1944."[79] The climax of the visit was a nighttime drive to Bonn and a secret meeting with Konrad Adenauer, former mayor of Cologne, then living under near house-arrest outside the city. They arrived shortly after midnight and left at approximately 3:00 a.m., coming and going through a back entrance, over a fence, and through shrubs and bushes— some quite thorny, as Shuster later remembered.[80]

But it was the train ride back to Holland that was most memorable. A few miles from the Dutch border a German customs policeman suddenly appeared and asked to see all passes. Shuster had no pass and did not want to show his American passport since he did not want to reveal his true identity. When the police demanded to see his papers, Shuster at first made believe he could not understand German, though he spoke it almost perfectly and knew almost no Dutch at all. Then, feigning understanding, he slowly took down his suitcase, lifted out all his clothes, and showed he had no contraband materials. When the policeman angrily rejected this, Shuster replaced the clothes, slowly and carefully once again, and then took out his billfold and showed the officer all his money. By this time the officer was becoming distinctly annoyed and Shuster was not sure what to do. Before he had to decide, fortunately, the train passed into Holland, the German police no longer had jurisdiction and disgustedly turned away, and Shuster got off at his proper stop, never in his life so glad to see Doris waiting.[81]

The Shusters were back in Vienna when the Nazis took over the city in March 1938, and their escape was harrowing. In February Hitler had forced the Austrian chancellor, Kurt von

Schuschnigg, to give Germany greater control over Austrian internal and foreign affairs but, on March 9, Schuschnigg decided to put the agreement to a vote of the people.[82] About the same time he asked Shuster to accompany a highly respected former government official through parts of Austria to encourage trade union solidarity against this move by Adolf Hitler. Shuster agreed, and the two of them eventually arrived at Graatz. Riding the elevator in one of the buildings, the elevator operator asked: "What do you think of the invasion?" "What invasion?" they inquired. "Hitler is in Vienna," he replied. He was not, of course, but the Nazis were taking over the city, the German army had entered the country, and Shuster decided to return to the capital immediately. It was not that simple, since Nazi youths frequently stopped their car and checked their papers, but they finally arrived at 6:00 a.m. Recalling those days, Doris remembered the horror of seeing a man killed in the street in front of her apartment, and remembered a kind of relief when the German army finally arrived and restored some measure of public order.[83]

George and Doris hurried that same day to visit the brilliant German author and theologian Dietrich von Hildebrand. Hildebrand had escaped from Nazi Germany, was now living in Vienna, and obviously had to flee again. His sister, an American citizen, had been able to get his furniture sent from Munich to Vienna, and the Shusters now agreed to purchase it, returning it to him whenever conditions permitted. They needed another signature on the purchase agreement, and the only person present that day was a young Czechoslovakian woman. Hildebrand refused to let her sign since he was sure she would be executed if the Nazis discovered it, and thus the furniture was eventually lost. In fact, Hildebrand himself barely escaped. He fled Vienna that day and the police arrived to arrest him the next morning.[84]

By this time, the American consul in Vienna had also ordered the Shusters to leave, by way of Czechoslovakia. George had wisely deposited his money in Basel and received from his account four hundred dollars at the beginning of each month. Since this was March 12 or 13, the Shusters still had quite a sum of money and, knowing they would not be permitted to leave with that amount, Doris purchased a set of Viennese china and had it sent to her in America, a set of china she prized for the rest of her life. (Others, of course, were not so fortunate. Shuster encouraged von Schuschnigg to withdraw his money also, but he delayed a day too long. The bank was taken over by the Nazis, and his account was immediately impounded.) The Shusters then drove through Czechoslovakia, Hungary, and Yugoslavia, and had a worrisome yet humorous experience attempting to cross from Yugoslavia into Italy. Very low on cash, they had managed with some difficulty to withdraw another five or seven hundred dollars from their account while in Yugoslavia, only to discover again that they could not take that amount out of the country. George was willing to lose it, but not Doris. She raised the hood of the car and hid most of it around the engine and under valves and wires. They got out of Yugoslavia successfully with this ruse but only a few feet away they faced the Italian border officials. These at first refused them entrance because they did not have enough money and might become charges of the state. Still within sight of the Yugoslavian officers and not yet safely in Italy, Doris feared to retrieve their money. As discussions continued another Italian officer stopped, listened to the conversation, and then said: "Don't be ridiculous! All Americans have money." The Shuster Pontiac probably looked like a Rolls-Royce to them, and the official gingerly waved them through.[85]

The Shusters went first to Florence, where they met Carlton and Mrs. Hayes and where George and Carlton discussed in detail both his project and the threatening scene in Eastern Europe. Leaving Doris in Florence, George traveled to Rome where, among other projects, he tried to lodge a protest against Cardinal Theodore Innizer of Vienna for having the cathedral bells rung on Hitler's entrance into the city, a distasteful act which Shuster never forgot. While in Florence, Doris thought she overhead two Germans discussing an impending invasion of Czechoslovakia, but George was convinced that she had misunderstood their conversation because her knowledge of German was limited. When the German seizure actually took place a short time later, they both agreed that she may have been correct.[86]

Before returning to the United States in August, George and Doris spent some time in Paris, and George also made a quick trip to England. He had already collected sufficient data for his dissertation on the English ode, and thus this visit was probably less connected with that. His purpose, in fact, was more to awaken the English to the real threat of Hitler on the continent, but in this he was disappointed. With Neville Chamberlain, most English seemed to feel that some kind of compromise, perhaps on the Munich model, was possible. On one occasion someone asked George explicitly how much the French were paying him to act as propagandist.[87] After the horrors he and Doris had witnessed, it was depressing not to be believed.

As they set sail again for the United States after more than twelve months away, Shuster viewed his trip with mixed emotions. On the positive side, he was confident that he now knew more about conditions in Germany than the vast majority of Americans, and he was undoubtedly correct. Furthermore, what he learned confirmed his earlier views and convinced him that his opposition to Fascism in Germany and in Spain had been justified. He had also been privileged to meet some of the most dedicated and heroic patriots he would ever know, many of whom would meet their deaths at the hand of the Nazi government they were courageously attempting to curb, and he cherished their memory for the rest of his life.[88] But negative feelings were equally strong. He had been generously allotted an office in the Vienna library and had kept many of his notes and documents there, and since he had no time to retrieve them before his hurried departure, he must have realized that this important documentation was lost forever.[89] And he was discouraged by so much indifference; time was marching inexorably toward world tragedy, and few seemed to care. But, ever the optimist, Shuster clung to the hope that, with the evidence he now had, he might help to awaken others to the threat he saw so clearly.

5

HUNTER COLLEGE
AND THE WAR YEARS
1938–1945

The book that Shuster had so long desired to write, and had researched at some personal danger in Europe in 1937–38—the history of the German Center Party to the rise of Adolf Hitler—was never to be written. Shuster worked over his notes sporadically in the months after his return from Europe, but Bruening, who was to be his collaborator, had moved to Harvard and close cooperation was not then possible.[1] In the meantime, Shuster became involved in other projects. In early 1938 Macmillan had published his *Brother Flo: An Imaginative Biography*, a delightful and only thinly disguised recounting of the eccentricities and lovable traits of the porter at Notre Dame's Administration Building, whom Shuster had gotten to know and enjoy during his student and teaching days there. Although the names were changed, the reader could not fail to recognize the portraits of Notre Dame's (Merrymount, in the book) fluent orator-president, Father John Cavanaugh, in Father Davidson; professors Maurice Francis Egan and Colonel Hoynes, in Michael Dominic Brady and Colonel Donovan; and even its famous football coach, Knute Rockne, in Vic Stoneman.[2] On his return from Europe Shuster collaborated with Joseph Bernhart in publishing *The Vatican as a World Power*, and with Robert Cuddihy in editing a volume of reactions in the United States to the death in early 1939 of Pope Pius XI, *Pope Pius XI and American Public Opinion*. That same year, Reynal and Hitchcock asked him to contribute editorial notes for a new English edition of Adolf Hitler's *Mein Kampf*, and this he agreed to do.[3]

A large part of his time in 1938 and early 1939, however, was spent completing the draft of his only novel, *Look Away!*, published that fall.[4] The story, set in mid-nineteenth century America, concerned a young Kentucky lawyer, Robert Cecil, who settled in southwest Wisconsin and there married the story's heroine, the beautiful Edith Treloar. When the Civil War broke out, he felt obliged to follow his conscience, take leave of his wife and son, and join the Confederate army in defense of states' rights. The book details the difficulty Edith experienced trying to manage their household and keep her family together without him. Robert is eventually sent behind the Union lines as a spy, is captured, and is audaciously rescued in part through the trickery of his wife. Reviewers agreed that the plot was only average and its development rather slow, but they praised the author's handling of subplots and especially several of the character portrayals. Both the *New York Times* and the *Saturday Review of Literature* chose to review it.[5]

Although *Look Away!* was clearly fiction, it contained much of George Shuster. The story took place in the farming area around Lancaster, land that Shuster knew and loved. The opening scene featured a devoted country doctor offering his services to the surrounding neighborhood, and Shuster knew that his own father had accompanied such a doctor on similar rounds as a young man. The Germans were proud to suffer in the war, seeing their fight to free the nation of slavery as a continuation of the desire for freedom of those who left Germany after the revolutions of 1848. And there may also be something of Doris in the attractive portrait of Edith—beautiful, charming, efficient, high-spirited, but with a touch of the mischievous and audacious also. The marital tensions which Shuster depicted as normal in the lives of the strong-willed Robert and Edith he may have known firsthand.

Despite these other interests, Shuster remained eager to complete his book on Germany. Almost each day in 1938 and 1939 evidenced the deepening and spreading evil of Hitler's totalitarian rule. Shuster's interviews and firsthand observations of the year before had given him insights and information few in the West could have, and he knew he was in a unique position to speak out. Yet he never found the time. In the late summer of 1939, to his complete surprise, he was offered the academic deanship and acting presidency of Hunter College in New York, at the time the world's largest college for women, and he could not refuse. He eventually joint-authored a short and popular history of Germany, but that was all the time his administrative duties permitted.[6] He confessed with embarrassment each year to the Carnegie Corporation that he still had nothing to show for the generous grant of nine-thousand dollars it had given him in 1936, and finally in 1945 he returned an unused balance of only one-hundred dollars and the project, for all practical purposes, was closed.[7]

Hunter College had been founded originally as Female Normal and High School in late 1869, primarily to train teachers for New York's expanding school system. It was located in lower Manhattan and, although the name was changed to the more prestigious Normal College of the City of New York even before classes opened the following February, it still occupied only an upper floor at Second Street and Broadway. The course of study was the regular three-year high school program. An elementary school for supervised teaching was established nearby, called at first Normal College Training School but soon the Model Primary School. Thomas Hunter, principal of Public School No. 35 on West Thirteenth Street, was named president, presiding over a college enrollment of several hundred and a faculty of ten.[8]

The city constructed a new building for the college on Fourth Avenue between 68th and 69th streets in 1873—"perhaps the ugliest building on Park Avenue," Lewis Mumford later called it[9]—and this permitted a beneficial expansion of the curriculum. Admission standards were raised, the program was lengthened to four years, and two separate tracks emerged, the normal or professional course for teacher preparation and a more strictly academic course for a general or liberal education. School assemblies were frequent, most days began with chapel service, and extracurricular activities of debating, glee club, bowling, tennis, and basketball gradually emerged. The course of study continued to grow and shortly after the turn of the century the programs had expanded to seven years, three of high school and four of either teacher preparation or the classical curriculum leading to the degree of Bachelor of Arts.[10] The need to balance the liberal and the vocational in the college's curriculum was a continuing challenge throughout its history, causing one commentator to recall the proverb: If a man finds himself with bread in both hands, he should exchange one loaf for some flowers, since the loaf feeds the body, but flowers feed the soul.[11]

In 1914 the name was changed to Hunter College to honor its first president, who had retired in 1906 after thirty-six years in office. By that time the college comprised separate academic departments of English, languages, history, mathematics, physical sciences, and pedagogy; summer and evening classes had been begun in 1910; the college budget was $500,000; and the total student enrollment was thirty-seven hundred. In the 1920s land was purchased and a Hunter College campus was also opened in the Bronx, comprising four separate buildings and expansive grounds by 1933. A Board of Higher Education had been established in 1926 to oversee the governance of both Hunter College and City College of New York (and Brooklyn College after 1930); an extension built on Lexington Avenue was proving far too small for the burgeoning main campus enrollments; full accreditation had been received for both classical and teacher preparation programs; and a Master of Science in Education program was proving popular. But in the midst of all this progress disaster suddenly struck. On February 14, 1936, the imposing Gothic structure on Park (or Fourth) Avenue caught fire, and this principal ediface of Hunter College was destroyed.[12]

By 1939 Hunter College was doubly a sprawling institution. Physically it was spread out on two campuses, one in Manhattan and one several miles away in the Bronx. In Manhattan, the Lexington Avenue addition had been untouched by the fire and remained in service. A building at 2 Park Avenue, between 32nd and 33rd streets was taken over also, and a college annex on East 32nd. The Model School (Elementary and Junior High) was housed temporarily in a building of Temple Emanu-el on East 65th Street, while the high school remained on East 96th, sixty blocks from the 32nd Street buildings. College administration in such facilities was a nightmare.[13]

At times the curriculum seemed equally sprawling. A student in the late 1930s selected her courses from between forty and fifty areas of specialization, grouped together generally as languages, social sciences, and physical sciences. Structurally, there was a prescribed base of courses, forty-six to sixty-three credits, including English, speech, foreign language, history, philosophy, science, and mathematics, which was intended to guarantee the liberal content of every student's education. Second, the student also selected twenty-four credits in the core subject, corresponding elsewhere to the student's major or concentration. Third, the student enrolled in twelve credits of enrichment courses, classes advisors determined would beneficially complement or broaden the core classes. The enrichment courses could be liberal or vocational classes and might be within the same academic department or outside it. Finally, the student completed her curriculum with the requisite number of optionals or electives, usually between twenty-six and forty-six credit hours. There were specializations also in pre-medicine, pre-journalism, pre-social work, and business, and in education the student could emphasize teaching in kindergarten and nursery school, elementary, junior high, or high school. In addition, the Evening and Extension Division offered a variety of courses, some for credit since they were taken by regularly enrolled students, and some without credit since they were intended only for the enrichment of the general public.[14]

The president overseeing this educational empire in the 1930s was Dr. Eugene Colligan. His background, unfortunately, had not been in higher education. Born in New York, he had graduated from Columbia College and had received the Ph.D. in history from Fordham University. He had taught in the Brooklyn public school system, had been a high school principal, and was then appointed associate superintendent of schools. He was still in his mid-forties when he was appointed to Hunter College in 1933.[15]

Despite the almost overwhelming obstacles it faced, especially the financial strictures of the Great Depression and the devastating fire of 1936, Hunter made genuine advances during the six years of Colligan's presidency. One major achievement was the complete revision of curriculum in 1937, clarifying the college offerings and simplifying the students' choices Along with this revision, the counselling and guidance services were upgraded, not only to assist students in course selection but also to offer support to those who found it necessary to seek at least part-time employment during these Depression years. Greek societies and sororities were popular at Hunter, but many felt, especially as financial difficulties of the decade increased, that they tended to exclude some social and economic groups. Thus a more general social organization, House Plan, was developed. As Hunter continued to grow, the old administrative structure and organization, maybe more adapted to the smaller and more closely-knit normal school of the past, seemed inadequate; in 1938 the by-laws were amended to provide for the election rather than appointment of department heads, the establishment of budget and personnel committees, and the creation of the position of academic dean to relieve the president of at least some of the day-to-day administration of the college. This last was especially necessary because, after 1936, Colligan had to become more absorbed in planning for the new Hunter College building at 695 Park Avenue.[16]

In fact, as the decade wore on the Board of Higher Education had become increasingly disenchanted with Colligan's performance. Colligan may have been a poor selection in the first place. His administrative experience had been weak, almost entirely in elementary and secondary education; he had never dealt extensively with a college faculty; his first experience in higher education administration was as college president; and some felt that he tended on occasion to administer the college as if it were high school. Furthermore, his appointment in 1933 may have been in part political, urged on an earlier Board of Higher Education by the leadership of Tammany Hall before reform Republican Fiorello La Guardia took office.[17] The democratization changes of 1938 seemed to indicate further dissatisfaction with the administration. And the job itself may have been impossibly demanding: a new building to plan and supervise; a budget to maintain despite the financial uncertainties of the Depression; and the daily administration of a large urban college, including an elementary and high school, now spread out over several buildings and several miles.

In June of 1939, at the close of the academic year, a committee of the Board of Higher Education—apparently without the knowledge of at least some Board members—approached President Colligan, expressing the Board's growing dissatisfaction with his administration and asking for his resignation. They gave him little choice. He could request and receive a year's leave of absence with full pay, and during that year submit his resignation, and in this way retain his full pension of approximately ten thousand dollars a year and avoid a public dismissal. If he chose not to accede, it was the intention of the Board to dismiss him; in this case he would lose his pension also. Colligan realized that the majority of the Board opposed him, and on June 20 he formally requested a leave of absence, citing poor health and the heavy demands of the position as the reason. The Board of Higher Education that same evening granted the request.[18]

But if Colligan's resignation was sudden and surprising, the announcement of his successor was even more so. On his return from Europe in 1938 Shuster had let it be known that he was interested in full-time college teaching if a suitable position were available. Historians Carlton Hayes and Harry Carman of Columbia, both friends, knew of this interest, and Carman was also a member of the Hunter College Administrative Committee of the Board of Higher Education. Discussions were quietly taking place late that spring and early summer, and eventually Shuster was invited by Hayes to tea with a small group at his home.[19] Carman was present, and also Ordway Tead, chairman of the Board of Higher Education. Shuster apparently thought, and hoped, that they would invite him to join the faculty, and was dumbfounded when they offered him the position of academic dean at Hunter and acting president in Colligan's absence. They made it clear that Colligan was not planning to return and that the appointment was intended to be long-term. If Shuster had any doubts or hesitations, he never expressed them in public. His appointment was announced on July 6.[20]

Why George Shuster? It was a question many on the faculty immediately asked, and so did many others throughout the country. His name had never surfaced in discussions of administrative posts in the past. He was relatively unknown but not necessarily unqualified. Hunter was primarily a liberal arts college, and Shuster was unquestionably a liberally educated man, widely read in literature, history, and philosophy, and a linguist, author, and respected commentator on world events. Having taught at Notre Dame and St. Joseph's College, he was not unfamiliar with college life and administration. Very important, he was also Catholic. The Hunter College presidency had traditionally been given to a Catholic, and this was especially important at this time when the

Catholic Colligan was being rather unceremoniously removed. To avoid extended controversy, the decision needed to be made quickly, and Shuster was available immediately. Finally, Shuster had known his share of controversies in the past, and had remained soft-spoken and in control through them; these qualities would be valuable in the new position.[21]

Carman later suggested that Shuster "was a natural for the job," but his appointment did stir up bitter controversy.[22] Although lauding Shuster's outstanding qualities, Dr. Joseph Klein of the Board of Higher Education felt compelled to note that Shuster lacked the Ph.D.:

> I am happy to vote in favor of the resolution appointing Mr. Shuster Academic Dean for one year and designating him as the Acting President during the year's absence of President Colligan. I would be less than frank, however, if I failed to state that I would be much happier about my vote if Mr. Shuster had his doctorate from a university of high standing and in a field of learning in which he was recognized as pre-eminent. It seems to me that if, as a matter of sound policy, our Board requires the Ph.D. degree for those who attain tenure in the rank of instructor, and, of course, of all those whose faculty status is in professorial rank, the person who is to be the supervisor, the guide and exemplar, even temporarily, of such a faculty should himself have a doctorate, in addition to possessing all of the other qualifications for the president set forth in our By-Laws.[23]

Others were critical of the haste with which the appointment had been made, as a letter to the *New York Sun* made clear:

> When, about a year ago, the then impending vacancy in the Brooklyn College presidency was announced, it was stated that an extensive search would be made for the best man for the position. The wording of the announcement gave the impression that even big shots like Dr. Hutchins of Chicago would barely qualify for consideration. A $21,000 job calls for the best talent available. It took over a year to fill that job.
>
> Now, without any time for search or deliberation, a choice for the possible Hunter College vacancy has been announced. According to the president of the Board of Higher Education, Mr. Shuster's qualifications are: (1) that he is a scholar (2) that he is a liberal (3) that he has a grasp of modern collegiate education policy, and (4) that his career as managing editor of a sectarian

weekly of limited circulation showed that he is a man of affairs. All these qualifications do not, in my opinion, necessarily imply that Mr. Shuster has the administrative ability required for the presidency of the largest women's college in the world. . . .

I would like to call to the attention of the Board of Higher Education that under the Hurley decision the presidents and faculties of the municipal colleges are in civil service just as much as the teachers in the public schools, and that the decision held that all positions in the civil service must be filled by competitive examination.[24]

A much stronger criticism came a few months later from Dr. Carmyn Lombardo, a member of the minority group on the Board of Higher Education:

With deepest personal regret I find myself unable to cast a favorable vote for the election of George N. Shuster as President of Hunter College.

Dr. Shuster is a splendid person who has my sincere respect and my action of tonight is in no wise a reflection upon him. The circumstances which force this decision are not of his creation nor is he connected with them in any manner, directly, indirectly or by implication.

At the Board meeting of November 20, 1939, I enunciated for the record a principle of fair-dealing which obtained then and obtains now. In executive session lasting over two hours I attempted to show this Board that a deliberate injustice was being done to one of our fine people, Dr. Eugene A. Colligan. I demanded that justice be done. None was forthcoming. I repeatedly requested that all information regarding the action against Dr. Colligan be made available to all the members of the Board rather than be limited to a few self-picked and self-constituted annihilators. My efforts were received in silence—a silence indicative of a brazen disregard not only of the rights of Dr. Colligan but also of the rights of each duly appointed member of this Board.

Legally, it is doubtful whether the Board has the right to ratify the decisions of a group of individuals who act without any specific or implied authorization of the Board. There was no free and full discussion of the reasons for the demise. On the contrary, after specific request, information was refused. We are accused of badgering the chair. On one solitary occasion when Mr. Barry asked for the date when the Colligan resignation was received, the answer was Nov. 1, 1939. What an utter disregard of the truth!!

The date, ladies and gentlemen, was sometime in June, 1939. The resignation was not voluntary but was forced under circumstances which made the actions of Europe's dictators resemble those of Caspar Milquetoast. One of our members in voting on the Colligan matter stated, "I reserve the right to re-open this case if I find that the resignation was not voluntary." Mr. Member, it was not!!

Further, to date, we know of no specific reason for the action. On the contrary we can point only to a splendid resolution of appreciation, voted by this same group of members which I am minded to compare with the truly sincere tribute paid Dr. Colligan by the Alumnae Association of Hunter College. The great mystery remains shrouded! The "strong men and women" of the Board of Higher Education will not talk!! In substance, we who are forced to these great lengths to defend a true democracy against so absolute a bureaucracy as exists in this Board, are told, for all intents and purposes, to go to blazes. I still call upon you to make known the truth. I still demand that justice be done and I shall continue to do so as long as I draw breath.

I feel confident that in the natural course of events the odious truth will be brought to light. Justice must prevail and when it does it will become clear that your actions were contrary to the public interest and not in accord with the high standard of principles which should characterize the procedure of any Board of Education.

I was constrained from voting in November. The then prevailing conditions still prevail and for this reason only I refrain from voting at this time. I feel you are doing Dr. Colligan's successor less than justice when you rush through an appointment before you have swept the dirt from your house.

To Dr. Shuster I express my apologies for dampening his hour of glory. He can be assured that at all times he will have my sincere and complete cooperation.[25]

Colligan agreed to vacate his office by August 28, and Shuster, at a salary of ten thousand dollars, began his year as acting president on September 1.[26] The year was primarily one of learning, but the great challenge was to learn while administering such a large urban college spread out over several buildings over two boroughs. One professor later recalled taking the subway out to the Bronx campus for one class, returning to the Park Avenue building for a second class, and then going around the corner to the 32nd Street annex for a third.[27] When administration went smoothly, the distances posed no special problems, but in times of emergency or changing schedules the necessary people were invariably either difficult to find or located in a distant building. The new administrative structures of 1938 were being implemented, and this also caused occasional complications. But most of these concerned greater democratization and the use of faculty personnel and budget committees and Shuster, with very limited administrative experience himself, probably found most of this faculty assistance quite congenial.

From his teaching at Notre Dame and St. Joseph's College for Women, Shuster had some familiarity with regular college structures and administrative procedures, but Hunter's Evening and Extension Session was new. According to the official *Bulletin of Information* for that year, its courses were taught at Hunter College, Central High School of Needle Trades, Julia Richman High School, Public School 30, the American Museum of Natural History, the Metropolitan Museum of Art, the Museum of the City of New York, Inwood Pottery, and the Lexington School for the Deaf.[28] Five thousand students were enrolled, most hoping to become better qualified for city employment in areas of social work, welfare administration, community organization, child care, teaching, housing, government administration, juvenile delinquency, crime prevention, guidance, and so on.[29] Shuster knew there were changes he would want to make, but his first year was spent in familiarizing himself with the various programs and services already offered.

That first year, in fact, was one of the busiest of Shuster's life. He attended regular meetings of the Board of Higher Education, developed close friendships with several of its members, and forged excellent working relationships with the other city college presidents. He and Doris attended what must have seemed an endless round of teas and open houses, but these gave the new president an opportunity to meet members of the faculty, administrative staff, and student body less formally, and gave all of them an opportunity to learn a little more about their new president.[30] Living within the approved budget was a major concern since the budget for 1939–1940 had actually been cut $213,000 from the amount recommended, and public protests had been staged at City Hall as a result.[31] A new principal for the Model School had to be appointed shortly after Shuster assumed office, and he must have felt even less certain of himself in this area than he did in matters of budget or extension programs.[32] And finally, the new college building was nearing completion and Shuster was charged with overseeing the myriad of details that construction of a $6 million building in the midst of a depression can offer.

Shuster's official review of that first year, submitted in the fall of 1940, was characteristically optimistic.[33] By that date, the massive new building at 695 Park Avenue had been completed and the whole downtown campus was again under one roof. There was still some crowding in faculty offices and in student lounges, and the Bronx campus lacked needed library and laboratory facilities, but these were minor problems after the splintered facilities of the past three years. Shuster had praise for the faculty, both in teaching and research, but noted too that classes were too large, that faculty members were expected to serve on too many committees, and that to put Hunter in step with other American colleges faculty rankings should be upgraded. Shuster was pleased with the student body but noted weaknesses also: "The woeful misuse of the English language in publications; the fuss over matters of no particular moment; and the tendency to split up into more parties than were dreamed of in the Weimar Republic."[34] The programs of both the Evening and Extension Session and the elementary and high schools needed further evaluation and, in fact, the very existence of the elementary and high schools in the college structure might merit consideration since more and more Hunter graduates were choosing careers other than teaching. Finances, of course, remained a major problem, and Shuster pleaded for additional funding.[35] The report closed with an appreciation of the advantages of Hunter's cultural diversity: "A school which is primarily a cross-section of our society, which is recruited from all races, all classes, all faiths, ought under leadership which possesses a measure of integrity and intelligence to inculcate both self-reliance and mutual understanding. We think that Hunter College has not been unworthy of the trust its opportunity implies."[36]

If the year was not sufficiently crowded with official duties, Shuster also had a personal obligation to acquit. A year before a member of the Board of Higher Education had questioned Shuster's selection because he lacked the Ph.D., and with all his other worries and responsibilities as acting president, Shuster finally managed to remove this obstacle. He had long completed his coursework at Columbia University, he had done the research for his dissertation both at home and during his trips to Europe, and thus it was just a matter of completing the dissertation and passing his final examinations. Actually, a slight complication developed when it was discovered that Shuster had neglected to request that his graduate courses at Notre Dame be accepted by Columbia for full credit, but this difficulty was eventually resolved. Shuster completed his final examinations in April and submitted printed copies of his dissertation to the library in early June; the degree was awarded shortly thereafter.[37]

Shuster's dissertation, published that year as *The English Ode from Milton to Keats*, was a major piece of scholarship. He had an excellent background in Greek and Roman literature, he had evaluated poetry for twelve years as editor of *The Commonweal*, and he worked closely with several excellent scholars at Columbia.[38] The dissertation discussed the influence of Pindar, Horace, and other classical writers on English poetry; traced the nature of the ode as crafted by Milton, Donne, Dryden, Pope, Swift, Burns, Coleridge, Wordsworth, Byron, Shelley, and Keats; and concluded that no single definition of the ode was adequate. But if the definition was elusive, Shuster's admiration was not:

> Certainly the ode form is more important now than it was when Tennyson died. The reason seems to be a very old one—that the flexibility of the ancient ode form is always a boon to the poet whose theme and feeling can find no outlet in the simpler lyric measures. True enough, the significance of theme and emotion is not now what it was in eras when the gravity of the Psalmist was inlaid into all English utterance. But though life may be a waste land or the scene of injustice demanding revolution of us all, the poet still rises with the mantle of the prophet about him. And on the scroll in his hands there is inscribed the ode.[39]

The reviewer in the *New York Herald Tribune* noted that Shuster "has sifted his data with critical discrimination and has thought about ode writing from the standpoint of the poetic technician, so that he enters into the solution of technical problems with a finely sympathetic penetration." "The pleasantest surprise," the writer continued, "is the added grace of witty comment which

constantly illuminates whatever it touches."[40] The work continued
to be cited in scholarly treatises forty years later.[41]

With the official resignation of Eugene Colligan as president
in November, the submission of Shuster's doctoral dissertation to
Columbia University the following spring, and the completion of
the new college building over the summer, formal dedication and
inauguration ceremonies could be planned for early October
1940. In fact, a Dedication Week was organized, with two days
devoted to the dedication of the new building and two days to the
formal inauguration of Shuster as president. But even as these
were being planned, a new crisis emerged. Building construction
was being assisted by a grant of $640,000 from the Public Works
Administration in Washington, and when the construction was
not completed by June 30, there was fear for a time that the
money, appropriated for the fiscal year ending on that date, would
be lost. Fortunately, an extension was granted.[42]

The formal ceremonies of dedication took place on Tuesday
afternoon, October 8. Hon. Stanley Isaacs, president of the
Borough of Manhattan, presented the new building, on behalf of
the city, to Chairman Ordway Tead of the Board of Higher
Education. A Dedicatory Ode was prepared by Robert P. Tristram
Coffin of Bowdoin College, and a magnificent new organ was presented to the college by the Associate Alumnae. Formal addresses
were delivered by Mayor La Guardia, by Professor Harry Carman
of Columbia University and the Board of Higher Education, by
Mrs. Walter Mack, Jr., of the Hunter College Administrative
Committee of the Board of Higher Education, and by Hon. John
M. Carmody, chairman of the Federal Housing Administration in
Washington. A reception was held in one of the lounges after the
ceremony, sponsored by the Associate Alumnae of the college,
and Shuster hosted a formal dinner that evening at the Savoy
Plaza Hotel. The following day was Student-Parent Day, open
house for the community, and the day was filled with tours
and exhibits and various class and department projects of interest
to students, parents, alumnae, and members of the New York
community.[43]

On October 10, in ceremonies beginning at 2:00 p.m.,
George Shuster was officially inaugurated as fifth president of

Hunter College. Ordway Tead, chairman of the Board of Higher Education, presided, and the invocation was delivered by Shuster's long-time friend Monsignor Patrick Barry, rector of Immaculate Conception Seminary on Long Island. The tone of the day was set in the opening paragraph of Mayor La Guardia's remarks. He apologized for arriving late but mentioned that it had been a very trying day at City Hall and yet he thought this occasion too important to delegate to another. "I did say to Dr. Tead," he remarked, "that I considered the ceremonies today of far greater importance than the mere dedication of a new building. We provided the building Tuesday. Today we give it its soul."[44]

Two major addresses were given by personal friends of Shuster—literary critic Van Wyck Brooks and Catholic philosopher Jacques Maritain. Brooks's presence was particularly gratifying. Shuster and he were near neighbors in Stamford, they enjoyed conversing on literary topics, and their wives met frequently and enjoyed each other's company. Brooks had suffered through a period of serious depression only a few years earlier. After many frustrating efforts, he apparently broke out of his depression while listening to a friendly conversation on American art one evening after dinner at the Shusters.[45] Brooks reviewed the state of contemporary American literature in his talk; lamented the pessimism, cynicism and despair of so many writers; and praised the exhilaration and optimism of others:

> In Robert Frost, in Lewis Mumford, to mention two of these, one feels a joyous confidence in human nature, an abounding faith in the will, a sense of the heroic in the human adventure, good will, the leaven of existence. All good things seem possible as one reads these writers. I remember a remark of John Butler Yeats, the father of the Irish poet. Thirty years ago, in New York, I used to see him every day, and one day he spoke of an old friend of his in Dublin, a judge who had retired from the bench. When someone asked this judge what remained in his mind, what had most deeply impressed him during his fifty years in the criminal courts, his answer was, "The goodness of human nature." The grand old Yeats, who also loved his species, quoted this with a smile of agreement, for although he did not take an easy view of life, he felt that a seasoned magistrate knew whereof he spoke. I have never forgotten this remark, and I have always felt that literature, if it is to carry out its

function, must contain this germ of faith, and that the greatest literature has always done so.[46]

Given Brooks's past depression, the words must have carried special poignancy for Shuster.

Maritain, then a visiting professor at Columbia, made a stirring plea for culture. The lights of culture were slowly going out in the lands of Goethe and Michelangelo, he lamented, and works of art were threatened by the devastation of war in France and England. America could be the savior, and institutions like Hunter had important contributions to make:

> Two things strike the foreign observer who visits America; this country appears to him as the privileged land of youth, and the privileged land of womanhood. Youth is honored here, and youth is served, especially in the colleges, in a more liberal generous way than in many other countries. Womanhood is honored here, and her liberty and dignity are respected in a more ample and uncompromising way than in many other countries. Women here have a deep sense of their own mission with respect to culture. The teaching of young women appears hence as a thing doubly important and significant in the American way of life.[47]

Shuster's inaugural address summarized his own philosophy of education. He began with a brief review of Hunter's history. "This institution was from the beginning a forward-looking place," he noted. "It was not only the first of the colleges to provide free higher education for women. It was above all the protagonist of fruitful innovations in academic orientation and method." Education was both liberal and practical, opinions and theories varied, but there was always a constant. Quoting the words of Emerson carved on the side of the new building, "We are of different opinions at different hours, but we may always be said to be at heart on the side of truth," he continued: "Those words seem to us the gist of the democratic social faith. The right to differ is the right to freedom. And yet this great and permanent privilege is meaningless unless one is committed unflinchingly to the quest for what is abidingly just, good, right, and true." Shuster spoke of his goals and ideals for the college, both its faculty and its students. "Those who form its staff," he stated, "must first of all be free men and women—persons of resolution and courtesy, afraid of nothing save subjection to error, pretense and dishonesty. And yet they must be humble, too, under the rule of service and scholarship." For students, "the question is not whether young people are to be taken too seriously or not seriously enough. It is rather, this:—how shall the grant of equality, upon which college life reposes, be accommodated to the reality of widely differing levels of experience and information? How shall the creative individuality of the student be associated with the measure of receptive obedience which educational routine requires?" His goal was to educate young women intellectually and prepare them also "for family life, home-making and the care of children." "It is a source of pride to us all," he closed, "that we serve a college for women, and we hope to serve it well."[48]

A dinner was held at the Hotel Commodore that evening to honor the new president, with a thousand guests attending, and the following day an academic symposium was held at Hunter on the subject: The Role of the College Woman in a Shaken World.[49] It had been an exciting and momentous week for both Hunter College and George Shuster, the college had received immense publicity, and the new president, with his Ph.D. in hand and a year of experience behind him, was eager for new challenges.

A major problem with which the new president had to wrestle, and one for which he had very little experience or attraction, was the continuing struggle with the budget. The college budget was part, but only a small part, of the city's budget. Thus it was buffeted by all the uncertainties of municipal budgeting during these last years of the Depression and years of World War II. The college budget had been $3.1 million for the 1938–39 academic year, and had been reduced to $2.9 million for the year Shuster served as academic dean and acting president. Although Shuster regularly requested more money, the budget did not reach the $3 million figure again until 1945–46, the first postwar year and a year of increasing inflation.[50] Such budget stringency presented serious problems for the president. Cuts in faculty positions were threatened almost annually, and some years were carried out; the position of academic dean was not filled when Shuster was promoted to the presidency, and over a dozen positions were dropped during the 1944–45 academic year. At the same time, new sources of money, mostly internal, needed to be found in part to cover increased costs in the new and more comfortable building. Besides the traditional library and science fees, a four-dollar book fee was charged to each student in the fall of 1940, costs for use of college lounges and the auditorium increased, and some food prices in the cafeteria doubled. Students transferring into the Evening Session were charged $2.50 per credit hour, and the following year a one-dollar admission fee was levied on all students to cover examinations and other administrative costs.[51] Shuster never felt completely at home with college budgets, and his assistants admit he felt even less comfortable sharing that responsibility with the pertinent faculty budget and personnel committees. Thus budgets remained one of the least attractive parts of college administration for him.

One of the more noticeable, and better publicized, changes during Shuster's first years as president involved the Model School. When the school moved into its new facilities on the third floor of the Park Avenue building, the name was changed to Hunter College Elementary School, probably to emphasize that this was an elementary school the equal of any in the city and not some model or reduced version. Other elements at first remained the same. The enrollment was approximately six hundred, both boys and girls; the program was eight years; and pupils had to be residents of Manhattan living below 86th Street. Applicants took the standard admissions tests. Pupils with IQ's of less than 100 could not be admitted, but no preference was given to those of superior intelligence. The school was still part of the college's teacher training program, and it profited now from being in the same building with the college departments of education, psychology, and philosophy.[52]

The major revision occurred the following year when the program was changed to one for gifted children. Fifty-four children, aged 3 1/2 to 5 1/2, and with IQ's of 130 and above, were enrolled in kindergarten in the fall of 1941. It was not to be an accelerated program but a broader and enriched one, adding to the usual curriculum visits to museums, broader learning in science, and even conversational French. Of that first kindergarten class, one had an IQ of 194, three were black, and nine were children of Hunter alumnae.[53]

The *New York Times* published an article "Our Youngest Intellectuals" one month into the program. The children had been divided into two classes: those aged three and a half to four and a half were "juniors," and those four and a half to five and a half were "seniors." Most seemed quite well adjusted and their superior intelligence was readily apparent. On the day the reporter visited, the pupils were in no hurry to end the session of pronouncing French names to go out to play. When one teacher began to explain the various colors of the rainbow, one youngster pleaded: "Don't waste so much time; we all know those colors." When a discussion of "warm" and "cool" colors centered on a picture showing flames, one boy suggested that blue was a "warm" color "because blue flames are hotter than yellow flames."[54]

At about this same time, the elementary school program was reduced from eight to six years. Each year a new class of exceptional pupils would be admitted into kindergarten and the oldest class of the former program would be graduated. Thus, after seven years, the whole elementary school program was composed of superior students. The former seventh and eighth grades were then added to the high school, housed in the older building facing Lexington Avenue, making it the first six-year high school program in the city. Since the elementary school was coeducational and the high school only for girls, the boys in grades seven and eight now had to transfer to other schools. Hunter College administrators did not consider this bad since the boys might elsewhere profit from gymnasium and shop facilities that were lacking at Hunter. By the fall of 1942, consequently, Hunter College Elementary School comprised six grades and kindergarten and was open to both boys and girls of exceptional abilities. Hunter College High School, next door, was a six-year program limited to girls. Both programs served in part as training opportunities for the college education and teacher-training programs.[55]

Major changes were also made in the Evening and Extension Division. When Shuster arrived in 1939, five thousand graduate and undergraduate students were enrolled in more than four hundred courses, and conditions across the country probably determined the areas of specialization and principal student interest: public service and social work, welfare administration, housing and community planning, crime prevention and juvenile delinquency, education, and teacher-training. Such vocational emphases continued throughout the war years, but interest in the humanities also ran high and the more traditional offerings in mathematics, history, English, classics, psychology, and philosophy were continually expanded. The most significant innovation within the division, however, was simply the upgrading of the courses. Since the vast majority of those taking classes in that division were part-time students holding full- or part-time employment at the same time, those courses were generally not of the same academic quality as those taken by the full-time students in the regular day and degree programs. In the spring of 1941 Shuster announced a revision. Evening and Extension Division courses would be reorganized to put them on an equal level with other courses, and the full-time college faculty would also be reorganized into traditional ranks of assistant, associate, and full professor, with comparable salary adjustments, to place it on a similar level with other colleges. With these changes, students in the regular degree programs could more easily take classes in the Evening and Extension Session, an opportunity which became more and more attractive as students were drawn into full-time war and defense employment after December 7, 1941.[56]

Since Hunter College hoped both to educate its students in the liberal arts and to prepare them for productive employment or public service, the entrance of the United States into World War II had a major impact on curriculum development, especially in the Evening and Extension Division. Non-credit courses in cryptography and cryptanalytics were added in the spring of 1941, and they proved so popular that advanced classes were added for the fall. With the attack on Pearl Harbor, courses were added the following spring in accident prevention and first aid, bacteriology, blood chemistry, nutrition and physical development, mechanical drawing, mathematics of map projection and navigation, meteorology, commercial geography, and recent developments in statistical method. Training in weather observation was added that same spring since a weather station could be ideally located atop the new skyscraper, and teacher training courses for nursing instruction were inaugurated that summer. By the summer of 1942 Hunter was one of only four women's colleges (Wellesley,

Smith, and Bryn Mawr being the others) participating in an Office of Education program offering specialized training in radio technology, drafting, physics, and basic engineering. Navigation and the economics of war and reconstruction were added that fall and specialized physical education courses, modeled after those employed in commando training, the following spring. Soon Hunter graduates were serving across the country as Army nurses, meteorological assistants, computation analyzers on engineering projects, and chemical researchers in war industries.[57]

By the spring of 1943, in fact, the war had caused a restructuring of the whole undergraduate curriculum. The Hunter College Chapter of the New York College Teachers Union a little earlier had suggested a two-year program designed precisely to train women for war occupations, with special emphasis on the vocations of draftsman, chemist, physicist, translator, mathematician, and mineralogist. The supporters felt that if Hunter did not voluntarily undertake such a revision, the military and the government would probably mandate it anyway.[58] Shuster did not agree. He saw the need for a basic revision of the curriculum since more women would now be leaving college after two years to enter the work force or public service, but he insisted that those two years should be in the liberal arts, as he said, "so that this generation will not face the post-war world minus intellectual preparation."[59] Accordingly, all students in freshman and sophomore years would now select a general area of concentration—science, social science, or languages; would study a basic liberal arts curriculum, including American history and either political science, economics, or sociology; and would not select a major until the junior year. If they left school after two years, they would still have a basic liberal arts education. If they returned to school later, they would already have an excellent preparation and need little more than their major courses for completion.

The most noticeable changes occasioned by the war at Hunter College were in the non-academic area. Within a week of the official declaration of war, Shuster appointed a college Defense Committee of both faculty and students to coordinate various defense activities. The modern, well-built structure on Park Avenue was designated as bomb shelter for schools in the surrounding area, teams of Hunter students were trained in fire-fighting and first-aid, and, since they hailed from all over the city, the young women were prepared to serve as an emergency messenger service also.[60]

On the social side, the students assisted the Alumnae Association in entertaining servicemen, especially on weekends. Hunter College Alumnae Hall on 55th Street was utilized for this purpose. The first floor was equipped for games and refreshments and the second floor for dancing, and students from each class volunteered to prepare refreshments, plan games, and serve as hostesses each Sunday afternoon. A major letter-writing campaign was organized about the same time. In March 1942 more than five hundred students volunteered to write letters in which they listed their hobbies and activities in order to be put in contact with servicemen of similar interests. The college committee maintained official contact with the army camps to coordinate the program. At the height of the campaign more than one thousand students were participating, and one girl was apparently writing twenty-eight letters each week.[61]

As students all across the country were being mobilized in various war drives, so too were the students at Hunter. They volunteered frequently as blood donors, although all those under twenty-one also needed parental permission. Various bond drives were sponsored, usually with some special goal or project in mind. An ambulance was purchased to assist the suffering of Europe as early as the spring of 1940, and two others were purchased in 1943. The students and alumnae combined to purchase a twenty-five-hundred dollar mobile hospital unit in early 1942, a one-thousand-dollar jeep was purchased later that year, and five LSM naval craft were financed in 1944. A scrap metal drive was sponsored in 1942, with major equipment from the older buildings being donated and the students contributing left-over keys, compacts, and lipstick containers from home.[62]

One of the college's more interesting and, considering its population, probably most unlikely programs was its farm assistance project. Maximum farm production was required for the war effort, and yet farm hands were at times scarce due to the draft and the demands of war industries. College women might be a solution since some farm work was not that strenuous and the students were free during summer. Eighteen Hunter students registered for the Volunteer Land Corps on Vermont and New Hampshire farms in the summer of 1942. Farmers were understandably skeptical because some of the women had never before been outside the city limits of New York, and one admitted that she "never saw a live cow except at the World's Fair."[63] But the program apparently succeeded. The first summer was spent picking berries, tomatoes, cherries, corn, and beans, and the following spring the college offered a course in the Evening and Extension Session on plant propagation, the care of seeds and plants, crop diseases, and similar gardening information. Hunter sponsored its own "Farm for Freedom" in 1943, under the direction of the Department of Biology, and approximately 250 students spent several summer weeks picking strawberries and weeding and cultivating vegetables on this and neighboring farms. These "farmerettes" lived together in camps or tourist facilities, were transported by truck to nearby farms at six o'clock each morning, and, as President Shuster noted, learned much, spent a very healthy summer outdoors, and contributed positively to the farm economy and the national war effort.

The greatest disruption of college life at Hunter occurred in early 1943 when the Navy assumed control of the Bronx campus as a training site for WAVES, the Navy's women's auxiliary. Originally called the Women's Naval Reserve Corps (WNRC), the WAVES (Women Appointed for Volunteer Emergency Service) was authorized by congressional legislation signed by President Roosevelt on July 30, 1942. The goal at that time was to create a department of ten to twelve thousand women to take over office, clerical, and laboratory positions and thus release that many sailors and naval officers for active duty. The WAACS (Women's Army Auxiliary Corps) had been established earlier, and the differences between the two were significant: WAVES could serve only in the United States, while WAACS could serve abroad; WAVES were part of the Naval Reserve and were under Navy rules and regulations, while WAACS were not that integrated into the Army; WAVES were paid salaries equal to men of the same rank, beginning at fifty dollars per month, while WAAC salaries began at twenty-one dollars; and the WAVES required a high school diploma for an enlisted member and a college degree for an officer, while the WAACS required only a high school diploma for an officer. The initial training program for WAVES was established that fall at Smith College, and Dr. Mildred McAfee, president of Wellesley, was named lieutenant commander.[64]

In early January 1943 Mayor La Guardia announced that, effective February 1, the Bronx campus of Hunter College would be used by the United States Navy as a training site for both WAVES and SPARS (Coast Guard). In fact, it would house the Navy's largest program. The four college buildings there contained office, classroom, dining, and recreational facilities, and the broad campus could accommodate drill and outside activities. Approximately twenty-five hundred recruits were scheduled to begin the six-week program on February 1, and a similar number later in the month. The campus could accommodate five thousand. The major difficulty, of course, was the lack of dormitory facilities; Hunter was not a residential college. The government thus requisitioned thirteen surrounding apartment buildings and agreed to move the six hundred families residing there at no cost. Some would be moved by the end of the month, and all by February 20. The twenty-two hundred students presently studying on the Bronx campus would be transferred downtown immediately, mandating larger class sizes and the utilization of additional space in Hunter College High School, Public School 76 nearby on Lexington Avenue, and in Roosevelt House on East 65th Street.[65]

The Navy program in the Bronx, dubbed the "USS Hunter," continued for three years. In all, more than eighty thousand WAVES were trained there, in addition to three thousand Women Marines and two thousand SPARS. The City of New York was reimbursed approximately half a million dollars a year for building rental and maintenance. With the close of the war in the summer of 1945, the Navy announced that the final class of recruits would be graduated that December or early 1946 and the buildings would be returned to regular college use in the spring. By that time the city had been doing without the use of seventeen apartment buildings used to house the WAVES, and Mayor La Guardia suggested that the Navy might still wish to retain these for use by veterans and their families upon demobilization. Four buildings, in fact, were returned to their owners almost immediately. Shuster and his staff began meeting with naval leaders soon after the start of the year to decide on a timetable for restoring the facilities to their original condition. Since the Navy's program was so largely academic, major renovations were not demanded. Locker rooms had to be restored as science laboratories and mess halls as student lounges, but the campus was scheduled to be available for full civilian use again by the fall semester. One Navy addition would be retained, Shuster noted; and the Home Economics Department in the future would have its own beauty parlor.[66]

An accomplishment of which Shuster was especially proud during these years was the purchase and utilization of Roosevelt House on East 65th Street. With the increasing demand for space in the new college building, especially after the transfer of the Bronx campus students downtown, there were few facilities for students to meet together and socialize either formally or informally, and Shuster considered such interaction and intercommunication important among such a diverse urban student population. Furthermore, he felt that religious development was just as essential as physical, intellectual, and social growth among the young, and Hunter College was able to provide little opportunity. It was not at all clear, however, what a public institution, financed almost entirely from city funds, legally could do to assist in religious development.

An attractive opportunity presented itself when President Franklin Roosevelt decided to sell the double apartment or town house he and his mother had lived in before his election as governor of New York. The building stood at 47–49 East 65th Street and housed two complete apartments of six floors each, with both opening onto the street through the same central door. With Sara Delano Roosevelt's death in late 1941, the president decided to put the house up for sale, asking sixty thousand dollars for it.[67] When leaders of the Hillel Foundation approached Shuster about possible use of facilities by Jewish students for their religious meetings and services, Shuster outlined his suggestion. He hoped that leaders of Catholic, Protestant, and Jewish bodies might unite to raise the necessary funds to purchase the Roosevelt home and then set up a corporation to own and operate it as a religious and social center for Hunter College. A small committee was immediately established—John S. Burke of the Altman Foundation (Catholic), Henry Monsky of B'nai B'rith (Jewish), Charles H. Tuttle of the Greater New York Federation of Churches (Protestant), and Aaron C. Horn as treasurer. Learning of Hunter's interest, President Roosevelt agreed to lower the price to fifty thousand dollars, and the committee immediately set about to organize a small fund-raising dinner at which ten thousand dollars was pledged. Fund-raising efforts continued, the full amount was collected by June 1942, and the house was signed over by President Roosevelt that summer.[68]

Renovation of the apartments began almost immediately. Some kitchen facilities were left intact in the basement, and other rooms were renovated for Student Self-Government and Athletic Association offices. The first two floors contained common rooms, which student groups could reserve in advance. President Roosevelt furnished one room as a library and donated books for it in memory of his mother. In building 49 Hillel Foundation by lot drew facilities on the third floor, the Newman Club on the fourth, and Protestant groups on the fifth. In building 47 House Plan had the fourth and fifth floors, and the Alumnae Association the sixth. The buildings also contained a game room, a meeting room for sororities, and offices for Toussaint L'Ouverture, the black student organization.[69]

The building was officially dedicated on November 22, 1943, as Sara Delano Roosevelt House but, because of the demands of the war effort, President Roosevelt was not able to attend. Eleanor Roosevelt was present and brought her husband's best wishes. "No houses could have a better background for the use they will now serve," she noted. "Always in both houses there was an effort to look on all human beings with respect, and to have a true understanding of the points of view of others."[70]

President Roosevelt himself had written a few days earlier:

> I feel that my dear mother would be very happy in the realization of the plans whereby the old home in East Sixty-fifth Street, with all its memories of joy and sorrow, is now to become Interfaith House—dedicated to mutual understanding and goodwill among students matriculating in Hunter College.
>
> It is to me of happy significance that this place of sacred memories is to become the first college center established for the high purpose of mutual understanding among Protestant, Jewish and Catholic students. I hope this movement for toleration will grow and prosper until there is a similar establishment in every institution of higher learning in the land, the spirit of which shall be unity in essentials; liberty in non-essentials; in all things, charity.[71]

It was left to Mayor La Guardia to have the final word. He noted that there had been "real progress" in interfaith and interracial understanding in New York recently, and then added: "Sometimes I try real hard to dislike somebody and just can't do it. There are only five or six people in the whole world I really dislike, and they all happen to be in Germany just now."[72]

A committee of prominent New York women—Mrs. Aaron Horn, Mrs. Charles Tuttle, Mrs. Victor Ridder, Mrs. James Picker, and of course Doris Shuster—was immediately organized to assist with continued fund-raising for the building and to arrange and sponsor appropriate events. The committee was originally called the Roosevelt House League, but out of deference to those unsympathetic to the president's political views, the name was later changed to the Association of Neighbors and Friends of Hunter College. The building was open from noon to 10:00 p.m. (midnight on weekends) and was in almost constant use. The religious groups, sororities, and House Plan held their regular meetings there; other groups sponsored teas, dinners, and dances; and various departments scheduled lectures and academic discussions. It was not unusual for between four and five hundred students and guests to use the building during the evening hours, under the at least nominal supervision of a faculty member being paid $1.50 an hour. With a rental fee of only fifty dollars, the building was also a very popular location for weddings. The various groups generally worked together harmoniously, although there was occasional friction when the Christian or Jewish groups decorated the common rooms for particular feasts, not realizing that the facilities were still reserved by the other group for a dance or party or academic discussion. With his appreciation of the place of religion in human life and growth, Shuster was particularly proud of his success in establishing Roosevelt House and making its facilities available to the students at Hunter College.[73]

If the changes at Hunter College were striking in the early 1940s, those in Shuster's own life were doubly so. He had always had some flexibility in arranging his teaching schedules at both the Huntington seminary and St. Joseph's College, and even at *The Commonweal* he could absent himself from the office on occasion if he needed greater quiet and freedom from interruptions for major writing projects. But with the presidency of Hunter, his time and his schedule were rarely his own.

The most noticeable change involved his residence. Because his new position would clearly involve extensive entertaining, he and Doris decided to sell their attractive but smaller home in the Glenbrook section of Stamford and purchase a much larger one on Shippan Point, along the city's shoreline. It was an impressive, three-story structure with a large parlor and dining room, additional bedrooms for guests, accommodations for a live-in maid, a curved driveway directly to the front door, and a pleasant yard in back for evening relaxation and George's favorite hobby, rose gardening. Because of Shuster's frequent evening commitments in New York City, he and Doris also took an apartment at the Carlyle Hotel on Madison at 76th Street, and often spent weeknights there. Their suite was well furnished and comfortable for cocktails, and the dining room downstairs was spacious, quiet, noted for fine food, and convenient for entertaining. The suite at the Carlyle may also have served to blunt some of the criticism that first year that Shuster held such an important—and high-salaried—city job and chose not to reside in the city itself, or even in the state, although Doris always denied that this was a motive. The city wanted George as Hunter's president, she insisted; he informed them that he was very comfortable living in Connecticut; and officials were willing to accept this. After giving up the apartment at the Carlyle, Shuster would occasionally take a room at the Players Club if he had either a very late or very early commitment, or occasionally both. He used that room most frequently after the late night hearings of the Enemy Alien Board in the early months of World War II.[74]

Shuster's daily schedule could vary, but it was always full. He continued to rise early, unusually early if there was some writing he wanted to do. Much of his writing was done at home, and he often found the quiet, early morning hours most conducive. He enjoyed a good breakfast, a heavy one on weekends, and either prepared it himself or waited for Doris, never an early riser, to join him. He took the train to work each morning, reading a book or articles or reports on the way, and friends were amazed at how much detail and precision he retained despite the crowds and jostling and distractions of the commuter lines. He usually arrived at his office close to 9:30 a.m. and, if no meetings or appointments were scheduled, began the day with the mail. He dictated replies to secretaries, and they were invariably impressed with the almost effortless beauty, grace, and precision of his language, letter after letter, with almost no correcting or revising. Personal letters and first drafts of reports he might type himself, with a two-finger style characterized more by speed than by accuracy. If he did not have a luncheon appointment, and he usually did, he would join a few faculty members at a nearby restaurant or coffee shop. The afternoons were usually taken up with appointments or meetings, and very often meetings in government, foundation, business, or educational offices downtown. He attended meetings frequently on the Bronx campus also. Usually he could leave the office between five and six o'clock and return home for dinner, but often there were evening benefits or dinners or performances to attend. On these occasions Doris would frequently come into the city in late afternoon and join him, spending the night then at the Carlyle.[75]

Shuster's heavy schedule at Hunter College, the long commute from Stamford, and his increasing involvement in other civic and educational projects posed serious challenges to his family life. Doris adjusted most easily. She loved New York, she loved to entertain, and she found her responsibilities and commitments as wife of the college president fulfilling. She enjoyed the theater, opera, and museums and, if her husband was occupied with conferences or meetings, she was comfortable with others or would go alone. She became increasingly involved with her own chosen interests—Roosevelt House and the Girl Scouts in New York, and the local Democratic Party and the Board of Education in Stamford—and she was willing to let George live part of his life and even travel without her. In fact, it was mutually satisfying. Doris loved to be active—entertaining, presiding, attending meetings, playing bridge, traveling—and George needed time for leisure, for reading, and for solitude. If his responsibilities as college president kept them apart more than they might have intended, both probably agreed it gave them opportunity to develop their own strengths and in some ways their own lives.[76]

It was not the same for Bobby, however. There was no question that Bobby loved his parents and knew that they loved him, but the relationship was less intimate. He was only five when they made their first trip to Germany, and he went to kindergarten in

Berlin while his parents traveled elsewhere. By the time he was fourteen he had made two more trips to Europe, had enrolled in different boarding schools there, often while his parents traveled again, and transferred schools at least once back in Connecticut. During his first year as president of Hunter, George and Doris often stayed at the apartment at the Carlyle, returning to Stamford only on the weekend. They hired a maid and house-keeper to look after the house—and Bobby—during the week. Like his father, Bob was tall and wiry. He went out for track in high school, but later could not recall either his mother or father ever attending a meet. After giving up the suite at the Carlyle, George still did not return home until late in the evening, after the rest of the family had eaten; he traveled much to attend meetings or give speeches; and he simply could not spend that much time with his family at home. Bob probably realized early that it had to be this way. If George had spent longer hours with Bob, or shared Doris's interests in visiting and the theater, he probably would not have had the time for his own writing and speaking and college responsibilities. Bob was left on his own frequently, and equally significantly, grew up very much with his mother. Doris was a very loving person, but one also with a strong will. Her very active personal life could not always include him, and, when it did, may have tended to dominate. She tutored him so well at home that on his return from Germany at the age of six he was admitted directly into the second grade; she chided him frequently for not writing from his boarding school in Berlin while she and George were in Vienna; and she took him systematically through the Louvre at the age of twelve, while George was in London, and was pleased that he was developing a taste in art all his own.[77]

Any loneliness that Bob might have experienced was miti-gated during the war years by the presence of two foster children in the Shuster household. With the near-disaster at Dunkirk in June 1940, and the growing threat of the invasion of England itself, the British government encouraged parents to send their children to greater safety with relatives elsewhere in the Com-monwealth. Since many did not have relatives elsewhere, Oxford University inaugurated a program of sending faculty children to the United States, with Yale University as the contact here. Felicity and Jenny Hugh-Jones, aged eleven and nine, and their two younger sisters, sailed across on Cunard Lines that June and arrived in Canada. Unknown to them, a second Cunard ship had been sunk during their crossing, and it was several days before their anxious parents learned that their four young daughters had not been killed. The four girls wanted to remain together, the youngest only three, and a family in Brooklyn, with six children of their own, agreed to take them, but this arrangement lasted only through the following spring. The girls spent the summer at camp, and after one or two additional experiments, the two youngest were entrusted to a family in New Haven and Felicity and Jenny were accepted by the Shusters. Parents in England contributed money to a fund at that time (which could not be taken out of the country during the war), and Yale reimbursed the host families for at least part of their expenses. Yale apparently was to be reimbursed through scholarships after the war. The Shusters accepted no money for the girls' upkeep; they did it simply out of charity. The arrival of the two girls caused a further change in lifestyle, because George and Doris now had to give up the apartment at the Carlyle and make Stamford their only home. George and Doris never indicated to the girls that they had caused any inconvenience at all, only that they were daughters they had never been able to have themselves.[78]

The two lively young girls added zest to the Shuster household. Felicity was most interested in music and the arts, Jenny in books and reading, and the three Shusters were interested in all. Bob was about five years older than Felicity, but the three got along as well as teen-age boys and girls do in the same family, and they remained close friends throughout their lives. The girls were treated as full members of the family: they went along when the Shusters visited neighbors, they had household chores to perform, and they were allowed to select one dish they did not have to eat (Felicity chose sauerkraut and Jenny eggplant). The girls finished primary school in Stamford and then boarded at Sacred Heart convent in the Bronx for high school, returning to Stamford each weekend. The weekends were particularly pleasant. On Saturdays the girls might help George tend his roses, work in his "victory garden" about a mile away, or during the fall, listen to a football game on the radio. The Saturday evening meal was always special, elaborate, and long, since during the week the rest always ate before George came home. The conversation was invariably stimulating because they all had read different things, and George was interested in what each one had to say. After dinner they would play poker, with each one risking twenty-five cents. Sunday morning was quiet time. No one was allowed up until time to prepare for Noon Mass. (Jenny later recalled that she had read quite a few books sitting in bed Sunday mornings until time to get up.) On the way home from Mass they would stop at a Polish bakery and buy fresh rolls for brunch. George loved to walk, and several other members of the family might join him for a walk along the beach on Sunday afternoons. To the girls he was always "Uncle George" and Doris was "Honey," the name George, Bob, and most of her closest friends called her throughout her life.

The girls remembered Christmases with the Shusters as particularly pleasant, especially because of the German tone to the celebration. On Christmas Eve there were always the usual last-minute things to do and, with all the family at home, the presents were wrapped that morning and afternoon. It was a day of abstinence for Catholics, and although dinner was a large meal, no meat was served—possibly oyster stew, fish, salads, and so on. After the meal, all would join to decorate the tree, always a large one standing in the front room. Then they exchanged and opened presents, and the family enjoyed the spirit of the season together until it was time for Midnight Mass. Christmas itself was a day of leisure and relaxation. Everyone rose late, not a problem after the long Midnight Mass and the excitement of the day before, and the hearty Christmas meal was served late in the afternoon. It was truly a day of rest and family sharing; all the rushing about and excitement over presents occupied the day before. These were occasions the whole family treasured deeply.[79]

During the war, unfortunately, such occasions were all too few. Shuster was not only attempting to guide a large municipal college during a difficult period and continue his writing as time might permit, but he was also being gradually drawn into government service. The first of his assignments was his appointment, along with Henry Pitney Van Dusen, later president of Union Theological Seminary, to New York's Enemy Alien Board II in 1942. The purpose of the board was to "screen" German, Italian, and Japanese aliens residing in the United States whose loyalty the FBI had some reason to suspect. Since the board met evening after evening at six o'clock in the Department of Justice Building on Foley Square and the sessions lasted until midnight, Shuster took a small room at the Players' Club; there was no time for daily trips back and forth to Connecticut. Several of the persons appearing before the board had unwisely joined suspect organizations or subscribed to some pro-Axis journal, but most were no threat at all, although one that came highly vouched for by many leaders of his community apparently later turned out to be a significant spy. The work of the board would have passed almost unnoticed by the public had not one of the persons called before it been the Italian opera star Enzio Pinza. Pinza was still an Italian citizen, he had apparently boasted of a citation he had received from Mussolini himself, and he had recently taunted a French singer that the Italians could defeat the French at any time. His marital indiscretions were an added source of public interest. He had been detained on Ellis Island in March, and the board heard his case in late May. Shuster and Van Dusen saw nothing threatening in his continued presence on the streets of America and promptly restored him to freedom.[80]

The government continued to establish Hearing Boards as needed throughout the country, and sometime later Shuster was assigned to a new board in Santa Fe. He thought it ironic that, fluent in German, he would be sent two thousand miles away to interview Japanese.[81] The board interviewed various first- and second-generation Japanese-Americans who had been relocated there from more sensitive areas along the Pacific coast. The board's principal responsibility was to ascertain whether a person's primary loyalty was to the United States or to Japan. For some, because of language difficulties, understanding the question seemed the greatest challenge. When one elderly gentleman struggled in vain to comprehend phrases like "undertake some action inimical to the best interests of the United States," the questioning attorney finally rephrased it: "The Emperor Hirohito calls you. He tells you, do something bad against the United States. What will you say?" The light of understanding suddenly appeared and the board had its answer: "Me tell him—got wrong number!"[82] Shuster enjoyed recalling this story in later years.

Throughout 1944 Shuster also did propaganda work for the Office of War Information. Most of this involved recording speeches for broadcast overseas, giving talks on the American educational system for English-speaking allies, or more often, preparing talks on American public life and war aims to be broadcast to the German people either behind enemy lines or recently captured by the Allies. Shuster often drafted his speech in English, on "Casablanca and Security for German People," for example, the Office of War Information would translate it, and Shuster would record the speech in German for later rebroadcast. Shuster not only had a fine command of the German language but was also a public figure already known to many in Germany; and he was thus able to inspire greater trust and confidence in his message.[83]

Probably the most satisfying government service Shuster performed during these war years was as a member of the General Advisory Committee of the State Department's Division of Cultural Relations from 1941 to 1945. The Division of Cultural Relations had been set up within the State Department in 1938 to further understanding and harmony chiefly between the United States and other countries of the Western Hemisphere through study and travel grants, faculty exchanges, and the support of libraries, schools, and other cultural centers.[84] In 1940 President Roosevelt appointed four committees to advise the State Department in its program of cultural relations: a Committee on Exchange Fellowships and Professorships, a Committee on Inter-American Medicine and Public Health, a Committee on Inter-American Cooperation in Agricultural Education, and a General Advisory Committee of the Division of Cultural Relations. The purpose of this last was "to advise the Department, through the Division of Cultural Relations, on general policy in the planning and execution of the program of cultural relations, and to serve as a coordinating body for the other advisory committees," and it was to this committee that Shuster was appointed on August 28, 1941. Other members of the committee included Waldo Leland of the American Council of Learned Societies, Archibald MacLeish of the Library of Congress, Beardsley Ruml of the University of Chicago, John Studebaker, the Commissioner of Education, and Vice President Henry Wallace.[85]

The committee was an active one and held two-day meetings in Washington three or four times a year. Topics frequently considered were the fostering of intercultural publications and translations, the exchange of personnel, desirable non-governmental programs, the utilization of foreign graduates of American colleges and universities, postwar cultural relations with China, and the educational rehabilitation of war-torn countries.[86] From his experience on the Enemy Alien and Hearing Boards, Shuster was especially concerned about the treatment of foreign nationals in the United States and the bitter prejudice against Japanese-Americans. On Shuster's recommendation the committee passed a resolution urging that some prominent official, even the president, send a letter to the national association of universities and colleges to remind leaders of their duty not to discriminate against Nisei students in educational institutions. With his long-time interest in German culture and education, Shuster was deeply concerned about the postwar rehabilitation of the educational systems in Germany and Austria and the eradication of Fascist and Nazi influences. As president of the world's largest college for women, he strongly favored the utilization of women graduates in various countries to promote international harmony and understanding.[87]

Shuster's most forceful presentation to the committee occurred in February 1942. He acknowledged that he was supposed to be speaking as chairman of a subcommittee, but since the subcommittee, because of the numerous other commitments of its individual members, had not been able to meet, the remarks he would make were primarily his own. He lamented once again the treatment of many foreign students on American campuses. They should not be presumed sympathetic to the country's enemies. They have become familiar with American public life and the American educational system and, if treated well, might serve America successfully as good-will ambassadors when they return home. He urged increased support for programs in comparative literature, both for American students and for foreign students studying here, and he singled out Columbia University's program for special praise. As a committed humanist, he also urged that the humanities and liberal arts not be overlooked in intercultural exchanges. In our emphases on economics and technology, he suggested, we "forget that the root of European nationalism, and of nationalism in the Americas as well, is primarily the product of linguistic and cultural differences," and thus attention to language and literature and culture is essential. In a time of war, national rivalries, and increased emphasis on technology and industrial production, this concern for the centrality of culture was an important contribution the Division of Cultural Relations could make.[88]

Despite his numerous other commitments, Shuster strove to find time for work on this General Advisory Committee of the Division of Cultural Relations. He supported its basic premise of international harmony through education and culture, and he was confident that it had exerted at least some influence on State Department policy. It was in part on the recommendation of this committee that the United States joined UNESCO, the United Nations Educational, Scientific, and Cultural Organization, and it was to UNESCO that Shuster was to devote so much time and effort over the next twenty years of his life.

6

PRESIDENT IN A TIME OF CHANGE
1945–1960

In one of his most enigmatic statements, George Shuster remarked in 1960 that one thing he had learned as president of Hunter College was that "you ought not to educate a women as if she were a man, nor to educate her as if she were not."[1] Precisely what he meant may not be clear, but it certainly conveyed his conviction, first of all, that women had a special and unique role to play in society and that education should help prepare them to assume and fulfill it successfully, and second, that this unique role was as important and challenging as that of men and thus the education of women was to be in no way less rigorous or scholarly. What made this educational challenge additionally exciting during Shuster's years at Hunter was that the role of women changed radically from those days of lingering Depression and high unemployment of 1939, through the demand for women defense workers in World War II and the immediate postwar years of baby boom and movement to the suburbs, to the early Civil Rights marches and the age of Sputnik in the late 1950s. Shuster viewed his responsibility at Hunter as a fascinating and exciting challenge, he acquitted it successfully, and he enjoyed it thoroughly.

One of the most satisfying aspects of his office was undoubtedly his contacts with students. Hunter students were indeed an interesting lot. In a 1939 survey the senior class selected as the greatest living men President Roosevelt, Albert Einstein, and the newly elected Pope Pius XII, adding support to the frequently repeated quip that Hunter was the largest *Catholic* women's college in the world. These seniors chose the *New York Times* as their favorite newspaper and, in humor magazines, preferred *Esquire* to the *New Yorker*. To demonstrate their diversity further, they named as favorite radio programs Charlie McCarthy, Information Please, and Philharmonic Symphony Orchestra, and their favorite foods were steaks and hot dogs. As ideal qualities in a man they listed "tall, dark, and handsome" first, a sense of humor second, wealth third, and intelligence fourth—not precisely the ordering to make a college president proud.[2]

Since Hunter was not a residential college, it would have been easy for Shuster not to become involved in student life, but he was determined that this would not happen. Realizing that faculty-student interaction in the classroom was the essence of college life, he attempted to offer one course himself each semester—English poetry in his early years and German politics or world affairs later. He was conscientious in attending Field Days on the Bronx campus, outdoor exercises and sports competitions, and the annual Sing on Park Avenue, competitive musical programs sponsored by each of the four classes. He had a special affection for Roosevelt House and was a frequent participant in social, academic, and religious events there. Never one to stand on his dignity, he allowed himself to be nominated for Ugliest Man on Campus in a fund-raising campaign. He gave a news briefing each week to the campus media, and even though he controlled and manipulated them at times, one editor recalled that he did it in such a "silky-smooth way" that they did not mind and they always departed with good quotes and headlines. He had occasional differences with student government leaders, as every president does, but one student recalled that "the chief advantage of being President of S.S.G.A. [the student government association] is the privilege of walking down to the Assembly Hall platform on the arm of President Shuster." And student contacts were a source of satisfaction, and at times humor, for him. He enjoyed retelling the story of the professor who asked his class on one occasion if anyone knew what extreme unction was. One student eagerly raised her hand and suggested that is was "a sacrament given to Catholics at the moment of death and on similar occasions." On days filled with the tensions and stresses of office, there were few more relaxing breaks for Shuster than sharing time and exchanging stories with interested, impressed, and admiring students.[3]

Shuster's relations with his faculty were equally satisfying. He had come to Hunter College relatively unknown and, with his limited academic background, was suspect to many, but he soon changed most reservations. He enjoyed the company of people with ideas, he loved to probe into their research interests, and the faculty appreciated this respect. He was not authoritarian and generally let the newly created faculty committees exercise their responsibilities and carry out their duties unhindered. Some, of course, were not supporters—faculty members denied promotion, administrators not retained, and many who simply did not like his less structured administrative style—but relations seldom became embittered, chiefly because, as one official suggested, he was a persuader rather than a fighter and disagreements consistently remained calmer.[4] In some ways, he remained one of the faculty, teaching a class, continuing to publish in his areas of expertise, and even finding time to act in faculty plays. As T. Tennyson Twinkle he attempted to woo the heroine by reading poetry in one play, he was the owner of a flophouse in another, and dressed in warpaint and feathers in a third, he portrayed a Chief Wannemucka, an "untutored savage" trying to arrange a tepee circuit for a young Indian maiden as a white princess. His initial entrances on the stage invariably brought on show-stopping applause.[5] The easy and friendly relations between Shuster and the faculty are suggested by the song "Prexy Shuster" sung to the tune of "Yankee Doodle" at his tenth anniversary celebration:[6]

PREXY SHUSTER
I
Prexy Shuster came to town,
Stayed at Hunter College,
Put a feather in our cap
With all his grace and knowledge.
Chorus
Prexy Shuster, stay with us,
We'll not let you rue it.
Mind the students and the staff,
And very well you'll do it.
II
Now a decade you have spent
Here with Alma Mater,
And all of us are well content
That you're our Almus Pater.

Chorus
Prexy Shuster, we all say,
What you want go *to* it.
Both the students and the staff
Will gladly let George do it.

As president and official representative of the college, Shuster's relations with the Board of Higher Education and with the public were excellent also. The Board had been publicly criticized for its removal of Eugene Colligan in 1939, and it hoped the controversy would not continue.[7] In fact, Shuster had made very few enemies in educational circles; he could be the epitome of charm and tact. During his twenty-one years in office few major problems at Hunter College came before the Board, and fewer of Shuster's own making. The college made excellent progress, and the Board was justifiably proud of its administration. Total enrollment increased approximately fifty percent; new programs were added, including education of the handicapped; standards were raised; programs like the Opera Workshop and the Concert Series attained national and even international reputation; and, very important, Shuster guided it all within budget.

Shuster's influence extended beyond Hunter College. The Board created an Administrative Council, consisting of the municipal college presidents, to act as an advisory body and coordinating committee in matters affecting all four institutions, and Shuster's advice was highly respected. By the late 1950s, of course, he had served in office longer than any of his colleagues, and his experience was especially valuable. He presided at Hunter for twenty-one years, serving under three Board chairmen and four city mayors. There is no evidence that the Board during that time ever thought of replacing him, and it was indeed sorry to see him leave in 1960.[8]

The relations between Hunter College and the public also remained good. There were disagreements and sources of friction occasionally—the paying of non-union wages to stagehands at high school stage productions and the effect of five thousand students on the residential life of Park Avenue—but these were relatively few. With its concert series and speakers program, Hunter became a cultural center for the city, and the public was properly proud of the distinguished artists, scholars, and statesmen who participated. Shuster appeared frequently at benefits and conferences and especially at interreligious programs, and his speeches were invariably thoughtful. As time went on, New York became increasingly proud of the positions he held and the honors he received—positions with the American Council on Education and the American Academy of Arts and Sciences, his appointment as Land Commissioner to Bavaria in 1950, and his appointment to the Executive Committee of UNESCO in 1958. His close relationship with the Roosevelts was a source of pride also, even for those who disagreed with the president's politics. Roosevelt visited the college shortly after Shuster's inauguration, and he continued to correspond on occasion on educational matters and to ask Shuster's assistance in finding employment for American or foreign scholars. Eleanor Roosevelt was particularly close to the college because of her interest both in Roosevelt House and in the education of women, and she spoke at the college frequently. If her schedule did not permit attendance in person, she often sent personal contributions to Hunter benefits.[9]

Shuster was proud to be associated with a school of Hunter's high standing and good reputation also. Another of his favorite stories concerned the time he was invited to an an educational conference where President Harry Truman was to speak. He apologized to the security agent at the door, explaining that he had forgotten his ticket of admission, and then identified himself as the president of Hunter College. "Go right in, Doctor," the agent responded. "My aunt graduated from your great institution." Nelson Rockefeller was following directly behind and had forgotten his pass also. He identified himself, but to no avail. "I don't care if you are Napoleon Bonaparte," the officer declared. "You can't get in here without a ticket!" Shuster stepped back and confided, as seriously as he could: "It's quite all right, officer. He teaches at Hunter." "In that case, Doctor," he replied, "of course, I'll let him in."[10]

Shuster undoubtedly had his deficiencies as an administrator. He had little training in finances, and yet the whole college budget of between two and five million dollars was dependent upon him. And a complicated budget it was. Most monies were appropriated by the city, but there were state and federally funded programs also, various student fees, and endowed accounts.

Shuster, in fact, was happy to allow Doris to handle family finances at times. But despite his personal distaste for finances, he made many budgetary decisions himself. He felt the area was too sensitive and too important to share with others, and he apparently did not make as good a use of his personnel and budget committees as he might have. There were few budget crises during the Shuster presidency, but many at the college felt that the money might have been appropriated and spent better had Shuster acted upon the advice of others more often.[11]

Another criticism of Shuster, probably equally accurate, was that he did not utilize standard administrative procedures well. He wanted to lead, he knew where he wanted the college to go, his instincts were generally excellent, but he often made decisions alone when others should have been involved. One dean recalled that it was not unusual for her to learn from faculty members of decisions Shuster had made in her area and about which he had simply forgotten to consult or inform her. It was basically a failure to communicate, a surprising deficiency in one who communicated and persuaded so effectively on personal and less bureaucratic levels. The fact that he occasionally did not utilize time-honored academic structures could antagonize those forced to work closely with him, but his graciousness and good will generally prevented such incidents from becoming major controversies.

Thus Shuster's administration was to an unusual degree a personal administration; personal diplomacy was clearly one of his greatest assets, but this had its drawbacks also. He allocated resources according to his own vision and goals, encouraging the fine arts and humanities but probably doing little for the morale of the scientists, who felt their departments were being neglected, if not actually "starved."[12] Shuster was not comfortable under a plethora of rules and regulations, although such rules and regulations might be necessary to assure some uniformity among the four municipal colleges. This could also leave his colleagues perplexed. Harry Gideonse, president of Brooklyn College, admitted that he did not disagree that often with Shuster's decisions but was never sure how Shuster arrived at them, what his vision for Hunter College really was, and whether the next decision would be wholly consistent. Shuster's more personal decision-making may in fact have left more orthodox and traditional decision-makers somewhat uneasy. In hiring new personnel to the faculty or staff, he at times ignored traditional procedures or committee jurisdictions, although once again his charm and graciousness generally prevented major confrontations. After seventy-five years Hunter College had accumulated a respectable set of bureaucratic procedures and Shuster, with little background in educational administration, intentionally or unintentionally overlooked them often.

But by almost any criterion Shuster's presidency was a grand success. For twenty-one years the college ran smoothly and even happily, with a minimum of crises during turbulent and changing times. Academic standards continued to rise, increasingly qualified faculty were attracted to the college, and the inauguration and expansion of various graduate programs enhanced the scholarly atmosphere of the whole institution. The school even took on more and more of the characteristics of the president himself. The curricular emphasis was clearly on the humanities and the liberal arts, although the fine and performing arts—music, painting, and theater—were given strong support. But American life was changing and women needed to be prepared not only for responsibilities in the home but for positions of trust and importance in government and business also. Thus vocational training became more available, although always subordinate to the humanities. Finally, isolationism was no longer an option for the United States after World War II—the transportation revolution and international dependencies made that impossible—and the environment at Hunter encouraged all, students and faculty alike, to adopt a more international point of view in politics, economics, and culture.

This international point of view was brought home to Hunter very realistically as World War II came to an end. The United States Navy had decided that the last class of WAVES would graduate from the Bronx campus in February 1946, and Shuster hoped that restoration of the college buildings to full academic use could be completed over the summer so a full contingent of students could enroll that September. But a new complication suddenly emerged that February. Throughout the war the Allied leaders had been making plans for the establishment of a United Nations organization to settle international disputes and preserve world peace, especially urgent now with the introduction of atomic weapons, and plans had been finalized at the San Francisco conference in the late spring and summer of 1945. By early 1946 almost all nations had ratified the UN charter and some agencies had already begun meeting in London. A permanent home was to be built in New York, but temporary facilities were urgently needed in order to permit the General Assembly, the Security Council, and the Secretariat to begin work immediately. James J. Lyons, president of the Borough of the Bronx, suggested the Bronx campus of Hunter College. The Navy was moving out that February, New York had excellent international communications, the facilities—over a hundred classrooms, two cafeterias, lounges, and a large gymnasium—seemed suitable, and, he suggested, since Hunter had gotten along without that campus during the war, it could surely do without it for a few months more. Shuster strongly disagreed. "Our educational facilities are strained to the utmost now," he remarked, "and under those circumstances the taking out of circulation of an educational unit as large as the Bronx unit would be nothing short of disastrous." Educational leaders were predicting that an additional twenty thousand veterans would seek college enrollment in New York state alone that September, and no one was certain where facilities could be found. Lyons understood Shuster's objections but did not agree: "I don't blame him; after all, he's an educator and he should be concerned about his school. However, I am not concerned about Shuster."[13]

The decision, of course, was not in Shuster's hands—nor even in the hands of the Board of Higher Education. Hunter College was a municipal school, the buildings belonged to the city, and the city could do with them as it wished. With prodding from the federal government, with a spirit of patriotism and good will, and with appreciation of the prestige it would bring to New York, the city decided to offer the facilities to the United Nations.[14] The original agreement was to extend only from February to May 15, 1946, to enable classes to resume on the Bronx campus in September as planned. With the United Nations moving in that early, however, the Navy was not able to complete the restorative work it had agreed upon, and Shuster recommended that the Board of Higher Education accept a lump sum from the Navy in lieu of this reconstruction, with the United Nations to be asked to cover additional expenses. The Board agreed. The lease was later extended to August 15, with rent approximately seventeen thousand dollars a month, and Shuster was delegated to work out with the United Nations and the city additional costs of renovations due to the sudden withdrawal of the Navy. The whole experience complicated Shuster's life during that spring and summer, and he certainly did not approve of some of the ways in which the transfer was handled, and yet he also was proud that the first meetings of the United Nations Organization were held in the facilities of the college of which he was president.[15]

The United Nations vacated the Bronx campus facilities that August, but further renovations were still necessary to return the buildings to full academic use, and as a result, classes could not begin uptown until October 14. By that time another major decision had been made. Because of the large number of returning veterans seeking to continue their education, usually under the GI Bill of Rights, the Board of Higher Education decided to admit male veterans to the Bronx campus under specific conditions: all had to be residents of one of the five New York boroughs and pass the standard admission requirements, all would attend classes in special afternoon and evening sessions, and only freshmen and sophomore classes would continue to be offered in the Bronx.[16] After that, the veterans could transfer to any other college in the city and receive a degree; Hunter College was still prohibited by its by-laws from granting degrees to males.[17]

When classes finally opened on the Bronx campus that October, there were 750 women and 500 men in the freshman class. (There had been no classes taught there since 1943, and thus there were no sophomores.) The women attended class from 8:40 in the morning until 2:00 in the afternoon, and the men from 2:00 in the afternoon until 7:00 in the evening. The average age of the male veterans was twenty-two, four years above the normal freshman age, and a few were as old as forty. Although they had been away from school for some time, they were also more serious, more mature, and their motivation was probably greater. They adapted to college life quite easily. They sponsored a spring dance the following May, selected a campus queen, and inaugurated their own newspaper, "The Hunter Mail."[18]

The steps toward coeducation did not stop there. With the great numbers of returning veterans and other students enrolling in New York city colleges after the war, it was increasingly difficult for the veterans at Hunter's Bronx campus to find openings and transfer elsewhere after their sophomore year. In the spring of 1947 Shuster announced that the Board of Higher Education had agreed to permit these 860 male veterans to complete their final two years of college at Hunter's Park Avenue campus, integrating that campus's day session for the first time. (Men had been admitted into the Evening and Extension Division earlier.) Shuster also announced that no special classes would be held for the men; they would simply be integrated within the student body. The decision was taken shortly after the women in a straw vote had voted, perhaps not surprisingly, three to one *against* the college becoming coeducational. By the spring of 1948 fifty-nine male veterans had completed their sophomore classwork in the Bronx and had transferred to Park Avenue. About 750 males remained in the Bronx for their first two years of college, and this number gradually diminished since Hunter stopped admitting male veterans in September 1948. The postwar admission crisis seemed to be declining.[19]

With the final class of veterans about to graduate in 1952, the Board of Higher Education made a further momentous change. Beginning in the fall of 1951 the Bronx division of Hunter College would become a four-year liberal arts college and would also be fully coeducational. The war veterans were no longer there, and thus space was available. City College of New York would begin admitting undergraduate women at the same time, and this might reduce the demand on Hunter. The population of the Bronx was growing rapidly and a four-year college there seemed necessary. Since the Bronx division was not a residential campus, relatively few changes would have to be made. A Dean of Men would be appointed, a locker room for men would be built in the gymnasium, and new teachers would be hired as increasing enrollments demanded. Borough president James Lyons admitted that he preferred establishing a completely independent four-year college but also admitted that that step would be much more costly. Beginning in the fall of 1951, consequently, men could enroll in the four-year college program on Hunter's

Bronx campus, and women could enroll either in the Bronx, if they preferred a coeducational program, or on Park Avenue, which would return to a single-sex campus with the graduation of the final five male veterans in February 1952. The freshman class of 1951 numbered twelve hundred, 450 women on the Park Avenue campus and approximately 600 women and 150 men on the Bronx campus. The last five male veterans to graduate from the Park Avenue campus received additional publicity since they were outnumbered by the women approximately 1000 to 1. They took it in stride. "They've treated us just like one of the girls," one quipped.[20]

Hunter College grew at a rapid but acceptable rate under Shuster's presidency. Total enrollment was approximately ten thousand at the time of his inauguration, about evenly divided between day students and the Evening and Extension Division. Enrollment dropped slightly during the war when more high school graduates went directly into war work or public service and when the Bronx campus was taken over temporarily by the Navy. Like most American colleges, Hunter experienced a sudden leap in enrollment immediately after the war as returning servicemen continued their education under the GI Bill of Rights. By 1960 the enrollment had grown to approximately fifteen thousand. Seven thousand of these were in the former Evening and Extension Division, six thousand in the regular undergraduate program, roughly half in the Bronx and half on Park Avenue, and the other two thousand in graduate programs. In 1950 the Evening and Extension Division was reorganized as the School of General Studies and was given jurisdiction over all non-degree and adult education courses and all non-matriculated students. The college budget attempted to keep pace with both inflation and increasing enrollment. In 1942–43, no longer a depression year and the last year before the Navy occupied the Bronx campus, the budget was $2.8 million; in 1959–60 it was $4.6 million. The sources of the Board of Higher Education's revenue had changed significantly also. In 1942–43, 91 percent of its budget came from city funding, less than 2 percent from state funds, and 6 percent from student fees. In 1959–60, only 56 percent of its budget came from city funds, student fees now accounted for 13 percent, and state funding had increased to almost 24 percent, chiefly in support of various teacher-training programs. Much of the expansion at Hunter took place on the Bronx campus, of course, with the conversion of that division into a four-year program. Shuster asked the Board of Higher Education to create the position of Dean of Administration and to appoint Dr. John J. Meng to it. Meng's responsibilities were to serve as Shuster's first assistant and, in practice, as acting president in Shuster's absence; to serve as chief executive officer of the Bronx campus and have his office there; and to serve as chairman of a newly organized Committee of Deans. The Dean of Men and Dean of Women in the Bronx would still handle day-to-day student contacts and decisions, leaving the Dean of Administration free for policy decisions, for long-range planning, for public relations in the Bronx, and especially for coordination with President Shuster on Park Avenue. As the four-year program in the Bronx progressed, a major concern was space. In 1955 Dean Meng turned his own comfortable office into a clinic and waiting room for the Department of Education, locker rooms were converted into science laboratories and the lockers relocated in tunnels between buildings, and even some corridor space was partitioned off to serve as classrooms. That same year the Board of Higher Education approved the construction of a $3.3 million combination classroom, library, and administration building, but it was not completed and ready for use until 1959.[21]

The physical and administrative changes at Hunter College during the Shuster presidency, however, were not as significant as the academic growth. Hunter had been a good school in the 1920s and 1930s—many educational leaders throughout the city and state in later decades were Hunter graduates—and it continued to advance under Shuster. For him, first of all, good teaching and scholarly publication by the faculty had to go hand in hand, as he wrote to the faculty in late 1942:

> We ought, as a college faculty, to place good teaching above all else. It is this alone which gives the student what she must have and wants to have—guidance that will help her to shape her own personal and intellectual life. But good teaching is not merely a kind of elocution, magnetism, or even devotion. It proceeds from fullness of knowledge enthusiastically treasured; and fullness of knowledge cannot be divorced from creative study of all that can

be found out about a given subject. It seems to me that such study will impel the individual to add something to the store of knowledge. Publication is not hackwork then, but a flowing-over of intellectual vitality. Doubtless one is impelled to earn the right to speak when one does a research essay, but one is driven above all by the desire to have one's own brain child born. That is why the College attaches value to publications. But it is not necessary that they have an immediate bearing on what one is actually teaching. The thing that counts is whether the child is alive.[22]

On the undergraduate level Shuster's educational goals were achieved chiefly through increased emphasis on the humanities and liberal arts and through the addition of what he called "vocational in-lays." When he assumed the acting presidency in 1939, the college was divided into eighteen traditional departments: art, biological sciences, business economics, chemistry, classics, education, English, and so on. With increased enrollments and growth of the college, several areas were split into separate departments under Shuster: biological sciences became biology, botany, and zoology; classics was divided into Latin and Greek; geology and geography separated, as did psychology and philosophy; and Romance languages became the departments of French, Italian, and Spanish. Four entirely new departments were created also: anthropology, Hebrew, home economics, and Russian.[23]

The core of the curriculum remained the humanities and liberal arts, and students took a majority of their courses in these areas. In an address to incoming freshmen, Shuster explained why the liberal arts were so central:

> They are studies, of language and literature, of mathematics and the sciences, of history and of the notable forms of social behavior— psychological, political, economic, sociological, anthropological, which if carefully pursued provide basic information, instruct in accuracy of thought and expression, and form judgment. With them the noble arts of music, painting, and sculpture are associated as forms of literature having their own lofty and distinctive being. We say not only that these constitute our legacy of human culture, but also that they are means through the use of which any one of us may attain unto a measure of personal cultivation.[24]

Shuster was proud of the fact that although Hunter was founded primarily as a normal school, as a school to train teachers, one could not major in education. The students took education courses and amassed sufficient credits to receive required state certification, but they majored in art, chemistry, English, history, or whatever area they were preparing to teach. Vocational in-lays fulfilled a similar purpose. Shuster and other college officials realized that Hunter graduates needed to find employment in an increasingly competitive and demanding job market, but they were determined that Hunter not become a professional or vocational school. Thus the liberal arts core remained, and in addition students could enroll in groups of courses that would help prepare them for a later career. "I have unashamedly urged all language and literature majors to take courses in typewriting and stenography," he admitted, "and I have just as persistently cajoled feminine students into finding out what a baby looks like, what has to be done to help it grow up, and what a strange sort of creature its father is likely to be." "It seems to me inconceivable," he concluded, "that a college exists in order to help young people fail in everything else than their classes."[25]

Major changes did take place in several departments during these postwar years and, not surprisingly, the Department of Education was one of them. Education programs had always been prominent at Hunter—it operated separate elementary and high schools to assist in teacher training—and with the postwar demand for increased schooling and the start of the baby-boom generation, the programs expanded even more. By the mid-1950s more than half of the students who graduated from Hunter were preparing to be teachers. By that time Hunter had begun receiving state funds (as distinct from city funds) for its educational programs and, with this assistance, fifth year and graduate programs were established. A Master of Arts in Teacher Education degree was begun to give post-baccalaureate students, both full-time and part-time, additional preparation for teaching specific academic subjects or for teaching specifically in elementary or secondary areas. Educational guidance was also a field of specialization. With New York state funds in support, this master's program had specific residency and citizenship requirements, and Hunter College then established a fee-charging Master of Science in Education program for those not meeting the above requirements or those desiring a more independent and less structured program. Preparing teachers for education of the physically and mentally handicapped became important parts of the education program during these years also.[26]

Nursing programs exhibited even greater growth and development. Nursing began at Hunter in 1943 when, at the request of the New York City Department of Hospitals, the then Evening and Extension Division established a graduate program for nurses already holding RN certification from city hospitals. Eventually this program was transferred to the Department of Education and became a Bachelor of Science in Education program with a major in Nursing. In 1953 Shuster hired Dr. Marguerite Holmes of Ohio State University to begin a four-year undergraduate program in nursing, a far more popular program nationwide. This new program, affiliated with Metropolitan Hospital, began by admitting fifty students each year. By the time of Shuster's retirement, enrollment had tripled. Before leaving office Shuster also approved establishment of a master's program in nursing, either for those who wished to enter nursing education or for those who desired advanced training in specialized areas. Shuster kept close to all of these programs, perhaps remembering his own father's interest in medicine. "He was wonderful," Dean Holmes later said of Shuster. "I was sorry to see him go. He was really responsible for nursing becoming such an important part of City University."[27]

Shuster deserves major credit for the School of Social Work at Hunter also. The demand for social workers was increasing in New York City and across the nation, and more and more young women were attracted to the field. Apparently without wide consultation, Shuster met with New York businessman Louis M. Rabinowitz in early 1955, and the philanthropist agreed to donate $106,000 over a period of four years to establish the Louis M. Rabinowitz School of Social Work. It was to be a two-year graduate program, with a total of sixty credits required for the master's degree and with four areas of specialization: social services, human growth and development, social work practice, and social work research. Field experience and practice were major components of the program. A fee would be charged, three hundred dollars a year, but this was only half the tuition charged at Fordham, Adelphi, Columbia, and NYU, and Shuster hoped to build up a scholarship fund for needy students. The program was an immediate success. Within two years it received its accreditation from the National Council on Social Work Education, it was soon admitting one hundred new students a year, and it was considered by some the finest program of its kind in New York. In 1969 a handsome new building was dedicated on 79th Street to house it.[28]

Most other departments were strengthened during Shuster's presidency also. Mathematics and education had traditionally been strong, and other departments—art, biology, classics, English, history, music, political science, and sociology—advanced through the establishment of solid graduate programs on the master's level. In his memoirs Shuster singles out English and history as deserving of special mention. It was probably the Art Department, however, of which he was most proud. The chair, Edna Leutz, became a close family friend, and Shuster had great confidence in her ability. He allowed her wider independence than he allowed most chairs, and he always seemed to find money in the budget for her needs. As a result, Hunter could boast of a truly outstanding department. Robert Motherwell and Gabor Peterdi joined the faculty in the 1950s, and Tony Smith in the following decade.[29]

Shuster realized also that education did not come entirely through formal schedules and classroom instruction, and he took advantage of Hunter's excellent location and his own broad contacts to invite outstanding speakers to the college. The Assembly Hall seated over two thousand and was ideal for the most popular of speakers. President Roosevelt, as noted earlier, visited Hunter in late 1940, and Mrs. Roosevelt did so on numerous occasions. Shuster always considered her, a New Yorker also, an important inspiration for Hunter students. Heinrich Bruening, former chancellor of Germany, spoke at Hunter, as did Georges Bidault of France and Dr. Leopold Figl, foreign minister of Austria. Jacques Maritain, philosopher and later French ambassador to the Vatican, not only spoke at Hunter but was appointed to the faculty. Thomas Mann, author of *The Magic Mountain* and *Joseph and His Brothers*, spoke in the Great Hall, as did Sigrid Undset and Dr. Manfred George, editor of *Aufbau* in Germany. Kirsten Flagstad visited in 1952. The Littauer Lecture series for one year, 1940–41, included noted historians Mary R. Beard and Harry Carman, Thurman Arnold, head of the anti-trust division of the

Department of Justice, Secretary of Labor Frances Perkins, and Charles C. Merriam of the National Resources Board. Under Shuster, Hunter was much more than an undergraduate college for young women, many of whom could not afford to study elsewhere. It was a center for the scholarly and academic-minded of all New York.[30]

Two other programs begun under Shuster, the Concert Series and the Opera Workshop, greatly enhanced the prestige of Hunter College. The Opera Workshop was the more strictly instructional of the two. Shuster had been in conversation with Fritz Stiedry, emigre German conductor and later conductor of the Metropolitan Opera, lamenting the fact that American youngsters did not have the opportunities and facilities for specific preparation for opera that their counterparts in Europe had. Shuster decided to establish such a workshop at Hunter, Stiedry agreed to serve as initial director, and Mrs. August Belmont helped secure modest funding. The workshop, which met in the evenings and on weekends, charged a fee of thirty dollars for a minimum of fifteen hours of instruction, and interested students arrived from all over the city. After Stiedry left for the Metropolitan Opera, the workshop was directed by Joseph Turnau, Rose Landver, and William Tarrasch, and included such instructors as Dr. Joseph Reitler, formerly of the New Vienna Conservatory of Music, Lothar Wallenstein of the Metropolitan Opera and the Civic Opera in Chicago, Enzio Pinza, whom Shuster had first met through his work on the Enemy Alien Board, and Hunter College's own alumna Regina Resnik. One of the workshop graduates of whom Shuster was particularly proud was, like Resnik, also a Hunter graduate, the brilliant and internationally acclaimed Martina Arroyo. In 1952 the Hunter College Opera Association was established to sponsor annual operas performed by students of the Opera Workshop.[31]

The Concert Series, one of Hunter College's proudest accomplishments, had its origin one evening at a celebration of Austrian independence when Lotte Lehmann introduced Shuster to Dr. Benno Lee, a European emigre impressario. Shuster was convinced that New York could only benefit from a first-class concert series, that Hunter College and its Assembly Hall were a most appropriate location, and although he was well acquainted with even better-known native and foreign musicians, he decided to launch it under Professor Lee. A fee was charged, attendance at first was sparse, but performances by Lehmann herself, Enzio Pinza, cellist Emmanuel Feuermann, and pianist Vladimir Horowitz soon attracted wide public notice. Shuster was embarrassed that he could offer such performers only a portion of their normal fees, but they too saw the benefit of making such music available. The quality of the performances was remarkable. The twelve concerts scheduled for 1948–49, for example, included pianists Artur Schnabel and Artur Rubenstein, violinists Joseph Szigeti, Erica Morini, and Jascha Heifetz, the Boston Symphony Orchestra, and singers Lily Pons, Enzio Pinza, and Marian Anderson. Whenever he was in the city Shuster served as host for the performances. He strove to accommodate such diverse personalities as the regal Renata Tebaldi, the reflective Elizabeth Schwarzkopf, and the tempestuous Hilde Gueden. Shuster's own favorites were probably Bruno Walter, whom he may have first met through the Enemy Alien Board, pianists Artur Schnabel and Artur Rubenstein, and Lotte Lehmann, a staunch supporter from the start. The Concert Series was not without its headaches— Carnegie Hall occasionally protested that city funds and the college's tax exempt status gave Hunter an unfair advantage—but it contributed to making Hunter College one of New York's more respected cultural centers. Shuster always considered it one of his most significant achievements.[32]

Shuster thoroughly enjoyed his years as Hunter College president and found them satisfying but, as with every college president, there were always items on his desk that he did not want to touch and wished would quietly go away. Many of these were minor, and later he could look back on at least some of them with a smile, but others had more merit.

For example, the new Hunter College building was at 695 Park Avenue, a residential area of fine and expensive homes, with the property of the Russian delegation to the United Nations almost directly across the street. The city requested that the Hunter students not use the Park Avenue entrance or congregate on that side. The women were understandably upset; they thought the directive insulting, but their protest remained mild.[33]

Another issue involved the leasing of the Bronx campus to the Navy. Some were opposed because blacks were not then accepted into the WAVES. However, the college had little influence in what the city decided to do with its buildings and even less on who was admitted into the military.[34]

A similar problem, more directly Shuster's responsibility, concerned the Model School, and this Shuster faced openly. In the 1930s the Model School was little different from other city grade schools and, like them, had territorial boundaries. During the early months of Shuster's presidency the school was changed to an institution for exceptional children. Then the requirement that pupils had to reside below 86th Street seemed to discriminate against black families, who often lived further north. After 1942 children were admitted solely on the basis of IQ testing and the 86th Street boundary was removed, although "pupils in Manhattan . . . will be given preference." The reason for that preference was that wealthy families from other boroughs could arrange for safe transportation of their youngsters to Hunter, and this might favor the wealthy in other boroughs even over the poor in Manhattan. For the same reason the city also paid the five dollar IQ testing fee of any family who would find this a prohibitive burden.[35] New York law also required that every grammar school have a monthly fire drill and that the school building be emptied, but Hunter petitioned for an exception since emptying its building involved perhaps four thousand students, science labs in session, students using the swimming pool, and, for many, twelve to sixteen flights of stairs. The Hunter building was much more than a elementary school and an exception to the regulation seemed in order.[36] An occasional bomb scare and armed robbery were of serious concern to the president also.[37]

Probably the most persistent and bothersome problem Shuster faced during his years as president was the question of censorship and freedom of speech. Shuster was liberal in this area personally, even assigning D. H. Lawrence to his classes at Notre Dame in the 1920s. He felt that a college campus was a proper environment for the exchange of ideas, and he was confident that the truth would eventually conquer and that no lasting harm would be done by the presentation of alien ideas, whatever they might be.[38] But there *was* the question of whether the presenters of such alien ideas should be able to use tax-supported city property as the podium from which to present them. In 1947, in the midst of growing concern over Communist infiltration and widespread debate over President Truman's Loyalty Program, the New York City Council considered the banning of all subversive and Communist organizations on city college campuses, specifically American Youth for Democracy. Shuster opposed any such action. He insisted that as long as there were Communists throughout the world, there would also be some on college campuses and that it was better to have them functioning openly in such organizations than underground or in front organizations where their activities would be more secret and other students might be more easily duped or deceived.[39] Shuster's tolerance, however, was not weakness; when a few instances of overstepping the bounds of academic freedom were reported to him, he reacted strongly. In a well-publicized letter to the faculty and staff in 1944, he called totally unacceptable and even subject to sanctions public assertions "that the Papacy and all Catholics are at heart advocates of nazism and fascism, and therefore anti-American . . . that the Jewish group is a 'race' different from and inferior to other groups in the community, and so unassimilable . . . that the Russian system of government and the Russian ideology are superior to our own, and gratuitously injecting propaganda to this effect into classroom discussion . . . that the Negro is an inferior being, who can legitimately be discriminated against, either economically or socially."[40] The Karl Marx Society was suspended in 1949, not because of its political or philosophical views, but because of attacks on religion contained in the literature it distributed.[41]

By 1951 the situation had changed. Eleven leaders of the American Communist Party had been found guilty in 1948 of advocating the overthrow of the federal government by force or violence, contrary to the Smith Act of 1940, and their conviction was upheld by the Supreme Court in *Dennis* v. *United States* in 1951. In 1952 Shuster warned the Young Progressives of America that many persons considered them sympathetic to Communism, and that in fact they might be manipulated by the Communist Party. The Board of Higher Education had prohibited the use of city college facilities by speakers under criminal indictment, and this was extended to persons convicted under the Smith Act also. Persons dismissed from city college faculties for cause were denied a campus forum. On the other hand, when some demanded pre-publication censorship of the student media after a student at Brooklyn College published a poem about an abortion undergone during an Easter vacation, Shuster opposed prior censorship. "We're not going to have it, period," he declared.[42]

One publicized incident during Shuster's presidency concerned leftist novelist Howard Fast. The Young Progressives of America invited him to speak in 1952, almost the height of anti-Communist concern and the senate hearings of Joseph McCarthy, and several persons petitioned Shuster to cancel the invitation. Shuster refused and allowed this self-styled "most widely read living writer on earth" to speak. Howard Fast, according to Shuster, was

> a writer of the most signal mediocrity, whose fuzzy thinking calls to mind a ball of moth-eaten yarn. . . . To assume that the college should not give a handful of students the opportunity to find this out for themselves, but should instead advertise its fear that such a speaker would undermine the sanity of the student body . . . is to suggest something not all the Fasts in New York could accomplish by themselves—namely, to give young people the impression that our country must rely upon the suppression of freedom of speech in order to maintain freedom.[43]

The most difficult problems Shuster faced during his presidency concerned conflicts with members of the faculty or administrative staff, and these were particularly trying because relations with them were normally pleasant and satisfying.[44]

One very delicate incident erupted in 1951, unfortunately while Shuster was serving in Germany as Land Commissioner for Bavaria. Dr. William J. Fordrung, professor in the Department of Physiology, Health and Hygiene and director of the medical office of the college, was accused by a faculty committee of conduct unbecoming a member of the Hunter staff, inefficient service, neglect of duty, and a "sensational and unwholesome" approach in his teaching of sex hygiene.[45] Fordrung's credentials were impressive. He had received his undergraduate degree from Fordham University in 1916, a master's degree from Columbia in 1920, a medical degree from Georgetown in 1923, and a law degree from Fordham in 1927. He had taught at both Fordham and City College before coming to Hunter in 1933. Acting President Eleanor Grady had received complaints from four students in October 1950 and immediately appointed a faculty committee to investigate the charges, as authorized by the college's committee on personnel and budget. Over the next five months the committee conducted 118 separate interviews with students, faculty, and with Fordrung himself, and recommended that further action be taken. A second faculty committee investigated further and recommended his suspension for the present and a formal trial before the Board of Higher Education. On June 18, 1951, Acting President Grady announced his suspension.[46]

The specific charges were that he had "failed to give the physiology department even a minimum degree of cooperation required by his position," had "failed to serve the college efficiently in that he has not maintained satisfactory working relations with its other departments and offices," had "devoted about 50 per cent of his class time to matters outside the syllabus of his hygiene course," had "a sensational and unwholesome approach" in his teaching of sex hygiene, and had attempted "to press upon students his own social, political, ethical, moral and religious views to the exclusion of beliefs held by large and well-respected groups in the community."[47] Fordrung, of course, denied the charges. "I have become the target of those people who seek to oppose the teaching of Americanism and morals," he declared. "I have tried to prove false, when the occasion arose, such concepts as free love and the use of the Kinsey report as the standard of new sex morality and the denial of the existence of God."[48] He admitted that he discussed in class "artificial birth control, criminal abortion, narcotic addiction, alcoholism, venereal disease, euthanasia, sterilization and a host of others similar in importance." Asked if he attempted to present both sides of controversial subjects, he replied: "There are no two sides to murder." In its report the committee suggested that Fordrung was, "directly or indirectly, teaching Roman Catholicism in the name of teaching morality," and that "morality had no place in the teaching of any subject-matter and should be left to the opinion of the individual student."[49]

The situation was delicate for Shuster on his return from Germany that December. As a fellow Catholic, he agreed with many of Fordrung's beliefs, but he realized that a municipal college classroom was not the place to advocate them. He thus set out to find a compromise and by late spring was successful.

Fordrung would be transferred to the medical office of the School of General Studies, he would be relieved of classroom teaching, he would retain his tenured status and prerogatives, and he would be restored to his full salary, retroactive to September 1, 1951. Both the Board of Higher Education and Professor Fordrung accepted this solution.[50] To complete the story, Fordrung, in fact, left Hunter College shortly thereafter, entered the seminary in New York, was ordained a priest at the age of seventy-five, and after assisting in various New York parishes, died there in 1975.[51]

The most disruptive controversy breaking out at Hunter College in the early 1950s, and on many other campuses across the country, concerned the presence of members of the Communist Party on the teaching faculty. Although the incompatibility between the American and Soviet political and economic systems had long been apparent, such differences had been minimized during World War II when Soviet-American cooperation was essential in the war against Hitler. When the war ended, the Soviet Union seemed reluctant to carry out wartime agreements, puppet governments were imposed throughout Eastern Europe, Russia built up a massive conventional (and, after 1949, nuclear) war-making machinery, and, as the sensational trials of Alger Hiss in America and Klaus Fuchs in England and the revelations of Igor Gouzenko in Canada demonstrated, sought to infiltrate and subvert the Western world.[52] President Truman launched his loyalty program in 1947, eleven leaders of the American Communist Party were indicted in 1948, several Communist-dominated unions were expelled from the CIO in 1949, and Senator Joseph McCarthy began his sensational charges of Communists in government in 1950. Communism had appealed to various American intellectuals in the 1930s and, as the McCarthy agitation increased in the early 1950s, concern grew that perhaps American schools and colleges had been tainted with Communist teachings. New York had provided for just such a situation. In 1939 the state legislature had passed a civil service law declaring that "no person shall . . . be employed in the public service as superintendent[s], principal[s] or teacher[s] in a public school or academy or in a state normal school or college . . . who . . . becomes a member of any society or group of persons which teaches or advocates that the government of the United States . . . shall be overthrown by force or violence."[53] The so-called Fineberg Law ten years later charged the respective boards of regents or of higher education with implementing this provision: "The board of regents shall adopt, promulgate, and enforce rules and regulations for the disqualification or removal of . . . teachers . . . who are ineligible for appointment to or retention in any office or position . . . on any of the grounds set forth in section twelve-a of the civil service law."[54] Spelling out responsibilities more explicitly, Section 903 of the city charter stipulated: "If any councilman or other . . . employee of the city shall . . . willfully refuse or fail to appear before . . . any officer, board or body authorized to conduct any hearing . . . or having appeared shall refuse to testify . . . on the ground that the answer would tend to incriminate him . . . his term or tenure of office or employment shall terminate."[55] Hunter College was soon the scene of investigation.

In the early fall of 1952, in the midst of the heated Stevenson-Eisenhower presidential campaign, members of the Senate Subcommittee to Investigate the Administration of the Internal Security Act visited New York to question several city college faculty members alleged to have been or still be members of the Communist Party. On September 24 Professor Bernard Reiss of the Department of Psychology at Hunter College refused to testify whether he was or ever had been a member of the Communist Party, basing his refusal on the Fifth Amendment's guarantee against self-incrimination.[56] On October 13, appearing before the same senate subcommittee, Professor Henrietta Friedman, instructor in Latin and Greek at Hunter for twenty-five years and faculty advisor for the Young Progressives of America, also refused to testify whether she was or ever had been a member of the Communist Party.[57] The senate subcommittee accepted this recourse to the Fifth Amendment, but their action put the two professors in violation of Section 903 of the city charter. The Board of Higher Education held formal hearings, examined the transcripts, and determined that indeed the questions asked had constituted an inquiry into the professors' official conduct, that they had refused to testify on grounds that it might tend to incriminate them, and that Section 903 had been specifically violated. By action of the Board of Higher Education, Professor

Reiss was relieved of his position at Hunter effective October 3, and Professor Friedman effective October 28.[58]

There was understandable opposition to these dismissals from both students and faculty, and Shuster addressed the issue openly in a public meeting. The dismissals, he insisted, were based on "the teachers' fitness to hold a government office, and not on the state education laws, the tenure statute, or principles affecting academic freedom." "Many may differ about its wisdom," he continued, "but as long as this and similar legislation exists, it is impossible for the Board of Higher Education nor [*sic*] the president of a city college to disregard it. If they did so, they would be guilty of a misdemeanor." In at least partial defense of the legislation he noted that "the dismissed persons are government employees, and service to the government of the state demands complete loyalty to the state and to the people of the United States." "It is a tragic thing to separate an individual from his academic profession, but it is also tragically true that the Communist ruthlessly disregards the freedom of others who do not share his beliefs."[59] At a municipal college Shuster could sidestep the question of academic freedom since faculty members were all public employees and were subject to all laws governing those holding jobs for the city or state.

But Shuster did not want such investigations to get out of hand or to interfere in any way with normal and legitimate activities of the faculty. During the course of the Reiss and Friedman investigations, and concern over them, he circulated an open letter of encouragement and support to Hunter personnel:

> Certain recent happenings which have resulted from inquiries into subversive activities by Government agencies may well give rise to quite unwarranted fears, and therewith to curtailment of educational activities which must be encouraged if public opinion in the United States is to remain vigorous and forthright. I have some reason to believe that these anxieties are not absent from the campus of Hunter College. This letter is an attempt to clarify the situation.
>
> The character of the Communist Party has led to the passage of legislation designed to curtail its potential influence. Hunter College and its sister institutions are affected in particular by the City Charter, Section 903 of which has been held by the courts to mean that failure to answer questions about membership in the

Communist Party when those questions are put by a duly constituted investigative body automatically leads to dismissal from
employment by the City. All this has been very well known for
some time. The Board of Higher Education could not, even if it
desired to do so, disregard this mandate.

There are, however, no laws and no rulings by the Board
which constitute any sort of limitation on the non-Communist
civic and intellectual interests of the faculty, with this exception:
attacks on the race or religion of any student are forbidden. This
does not mean that a chance remark or an expression of opinion on
a controversial subject will be made an issue. Your College administration will defend to the uttermost any member of the staff from
suspicion or retaliation except in those instances in which a
chronic seizure of vocal prejudice is indicated.

In every other respect the faculty should not only feel entirely
free to act as responsible citizens but, indeed, must be convinced
that such conduct is indispensable. When I hear that younger
members of the staff, particularly those without tenure, are warned
not to act as faculty advisers to student clubs having a political
character, I am deeply shocked. No victory the Communist Party
could possibly win in this country would be more decisive than
would be success in depriving younger instructors of an opportunity to give the leadership which only they can provide. After one
has reached a certain age one acquires for students a manifest
august dignity which usually consorts poorly with what they look
upon as club life. We must therefore rely on our less venerable colleagues for assistance in this vitally important matter. . . .

I came to Hunter in 1939. Since then I have sometimes been
troubled and occasionally annoyed. But nothing that has been said
about the College in all these years is more disturbing than are the
reports alluded to above. I shall hope they are not true. And I shall
look forward to receiving evidence to that effect.[60]

Even more controversial suspensions took place two years
later. Professor V. Jerauld McGill of the Department of
Psychology and Philosophy, Professor Louis Weisner of the
Department of Mathematics, and Professor Charles W. Hughes of
the Department of Music were all dismissed from their faculty
positions at Hunter College by the Board of Higher Education on
October 1, 1954. The specific findings against all three were that
they were at one time members of the Communist Party and had
not terminated that affiliation in good faith, that they had failed to

cooperate with the Board's investigation into their conduct earlier that spring, and that they had conspired to conceal information during that investigation. McGill was further charged with giving false testimony before a state investigative body in 1941 and before the Senate Internal Security Subcommittee in 1952.[61] Such actions were cause for dismissal under the Civil Service Law of 1939 and the Fineberg Law of 1949.

During the investigation, all three admitted that they had at one time been members of the Communist Party—McGill from 1936 and Weisner and Hughes from approximately 1938—but McGill insisted he had left in 1941 and Weisner and Hughes, without giving specific dates, stated that they were now no longer in sympathy with Communist beliefs. Weisner and Hughes testified that they did not know at that time that the Communist Party advocated the overthrow of the government by force, and McGill stated that he personally "never believed or advocated the doctrine that the Government of the United States should be overthrown by force or violence." He further testified that he never heard any member of his unit advocate violence. All three denied that they had conspired to withhold information from the Board, but that they had decided, as individuals and as matters of conscience, not to identify other members of their cells while they were in the Party.[62] Said McGill:

> I could not, in conscience, reveal the names of the few persons who had been members during the period 1936 to 1941, for they had violated no laws, nor done any harm I knew of, and their motives and activities had been mainly anti-Fascist.[63]

Concerning the charge of perjury, he noted:

> The charge that I misinformed the Rapp-Coudert Committee as to my membership in the spring of 1941 is true. People at that time were suddenly required to state under oath whether they belonged to a party that was legal, and I made a serious mistake in following the advice of the lawyer assigned to me by the Teachers Union.[64]

McGill insisted that he may have made innocent mistakes in the 1930s but they were not reason for dismissal now:

> I became a Communist in the Nineteen Thirties, together with hundreds of thousands of my generation because, like them, I feared that Hitler might dominate Europe and the world, and that

a new world depression was on its way, entailing unemployment, intolerance and oppression. I turned away from Communist ideas when I realized that in practice they were incompatible with my conception of human values.[65]

In October 1955 Shuster addressed an open forum of faculty members and students and discussed the recent cases with them. He explained that a Communist Party cell had apparently existed at Hunter from 1935 to 1955. It probably never contained more than ten or twelve members, and it was discovered only during the recent Board of Higher Education investigations. Two of the most prominent members had left before 1938 (one of whom was probably Bella Dodd, although Shuster did not mention her by name) and five others—Professors Reiss, Friedman, McGill, Weisner, and Hughes—had recently been dismissed. "These were five very difficult, trying tragedies," he admitted, "which those associated with them will never forget." He outlined the procedures leading up to the dismissals—an initial private investigation by a committee of the Board of Higher Education, then a questioning before the full Board, then an administrative hearing with defense attorneys and with the initial investigative committee as jury, and a final decision by the Board which could always be appealed through the courts. Shuster expressed confidence that the cell at Hunter had now been destroyed, and seemed satisfied with both the procedures and the outcome. "Everyone makes mistakes," he declared, "but I cannot see how persons can continue to maintain affiliations with the Communist party when the efforts of that party are so obviously and appallingly evil."[66]

The cases, however, were far from closed. Professor Weisner decided to submit his resignation from the Hunter faculty, and it was accepted by the Board of Higher Education, effective September 27, 1954.[67] Professor McGill announced immediately that he was appealing his dismissal through the courts, but his appeal was eventually lost. He had publicly admitted that he had given false testimony under oath before the Rapp-Coudert Investigating Committee in 1941, and the courts determined that this constituted conduct unbecoming a municipal college instructor and was grounds for legitimate dismissal.[68] The case of Professor Hughes, however, continued for several years.

The findings against Hughes in 1954 had been twofold: that he had been a member of the Communist Party in the past and had not terminated that membership in good faith (but only nominally, to escape further consequences); and that in refusing to identify other cell members he had conspired to conceal information and had failed to cooperate with the Board of Higher Education's investigation. To the first charge, of membership in the Communist Party, New York Supreme Court Justice S. Samuel Di Falco first ruled that Hughes had received a fair hearing under the Education Law and thus was not entitled to reopen the case under Civil Service Law. This was overturned on appeal and a new trial ordered. At this trial it was determined that Hughes could not be dismissed under anti-subversive laws because, in fact, he had broken connections with the Communist Party in good faith in 1941, long before his dismissal and before the enactment of the law. In 1958 this decision was upheld on appeal.[69]

At the same time, Hughes appealed to New York State Education Commissioner James E. Allen that faculty members should not be expected to identify other cell members and that failing to do so should not constitute grounds for dismissal. Allen agreed and stated that compelling teachers to become informers "would do more harm than good and that this type of inquisition has no place in the school system."[70] Allen admitted that during the investigation Hughes had refused to answer questions even about the size of the Hunter College cell, but that this was because he considered it "an approach to naming names." Allen's determination was challenged, but the State Court of Appeals upheld it. It did not say it agreed with the decision, but only that the Commissioner's decision was not "arbitrary" and thus deserved to stand.[71] The case was then returned to the Board of Higher Education, its investigative committee presented again the questions it had asked earlier, except for specific names, and Hughes acknowledged that there were probably eleven members in his Communist unit at Hunter College over all, with a maximum of seven or eight at any one time. He admitted that one member of that earlier cell was still at Hunter College, but he did not identify him or her and it was later confirmed that that person had earlier been cleared of present Communist Party affiliation. The investigative committee was satisfied with Hughes's new responses, saw no grounds now for dismissal in light of Commissioner Allen's determination, and recommended Hughes's reinstatement. In July 1959, just a few months before Shuster's retirement from Hunter College, Hughes was reinstated to his position as associate professor of music, with accumulated back pay of fifty-four thousand dollars, less whatever monies he had earned since his suspension.[72]

The investigations and determinations under section 903 of the city charter and the Fineberg Law were completed at Hunter before Shuster left office. Five faculty members had been dismissed, although one had technically retired first. Altogether there had been sixty-five hundred persons working in the four municipal colleges at that time; 122 of these had been investigated by the Board of Higher Education. Sixty-three were either cleared of the allegations or had their cases otherwise closed; eighteen were subject to further investigation but chose to leave the college system before being questioned, and thirty-nine were either dismissed or resigned.[73] Despite the wide publicity and controversy at the time, the five cases at Hunter were only a small percentage of the total.

If some persons thought Shuster too accommodating and cooperative with the Board of Higher Education and various governmental investigative agencies in their search for Communists on college campuses, at least one prominent official thought him not accommodating enough. In a speech in New York on March 19, 1953, Shuster had urged Senator Joseph McCarthy to moderate some of his investigative procedures. He admitted that it was "better that the watchdog on the lookout for subversives in government growl too much than that he bark not at all" but the delving into past activities and mistakes of often well-intentioned persons was not always healthy.[74] "The constant opening and shutting of the Pandora's box of moods, convictions, assumptions and slogans which was America in the days when the rest of the world was being carved up by two opposing and equally vicious tyrannies," he suggested, "is an extremely dangerous business from every educational and psychological point of view." Referring to the national publicity and ferment resulting from the McCarthy hearings, Shuster even suggested that universities might investigate the senator's tactics and procedures and report on them to the American people.[75]

McCarthy was not long in responding. He wrote Shuster that his criticism was weakened by "your failure to join with millions of Americans in fighting Communism in our great public education system." The senator noted that Professor Friedman had been named earlier as a Communist Party member but "you made no move to discharge Mrs. Friedman and it took a Senate investigation by the Internal Security Subcommittee in October, 1952, to force action by the New York City Board of Higher Education."[76] He also criticized Shuster for allowing Howard Fast to speak at Hunter the year before.

Shuster answered immediately: "I was fighting communism before Mr. McCarthy woke up to the peril."[77] Concerning the Freidman case, Shuster admitted that the case had first come to his attention in 1950. He said he had investigated then, had only a statement of an FBI agent that she had been a Communist Party member, and that the counsel for the Board of Higher Education said that no action could be taken at that time without some corroborative evidence. When Professor Friedman refused to answer questions before the senate investigative subcommittee, she was clearly in violation of New York law and was immediately dismissed. Turning to the Howard Fast controversy, he insisted that the decision to allow the writer to speak at Hunter was not his alone but also that of the faculty, but he still defended the judgment, as he had at the time. "Mr Fast was invited to make a nonpolitical speech," he noted. "He made a fool of himself and provided the best kind of anti-Communist propaganda."

Few university officials across the country took public issue with Senator McCarthy during these days, and Shuster's altercation was recalled by at least one teacher six years later:

> Surely those of us in the teaching profession wish Dr. George N. Shuster well in his decision to retire next year. The world of letters will profit from his writings as the world of education profited from his years of service as a great leader in a field which too often has been subject to unjust and unfounded criticism.
>
> Personally, I will always be grateful to George N. Shuster for the courage he showed in his forceful stand against the McCarthyite forces which sought to destroy some of the foundations of academic

freedom. Few of us were willing to stand up and be counted during
those dark days. George N. Shuster chose to be among those who
could, and did, stem the tide of fear. He spoke out fearlessly and
we all are freer men for his having done so.[78]

Shuster presided over truly momentous years at Hunter
College. The city colleges had been reorganized in the late 1930s,
giving faculties and faculty committees greater influence in form-
ing policy and administering the institutions, and George Shuster,
as unauthoritarian as any successful administrator could be, had
few conflicts with his faculty committees and implemented the
new directives well. World War II caused major disruptions on college campuses across the country, and at Hunter, too, especially
with the WAVES occupying the Bronx campus, but Shuster successfully integrated war and vocational training into the curriculum without compromising fundamental liberal arts education.
Major changes took place after the war—steadily increasing enrollments, coeducation on the Bronx campus, the inauguration of
highly respected graduate programs—and Hunter's prestige continued to increase. Its program in art, training in opera, and its
Concert Series were nationally and even internationally known.
Investigations of Communist infiltration of college faculties caused
disruptions all across the nation, but Shuster presided over relative
calm and harmony in the volatile situation at Hunter. Kindly,
friendly, and almost invariably pleasant, Shuster was popular and
respected year in and year out by faculty and students alike.

As time went on, Shuster was given greater recognition and
honor by his educational colleagues off campus as well. There
were few major scholarly conferences or conventions that did not
list George Shuster prominently on their program sometime during his presidency. The list of his academic honors and awards is
impressive and almost endless. Citing only the most prestigious,
he was elected a Fellow of the American Academy of Arts and
Sciences in 1950, was selected to deliver the National Catholic
Educational Association's Gabriel Richard Lecture in 1952, was
awarded the Butler Medal in Silver by Columbia University in
1953, was elected to the Board of Trustees of the Carnegie
Endowment for International Peace in 1954, received the Insignis
Medal for outstanding service to humanity from Fordham
University in 1959, and was given the Laetare Medal as an out-
standing Catholic layman from the University of Notre Dame in

1960. He was awarded honorary degrees from institutions as diverse as Columbia University in 1954, New York College of Music the same year, Jewish Theological Seminary in 1956, Loyola University in 1957, University of Freiburg in 1957, and the Free University of Berlin in 1958.[79]

By late 1958 Shuster decided it was time to resign his position at Hunter. He had thought of resigning on other occasions, but the Board of Higher Education had always been so understanding and accommodating in his requests for leaves of short or longer periods of time to accept other public assignments that he felt ungrateful in leaving so soon after. But except for annual meetings of the Executive Committee of UNESCO, Shuster had not been out of the country that much since early 1956, and he was now satisfied that he had served the Board consistently and well.[80]

Other questions undoubtedly weighed into his decision also. One of them was the creation of the position of chancellor. By the late 1950s all four municipal colleges—Brooklyn, City College, Hunter, and Queens—were undertaking broader programs in graduate education, and rather than face costly and unnecessary duplication of efforts and programs, the Board desired some office of oversight and coordination. At first the Administrative Council, consisting of the four college presidents, was set up for the purpose, with the chairmanship revolving among them. By 1955, however, the Board was convinced that something further was needed and decided to establish the position of chancellor to chair this Administration Council and to serve between the Board of Higher Education and the individual college presidents. A sum of $100,000 was appropriated for the expenses of the office two years later, with the salary set at $25,000—the same as that of the four presidents—and, to lessen any fears on the presidents' part, the Administrative Council was appointed by the search committee to recommend a suitable candidate.[81]

Needless to say, no candidate was found. First, some believed the salary was too low to attract a truly outstanding educational administrator. None of the four college presidents would probably have been interested in the added responsibilities at no increase in their own salaries, and yet it may have been indelicate to offer the new chancellor more than the college presidents were receiving. Second, none of the presidents probably favored the position in the first place. They feared that, at best, it would lessen their direct access to the Board, which they all enjoyed, and, at worse, reduce them to positions analogous to deans under a kind of super-president. The members of the Board of Higher Education, finally, were not unanimous in precisely what authority the chancellor should have, and that was probably another reason why exceptionally qualified persons hesitated to apply.

Close friends of Shuster insist that he could have had the position of chancellor had he wanted it, and others suggest he was not offered it and was not seriously considered. Both may be correct. Shuster was the oldest of the four presidents in terms of service, he had the confidence of the presidents and the Board of Higher Education, he was chairman of the Administrative Council during much of its search, and he believed in college autonomy and would not have interfered with the individual presidents in the administration of their colleges. Shuster, in fact, may have been an excellent candidate. On the other hand, he was opposed to the establishment of the position and was letting it be known that he was seriously considering retirement. The Board thus possibly eliminated him early as a candidate, although undoubtedly with reluctance. But by late 1958 it was clear that eventually a chancellor over all four colleges would be appointed, the position of college president would in consequence be changed, and this undoubtedly added to Shuster's determination to retire.[82]

Other changes being discussed also concerned Shuster. The first generation of "baby boomers" was coming of college age, a college degree was becoming more essential for adequate employment, and colleges were being urged to expand their enrollments. At the same time, grade and high schools (and colleges) were being increasingly criticized for lowering their academic standards and for promoting and graduating students who could not meet basic requirements. (*Why Johnny Can't Read* was a popular book in the 1950s.) There was more and more talk in New York about establishing an open-admissions policy in the municipal colleges and giving each college less autonomy over who would or would not be admitted. Shuster was firmly in favor of education of the poor and of minorities, he was justifiably proud of Hunter's accomplishments in these areas, and his vocational in-lays assisted those seeking careers outside the field of education after graduation. But his own educational standards and devotion to the liberal arts remained high, and he was concerned about what the new directives and new procedures might entail. Nearing twenty years in office in late 1958, he decided that that was a challenge a younger man might better face.[83]

None of these, however, was the determining motive. His main reason, in fact, was simply those twenty years. He would have served as president for two full decades, they had been very challenging and satisfying years, he had accomplished most of what he wanted, and he was proud of the developments he had guided. Furthermore, his health was still good, there were several other challenges he knew he could accept and especially several other books he wanted to write, and on January 6, 1959, he officially submitted his letter of resignation to the chairman of the Board of Higher Education:

> I am taking this opportunity to inform you and your distinguished colleagues of the Board of Higher Education that both wisdom and valor suggest that I request to be relieved of my duties as President of Hunter College as of January 31, 1960. . . .
>
> I came to Hunter College after a rather strenuous career elsewhere, and I shall soon have served as President during two decades. As a result there have developed any number of ties with the community and the nation which, though they may have enhanced in some measure the prestige of the College, have become very complex, time-consuming and burdensome. I therefore think it desirable that a younger man less involved in these things take over the leadership of a constantly growing college.
>
> Nor would it be honest to deny that all my life I have been tormented by twin demons. In the first place, I cannot stop writing. This is a disease as chronic and ravaging as malaria. Then, too, I feel a deep desire to concern myself, with what strength will remain, with the basic situations and ideas which are shaping the future destiny of mankind.[84]

With reluctance and regret the Board accepted his resignation, as of January 31, 1960; granted him a terminal sabbatical leave of absence until August 31, 1960; and appointed Dean John Meng as his successor.[85]

Hunter College, of course, did not let Shuster go quietly. A committee to plan an appropriate celebration was quickly appointed, with the Shusters' close personal friend, Dr. Ethel Berl of the Department of Education, as executive secretary, and it soon organized a threefold tribute. It first commissioned a portrait of Shuster by New York artist Stephen Csoka to hang in a prominent and honored place on the Hunter campus. Second, it authorized the publication of a collection of some of the more prominent addresses of Shuster during his years at Hunter, *Education and Moral Wisdom*. Third, a Shuster Faculty Fund was established to assist Hunter College faculty in their continuing research projects. The Rockefeller Foundation and James and Evelyn Picker, who had earlier contributed generously to the renovation of Roosevelt House, made large donations, and by the time of Shuster's actual retirement the fund had reached sixty thousand dollars.[86]

A special and very unexpected tribute came to Shuster that final year also. He had announced his retirement plans in January 1959, and one of his last and most rewarding functions as president was to preside at the dedication of the new administration-library-classroom building on the Bronx campus. The building was urgently needed, especially after the decision of the Board of Higher Education to transform the campus into a full four-year, coeducational college, and the sum of $3.3 million dollars was appropriated in 1955. The building progressed more or less on schedule and was due for formal dedication on October 26, 1959. When Shuster arrived for the dedication ceremonies, he noticed that a rather unsightly square of cardboard covered the cornerstone, and he thought of asking the building's architect, the distinguished Marcel Breuer, to remove it before the guests arrived. But he knew that Breuer could not have missed noticing it himself and presumed that it was probably hiding a mistake even more unsightly. It was only during the ceremony that the obstruction was removed and Shuster, taken completely by surprise, was aware that the magnificent new building was being dedicated to him. Shuster Hall is still a proud possession of the municipal college system.[87]

The climax of the farewell celebrations was a special academic convocation held at Hunter on the afternoon of January 26, 1960. It took place in the impressive assembly hall where Shuster had hosted so many convocations, commencement ceremonies, and presentations in his Concert Series, and two thousand students, faculty, and personal friends attended. The Shuster Faculty Fund was officially announced at that time and his portrait, which was to hang prominently in Shuster Hall on the Bronx campus, was unveiled. Shuster had asked that there be no personal gifts, but the College did make an exception for only the third time in its long history and awarded him an honorary degree of Doctor of Humane Letters for his championing of freedom of the press, his dedication to the teaching of the young, and his "concern for freedom and for the worth of the individual." Prominent persons graced the platform to honor him. Chairman of the Board of Higher Education Gustave Rosenberg presided, twenty-nine college presidents attended, and Mayor Robert Wagner added words of tribute. Cardinal Francis Spellman of New York, who did not always agree with Shuster's liberal views, was on stage, as was Eleanor Roosevelt, whom Shuster introduced as "the only unpaid member of the Hunter faculty." When Shuster mentioned informally to Spellman that he thought it wise for senior college administrators to step aside for younger persons, the cardinal was reported to have replied that he was happy his own organization did not have the same policy. After their celebrated disagreement over federal aid to education in 1949, when Cardinal Spellman referred to Eleanor Roosevelt's record as one "unworthy of an American mother," it was noted by several that it was only someone with the broad appeal and friendships of a George Shuster who could attract both of them to the same stage.[88] In his brief remarks, responding to the honorary degree, Shuster paid tribute to higher education for women:

> It has taken us a fearfully long time to see that however great may be the intellectual sacrifice woman must bring by reason of her primordial function as the bearer of life, there is no reason at all why her share in the community of scholars and artists should be of a lower order than is that of man.[89]

Henry T. Heald, president of the Ford Foundation, summarized Shuster's contributions in his principal address:

> It is men like George Shuster—men who have come forth publicly as tribunes of learning—who have kept our colleges as

places where free opinion has not surrendered to fear, where liberal knowledge has not been adulterated by vocationalism and where cherished values have not been compromised to expediency.[90]

In his formal letter of resignation Shuster had noted that "it will be a gloomy day for me when I leave an office to which so many people, young and old, in trouble or glorious because of an absence of trouble, have come to talk things over."[91] The day of his departure did have a touch of gloom, precisely because it meant saying goodbye to people, young and old, he had come to enjoy and love very much, but it was also a day filled with deep satisfaction in the realization of a job well done.

7

THE EMERGING NATIONAL FIGURE

In defense of the travels and numerous off-campus commitments of another university administrator, Shuster once suggested that any college president who was not widely visible away from his campus would soon not be very visible on his campus either.[1] His point was clear. College presidents had to be active and recognized nationally—meeting with alumni, strengthening relations with public officials, attending fund-raising functions with benefactors, addressing national meetings and conferences, and simply broadening their own education and worldview—or they would almost certainly not be retained long as the college's chief administrator. During his more than twenty years as president of Hunter, Shuster became increasingly recognized and active off-campus, almost too much at times. He spoke at professional and educational conferences, took part in government panels and symposia, and delivered baccalaureate and commencement addresses across the country. He published widely in national journals on American Catholicism, the state of education, the treatment of Germany, and international affairs. He found time also to accept various public and government appointments: he chaired a War Department Committee interviewing German prisoners of war in 1945, was a member of a University of Chicago Commission on Freedom of the Press, served on a National Committee on Segregation in the Nation's Capital, was president of the American Council on Germany, undertook several important studies for the Ford and Carnegie Foundations, was Land Commissioner for Bavaria with the American occupation in 1950 and 1951, and represented the United States on the Executive Board of UNESCO in Paris. At times, the Board of Higher Education must have feared that he was almost too visible away from Hunter.

As president of such a large municipal college, Shuster was invited most often to comment on the strengths and weaknesses of American education. His basic message was always the same: the purpose of education was intellectual, the training of the mind; courses in the humanities and the liberal arts had to be central; and all other goals remained secondary. "The core of the liberal arts college is sound," he stated at an annual meeting of the Association of American Colleges.[2] "Arts, literatures, philosophies and sciences must survive in the minds and hearts of women, though they may need restatement now." To the United Parents Association of New York City—at least some of whose members must have been concerned primarily with job opportunities for their children—he declared bluntly:

> We need a philosophy which will not endorse acceptance by our best young people a year after graduation of the decision that their idealism—their desire to be of service and their eagerness to be intellectually active—has been a great mistake. We need a philosophy which will make it wholly clear that acquisition of the goods of the mind is harder than getting hold of the goods of the body. And we need above all a philosophy which will contend that the goods of the mind are the only true riches—that Socrates was right when he said that a miserable man was better than a contented hog.[3]

He insisted elsewhere that such intellectual discipline and study of the liberal arts needed to begin even in high school:

> Since mathematics and the sciences will pretty much take care of themselves when properly taught (which unfortunately is not too frequently the case), the real problem is often how to formulate properly instruction in poetry, literature, the arts, and philosophy. Prior to leaving high school the boys and girls I have in mind should certainly have been helped to gain knowledge of and insight into Homer, Virgil, Dante, Shakespeare and one major English or American novelist. They ought likewise to have studied in class one good short introduction to philosophy, have read the Nicomachean Ethics and selected Dialogues of Plato. If I had my way, they would also have concerned themselves in detail with at least one great artist—Giotto, perhaps, or Michaelangelo, or if you prefer the Northern culture cycle, Durer or Rembrandt. Naturally a feeling for genesis and progression in all forms of historic time will be stimulated by the teacher through imaginative sketching in of the background against which personages and themes loom up.[4]

To those who protested that such a regimen was too rigorous, Shuster had a ready answer: "If a youngster can be held to a rigid schedule while training for football squad, why not when he prepares for the intellectual life."[5]

Shuster's educational theory always had place for "vocational in-lays" also, courses designed to prepare the student not for a job but for life as a mature, responsible, and effective adult. "Every student should develop a modest competence in typewriting and stenography," he stated in Baltimore in 1942.[6] "The college should provide training in automobile driving, and wherever possible in aviation. As many students as possible should be taught first aid, and the elements of chemistry. No girl should [be] permitted to graduate unless she can show that she has improved her physical health at least as much as she has improved her mind." He acknowledged during the war that colleges might introduce a few new courses appropriate to the emergency— Hunter would offer classes in cipher analysis, blood chemistry, and military German—but they should not attempt to prepare students specifically for defense employment. "For if women are needed as air raid wardens or spotters, if girls must be enrolled in defense industries for the duration, there is little we can do to prepare them," he insisted.[7] "The campus is not the place to learn how to operate a milling machine."

This training for a responsible future had also to include growth in principles, even in religious belief. He lamented the fact that public education had been so divorced from religion:

> The Law also limits freedom of instruction, particularly in the sense that anything smacking of religious exhortation is taboo. Personally I consider this ban an anachronism. It is of course undesirable that students belonging to different churches or creeds be subjected unilaterally to teaching which incorporates the dogmas of any one church or creed. But just why one should be so squeamish about the presentation of religious views to students who desire to see such views expounded remains a mystery.[8]

His own recommendation was clear:

> May we soon cease apologizing to young people for religion, for dedication of the spirit to counsels of sacrifice and altruism and for communion with the spiritual thinkers of all eras. Such apologies stamp us as doddering ancients. Young people see almost instinctively that we are in the mess we are in precisely because there were

question marks behind everything, even the simplest and most manifest of things. Hitler began by waging war on the professors and the intellectuals. He won that first and critical contest because the professors and the intellectuals were labeling and classifying ideals rather than standing by them.[9]

At a special centennial convocation at the University of Dayton, a Catholic institution, he spelled out his views in greater detail:

A great and true faith is uniquely aware of reason and mystery alike. On the one hand it cherishes reason, which is the true glory of the university—reason which may be speculative, or practical, humanistic as well as scientific, philosophical or religious in its orientation. It is man finding out, judging, comparing, planning. Yet there are vast realms of being which reason cannot explore. The human spirit is able to reach down and touch the floor of the universe, but it must take the cellar for granted. It can likewise place its hand on the ceiling of human destiny and therewith know that God exists, but it is unable to fathom the hidden things which rest in the Divine counsel. To fancy that reason is all of man's strength is just as limiting as is the denial of reason's existence.[10]

The great advantage of a religious institution was that it not only could study religion but also practice it:

And so I have long since come to the conclusion that the university must also pray. There must be associated with its realistic consciousness of its own worth the humility of insight into the fact that the order of reason it seeks to establish upon the earth will depend for its realization upon how much goodness is Divinely infused into the evil which is native to man—the evil which in our time towers so huge and monstrous as to frighten all. The University can only ask fervently that there may be not only a new birth of freedom but also a resurrection of virtue. . . .

Therefore to kneel every morning and evening, as this your university does in prayer of gratitude and dedication, is to supplement the godly business of the academic day with that yearning for the rain of eternity which alone can make time flower. Of course we know that this kneeling is not enough, but that the issue will depend upon the extent to which gratitude and dedication are carried not only into life but into every hour and moment of life, and upon the individual's ability never to cease growing and inquiring even while he remains conscious of the limitations of the waxing and waning, the questioning and answering, of man. . . . Carrying on with confidence but not with pride, with integrity but not with self-esteem, with a desire for what is useful but also a yearning for what is holy, may you move forward to the end of another century in the steadfast hope that through what you do God will in some measure bless you, our country and all mankind.[11]

Shuster continued his work as Catholic publicist or apologist also, work which he had performed for twelve years at *The Commonweal* and especially in writings like *The Catholic Spirit in America*. In 1938, the year after he left *The Commonweal*, George Seldes, leftist-leaning news reporter and commentator on world events, published an article critical of Catholicism in *The New Republic*.[12] He accused the church of hostility to liberty and personal freedom and of too often siding with those engaged in oppression. In Spain, Seldes suggested, the church was on the side of Franco and totalitarianism; in Mexico and Austria she favored the military, wealth, and big business; she supported militarist Japan in its conflict with the Communists in China; and the pope had not opposed Italy's invasion of Ethiopia three years earlier.

Shuster replied in the same journal. "During the past eight years," he noted, "I have been abroad a good deal, and may perhaps safely suggest that few Americans have been in closer touch with men and women whose business it is to know the Catholic situation."[13] He reminded Seldes that Catholics, in fact, were not unanimous in support of Franco, either in the United States or around the world. In Spain itself, a predominantly Catholic country, there were Catholics on both sides. The Vatican and the Spanish hierarchy had feared that the Spanish Communists, as they had done in Germany several years before, were hoping for a popular uprising, further violence, and eventually a Communist victory, and church leaders preferred Franco to such a bloodbath and Communist takeover.

But Shuster's main argument was that Spain, because it was so unique, was not representative of church policy at all. The rest of Europe was much more typical. With the danger of Nazi oppression at their borders, Catholics in Switzerland, Belgium, and the Netherlands were strong in their defense of liberty; Pope

Pius XI had issued an encyclical against Fascism in 1937 and had repudiated its racist theories; and Catholics in Germany itself had suffered from Nazi oppression and had often been heroic in defending their own liberties and those of other persecuted minorities. Shuster was embarrassed that Father Coughlin in Detroit and writers for the *Brooklyn Tablet* mouthed Fascist slogans all too often, but he insisted that these were rare exceptions ("gibberish worthy of a fat individual in Henry IV") and that the record of the church in defense of liberty and individual freedom worldwide was quite good.[14]

In an article published the following year in *The American Scholar* Shuster lamented again that some Catholics in America, especially those influenced by Father Coughlin and the *Brooklyn Tablet,* had been less than sympathetic to the plight of European Jews, but he insisted that these were in no way representative of their fellow religionists. The title of the article, in fact, was "The Conflict Among Catholics," and he repeated that the church's official position was otherwise.[15] "As one who has been something of a specialist in recent German history," he noted, "and has for that reason been in constant touch with Roman authorities since 1932, I can assert categorically that neither the present Pontiff [Pius XII] nor his predecessor [Pius XI] was even for a single moment in doubt that the rise of Nazism was a grave menace to Christianity."[16] "When the present Pope, then Cardinal Pacelli, visited the United States as the guest of the late Mrs. Nicholas Brady," Shuster continued, "he talked with me in German for some time and said earnestly that the Holy See was more concerned over the situation in Germany that [*sic*] it was over anything else troubling the world, and that it viewed with the deepest alarm the peril to religion that had become incarnate in the Nazi movement."[17]

America's entrance into World War II and the need for national unity curbed much interreligious criticism from 1941 to 1945, but suspicions and accusations broke out again in the postwar world. Protestants and Other Americans United for the Separation of Church and State was founded in 1947, and Paul Blanshard published his highly critical *American Freedom and Catholic Power* in 1949. In an article in *Harper's Magazine* later that year, Shuster responded.[18] He admitted that many Catholics held serious suspicions of Protestants but stated that these were wrong. Catholics realize they make mistakes, he noted, and that is why they examine their consciences daily and go to confession regularly. Addressing Blanshard's allegations, Shuster insisted that if Catholics seemed different from other Americans it was not because they were Catholic but because of their Irish, German, Italian, Spanish, and other immigrant backgrounds; America, after all, was a melting pot and an amalgam of various cultures. He admitted that the church was clerically dominated, but noted also that clerics were as divided on most political, social, and economic issues as laymen were. The Catholic school system sprang up, he insisted, only when the public school system became wholly secularist, contrary to our early national traditions, and some form of released-time compromise might in fact be acceptable now to both sides. To the charge that Catholics were attempting to impose their moral views on others, Shuster responded that any anti-contraception legislation passed in Massachusetts and Connecticut was done only by democratic process and legislative vote. Shuster's close friend Father John Ryan had recently stated that the rights of minorities could be curbed if Catholics became the majority, but Shuster responded that this opinion was not supported by most Catholics at all. As Shuster had written nearly twenty years before: "Really there is only one thing to be said in conclusion: We Americans can live tranquilly together, with no just fear of 'Catholic domination.'"[19]

Shuster was not uncritical of his church, of course, and his comments could be harsh, as in the *Harper's* article:

> Yet there is about many Catholic churches, in town and country, a fearful quantity of ten-cent-store arabesque—inane statuary, painted glass dripping sentimentality, vestments made for thin people on fat people, and music designed to make one wish the singers would join the angelic choir without delay. And if, as may well happen, all this is topped with a sermon combining a curiously ungrammatical orthodoxy, pot-shots at the rest of the world, and invitations to participate in varied gambling events, it can easily be that what is suggested is Coney Island on a religious binge.[20]

Despite these glaring deficiencies, however, Shuster saw much to admire in American Catholic culture. It was a fusion of elements brought over chiefly from Europe, elements acquired from the environment here, and elements adapted unconsciously, and perhaps unknowingly, from others.[21] The elements brought from abroad seem to have worn best: the Spanish architecture of California, the German churches of Minnesota and Wisconsin, and even some French architecture, as in the Administration Building with its Golden Dome at the University of Notre Dame. Because most American Catholics, at least in earlier years, were of immigrant background and were absorbed with eking out a livelihood in their new land, they had little time for, and often little appreciation of, literature, the arts, and scholarship. They were left primarily with the literature of their co-religionists in Europe— Chesterton and Belloc, Newman and Greene, Mauriac and Bernanos, Sienkiewicz and Guardini. But Shuster reminded his readers that the likes of Nathaniel Hawthorne, Henry Adams, T. S. Eliot, and Francis Parkman had all spoken admiringly of things Catholic on occasion.

The core of Catholic culture, of course, was religious and spiritual. "[All] these things and more added together," Shuster continued,

> do not really tell us what American Catholic "culture" is. This can only be described as something to be sensed rather than defined. It is the relative, always limited, inexhaustibly rich and yet on the other hand necessarily circumscribed, awareness a huge toiling population, which at its fringes achieves a measure of prosperity, has of the place of sacramental mysteries in daily life. . . . What is so glorious here, and no doubt also so little comprehended, is that a free and in no sense class-bound working population has compelled an environment which moves in a different direction from the Catholic direction to build a fence round a place inside which a sacred fire burns.[22]

Catholic office-workers, Shuster stated, give up part of their lunch-hour to attend Mass on Holy Days, even fasting the while, and working people contribute to poor boxes and CARE packages for persons never seen. Despite deficiencies in American Catholicism, Shuster concluded, "our people has drunk in the smell of the stockyards without losing hope; it has worked in the coalmines and kept its faith; it has stood all day and night in the heat of the steel mills without abandoning charity. It is a great people."[23]

One area of continual lament for Shuster was the lack of harmonious cooperation between Catholics and Protestants in

America. In a 1948 article, "The Contemporary Situation: As a Catholic Sees It," he noted the unfortunate stereotypes on both sides: Protestants viewing Catholics as living in some kind of authoritarian bondage to Rome, and Catholics still referring to Protestants as heretics or worse.[24] He emphasized the fact that the beliefs and goals that bound peoples together were much more central and decisive than those which separated, and he pleaded for greater understanding. The common experience and suffering of World War II, he suggested, should make this more attractive and more urgent. He even had specific suggestions:

> I wish there were some way of building a church so that one end of it would be Presbyterian and the other end Catholic. I wish the YMCA were a joint Catholic-Protestant enterprise, with differing religious services for each group. I wish you could find the clergy together elsewhere than on the golf course, though even that neighborliness is better than none.[25]

As Shuster emerged more and more into national prominence, he did not hesitate to express strong opinions on national and international affairs. In the late summer of 1941, several months before the United States entered World War II, he defended President Roosevelt's foreign policy against attacks by Republican Senator Gerald Nye of North Dakota. With the revision in neutrality legislation in 1939, the sale of U.S. destroyers to Great Britain, and the lend-lease program to the Allies, Nye suggested that the United States was being dragged into the war. He also opposed aid to brutal, atheistic Russia. Shuster, speaking in behalf of Loyal Americans of German Descent, insisted that Nazi totalitarianism was the supreme danger that had to be checked.[26] Hitler had already destroyed much of what Germany had meant to Western civilization; he had little tolerance for religion or democracy; and by absorbing the U.S.S.R. and defeating Great Britain, he hoped to relegate the United States to a subordinate position in world affairs. The policy of President Roosevelt, according to Shuster, was precisely the right one, midway between appeasement and war. Because of Hitler's threat to the freedoms and liberties Americans hold dear, the nation should be eager to assist all those resisting him, and in this sense America was not being dragged into England's war but England was already fighting a war to assist and defend America. Shuster had no sympathy for the Communist regime in Moscow, but he insisted that the Russians themselves were a good and religious people and, with the invasion of their homeland by Hitler that summer, there was no doubt whose side we should assist.

Shuster had always considered Adolf Hitler an aberration and Nazism an imposition on German character and culture, and he looked forward to the day when postwar Germany could return to its honored place in the ranks of Western civilization. He was thus deeply disturbed with the Yalta Conference in early 1945 and Roosevelt's agreement both to a division of Germany and to the growing influence of the Soviet Union in Europe:

> For whatever else this Conference has accomplished it has endorsed a division of Europe into two spheres of influence, the one of which, namely the Russian, is to include a large and populous section of Germany, as well as nearly all the nations of Eastern and Southeastern Europe, and the other of which is to be subject to Anglo-American domination. In the second place, the only realistic international organization which has so far been established is an organization [reparations commission] which is to determine what drafts of labor and materials are to be exacted from Germany; and the headquarters of that organization are to be in Moscow. We shall therefore have to look the issue of slave labor squarely in the face. In the third place, the kind of government to be set up in the Russian part of Germany has already been created. It is a government such as Radek dreamed of in 1919—a union of generals and Communist Party functionaries.[27]

Shuster noted that many things would need to be done in Germany immediately after the war—locating and punishing Nazis, provisioning an army of occupation, revising the code of jurisprudence and legislative statutes, administering relief, establishing an effective agency of public information, and eventually creating a new German government—but he seemed confident that these could be accomplished. It was the division of Germany that caused him greatest concern. Germany, east and west, was an economic unit, and this unity was now being sundered—rural from urban and agriculture from industry. Shuster saw the artificial redrawing of national boundaries at Versailles as a major cause of the European discontent in the 1920s and 1930s, and he feared that the divisions of Germany agreed upon at Yalta could only add to economic hardships and be the source of further crises.

"If you argue that armament control must be our first thought," he insisted, "remember that wars are always begotten these days by dissatisfaction upon a corroding and purposeless economic life."[28]

Despite these criticisms, Shuster remained a strong supporter of President Roosevelt. He realized that the president represented the hopes of millions throughout the world, was deeply saddened by his sudden death three months after Yalta, and thought it particularly fitting that young women of New York brought flowers to brighten the rooms of Roosevelt House that the president himself had once called home.[29]

If Shuster was concerned over the conference at Yalta in 1945, he was equally disturbed over the trials at Nuremberg the following year. "The fact that bad men got what was coming to them is beside the point," Shuster stated.[30] "The three evil geniuses of the movement"—Hitler, Goebbels, Himmler—were not there to stand trial with their underlings. Furthermore, the punishment meted out to military men like Generals Jodl and Keitel was also of concern. "We may as well admit that probably not a single responsible American officer, from General Eisenhower on down, has failed to gulp at the sentences imposed. . . . When soldiers fail to do what they are told, there will be no more soldiers."[31] As a former soldier himself, this was a dilemma Shuster was hesitant to have anyone confront.

But Shuster's principal qualm concerned the patent inequality of the whole procedure. "The only chance democracy has to create a reign of peace and reason is by establishing law," he noted.[32] "Now the trouble with Mr. Jackson's [Associate Justice Robert Jackson, the U.S. representative at the trials] attempt to help create such a law was from the beginning that it rested upon the assumption that a war-time mirage could be trusted. That is, the court was convened in the belief that the only atrocities were nazi atrocities, and the only menace to peace the nazi menace." What about Russian crimes in 1918? What about Soviet activities in Eastern Europe in World War II? What about mutual guilt in the Stalin-Hitler Pact of 1939 which the Nuremberg trials brought into the open? And yet a Russian judge sat equally on the bench. As Shuster remarked sadly but perceptively: "Everyone knows that if another war broke out now, the question to be asked in the

end would not be 'who started it?' but 'who won?'"[33] The lesson
of Nuremberg was supposed to be that might does not make right
and that the rule of law must be obeyed, and yet the example of
Nuremberg was the opposite. Russian atrocities were not on trial
because Russia had been on the winning side.[34]

Shuster's comments on the Nuremberg trials were particularly significant because he had personally interviewed several of
these same Nazi leaders as chairman of the War Department's
Historical Commission in the summer of 1945. A letter of invitation from the War Department's Troyer S. Anderson outlined the
commission's purpose:

> A short time ago it occurred to us in the Historical Branch
> that a unique opportunity to enrich our knowledge of the history of
> our times exists in the fact that numerous former German officials,
> both civilian and military, are now our prisoners of war. These
> men have information about the inner history of the Nazi regime
> which, under the best of circumstances, could never be fully recap-
> tured from documents. . . . If, however, we can tap the memories
> of leading participants, we can minimize this imperfection and
> shed light on many things which, otherwise, may remain forever
> obscure. . . .Of course we realize that there are some disadvantages
> in immediate interrogation, that some men, for instance, will lie to
> us because fearful of their personal fate. However, after making
> due allowances for these difficulties, we feel something can be
> learned from immediate interviews which the historical world can-
> not afford to miss.[35]

The Department decided on a commission of six members—Dr. Frank Graham of Princeton, Lieut. Col. Oron Hale of
the University of Virginia, Maj. Kenneth Hechler of Columbia,
Dr. John Brown Mason of the Hoover Library at Stanford, Col.
John J. Scanlon of the Office of the Director of Materiel in
Washington, and Shuster as chairman. The commissioners were
selected for their expertise in military affairs, in economics, in the
political and administrative history of Nazi Germany—and for
their knowledge of the German language. The interviewing continued from July to November, slightly longer than the originally
planned ninety days, and each civilian on the commission was
paid twenty-five dollars per day.[36] The commission members

separated into groups, interviewed in various centers throughout Europe, and were guided by specific questions the War Department wanted addressed, although they were also free to range as widely as they wished as the interviews progressed. The interviews were conducted in German unless the German official spoke English fluently, long-hand notes were taken during the interviews, and summaries of the interrogations, in greater or less detail, were then submitted to the War Department.[37]

The assignment could not have come at a less convenient time for Shuster. Germany had surrendered unconditionally on May 8; the WAVES were still occupying the Bronx campus of Hunter but were preparing to leave near the end of the year; the controversy over temporary quarters for the United Nations in New York had not yet arisen but Shuster and all college presidents were working against the clock to prepare curricula, classroom space, and living facilities for the millions of returning veterans and temporary defense workers who would soon be crowding to college campuses. Shuster did not need a full-time assignment for three or four months in war-torn Europe, but he eventually accepted. He arranged for the necessary briefing trips to Washington, received the two sets of required shots, was measured for an officer's uniform (without rank), and prepared to depart shortly after college commencement.[38]

Shuster himself interviewed more than twenty-five of the one hundred seventy individuals from July 20 through October 3, including Admiral Karl Doenitz, Hitler's successor as head of the German state and the one who authorized the final German surrender; Hermann Goering, commander of the Luftwaffe and Hitler's close friend and associate; General Heinz Guderian, commander of the Russian front; Field Marshal Albert Kesselring, commander both in North Africa and on the western front; Franz von Papen, Bruening's successor as chancellor of Germany in 1932; Joachim von Ribbentrop, German Foreign Minister from 1938 through World War II; and Alfred Rosenberg, administrator of several Eastern European territories occupied by the Germans.[39] Some of the topics he investigated were specific military strategy, political decision-making within the Nazi bureaucracy, the decline of the Center Party and the rise of National Socialism (a subject about which Shuster still hoped someday to write), and also the attitude of German Catholics, both the laity and the hierarchy, toward the Nazi regime.

One of Shuster's earliest interviews was with Franz von Papen in a detention center in Luxemburg. With the German economy reeling from the worldwide economic collapse of 1929, von Papen had succeeded Bruening as chancellor of Germany in mid-1932, but, unable to ward off challenges from both the Communists on the left and the National Socialists on the right, he resigned in five months, later convincing the aging President Paul von Hindenburg to form a government with Adolf Hitler as chancellor, at least in name. Shuster thought the interview frank and honest, and his final evaluation of the fallen leader was perceptive. "More than any other German of his time," Shuster wrote, "he pitted his wits against those of Hitler. The trouble was not merely that Hitler's were of very much better quality but also that generals and others relied upon by Papen to redress the balance were even more unintelligent than he."[40]

General Guderian's observations about the Russian front were enlightening. The reasons for the German attack on Russia, he believed, were threefold: most important, the German dislike and even hatred of the Russians; second, the need for raw materials like grain, cotton, ore, and coal (but since these had already been arranged for by treaty, this was not a primary cause); and finally, the desire for German predominance in Europe.[41] Himmler also had the idea to colonize part of Russia with Germans, but Guderian called this "sheer lunacy." Guderian confirmed that Hitler did not often discuss major decisions with political or military advisors beforehand. The general showed a genuine respect for his enemy. Russian military leaders were probably too inflexible and fought too strictly by the book, but the average soldier was an excellent fighter. Many of the Russian people seemed to see some hope in the German advance and maybe relief from the sufferings of Stalinism, but German administration of these captured territories soon turned the citizenry hostile. Guderian confirmed that all along the Russian front he saw no evidence of a Soviet build-up or preparation for an attack against Germany. The general had no praise, finally, for Col. Claus von Stauffenberg's unsuccessful attempt on Hitler's life in July 1944.

Placing the bomb in a briefcase and walking out of the room admitted too wide a chance for failure. The truly courageous act would have been to shoot Hitler face to face that day with a pistol.

The interview with Goering was particularly memorable. Shuster was probing for specific reasons for Hitler's declaration of war on the United States, suggesting that "theoretically it was quite possible that if Hitler had spoken the next day [after Pearl Harbor] in terms disavowing any desire to be at conflict with the United States the whole weight of America would have been brought to bear on the Pacific theatre." Goering "was startled and said that if he thought this were true he would hang himself immediately."[42] Shuster noted lightly that with all the guards and precautions of his confinement that might be quite difficult to accomplish. With a slight smile, Goering responded, "A man can take his life any time he wants to."[43] Shuster remembered these words vividly when it was revealed a few months later that Goering had in fact committed suicide in an even more closely guarded cell during the trials at Nuremberg.

Of all the German leaders, Shuster had least personal regard for von Ribbentrop. Von Ribbentrop had joined the Nazi Party only because von Papen had no position for him in his government, and he soon rose under Hitler to be ambassador-at-large, ambassador to Great Britain in 1936, and then foreign minister from 1938 to 1945, both feared and honored on the world stage. Shuster found him obsequious and self-serving. He insisted that he had known nothing of some of Germany's major war-time decisions and that Hitler acted mostly alone. He admitted that he could not have dissented from Hitler since that could be interpreted as treason and he would have suffered the fate of others. Shuster could not help adding at the close of the interview: "Ribbentrop is a thoroughly lifeless, spineless, supine and maleficent dolt."[44]

Admiral Doenitz, on the other hand, was more sympathetic. It was on April 30, 1945, that Doenitz had received word that, with Goering and Himmler fallen from favor, Hitler had appointed him successor and authorized him to take whatever steps the situation demanded. The following day Hitler committed suicide. The military situation, Doenitz knew well, was disastrous. The German armies were in retreat on almost all fronts, the Navy had lost most of its heavy surface ships, the air force was only a fraction of its earlier size, transportation and communications among the various fronts were being cut, and millions of civilians were fleeing to the west before the Russian advance. Doenitz was eager to end the war, but the Allied policy of unconditional surrender, announced at Casablanca in 1943, was an obstacle. Doenitz knew how the Russians were treating German captives, and he insisted that he could not consign his people to that fate. Furthermore, he might agree to surrender to all the Allied military leaders, wherever they were, but he could not enforce it and guarantee that the military and civilian populations would not continue to flee the Russians. His plan then was to surrender in the West as soon as possible and delay capitulation in the East until more and more could flee. On May 5 Doenitz authorized Fleet Admiral Hans von Friedeburg to surrender all German forces in Denmark and Holland to Field Marshall Bernard Montgomery of Great Britain, and the following day Doenitz sent General Alfred Jodl to offer General Eisenhower the surrender of all troops facing the Americans. Eisenhower had approved the surrender to Montgomery the day before as a "tactical" surrender, but now insisted on total capitulation on all fronts. Jodl explained Doenitz's reasoning and the situation on the Russian front, but Eisenhower was adamant. He did, however, allow an additional forty-eight hours for formal ratification and complete notification along all fronts, and Doenitz realized that this was all the time he could buy. The final capitulation was signed in Berlin on May 8 and went into effect officially the following day.[45]

To understand better the growth and influence of Nazism in the 1930s, and certainly to satisfy further his personal interest in the church in Germany, Shuster also conducted a series of interviews on religious opposition to Nazism in western Germany. He interviewed more than a dozen religious leaders, including the archbishop of Cologne, the bishop of Muenster, the abbot of Maria Laach, and several active political figures. On the Protestant side, the Confessional group generally stood firm against Nazi interference and suffered much because of it. Others seemed to find ways to accommodate to government demands, as did many of the theology faculty of the universities of Bonn and Heidelberg, and these "German Christians" suffered less. On the

Catholic side, opposition to Nazism was expressed chiefly in the dissemination of pastoral letters by the bishops, in the work of Catholic youth groups, and in the activities of the Catholic Worker societies. Many Catholics accepted Nazi insignia out of compulsion or to retain their employment, and most of those interviewed seemed to feel that the German bishops in fact should have spoken out much more.[46]

Shuster interviewed one former Catholic priest who, at the urging of Himmler, had renounced his vows, married, and drafted attacks on the Christian churches to be used after the German victory. The man was near despair and kept pleading with Shuster: "What will happen to me? Will they kill me? . . . You must not let them kill me. I am afraid of what will happen to me when I die!" "It was a gruesome experience," Shuster admitted, "which opened up a view of the depths of a tortured spirit."[47]

Completing his interviews in Germany, Shuster went to Rome to discuss with officials there the possibility of doing research in the Vatican Archives on this topic of the church, Nazism, and the war. During a private audience Pope Pius XII spontaneously offered to open all Vatican records to him for a serious and scholarly study of that controversial topic. Shuster was most grateful but admitted that he personally might not have sufficient time but that the study could certainly be done by another. In that case, the pope suggested, he would have to withhold permission until he knew for certain who that person might be.[48] Shuster realized that a golden opportunity had been lost.

A lighter side of the trip into Italy was provided by Shuster's driver. Shuster had suggested that the trip from Germany could be very educational and thus asked the transportation officer if some erstwhile college student in the military might be available. The driver assigned him was pleasant enough but seemed devoid of any cultural interests, came equipped with a spyglass and a mouth organ, and preferred to be called by the name of his home state, Tennessee. When he drove Shuster to the Vatican on their first day in Rome, Shuster suggested he might wish to spend the hour or so walking through St. Peter's Basilica. "Naw, sir," he replied. "I just don't care much for churches." Shuster had him drive him over to the Protestant cemetery so he could visit the graves of Keats and Shelley, but Tennessee stayed in the car, not much interested in "dead men." Coming across an ancient aqueduct outside of Naples, Tennessee asked how old it was. Shuster thought he detected some slight interest, said it was probably two thousand years old, and asked Tennessee if he wanted to look around. "Naw," he replied. "It ain't got no modern improvements." Shuster's only success at cultural enrichment may have come at Pisa. Driving into the city on a beautiful moonlit night, Shuster proudly pointed out the famed Leaning Tower. With a least a modicum of enthusiasm, Tennessee acknowledged: "Well, sir, the doggoned thing sure does lean!"[49] Shuster was never sure whether the selection of Tennessee had been deliberate or random.

The historical commission's interviews remained classified for several years but, in the meantime, they assisted War Department officials in understanding the growth and operation of the Nazi government before and during World War II, and they gave Shuster a deeper understanding of wartime Germany, an understanding which prepared him better for his eighteen months as Land Commissioner to Bavaria in 1950 and 1951.

Conducting interrogations in Europe for the War Department in the summer of 1945 forced Shuster to interrupt, if only briefly, work on another, and better known, commission to which he had been appointed a couple of years before. In December 1942 Henry R. Luce, of Time, Inc., suggested to Robert Hutchins, then chancellor of the University of Chicago, that he appoint a commission to study "the present state and future prospects of the freedom of the press" in the United States.[50] Hutchins and Luce both feared that freedom of the press, one of the pillars of the American way of life, might be endangered either from internal weaknesses in the media itself or from government interference or private pressure groups from outside. Luce agreed to contribute $200,000 from Time, Inc., to assist the commission, and the Encyclopaedia Britannica eventually added another fifteen thousand.

This Commission on Freedom of the Press boasted an impressive membership. In addition to Hutchins and Shuster, it included philosopher William Ernest Hocking and historian Arthur Schlesinger from Harvard; Zechariah Chafee, Jr., from the Harvard Law School; economist John Clark of Columbia; John Dickinson, professor of Law at the University of Pennsylvania;

political scientists Harold Lasswell of Yale and Charles Merriam of the University of Chicago; anthropologist Robert Redfield, also of Chicago; Archibald MacLeish, poet and former librarian of Congress; theologian Reinhold Niebuhr of Union Theological Seminary; and Beardsley Ruml, chief executive officer of Macy's and chairman of the Federal Reserve Board of New York.[51] The commission held seventeen plenary sessions over the next three years, studied 176 staff documents, interviewed fifty-eight persons, authorized its staff to speak with 225 others, and in early 1947 published its findings and recommendations in a report entitled *A Free and Responsible Press.*[52]

The findings of the commission were not earth-shaking, and Hutchins admitted as much. "The most surprising thing about them is that nothing more surprising could be proposed," he acknowledged.[53] A disappointed Henry Luce was much more blunt. He called the commission's analysis of media conditions "in various respects, elementary, naive, superficial, uncritical and obsolete," and he was equally critical of the report's theoretical framework. "As to the general philosophical treatment of the problem," he wrote Hutchins, "I give your distinguished Commission a gentleman's "C" and no more. In this area, which I regard as the most important of all, I believe that each member of the Commission could have done a better job by himself than has been done for or by the whole Commission."[54] Frank Gannett of Gannett Newspapers called the report "erroneous, inconsistent, ineffective, and dangerous," and Robert McCormick said he would not have time to read these "outpourings of a gang of crackpots."[55] Many newspapers gave the report little publicity at all, although this might have been in part because of the criticisms levelled at the newspaper industry.[56] Still, the considered judgments of such a distinguished panel on this important topic could not be ignored.

The commission concluded that any major threat to freedom of the press in America did not arise from government interference, as it clearly did in totalitarian states like Nazi Germany or Communist Russia, but from problems within the media itself. The commission enunciated five responsibilities the press and other media were called on to acquit: first, to provide a "truthful, comprehensive, and intelligent" account of events, presenting fact as fact and opinion as opinion, and withholding no information essential for accuracy; second, to provide a "forum for the exchange of comment and criticism," publishing views different from its own and revealing the sources of its information and judgments; third, to provide an accurate and "representative picture of the constituent groups in the society," not presenting various groups in unfavorable stereotypes; fourth, to provide a "clarification of the goals and values of the society"; and fifth, to make its information and its contributions available to all in society, not just to a select few.[57] Although the commission saw no present threat of government interference, it did fear that if the press and other media did not fulfill these responsibilities well, the government might then feel the need to intervene. It was the commission's judgment, in fact, that the press was not fulfilling its responsibilities well. "When we look at the press as a whole," the commissioners declared, "we must conclude that it is not meeting the needs of our society. The Commission believes that this failure of the press is the greatest danger to its freedom."[58]

The reasons for this relatively poor performance, according to the commission, were several. The press, first of all, had become big business, and as in many other big businesses, power was being concentrated in fewer and fewer hands. The number of newspapers in America was declining, many belonged to the same chain, and most subscribed to the same news services. There were only eight large magazine publishers and four major radio networks. On the local level, radio and newspaper news services were often linked. As a result of this concentration of power, competition was drastically reduced and newspapers could publish unbalanced or even inaccurate accounts often without fear of challenge or contradiction. Second, in order to attract the greatest number of readers, the press often emphasized the unusual and the sensational—"night-club murders, race riots, strike violence, and quarrels among public officials"—rather than equally important but perhaps less exciting occurrences. Third, the press at times shirked its responsibility out of fear of offending particular groups. Newspapers took into account the personal views of the owners, the sensitivities of various religious and ethnic groups, and the concerns of major advertisers. The media, finally, tried to appeal to the majority, the masses, and then often settled for the lowest common denominator in quality.[59]

The commission's final recommendations were moderate. It recommended that present libel legislation be greatly simplified and that advocacy of revolutionary changes in American government be prohibited only in situations of "clear and present danger." It urged the media to present a wider diversity of views, to offer programs of higher cultural and artistic value, and to be less influenced in programming by advertisers. It advocated, finally, the establishment of additional libraries, schools, and other institutions to complement the educational and cultural activities of the media, and the establishment also of an independent agency charged with appraising and reporting annually on the performance of the media in the United States.[60]

Shuster did not play a particularly prominent role in the commission's deliberations. He attended all but three of the seventeen plenary sessions, he chaired the subcommittee on pressure groups and economics, but his influence on the final report was much less than that of Hutchins, Niebuhr, Hocking, Lasswell, or MacLeish.[61] When the Commission began discussing whether the postmaster general should have approved second-class mailing privileges to *Esquire*, Shuster interjected that the mailing privileges of one risqué journal, which he admitted he had never read, was far from crucial to freedom of the press.[62] He also objected to a statement that "free expression" was the "promoter and protector of other liberties." He noted that in northern Bavaria before the war a "purse could be left on a bench and found again intact hours later," and "a pretty young woman could sleep all night in the open without fear of assault or even insult," but if anyone attacked the Mother of God in print, they had better leave town immediately. On the other hand, he reminded his colleagues, New York enjoys complete freedom of expression and yet "nobody can venture into Central Park of nights without a police escort."[63] He was also quick to point out the revolutionary changes taking place in the media industry, the dominance of telephonic and televisual communication:

> I often say that the difference is just as great as was the difference between the oral tradition, preceding printing, and the coming of printing, because the arrival of printing simply removed oral tradition as an educative factor. The new visual education, together with auditory education, is bound to make our purely literary education look as outmoded to the youth of the future, unless we do

something about it, as oral tradition was outmoded through an age which brought up printing. . . .

We don't know too much about it, but it is fair to say, I think, on the basis of what is now known, that this is bound to be the most revolutionary influence that has come into the shaping of the human mind since the introduction of printing.[64]

A major concern for Shuster, one which he emphasized as chairman of the subcommittee on pressure groups, was that the media comprised an enormous business. Unfortunately, he also thought it was a business poorly run. "I think that if Ruml ran Macy's the way AP runs AP," he stated, "they would have been in bankruptcy long since."[65] As a business also, the media were greatly influenced by what the public and pressure groups wanted. Tabloid newspapers were proliferating and catering to the desire for the sensational and the salacious, and older, more reputable papers were tending in that direction also or faced loss of readership. Shuster suggested that most Americans could identify Dorothy Lamour's sarong but few the Atlantic Charter.[66] Americans were still friends and allies of the Soviet Union in 1945 and 1946, and perhaps that was why little was being said about Russian control of Poland or Eastern Europe.[67] Returning to a subject he knew well, Shuster noted that "during the Spanish Civil War, nobody could defend Franco in the daily press of New York; but in the Catholic press, nobody could criticize him."[68]

When some singled out the Catholic church's Legion of Decency for criticism, however, Shuster dissented:

> The Legion of Decency is an organization with which I find myself, personally, often in disagreement, but its purpose, I think, is a legitimate one. The Legion of Decency serves the people who, rightly or wrongly, believe that an occasion of sin is an occasion of sin, and who also belong to a church which, in the opinion of those who are its members, has a right to point out what is an occasion of sin.
>
> If it does that, and does that only, I don't see how it is violating a proper social function of that kind of organization in our society.[69]

Shortly after this work was finished and the report published in the spring of 1947, Shuster took on what could have been an even more controversial assignment.[70] In late 1946 the Social

Science Research Council (which had sponsored Shuster's research in Europe in 1937 and 1938), the Rosenwald Foundation, and several other research organizations decided to investigate the problem of racial segregation in Washington, D.C. They saw the inconsistency of preaching the virtues of the democratic way of life to war-torn nations of Europe and Asia while tolerating countless forms of discrimination in the nation's own capital. A research committee was soon assembled, including Will Alexander, Robert C. Weaver of Chicago, and sociologist E. Franklin Frazier of Howard University, and an investigation of actual conditions in Washington was undertaken from January to July of 1947. A national committee of prominent and respected citizens, the National Committee on Segregation in the Nation's Capital, was also established to sponsor and give the study greater prestige. Shuster agreed to serve as chairman.[71]

Shuster later noted at least one reason for accepting this position. He recalled that each year Hunter College graduated large numbers of qualified young black women, many of whom migrated to Washington during the war years in search of employment. "Conditions of discrimination were so intolerable for these girls," said Shuster, "that many of them were forced to return."[72] He recalled one case in particular, when a former editor of the Hunter College newspaper was forced to walk ten blocks for her lunch each day because she could not be served even in the government cafeteria.

Shuster had few responsibilities until the final report was completed. The research staff collected data on segregation and discrimination in almost all areas of Washington life, some data were screened out as too personal or too exceptional for inclusion, and then the material was turned over to Kenesaw M. Landis II, a member of the National Committee, a lawyer, and a syndicated columnist, for the actual drafting. As each draft was completed, it was returned to members of the original research committee, and especially to Doctor Frazier, for comments, criticisms, and suggestions. Even as the report was being drafted, the material was having an influence. Some of the committee findings had been shared with the President's Committee on Civil Rights, which President Truman had appointed in late 1946 and which had reported back to him the following October, and the committee's findings had also been utilized in a legal brief in the city's restrictive covenant cases before the United States Supreme Court. After several last-minute delays, the committee report, entitled *Segregation in Washington*, was released at a well-publicized luncheon in the Willard Hotel on December 10, 1948. It was only the second time in recent memory, according to one observer, when black and white Americans had been served together in a major Washington restaurant. Shuster and three other members of the committee also met with President Truman that morning and presented him with a copy of the report.[73]

The committee's report told a tragic story. Segregation and discrimination touched almost every aspect of life in Washington and were contradictory in their senselessness. Black Americans could not be seated in most restaurants and coffee shops, but black citizens from other countries often could. There was no segregation on public transportation and black and white passengers sat wherever they pleased in city buses, but no blacks could be hired as drivers, even during the wartime labor shortage. In commercial theaters blacks could act on stage but not be seated in the audience, while in Constitution Hall blacks could attend performances in the audience but not appear on stage—and thus the brilliant Marian Anderson was denied the use of those facilities in 1939. In education, black schools were so crowded that some junior high pupils could attend only part-time and in split-shifts while eighteen hundred spaces were unutilized in white schools. Even pet cemeteries were segregated, and one would bury dogs of white owners but not of black owners, the proprietor admitting that the dogs probably would not mind but the white customers might. As the report noted, segregation was not just a "Negro problem" but a "white problem."[74]

According to the report, the origins of the tragedy were just as strange as its manifestations. In the decades after the Civil War all persons could vote in the District of Columbia, black Americans "served as Register of the Treasury, Auditor of the Navy, as Consul, Collector of Customs, and in many other responsible posts at home and abroad," and an 1872 law assured black Americans "equal rights in restaurants, hotels, barber shops, and other places of public accommodation."[75] That law apparently was never repealed but was simply dropped or left unmentioned when the District's legislation was codified at the turn of the century. Segregation in government employment may have begun under President William Howard Taft (1909–13), but it became official federal policy only under his successor, Woodrow Wilson. President Wilson himself may not have been to blame, but the District of Columbia was governed principally by congressional committees and congress at this time came under the influence more and more of segregationist southern Democrats like Hoke Smith of Georgia, "Pitchfork" Ben Tillman of South Carolina, and James K. Vardaman of Mississippi. Employees were segregated by race in most government offices, Black Americans were relegated to more menial and lower-paying jobs, and the increasing racial tensions finally culminated in the bitter riot of 1919. Some progress had been made during World War II—such emergencies often cause relaxation in existing laws and customs—but the committee found postwar conditions still deplorable.[76]

The committee laid major blame for this tragic situation on two sources: business and real estate executives on one hand, and the federal government on the other. The local real estate board, made up chiefly of banking, insurance, and other business interests, insisted on segregated housing in the District—at least until early 1948 when restricted covenants were declared unenforceable by the Supreme Court—for the simple reason that such housing brought greater profit.[77] The Washington Real Estate Board Code of Ethics stated openly that "no property in a white section should ever be sold, rented, advertised, or offered to colored people."[78] Expensive and even luxury housing was then constructed in these restricted areas and higher prices charged. As blacks were crowded into narrower spaces elsewhere in the city, two developments took place in prices there. More people and families moved in and thus the real estate owners made greater profit, and housing prices increased rapidly since lodging elsewhere was unavailable. Segregated housing, the source of so many other evils in the city, was continued because it seemed most profitable to real estate executives.[79]

But the federal government received stinging criticism also. During the war, one office found it necessary to hire two black women in its typing pool, and the supervisor later boasted that she had avoided any conflicts and friction simply by placing the two new typists behind a screen. Happily, that solution was overturned as soon as it was discovered.[80] The Federal Housing Authority guaranteed loans for segregated housing, the District's Planning Commission planned no integrated public housing "until the community is ready," and federal funds assisted many private hospitals in the city which limited the number of nonwhite patients and excluded black physicians.[81] All this was especially reprehensible in the nation's capital because, although there might be disagreement over the federal government's authority to intervene in the civil rights area in the individual states, all agreed that congress had full jurisdiction over the District of Columbia. Congress had no excuse.[82]

The report did not cause as much public controversy as might have been expected because the committee limited its scope to fact-finding, to describing the situation as it then existed, and it left to a continuation committee the task of drafting specific proposals to remedy the evils the report uncovered.[83] Shuster himself, however, evoked controversy with remarks he made at a forum sponsored by the Catholic Interracial Council in New York in early January 1949. He admitted that conditions were deplorable. "Until I actually witnessed some of the situations that are now published in the committee's report," he stated, "I would never have believed such conditions could exist anywhere in the U.S., let alone in the capital city."[84] Realizing that a basic source of segregation and discrimination was the greed of land owners and real estate executives, he did not look to congress for the full solution. "Legislation alone will not remedy this situation," he suggested. "Only a complete awareness by the American people of the evil of these conditions can really change this discriminatory picture." But bleak and devastating as the picture was, Shuster, as always, found reason for hope. "The number of organizations and individuals that have come forward and expressed an interest in this work has been a complete surprise to me and a great source of encouragement," he declared. "When I witness the great number of people interested in this report, I am convinced that tremendous progress has been made in this country since the outset of the interracial movement. A kind of revolution has taken place in the hearts of Americans and awakened them to the principles of democracy and their Christian ideals."[85]

By seeming to de-emphasize the role of congress and legislation in the problem, Shuster opened himself to criticism. The
Washington Afro-American subtitled its account, "Dr. Shuster Tells
Catholic Council That School Segregation Is Not Basic Cause,"
and stated that he had "brushed aside the often-repeated charge
that Washington's jim-crow school system lies at the root of its
segregation and discrimination."[86] Ida Fox, executive secretary of
the Council for Civil Rights in the Nation's Capital, was disturbed
that the committee's report had traced the legislative history of
segregation in Washington and had noted that Congress had jurisdiction over civil rights in the city, and yet Shuster's speech
seemed to suggest that legislation was not the answer. Fox wrote
directly to George K. Hunton of the *Interracial Review* for his
"own account of what he [Shuster] said and your own interpretation of what you think he meant." She was reassured that Hunton
had liked the talk "from the beginning to the end" and that in
reply to a question, Shuster had insisted "that Congress would
have to pass needed legislation."[87] Shuster was familiar with
Jewish ghettos in Nazi Germany and the realization, through his
work on this committee, that an inhuman racial ghetto existed
even in Washington, the "Symbol of Democracy,"[88] was particularly disturbing.

As Shuster's prestige as an educator and commentator on
world affairs increased in the postwar years, he was invited to join
more and more national boards and committees. He served with
labor leaders David Dubinsky, Matthew Woll, and other prominent citizens on the American Committee for a Free Spanish
Republic in 1945 and urged the withdrawal of United Nations
recognition of Franco's government as a peaceful way of restoring
democracy to that nation.[89] In 1948 he succeeded radio commentator Edward R. Murrow as chairman of the Board of Trustees of
the Institute of International Education, and he joined the
Connecticut State Board of Education under Governor Chester
Bowles.[90] Shuster's good friend, Mrs. Ordway Tead, was
appointed president of Briarcliff Junior College, later Briarcliff
College, in the 1950s, and she convinced Shuster to join her
Board of Trustees for two three-year terms.[91] The James Picker
family had been generous to Roosevelt House at Hunter College
since 1943, and when the Picker Foundation asked Shuster to join
its five-man Board of Directors in 1956 and assume its presidency

three years later, he could not refuse. The Picker Foundation made sizeable grants both for research in radiology and for graduate and undergraduate scholarships, and Shuster was pleased to have a part in such awards.[92] With his interests in education and the media, Shuster in 1957 accepted election to the Board of Trustees of the Broadcasting Foundation of America, an agency established by the Regents of the University of the State of New York to sponsor educational and cultural radio and television exchanges between the United States and Western Europe and the Far East. It was constantly seeking outside financial support, and Shuster's wide educational and foundational contacts were highly esteemed.[93]

One other public office, which Shuster may have quietly eased himself away from, was the senatorship from Connecticut in 1949. Ex-governor Ray Baldwin, a Republican, had been elected to the senate in 1946, but was becoming increasingly disenchanted with Washington politics, in part because the Taft Republicans controlling the senate considered him too liberal and he thought denied him prestigious committee assignments. Baldwin was also having difficulties with the State Republican Party in Connecticut.[94] In April 1949 Baldwin approached Connecticut Governor Chester Bowles, a Democrat, with an offer to resign his seat in the senate if Bowles would appoint him chief justice of the state supreme court instead. The offer was particularly attractive since it would allow Bowles to appoint a Democrat to the senate as his replacement. Bowles eventually accepted the proposal, although by mutual agreement the appointment was as associate justice rather than chief justice, and the question then arose of whom Bowles should appoint to fill out the final three years of that term.

Bowles' memoirs list Shuster as one of the candidates he considered, and several of Shuster's friends felt the offer was probably there for the taking.[95] Shuster and Bowles were close political allies at this time, but there were also excellent reasons for not appointing Shuster.[96] Although he had lived in Connecticut for twenty years, as president of Hunter College Shuster was probably considered a New Yorker by most. Connecticut's other senator, Brian McMahon, was a Catholic also, and the Democratic Party in Connecticut might face added opposition if both were Catholic. Finally, Governor Bowles would be running for re-election in 1950, the competition for campaign funds within the state would be keen over the next few years, and selecting some-one of independent wealth for this appointment had definite advantages.

In the midst of all the discussion Shuster let it be known that he did not wish to be considered. There is no doubt that he was enjoying his work at Hunter, especially as times were returning to normal in the postwar years and Hunter was open to new chal-lenges and exciting opportunities. The fact that most of his con-tacts and even interests were in New York rather than in Connecticut may have been another consideration. A major rea-son was also finances. He was not wealthy and was concerned how he might maintain homes in both Connecticut and Washington in the style expected of a United States senator. He noted also that, "to the constant regret of my wife," he was an independent in politics, possibly due to the early Wisconsin influ-ence of Robert LaFollette, and he was determined to retain his independent status.[97]

A further reason, however, may have been more personal. Shuster's son, Robert, had had a difficult youth. His early educa-tion had been irregular, due in part to the three trips the Shusters had made to Europe in the 1930s, but he had unusual talents in music and by his late teens was taking advanced lessons in violin, piano, and especially voice. After graduating from high school, he enrolled at Columbia University, his father's recent alma mater, but he attended classes irregularly, received unsatisfactory grades, and dropped out of college for two full years. He eventually returned to Columbia and graduated in 1948. Early the following year, however, he was arrested in Connecticut on a minor morals charge and avoided sentencing only by agreeing to undergo psy-chiatric help at a Hartford clinic.[98]

Shuster was deeply embarrassed by his son's behavior, but he remained optimistic that his problems could be cured. He or Doris wrote to Bob several times a week, and George turned to prayer with almost every letter. He wrote that April:

> I shall pray harder than ever during this Holy Week for you. It is a wonderful week, from the point of view of the liturgy and its mean-ing. If only there were time in which to follow everything closely, as

I once was able to do. At any rate I shall continue to believe and hope that Christ will keep you in His very special care and that as a result of all your trouble and aberrations you will become stronger and deeper than most men are.[99]

Several months earlier he had written:

But it is above all necessary to be at peace with yourself, and that is the greatest of problems. However different from other people one may be it is clear—as clear as anything can be—that all people are alike in the presence of God. Only Universal Goodness and Love can make any of us loveable. That is why one's relationship to God must take precedence over all else, however reluctant we may be to concede that this is true. . . .And so I hope that nothing will keep you from Mass on Sunday, or from some little prayer at morning and evening. There is nothing that prayer cannot triumph over, even though our own merits may seem slight in our own eyes.[100]

Bob's arrest received almost no publicity at the time, but Shuster may have feared that the whole incident would have been unearthed if he had accepted the senatorial appointment and had to run for re-election in 1952. Bowles eventually appointed William Benton.[101]

Whatever his motives for withdrawing, Shuster was certainly becoming more attracted to public life, a deliberative body like the United States senate would seem to have suited his talents well, he and Doris would have found Washington social life most congenial, and for the rest of his life, he must at times have looked back on his quiet withdrawal at least with mixed feelings. It in no way removed him from the public stage, however.

8

THE RECOVERY OF GERMANY
1945–1960

Of Shuster's numerous off-campus activities during his years at Hunter College, clearly the most absorbing were his interest in the recovery of Germany and his work for the United Nations Educational, Scientific, and Cultural Organization (UNESCO). Even as the war continued, Shuster began to advocate the rehabilitation rather than the destruction of postwar Germany. In an article in *Foreign Policy Reports* in 1943, he emphasized that many Germans hated Nazism and were no different from Americans or other persons throughout the world.[1] "Therefore," he continued, "all fantastic schemes for 'educating' the Germans and teaching them 'democracy' are not worth a moment of serious consideration. The Germans who will be freed from the Nazi strait-jacket love freedom as much as we do, and they have reason to hate war even more than we do."[2] An added challenge would be to uplift and maintain German morale after the war since the people would be despondent over the abuses of their leaders. Shuster suggested four major steps in postwar reconstruction. First, contrary to World War I, there should be nothing vengeful this time. Criminals should certainly be punished and all stolen and confiscated booty should be returned, but Germany should not be splintered into autonomous states. Fifteen months before Yalta he warned: "Above all, we ought not to underwrite the cession of East Prussia to Poland, possibly by way of compensation for the seizure of certain Polish territories by Russia."[3] Second, Germany must not be permitted to rearm, but its postwar economy should be directed almost exclusively toward survival and rearmament will not be a major concern. Third, German industry must be demobilized but not destroyed, since the country needs to be put

225

back on its feet and made economically self-sufficient again as early as possible. Finally, a new government must be established, free of Nazi influence certainly, but free of Stalinist domination also.[4]

In a speech before the Association of the Junior League of America that same summer, Shuster made a plea for the establishment of some kind of postwar world government. He took as his text Horace Walpole's remark to Voltaire: "The admirable letter you have been so good as to send me is a proof that you are one of those truly great and rare men who know at once how to conquer and to pardon."[5] The victors in World War I, according to Shuster, knew how to conquer but not to pardon, and this time the world must do both. "And as we were mistaken then we shall be mistaken again if we assume that mere possession of military strength will automatically guarantee the peace," he declared. "The only possible foundation for peace in the world is law and respect for the law, is an institutionalized world government based upon the consent of the governed to the integrity and immutability of principle."[6] World government was not the sole solution, of course, and Shuster had other recommendations to urge: the disarming of the Axis powers, the establishment of temporary military governments, the continuance of lend-lease to all devastated nations, the setting up of effective agencies to control credit and finances, and programs to restore maximum employment.[7] But world government was the key to any lasting peace and stability, and Shuster felt that three steps were essential to make such a government this time a success. First, the structure of any world organization must be widely discussed and commented on beforehand. Not every nation's suggestions could be taken, of course, but they could be listened to and eventually majority vote must decide. The organization must not be the private brainchild of only two or three world leaders. Second, the United States must be firmly committed to such a world organization and world court; only this can make them successful. Third, churches, labor unions, schools, scientific organizations, and similar agencies must become more internationally minded and reach out to both the Old World and the Orient and in this way help to unite and bind all nations closer together. For Shuster, the major question was whether the United States would have the dedication and the discipline to make the effort to save the postwar world.[8]

Shuster was particularly concerned as the war ended with the divisions and partitioning of Germany. He was convinced that the almost arbitrary drawing of boundaries in the Treaty of Versailles was a major cause of discontent and political and economic instability between the wars and ultimately of the failure of the peace, and he did not want to see the same mistake made again. In a speech before a senate subcommittee in Washington even before the war ended, he stated his view that the agreed upon division of Germany was the major failure of the Yalta Conference.[9] After the war, demand for the partitioning of Germany came from two main sources: the Soviet Union, which sought additional friendly and even submissive governments in eastern Europe, and those in the West who saw partitioning as a means of preventing the return of Germany to war-making potential once again.[10] Shuster admitted that dividing Germany would reduce any war-making potential, but it would cause even more serious problems. Economically, Germany must be restored to self-sufficiency and independence as soon as possible since the United States could not be expected to send massive shipments of food and supplies indefinitely. Only a united Germany—the farm lands of Saxony and Thuringia, the industry of Bavaria, the mining of the Ruhr valley, and the shipping of Hamburg and Bremerhaven—could guarantee this self-sufficiency. Politically, such a division simply could not last because the people themselves were opposed and were bound together by too many ties of language, culture, and history. Shuster's solution to the problems of postwar Europe was twofold: a unified and self-sufficient Germany under a strong and centralized government, and a federation of all European nations, cooperating with and complementing each other in the building of a stronger and more stable Europe.[11] The Marshall Plan of economic aid to Europe, announced by Secretary of State George Marshall only a few months later, was at least a partial step toward the fulfillment of Shuster's second hope.

In a speech in May 1949 Shuster gave his evaluation of German recovery so far. He admitted that the problems seemed overwhelming: once powerful Germany was in a state of almost complete economic paralysis at war's end; many were demanding even greater suffering as punishment for wartime abuses; Russia had its own agenda and refused to cooperate; France was not sympathetic to a full reconstruction of Germany; and approximately fourteen million refugees from eastern Germany had fled to the British and American zones and seriously complicated a situation almost hopeless at the time.[12] Our policy was still to democratize and eliminate the elitism in the German educational system, but many in Germany were convinced that the German school system was already superior to that of the United States. The Germans also realized that they were increasingly pawns in the East-West rivalry, and they were not hesitant about offering to bargain with the Soviet Union if it would reduce restrictions in the Russian zone or bring additional favors from American officials.[13]

As always, Shuster had specific recommendations to offer. Americans needed to realize that many Germans still harbored ill feelings for what must have seemed to them almost wanton bombing of churches and libraries and museums, and occupation officials needed to be culturally more sensitive. Second, Shuster urged caution in interfering in educational matters and warned against what he called "all unnecessary and piddling educational reforms."[14] He hoped that Americans would be successful in raising private funds to help rehabilitate German education, as they had done in the Philippine Islands. Finally, he thought much better use of the Voice of America could be made in the presently divided and despondent Germany. Shuster closed with a mild warning: "In short, it is too early to rejoice and not too late for hope. But the clock will not stand still."[15]

With Shuster's vast knowledge of German affairs, it was not surprising that he was drafted into public service. Even before his selection to head the War Department's Historical Commission to interview Nazi leaders in the summer of 1945, he was sought by the Office of War Information apparently to direct its agency in postwar Austria. Elmer Davis, director of the Office of War Information, wrote to Shuster on February 26 and outlined a challenging opportunity.[16] After the war Austria was to continue as an independent nation, and it was hoped that it would play an important role in the establishment of world peace and liberty. America was clearly the country that could lead best in this direction, better than the Soviet Union, and yet Austria might be less than friendly with the United States, at least initially, due to the "necessary but painful operations of the strategic air force." The

Shuster's parents, Anton and Elizabeth Schuster.

Young George served mass at his home parish in Lancaster, Wisconsin.

The president of Hunter College was a popular actor in faculty plays.

As land commissioner for Bavaria, 1950-51, Shuster advised High Commissioner John J. McCloy (center) on conditions in the largely Catholic area.

Any tips received at this luncheon in the Hunter cafeteria benefited World University Service.

Left to right: Margaret Rendt, Doris Shuster, Eleanor Roosevelt, and George Shuster. Mrs. Roosevelt was a frequent speaker at Hunter.

Dr. Leopold Figl, Austrian Foreign Minister, presents the Grand Gold Medal of Honor to Shuster.

Left to right: Notre Dame President Theodore Hesburgh, Cardinal Giovanni Montini (the future Pope Paul VI), and 1960 Laetare Medal recipient Shuster. Dr. Thomas Dooley is in the background.

Shuster returned
to Notre Dame as
special advisor to
the president in
1961.

Photo courtesy Bruce Harlan

Notre Dame Archives

Shuster at home in his study.

publicity work of the OWI, Davis admitted, "will require intelligent, tactful and sympathetic handling." He closed with a final plea: "It is going to be a very tough job indeed, and we believe that you are the man to undertake it. With full appreciation of the responsibilities you are carrying now, I hope you may conclude that for the limited period in which our office will continue in operation, the job we are asking you to undertake is the more important."

Negotiations progressed sufficiently that the Board of Higher Education discussed a possible leave of absence, but Shuster eventually declined the offer, apparently for health reasons primarily. "When I first talked with Mr. Barrett and Mr. Ginsberg," he informed Davis on May 15, "I thought it would be practicable for me to undertake the work in Austria, despite a somewhat problematical health situation. . . . But the bad weather of the past month brought on a series of colds and nasal infections which conspired with the very heavy load I am carrying to wear me down. I simply have to have a month's rest and some sunshine before I can possibly be ready for such an assignment as the one you had in mind for me." The war by that time was over in Europe, someone was needed almost immediately, and thus Shuster declined. By this time Shuster was also disturbed by the divisions of Germany and Austria agreed upon at Yalta, but this was not determining. "I shall also confess," he noted, "that I have been troubled by recent public statements concerning our policy in Europe. But of course had these been the sole causes of my disaffection, I should have got on the train and gone to Washington to discuss the problem with you."

Whatever Shuster's reasons for declining the appointment to Austria in 1945, they were no longer present five years later, and in the summer of 1950 he accepted the appointment as land commissioner or governor of the German province of Bavaria. The Yalta meeting of Roosevelt, Churchill, and Stalin had finalized plans to divide Germany temporarily into four zones, presided over by the United States, Great Britain, France, and the Soviet Union. The city of Berlin, entirely within the Soviet zone, was similarly divided into four sections. These partitions and military governments were to remain only until stable civil governments, devoid of all Nazi influence, could be established. At that time national elections were to be held, a central government was to assume control, and the occupying powers were to depart. The United States zone was comprised of the three German states of Bavaria, Hesse, Wuerttemberg-Baden, and later the port city of Bremen, and for the first few months was governed by General Dwight D. Eisenhower. He was succeeded as military governor by General Joseph McNarney, then by General Lucius Clay from 1947 to 1949, and finally by John J. McCloy, under whom the office was changed to civilian high commissioner. Under each of these, there was also a land commissioner or state governor for each of the three states, and in 1950 George Shuster was appointed land commissioner for Bavaria.

The announcement of Shuster's appointment did occasion public protest. The issue was Shuster's writings on Germany in the 1930s and whether they indicated pro-Nazi sympathies or even anti-Semitism. Shuster had been called as a witness on behalf of Victor F. Ridder, publisher of the German-language New York daily *Staatszeitung*, in 1945, and the opposing lawyer, Louis Nizer, confronted him with quotations from his earlier writings:

> Q. I read to you from page 40 of *Strong Man Rules* by Shuster. I take it you will acknowledge that is your book?
> A. With pleasure, Sir. . . .
> Q. Now I will continue and I will re-read it so we will have the continuity: "Hitler is a politician of whom it might be said that if he had not existed, it would be necessary to invent him. Hitler is our friend, the old soldier, destined to go down in history as a cross between Hotspur and Uncle Toby and to be immortal as either." Do you recall writing that sentence?
> A. Yes.
> Q. I re-read: "Hitler is not a German. Hitler is and has been a greatly perplexed, honestly inquiring and quite unsteady young man." Do you recall writing that sentence?
> A. Yes, Sir. . . .
> Q. Let me read from page 56 of your book and then I will show it to you, Doctor: "Frankly, I think that the record tends to show the United States the most militaristic of Western peoples. At least, there is no other which has fought so many wars from which it could have abstained." I show you that on page 56 and ask if you wrote that in 1934?
> A. Yes, Sir. . . .

Q. Let's see if you meant that "very good people who stagger under heavy blows feel that the great man wanted otherwise, and that subordinates frustrated his benevolent designs." The words "the great man" referred to Hitler in that sentence, didn't it?

A. Oh, of course. I point out to you again, Mr. Nizer, as you are well aware, the device of irony is a customary one in literary composition. . . .

Q. You say that you never said in that speech that Hitler "certainly is no monster"—you never said that in your speech?

A. I might conceivably have said that Hitler was no monster.[18]

This exchange with Nizer had had its effect even in 1945. A few weeks later Shuster prepared to depart for Europe as chairman of the War Department's Historical Commission, and at the last minute discovered that his passport was being held, apparently because a State Department official was concerned about his "pro-Nazi past."[19] It took the intervention of Assistant Secretary of War Robert Patterson finally to cut through the difficulty.

The issue refused to die, however. While traveling throughout Europe to conduct the War Department interviews, it was suggested that he also visit Austria. The American military commander there, General Mark Clark, heard of the possibility and sent a cable back to Washington, stating in part:

Political advisor here states some time ago informal application was made for Shuster to enter Austria and application was disapproved.

If Shuster has left U.S. for Austria information is desired concerning source of his authority.

If he is still in U.S. desire that he be not, repeat not, permitted to come to Austria.[20]

Assistant Secretary Patterson's office cabled back immediately, giving Shuster his full confidence and support, Clark replied with an apology and a personal invitation for Shuster to pay him a visit, and the controversy was forgotten.[21]

But these were minor disturbances compared to the flareup that erupted with Shuster's appointment as land commissioner in 1950. On the day that the Hunter College staff honored him with a tea and congratulated him on his new assignment, between ten and thirty members of a "Student Conference for a Labor Youth League" carried picket signs outside the college's 68th Street

entrance and protested Shuster's appointment as a step in the
"renazification of Germany."[22] None of these were Hunter
College students apparently. About that same time, a poster with
the banner headline "NO MORE CREMATORIUMS" urged
the public to protest a "Hold Berlin" rally at Town Hall at which
one of the speakers was to be George Shuster, "long time admirer
of Hitler" and "a spouter of vicious racist ideology." "Schuster,"
the poster noted, misspelling his name, "will never be able to
establish democracy in Germany but only an agent for renazification." "Protest the Appointment of Shuster," the poster closed.[23]
Walter Winchell attacked the appointment in his column in the
New York *Daily Mirror* also, basing his opinion chiefly on the
Nizer interview.[24]

The protest that hurt him most, however, was probably one
which originated at least in part from his own Hunter College students. They could not be expected to be familiar with the whole
context of his writings and activities, and they could not help but
be disturbed by statements taken out of context. Their protest
began:

> As a group of students at Hunter, we are disturbed by the recent
> resurgence of German fascism, particularly in Bavaria, the birth-
> place of Hitlerism, and feel that any doubts about the nature of Dr.
> Shuster's political and social attitudes are of great importance in
> view of his appointment. We have undertaken therefore, to state in
> detail, within a coherent context, what we have found regarding
> Pres. Shuster's views on Germany . . . the fascist movement . . .
> and the Jews.[25]

They then repeated some of the by then familiar quotations
on Hitler from Shuster's writings of the 1930s and added other
references to Jews and their treatment: "On the other hand, one
cannot help thinking that Jewish errors have been several and sizable."[26] "The besetting sin of the German Jew has been vanity.
Accustomed so long to a position of social inferiority, he could
not and still can not resist the dangerous spell of limelight."[27]
"The rise of Jewish professional classes, notably doctors and
lawyers, also aroused jealousy which was often combatted rather
tactlessly. Jewish speakers talked far too much; Jewish newspapers
were inordinately lavish in their use of colored ink; and successful
Jewish families could seldom keep their prosperity a relative

secret."[28] "No doubt much too much has been written about 'atrocities' but there is a sense in which those who care for Germany cannot talk about them excessively. As individual crimes they are no more serious than many incidents which have occurred in the U.S. during times of war hysteria, Ku Klux Klan excitement, labor trouble or racketeering."[29]

Shuster answered these charges in a letter to his faculty as he departed for Germany. He reminded them that he had been one of the early members of the National Conference of Christians and Jews (or Jews and Christians, as it was known in the 1920s), a member of its Committee on the Rights of Religious Minorities, and later a member of the American Jewish Committee. In 1934 and 1935 he was one of the organizers of the American Catholic Committee for Refugees and the American Christian Committee for Refugees, and in 1935 he urged Catholic cooperation with Jews in boycotting the coming Olympics in Berlin in protest against German policies of discrimination. He had been an editor of *The Commonweal* magazine for twelve years and had written often against the totalitarian regimes of Mussolini, Hitler, and Stalin; he thought he had been one of the first Catholics to write against Father Coughlin and his trend toward Fascism; and he resigned from *The Commonweal* rather than compromise his opposition to General Franco in Spain, "an ally of Nazism."[30]

He addressed the question of his three books on Germany directly. The first one, *The Germans*, was published before Hitler came to power and was yet sufficiently critical that the German translation was suppressed by Propaganda Minister Goebbels and the German publisher was told to leave the country. *Strong Man Rules* was written hurriedly in late 1933, in part because Shuster was shocked by the prevalent anti-Semitism at that time and was convinced that Christianity would soon face the same fate. He clearly had underestimated Hitler, but there was no way one could have foreseen the surprising events of the next few years. The purpose of *Like a Mighty Army* (1935) was to demonstrate that Nazism's war was not against Judaism only but against Protestantism and Catholicism also. In none of these books did Shuster claim that either Jews or Christians were free of blame, but with this work he began to cooperate more urgently with Jewish relief and become more insistent in his warnings to fellow

Catholics. His close friendship with Rabbi Stephen Wise and his cooperation with the American Jewish Committee dated from this time.

Shuster's defense was convincing to most. His writings over a period of at least twenty-five years had been overwhelmingly on the side of freedom and liberty—so much so that many of his co-religionists considered him too liberal—and opposed to all oppression and totalitarianism. His analysis of the German political situation in the early 1930s in many respects had been mistaken, but no more so than those of other equally respected commentators. If his attempts had irony or even humor, some of his remarks were clearly too flippant, although even those were written before the evil of Hitler's policies was fully evident. He had witnessed personally the Nazi take-over of Vienna in 1938 and the degradation inflicted on the Jews at that time, and he admitted that he could never view prejudice in the same light again. Shuster was confident that anyone viewing his overall record, both his writings and his other activities, would decide overwhelmingly in his favor. The Hunter faculty seemed to agree. More than three hundred letters and signatures of support and congratulation arrived at his office before his departure.[31]

If Shuster was pleased to be leaving behind much of this controversy when he departed New York in late June, he would certainly encounter more when he arrived in Bavaria. This time the controversy did not concern him but the mission itself. Of the three American states, Bavaria was clearly the most troublesome. It had one-half the population, one author suggested, but three-fourths of the problems.[32] Geographically, it was somewhat isolated from the rest of Germany by the Alps to the west and the highlands in the north and had often been allowed to go its separate way. Populated largely by peasants and farmers, and predominantly Roman Catholic, it remained conservative politically. Disliking the socialist policies emanating from Berlin between the wars, and even more so the Communist doctrines of Russia to the east, many Bavarians had preferred National Socialism. This isolationist, conservative, and even Nazi past would not make American reconstruction easier. As the same author noted, "Bavarians were proud of their ways and increasingly determined to maintain them."[33]

Much of Bavaria had been liberated by General George Patton's Third Army in the closing weeks of the war, and Patton was then named the area's first military governor. He served for six months, from April to October 1945, and like most other assignments he undertook, his governorship was controversial.[34] After almost six years of war in Europe, and with increasing revelations of Nazi atrocities, the major concern of American occupation policy was the removal of all Nazis from positions of influence and even the punishment of Germany for the horrors of World War II. Patton did not disagree with this policy, but he had an additional goal, and perhaps of greater priority: the halting of the Russians, whom he had come increasingly to despise, from any further expansion in central Europe. This stance also put him in some conflict with his military superior, General Dwight Eisenhower, Supreme Allied Commander, whose relations with his Russian counterpart, Marshal Georgi Zhukov, were good. When a Russian general during a joint visit to Berlin invited Patton for a drink, Patton reportedly ordered his protesting translator to respond word for word: "Tell that Russian sonuvabitch that from the way they're acting here I regard them as enemies and I'd rather cut my throat than have a drink with one of my enemies."[35] In selecting a civil government to work under the American military, Patton's staff asked for recommendations of Munich's Catholic archbishop, Cardinal Michael Faulhaber, and Protestant Bishop Hans Meiser. At least Faulhaber recommended Fritz Schaeffer, leader of the Bavarian Peoples' Party before 1933 whom the Nazis had imprisoned for a time, as minister-president, and Patton made the appointment. Schaeffer, a Catholic, appointed a government of prominent conservatives who may have been more concerned with checking the spread of Communism than with removing Nazi influence from public life. Schaeffer feared that wholesale removals of public officials would leave civic administration in chaos, but Eisenhower intervened and insisted that the denazification program must be implemented immediately. Eisenhower's patience was wearing thin; in late September Schaeffer was ordered replaced as minister-president by Wilhelm Hoegner, and a few days later Patton himself was replaced.[36]

With the departure of Patton, the Third Army relinquished its jurisdiction, and the Office of Military Government-Bavaria

(OMGB) was established, with General Walter Muller, Patton's long-time associate and Third Army Supply Officer, as first commander.[37] It was during Muller's tenure in Bavaria from October 1945 to November 1947 that American policy toward the reconstruction of Germany was formulated, often in conjunction with the other three occupying powers: complete disarmament and demilitarization, the removal of Nazi officials from positions of influence, the eradication of all Nazi laws and regulations, strict supervision of industrial growth, radical reform and democratization of the educational system, a policy of non-fraternization between the occupying and defeated peoples, and the gradual restoration of self-government under close American direction. Supreme Headquarters, Allied Expeditionary Forces (SHAEF), which coordinated the Western Allies' military activities in the European theater during the war, was superseded in 1945 by the Office of Military Government, United States (OMGUS), presided over successively by Eisenhower, McNarney, and Clay. From 1947 to 1949, Clay then served as both military governor of the American zone and as American representative on the four-power Allied Control Council (ACC), which met in Berlin to coordinate occupation policies.[38]

Significant steps toward the reconstruction of Bavaria were also made during Muller's tenure, but always at an agonizingly slow pace and amid public controversy. A new constitution was approved for Bavaria in the fall of 1946, the first state to have one, but only after an earlier draft had been disallowed by OMGUS because it gave the state too much autonomy and almost independence from the rest of Germany. The first elections were held that same year, and the Americans were gratified that so many of their earlier and temporary appointees emerged victorious. But denazification still remained most thorny. Many persons had joined the Nazi party (nominally) only to retain their civic jobs, as school teachers or postal workers, for example; the reviewing process was often long delayed because judges and other reviewing officials had not been cleared themselves and were temporarily suspended; some leading anti-Nazis were also Communists, and neither the Americans nor the Bavarian leaders were anxious to appoint them to public office; some officials remained in internment camps up to two years before their cases were heard, clearly "guilty until proven innocent"; and the delay in getting a civil administration in place and functioning was delaying the whole economic, political, and social reconstruction of the area. Progress continued to be made, but many saw the irony of channelling millions of dollars of Marshall Plan assistance to Germany while major delays in approving officials for important public and private employment continued to retard the nation's own economic recovery.[39]

The most significant advances in the reconstruction of postwar Germany took place under General Muller's successor, former Michigan governor Murray von Wagoner, from November 1947 to September 1949. During this period the major goals of the denazification program were accomplished; the new West German constitution or Basic Law was ratified in the spring of 1949, and the new Bonn government under Konrad Adenauer began operating; and, as a step toward civilian American presence in Germany, General Clay at that same time was succeeded as military governor by former Assistant Secretary of War, John J. McCloy. But problems continued, and Wagoner had more than his share of conflict. Reparations were still demanded, but there were always disagreements over precise amounts and dates due; the celebrated "Great Potato War" of late 1947 broke out when both the native population and the recently arrived Displaced Persons laid claim to the limited Bavarian potato crop; and the Bavarian civil service system—efficient but also entrenched and elitist—seemed immune to democratic reform. Many of these officials were Catholic, they had not been Nazi in their sympathies, and they felt the Americans had no right to interfere.[40]

Wagoner's most delicate challenge, however, was the reform of the educational system. In the German system, even before the Nazis took over, all children attended the same common schools for the first four grades. Some pupils, the more talented and often more wealthy, were then enrolled in college preparatory schools and the *Gymnasium*, and the others, the majority and often the poorer, were enrolled in trade schools and given vocational preparation. For American officials, this system was much too elitist. They urged free, compulsory, full-time education for all to the age of fifteen (vocational schooling was often only part-time); continued education, at least part-time, for all until the age of eighteen; high school education reorganized as general education, not exclusively college preparatory; greater opportunity for all to attend college; and university education required of all teachers, even elementary. German officials objected. They felt that all children were not equally talented and thus should not be given the same education, that college preparation and language classes should begin at approximately age ten, and that extending school years was unwise since young men were desperately needed in Germany's struggling industry. Cardinal Faulhaber objected that such strict regulations and requirements seemed to be interfering with the parents' right to control their children's education. It was pointed out, furthermore, that the objections of the Americans could be raised against similar school systems in other European democratic nations also. Finally, some Americans objected to the presence of "confessional" schools, state schools more or less exclusively for Catholic or Protestant youths, but this arrangement was allowed to stand.[41] The most serious frustration of Wagoner's administration was probably his inability to solve this educational conflict.

In this situation, the selection of George Shuster as Wagoner's successor had much to commend it. Shuster, first of all, was of German ancestry and fluent in German, was familiar with the German situation from his earlier visits, and had a deep respect for German culture and the German people. "I do know Munich and Bavaria very well, indeed," he had written in early 1950. "As a matter of fact, there is probably no single town in the country which I have not at some time visited."[42] Second, Shuster was Catholic, Bavaria was Catholic also, and many of the military government's conflicts had been with Catholic leaders, especially Shuster's long-time friend, Munich's Cardinal Faulhaber.[43] Third, Shuster was an educator, and a major disagreement concerned the reconstruction of the educational system. Fourth, Shuster had the almost ideal temperament for a position of conflict. A social and philosophical liberal, he was open to new ideas, was a good listener, and seldom became ruffled or lost control. And, finally, at least from his work on the Historical Commission, he was acquainted with both Robert Patterson and John McCloy, and they had confidence in him. McCloy later affirmed that he was especially impressed with Shuster as "a man of character," and perhaps he was conscious of the criticism of other officials assigned there. Shuster himself later lamented that they were too often "lechers, traffickers in women, manipulators of the black market, petty protagonists of illiteracy, and fools."[44]

By the time of Shuster's appointment, several important changes had taken place. McCloy had succeeded Clay as military governor in May 1949, and in September the whole administration switched from a military to a civilian operation: the Office of Military Government, United States (OMGUS) was changed to the High Commission for Germany (HICOG), and the headquarters were moved from Berlin to Frankfort, the military governor in Bavaria became the land (or state) commissioner, and final jurisdiction was transferred from the Defense Department (formerly War Department) to the State Department. When Wagoner resigned that September also, his assistant, Clarence Bolds, agreed to stay on as acting land commissioner until a successor could be appointed. McCloy returned to the United States the following spring and offered the position to Shuster. The Board of Higher Education agreed to give him a leave of absence for the 1950–51 academic year and appointed Dean Eleanor Grady acting president. Shuster presided at commencement ceremonies that spring, he and Doris made final preparations throughout that June, and they sailed from New York on Cunard Line's "Caronia" on June 30, along with Bing Crosby, whose autograph they collected on a July 4th menu. At twelve thousand dollars for the year, Shuster was taking a cut in salary, but money never seemed of special concern.[45]

An official government directive noted that the land commissioner "serves as principal representative of the High Commissioner and of the United States government in his Land . . . recommends action under the reserved powers to the High Commissioner . . . in cases of emergency where responsible German authorities are unable to maintain law and order, takes such steps as may be necessary to do so . . . and coordinates and supervises the execution of all U.S. or High Commission programs within the Land."[46] Shuster himself defined his assignment as "to serve as a kind of regent 'ex partibus infidelium,' "[47] and he was probably not far wrong. His responsibility was not to originate policy but to represent High Commissioner John McCloy and the American government in Bavaria and carry out their policies, to resolve sources of friction between the German people and the occupying forces, and to prepare for full German independence and self-government while maintaining close ties with the West.

Events on the other side of the globe, however, suddenly cast Bavarian concerns in a different light. On June 25, five days before the Shusters departed for Germany, North Korean troops invaded South Korea, the focus of the East-West confrontation suddenly shifted to the Korean War, and in November the flood of Chinese troops entering the conflict confirmed that it was a war the East was determined the West would not win. The war was especially ominous for West Germany. Like Korea, Germany was divided between East and West; like South Korea, West Germany feared an armed invasion from a Russian satellite, in this case, East Germany; but unlike South Korea, West Germany was demilitarized and, of itself, defenseless. Thus questions of the rearming of Germany, the subsequent integration of a German army into a European Defense Force, and the reconstruction of Germany's heavy industry, possibly coordinated with France in the Schuman Plan, took on much greater importance.[48]

Shuster arrived at McCloy's headquarters in Frankfort, on July 7, and met with McCloy the following afternoon. He attended his first staff conference with McCloy and other land commissioners on the eleventh, had dinner with McCloy on the twelfth, and attended his second staff conference on the eighteenth. He then left Frankfurt for Munich and officially assumed his duties as land commissioner for Bavaria, replacing Clarence Bolds, on July 18.[49]

The Shusters' personal residence in Munich, originally built by one of Hitler's cabinet ministers, was most comfortable—"the most desirable requisitioned house I ever saw in Munich with one exception," a former occupation official remarked.[50] McCloy was less reserved. "Here are some fleeting shots of your new home," he had written earlier. "I understand it was formerly occupied by the mistress of one of the most prominent Nazis in Bavaria, so I'm sure it is in exquisite taste."[51] Servants' quarters were on the third floor (with bath) and there were three family or guest bedrooms on second. The basement contained laundry and utility rooms, a "bier stube," and a projection room with an excellent 35-millimeter projector. The first floor contained ample living, cooking, and dining areas, and at one time at least six servants were in attendance. Such ostentation and display had been increasingly resented by the German people, and by the time of Shuster's arrival probably only two servants were provided. A pleasant garden and lawn were attached to the house, allowing George to indulge occasionally his love of flowers and allowing the family dachshund, Kleiner, additional freedom to roam. The home was sufficiently spacious for the formal entertaining the Shusters enjoyed so much and yet most comfortable also for quiet evenings alone, reading or listening to fine music.[52]

As noted, the office that George Shuster assumed that summer was not as important as the title land commissioner or state governor might imply. American policy toward Germany was formulated either in McCloy's office or in Washington, both far removed from Shuster's office in Munich, and the whole occupation structure of high commissioner and state governors was gradually being transformed toward the more regularized status of American ambassador and consuls, with more authority transferred to local German officials. On the other hand, the position of land commissioner was not without influence. Shuster was the intermediary between American policy-makers in Frankfurt and Washington and the recently elected Bavarian State government of Minister President Hans Ehard and the State Assembly or *Landrat* in Munich. He advised McCloy (and, through him, Washington) on conditions in Bavaria and on the concerns of the Bavarian government, and he was charged with implementing the policies McCloy forwarded. After five years Bavarians were becoming quite restless with continued American occupation, they felt that Germany had progressed sufficiently to be restored to full autonomy and independence, and disagreements and friction between Germans and Americans were to be expected. It was Shuster's responsibility to continue implementing American policy and to keep disagreements to a minimum. He corresponded frequently with McCloy and attended weekly staff conferences in Frankfurt, he kept in close contact with Minister President Ehard and other Bavarian officials in Munich, and he enjoyed touring the area and learning of conditions firsthand.[53]

Shuster addressed the people of Bavaria by radio, in German, within a week of his arrival. He began by apologizing that the radio reception might be poor in some areas, and he noted that the possibility of setting up a new and stronger frequency was already being considered by High Commissioner McCloy. The purpose of the address was to assure his listeners of his affection for the state of Bavaria and of his confidence in the goodness of the Bavarian people. "As far as my family relations are concerned," he noted, "let me say that my paternal grandmother descends from Bavaria and that my great-grandfather was one of those Germans who sought and found a new home in America in 1848."[54] He acknowledged that there were many who, "in the face of Gestapo and terror methods, were courageous enough to stand up against the Hitler regime and its false teachings." He mentioned by name several prominent Bavarians whom he had first met in the 1930s and whose memory he still cherished. He singled out three groups as "a great part of Germany's true pillars of liberty and human dignity: the workers' associations and trade unions, the churches—the Catholic as well as the Protestant church—and, partly, at least, the German universities," and he affirmed his confidence that Germany was now prepared to "share in the formation of a world which can economically, culturally and morally defy all forms of totalitarism [sic] and uphold liberty and human dignity."

One of the earliest, although certainly not among the most serious, controversies Shuster faced as land commissioner concerned hunting permits and the regulation of arms. It was American policy that Germany was to be totally disarmed during this postwar period, even to fowling pieces at times. On the humorous side, many Bavarians whose guns had been confiscated were overjoyed with the news of Shuster's appointment. As president of Hunter College, they thought he was director of a famous academy for hunters, a *Jaegerakademie*, and would be especially sympathetic to their petitions for a restoration of sporting arms and hunting permits.[55] Although the hunting laws were not significantly changed during Shuster's tenure, the whole context of discussion was altered. With the North Korean invasion of South Korea in June 1950, the threat of similar aggression in Europe loomed larger, America did an about-face and urged Germany to rearm militarily and join the NATO forces, and eventually this was accomplished.[56] A more frequent complaint concerned American occupation personnel, with guns, trespassing and hunting at will on private German property. Shuster recommended that limits be imposed and that compensation be granted the property owners, and he admitted also that the Americans at times were simply inexcusably unruly, as when soldiers on one occasion fired at the local game warden.[57]

Another early, and continuing, source of tension, over which Shuster had no control, was the shortage of coal. Bavarian porcelain, glass, and other industries needed coal. Bavaria mined little itself, and Shuster was constantly being presented with urgent requests and petitions.[58] Coal might be available from German mines outside Bavaria, but this internal trade was the responsibility of the German central government. Coal might also be imported from neighboring Czechoslovakia, but that country often demanded scrap iron in return and the Western Allies hesitated to approve the export of such potentially military materials. Although he had no direct jurisdiction in the area, Shuster was urged by the land government and Bavarian industrialists to use his influence with both the central government and higher American officials, and, although the problem continued to the end of Shuster's term, stop-gap remedies were generally found.[59] The land commissioner's position was often one of mediator, and this was the role Shuster filled best.

One of the important qualifications Shuster brought to his position as land commissioner was his wide experience in the field of education. The educational conflicts surfacing periodically during the Wagoner years did not become burning issues under Shuster, and the new land commissioner perhaps deserved major credit. The Bavarians had already accepted the denazification program, in both textbooks and in teaching personnel, and the principle of free public education for all, although in some places this might have to be implemented gradually. Continuing concerns were the use of public funds for religious or confessional schools, the inclusion of more social science courses in the curricula (for greater civic responsibility), university education for even primary education teachers, and the drill-mastering techniques emphasized in many German schools. Shuster handled these issues diplomatically. He assured the Bavarians that, whatever system worked best in America, the German confessional schools would not be touched.[60] The Germans were willing to accept courses in economics and political science in their curricula and to raise the requirements for teachers' licenses in the primary grades, and Shuster admitted that drill-mastering and memorization might be the better teaching methods in some subjects.[61] Almost all were in favor of increased student and teacher exchanges between Germany and the United States.[62] Bavaria's feisty minister of culture and education, Dr. Alois Hundhammer, later declared:

> When Professor Shuster came over to us, peace was soon restored between us and the occupation forces. We retained our confessional schools. When we discussed our new Bavarian constitution in 1946 I had already taken a firm, definite stand in favor of our confessional schools. At that time I was chairman of my party [Christian Social Union] in the *Landtag* and had a strong influence on the committee in charge of the draft of the constitution. So with the arrival of Dr. Shuster, our school troubles were settled.[63]

The American denazification program continued to be a source of some tension. Within a month of his arrival in Munich, Shuster received a letter from the high commissioner's office requesting information on the progress of the denazification program so far.[64] The goal was clear—to assure that the hated Nazi doctrines of Aryan supremacy and state domination no longer permeated German society—but one of the means employed, the barring of former Nazis from public office, was difficult to apply. Many persons with experience in public life had held civic office during the Nazi era, maybe as school teachers or postal clerks, and had registered as party members only to retain their jobs and livelihoods. Many of these were now barred from office, whatever their current views toward Nazism might be.[65] The denazification program had also been placed in the hands of German agencies, and German courts and many Americans felt that these were too lax.

Shuster's reply to the high commissioner's question has not been found, if he felt qualified to reply at all that early in office, but his view was moderate. He was convinced that most confirmed Nazi officials had already been discovered and barred from office by 1950 and that the cases still pending involved mainly nominal party members. He was in favor of returning more local decision-making to German departments and courts, even if some minor abuses might result. There were, of course, isolated disagreements over individual officials whom the American occupation forces wanted removed and the Bavarian government wanted to retain, but the denazification program in Bavaria during Shuster's tenure generally proceeded without major incident.[66]

Another source of occasional tension was the decartelization program. American occupation policy was to bring greater political and economic democracy to Germany after years of Nazi rule, and in the economic sphere, this meant breaking up some of the larger monopolies and cartels, both to limit war-making capacity and to make trades and professions more accessible to all citizens. As in education, the goal was to make German trades and professions less elitist. The responsibility of the Bavarian Decartelization Department was a heavy one, complaints were numerous, and procedures were complex. In most cases, as Minister President Ehard explained to Shuster, investigations had to be made into the "formation of prices and costs, marketing systems, and organization of sale as well as into terms of payment, business and delivery."[67] Even in his last full month in office, November 1951, Shuster was investigating, at the insistence of McCloy, charges that the Bavarian Chamber of Pharmacists had been granted too broad authority to limit access into the pharmaceutical profession.[68]

Probably the most troublesome source of conflict coming before Shuster during these years—troublesome because it was most frequent, had deeply upsetting consequences in the lives of the citizens, and was often left to Shuster's own decision—concerned the requisitioning of private homes and lands for occupation use. Private residences and office space, often the best the area had to offer, were requisitioned by American officials, and if this created serious hardship for individual families or businesses, it was considered no more than an unfortunate consequence of war. But by 1950 the war had been over for five years, Germany had been restored to some degree of political and economic stability, and yet the requisitioning of Bavarian property continued. The problem was especially acute because more and more refugees were arriving from the Communist-dominated East and lodging had to be provided for them also. Bishop Aloisius Muench, the Vatican's representative in West Germany and former bishop of Fargo, North Dakota, was especially concerned about the moral climate of postwar Germany and alluded to this problem in one of his annual reports to the American bishops:

> In Bavaria, whose population was increased by 33 per cent through the influx of expellees and refugees, there is a lack of 650,000 homes; approximately 125,000 couples in Bavaria must live apart for lack of even a room; in all West Germany there are about 335,000 such married couples.[69]

In this situation, American occupation of the already greatly over-extended facilities could only add to the aggravation. In meeting after meeting Shuster reminded HICOG officials that this was a continuing and major obstacle to friendlier German-American relations, but the problem was far from easing.[70] With the outcome of the war in Korea uncertain in the fall of 1950, additional American troops were assigned to Germany to prevent similar aggression there. Shuster reluctantly notified Minister President Ehard: "In order to obtain the facilities necessary to accommodate new troop units, we shall have to ask that certain installations now under US Army requisition, but housing residual displaced persons, be evacuated and made available for army use. The Office of the United States High Commissioner has instructed that the following properties be evacuated by November 1, 1950: . . .".[71] As the troop build-up continued, Shuster found it necessary to approve the requisitioning of more land—for a new military base, an addition to base facilities, a shooting range, a more effective radio tower, and so on.[72] When the army requested additional facilities for carrying out its responsibilities, it was difficult for Shuster to decline. Occasionally he did, however, or demanded at least a reconsideration.[73]

The majority of the conflicts concerned houses that had been requisitioned for three, four, or five years, and which the original families now wanted returned so that they could begin their lives anew. Bishop Muench forwarded one case of an elderly couple whose house had been taken from them in 1946 and who had been living in a poorly equipped garden house since then. Their health was not good, the bishop noted, the gentleman froze his leg during one winter, theirs was the only house in town still requisitioned, and, in fact, it was only sporadically utilized by the Americans.[74] Shuster had the case investigated and replied to McCloy that, although the situation as the bishop described it was essentially true, the house was still needed. It was being utilized by army intelligence, different personnel did use the facility from time to time, and the house could be empty during intervals. Despite the serious hardship to the owner, Shuster agreed that switching sites for intelligence operations at this time would not be in the best interests of occupation goals.[75]

Other petitions, of course, were less serious. Official regulations forbade any alterations in requisitioned houses that would be a liability when returned to the original owner, and one owner protested when the occupation officials installed an additional bathroom in her home. It was decided that this enhanced rather than reduced the value of the home and was thus approved.[76] Another owner was granted permission to continue to harvest fruit growing on his property even though the house had been requisitioned and was being occupied by American personnel.[77] Through it all, Shuster kept his sense of humor. He reported at one staff conference that he had made a short radio broadcast on July 4 on the significance of that day, "and I received one piece of fan-mail—in the form of a telegram in honor of Independence Day, 'As a result of listening to your speech, I now request you to give me back my house which has been requisitioned.'"[78]

The heart-rending refugee problem involved much more than housing. Millions of displaced persons and expellees were seeking asylum in West Germany, two-fifths of them in Bavaria, and the issue was unfortunately further complicated by the fact that many were Jewish and not always welcomed by the local population. Others were suspected of being Communist infiltrators attempting to foment opposition and discontent.[79] Shuster himself was continually concerned with this tragedy—forwarding official directives, requisitioning living space, mediating conflicts, and attempting to unravel questions of legitimate or illegitimate immigration.[80] Mrs. Shuster became directly involved also, adopting the crisis as a personal concern. Within two months of her arrival in Munich, she called a meeting at her home of officers of the German-American Women's Club and of various other local women's organizations. She noted that the refugee problem needed serious attention, that the needs of children were especially urgent, and that their long-range goal should not be direct relief but rather methods of helping the refugees help themselves.[81] At a second meeting less than a month later the group considered various programs for possible adoption: recreation homes for refugee mothers (and others) needing relaxation but unable to afford it; sewing gatherings of both German and American women; parties and special festivities for youths and the elderly living in institutions; and a traveling lending library for the institutionalized.[82] For the group's third meeting, held again at the Shuster residence, State Secretary for Refugees Dr. Wolfgang Jaenicke was present, and he approved the goals the committee had adopted. The group, eventually named the Good Neighbor Committee, organized itself into teams of one German, one American, and one refugee to visit the approximately twenty-five refugee camps in the Munich area and decide how best to inaugurate the projects.[83] The committee implemented its projects and sponsored a well-publicized Good Neighbor Week in the summer of 1951 both to raise funds for continuing works and to demonstrate, through combined social, cultural, and athletic events, increased harmony between Germans and Americans. In the mayor's official proclamation Mrs. Shuster was given special credit.[84]

Policy questions and crises were not the only concerns that crossed the land commissioner's desk, and much of Shuster's time was occupied with more or less routine administrative duties, some more challenging and satisfying than others. He made a weekly trip to Frankfurt for a staff conference with Commissioner McCloy and the other American land commissioners, and this was generally followed by lunch and often a private appointment with McCloy to discuss uniquely Bavarian concerns.[85] Back in Munich Shuster held regular meetings with his own staff, the heads of the various divisions he controlled—economic affairs, political affairs, legal affairs, labor affairs, intelligence, public affairs, and field operations. In the Field Operations Division, a United States Resident Officer was assigned to each county or *Kreis*; these officers submitted periodic reports to Shuster on activities in their jurisdictions and met with the land commissioner as need arose. Most questions, of course, were handled through routine correspondence. Shuster met frequently with Minister President Ehard and members of his cabinet and staff and found occasions to travel throughout Bavaria, both to meet local German officials and to be seen by the local populace. Shuster was accomplished in public relations, and he met frequently with both German and American reporters. There were dinners and other social events to attend, and often to sponsor, but the Shusters had become accustomed to these at Hunter and they generally found them both relaxing and enjoyable. During his eighteen months in Bavaria, Shuster apparently returned to the United States only once, for a few weeks in the early summer of 1951, chiefly to fulfill a few responsibilities at Hunter and meet with various government officials in Washington.[86]

But even Shuster's daily administrative routine involved the mediation of ever-emerging disagreements, often relatively minor but always time-consuming. Anti-government and anti-American posters appeared periodically, often at times of political unrest, and the land commissioner had to decide which were acceptable and which to be confiscated. Communist-inspired parades and demonstrations were monitored also.[87] The city of Bamberg opposed the reconstruction of a bridge which the American forces considered necessary and this controversy continued for several months.[88] Some issues, at least in retrospect, must have brought a smile to Shuster's face: he got into a disagreement with a local bishop over how long bells should ring at a local festival; he heard complaints that American fishing was denuding Bavarian streams of trout; and he had to intervene to assure that local licensing practices were not too severely curtailing hog production.[89] Other issues were deeply personal: requests of Americans to marry native Germans; applications to adopt German children; and jurisdiction over paternity suits lodged against American service-men.[90] As Cold War tensions between East and West increased during the Korean War, there were incidents along the border separating Bavaria from Czechoslovakia and even an occasional shooting.[91] The State elections in the fall of 1950 were trouble-some but Shuster was powerless to assist. The conservative Christian Social Union of Minister President Ehard won sixty-four seats, but the rival Social Democratic Party won sixty-three, with seventy-seven others scattered among three remaining parties. The brilliant but authoritarian Dr. Alois Hundhammer insisted upon the Ministry of Culture but the Social Democrats would not accept a coalition with him. Shuster kept the high com-missioner informed as negotiations progressed, and eventually a CSU-SPD coalition was established, with Hundhammer sitting out and joining the opposition.[92] The establishment of a stable and effective state government was of particular concern to

Shuster because another of his responsibilities throughout 1951 was the gradual reduction in American personnel in preparation for transferring more and more responsibility to local officials and reducing the land commissioner's office to the status of a Bavarian consulate. This project was completed under his immediate successor, Professor Oron Hale.[93]

When Shuster finally left the land commissionership in December 1951, after an extension of six months from his original agreement, it was with a sense of satisfaction. The assignment had been fraught with difficulties and controversies—differing American and German views of democracy, conflicts with Bavaria's Catholic hierarchy, resentment over America's continuing occupation—but Shuster had managed to keep them to a minimum and had brought the occupation well along toward its goal of final withdrawal. His contributions were widely recognized. The mayor of Kulmbach wrote favorably to President Truman, and Bishop Muench recalled another tribute and then added: "What the writer says about the warm place you have made for yourself in the hearts of Bavarians corroborates what I have repeatedly heard about you and your outstanding work in Land Bavaria."[94] Commissioner McCloy, Oron Hale, Shuster's deputy and successor, and French statesman Jean Monnet all praised his work.[95] Later judgments have not differed. Harold Zink, former chief historian for HICOG declared in 1957 that "the outstanding *Land* commissioner was Dr. George N. Shuster who was loaned by Hunter College where he served as President to fill the post in Bavaria," and twenty years later Edward Peterson stated in *The American Occupation of Germany* that "one could regret that America sent so few administrators with Shuster's qualifications and that five years of the occupation passed before he could be used. . . . He has since been praised by all as the ideal representative."[96]

When Shuster returned to Hunter College in December 1951, his interest in Germany in no way subsided. In fact, it was only intensified from his firsthand acquaintance with Germany's serious problems but also extraordinary potential. "I do not think the average German has grasped the essential issues in the world about him," Shuster commented shortly before his return. "He is confused by Russian propaganda, as well as our attempts to retaliate against that propaganda and the average German has thus been unable to formulate his own position in his own mind."[97] Shuster found ways almost immediately to help improve U.S.–German relations, to clarify American policy for the German people, and to help educate Americans on the dangers and opportunities existing in Central Europe, and many of his efforts were channelled through the American Council on Germany.

The American Council on Germany might have been a distant successor of the Loyal Americans of German Descent. Founded by Shuster and others in July 1941, this earlier organization sought to demonstrate the opposition of the majority of German-Americans to Nazism and Nazi aggression, to profess loyalty to American principles as World War II approached, and to help deter others from support of Adolf Hitler. The timing was significant. Hitler had assumed power in Germany in 1933, the American Nazi Party had been founded in 1935, and Germany had unexpectedly invaded the Soviet Union in June 1941, leading some anti-Communist Americans to side with Nazi Germany. Robert Wagner, Jr., New York state assemblyman and future mayor of New York, was president of the new organization and Shuster chairman of the board of directors.[98]

Over the next twelve months the organization, usually in the person of Shuster, sent telegrams of support to President Roosevelt, distanced itself from Charles Lindbergh and others opposed to American policy, and issued other public statements of loyalty. But with American entrance into the war in December 1941—and with Americans of German background like Dwight Eisenhower, Chester Nimitz, Carl Spaatz, and Walter Krueger leading that fight—the loyalty of German-Americans was rarely questioned, and the organization gradually faded from existence.[99]

Plans for the formation of the American Council on Germany were begun in early 1952, shortly after Shuster returned from Bavaria, and he committed himself to serve as president that April.[100] The council's stated goals, drafted by Christopher Emmet, the executive vice president and actual founder of the organization, were the dissemination of information on America to the people of Germany, the dissemination of information on

Germany to the people here, sponsorship of visits of prominent Germans to the United States, and circulation of articles by members of the council itself. Eventually General Lucius Clay was recruited to serve as honorary chairman, Mrs. John McCloy served as vice president, and Russell Bourne, Dr. James Conant, Professor Carl Friedrich, Father John LaFarge, S.J., and publisher Henry Regnery were among the members.[101]

The council remained true to its objectives. From 1952 to 1953 it circulated materials to assure the German people of continuity in American foreign policy, even with the change of parties after the election of Dwight Eisenhower; it publicized the qualifications of Dr. James Conant of Harvard as McCloy's successor in Germany; and it helped sponsor visits of Chancellor Konrad Adenauer and Berlin Mayor Ernst Reuter to the United States.[102] In 1955 the council supplied its counterpart in Germany, the *Atlantik-Bruecke* (Atlantic Bridge), with explanations of American foreign policy during the bombardment of the off-shore islands of Matsu and Quemoy by the People's Republic of China.[103] Public controversy broke out in late 1957 when former State Department official George Kennan suggested, in the Reith Lectures over the British Broadcasting Corporation, that the United States should disengage itself from some of its worldwide commitments, even if that meant that some countries might then drift into the Communist orbit. Former Secretary of State Dean Acheson responded heatedly that any such disengagement and return to isolationism would simply be a reversion to the mistakes of the post–World War I years, and the American Council on Germany, although slightly apprehensive about jeopardizing its non-political, tax-exempt status, helped publicize Acheson's assurances in Europe.[104]

The most significant of the council's activities, however, were accomplished through the generous and continued assistance of the Ford Foundation. Shuster was already well known to Foundation officials, and he had been hired early in 1952 as a consultant on a project for funding refugee assistance in Germany.[105] Beginning in 1955 Shuster, as president of the American Council on Germany, applied for and received almost yearly grants to assist the council's projects. That first year the Foundation granted the council five thousand dollars to sponsor a study of democratic institutions in Germany, and the following year seventy-five hundred dollars to defray travel expenses for American and Japanese scholars to attend an international conference near Bonn on Soviet political and economic policies.[106] In 1958 the council was awarded grants of four thousand dollars to sponsor a visit to the United States by Berlin Mayor Willy Brandt, and twenty-three thousand dollars to establish a summer institute in Munich for young American and Western European students to study Soviet policies.[107]

The American Council on Germany and the Ford Foundation also cooperated in sponsoring six American-German conferences, held almost alternately in the United States and Germany from 1959 to 1970.[108] The first conference, held in Bad Godesberg in 1959 and co-sponsored by the *Atlantik-Bruecke*, was a striking success. The American delegation included three senators, three congressmen, and leading diplomats Dean Acheson, John McCloy, and James Conant. On the German side, President Heinrich Luebke and Chancellor Adenauer attended the opening session and Berlin Mayor Willy Brandt was a member of the official delegation. The meeting was front-page news in the *New York Times* for two days.[109] The second conference, held in Washington in mid-February 1961, was addressed by both Secretary of State Dean Rusk and German Foreign Minister Heinrich von Brentano and gave the German representatives an opportunity to meet, both formally and informally, with officials of the new Kennedy administration. The timing of the third conference, mid-November 1962, again in Germany, was equally important. Premier Khrushchev had renewed Soviet threats toward Berlin after his capitulation in the Cuban missile crisis that October, and the presence of General Clay, former Secretary of State Christian Herter, and former Ambassador to Germany James Conant in Berlin helped confirm America's resolve not to withdraw. The fourth conference was held again in Berlin in 1964, the fifth in Washington in 1967, and the sixth in Bonn in 1970.[110] By 1970, however, Shuster had been living away from New York and the headquarters of the American Council on Germany for ten years; his health, at age seventy-six, was beginning to fail; and he was taking a much less active part in council programs and affairs.

A final cooperative effort between Shuster and the Ford Foundation, this time without the involvement of the American Council on Germany, greatly benefited the Free University of

Berlin. The original and respected University of Berlin, founded by the famed Wilhelm von Humboldt in 1810, was claimed after the war exclusively by Soviet authorities, who insisted that it was an institution of the province of Brandenberg (the Soviet zone) rather than the city of Berlin (under joint Allied administration). The majority of buildings were in the Soviet sector of Berlin also. Dialectical materialism and anti-American propaganda permeated the institution's teaching, and early protests by students accomplished nothing. In the spring of 1948, however, three students had been dismissed from the school for anti-Soviet activities and they appealed to the American authorities to set up another university where a freer exchange of ideas could take place. American Cultural Advisor Herman Wells was supportive and General Clay, although apprehensive about increasing East-West tensions, gave his approval. American officials allocated several rooms for early administrative work, a call went out for donations of books, and growing numbers of students and professors expressed a willingness to defect from the older University of Berlin, now called Humboldt University. Classes opened that fall for approximately two thousand students, but the future was still uncertain.[111]

Prospects brightened considerably in July 1951 when the Ford Foundation approved a grant of $1,309,500 to the Free University for construction of a combined library, lecture hall, and student dining building and for inaugurating an extension service.[112] When this work was completed, Ford Foundation officials in 1954 decided to hire a consultant to study and report on this earlier grant and evaluate the potential of the whole university. Shepard Stone of the Ford Foundation explained the selection of George Shuster:

> The choice of Dr. Shuster was based on the fact that he is highly respected and widely recognized in Germany, where as a scholar and diplomat he had previously made a deep impression. His performance as Land Commissioner of Bavaria under High Commissioner McCloy was outstanding. His knowledge of German universities is extensive. He speaks German fluently. Moreover, here at home he enjoys a solid reputation.[113]

A grant of ten thousand dollars was made available, the Board of Higher Education approved his absence from Hunter for the necessary two months, and George and Doris prepared to leave for Germany shortly after Christmas of 1955.[114]

Shuster spent most of January and February of 1956 in Berlin, and he submitted a thorough report to the Ford Foundation on his return.[115] He found the buildings and physical facilities of the institution adequate, but the science laboratories needed upgrading and further expansion would soon be necessary. He had high praise for the university rectors but admitted that the practice of changing almost every year, allowing each rector to continue scholarly research, rendered continuity difficult. Student enrollment provided the greatest challenge. Increased interest in job-related fields like engineering seemed to reduce the importance of the Free University, whose strength was in the humanities, but almost one-third of the institution's eight thousand students still came from the East and the opportunity for beneficial influence on them was unique. The faculty was satisfactory but aging, and the university had to attract highly qualified professors from West Germany and also educate future faculty itself. Despite such shortcomings, Shuster concluded that the university possessed an unusual opportunity to counter Eastern European influence and deepen Western and democratic principles in Germany and thus its humanistic education deserved to be strengthened.

Shuster made several recommendations.[116] First, he recommended the construction of a *Studentendorf* or "student village" near the university where students from a distance (especially the East) could find not only lodging but, more important, guidance and intellectual exchange and comraderie. Second, he recommended the establishment of two professorships to attract highly qualified and German-speaking professors from the United States each year. Two research fellowships to enable younger German scholars to study in the United States each year should be established also. Third, a new building was needed for the *Osteuropa-Institut*, the East European Institute, a center for the study of Russian and East European affairs strategically centered in Berlin. Fourth, Shuster recommended an annual grant of thirty-five thousand dollars for additional library resources. Finally, he listed a series of smaller and miscellaneous grants that, while not essential, would still be most beneficial.

The Ford Foundation accepted several of Shuster's recommendations and, during a visit of President Theodor Heuss to the United States in 1958, surprised and honored the statesman with a gift of one million dollars to the Free University in his name. The money was to be utilized over a five-year period to upgrade the tutorial system in a newly constructed student village, to promote faculty and student exchange programs with the United States, to expand research and training in several affiliated institutes, and otherwise to assist various international programs.[117] Shuster was justly pleased. "The Foundation is grateful to you for the advice you gave in connection with the grant to the Free University," one official wrote. "As you know, your report was the basic factor which led to our positive decision."[118] Shuster was also appointed to a three-person advisory committee to be of assistance to the university in carrying out the terms of the grant, and a grateful institution later that year bestowed on him the Honorary Citizen Award of the Free University of Berlin.[119]

This award from the Free University was only one of several he received in recognition of his many contributions. In 1951, during his months as land commissioner, he was given Student Honorary Membership at the University of Munich; in 1955 he was awarded the Great Gold Medal of the Republic of Austria; that same year the Great Cross of the West German Federal Republic; and in 1957 the Austro-Hungarian Mariazell Medal. In 1962 he was given the Columbus Gessellschaft Medal from the city of Munich, and he was made an Honorary Citizen of Munich ten years later.[120] Shuster at times seemed indifferent to honors and awards but, after earlier criticism of his views regarding Germany, he must have been grateful indeed for these marks of appreciation and recognition from German-speaking peoples for his years of effort on their behalf.

9

UNESCO:
CONFLICT AND PROMISE

One of the most significant achievements of the General
Advisory Committee of the State Department's Division of Cultural Relations, of which Shuster was a member from 1941 to
1944, was, ironically, to prepare for its own demise. The purpose
of this committee had been "to advise the [State] Department,
through the Division of Cultural Relations, on general policy in
the planning and execution of the program of cultural relations"
with other countries, chiefly in the fields of travel and study
grants, faculty and student exchange programs, and the sharing of
library and other informational resources.[1] Throughout 1943 the
committee discussed the need for the educational and cultural
reconstruction of Europe (and other areas) after the war—
libraries and museums were being destroyed, works of art had
been stolen, and funding for education clearly would be scarce—
and in early 1944 it urged the United States to join with other
nations in meeting this challenge:

> In particular the Committee would give special emphasis to
> the recommendation that the United States Government establish
> as an ultimate goal the creation of and full participation in "a per-
> manent international agency for educational and cultural relations,
> within the framework of such world-wide organization of nations
> as may be effected."
> As an immediate step the Advisory Committee recommends
> that the United States Government cooperate in the creation of a
> United Nations provisional commission on educational and cul-
> tural reconstruction and that as soon as created it assume member-
> ship therein.[2]

State Department officials were already discussing the establishment of such a postwar organization, and of American

257

participation in it, and the planning of the General Advisory Committee was at least temporarily curtailed until it was evident what the outcome of those discussions might be. The committee was not reappointed for the 1944–45 year and, in fact, did not meet again.[3]

Discussion of such an organization had been taking place on several levels. The Conference of Allied Ministers of Education (CAME), meeting in London in the fall of 1943, had recommended such a step and had called a second meeting for April 1944 to discuss it further. The League of Nations' International Institute of Intellectual Cooperation, several national governments, and even the fledgling United Nations Organization were also discussing preliminary plans, and finally, in mid-July 1945, the new Labour Government in Great Britain announced that a meeting to plan or establish such a body would be held in London that fall.[4] In late October Shuster was appointed an official advisor to the United States delegation.[5]

The timing once again could hardly have been worse. World War II had finally ended (the Japanese had surrendered on August 14) but the WAVES would be occupying the Bronx campus of Hunter College for one more semester. Shuster had recently returned from three months in Europe as chairman of the War Department's Historical Commission to interview the defeated Nazi leaders, and Robert Hutchins's Commission on Freedom of the Press was beginning to draft its final report. But Shuster was deeply interested in international cultural and educational exchange, he was convinced that he had solid contributions to make, and he immediately accepted the appointment.[6]

The scheduling, however, was too tight. Shuster's sinus condition had flared up. In fact, he had declined the assignment to Austria that spring because of it, and it had been aggravated by his recent flights to and around Europe for the Historical Commission. This time he decided that he had to go by boat.[7] But a series of meetings was scheduled for the American delegation in Washington for late October, and the conference was to open in London on November 1; there was clearly no allowance for a boat trip across the Atlantic. Shuster attended the meetings with close to twenty other members of the American delegation in Washington on October 26 and 27 to discuss the general purpose and goals of the new organization and the draft constitution then in circulation.[8] While others prepared to fly to London in the following two days, Shuster returned to New York; on November 1 he sailed on the SS *Argentina*.[9] With ships arriving from Europe daily, bringing U.S. military personnel home after the war, it was not difficult to select a ship leaving for Europe at a convenient time. But Shuster did miss the first week of the conference and arrived in London only in time for meetings on November 8.[10]

Although Shuster was only an advisor to the American delegation and took full part only in meetings of the American commission before and after the official conference sessions, he had to have been pleased with the conference results. With all the opportunities for major and even irreconcilable disagreements among the participants, and with the obstinacy of the Soviet Union in boycotting the conference entirely, the fact that the organization was established at all was a major accomplishment. UNESCO was to be both a governmental and a non-governmental organization—only national governments could be members of UNESCO but each country also had to have a National Commission with both government and private representatives, and these National Commissions were to help select and advise the official national delegates.[11] The constitution adopted in London vacillated somewhat on the question of the new organization's responsibility toward world peace, but such vacillation was probably necessary. Article I stated that the "purpose of the Organization is to contribute to peace and security," while the Preamble cited as objectives both "international peace and . . . the common welfare of mankind."[12] Shuster agreed that peace was essential, but so also was the furtherance of culture and education—"the common welfare of mankind"—even if peace were not in danger. The delegates also discussed the new organization's responsibility for rebuilding the educational and cultural facilities of war-torn countries, but the American position remained firm that UNESCO must not become primarily a relief agency, that such postwar rebuilding efforts could best be undertaken by specifically relief and reconstruction agencies, and that UNESCO must never lose sight of its longer-range goal of international educational and cultural exchange.[13] In daily meetings of the American delegation, Shuster emphasized the need for American assistance in the reconstruction of these educational programs in Europe and Asia, but he also agreed that UNESCO was not the proper vehicle. He also saw the need for large contributions from private sources in the United States, and in fact, over the next fifteen years he would be instrumental in directing several Ford Foundation awards to precisely this purpose.[14] Finally, the London Conference also added the world "Scientific" to the organization's official title, "United Nations Educational, Scientific and Cultural Organization," in part because international organizations of scientists had already achieved a commendable degree of cooperation on which to build, and also because the dropping of the two atomic bombs on Japan three months earlier seemed to make scientific cooperation and harmony much more urgent.[15]

Despite disagreements among the various national delegations, Assistant Secretary of State William Benton proudly emphasized the conference's three major accomplishments in his final report. First, the *Constitution* for this agency of international educational, scientific, and cultural understanding and cooperation had been overwhelmingly and enthusiastically approved. Second, Paris, long a center of international intellectual and cultural achievement, was selected as the new organization's permanent home. And third, a smaller preparatory commission had been established—and it had begun meeting the very day the plenary conference adjourned—to begin preparing an agenda for the new organization's first meeting the following year, and also to study both the wartime destruction and the educational and cultural reconstruction needs of the various member nations. "I believe it would be a mistake for us in the Department to minimize the potential significance of UNESCO," Benton wrote. "True, it may not reach the stratosphere. But the hopes of millions of people are centered in it."[16] Shuster's own evaluation was equally positive. "It seems to me that this delegation did what it was supposed to, and incidentally enjoyed doing it," he wrote Benton. "This should be a real feather in your cap."[17] Delegation Chairman Archibald MacLeish praised Shuster's contributions also:

Dear George:
I think I am to see you in a day or two when I shall have a chance to tell you how grateful I am to you for what you did in London. This must serve until then to say that I have thought often of the new and

fresh and affirmative point of view you brought to the discussions of the Delegation and the strength it gave us all to know that you were there and that you felt as you did.[18]

One of the first responsibilities to be faced after the American delegation returned from London was the establishment of a United States National Commission for UNESCO. The UNESCO *Constitution* was intentionally vague, stipulating only that the national commissions were to include both government and non-government representatives, that they should be consulted before the nation's UNESCO delegates were chosen, that they were to serve as advisors to both governments and national UNESCO delegations, and that they were to serve as "agencies of liaison" between UNESCO and its various constituencies.[19] Much of the discussion concerned the size of the commission since the larger the membership, the more representative the commission might be, but also the more cumbersome and less efficient. The method of selection was debated also. Some feared that if the State Department chose the members, the commission might be too subservient, almost an adjunct of the State Department, and not sufficiently represent the scholarly and educational community. Others felt that scholarly professional organizations were too numerous, too diverse, and perhaps too fraught with vested interests to acquit the responsibility efficiently.[20] Shuster had at first feared too much government control, but apparently came to the conclusion over time that other methods were just not practical.[21] When James Marshall of the American Association for an International Office for Education wrote to ask his support for a procedure of less government influence, Shuster declined:

> I have read your letter with great interest and am sorry that I still feel that the machinery you outline is too cumbersome to work. This may not be true but you will have to forgive me for thinking that it is. I do not, of course, wish to oppose any views that you may have on the matter but would appreciate it if you did not associate me with them. Perhaps I can be converted slowly, but at the moment I am deep in heresy.[22]

As congressional debate continued into the summer, Shuster telegraphed his own opinion to Senator James Murray:

Experience indicates education best served by authorizing Department of State to designate members of cultural commissions. I sincerely believe this the best policy also for UNESCO National Commission. Public pressure by organizations of great prestige surely adequate to correct possible mistakes and oversights by Department. Other method too cumbersome.[23]

The method eventually agreed upon was a compromise and Shuster found it agreeable—or at least he expressed no criticism at the time. The membership of the commission was set at one hundred, with sixty nominated by various educational, professional, and religious groups, and the other forty appointed by the State Department as federal, state, and local government and "at large" representatives. This was provided by congressional law of July 30. In early September Shuster was selected as one of the Department of State appointees.[24]

The work of the commission began immediately. One of its major responsibilities was to advise the State Department in the selection of delegates to the UNESCO General Conference and, since UNESCO's first conference was already scheduled for November, no time could be lost. In his letters of appointment Assistant Secretary Benton asked each member of the national commission to submit five names for possible selection, and he also scheduled the first meeting of the National Commission for September 23.[25] At the close of that September meeting the State Department selected its ten-member delegation to the Paris conference. The five voting members were Assistant Secretary Benton, former Assistant Secretary Archibald MacLeish, Arthur Compton of the University of Washington, Anne O'Hare McCormick of the *New York Times*, and George D. Stoddard of the University of Illinois. The five non-voting members were former Office of Price Administration head (and former Benton business partner) Chester Bowles, Milton Eisenhower of Kansas State University, Charles Johnson of Fisk University, Anna Rosenberg of the Office of War Mobilization and Reconversion, and George Shuster.[26] Shuster at first hesitated to accept, concerned whether a representative of the Catholic educational system might not be better. "What troubles me about the situation is that I am sure the Catholic education group would not feel that I represented it. Of course there is no opposition to me but rather a frank sincere feeling of friendship. In their view, however, I am totally outside their own educational system and so not representative."[27] The State Department, however, remained with its initial choice.

The Paris meeting, UNESCO's first General Conference, was almost a microcosm of the organization's whole existence—successful in some areas, unsuccessful in others, and controversial in most. On the positive side, the American delegation was highly respected and its lead was followed by many on key issues, and, most important, the fundamental goals of the organization—peace, security, and international educational and cultural understanding—did not get sidetracked or lost under a plethora of petty nationalistic concerns. Even the budget conformed to American desires, except that on two occasions directives arrived late from Washington and Benton was unsuccessful in reversing provisions he had earlier accepted.[28] On the negative side, the conference was much more political than the Americans anticipated, with both France and Great Britain apparently hoping to recover through UNESCO some of the prestige and world stature they had lost through the war. The British campaigned hard for a British director-general and, once they were successful, for an increased budget for his use. France, already successful in locating UNESCO headquarters in Paris, sought to fill staff positions with French employees and link UNESCO procedures more directly to French agencies, the French franc, and so on. Benton later admitted that, although the American delegation represented scholarly and cultural interests well, it was probably weak in political and diplomatic expertise.[29]

The major controversy of the conference concerned the election of England's Julian Huxley as first director-general. Huxley was a scientist and author of international reputation, and Great Britain, because UNESCO had developed from recommendations of the Conference of Allied Ministers of Education in London, felt it merited the first director-general. The American delegation strongly opposed Huxley, in part because he had almost no administrative experience and in part because of his outspoken atheistic views. MacLeish, on the other hand, called him a "deeply religious man who has not yet found God."[30]

Unfortunately, the Americans could not agree on a candidate of their own. Some preferred Archibald MacLeish, a writer of international reputation, fluent in French, and head of the

American delegation to the London conference the year before, but Shuster and others were not confident of his practical judgment. "Archibald MacLeish is a very fine chap," Shuster had written earlier that summer, "but, having been associated with him on a number of occasions, I feel that his ideas are so nebulous and his ability to grasp reality so limited that it would be a mistake to commit so important a business as America's share in the work of UNESCO to him."[31] The State Department candidate was Francis Biddle, former attorney general and a judge at the Nuremberg trials, but even in the American delegation several opposed him as too political and almost unknown in the international educational and scholarly community.[32] With no other truly viable candidate, the election then went to Huxley almost by default, but the Americans were at least successful in limiting this first term to two rather than six years.[33]

Shuster's own evaluation of the conference was positive. He agreed that the American delegation had been well chosen and had been highly respected by other delegations, especially those of Holland, Belgium, China, and Czechoslovakia. He thought the greatest achievement of the conference had been the successful linking of the twin goals of freedom of information and service to peace, and the emphasis these two were given in conference deliberations. On the negative side, the American delegates probably met too much among themselves and not enough with other delegations ("perhaps we spent too much time going into huddles and trying quarterback sneaks," he suggested), and he lamented Huxley's rather narrow philosophical view. Shuster hoped Americans would now take cultural exchange much more seriously. "I need only refer to a fact which you know far better than I do," he noted to Secretary of State James Byrnes, "namely that we have four cultural relations people in Roumania, while the Russians have at least four thousand." Despite the major tasks still to be done, Shuster's respect for UNESCO and its purpose remained high:

> We are going to try to limit a dangerous and potentially destructive cultural imperialism by setting up a rival empire of the human mind. Such an empire must have freedom and a sense of responsibility. Its function is not so much to keep the peace as to transform narrow nationalistic cultures into cultural activity having a world view, and therewith a pacific, understanding-building view.[34]

Shuster had been appointed to the United States National Commission for UNESCO for a one-year term in 1946, and he was reappointed for three years in 1947. Commission activities soon occupied more and more of his time—together with his work with the Hutchins Commission, the Committee on Segregation in the Nation's Capital, and his efforts to return Hunter College to postwar conditions, including coeducation.[35] The national commission for UNESCO had a membership of one hundred and thus, for the sake of efficiency, much of its work was done through committees. Shuster was appointed to the Interim Committee on Program Assignments in February 1947, to the Committee on Nominations in both 1947 and 1948, to the Information Committee in 1948, and in 1949 to the Program Committee again and to the chairmanship of a new Committee on Educational Reconstruction.[36] Dr. Huxley also appointed him UNESCO representative to a United Nations Subcommission meeting on Human Rights in 1947, and in 1948 he was elected to the Executive Committee of the United States National Commission.[37] The challenge for Shuster was not only to find time for the additional work but especially to fit the additional meetings, only rarely in New York, into his already overcrowded schedule.

The first conference of the National Commission for UNESCO after the General Conference in Paris was held in Philadelphia in March 1947. The organizers were eager to have one session on philosophy and the humanities, in part because the physical and social sciences and educational reconstruction seemed to have been given major emphases so far, and Shuster was asked to preside and to present basic ideas for discussion.[38] He had apparently presented some personal reflections to the American delegation in Paris, but these were never brought, at least in their original form, to the conference floor.[39] What Shuster advocated was, first, that UNESCO undertake a broad-based comparative study of civilizations—their individual goals and aspirations, their contributions to other cultures, and possible sources of misunderstanding with other peoples—and, second, that scholars from various disciplines in the humanities—philosophy, linguistics, history, literature, anthropology, and so on—all contribute to such a study.[40] His remarks suggested at least one way the humanities might assist in furthering international understanding, and Milton Eisenhower, chairman of the National

Commission that year, sent him a note of appreciation when the conference closed.[41]

Shuster attended the commission's meeting the following year in Boston.[42] By this time, September 1948, the Cold War stalemate between East and West had hardened, the Berlin airlift was under way, Stalinist governments had been established in most Eastern European nations, and the flood of refugees from East to West had reached crisis proportions. Shuster viewed the situation as a twofold challenge, which UNESCO must embrace. "The first is the chance to champion vigorously the cause of those refugees from the East who are classified as D.P.'s," he stated. "In many instances they constitute the sole hope for the survival of a national culture or it may be even the survival of a vital part of what we call Western Civilization."[43] As the culture, the religious traditions, and the aspirations of so many peoples in Eastern Europe were in danger of being suffocated, this national spirit might still live on in refugees if conditions were conducive. Secondly, a similar crisis faced the peoples of Eastern Germany. Millions of them were fleeing to the West, either because their land had now been incorporated within the new Polish boundaries or simply because they preferred not to live under the East German regime. Thus their culture and traditions were in danger of being lost in this sudden and at times violent uprooting. For Shuster, these issues were much more worthy of UNESCO's attention than some of the scientific investigations Huxley seemed to be encouraging. "It seems to me that the peoples of the whole world would listen to UNESCO with far greater interest if it vigorously attacked vital issues of this kind and did not lay itself open to the accusation that its program was a compound of an inquiry into sex at high altitudes and the suggestion that contemporary music be given priority in such catalogues as Mr. Huxley may sometimes publish," Shuster declared. "I will not demean the value of these enterprises but I am certainly convinced that if the organization is to succeed and prosper it must be just as concerned with the conservation of human and social values in the aftermath of the war that gave UNESCO birth as it is with observing the flights of birds around Heligoland."

At the next meeting of the national commission, in Cleveland in February 1949, Shuster was asked to chair a session on educational reconstruction. He was soon after named chairman of a standing committee on educational reconstruction, and much of his work for the national commission over the next eighteen months was done in this area.[44] Shuster admitted that the title "Educational Reconstruction" was unfortunate. "The name of the Committee is a misnomer and will be changed," he wrote. "What it does is to correlate as much as possible the work of volunteer agencies in the United States which are interested in doing something to help bring about a revival of education and of general culture in a world sadly undermined by war and disturbance. It also tends to initiate some projects."[45]

The major project of the committee's own initiative may have been Shuster's suggestion in mid-1949 that approximately fifty universities be found to donate one thousand dollars each to a fund to assist the publication in war-torn countries of worthwhile and scholarly works that would not be profitable to publish commercially. The proposal was accepted by the committee and was warmly praised (and accepted) by UNESCO's new director-general in Paris, Jaime Torres Bodet.[46] Shuster, as committee chairman, immediately undertook to promote and publicize the project, and he sought to convince Richard Simon of Simon and Schuster Publishers to head the program.[47] Simon hesitated because of other commitments at the time and before the complication could be resolved, Shuster was forced to resign in order to accept appointment as land commissioner for Bavaria. But the project was eventually adopted by UNESCO's ruling body in Paris.

The other major project of the committee was the encouragement of private groups and organizations to assist in educational reconstruction around the world. Basic educational needs for pencils, pens, paper, blackboards, and so forth, had already been met in most countries, although not in all, by 1950, but books, laboratory equipment, art supplies, musical instruments, shop machinery, and so on, were still in great demand. For example, ninety-five percent of the books in school libraries in the Philippines had been lost, and ninety-nine percent of the books in the bookstores of Poland.[48] Shuster asked all organizations affiliated with the national commission to sponsor one undertaking in educational reconstruction—donate a sum of money, provide a collection of books, equip a physics or chemistry laboratory, or formally affiliate with a library or college in need in one of the recovering countries—and he promised that his committee would assist in every way possible. He scheduled two smaller meetings at Hunter College in late 1949 and early 1950, and a full committee meeting for Washington in February 1950, and he encouraged all commission members to publicize the program as widely as possible.[49] The committee itself systematically circulated information about the programs it was sponsoring: personnel training and fellowships, library and laboratory needs, requests for vocational equipment and audio-visual aids, fine arts equipment, sponsorships for needy students, and monetary needs almost everywhere. The needs were particularly urgent because more than $200 million in money, goods, and services had been sent abroad in the three years after the war through the Commission for International Educational Reconstruction, and the United States National Commission for UNESCO had now undertaken to carry on this work.[50]

In his official report on the Paris Conference in 1946, Assistant Secretary of State Benton had noted: "If two or three of the leading members of the American delegation—such as President Stoddard of Illinois and President Shuster of Hunter—could be prevailed upon to travel for three months this coming summer, on behalf of the State Department . . . this could prove tremendously helpful."[51] Shuster was not able to travel abroad for three months that summer, but he did devote much time in 1947, and later, publicizing UNESCO's work. In an address before the Association of American Colleges in Boston in January 1947, he pointed out how organizations like UNESCO could facilitate the exchange and sharing of what was best in each country, and he suggested that greater attention be given to means of mass communication—radio, film, newspapers, and libraries. "If fifty per cent of the talent and funds about to be expended by various countries on propagandistic broadcasts to foreign lands," he stated, "could be turned over to a World Radio Foundation associated with UNESCO so that the peoples of the earth could be introduced to each other in terms of what is finest in their cultural achievement, a road to understanding would be cleared which might—not immediately but in the end—lead to peace in the hearts and minds of men."[52] In an address before the Foreign Policy Association in New York one month later he had particular praise for the national commissions, the liaisons "between UNESCO and the more or less organized cultural life of the peoples." "These Commissions have a great work to do," he insisted. "Through them the virility of each nation's intellectual life can filter to the Secretariat, and in turn the achievements of the Secretariat can be incorporated into the thinking and acting of each people."[53]

In early April Shuster was back in Boston to address the convention of the National Catholic Educational Association. This was probably his most important address of the year, since many Catholics were quite suspicious of the leftist and even irreligious views of some UNESCO leaders and it was hoped that Shuster might be able to calm the fears of his co-religionists. "The goals of honesty and freedom have been before UNESCO from the beginning," he stated, in outlining its purposes:

> The organization is committed to fostering the free flow of communication; to promoting the sharing of knowledge by scholars in all fields of enquiry, across national boundaries; to placing at the disposition of less well-educated peoples the educational methods best calculated to insure their mastery of pedagogical and technological skills; to overcoming the handicaps imposed upon countries harassed by war, in the belief that educational retrogression is dangerous to the peace of the world community; and to the gradual development of the cooperative use of the great mass media of communication for the purpose of diffusing knowledge and understanding.[54]

Compared with the tremendous opportunities before UNESCO, the foibles of temporary leaders were not that significant. "Surely our glances should be focused on such matters rather than on whether Mr. Julian Huxley is secretary general of the UNESCO," he suggested. "Mr. Huxley is only a minor authority on birds and an equally minor menace to them or to anybody else." Much more important was the role Catholics could play in postwar reconstruction:

> There are in Western and Central Europe no energies other than those of Catholicism capable of assuming leadership in resisting the onward sweep of totalitarianism. The reasons are twofold. First, every other important group is in some manner allied either with Capitalism, in the predatory sense, or with Marxian philosophy. Second, other groups will follow Catholic leadership if it is

offered. If then there is to be any debate with Russian Communism in terms which Europe can understand, it will be a debate in which Catholics are protagonists. I have no doubt they can win it, provided they really want to.

When Congress seemed hesitant to appropriate additional funding for the State Department's Office of Information and Cultural Affairs, Shuster wrote directly to New York's influential Cardinal Francis Spellman:

> Your Eminence knows that I have myself urged a far flung Catholic effort in this direction. But until that can be organized and put into operation, we must I think look upon the activities of our Government as absolutely essential. Of course, some criticisms have been levied against the Office of International Information and Cultural Affairs. On the other hand, having had a great deal of opportunity to see some of the things that are being done and to know people in charge, I am absolutely convinced that on the whole this Office is doing precisely what we should like to see it do.
>
> I am, therefore, hoping that it will be possible for Your Eminence to indicate in some appropriate way, support of the work being done in this field by the Department.[55]

Recognizing his very limited knowledge of the physical sciences, Shuster saw the irony in his invitation that spring to address the national meeting of the American Chemical Society in Atlantic City. But his message was the same: international cooperation and understanding through organizations like UNESCO can not only assist in avoiding international conflicts and preserving peace but also channel the talents and resources of various nations more effectively toward bettering the conditions under which the peoples of the world live. He was optimistic that the people of America were eager to assist. He mentioned that during a recent speech in Chicago a lady asked him in public where she might send food parcels and other items, and he volunteered to send her addresses if she would send him a letter, and more than a hundred others wrote for addresses also.[56] Later that year Shuster published an article in *Survey Graphic*, explaining to a wider public the goals of UNESCO and suggesting that increased international understanding could only result in greater appreciation of non-Western cultures and a lessening of racial prejudice and ignorance among peoples.[57]

Shuster resigned from the national commission when he was appointed land commissioner for Bavaria in the spring of 1950, but he accepted reappointment to another three-year term on his return to the United States, this one effective through 1954.[58] He plunged into the work immediately. Before leaving for Germany he had been approached about holding the third National Conference on UNESCO at Hunter College in the fall of 1951— the first had been held in Philadelphia in 1947 and the second in Cleveland in 1949—and he had agreed. The location seemed ideal. New York was accessible from every part of the country, and Hunter College housed a 2000-seat assembly hall or auditorium, a 650-seat theater, a smaller high school auditorium, various lounges and classrooms for meetings and smaller discussions, and a cafeteria that could conveniently provide meals. Roosevelt House could be available for receptions and cocktail parties.[59] Plans were finalized with Acting President Eleanor Grady during Shuster's absence in Germany, the date was eventually changed to late January 1952, even more convenient since the college would not be in session between semesters, and Shuster thus turned his attention to it almost as soon as he stepped off the boat that December.[60]

The gathering was a six-day affair. The National Commission held its meeting on January 26–27 and the five-day National Conference began on January 27 and continued through January 31. On the opening day, January 26, Dr. George Stoddard, president of the University of Illinois and chairman of the United States National Commission, spoke, as did UNESCO's director-general from Paris, Jaime Torres Bodet. Torres Bodet, former minister of education in Mexico, urged the establishment of training centers for educational leaders and announced that the first such center was being opened in his native Mexico and the second probably in Egypt.[61] Other topics discussed were the world refugee problem, freer access to information in all countries, discontent with foreign rule throughout many African nations, and suggestions for the possible easing of East-West tensions.[62]

Shuster's part in the conference attracted little public attention. He participated in a discussion, "The Spiritual and Cultural Dimension of the Problem of World Community," and delivered an address entitled "The Nature of the Challenge," an effort to direct attention from the general purpose and goals of UNESCO to practical programs that the American people might undertake here and now.[63] But most of the time Shuster was involved in behind-the-scenes administration, assuring that necessary facilities were available and that the sessions proceeded as efficiently as possible. For weeks thereafter, he received letters of congratulations on the fine meeting. "I am firmly convinced that on the whole this Conference attracted more attention and received more complimentary comment than any other which the organization has sponsored," he wrote. "So far I have encountered only one negative critic, and I am sure that his opinion is based upon the fact that the study group he attended was not the most sprightly one."[64]

On his return to the United States in December 1951, Shuster faced a very difficult year as president of Hunter College and, after the National Conference in January, UNESCO activities had to compete with other urgent demands. The Bronx campus had been fully coed for one semester now; Professor Fordrung had been suspended from his teaching duties in June, and Shuster was attempting to work out a compromise settlement; and two faculty members, Bernard Reiss and Henrietta Friedman, refused to testify before government investigating committees that fall.[65] In the midst of all this, however, Shuster was drawn into the debate over one of UNESCO's most controversial projects, the publication of a *History of the Scientific and Cultural Development of Mankind*. The idea had originated in the General Conference of 1947. The Conference of 1950 had authorized the appointment of an International Commission to undertake the project, and Director-General Torres Bodet had appointed the commission members and international editors of the projected six volumes. The motivation behind the project was that most national histories were biased in that nation's favor, that its national leaders were heroes and other nations' leaders were either ignored or their accomplishments de-emphasized, and that a new and objective history could only add to international understanding, a principal goal of UNESCO. The project met with controversy from the start. Many were disappointed that their own favorite historians had not been selected, others were concerned that any work produced by such a diverse group of international scholars would necessarily be bland and too much a compromise, and Catholics were especially fearful that religion would not receive satisfactory treatment.[66]

Shuster felt that these were controversies the struggling UNESCO did not need and should have avoided. "Personally, I have long since thought," he wrote, "that it was a mistake for UNESCO to embark on publishing projects of its own for the reason that one can, with such projects, seldom please everybody and is inevitably obliged to displease many."[67] In March 1952 he was asked by the general editor to become a corresponding member of the commission, but he diplomatically declined.[68] Two months later he confided his objections to a UNESCO colleague:

> Perhaps you may be interested in some quite personal reflections about the History which UNESCO is planning. When I returned from service in Bavaria during December last, I learned to my amazement that this idea had been adopted by UNESCO and that an editorial chairman had been selected in a most casual manner. In this first place, I expressed myself as being extremely critical of any publication program undertaken by UNESCO itself. I have always felt strongly that while this organization might well subsidize studies designed to promote international cultural cooperation, it was unwise for it to embark on such studies of its own initiative.
>
> Secondly, I thought—and still think—that if so ambitious an undertaking as a Cultural History of Mankind was to be supported, the major national associations of historians should be brought into consultative relationship, so that after careful thought the best possible editorial board could be selected. The haphazard way in which American participation, at least, was assured seems to me from the professional point of view rather surprising.
>
> At the present time, if the outcome is to be at all favorable, I think each of us should speak our minds frankly, less no doubt from a confessional point of view than out of sincere critical concern lest the scholarship of the free world stand convicted of producing something of which UNESCO will in the long run be embarrassed to acknowledge as its cultural offspring.[69]

Despite other demands, Shuster did consent to accept appointment to both the executive committee and the program committee of the national commission, but the additional meetings these entailed were usually held in New York or Washington.[70]

Still a staunch supporter of UNESCO, he met on one occasion with officials of the American Legion in an effort to dispel their fears about UNESCO's goals and activities, and he addressed a personal letter to President Eisenhower shortly after his inauguration to suggest reasons why the new administration should give support and encouragement to UNESCO's work:

> First and foremost is the fact that by working with a body of men and women who represent nearly all the free peoples, our own American representatives can and do mitigate the fears of other nations that the United States has embarked on a program of cultural imperialism. . . .
>
> Second, I should like to stress what is being done to marshall the resources of private groups in order to help education in war-torn or backward countries solve some of its problems. . . .
>
> Third, let me say that UNESCO is the only international agency in which all the cultural forces of the world are represented. It brings together representatives of the great religious bodies, of the various fields of social science and of those agencies which, like libraries and museums, provide the materials which a culture needs in order to flourish.[71]

On the other hand, when some in the State Department sought to delay publication of a UNESCO pamphlet that countenanced interracial marriage and noted that "in the United States, some groups of Northern Negro recruits, when tested by the Army during World War I, were found to be superior to groups of Southern whites," Shuster sent a letter to protest what seemed like censorship.[72]

In mid-September 1953 Shuster attended the Fourth National Conference on UNESCO in Minneapolis and delivered a summary address toward the close of the conference that was very well received.[73] The most significant event of the conference for Shuster personally, however, was his selection for the next year as chairman of the national commission. He had been in telephone contact with the State Department earlier that month, and on September 10 he received an urgent telegram from Secretary of State John Foster Dulles: "Earnestly hope you will accept the key role of chairman of the National Commission for UNESCO. Your leadership greatly needed in this field."[74] The decision needed to be made at the National Conference the following week, and Shuster wrote immediately to the chairman of the Board of Higher Education, Hon. Joseph B. Cavallaro. Cavallaro sought the advice of several other Board members; they all agreed that accepting the position would be good for Shuster himself, the city colleges, and the nation. The Board's approval was wired to Shuster in Minneapolis on September 16, and he was elected soon after.[75]

Very early in his term as chairman, Shuster wrote to a friend: "For me right now UNESCO is synonymous with headaches." Unfortunately, the situation did not change.[76] Shuster hoped the Eisenhower administration might take greater interest—"The desire of the Department to give new life and direction to UNESCO is of course commendable," he wrote to Cavallaro— but he was not certain.[77] Secretary of State Dulles was the key:

> The good thing about the Department seems to me to be that for the first time in a long while there is a Secretary to whom the responsibility for the conduct of foreign affairs is actually entrusted. But so far as I can tell, everybody else's job is either to buy tickets for him when he goes abroad or to spread the carpet for him when he comes back home. My conclusion is that until the Secretary decides that cultural exchange, etc., are matters on which he should concentrate, no one else is likely to do so.[78]

Shuster's fears were justified. Officials of the cultural affairs and public affairs divisions, with which the national commission worked most closely, were often promoted or transferred, and the newer persons were not always an improvement.[79] The Republican Party had campaigned in 1952 on charges of Communist infiltration in government, especially in the State Department, during the Truman presidency, and Senator McCarthy was keeping such charges alive. Since many feared leftist infiltration in UNESCO's activities, there was an effort to require government clearance for all national commission members and even its staff. Shuster complained frequently that such clearance was often either needlessly denied or too long delayed and that qualified officials simply withdrew their applications.[80] Shuster addressed a particularly critical letter to Dulles. He complained that "considerations arising out of the search for security make progress virtually impossible" and, in another case, "the obstacles are so numerous that surmounting them seems out of the question."

One of Shuster's nominees had been recommended by three respected generals, and yet could not get clearance. "If a man who served his country with skill and success on the Berlin firing line cannot be trusted to serve the United States National Commission," Shuster declared, "one is left wondering whether anybody not wholly inert and inept can be found for the job."[81] The commission was never able to convince Eisenhower and Dulles of UNESCO's importance. With the world at times poised for war—"brinkmanship," Dulles called it—Secretary Dulles was much more interested in diplomatic than cultural matters, and he may even have been out of sympathy with basic UNESCO aims. UNESCO officials sought to compromise differences and harmonize views between East and West, but Dulles seemed adverse to compromise. In his Cold War analysis the West was correct and the East wrong, and the solution of the conflict was not in compromise or the harmonizing of differences but in the East admitting its error and accepting the West's positions. Without the support of Dulles, little could be accomplished.[82]

The uncertain relationship between the State Department and UNESCO was further complicated in 1953 when Luther Evans, Librarian of Congress, was elected director-general. With the State Department wavering in its support and at times openly critical, the election of an American as director-general could prove embarrassing. When confiding his difficulties to former Assistant Secretary Benton, Shuster acknowledged this openly: "The fact that Luther took his job against the wishes of the State Department is now, alas, playing a part in the proceedings."[83] The National Commission strove to be loyal and cooperative with both UNESCO and the State Department, and any widening of a split between them could only make life more complicated for the commission chairman. In April 1954 the Soviet Union widened that split considerably by suddenly reversing its uncompromising policy of eight years and officially joining the organization.[84] Most Americans, if they thought about it at all, were probably highly suspicious of the Soviet decision, as they were highly suspicious of most Soviet decisions at the time. Shuster agreed. "In my opinion, the Russians are not likely to place great stress on UNESCO activities *per se*," he had confided to Benton in early June, "though they will undoubtedly attempt to block various activities in Europe and Asia which run counter to their program of action."[85]

In an address before the National Education Association that summer, Shuster cautioned all freedom-loving peoples to watch Soviet activities in UNESCO carefully and "stand ready to resist any sudden moves to undermine UNESCO's effectiveness."[86]

Evans, however, did not agree, or at least he insisted in public that he did not agree. "I think I must assume," he wrote Benton, "that they [the Russians] intend to devote their efforts to the advancement of the purposes of the Organization and that they will co-operate in the same way as other Member States."[87] He was especially concerned that Shuster, chairman of the United States National Commission, was questioning Soviet motives:

> I am informed that, with very minor exceptions, the only action the Soviet Union's representative has taken in the Economic and Social Council concerning Unesco has been to [listen] to its reports in complete silence. As soon as I have all my data together I will write Shuster a letter setting him straight on this business, because all he can do by repeating such statements is to make it more difficult to secure Russian co-operation in Unesco, a co-operation which up to now they provide evidence of wishing to give. A heavy and shameful guilt will rest on those who first throw cold-water stones in Unesco's glass-house.[88]

During his year as chairman of the national commission, the UNESCO secretariat in Paris inaugurated a series of conferences on cultural ties between the Old World and the New, one of which was scheduled for that summer in Sao Paulo, and Shuster was asked to be the North American spokesman. He agreed, and his speech on cultural ties between nations must have been one of his favorites to prepare (although images like "shark-infested cities" must have posed challenges for the French and Spanish translators).[89]

Shuster began by noting the debt the New World owed the Old in home-building and architecture: English influence in Salem and Charleston; French in Quebec, Montreal, and New Orleans; German Romanesque in the Middle West; Spanish throughout the Southwest; and comparable influences throughout Latin America.[90] Religion was vitally important for Shuster, and the ties were close:

> Early there came to North America the Franciscans of Spain and the Jesuits of France, of whom scholars from Parkman to Bolton

have paid tribute. Then other strands were woven into the cord—
Anglican, Puritan and Methodist from Great Britain, Catholic
from Germany, Italy and Poland in particular, Jewish from Central
Europe, Calvinist and Lutheran from many lands. . . . Beyond all
this one may say that no powerful moment in European religious
thought has failed to leave its imprint on these lands. The Oxford
Movement of the mid-nineteenth century left its stamp on New
England and New York. Transcendentalism, moving away from
religious custom, busied itself with the study of German idealism.
Even today it is religious thought which is the most coveted of
imported intellectual wares. One has only to select a number of
names at random—Albert Schweitzer, Martin D'Arcy, Jacques
Maritain, Karl Barth, Nicholas Berdyaev, Aldous Huxley, Martin
Buber among them—in order to see how very much alive this
interchange is.

The same might be said also of philosophy, history, and the
social sciences. But gradually in the nineteenth century the Old
and New Worlds began to go their separate ways, with the New
regularly influenced also by differing Native American cultures
from Hudson Bay to Terra del Fuego. One major difference at
present, Shuster took pains to point out, was that some in Europe
clung to dialectical materialism while the American experience
seemed a clear refutation of Marxist theory. Americans view the
predictions made in *Das Kapital*, Shuster suggested, like "forecasts
of rain prior to a week of glaring sunshine." In the material and
social orders the United States has made extraordinary advances
and the average American enjoys a level of health, wealth, security,
leisure, and independence that is the envy of many. But Americans, Shuster noted, realize that life is more than material and they
can learn from the spiritual and cultural foundations of European
civilization. In bringing the Old World and the New into closer
harmony, Shuster insisted in his conclusion, UNESCO could
play a significant role, because it was founded on a common belief
in human rights:

> For it is this concept which, however diversely interpreted or
> understood, is the greatest legacy we hold in common. Not merely
> have we written it into law, so that from Hudson Bay to Cape
> Horn the codes are based on recognition of man as a creature
> endowed with inalienable rights—a recognition to which, we grate-

fully admit, we should never have arrived had it not been that the conscience of Europe had earlier, in the aftermath of struggle and ceaseless quest for purification, written it into the Common Law. . . . Sacred to us it is anew, not primarily because it is in danger but because we as peoples could not be joined together in the West unless we knew that reverence for it abides as the sole basis of our faith in the emerging moral solidarity of mankind.

Almost immediately on Shuster's return from the UNESCO meeting in Sao Paulo, he turned his attention to final plans for his last responsibility as commission chairman, presiding over a meeting of the national commission in Milwaukee in mid-October. The two-and-a-half day meeting was well attended and the topics discussed were challenging: implications of Soviet membership in UNESCO, how local communities participate in UNESCO activities, commentary on UNESCO's announced program for next year, and America's stake in the progress of less developed nations.[91] But it seemed somehow inevitable that Shuster's term would close in controversy, and that the controversy would center on Luther Evans. The federal government's purge of suspected security risks was at its height—J. Robert Oppenheimer had recently been denied Atomic Energy Commission clearance and John Carter Vincent and John Paton Davies had been removed from the State Department—and the State Department wanted eight Americans on Evans's UNESCO staff in Paris removed as security risks also. With the Soviet Union now in UNESCO, it was a particularly thorny issue, and Evans demurred. He agreed that four of them would not be reappointed when their terms expired, but the other four had no fixed terms, Evans was not certain he had authority to terminate them, and he announced that he would continue his investigations.[92] The national commission, meeting in closed session, supported Evans and recommended only that, after his investigation, the director-general seek from the General Conference whatever authority he needed to carry out his responsibilities. Shuster noted also that the officials were mostly in minor positions.[93] But once again, with loyalties to both UNESCO and the State Department, he was caught between. When his three-year term on the national commission came to an end at the close of the meeting, and when

Maj. General Milton G. Baker of Valley Forge Military Academy was selected to succeed him as chairman, Shuster must have expressed a sigh of relief.[94]

In 1958 Shuster returned to UNESCO affairs again, this time more deeply than before. Having decided that summer to resign the presidency of Hunter College in 1960, he accepted appointment in May as the United States representative on the twenty-four member Executive Board of UNESCO, in July he was reappointed to a two-year term to the United States National Commission for UNESCO, and in August President Eisenhower appointed him one of four voting delegates to the Tenth General Conference of UNESCO, scheduled to open in Paris early in November.[95] Acknowledging a friend's congratulations on his appointment to UNESCO's Executive Board, Shuster noted: "I gather that I have put my foot into something that resembles a more or less amiable combination of hornet's nest and barrel of molasses,"[96] and he was not far wrong. He was not able to attend his first Board meeting (the 51st Session) in mid-September in Cologne and Brussels because it conflicted with the opening of the new school year at Hunter, and the 53rd Session was scheduled immediately following the UNESCO General Conference in Paris and, after being away for approximately a month, he did not remain for that one either.[97] When a South American candidate for chairman of the Executive Board, Paulo E. de Berredo Carneiro, was defeated, he took out his anger on the United States, and especially on its delegate to the Executive Board for his absence from those meetings. "Carneiro proved to be a very poor loser," an official notified Shuster:

> He attacked the U.S. directly on the following morning, charging us with persistent truancy in Executive Board sessions and referred in a subsequent private conversation to your absence at the 51st and 53rd sessions of the Board and the Administrative Commissions. This attack was evidently no more than an attempt to screen his disappointment and fury over his defeat, for the next ten minutes of his tirade was spent in accusing us of making "common cause with our enemies" and letting down our "Latin American friends."[98]

It was unfortunate that relations between Shuster and Carneiro could not have begun more favorably, because Carneiro was at the center of one of UNESCO's major controversies over the next twelve months, with Shuster again on the opposing side. Carneiro had earlier been named president of the UNESCO commission to oversee the writing of the *History of the Scientific and Cultural Development of Mankind,* a project Shuster had opposed as far back as 1952, and the project was now encountering serious difficulties.[99]

The first difficulty concerned the chairman of the editorial committee, Professor Ralph Turner of Yale. Some were critical because they disagreed with his approach to history (which they thought did not sufficiently emphasize the role of religion in historical development), but more serious objections concerned the state of his health and the slow progress the project seemed to be making.[100] Shuster and the American delegation recommended that a broader committee of historical consultants be established as a face-saving way of replacing Turner, but Carneiro would agree only if Turner were on the committee also.[101] Carneiro realized that progress had been slow, however, and that additional funding might be required before completion, and he turned to Shuster for assistance. The State Department did not want the United States placed in any position of responsibility. "It was made very clear to Mr. [Henry] Kellermann [United States permanent representative to UNESCO]," a State Department official wrote Shuster, "that given the 'achievements' of the International Commission to date, there was no chance you would pull their chestnuts out of the fire by endeavoring to obtain a grant from American foundations thus jeopardizing your own reputation, prestige and good relations with the foundations."[102] When Turner suffered a series of strokes early in 1959, the project was necessarily delayed further.[103]

A second serious difficulty emerged when the Soviet Union's delegation to UNESCO raised major objections to Volume VI of the *History* (The Twentieth Century) and demanded major revisions. The Russians pointed out that Socialist countries across the world then numbered approximately one billion people and yet were not given "proportionate space and attention" in the volume.[104] The Western countries were given greatest credit for advances in science and engineering while in certain branches, the delegation insisted, "the USSR had already outstripped the most advanced capitalist countries." The reference to Sputnik two years earlier was clear. Western democracies were credited with eliminating many social inequalities but "at the same time they [the authors] say nothing about the acute class contradictions, mass chronic unemployment, and racial discrimination existing in capitalist countries." The Russians objected to the treatment of the "national liberation" movements taking place in various developing nations. Shuster and other UNESCO officials agreed that such views could in no way be forced on the original authors, and Shuster even wondered if the whole project might not be conveniently terminated. "Perhaps we ought to consider with due care whether our policy ought to be easing the project quietly into its grave, but salvaging what we can of the earlier volumes," he wrote a friend. "I am also afraid that any attempt to do what the Russians ask would create an even greater scandal here than would dropping the whole business."[105] It was eventually decided that the authors themselves would retain final control over the text, but that differing comments and views could be contained in the notes.

A final and later concern of Shuster, and perhaps the most serious for him as an academician, was the fact that many early reviews of the work were negative.[106] The six volumes, published serially from 1963 to 1975, were praised for the scholarly research and well-supported judgments of the individual authors but were criticized because too many authors, editors, consultants, and committees had a hand in the final product. "This is not the way to write history well," a reviewer noted of Volume I. "Our sympathies go out to the two authors who have suffered from a process of supervision, collaboration, assistance, reference and consultation."[107] "Committee history is a contradiction in terms, the effort foredoomed," an English reviewer remarked of the same volume. "It is very sad to observe so many distinguished scholars allowing themselves to be drawn into such a project."[108] "What has emerged from the crosscurrents of collaborative authorship is not the refined gold of historical truth, shining in magnificent purity and purged of error and bias," wrote William McNeill of Volume VI. "Instead we have an unwieldy, uneven book in which the authors resolutely straddled or avoided every important issue and still provoked an unremitting drumfire of dissent from the official experts who read and, particularly in the Russian case, disapproved of what had been written."[109] George Shuster had opposed the *History* from the beginning but, as one of the highest UNESCO officials from the United States, was not able to escape embarrassment as the project reached completion.

In late 1958 Shuster attended the Tenth General Conference of UNESCO, held in Paris from November 4 through December 5. He was one of four United States delegates appointed by President Eisenhower several months earlier, but he apparently played no prominent role.[110] The major accomplishment of the conference was the election of Italian scholar Vittorini Veronese to succeed Luther Evans of the United States as director-general. There was some ironic, off-the-floor maneuvering when the Soviet delegation suggested the United States renominate Evans for a second term, apparently preferring the American to the lesser known but strongly anti-Communist Catholic Veronese.[111] The United States delegation showed no interest. The only excitement for Shuster was the criticism he received from some disgruntled delegates for his absence from the Executive Board meetings immediately before and after the General Conference.[112]

Shuster did attend two meetings of the Executive Board in 1959, the 54th session in June and the 55th in late November and early December, both in Paris, and he was soon exerting significant influence. Finances were a major concern for the Executive Board since it was charged with drafting a two-year budget for the General Conference's approval, and they were an equally major concern for Shuster since the United States contributed approximately thirty percent of the total UNESCO funding (the Soviet Union thirteen percent, Great Britain seven percent, and France five percent) and there was growing opposition in Congress toward financing programs of which the United States might increasingly disapprove. The two-year budget was in the area of twenty-five million dollars, the director-general requested an increase of fifteen percent and an unallocated reserve fund, but Shuster insisted that his government would support no more than a ten percent increase and did not approve of unspecified accounts. American wishes, often with some disgruntled feelings, generally carried.[113]

Other issues before the Executive Board that year were the embarrassing delays in the *History* project, the need to regularize UNESCO procedures so that delegates had sufficient time to consult their governments before decisions were taken, the danger of focusing exclusively on immediate needs and losing sight of UNESCO's longer-range programs, and the increasing urgency to save the three-thousand-year-old Nubian monuments threatened by flooding along the Nile.[114] But Shuster's major contribution to the December session was his response to a Soviet resolution that if the world would accept recent disarmament proposals put forth by the Soviet Union, more money could be available for UNESCO, and therefore UNESCO should radically revise its present programs and the United States and the Soviet Union should begin to meet at the highest levels to plan for a new era of peaceful coexistence. Shuster began his extended response by praising the Russian people, with whom all Americans wished to live in peace and harmony, by paying tribute to Tolstoy and Dostoyevsky, "the two greatest masters of the human spirit of their age," and by commending the Soviet government for joining UNESCO, even at a late date. Shuster agreed that any progress on the disarmament front could release larger funds for combatting poverty and illiteracy throughout the world, but UNESCO already had various programs in place and he saw no reason to terminate such activities and begin anew in some totally different direction. He was especially opposed to any suggestion of summitry, of top-level United States–Soviet meetings to deliberate current educational and cultural questions. The concept of UNESCO, he insisted, was that of a family of nations, with even the smallest nation having an equal voice in discussions and decisions, and it was not for the United States and the Soviet Union to impose solutions on the rest of the world. He further opposed any idea of East-West parity in such meetings or discussions since capitalist and socialist countries were not that conveniently divided and Eastern and Western bloc countries were certainly not equal in number. Shuster concluded his remarks with the recommendation that both he and his Soviet counterpart consult with their governments and bring before the next General Conference a list of particular goals and programs their countries wished to see UNESCO adopt. This might furnish additional momentum for UNESCO's work and also remain within the organization's operation. Shuster had introduced his proposal

with the words of Lincoln: "With malice toward none, with charity for all, with firmness in the right as God gives us to see the
right, let us finish the task we are in."[115]

Secretary of State Christian Herter, who had earlier that year
succeeded John Foster Dulles in that office due to the latter's
increasing debilitation from cancer, praised Shuster for "the distinguished manner in which you represented the United States at
this Board session." He appointed Shuster to the United States
delegation to the 1960 UNESCO General Conference and urged
him to stand for reelection also to the Executive Board. "Your
account of the consideration of the Soviet proposal on disarmament and peaceful coexistence has particular value at this time,"
the Secretary continued, "since a definite pattern of USSR initiative on these issues is emerging in various international forums.
You and the other members of the United States Delegation are
to be commended for the effective manner in which you met these
issues. The wide support accorded your presentation of the
United States position is a tribute to your position of leadership
on the Executive Board."[116]

Shuster's work for UNESCO the following year, 1960, was
not demanding. It was the final year of the Eisenhower administration, and the United States was thus proposing few new initiatives. UNESCO itself was less active than before due to the
deteriorating health of Director-General Veronese.[117] Shuster
urged the national commission to continue its interest in safe-
guarding the threatened Nubian monuments, and in February he
invited Laurence Rockefeller to become a member of an international committee under UNESCO to work toward the same
goal.[118] He sought to get Americans appointed to the UNESCO
Secretariat in Paris, but his efforts were often frustrated. Positions
were to be apportioned among the member states in proportion to
their budget contributions and, as new states joined UNESCO
and made their contributions, they also had first claim to available
positions. UNESCO salaries were not always comparable to those
in the United States and academic personnel hesitated to leave
their faculty positions for three or six years at UNESCO, realizing
that they would be far behind others in their disciplines on their
return.[119] Shuster also attended three meetings of the Executive

Board that year—one in April, one in late October-early November, and a two-day session in mid-December—but the issues were routine and Shuster's intervention rarely crucial. He took an active part in budget deliberations, continued to urge assistance to the Nubian project, encouraged greater efficiency in UNESCO procedures, and expressed growing concern over the *History* project. On a subject that would become even more prominent the following year, he proposed an increase of one million dollars over the recommended budget to provide additional educational assistance to the nations of Africa, many of which were in the process of gaining political independence, and the United States agreed to contribute almost the total sum.[120]

The year 1961 dawned in a spirit of hope and optimism. Although Shuster had been favorably impressed with Secretary of State Herter personally, he felt the Eisenhower-Dulles foreign policy too strongly opposed contact and cooperation with the Soviet Union and other Communist nations and thus never gave enthusiastic support to UNESCO activities.[121] But the inauguration of President John Kennedy that January offered promise. His administration seemed more innovative, his inaugural address offered friendship and cooperation to all, and his close advisors included respected scholarly leaders like McGeorge Bundy, Dean Rusk, and Arthur Schlesinger, Jr. Unfortunately, the promise for UNESCO soon gave way before the harsh realities of world politics. The president's domestic program encountered strong opposition in congress, the Bay of Pigs disaster was a personal and national embarrassment from which he continually sought to recover, and his meeting with Soviet Premier Nikita Khrushchev in Vienna that June left the world even more fearful of a nuclear confrontation. "It will be a cold winter," a visibly shaken president remarked at the summit's close, and bomb shelters began to proliferate ominously across the country that fall.[122] UNESCO projects were afforded much less attention.

George Shuster that year had decided to accept the invitation of Notre Dame president Father Theodore Hesburgh, C.S.C., to return to Notre Dame as assistant to the president and director of a major new institute, the Center for the Study of Man in Contemporary Society, and it was from his new location in South Bend that he attended Executive Board meetings in late

spring and fall.[123] Like the Kennedy presidency, the sessions
began with hope and promise, with Africa the scene of major
interest. The United Nations had intervened in the Belgian
Congo in 1960 to prevent the further spread of civil war, and
probably to forestall Soviet intervention, but the educational system was totally disrupted in the turbulence. The United States,
through UNESCO, had contributed one million dollars for
African education the year before, but it was uncertain whether
Belgian educators would return, or be welcomed. In May 1961
UNESCO helped sponsor a Conference on African Education at
Addis Ababa, which Shuster later said constituted "one of the
most significant efforts in UNESCO history."[124] The conference
suggested that 450 million dollars would be needed for African
(sub-Saharan) education in the two-year 1965–66 period, and
one billion dollars by 1970. The African nations themselves could
never appropriate such sums. Other countries would need to
assist, and UNESCO might be the agency to coordinate such
efforts. UNESCO might also play a major role in training educational administrators, providing textbooks and other educational
materials, building physical facilities, and educating classroom
instructors. Educational systems in Africa seemed a golden
opportunity for UNESCO, with the Ivory Coast, Guinea, Ghana,
Nigeria, Cameroon, and Zaire among those gaining independence in recent years, and Burundi, Tanzania, Rwanda, Kenya,
and Uganda in the near future.[125]

At the next meeting of the UNESCO Executive Board that
spring, Shuster had high praise for the Addis Ababa conference,
was pleased that the United States had sent official observers, and
insisted that the United States "considered that it received in
exchange things of great value" for the assistance it gave other
countries. The United States gave material assistance to developing nations but expected to receive in return, and almost always
did, inspiration and wisdom from the countries it aided.[126] When
offering such aid, Shuster noted, the United States did not want
to impose American ways, because it was important for each
nation to retain its own culture and unique contributions. Shuster
urged other delegates to assist in the Congo education program,
expressed the hope that the Addis Ababa conference might be a
first step toward a permanent conference of African Ministers of

Education, and strongly supported a resolution opposing colonialism.[127]

After fifteen years UNESCO projects were so scattered and diverse that questions about control and budgetary oversight were understandable. At that 59th Session of the Executive Board, in addition to the major discussion of assistance to African education, the delegates deliberated on an educational conference scheduled for Chile, an academic training center in Beirut, a physics center in Brazil, an international meeting on oceanography, continued efforts to safeguard the Nubian monuments, a reduced budget allotment for the Republic of China, geographical distribution of the Secretariat staff, USSR delays in meeting its budget commitment, and the rising cost-of-living index in Paris, UNESCO's headquarters.[128] Despite obvious problems, Shuster urged the new secretary of state, Dean Rusk, to continue American support. "The program of UNESCO has developed in almost startling fashion," he wrote. "It is today unquestionably one of the great educational agencies of the world. . . . I think the organization will carry on somehow, simply because it must do so. There is no imaginable substitute for it."[129]

One immediate follow-up of recent Executive Board meetings and their emphasis on African education was the scheduling of a National Conference of the United States National Commission to meet in Boston that October on the theme "Africa and the United States: Images and Realities." Two thousand delegates, one hundred of them from Africa, attended the four-day conference. One of the principal speakers was Assistant Secretary of State for African Affairs G. Mennen Williams. Shuster had accepted appointment to another three-year term in 1960 and chaired one of the plenary sessions.[130] The question of United States relations with less developed nations was a delicate one, and while Shuster was honest enough to admit American failures in the past, he was also a government official responsible for defending American policies:

> It may be that some French primary school teachers in Africa did say naughty things about Americans. But after all, in most parts of that Continent our missionaries and sometimes their wives were giving a demonstration of the opposite. Perhaps also we now

and then played haughty in the Orient. But we did turn the Boxer Indemnity into a scholarship fund for the Chinese, we did make friends of the Philippinos and give them their independence, and on the whole—until Pearl Harbor—our relations with the Nisei were very good.[131]

Shuster attended another meeting of the UNESCO Executive Board in Paris that fall, and he and Doris followed it with a trip through Egypt to view the Nubian monuments and to survey the danger firsthand. He called the visit "extraordinarily interesting."[132] By the following spring, however, he had decided to resign, chiefly because his new work at Notre Dame was becoming increasingly time-consuming.[133] He attended the 61st Session of the Executive Board in May 1962 and must have found it typical of the successes and frustrations of the whole organization. In any voting that took place the side favored by the United States generally won, but by ever narrower margins, perhaps as additional countries from the Third World were admitted into the organization. There was the usual maneuvering and verbal sparring with the delegates of the Soviet Union and other Eastern European nations, and Shuster refused to permit unsubstantiated charges against countries of the West to remain in the official minutes unchallenged. Inefficiencies in the American organization remained evident also. With the early resignation of Director-General Veronese because of ill-health, a new director-general was to be recommended by the Executive Board. Shuster was informed late in the preliminary discussions whom the State Department wished to propose. None of the American delegates in Paris knew the man personally—all they had to go on was a mimeographed account of his career—and it was no wonder they could make no convincing case for his selection.[134]

Secretary of State Rusk accepted Shuster's official resignation that summer with regret:

> I am sorry to learn from your letter of your decision to step down as the United States member on the Executive Board. You have long and ably supported UNESCO and have represented our government with distinction in that organization, a service for which the Department is indeed grateful. I regret that you will no longer be officially representing us, but I feel confident that, as a

member of the U.S. National Commission, you will continue to take an active interest in UNESCO affairs and that your counsel and wisdom will be available to us when needed.[135]

There was some confusion over Shuster's resignation from the Executive Board—he had officially notified Secretary Rusk in June 1962, but apparently did not notify the Executive Board itself until Rusk had a successor to propose for election by the Board—and Shuster agreed to attend one final meeting, a joint session in Paris and Istanbul in late summer.[136] Conflicts with the Soviet delegation continued—generally over budgets, the admission of North Korea, North Vietnam, East Germany, and the People's Republic of China into the organization, and the dominating influence of the Western powers—and disagreements over a successor to Veronese at times bordered on the hostile. The United States decided to support the Dutch candidate, but Holland itself seemed hesitant ("in general played it as if they were wrangling for a bid to come to a dance," Shuster described it) and with as good a grace as possible eventually agreed upon Deputy Director-General Rene Maheu of France.[137] Shuster admitted that the discussions at times were unpleasant, but he enjoyed the visit to Turkey. "It is to be feared that Mrs. Shuster came back with too many 'souvenirs,' thus endangering the family budget," he noted. "But they will help us recall memorable experiences."[138]

As Secretary Rusk noted in his letter of mid-July, Shuster was able to continue his work for the United States National Commission, but only on a limited basis. He accepted committee assignments as offered, occasionally with humor. "It will no doubt be all right," he informed the chairman that February, "to keep on thinking that I can do something useful for the Sub-committee on Special Conferences and Seminars."[139] He could not attend the fall meeting of the national commission in 1962 because, as he explained to one of the officials, "unfortunately, my sojourn in Turkey, otherwise very memorable, brought with it an amoebic infection which has caused me considerable difficulty."[140] His term of office on the national commission was completed at the close of a meeting in Chicago that November 1963, and since he was ineligible for reappointment (having served two consecutive terms), his UNESCO activities came to a close.[141] He was succeeded on the Executive Board by his close friend

William Benton, and Benton hoped to benefit from his counsel. "I hope you will give me your continuing guidance," Benton wrote. "Your frank comments. If you ever want to come to Paris, I shall gladly pay your round trip expenses. We won't have to rely on the State Department."[142] Although Shuster did attend an occasional meeting of the national commission over the next decade, there is little evidence that he was able to find time to be of direct assistance.

During these latter months, however, Shuster was becoming an elder statesman of America's UNESCO involvement, and he did not neglect opportunities to offer comments and criticism. He had earlier felt, but without overwhelming confidence, that the commission (one hundred members) was too large, and by the 1960s he was sure that was true.[143] To retain the interest and support of one hundred academic leaders each would have to be given ample time to speak and comment, and the resulting ideas were almost certainly to be too numerous and too wide-ranging effectively to guide national policy. "The Department could of course use it for some sort of annual White House Conference," Shuster noted, "though I have never felt that these accomplished very much."[144] But excellent potential was there and reducing the size of the membership was one way to achieve it. A second need was to give at least the officers of the national commission direct assess to policy-makers in the State Department. Shuster realized that American policy toward UNESCO was influenced by broader political and diplomatic considerations than the State Department could make public, but access to higher State Department officials would ensure that the expert advice from the national commission was actually being heard rather than being shunted aside at some lower level.[145]

In January 1961 Shuster had sent a long letter to the Secretary of UNESCO's Executive Board, recommending changes which he believed would render that body more efficient. His concern was genuine since Executive Board meetings took approximately three months of his time each year. He recommended, first of all, that the constitutional responsibility of the Executive Board be adhered to consistently, that it serve as an agency of review for the General Conference. Proposals could still be submitted at any time to the director-general, but that official should then route them through the Executive Board, meeting three times each year, for approval and refinement before deliberation and voting by the General Conference. This should greatly streamline the procedures of the General Conference in its biennial meetings. In emergencies, and by a two-thirds membership vote, the conference could always take up matters not submitted through the Executive Board.[146] By better controlling the agenda, the Executive Board could assure that long-range planning would not be shunted aside by immediate needs and crises. Shuster had suggestions, too, for streamlining Executive Board procedures, especially assuring sufficient time for considering formal proposals. He acknowledged that there would always be divisions on the Executive Board—between richer and poorer nations on budget matters, between East and West on political and public relations issues—but he urged that steps be taken to cut back on political harangues and speeches delivered only for public relations value back home. "Except for one or two people," he warned ambassador Benton a little later, "the Board consists of talkative snails each one of which is trying to settle down on a special leaf. After a while one gets used to this but at first it can prove exasperating."[147] Shuster also advised the State Department that the positions of permanent United States representative to UNESCO and the United States representative on the Executive Board, held by Henry Kellermann and Shuster until then, be combined into one position, with the rank of ambassador, and this was done with the appointment of William Benton as Shuster's successor.[148]

Shuster's most extensive commentary on UNESCO and its work was a book he published for the Council on Foreign Relations in 1963, as he was bringing his service to that organization to a close: *UNESCO: Assessment and Promise*.[149] He had first approached the Ford Foundation in late 1961 about sponsoring such a study: "After all probably very few people have as much experience as I have had with the development and growth of the organization."[150] Shuster met with members of the Council on Foreign Relations a few months later, and the council agreed to sponsor the book and pay Shuster three thousand dollars in lieu of royalties. Shuster in turn agreed to complete the book, approximately one hundred pages, within three months, and to meet with the council to discuss the book and its findings once or twice before publication.[151] This in fact was done, and the book was also discussed at meetings of the United States National Commission for UNESCO.[152]

Shuster began his study optimistically. "I am one of those," he wrote in the Preface, "who believes that UNESCO is an international organization which can be and is very helpful in realizing not merely some of the humanitarian objectives we in this country respect, but also several of the hopes which are implicit in our foreign policy."[153] He acknowledged, here and elsewhere, that the organization was the target of much criticism in America—for recommending variations in the present educational system, for emphasizing international rather than national political loyalties, and for treating democratic and totalitarian nations equally—but he insisted that most criticisms were ill-founded.[154] On the other hand, there were serious issues the organization needed to face. UNESCO policies were necessarily inconsistent, he suggested, because new member states were always being added and gaining in influence and because the quality of the delegates also continued to change, and these were problems the organization needed to address. Some unwise projects, he admitted, had been undertaken, and others had not been efficiently controlled, but he did not believe that such embarrassments were numerous.[155] UNESCO's goals were good, but for Shuster, the major problem was recruiting satisfactory personnel to staff the central office and administer the programs. Because of lower salaries, Americans rarely competed for lower-level positions, all member nations had to be represented proportionately on the secretariat staff, and few academic leaders wanted to leave important educational positions for temporary service in Paris, especially service often heavily influenced by political considerations and compromise.[156] Shuster's major criticism of UNESCO may have been simply that its generally worthwhile programs were not being effectively administered under present procedures and with present personnel.

Despite the controversies and frustrations, UNESCO's accomplishments were not insignificant. The emphasis given to education and the financial assistance offered to poorer nations were excellent. UNESCO had undertaken a Major Project on the Extension and Improvement of Primary Education in Latin America; had established regional education centers in Bangkok, Bandung, New Delhi, and Manila; and had recently sponsored well-publicized conferences in Karachi and Addis Ababa. An

International Copyright Convention had been secured through UNESCO and an International Geophysical Year (1958) proclaimed. A project for research in arid land and soil improvement had yielded some benefits, as had projects to combat illiteracy, and the Major Project in East-West Understanding was improving international friendship and appreciation. UNESCO was also continuing the worthwhile works of the International Institute of Intellectual Cooperation, chiefly in the area of publications.[157]

After seventeen years of close collaboration, Shuster's final evaluation was modest but optimistic:

> There can be no question as to the significance of the role which as a result has been assigned to UNESCO. All the old jibes are now pointless. It is not an odd collection of intellectuals otherwise unemployed, or a society talking about peace when this is a mirage, or a household of ambassadors of good will conversing with each other. It is, above all, a forum in which those who have needs in the broad realm of education are able to present them, and where others decide whether the response can, in some sense at least, be a common response. It is the only means humankind has of seeing whether the two worlds now miles asunder—that associated with us and that in fief to Moscow and Peking—can cooperate at all within the broad framework of education. UNESCO would have to be created if it did not exist.[158]

10

RETURN TO NOTRE DAME

When George Shuster left Hunter College in February 1960, it was to a somewhat uncertain future. As he had written to the Board of Higher Education when announcing his resignation, there were two major desires he still wished to indulge: first, he had long been attracted to writing and yet had found little time to pursue it during the past twenty years; and second, he hoped to use his experience to influence in even a modest way national and world affairs.[1] But from what platform, from what office, would he do this, and, more mundanely, from where would he derive sufficient income to support Doris and himself through their declining years?

The immediate future was not a serious concern because the Board of Higher Education had granted him a terminal leave of absence for seven months and thus he would remain on the Hunter College payroll through August.[2] Those months would be busy ones. In early 1959 he had agreed to chair a committee of the American Council on Education to report on the availability of courses in non-Western cultures in American colleges and universities, and the report was due by the end of 1960.[3] He had also signed on with Robert Hutchins's Fund for the Republic in Santa Barbara and had agreed to head a New York office, which would be concerned mainly with raising funds for the various projects Hutchins hoped to sponsor.[4] From early April until May 6 he was in Paris for a UNESCO meeting, and he returned to Munich to attend the International Eucharistic Congress in August.[5] Immediately upon his return from Munich, he also agreed to chair a committee to make recommendations for an exhibit on American education at the New York World's Fair in 1964.[6] Finally, by mid-1960, Rev. Theodore Hesburgh, C.S.C., president of the University of Notre Dame, had convinced Shuster to return to

Notre Dame as assistant to the president and contribute his unique talents and experiences in strengthening and upgrading the academic level of his alma mater.[7] Once he returned to Notre Dame, Shuster never left.

In 1958 the American Council on Education had decided to undertake a nationwide survey of American colleges and universities to determine what courses in non-Western cultures were at present available to students, expanding on a narrower study completed by Robert Byrnes of Indiana University: *The Non-Western Areas in Undergraduate Education in Indiana.*[8] The Hazen Foundation provided a grant of twenty-nine thousand dollars, and in 1959 George Shuster agreed to chair a small committee that would conduct the survey, analyze the data collected, and draft an official report. The committee and research staff were quickly assembled, survey questionnaires were agreed upon and mailed, and Shuster himself spent much of the spring and summer of 1960, after turning over the presidency of Hunter College to his successor, visiting selected universities and learning firsthand of the difficulties encountered and the successes achieved. Although Shuster had an office in Manhattan for his Fund for the Republic work, he decided to work out of his home in Stamford for the ACE project. He accepted a salary of seventy-five hundred dollars as director, and hired his wife, a legal secretary before their marriage, for stenographic and typing assistance.[9]

By the end of 1960, most of the research was completed and, in a meeting of members of the committee with ACE officials in early March, 1961, a general outline of the report was agreed upon. By this time, however, Shuster had returned to full-time work as Father Hesburgh's assistant at Notre Dame—more than full-time he sometimes thought—and the drafting was constantly interrupted. On one occasion, when Doris was away, a finished chapter was somehow lost in transit between Shuster and a typist and it had to be completely redrafted.[10]

Shuster's final draft was not submitted to the council until December 1963.[11] Emphasizing the obvious, the report noted that World War II and its aftermath, the Cold War confrontation between East and West, had brought the nations of the world into much closer contact with each other, and yet Shuster's survey and campus visits suggested that all schools were not responding equally well to this new demand and new opportunity. The task was not at all impossible, Shuster insisted. Even very young Americans were at least minimally world conscious—Volkswagon, Suez, the Korean War, and Khrushchev were all familiar names— and just as American schools in the past had prepared students well for citizenship in a democratic society, so might they now prepare students for an international society. For Shuster that did not mean dropping any subjects now being taught, but only broadening them or adding others. He thought changes could be made most easily in the areas of literature and the fine arts, and probably less easily in history and philosophy. Western emphases there seemed particularly strong. Shuster suggested that all undergraduates might be required to study one society other than their own before graduation and that Ph.D. programs include minor concentrations in other civilizations. He admitted that producing satisfactory textbooks would not be easy, recalling his own dissatisfaction with UNESCO's *History of Mankind*, and despite his friendship and even admiration for Robert Hutchins, he judged the so-called Great Books not a feasible vehicle because they too were almost exclusively Western.[12] Shuster's final report—submitted within ten days of President John Kennedy's assassination and amid growing concern about campus unrest, the revolution in civil rights, and the escalation of the war in Vietnam— received little public attention.

One major distraction from this work on the council's report in the late summer and early fall of 1960 was a commitment Shuster made to help plan an educational exhibit for the New York World's Fair of 1964. Robert Moses, president of the World's Fair Corporation, wrote to Shuster that August, asking him to select a small committee and jointly draft a proposal of not more than five thousand words for an exhibit portraying "progress in education and democratic institutions." A budget of thirty thousand dollars was allotted and a deadline of November 1 was stipulated.[13] Shuster immediately accepted, selecting four others for his committee and naming Robert Hutchins, Marcel Breuer, John Meng, and others as consultants.[14] The report was completed by the end of October and returned to Moses on October 29. The proposal recommended a building of two stories, two hundred by one hundred feet. There were to be eight rooms in all, divided into two groups of four, one portraying educational institutions and the other the developing characteristics of education. For the former, one room each would be devoted to elementary education, the high school, the college, and the university, with photographs and artifacts showing the history of each, individual leaders, and major accomplishments. The four rooms portraying the developing characteristics of education were devoted to the development of the teaching profession, the town meeting then and now (from town meetings to educational TV), education and the person (educational counseling, physical education, exchange programs), and support of education (both private and public financial assistance).[15] Shuster worked conscientiously on the project, found the discussions worthwhile and challenging, but unfortunately the committee's final recommendation was not accepted by the World's Fair Corporation.[16]

Shuster's work that year for Robert Hutchins's Fund for the Republic may have been similarly unproductive. His acquaintance with Hutchins was long-standing: they had undoubtedly met at academic meetings and conventions while Shuster was president of Hunter and Hutchins was heading the University of Chicago; from 1943 to 1947 Shuster was a member of Hutchins's Commission on Freedom of the Press; and more recently they were serving together on the Board of Directors of Encyclopedia Britannica.[17] The Fund for the Republic had been established in 1952 with a grant of approximately fifteen million dollars from the Ford Foundation to "defend and advance the principles of the Declaration of Independence, the Constitution, and the Bill of Rights." Specific topics it intended to investigate in this era of Senator McCarthy included the procedures of congressional committees themselves, loyalty programs, immigration policies, blacklisting, censorship, segregated schools in the South and segregated housing in the North, and the plight of Native Americans. Shuster had been named to the first Board of Directors in the early 1950s.[18]

Shuster played a significant role in the Fund's activities throughout the decade. At the first meeting of the Board of Directors, he was elected to its planning committee, he interviewed prospective candidates for the presidency, and he served as acting president of the Fund on one occasion.[19] More significantly, it was Shuster who recommended the most important decision the Fund made: the establishment in 1956 of the Center for the Study of Democratic Institutions. The Fund had sponsored numerous projects, but they were diverse and almost autonomous, and Hutchins and the Board of Directors feared that, because of their autonomy, they were probably not having the unified educational impact originally intended. It was Shuster who recommended the establishment of an institute to investigate and discuss what were called the Basic Issues, the "political and moral principles underlying civil liberties and civil rights" as one author has defined them, and the Fund shortly thereafter purchased property in Santa Barbara, California, and, patterned only slightly after the Institute for Advanced Study at Princeton, set up the Center for the Study of Democratic Institutions.[20]

By late 1959 the center had a small but full-time support staff, a nucleus of resident fellows, and a program of distinguished visiting fellows, and the work it was doing was attracting public acclaim. A major problem, however, was that the Fund's original grant from the Ford Foundation was rapidly diminishing—it was then down to approximately four million dollars—and thus the future of the center was in some doubt. Because Shuster had been associated with the Fund from its beginning and had been one of the prime movers for the establishment of the center, it would have been difficult for him to decline Hutchins's invitation to join the center for one year after his retirement from Hunter and help solicit foundation support for the center's projects. At that time Shuster had made no long-range plans for the future, he had good contacts with various foundations in New York, and the post would give him an additional year in which to accept a more permanent position. Hutchins opened an office for him on East 54th Street in New York but his work for UNESCO, the American Council on Education, and the World's Fair Corporation occupied much of his time and he was in fact unable to add large sums to the Fund's coffer during that year.[21]

Shuster was only sixty-five years old in 1960, in relatively good health, well respected in religious and educational circles, and he had accepted the position with the Fund for the Republic only temporarily. Permanent job offers continued to mount. Doris later recalled that he came home one evening from his

Fund office and remarked: "You know, this has been a lost day. I wasn't offered a job."[22] From all his work with the Ford Foundation, especially with the Free University of Berlin, the American-German Conferences, and the Fund for the Republic, he probably could have taken a position there, and this was the office Doris would have preferred.[23] But the offer that Shuster eventually accepted came from Notre Dame. One evening after work, while George and Doris were enjoying a cocktail before dinner, Father Hesburgh called from Notre Dame. The conversation lasted almost two hours, and Doris kept the dinner waiting. Father Hesburgh explained that Notre Dame was in a position to become a truly first-rate academic institution, that private and public funding was available for respected research, and that he himself was committed to remain as president to see these efforts bear fruit. George finally hung up the phone and turned to Doris: "Can you imagine that after all these years I'm asked to go back to Notre Dame?"[24]

The surprise was warranted. Shuster had been hired on the Notre Dame faculty in 1919 by then-president Father James Burns, C.S.C. Father Burns had taken steps to terminate the high school or preparatory program, to divide the university into separate colleges under more autonomous deans, and especially to undertake a massive fund-raising drive to help upgrade both the physical facilities and the quality of the teaching and research. Young Shuster had found all this exciting. But after only three years, Father Burns was unexpectedly removed from the presidency by his religious superiors, and his successor, Father Matthew Walsh, C.S.C., did not seem to share the same high scholarly ideals—at least not in Shuster's eyes—and Shuster left his position and went to New York in 1924. The following year he published two articles in *America* and *The Commonweal* highly critical of Catholic higher education in general and of Notre Dame specifically.[25] Many at Notre Dame never forgave him for this public criticism of his alma mater. The offer to return was indeed a surprise.

But Hesburgh either decided it was time to forgive and forget, or more probably, agreed that many of Shuster's charges had been justified. In late March Notre Dame announced that it was awarding Shuster its prestigious Laetare Medal, an award established by Father Sorin in 1883 to honor each year an American

Catholic lay man or woman who had attained unusual success in his or her chosen profession. Recent recipients had included Governor Alfred E. Smith, actress Irene Dunne, labor leader George Meany, Ambassador Clare Boothe Luce, and Irish tenor John McCormack. President John Kennedy would receive the award the following year. The announcement of the award was made on the Fourth Sunday of Lent, Laetare Sunday, March 27 in 1960, but the medal was conferred during impressive commencement ceremonies on campus early in June. Sharing the stage that day with Shuster were President Dwight Eisenhower, the university's commencement speaker, and honorary degree recipients Cardinal Giovanni Montini, archbishop of Milan and future Pope Paul VI, and Dr. Thomas Dooley, missionary doctor in Southeast Asia.[26] It was a most memorable day, but many still felt that Notre Dame had delayed too long, that Shuster had been at the height of his profession either at *The Commonweal* or at Hunter College, not after his retirement from both.[27]

If Notre Dame's offer of a position was a surprise, so to many of his friends was Shuster's acceptance. Doris certainly would have preferred that they remain in New York, and she was still hurt by Notre Dame's earlier criticism of George and by the long delay in awarding the Laetare Medal.[28] Shuster's close friend, Saul Alinsky, wrote from Chicago:

> I get torn by ambivalent feelings whenever I think of you in South Bend. First, I am overjoyed at the proximity and to know that I shall be seeing you frequently (and if you avoid Chicago I shall repeatedly invade South Bend) and then I get feelings of melancholia thinking of you trying to do what you will be doing in a matrix controlled by and permeated by "Cheer, cheer for Old Notre Dame" and "Hold that Line." They say that every time there is a change of a football coach it has always been a question as to whether they are going to get rid of the president or the coach, and some say that Paul of Tarsus had a push-over organizing the Roman Catholic Church compared to the ordeal of a scholar faced with the South Bend intellectual jungle of tackles, guards, full-backs and T formation. . . . This is one time I desperately hope that all of my information is completely wrong.[29]

But the return to Notre Dame was not at all difficult to explain. In fact, it was almost natural, the culmination of his life's work. Shuster always felt comfortable and at home in an academic environment. Even when working almost more than full-time at *The Commonweal* he still taught part-time at St. Joseph's College for Women and at Immaculate Conception Seminary at Huntington, and it was understandable that he might prefer to spend his final years on a college campus. After twenty years as a college president, he was certainly convinced that he had something important to contribute. Shuster was deeply religious and devoted to Catholicism, and he knew he could serve his church well through Catholic education. And Father Hesburgh's goal of raising Notre Dame to the front ranks of American higher education did not seem unrealistic. From 1948 to 1958 Notre Dame had raised a most impressive twenty-five million dollars from outside sources; the Ford Foundation had awarded a three million dollar grant in 1957 to assist its academic programs; and in 1960, along with Johns Hopkins, Vanderbilt, the University of Denver, Brown, and Stanford, the University of Notre Dame was singled out for a grant of six million dollars from the same Foundation, in part for faculty development.[30] With such support, the possibilities for major progress seemed exciting; that this challenge came from Shuster's own alma mater made the invitation all the more attractive.

The offer that Shuster accepted from Notre Dame was neither clear nor precise. His position was to be assistant to the president, and he was assigned an office in the Administration Building, close to that of Father Hesburgh. His principal work was to be assisting the advancement in scholarship chiefly in the humanities and social sciences, especially by helping to locate necessary funding for scholarly research and uninterrupted study. For this a new institute or center was soon created, the Center for the Study of Man in Contemporary Society, with Shuster as the first director.[31] The distinction between the two positions, assistant to the president and director of the center, was not always clear and would eventually cause confusion, and even embarrassment, when a successor as director was needed. But if the position Shuster assumed at Notre Dame was not precise, it was indeed firm, and he began his work in early 1961. For the first several weeks he lived in the Morris Inn, a comfortable hotel recently built at the entrance of campus by a Notre Dame alumnus, while Doris remained in Stamford, putting their large home up for sale.

In early spring Doris moved to South Bend also, and they rented a home on East LaSalle Street, approximately a mile from campus. After a brief search, they located a rather spacious ranch-style home for sale in a quiet residential area on the southern side of town, at least three miles from the university. George, Doris, and their pet poodle, Bonnie, moved there in late spring, and Doris immediately began serious renovations.[32] The adjoining garage was turned into an enlarged kitchen, and a new garage was added on the other end of the house. The backyard was spacious enough for George to pursue his hobby of rose-gardening and also for the construction of a small swimming pool, which Doris used regularly during the summers.

Shuster's original intention—and hope—was that a single donor might be found to endow the center's activities. Several possible individual and corporate donors were approached in the spring and summer of 1961 but all eventually declined.[33] Father Hesburgh had immediately made $200,000 available from university funds, and Shuster made use of this to inaugurate programs which could then apply for outside funding more successfully. Within a few years Shuster's close friend and fellow alumnus, Jerome Crowley of O'Brien Paint Company, provided the center with a grant of fifty-thousand dollars to be used as "seed money" to assist faculty research over the next three years in the humanities, social sciences, law, and business administration. At the close of the three-year period, a second grant of ninety-eight thousand dollars was awarded for the next seven years. Since one of Shuster's primary goals was the initiation of additional research in the humanities and social sciences, the O'Brien Fund was particularly beneficial.[34] But since no major endowment had been procured for the center, much of Shuster's work as director was the solicitation of smaller funds to finance individual projects the faculty wished to pursue.

Shuster's efforts benefited greatly from the construction of two new buildings, one already underway in 1960 and the other only an uncertain dream. Construction was then moving forward for the new, fourteen-story Memorial Library (now the Theodore M. Hesburgh Library), the largest college library building in the world at the time of its completion in 1963. The structure could house three million volumes, 250 faculty members would have offices there, and Shuster himself would preside over research and administrative offices occupying the whole of the eleventh floor. Shortly after his arrival, Shuster began cooperating with Father Hesburgh and Academic Vice President Father John Walsh, C.S.C., in efforts to secure from the Kellogg Foundation a grant for construction of a Center for Continuing Education on campus. Such a modern conference center, with seminar rooms, translating services for international gatherings—and connected by an underground walkway to the living accommodations of the Morris Inn across the street—would be of great assistance to the various programs and conferences Shuster hoped to sponsor. In fact, the official proposal to the Kellogg Foundation emphasized the close collaboration envisioned between such a facility and Shuster's programs under the Center for the Study of Man in Contemporary Society. Shuster was one of the happiest of Notre Dame's officials when the grant was finally approved.[35]

One of the earliest efforts to attract a major research grant to Notre Dame was a success and brought a measure of national acclaim to the university, but the final research also met with serious criticism. The Carnegie Corporation of New York had expressed an interest in sponsoring an in-depth study of Catholic elementary and secondary education in the United States, both strengths and weaknesses, similar to the study of public education recently undertaken by former Harvard president James B. Conant.[36] Father Hesburgh and Shuster agreed that such a study would be valuable, and also that it could be most successfully undertaken by a Catholic university, and by August 1961 Shuster had a specific proposal to present to the Carnegie Corporation. The scope of the study would be both elementary and secondary schools, and areas to be investigated would include differing goals of students, teachers, and parents; available resources; administrative structures; pertinence of the curricula; and level of academic achievement. Researchers would utilize whatever sources were available: studies already undertaken by other colleges and universities, statistics available through the National Catholic Educational Association, and especially questionnaires drafted specifically for this study. Shuster thought the study could be completed in three years, and he even volunteered to resign his UNESCO position in order to devote more time to it.[37]

Carnegie officials were impressed with the proposal, pared approximately fifty thousand dollars from the projected budget, and announced a grant of $350,000. Shuster immediately hired Dr. William Conley of Marquette University as director and Reginald Neuwien, former superintendent of schools in Stamford, Connecticut, as associate director; collected an impressive National Advisory Committee of church leaders, educators, and business leaders; and began work enthusiastically. Before long, however, problems emerged. Thirteen dioceses had been singled out for in-depth studies, but data arrived irregularly from some. Computerization of the data was slow because Notre Dame was not far advanced in this technology. Conley resigned in 1963 to assume the presidency of Sacred Heart College in Bridgeport, and Neuwien was promoted to replace him. There were serious disagreements over the quality of the questionnaires and other instruments being used, and Notre Dame's own Education Department decided not to be a part of it. Carnegie officials themselves realized that the study was not going smoothly but decided it was better not to interfere. In fact, when Shuster requested additional money to expand the study to school finances, another forty-six thousand dollars was forthcoming.[38]

The final result, published in 1966, was a report of some 328 pages, entitled *Catholic Schools in Action: The Notre Dame Study of Catholic Elementary and Secondary Schools in the United States.*[39] Divided into eight chapters, the study examined enrollment trends and the adequacy of present facilities, the availability and qualifications of teachers, the training of religious men and women for classroom work, the success of religious instruction in the schools, the values students absorbed there, and evaluations of the present school system by both the students and their parents. Many of the report's conclusions were not striking, nor were they unexpected, but at least now they were supported by hard evidence. The study revealed that only one-half of eligible Catholic grade schoolers were in Catholic schools and less than one-third of those of high school age, that learning potential was good but that this was due in part to the system's selectivity, that the economic and professional status of lay teachers was not high and that turn-over was rapid (an average of about four years for women), that the curriculum in smaller schools was often quite restricted, and that the religious learning of school graduates was only at the "conventional level."[40]

Most reviewers had praise for the significant data the study had collected. The *New York Times* called it "probably the most extensive study of the parochial schools ever undertaken in the United States" and the reviewer in the *Harvard Educational Review* noted that such data were especially significant since the Catholic school system was in no sense a monolith, that each diocese was almost autonomous, and that statistics from different dioceses were not earlier available.[41] Beyond this, the praise was limited. Some critics insisted that the decision to avoid both evaluations and comparisons with the public educational system greatly reduced the study's value.[42] But the harshest critics charged that the collection of data was too haphazard, the instruments used too unscientific, and the respondents not representative. The source of the difficulty was thought to be either that parts of the study were simply done too hurriedly or that too many on the staff, especially Shuster and Neuwien, were educational administrators rather than experts in social science technology.[43] The review of Daniel Callahan, a Catholic, was especially harsh:

> The Notre Dame study, while useful, is marred by blatantly sloppy methods of data collection and evaluation. It is better than nothing, but it seems incredible that a university with the resources of Notre Dame should have tolerated such ineptitude.[44]

Much more successful was Shuster's assistance in building up a Latin American Studies program at Notre Dame. Notre Dame's interest in the Latin American area was not new. As a widely known Catholic university, Notre Dame had long attracted students from Central and South America. In the 1880s, the university's noted scientist, Father John Zahm, C.S.C., used to recruit students during research trips south of the border, and in 1884 they returned on the "First International Train from Mexico City to Notre Dame."[45] Father John O'Hara, C.S.C., first head of the Department of Commerce in 1920 and president of the university in the 1930s, had spent part of his youth in Montevideo, where his father was consul, had inaugurated programs in Foreign Commerce, especially with Latin America, and had continued Father Zahm's recruiting efforts in the various countries he visited.[46] By the 1950s the La Raza Club, composed of Latin American students, was a prominent campus organization. But although Latin American history was offered and there was a Latin American orientation to several courses in economics, political science, and commerce, no broad Latin American Studies program had yet been adopted.[47] University officials were convinced that this was an area where Notre Dame could and should have an impact, and Shuster joined the effort.

Notre Dame's original proposal, drafted by Shuster and Latin American specialists on the faculty, was broad and unusual. "Of course the underlying idea is that *change* is the dominant note in Latin America today," Shuster wrote his good friend William Benton, "and that one cannot follow that change in any other way than continuously."[48] One part of the proposal, therefore, was to support approximately 120 Catholic leaders and intellectuals throughout Latin America who would send back to Notre Dame information and important data on the changing political, economic, and social scene in various countries. This information would then serve as a research base for graduate dissertations or other scholarly monographs. Notre Dame faculty members would maintain mutually beneficial contacts with colleagues in Latin American universities. As interest increased, the university's Latin American course offerings would be expanded and graduate fellowships could be added. Shuster envisioned that the cost of the program, including administration, would be $175,000 annually, and he hoped for an initial grant to support the first five years.[49] He thought first of the Ford Foundation and, contacting its officials that May, only a month after the disastrous Bay of Pigs invasion, he remarked that American officials had obviously misjudged the Cuban situation and a program like the one recommended could perhaps supply more accurate information.[50]

To demonstrate Notre Dame's serious interest even while the proposal was being drafted, Shuster helped sponsor a major symposium at the university on the subject of religion and social revolution in Latin America. He estimated that the cost would be close to twenty thousand dollars, including travel, honoraria, and hospitality, but when the Rockefeller Foundation offered only seven thousand (for travel and honoraria for the nine invited speakers) Shuster agreed that his office would cover the rest. The conference was that important, he thought, for getting the Latin American program under way.[51] After extensive planning, the symposium took place in April of 1963. Shuster welcomed the guests in the name of the University of Notre Dame and provided the introductions. The Argentine Ambassador to the United States, Honorable Roberto T. Alemann, was a luncheon guest, and the conference speakers included Professor Arthur Whitaker of the University of Pennsylvania, Eduardo Frei Montalva of the Chilean National Senate (later president of Chile), Auxiliary Bishop Marcos McGrath, C.S.C., of Panama, Emilio Maspero of the Latin American Congress of Christian Labor Unions, and Simon Hanson, editor of *Inter-American Economic Affairs*.[52] The conference papers were eventually published as *Religion, Revolution, and Reform: New Forces for Change in Latin America*, and most reviewers praised the book, and the conference, for emphasizing both the centrality of the church, for good or for ill, in any Latin American reform, and the necessity for the church to become more open and flexible if its influence was to be constructive.[53]

Shuster in the meantime was continuing discussions for a major grant with the Ford Foundation, and in mid-1963 Foundation officials suggested that provision for collaborative efforts with other universities might make the proposal even more attractive.[54] This suggestion met with immediate acceptance from both Shuster and Father Hesburgh, and they drew up plans for a so-called Triangular Conference, a seminar of scholars and university officials from the United States, Latin America, and Europe, to study some of the major social problems confronting Latin America. After further discussions the Ford Foundation and the Agency for International Development each contributed fifteen thousand dollars, and the first of the proposed conferences was held in Santiago, Chile, in February 1965.[55] The conference succeeded in bringing together an interested and talented group of scholars. They discussed various problems needing research and investigation, and they reached at least initial agreement on the roles the three councils in Latin America, the United States, and Europe might play. These contacts continued, especially between sociologists, economists, and political scientists at Notre Dame

and scholars in Peru and Chile, but further Triangular Conferences were not held. The Latin American participants apparently
wanted the organization headquartered in Latin America, but
Father Hesburgh and Shuster insisted that essential funding from
American foundations would be forthcoming only if the organization were centered here.[56] Despite the differences, the contacts
continued and became an important component of Notre Dame's
Latin American Studies program.

By late 1963 the efforts of Shuster and Father Hesburgh
began to bear fruit, even more than they may have hoped. In 1960
the Ford Foundation had offered Notre Dame six million dollars
for academic development on condition that Notre Dame raise an
additional twelve million dollars within three years, which the university promptly did. In December 1963 the Foundation offered a
second six million dollar grant under the same conditions. Notre
Dame immediately accepted and inaugurated a "Challenge II"
program to raise the desired twelve million dollars. Father
Hesburgh announced that part of the money would be utilized for
the Latin American Studies program.[57] Five months later the
Rockefeller Foundation awarded Notre Dame a grant of $210,000
for Latin American Studies, specifically $150,000 for salaries of
additional faculty and $60,000 for travel and other expenses to
facilitate collaboration with Latin American universities.[58]
Professor John Kennedy, a political scientist and Latin American
expert, was hired from the University of Virginia as director, and
the program expanded through the departments of history, economics, sociology, and political science. As deans and heads of
departments took over responsibility for the program's administration, Shuster's influence declined. But what he had helped to
found in the 1960s reached full fruition in the early 1980s when
the Helen Kellogg Foundation gave the university ten million dollars for international studies, and the emphasis in this new
Kellogg Institute was immediately focused on Latin America.[59]

By the time these major grants from the Ford Foundation
and Rockefeller Foundation were announced in late 1963 and
early 1964, Shuster's position in Notre Dame's official academic
hierarchy was well established. He had been hired in 1961 to assist
the university's research efforts in the social sciences and humanities through a Center for the Study of Man in Contemporary

Society, but in the early years at least, the center had no permanent home except in Shuster's small office close to Father Hesburgh's in the university's Administration Building. Shuster, in fact, made light of his sparse quarters. "When someone asks," he wrote for an alumni publication, "where the Center for the Study of Man in Contemporary Society is, I answer, 'In Father Hesburgh's head and mine.' That would seem to indicate that the second part of the housing leaves very much to be desired."[60]

Despite lack of adequate physical facilities at first, the center's place in the university's educational enterprise was clear. Shuster and others insisted that education necessitated a "two track" approach. The first track, which Shuster acknowledged also needed strengthening at Notre Dame, comprised traditional academic programs and components—students, faculty, resources—associated with standard college curricula and the classroom experience. The second track called for the establishment of exciting new projects and approaches, chiefly in the areas of theology, philosophy, law, the social sciences, history, literature, and business, where the university might undertake specialized research, sponsor scholarly symposia, and support new initiatives in solving emerging social problems. As a private Catholic university—free of restrictions from state legislatures and able to bring strong ethical, moral, and religious considerations to its investigations—Notre Dame could make unique contributions to the field of scholarship. Shuster always insisted that the two tracks were not in opposition, nor did the second in any way supersede the first. In fact, the second could attract more brilliant faculty to Notre Dame and the classroom experience, on both the graduate and undergraduate levels, could only be better because of it.[61]

In addition to the Carnegie Study of Catholic Elementary and Secondary Education and the strong support of a Latin American Studies program, the center sponsored numerous other research projects and academic conferences in its early years. In the area of theology, the center supported national conferences on religion and education; it received financial support from New York's Cardinal Francis Spellman and others to publish a series of theological works, called the Cardinal O'Hara Series after Notre Dame's one-time president and later cardinal-archbishop of Philadelphia; and it sponsored a pilot program, again with outside funding, to bring biblical stories to television. In philosophy it funded studies of artificial intelligence, studies later supported by the National Science Foundation. In this era of the emerging nations of Africa, the center sponsored a conference in 1961 on the role of mission schools in the development of education in Africa, and it later helped establish an African Studies program at the university. With major funding from the Lavenburg-Corner House, the Department of Health, Education, and Welfare, and eventually the Office of Economic Opportunity, the center assisted Professors Bernard Lander of Hunter College and Hugh O'Brien of Notre Dame in their studies of juvenile delinquency and of vocationally handicapped youths and in their investigation of the effects of social services on the poor. In early 1964 the center co-sponsored an important "Galileo Quatercentenary Congress, 1564–1964" at Notre Dame, and the papers delivered there were later published in the well-reviewed *Galileo: Man of Science*.[62]

One of Shuster's earliest fund-raising projects on his return to Notre Dame, and one that must have caused him much personal anguish, was his effort to revitalize the university's Maritain Center. Jacques Maritain, a convert to Catholicism and the twentieth century's most highly respected proponent of the philosophy of St. Thomas Aquinas, had visited Notre Dame frequently and had been persuaded to donate to the university a quantity of his books, manuscripts, and personal correspondence. The university had set aside space in its new Memorial Library for a Maritain Center. Its purpose was to house this collection and to encourage further study of Maritain's philosophy and eventually to publish a complete edition of his works.[63] Although Shuster, especially in his earlier years, had had serious reservations about Thomistic philosophy, he and Maritain had been friends since the 1930s, when both were opposing European totalitarianism and Shuster was attempting to make such European Catholic authors better known in America through the pages of *The Commonweal*. Funding was needed to provide the Maritain Center with a director and secretary, to grant fellowships to students desiring to pursue the philosophy of Maritain, and ultimately to bring forth a complete collection of his works, and Shuster was asked to take on this assignment.[64]

With the philosophy of Saint Thomas losing its support and adherents, even on Catholic campuses, Shuster realized that funding for any narrow vision of the Maritain Center would be difficult and, in his promotional materials, he attempted to broaden the center's purpose to include also Catholic-Protestant dialogues, Christian-Islamic projects, symposia on religion and science, and so on, projects he hoped would attract outside funding. But Maritain himself objected. The Maritain Center was to be concerned specifically with his thought and teaching, and he was not willing to lend his name and his support if this purpose were diluted. "It is crystal clear," Maritain wrote Shuster,

> that the University, in general, and especially the Department of Philosophy, remain in this regard [the purpose of the center] out of the picture. They may teach any kind of Thomistic or non-Thomistic philosophy they please. . . . But it is crystal clear, also, that as far as the Maritain Center is concerned, this particular place, to which I have accepted to have my name attached has only to do with the study and development of my own philosophy and interpretation of living Thomism: and this means a *real*—that is, modest, patient, immune of any publicity purpose, intellectually profound, dedicated and at long-range work—of understanding and training, and steady effort of ploughing and studying, (at least for the time being).[65]

Shuster answered as diplomatically as he could. He admitted that in recent months he had been committing more time to the Maritain Center than to any other project on his desk. "No one could be more anxious than I," he pleaded, "to make it an effective force in American life, and indeed in the cultural life of mankind generally." He was convinced that the center could have two purposes. The first would be the training of students in Maritain's philosophy and the editing of his works—and Shuster admitted that funding for these would not be easy. "The second point of view," he added, however, "is to consider those aspects of your thought which have very great significance at the present time when the plight of man and society is so dire. Here the objective would be to carry forward certain seminal trends in your thinking in the same creative way you so brilliantly exemplified." Shuster then listed several of these intercultural projects he had in mind. But Maritain was not convinced, encouraged perhaps by Thomists at Notre Dame who did not wish to see the purposes of the center expanded. Shuster had to rein in some of his more expansive projects and the large donations he was seeking never materialized.[66]

As Shuster's broadened plans for the Maritain Center met with both increased opposition and minimal financial interest, he turned his attention to an even loftier project, but one which might also accomplish his earlier goals—an Institute for Higher Religious Studies. Shuster was convinced in the early 1960s that the timing was excellent. The Second Vatican Council in Rome was spawning ecumenical dialogue across the world, and in the United States the election of President John Kennedy was helping break down Catholic-Protestant antagonisms. Shuster envisioned an institute where Catholics, Protestants, Moslems, Jews, and others could come together, even for extended periods of time, to understand one another better and especially to work cooperatively to resolve the serious social problems the world was facing.[67]

The vision was indeed a large one. Architectural plans were drawn up for an impressive building complex on the side of one of the two small lakes at the edge of campus, with a pleasant walkway extending out to a nearby island. The main structure would be a ten- or eleven-story residence building, with suites for up to forty visiting fellows and with additional facilities for dining and recreation and a rooftop terrace. Connected buildings would be smaller, two stories in height, and contain administrative offices, seminar rooms, and study facilities.[68] Shuster even drafted a set of by-laws for the institute:

> The Institute has been established by the University of Notre Dame in order to promote studies in depth of those areas of inquiry, social policy and action, and historical re-evaluation which reveal a convergence of Religion with other disciplines. It will seek to achieve its aims in three principal ways: (a) by providing opportunity for mature scholars to remain for limited periods of time; (b) offering such scholars the means to become identified with the ongoing teaching and research at Notre Dame, if they so desire; and (c) making it possible for a group or "team" of scholars to deal with a problem of importance.[69]

The proposed cost would be large. Shuster informed Notre Dame's Associate Board of Lay Trustees that the physical facilities would run to approximately $3 million and an additional $10 million would be needed for an operating endowment. Five members of the Board's Development Committee immediately pledged a total of more than $125,000 on the condition that the university raise an additional $75,000, enabling the Ford Foundation

Challenge grant to contribute another $100,000. With the $300,000, the proposed institute could be officially announced and programs developed while additional funding was sought.[70]

Initially, good progress was made. Professor James Kritzeck, an expert in Islamic religion and culture and a member of the Institute for Advanced Study at Princeton (and the person Shuster had earlier hoped to attract to the Maritain Center) was appointed director, and Howard Phalin, a Notre Dame alumnus and chairman of the board of Field Enterprises in Chicago, pledged a further $300,000.[71] One or two visiting scholars were attracted to Notre Dame for extended periods, especially Dr. Charles Malik of Lebanon, and very worthwhile intercultural conferences and discussions were held, but the institute itself never became a reality.

The reason for the institute's eventual demise was threefold. First, despite Shuster's best efforts, donations on the required scale were simply not forthcoming. Second, the institute's director, Professor Kritzeck, although a well-respected scholar, was not effective in organizing programs and in fund-raising efforts. By the end of the decade Shuster himself became more directly involved and personally took over more of the development and public relations responsibility, but by then it was too late. And finally, at approximately the same time, Pope Paul VI asked Father Hesburgh to take on the responsibility of establishing an ecumenical house of theological studies outside Jerusalem, and this diverted attention and even financial resources away from Shuster's institute and fulfilled in large part the mission Shuster had in mind. Various intercultural and ecumenical projects continued at Notre Dame, and even expanded, but the highly publicized Institute for Higher Religious Studies never left the drawing board.[72]

Of all the projects Shuster sponsored as center director, he would undoubtedly have judged his support of population studies the most significant. The studies did not have the immediate impact he may have hoped, but their long-range effects were significant, and they certainly influenced Shuster personally.

Notre Dame's, and Shuster's, entrance into this field, at least on the level that eventually developed, came about almost accidentally. Cass Canfield of Planned Parenthood had been corresponding with Father John A. O'Brien at Notre Dame about the possibility of holding a national conference in New York on family planning. O'Brien showed the letter to Shuster, and Shuster suggested an alternative. To have the desired impact, Shuster noted, the conference would have to have respected Catholic priests and laity as participants. These would need the permission of the Archdiocese of New York to participate there, and Shuster was sure it would not be given. He recommended, as an alternative, that the conference be sponsored at Notre Dame, with whichever participants O'Brien and Canfield wished to invite. "This arrangement would enable prominent Catholics to attend without difficulty," he stated. "For any problem involving participation in a meeting sponsored by Planned Parenthood would have been removed."[73]

Canfield immediately agreed, the Population Council of New York assisted with five thousand dollars, and the dates January 11–12, 1963, were set. Canfield himself suggested three questions for discussion:

1. What is the general thinking from various viewpoints on the "population" problem, its extent and probable consequences?
2. What are the beliefs of the different faiths concerning the regulation of family size in the context of responsible parenthood, and to what extent is there agreement here?
3. What are the opportunities—among religious groups themselves, and between religious groups and the Planned Parenthood organization—for co-operative thought and action on these vital matters.[74]

The conference accomplished precisely what was intended. Twenty-four participants attended, about half from universities; others included James Norris of Catholic Relief Services, Alan Guttmacher of Planned Parenthood, Frank Notestein of the Population Council, Leland DeVinney of the Rockefeller Foundation, and Oscar Harkavy of the Ford Foundation. Dr. Richard Fagley of the Commission of the Churches on International Affairs summarized the Protestant view, insisting that *responsible* parenthood is essential, that family limitation should be evaluated according to motives rather than means, that limitation is acceptable if not injurious to the child or contrary to the wishes of either spouse, and that abortion is condemned as the taking of human life. Father O'Brien summarized the Catholic position—that marriage is above all a sacrament and a holy state, that procreation is a clear biblical mandate, that Pope Pius XII had approved the rhythm method even for a lifetime, and that no religious group should impose its teachings on any other group. Doctor Guttmacher presented the Jewish viewpoint, noting that the Talmud permits contraception under some conditions, that Catholic and orthodox Jews hold similar views on contraception, and that some rabbis approve of the pill and others do not. Dudley Kirk of the Population Council spoke on the current research in demographic studies, and Oscar Harkavy outlined what studies sponsored by the Ford Foundation were discovering. Open discussions centered around religious agreements and disagreements, the impact of population growth on different countries of the world, the need for more convenient and more accurate testing of the ovulatory cycle, and the role of government in such intimate family decisions.[75]

Because such discussions were politically delicate, especially for the Catholic participants, Shuster had agreed that publicity would be minimal. Nonetheless, the conference was so successful and the exchanges so beneficial that he immediately sought additional funding to schedule further sessions.[76] The Ford Foundation, which had sent a representative to the first gathering, approved a grant of twenty-one thousand dollars in the summer of 1963 to support three additional conferences over the next two years.[77] The first of these was held, again at Notre Dame, in early September 1963, with only Catholics participating and with the agenda limited to clarifying the Catholic position. According to Shuster, the conclusions were that there were differences of opinion among theologians over whether the present Catholic teaching on contraception was immutable [the papal encyclical on birth control was still five years away]; that American Catholics, as in Britain, need not oppose contraception clinics as long as rhythm clinics were established also; that population problems in our urban areas and in many foreign countries were becoming critical; and that programs in education were an urgent need.[78]

A later conference, held in March 1965, was the most significant of all, and also the most controversial.[79] Almost forty attended and they drafted a statement to be sent to the papal commission earlier established to advise the pope on his proposed birth control encyclical. The conferees acknowledged the urgency of the question. "The crisis of world population," they wrote, "the demands of responsible parenthood, and the more subtle but no less imperative requirements of conjugal love which give rise in many instances to grave moral dilemmas, all attest to this urgency." They further acknowledged that, for them, past norms "are not definitive but remain open for further development." Past arguments, they continued, "do not manifest an adequate appreciation of the findings of physiology, psychology, sociology and demography, nor do they reveal a sufficient grasp of the complexity and the inherent value of sexuality in human life." The key paragraph read as follows:

> The majority of the members were of the opinion that there is dependable evidence that contraception is not intrinsically immoral, and that therefore there are certain circumstances in which it may be permitted or indeed even recommended. While marriage is ordered to procreation, the individual acts which express and deepen the marital union need not in every instance be so ordered. For procreation in the full sense (*bonum prolis*) includes the Christian rearing of the child in a well-regulated harmonious environment of love. This environment may demand the continuance of sexual communion even if a new pregnancy cannot be responsibly undertaken.[80]

It was indeed an extraordinary document, a dissent from current church teaching, signed by thirty-seven of the most respected Catholic priests and laity in the United States. Two reservations, however, need to be noted. Several more conservative or traditional American theologians, although equally esteemed and respected—Msgr. Austin Vaughan, Father John Ford, S.J., Father Anthony Padovano, and Germaine Grisez—either had not been invited or had chosen not to attend.[81] And the crucial paragraph also stated that "the majority of the members were of the opinion," indicating that even among those who signed the statement, there were apparently some who disagreed.

Public controversy erupted five months later. Shuster had sent a copy of the statement confidentially to the papal commission through its secretary, Father Henri do Riedmatten, O.P. In fact, Father Hesburgh was on his way to Rome at the time and delivered it personally. After several months it was discovered that the document had still not been circulated to the commission members. When he was approached in Rome, do Riedmatten indicated that he had not received enough copies. A priest visiting in Rome then volunteered to make sixty copies for the commission on a mimeograph machine at his disposal. On his way to the Vatican to deliver the copies, however, he met John Cogley, religion editor of the *New York Times*, and Cogley informed him that, although he already knew about the Notre Dame document, he wanted a copy to check his facts. On September 28, 1965, the document was made public through the *New York Times*, with all signers identified.[82]

This revelation caused consternation back at Notre Dame and elsewhere across the country. The conferees had agreed that the document was to remain confidential and that the identities of the signers would not be made public, and for a time the source of the leak was unknown. Shuster immediately contacted all the conferees by night letter: "Following talk with Father Imbiorski [Walter Imbiorski of Chicago, one of the conference convenors] I have taken the following position. The University sent the Commission a confidential letter. This letter is now the sole property of the Papal Commission itself. You may wish to follow this policy. We here are unaware of the Cogley source."[83] After learning that a priest-friend was the source of the leak, Shuster was forgiving but embarrassed. The revelation, he wrote Father Hesburgh, "clears up the mystery of the release of the Statement. I am not blaming him, but still what a thing to do! We had not asked the signers whether they agreed to that release. This is the truly embarrassing thing about the episode."[84]

Three additional conferences were eventually held, sponsored chiefly by a second generous grant from the Ford Foundation, but their impact was limited. In December 1965 Shuster invited a small group to attend a two-day gathering on campus chiefly to hear a report from Professor William Liu of Notre Dame's sociology department on a population studies program the university was undertaking, and especially to receive reactions and recommendations. The university sponsored a conference the following September, chiefly for public officials, on the subject of population and public policy, but since the United States Senate remained longer in session that summer, only the invited members of the House of Representatives could attend. A final conference was held in December 1966, and those papers were eventually published under the title *Family and Fertility*.[85]

One of the topics that surfaced during every conference was the urgency of the population problem in other countries, especially poorer ones, and Shuster encouraged studies abroad also. The Population Conference of September 1963 had raised the question of the attitude of British Catholics toward contraception clinics there, and the following year Shuster's center received a grant of nine thousand dollars to enable Notre Dame sociologist Donald Barrett to study rhythm clinics in Great Britain more thoroughly.[86] A few years later Professor William Liu undertook a study of population attitudes and trends in the Philippines, not without some controversy over the validity of his data due to lack of sophisticated techniques in some of the less developed areas.[87] And, finally, in 1965 the Agency for International Development awarded Notre Dame a grant of approximately $550,000 to study "Family and Fertility Changes in Latin America" over the next three years. This project ran into controversy also when some accused the investigators of encouraging family planning, local authorities protested to the State Department, and funding was almost abruptly terminated. Direct correspondence between Shuster and Secretary of State Dean Rusk eventually worked out a satisfactory solution.[88]

On July 25, 1968, Pope Paul VI issued his long-awaited encyclical on birth control, *Humanae Vitae*. He noted the serious economic hardships suffered in many countries because food supplies were not keeping pace with expanding populations, and he urged greater scientific investigation and scholarly research toward solving such dilemmas. But he also reaffirmed the church's traditional prohibition of artificial contraception, although continuing the church's approval of the rhythm method of natural family planning, limiting sexual intercourse to those periods when conception would not result.[89]

Shuster was disappointed with the papal statement and gave his view in the syndicated column he was then contributing to several diocesan newspapers. He noted that the church's position on marital ethics had developed during centuries when high infant mortality kept the population limited, but increased populations and food shortages now made hunger and starvation stark realities and the proper care and education of children in some places impossible. He then asked for a temporary relaxation of the church's ban on artificial contraception:

> What I argue for with all the strength I possess is that the present grave situation in which human society finds itself must be taken into account realistically. . . .
>
> Can we not urge that "natural law" is not applicable in the state of nature which we of the present unfortunately call our environment? When poverty and ignorance have been alleviated another day will have dawned.
>
> Can we not ask that when the rhythm method has been perfected, the discussion can proceed in an entirely different mode? . . .
>
> In short, we would not ask the Pope to alter his moral position, nor would we question the privilege of the magisterium. We would merely ask that he grant what is entirely within the scope of his authority to grant and suspend for a time demands on the laity throughout the world which they cannot possibly meet.[90]

Ever the mediator, Shuster also sought to save what he could of a disappointing situation. William Draper of the Population Crisis Committee met with Father Hesburgh that fall and suggested that the Committee would be willing to seek a grant of one million dollars to finance a three-year scientific study of the rhythm method and especially of ways of making it more effective. He suggested further that such a research institute be established at Notre Dame and that Pope Paul VI be asked to support it publicly since his encyclical had explicitly urged scientists to advance this natural family planning method. Hesburgh agreed that the idea was sound and asked Shuster to represent him in the project.[91]

After further discussions and correspondence, Draper, Shuster, and Eugene Power, a regent of the University of Michigan, flew to Rome in mid-December to speak with Vatican officials and solicit papal approval of the project. Shuster found the meetings encouraging. The officials they spoke with were not at all agreed on the wisdom of some parts of the encyclical, and they hoped to distance themselves somewhat from the harder-lined reaction to dissent taken by Cardinal Patrick O'Boyle of Washington and Cardinal James McIntyre of Los Angeles. Draper's proposal met with strong support, although these were all lower-level officials, and Draper, Shuster, and Powers then agreed on the next steps toward implementation. First, they would redraft the proposal in the form of a letter to be sent to the pope over Father Hesburgh's signature, asking for official support. Second, the research should be done through a Foundation for the Study of Human Reproduction, and Notre Dame, with its departments of biology, social sciences, and theology, seemed to be an excellent location for it. Finally, the foundation should be under the supervision of an independent board of trustees, with Hesburgh as chairman and Shuster as secretary, to award specific grants for research in this area.[92]

The Draper proposal was then redrafted, and Father Hesburgh sent it on to Pope Paul VI through Secretary of State Cardinal Amleto Cicognani, former Vatican representative in Washington:

> The Foundation, jointly sponsored by Notre Dame University and the Population Crisis Committee, will do all in its power to respond to Pope Paul VI's Encyclical, *Humanae Vitae*, which asked science to make the rhythm method of birth control effective. . . .
>
> When adequately financed, the Foundation will undertake a scientific and carefully documented research program, intended to find and pinpoint practical and generally useable means to recognize and if possible predict the specific time of ovulation and thereby to identify unmistakably the so-called "safe period" of the monthly cycle."[93]

Hesburgh's covering letter asked again for explicit Vatican approval and financial support. He noted that even a small Vatican contribution would make it easier to solicit additional financial support in the United States, and since many considered the recent encyclical principally negative, such a contribution would also be a very public, positive step.[94]

The plan unfortunately never materialized. One reason was that, during this first year of Richard Nixon's administration and the escalation of bombing in the Vietnam War, Father Hesburgh— and most other university presidents—were forced to devote so much attention to campus unrest. Shuster wrote to Draper early that July:

> For some time I have been trying to tie Father Hesburgh down with reference to the proposal you initiated and in which he took a

great interest. But over the past months he has been so concerned with student problems that it has literally not been possible to get him to think about other matters. This concern has taken a great deal out of him.[95]

But the major difficulty had nothing to do with Hesburgh. Cardinal O'Boyle of Washington and Bishop John Wright of Pittsburgh had developed a similar idea of raising one million dollars to sponsor programs to improve the rhythm method. And Wright had recently been elevated to the College of Cardinals and given a position in the Vatican. It was now clear that if the Vatican supported any program, it would be the O'Boyle-Wright proposal rather than the Shuster-Draper plan. And it was Vatican approval that would have given the Notre Dame project special prestige and probably assured its fund-raising success.[96]

In his private correspondence throughout the 1960s, Shuster gave his own views on the question of contraception. Shortly after the first Population Conference in 1963, Shuster wrote to a Jesuit friend:

> It seems to me that our Theology ought to be restated. All we have to do in my opinion is to read St. Paul and consider very carefully what he said on the subject and stop talking about the Natural Law as if it were something which drew a sharp distinction between one form of birth prevention and another. It just doesn't. All we have to go by is that the Popes look on Onan as a rascal and approve the use of Rhythm for a variety of reasons in various circumstances. This is binding on us and will remain so until it is otherwise decreed. . . .
>
> What if rhythm doesn't work? We all know what happens. But I am personally persuaded that the pill offers an acceptable solution provided it is really made a matter of moral counseling. I should not wish to see married couples resort to it of their own accord because it does unquestionably involve factors which are not present in the use of Rhythm. On the other hand, granted reliable indications that the Rhythm method cannot be relied upon and the desirability of family increase is not present, I believe it would be admissible on moral grounds. And I hope that before the Council [Vatican II] goes out of business it will say so.[97]

Shuster rejected as both impractical and even untheological the idea that, if rhythm did not work, abstinence was the only moral alternative. He returns to St. Paul:

What he says about sex and marriage is frank and to the point. He says that sex is a very powerful drive, and that if one can't fend it off the thing to do is to get married. And indeed if we are frank there is no other good reason for marrying. Women and men were never meant to live together for any other purpose.

Those who recommended celibacy and abstinence in marriage were wholly unrealistic: "In other words, they assumed that marriage would somehow abrogate the only reason why it exists."

Shuster was also strongly critical, again in private, of the church's practice of denying the sacraments, especially the eucharist, to those resorting to contraception:

> But I think I am prepared to say that the manner in which the priests of this country have been instructed to deal with contraception in the confessional is one of the scandals of our ecclesiastical history. It is true that the unworthy . . . should not, as St. Paul said, partake of the Lord. But if this be the case . . . it seems a very narrow theology of Penance which eliminates from consideration what the penitent's concept of his unworthiness is. He may, for example, be in a position where he can neither abstain from the "marriage act"—a phrase which I detest—nor seriously endanger the health of his wife by inducing another pregnancy. The inability to abstain may be a weakness, though I am not sure it is, but the refusal to endanger the wife's health is a virtuous action.
>
> If these things be true, surely the aim in the confessional should be to suggest that the weakness, if again it be one, can be overcome through the fullness of Eucharistic grace. How anyone could ever believe that the weakness could be surmounted by closing the door to the sacramental life has always been beyond my comprehension. This is not a new view. I argued it with moralists in a major seminary thirty years ago.[98]

When the encyclical was finally issued in 1968, Shuster was critical, but only moderately so. He wrote a friend the following month:

> We are having rather saddened days. I don't believe that any of us were prepared for the Encyclical as written, especially the parts urging States not to foster birth control methods of which he disapproves—I think he is on an uncharted island on that one—but his basic purpose does deserve more respect than many Catholic theologians and journalists are giving it. He makes a strong case for the sacredness of life and against unrestrained libidos; which

indicates that a sense of the holy is still alive in the Church. I can only wish that he had said what he wanted to say and then added that in view of the population problems he was granting an indult for twenty years, at the end of which time the Church could reassess the situation.[99]

He remained with this recommendation of an indult and explained it further two years later:

> Very briefly. Like so many other teachings of the Church in the field of morals that about contraception is also governed by the conditions under which it must be obeyed.
>
> Thus killing is a crime, but killing in self-defense is not. Stealing is wrong, but not if the thief is starving. These and other actions are governed by indults. In the case of contraception, the distribution and use of the pill or the coil has been sanctioned, for instance, in the case of nuns threatened with rape by incoming Russian soldiers. My contention, and I believe it strongly, is that if child-bearing makes the problem of starvation greater, or creates a grave threat of population surpluses, an indult would seem to be permissible, especially since the alternative provided by Pius XII, namely the rhythm method, was itself an indult.
>
> If the rhythm method were practicable, or if abortion were not the only real alternative provided, the situation might be different.[100]

By the time this letter was written, March 1971, Shuster had long left his position as director of the Center for the Study of Man in Contemporary Society. He was already sixty-six years old when he returned to Notre Dame in 1961, and he may have originally agreed with Father Hesburgh to see what he could accomplish in five years. At least he had been given a five-year budget of $200,000 when he began.[101] He was bothered apparently by no more than the usual aches and pains of a near-seventy-year-old during most of this time, but other afflictions gradually began to slow his pace. They could not dampen his humor, however. He wrote a friend in the fall of 1966: "I stupidly stumbled and fell on my not too minute proboscis with consequences that might have been anticipated."[102] The fall also loosened a few teeth. Arriving in New York two months later to address a conference sponsored by the Department of Health, Education, and Welfare, he suddenly took sick in his hotel room and called his son to rush him to his former doctor at Stamford Hospital. He feared kidney stones, but it turned out to be a urinary tract infection. "Nobody has ever been pumped fuller of wonder drugs or made to pose for more x-ray pictures. But at least I know that I do not have heat flashes, TB, leukemia, or St. Vitus Dance. Nor am I in much danger of helping to increase the population."[103] His eyesight began to fail and he suffered an infection in 1972 and even wore a patch over one eye a few years later.[104] He was relying more and more on Doris, especially for driving, and she was experiencing similar mishaps. In late 1968 she also fell and broke some blood vessels in one arm; a year later she was hospitalized for a time with a painful back injury; and shortly after recovering from that, she fell again and dislocated a shoulder. In early 1970 George and Doris spent a full month in Hawaii, in part to recover from various afflictions.[105]

One problem with Shuster retiring as director of the center was that he wore so many hats that it was not clear precisely which responsibilities he was acquitting as director. He was primarily concerned, as director, with sponsoring research and conferences in the humanities and social sciences, but as assistant to the president he was a member of the university's officers group or council of vice presidents. And as close personal advisor and confidant of Father Hesburgh he carried out whatever other responsibilities the president desired. Shuster hoped to leave the center at the close of 1967, but negotiations with his chosen successor broke down, with some bitterness, over the requirement to earn tenure through an academic department and over membership in the officers group and other decision-making bodies.[106] The present close relationship between Hesburgh and Shuster could not be duplicated with another. Eventually, Father Ernest Bartell, C.S.C., chairman of the department of economics and an expert in private school financing, was named associate director with Shuster, and then director in 1969.[107]

When Shuster first raised the question of his retirement in 1967, Father Hesburgh sent him a heartfelt letter:

> As I have told you many times in the past, there is a place for you at Notre Dame, a very important and fruitful one, as long as you desire to be involved and as far as I am concerned, this can be on your own terms. I deeply believe that many of the things you do

here defy any kind of organizational chart because they are personal, inspirational, and visionary. We deeply need all three of these functions if the University is to reach its full stature and if young men are to be encouraged as well as older faculty members kept from going to seed. Students, too, need some of the wisdom you disburse so freely and so generously to them. And, needless to say, I am always grateful for your abundant help in so many areas.[108]

General as this letter was, it was probably as specific as it could be in describing the broad variety of contributions Shuster made to Notre Dame throughout the 1960s. He assisted Dr. Stephen Kertesz of the Committee on International Relations in his sponsorship of conferences and publications, he co-sponsored with the Catholic Academy of Bavaria a conference on Freedom and Authority, and he supported students in their "Little United Nations" project on campus. He helped establish faculty committees in the humanities, the social sciences, and education to encourage scholarly research and publication. He encouraged experimental programs in the university's freshman humanities classes and the collegiate seminar, a modified Great Books program. He helped work out a financial arrangement to bring the valuable library of philosopher Elias Dennissoff to campus, he sat on the Board of Editors of the University of Notre Dame Press, and he sought funding for art gallery brochures. With his long association with Phi Beta Kappa at Hunter College, he helped establish a chapter at Notre Dame in 1968, and he was part of a four-man team that visited alumni groups across the country to solicit donations to match the Ford Foundation's Challenge Grant. Month by month he continued to channel small but significant amounts of start-up money to enable faculty members to expand their research interests.[109]

As Shuster's advice and counsel became more valued by university officials, Father Hesburgh decided to appoint him to the university's Associate Board of Lay Trustees in 1963. This board, made up primarily of lawyers and business leaders, was charged principally with investing and administering the university's increasing endowment, but it served to advise and assist the university administration in other areas also. Shuster wrote his friend, Father John J. Cavanaugh, C.S.C.: "I continue to be mystified by my appointment to the Board of Lay Trustees," but he worked well with these other national leaders and brought years of educational experience to the Board's deliberations and decision-making.[110] Nationwide fund drives were successfully inaugurated and, with matching millions from the Ford Foundation, large sums of money became available. New building projects were approved, curriculum revisions were undertaken, and the Catholic character of the university had to be safeguarded as the drive for academic excellence continued.[111]

Clearly the most important decision affecting the Associate Board, and the whole university, occurred in 1967. In the aftermath of the Second Vatican Council, the Congregation of Holy Cross, which had founded the university in 1842 and had continued to own it for 125 years, decided to divest itself of this institution and turn its control over to a predominantly Lay Board of Trustees. Most of the members of the Associate Board, including Shuster, were named to the new Board, and the Associate Board was abolished. Shuster was also named chairman of the new Board's Education Committee, later changed to Faculty Affairs Committee. The purpose of this committee was "to establish a mutually beneficial liaison between the Board and the Faculty of the University." It was not to be an appeals board or concern itself with day to day administrative decisions, but to be concerned "with broad issues of academic policy about which it believes the Board of Trustees should be informed so that it can exercise appropriate leadership."[112] Shuster remained on the Board until 1971, an important voice of academic experience during the difficult and highly significant days of the 1960s.

At Notre Dame, and all across the country, the most serious problem confronting the university administration and Board of Trustees was the growing unrest among the student body. The causes of the unrest were several—a participation in the broader civil rights movement of the 1950s and 1960s, growing opposition to the escalation of the Vietnam War, impatience with the nation's apparent inability to solve its urban problems, and especially the increasing impersonality of college campuses as universities almost suddenly burgeoned into enrollments of thirty, forty, or fifty thousand. Although the discontent and agitation at Notre Dame never turned violent, the campus was not spared. In early

1969 Father Hesburgh received national acclaim and a letter of praise from Vice President Spiro Agnew for his "fifteen-minute rule," ordering the suspension from school of any student demonstrating in a way that blocked the ongoing activity of a university office for more than fifteen minutes.[113]

As might be expected, Shuster felt that the problem of student unrest, the competing demands of students and policies of administrators, could be solved only through mediation and rational discussion. In the wake of unrest at Berkeley in 1965, he had shared his thoughts with philosopher Sydney Hook:

> In my own experience, only three measures help. First every campus should have a joint Faculty-Student Committee composed of members chosen through election. Second, this Committee should meet regularly with the top administrative officers. Third, it should report to the Faculty at stated intervals, so that in a crisis its judgment will be welcomed and trusted.[114]

Three years later, after several demonstrations on campus, the Board of Trustees approved the establishment of a very similar committee, a Student Life Council, composed of equal representation from the faculty, the administration, and the student body.[115] When a sit-in occurred a few months later, Shuster praised Father Hesburgh's attitude and analysis, but also lamented that mediating bodies were not used:

> It seems to me that the point you make in your letter is the absolutely correct one. We are not debating the issue whether the CIA is morally indefensible or whether somebody may peacefully assemble to protest against it. The only issue is, as you say, that of freedom.
>
> But I must admit that it seems to me too bad that the governing bodies of the University were not assembled at the very same time the sit-ins began. I know that you weren't here and cannot therefore be burdened with responsibility. Instead we had a kind of spectacle one would hardly have expected at Notre Dame— a Mass, harangues, filthy bodies, etc.[116]

In an effort to improve faculty, student, and administration relations himself, Shuster periodically invited groups of student leaders to his home for lunch or dinner, with a corresponding number of faculty and administrators. Serious questions may never have been resolved, but the pleasant conversation and

Doris's excellent meals certainly demonstrated that at least this university official was listening and deeply cared.[117]

One of the sources of campus unrest was the growing involvement in the Vietnam War, and Shuster's views of that conflict were mixed. As the troop build-up began in 1965, he lamented its effect on national outlook:

> Vietnam may or may not be the place for us to be. . . . But beyond any doubt one effect of being there is to make our peers in the world, friends and foes alike, think that because we are so bogged down in Vietnam we have no time left for taking real initiatives elsewhere. There has been no serious approach to Western Europe, and indeed no steam has been put behind disarmament. I should think that just because we are in Vietnam, we should redouble our efforts on every other front.[118]

As the bombing north of the seventeenth parallel increased, Shuster's ambivalence became clearer:

> It does no good to argue any more about the Vietnam war. For my part I have been able to justify our presence there only on two grounds—first, that a Communist victory would probably wipe out the emigres from the North, and second that the Mekong Delta is so vitally important to the future development of Southeast Asia that if at all possible it should not be permitted to fall into Communist hands. But whether these things are important enough to justify the losses we are suffering and inflicting is a question I leave for others to decide.[119]

He stated the same opinion, although more philosophically, to his friend James O'Gara of *The Commonweal* six months later:

> At any rate there arises a grave question: can human rights be defended in the final analysis without recourse to force? To me the answer seems clear. They cannot be. The supporting testimony is already contained in the Book of Revelations. . . .
> Yet it is part of the dark tragedy of the human situation that once recourse is had to force in Caesar's world it is difficult if indeed not sometimes impossible to make it function within the context of justice. Thus the campaign against Hitler spilled over into the bombing of Dresden, the expulsion of the Sudeten Germans and by implication the rain of death on Hiroshima. . . .
> There is no easy way out. One need not swallow the whole of Reinhold Niebuhr's favorite thesis in order to contend that while

we cannot have rights without the use of force, it is in like manner
tragically hard to employ force within the bounds of justice. But
there is no excuse for failing to try. . . .

Therefore it seems to me quite evident that so long as the
purpose of armed intervention was to reckon with these facts and
to attempt on the one hand to protect human rights while on the
other hand assisting those protected to strengthen the frail structure of democratic government there was no reason why the
Christian conscience should dissent. Indeed, I would contend that
it should agree. . . .

Today there are some, and often in high places, who talk as
their predecessors did about Hiroshima and the bomb. Their con-
tention is that world public opinion can safely be told to go to hell
while we go "all out." Maybe so. But certainly if the Christian conscience in this country is alive at all it must say that bombing tar-
gets in North Vietnam is unjust, regardless of how beneficial or
perilous they may be. If we do not speak now we shall confront the
repetition of Dresden and Hiroshima. I think that all of us, regardless of how we may differ about the Vietnamese situation in its
entirety, could agree on this point and make ourselves heard in
some unison.[120]

Although Shuster had serious reservations about several military decisions taken in Vietnam, he had no sympathy with those
anti-war protestors who wanted to see all R.O.T.C. [Reserve
Officers Training Corps] programs dropped from college campuses. He expressed his view to the secretary of the Academic
Council at Notre Dame:

I sincerely hope that no action will be taken to lessen the impact of
the R.O.T.C. at Notre Dame. . . .

I have been observing and even sharing in the foreign affairs
of the United States for a long time. It may well be that I have
worked for the cause of peace as much as anyone of my period. But
I do not feel that it is anywhere in sight. We as a people will doubtless need trained military leaders as much as we do now.[121]

When World University Service adopted a resolution in
1970 that universities should sever their relations with R.O.T.C.
and the military, Shuster sent a strong response:

I therefore request you to remove my name from any list of
directors, honorary or otherwise, as of this date. . . . I am not at all
in sympathy with the stand the directors have taken, and so wish
you to note my disassociation with them immediately.[122]

One early example of campus unrest at Notre Dame, and an example undoubtedly embarrassing for Shuster, was a movement among some student leaders to have Father Hesburgh removed as president—and replaced by George Shuster! In February 1963 the lead editorial in the student magazine, *The Scholastic,* began:

> Now that the student romance with Fr. Hesburgh is over, the necessity of evaluating the administrative power structure and prevailing modes of thinking is evident. For reasons that will become obvious we feel that it is imperative that Fr. Hesburgh be removed from his post as President and be designated Chancellor. For the Presidency we would advocate that a renowned lay educator of the stature of George N. Shuster, presently special assistant to the President, be appointed to govern the internal affairs of the university.[123]

The reasons behind their suggestion seemed twofold. First, Father Hesburgh was so occupied with commitments away from the university—Atoms for Peace Conferences, Carnegie Corporation work, the Peace Corps, the Civil Rights Commission, and so on—that he seemed unable to devote the requisite time to guiding the internal affairs of a university which, to his credit, he had brought to such national prominence. Second, Father Hesburgh's adult life had been spent as a priest and a member of the Congregation of Holy Cross, subject to obedience to superiors, and the editorial suggested that the way to run a religious order was not at all the way to run an academic institution.

In the following issue Shuster wrote his reply. "Now that a student romance with a man of my 'stature' seems to have begun," he noted, paraphrasing the earlier editorial, "it may be appropriate for the somewhat reluctant partner to reply."[124] He dismissed any personal consideration immediately. "Why did I come to Notre Dame?," he asked. "Obviously not to be president, since I could have kept right on being one." Then he analyzed the arguments of the students' editorial and found them all wanting. Whatever you call him, president or chancellor, only one person can be at the top and make the final decisions, and that person, in fact, has to be away from campus much of the time. It is only that way that the president or chancellor can attract funds and professors and national prestige. Since priests who were serving as deans and department chairmen were performing as well as laymen in similar positions, there was no reason to suppose that a layman would have greater success as president. Furthermore, it had been the Congregation of Holy Cross that had founded and built the university to its present stature, the Congregation certainly had rights at the university, and probably only a member of that religious community could be successful in soliciting the large contributions necessary to continue its progress. There were problems at Notre Dame as there were on every college campus, Shuster admitted, but in a few years, he predicted, these same students will look back and recall that "there was something luminous, living and persistent in the spirit of Notre Dame."[125]

As Notre Dame continued to develop throughout the 1960s—construction of new buildings, increased undergraduate enrollments, expansion of graduate programs, and a rapidly expanding budget—Shuster admitted that the administrative structure might need revision, but he rejected the chancellor-president arrangement. "For my part," he wrote, "I have always favored the Columbia University arrangement, which flanks the President with a Provost," and a few years later, this was precisely the new structure the Board of Trustees established.[126]

The creation of the office of provost was not the only change undertaken at Notre Dame with the recommendation of Shuster during these turbulent days. In the spring of 1968, perhaps at the suggestion of the Board of Trustees, Father Hesburgh asked Shuster and Dean of the College of Arts and Letters Father Charles Sheedy, C.S.C., to draft a statement or position paper on the state of student life on campus. Shuster drafted the statement himself, incorporated additional suggestions of Father Sheedy, and forwarded it on to the president.[127]

The statement noted that several factors were influencing student climate on college campuses across the country: the rapid increase in college enrollments; fewer rules and regulations, with consequently more freedom; fewer serious worries by students about the future since the country seemed prosperous; and a sense that society was failing (the Vietnam War might be one illustration) and thus anti-establishment stances were popular. The sources of discontent varied only slightly at Notre Dame. The rules and regulations had recently become more liberal; the residence halls were overcrowded and consequently less orderly; there were problems in the food service, and since the university managed it, it received the criticism; and relations with women on the still all-male campus were limited and the behavior of the men probably more boorish.

Shuster and Sheedy rejected the demands of a recent student assembly—that rules and regulations be made by students alone and that all judicial boards be composed exclusively of students—but they made their own specific recommendations. In the area of academics they admitted that with the recent emphasis on faculty research teaching might be losing some of its priority, and that with a possible over-emphasis on grades (to remain in college or enter graduate school or not be drafted to Vietnam), some elective courses might be permitted on a simple pass-fail basis. In the area of residence life the report noted with favor that additional residence halls were being constructed and the dining facilities enlarged. On the administrative level the report noted that the president seemed to be involved too early in student disputes (the creation of the office of provost would soon mitigate this); it suggested that some form of student, faculty, administration council be established to oversee student life; that a more professional method of selecting and training hall rectors be devised; that the campus judicial system pay more attention to student rights and adopt more open procedures; and that the emphasis in the Student Affairs area be not on discipline and prevention of abuses but on positive cooperation with students in providing a more comfortable and pleasant living environment. Over the next few years a pass-fail system was in fact instituted, the office of provost was created, the Student Life Council was set up, wider student rights were incorporated in the student manual, the number of students in each residence hall was significantly reduced, a new team was appointed to the Student Affairs area, and the university began admitting undergraduate women to its student body in 1972.

This decision to admit undergraduate women—to "go coed," as the phrase of the time expressed it—was one of the most important, but also most controversial, decisions taken during Shuster's years as a Notre Dame administrator. Many traditionally all-male colleges, both religious and others, had begun admitting women during this period—Boston College, Georgetown, Yale, Rutgers, even the military academies eventually—and Notre Dame was following a trend. Single-sex high schools were fewer in number, and students were more comfortable with coeducational classrooms; the admission of women, a formerly unutilized pool of applicants, would significantly raise the academic level of the student body; educating men and women together seemed a better preparation for working together after graduation; and with more and more smaller Catholic women's colleges forced to close— chiefly due to financial difficulties—there would be fewer options in Catholic education for women if traditionally male institutions did not change.[128]

Convinced of the cogency of many of these arguments, Notre Dame and neighboring Saint Mary's College had begun cooperative programs by the middle of the decade. There were clear advantages in women and men learning together, and it seemed financially wasteful to duplicate at least marginal programs on each campus. A so-called "co-exchange" program was begun in the fall of 1965, permitting a limited number of upper-division students to take classes on the other campus. Some language and science classes at Notre Dame could accommodate additional students, and Saint Mary's undergraduate education program could be very beneficial for Notre Dame students seeking a teaching career. A shuttle bus was established between the two schools, approximately a mile apart; regular meetings of administrators from the two schools took place; all financial adjustments were postponed until additional data were available; and, by the end of the spring semester, approximately two hundred students from the two schools were participating in the co-exchange program.[129]

With the popularity and success of this "co-ex" program, the year 1966 witnessed two further developments in intercampus cooperation. The first was that, as a result of discussions at the spring meeting of the Executive Committee of Notre Dame's Associate Board of Lay Trustees, Father Hesburgh asked Shuster to draw up a tentative master proposal, the "best possible plan for future intellectual cooperation between the two schools." Shuster later acknowledged that his selection had merit: he had been president of a women's college for twenty years; he was quite familiar with the "cluster college" idea; and he was personally close to Saint Mary's College since his wife was a Saint Mary's graduate, he had been married on that campus, and they had maintained close contacts with the college ever since. Shuster accepted the assignment but noted also that "this one will require courage akin to that demanded of a sheriff in a western movie."[130]

Shuster then asked a member of the Notre Dame sociology department to draft a questionnaire to send to students and faculty of both schools in order to gauge present sentiment and to elicit suggestions for further cooperative steps. The questionnaire became an immediate source of controversy. Some questions seemed condescending—should members of the Saint Mary's faculty be encouraged to cooperate in research projects with the Notre Dame faculty—and others might have seemed a veiled threat—whatever the relationship between Notre Dame and Saint Mary's, should Notre Dame establish a small experimental college for women on its own campus. Many at Saint Mary's considered the questionnaire "obviously biased, very confusing, and blatantly talking down to St. Mary's." In the opinion of one faculty member, the "cow had already been sold and a decision was needed only as to how it should be cut up." Shuster immediately tried to reassure his Saint Mary's colleagues. He stated that one purpose of the questionnaire was "to try to shock people into telling us what they think" and after that they could better decide what steps to take next. He also admitted that no questionnaire could be completely satisfying and that was why this one encouraged written comments also. He felt that some opponents were focusing on the details and losing sight of the broader, more important issue. "What Notre Dame wants," he insisted, "is for St. Mary's as a component part of Catholic education to be the best and for better relations to exist between the students."[131]

A second development in 1966 was the establishment of an official "Notre Dame–St. Mary's Co-Exchange Committee," a fifteen-member committee appointed jointly by the two college presidents. A Saint Mary's representative, Dr. Francis Benton, was elected chairman, and Father David Burrell, C.S.C., of Notre Dame, was named secretary. Shuster was a delegate from Notre Dame. The committee sought to mitigate any fears either faculty or staff might have about a closer affiliation between the two schools and, after requisite study, recommended steps toward closer collaboration. The representatives met with department chairs on each campus to solicit suggestions and be advised of possible difficulties; they studied the feasibility of shared library privileges immediately and the connecting of the two telephone systems; and they closely monitored the co-exchange program of shared classes. In December Shuster sent a personal report to Father Hesburgh:

> The purpose of this one is to report on what has happened in the area of St. Mary's-Notre Dame relations. Father Sheedy has done very well, indeed, with the co-ex program, and I shall say no more about that except to report that it seems to be achieving greater stability and awakening wider student interest.
>
> I had three exploratory sessions, the first of which was with the Co-Ex Committee. We went over the questionnaire and I think achieved a goodly measure of agreement. . . .
>
> My talk to the St. Mary's Board of Trustees went extremely well. Sister Renata [former president of Saint Mary's] played devil's advocate but the tide in favor of cooperation was overwhelming.
>
> About a week ago I went over and talked to the Faculty. It was rather an ordeal, because a handful of dissidents dominated the discussion. But I believe the response was rather affirmative even so.[132]

In early 1967 Shuster wrote an article for the student weekly, *The Scholastic*, in which he outlined his views on current negotiations. "What is meant by affiliation between St. Mary's and Notre Dame?," he asked. "No one is thinking of absorption, coeducation, or second-class citizenship on either campus. We have in mind rather a condition of cooperation into which both institutions can grow, undertaking jointly the educational and administrative tasks which they cannot do as well separately." One motive for such affiliation was obviously financial; it was becoming increasingly expensive to maintain duplicate libraries and laboratories and to hire top faculty on two campuses. Second, Shuster suggested, "the college can no longer be wholly segregated sexually. Training boys and girls separately at the secondary level may be wise. . . . Most American colleges today, however, are more directed toward graduate schools than toward secondary schools; and graduate schools are almost necessarily coeducational." Another advantage of affiliation was the improved social situation.

"Herein undoubtedly lies one of the greatest potential benefits of affiliation," he wrote. "Thinking together is a great improvement over one-sided clowning. Social relationships can be educational in the best and most personal sense of the term." But Shuster insisted that any form of absorption was not his goal at all: "You may ask: why not go co-ed and be done with it. I am persuaded that colleges for women have a wholly warranted role in contemporary life, provided they develop in addition to the program in the liberal arts forms of preprofessional education suited to the special needs of women."[133]

In a private memorandum written at about that same time, Shuster reiterated the advantages he saw in closer collaboration, and he reviewed the progress of the negotiations so far. He noted that while the Notre Dame faculty seemed to be taking the co-ex program and affiliation discussions almost in stride, the Saint Mary's faculty was obviously apprehensive. And Shuster admitted that the grounds for Saint Mary's hesitancy were real. There was certainly danger, first of all, of Saint Mary's losing its identity as a relatively small and intimate liberal arts college for women. Second, it was possible that most advanced courses would be taught on the Notre Dame campus (with the larger library and more extensive laboratory facilities) and the beginning courses at Saint Mary's, with negative effects on Saint Mary's image and identity. Third, research might tend to dominate in this combined educational program, thus modifying Saint Mary's traditional concept of itself as primarily a teaching institution. And finally, some feared that the more liberal orientation of Notre Dame's department of theology might "overwhelm more conservative St. Mary's."[134]

Negotiations between the two schools continued throughout the summer and fall of 1967, sometimes smoothly and sometimes under strain, and the extent of the strain became apparent in November with the announcement that Sister Mary Grace, C.S.C., Saint Mary's College president, was being removed from her position midway through the academic year. Although other issues were undoubtedly involved, Sister Mary Grace emphasized only one. "I believe that I was relieved as president because of the wish of the board (the Trustees of St. Mary's) that a merger with Notre

Dame proceed much more rapidly," she stated. "The faculty opposes merger, and I am supporting them." She also singled out George Shuster and stated that he had been pushing the Saint Mary's trustees to conclude definite arrangements by the spring. "This," the news release affirmed, "was one of the reasons she opposed the move." Shuster denied that any deadline had been set and insisted that "there has been no use of the word 'merger.'" To emphasize this point further, Shuster read from a joint Co-Ex Committee statement that "the University of Notre Dame and St. Mary's College are two autonomous but cooperating institutions" and that "each has and will continue to have its own board, administration, faculty and student body." Shuster had earlier been critical of what he considered Sister Mary Grace's vacillating leadership, but he insisted that he had no hand in her dismissal. "I had absolutely nothing to do with the affair," he confided to a friend.[135]

Msgr. John J. McGrath, an expert in canon law, was appointed to succeed Sister Mary Grace as president—the first non-sister ever to hold that office—and despite differences of opinion, affiliation continued. The speech and drama departments were merged into one, the two departments of sociology began making joint faculty assignments, Saint Mary's students were permitted to utilize Notre Dame's counseling and career placement services, and a joint student newspaper, *The Observer*, began publication. For a time there were discussions of the possible relocation of a third Catholic college in the area—meetings were held with officials of Barat College for women in Lake Forest, Illinois—but nothing came of these negotiations. In early 1969 a joint Notre Dame–Saint Mary's Dual Council was set up with both presidents and the chairmen of both Boards of Trustees as members, and in May that council released a statement that the ultimate goal of the two schools was that they should become "substantially coeducational with each other." Saint Mary's would double its enrollment to twenty-five hundred by 1975, making the proportion of men to women then approximately two-and-a-half to one, and the council envisioned "one educational entity, with the preservation of the individuality and integrity of Saint Mary's College as a women's college."[136]

With the new Dual Council providing leadership, affiliation progressed rapidly. Discussions aimed at closer collaboration were held on almost every level, and two outside consultants, Professor Rosemary Park of U.C.L.A. and Professor Louis Mayhew of Stanford, were hired to draft a master plan of collaboration. The Park-Mayhew Report, completed in December, noted that for financial reasons it was unwise for the two schools to remain totally separate, but it also cautioned against any "precipitous action" in the direction of a merger. It recommended that "Saint Mary's College should join the University of Notre Dame as a separate and distinctive entity operating within the larger university framework," and it recommended further that this affiliation take place by May of the following year. By the time this report was released, however, important administrative changes had taken place on both campus. At Saint Mary's, Monsignor McGrath had died suddenly of a heart attack that summer and had been replaced by Sister Alma Peter, C.S.C., formerly academic dean; at Notre Dame, Father Hesburgh had appointed Father James Burtchaell, C.S.C., to the newly created post of provost, the chief academic officer and acting president in Hesburgh's absence. Some administrators, chiefly at Notre Dame, became convinced that the Park-Mayhew proposal could still sanction much costly and perhaps unnecessary duplication, and the two Boards of Trustees decided to go further. The chairmen of the two boards and the two presidents signed a "Joint Policy Statement on Unification" on May 14, 1971, at Saint Mary's College. The statement was clear and explicit. "The two institutions have agreed to a unification," the statement declared, "which will create a center of total educational opportunity that could not be achieved by either institution alone." Only broad financial and administrative guidelines were given but the "ultimate goal" was clear: "a single institution with one student body of men and women, one faculty, one president and administration, and one Board of Trustees." Complete unification was to take place by the close of the 1974–75 academic year, and the name "Saint Mary's College of the University of Notre Dame" was to remain as the college of record for all women undergraduates.[137] Affiliation had accelerated dramatically since those tentative steps in 1966.

As discussions continued to implement the "Joint Policy Statement on Unification," however, fundamental disagreements soon emerged, so fundamental, in fact, that on November 30, only six months after the agreement had been signed, the Boards of Trustees of the two schools announced that the negotiations were being halted and unification cancelled. The two schools did agree to continue the co-exchange program and other social and cultural cooperative activities. Convinced that educating men and women together was still the better decision, Notre Dame also announced that it would embark on coeducation alone and would begin admitting a limited number of undergraduate women the following fall.[138]

Although Shuster was a member of the Dual Council established in early 1969, the two presidents and board chairmen exerted major influence, and Shuster's role in the negotiations declined. He was undoubtedly not pleased with the ultimate resolution, but it is not clear precisely why. He may have felt that the step to full unification had occurred too quickly, before Saint Mary's faculty and staff had been fully persuaded, or he may have preferred the Park-Mayhew recommendation, preserving the identity of Saint Mary's and at least some advantages of single-sex education. The deteriorating relationships were also reflected in his own home, with his membership on Notre Dame's Board of Trustees and Doris's membership on Saint Mary's Board of Associate Trustees. On December 2, 1971, just two days after the unification was officially cancelled, Shuster announced his intention to resign from Notre Dame's Board of Trustees. One reason, he stated, was his advancing age and declining health. A younger person, he was sure, could contribute much more. But the recent negotiations were also a factor. "In the second part," he admitted, "my request is based on the fact that I cannot for several reasons be anything but neutral about the relationships between St. Mary's and Notre Dame."[139]

Although Shuster remained at Notre Dame for the rest of his life and retained an office and secretary on campus, his official responsibilities steadily declined with his resignation from the Center for the Study of Man in 1969 and the Board of Trustees in 1971. His contacts with foundation officials remained invaluable, and he was consistently called on for advice by faculty members drafting proposals for funding. Enjoying academic discussions and the company of scholars, he continued to invite student and faculty groups to his home for pleasant drinks, fine food, and intellectual exchange. Above all, he remained a valued advisor to Father Hesburgh. As Hesburgh's own commitments broadened and as the university he guided expanded and became more complex, he continued to turn to Shuster for advice and independent judgment. Hesburgh often referred to him as his "Father Confessor."

Shuster's years at Notre Dame certainly had their disappointments. Funding for favorite projects, like the Institute for Higher Religious Studies, never materialized; he lamented the strained relations with Saint Mary's College resulting from the failed merger talks; and Father Hesburgh's strong but very personal leadership style occasionally made longer-range planning less certain. But the years had been good ones, both for Notre Dame and for Shuster. During those ten years since 1961 the university had grown from a student enrollment of 6600 and a faculty of 480 to an enrollment of 8500 and a faculty of 650. The annual budget had increased from $18 million to $55 million, and the endowment had tripled from $26 million to $75 million.[140] The period of student unrest had been survived without serious disruption or scars, academic standards had continued to rise, research money had flowed in as never before, the step to coeducation had been taken, and university governance had been transferred to a predominately lay Board of Trustees. If Shuster had left Notre Dame disillusioned and even angry in 1924, he could look back on his contributions in the most recent ten years with a sense of deep satisfaction.

11

ELDER STATESMAN

Although Shuster's various responsibilities at Notre Dame, both as assistant to the president and as director of the Center for the Study of Man in Contemporary Society, absorbed the major portion of his time and energy throughout the 1960s, he continued his work off-campus as well. His draft proposal for an educational exhibit for the 1964 World's Fair had been submitted in late 1960, his resignation from the Executive Committee of UNESCO was accepted in the summer of 1962, and his study for the American Council on Education was completed in 1963, but other commitments soon followed.[1] He was highly respected after long years of service to education, to his church, and to public life; he knew he still had much to contribute, and when new opportunities in the national or international arenas arose, he found it difficult to decline.

One commitment that continued, although on a limited scale, was his work with Robert Hutchins's Fund for the Republic and Center for the Study of Democratic Institutions. Shuster had been associated with the fund since its inception in 1952, and he served in the center's New York office almost full-time throughout much of 1960. He continued on the center's board of directors through 1965, although he was able to attend few board meetings in the center's beautiful headquarters in far-off Santa Barbara. The conferences and seminars he did attend, however, were memorable for their lively intellectual exchanges. "I do remember especially the debates between John Courtney Murray and Reinhold Niebuhr," he later recalled. "Both were great men and eminent theologians but they could not agree about anything."[2] He also took part in a well-publicized conference on the recent encyclical of Pope John XXIII, *Pacem in Terris* ("Peace on Earth"), sponsored by the Center for the Study of Democratic

343

Institutions in New York in 1965. A gathering of more than two thousand was addressed by Vice President Hubert Humphrey, Chief Justice Earl Warren, United Nations General Assembly President Alex Quaison-Sackey, Secretary-General U Thant, and Nicolai N. Inozemstev of the Soviet Union, all considering ways to prevent the Cold War from escalating into a nuclear holocaust. Although Shuster thought his own panel the worst, his final evaluation to Hutchins was positive: "I thought that the *Pacem in Terris* meetings were also in the main very good. To my mind the talks by Phil Jessup and Paul Tillich were the best of the lot."[3]

Shuster likewise continued his work for the Lecomte du Noüy Foundation. This foundation had been established by the widow of Pierre Lecomte du Noüy, the evolutionary scientist and author of *Human Destiny*, shortly after his death in 1947, and Shuster, along with Jesuit Father John LaFarge and biochemist Ralph Wyckoff, was a founding member. The Board of Directors had increased to seven or eight over the years, and as long as Shuster was president of Hunter College, their meetings had been held in the college board room. The principal activity of the foundation was the awarding of a prize of two thousand dollars every other year for the best book published in the area of science and religion, and Madame du Noüy herself always took an active part in these deliberations. The foundation also sponsored occasional seminars and conferences, the most prominent of which was one hosted by Shuster at Notre Dame in 1967 to commemorate the twentieth anniversary of the publication of *Human Destiny*. The speakers included scientists, philosophers, and theologians, and were almost equally divided between Americans and Europeans, and the papers were eventually published as *Evolution in Perspective: Commentaries in Honor of Pierre Lecomte du Noüy*, with Shuster as co-editor. In a letter to philosopher John Smith of Yale, Shuster succinctly summarized the conference's success: "New light was thrown on the life and work of Pierre Lecomte du Noüy, we promoted Franco-American amity, and we did listen to some quite brilliant statements."[4]

Throughout the 1960s Shuster also served on the Board of Editors of *Encyclopaedia Britannica*, and on the Advisory Board of Encyclopaedia Britannica Films, and these positions continued or renewed old friendships. William Benton, under-secretary of state at the time of the founding of UNESCO and a major contributor to the publication of the report of the Freedom of the Press Commission, had purchased both organizations in the 1940s. *Encyclopaedia Britannica* was then associated with the University of Chicago, where Benton was serving as vice president and Robert Hutchins, later of the Fund for the Republic, as chancellor. In 1960 the Center for the Study of Democratic Institutions in Santa Barbara, with which both Hutchins and Shuster were affiliated, agreed to assist in planning a revised edition of the *Encyclopaedia*.[5] Shuster was able to take an active part in board deliberations since most meetings were held in nearby Chicago. Perhaps because so many of the contributors to the revised edition were his friends, Shuster's criticisms, though firm, were gentle. Hutchins drafted the major article on education, and Shuster prefaced his comments with the following:

> At any rate I need not tell you that I have long since appreciated your views on educational problems, and that it is unnecessary to repeat what I have already written. Nevertheless this "roof article" does not seem to me designed to serve its purpose as well as you doubtless wish it would, and so I shall express some dissent.[6]

Four pages of criticism followed.

His response to John Cogley's draft on religion was similarly gentle: "John is a very gifted person, and I am sure he can do better than this. It would be a pity if he did not make the attempt."[7]

Because he was so widely read in so many fields and had years of experience as author and editor, Shuster was relied on heavily for advice and criticism. He found the work both challenging and enjoyable, and he certainly appreciated the board's generous stipend, $750 per meeting in 1966. Encyclopaedia Britannica Films produced educational films for classroom and other uses, and Shuster found this participation in educational innovation satisfying also. He attempted to resign from the *Britannica* earlier in the 1960s, but Benton would not hear of it. Finally, in 1972, with Shuster approaching seventy-eight, Benton agreed that a younger director might be appropriate.[8]

Shuster's public service had generally been confined to either the United States or Europe. He was a well-respected educational leader at home, and since his principal foreign languages were French and German, his foreign assignments usually led him toward Paris, Munich, or Vienna. Except for brief visits to Turkey and Egypt, even his UNESCO work rarely took him outside of Europe. In the mid-1960s, however, his attention was turned seriously toward Latin America. Ten years earlier he had made a comprehensive evaluation of the Free University of Berlin for the Ford Foundation, resulting in a grant of one million dollars, and in 1963 the same foundation asked him to undertake a similar study of the Catholic University of Peru.[9] Shuster had some familiarity with Latin American education through his efforts to establish a Latin American Studies program at Notre Dame, and he readily accepted the foundation's invitation.[10]

The Catholic University of Peru was that country's oldest and still its principal private university, with a student enrollment of approximately five thousand, divided among twelve faculties and institutes. A dynamic new rector had been appointed in early 1963, Father Filipe MacGregor, S.J., formerly provincial superior of the Jesuit order in Peru. Ford Foundation officials thought the university had excellent potential—it had a substantial but partially frozen endowment, a young but mostly part-time faculty, much goodwill and popular support throughout Lima, and an enthusiastic and far-sighted rector—and it asked Shuster to chair a committee to make a thorough study of the institution. The purpose of the study was threefold: 1) to advise the foundation whether it should assist the university, and if so, what form such financial assistance might take; 2) to produce a document outlining the strengths and weaknesses of the university, which could be of assistance to Father MacGregor and his academic assistants in future planning; and 3) to recommend to the university how it might successfully apply to other foundations and loan-making agencies for additional assistance.[11]

Shuster and his colleagues, one from the University of Chicago and two from the Catholic University of Santiago, Chile, visited Lima in early 1964 and then sent Father MacGregor a long and detailed questionnaire on the present state of the university: financial status, administrative structure, organization of the faculties and departments, teacher training opportunities, faculty-student relations, public relations, and the predicted size of the applicant pool in the years to come. There were unexpected delays in collecting the information. Father MacGregor was away from campus for six weeks that spring and then collapsed at his desk during the summer—from the additional work the questionnaire imposed, Shuster always feared—and Shuster was not able to make his second site visit until November. At that date his two South American colleagues could not join him, but he was accompanied instead by Professor John Kennedy, fluent in Spanish and director of Notre Dame's Latin American Studies Program. By this time other developments were occurring also: Cardinal Richard Cushing of Boston pledged two million dollars to the university for needed construction, and Father Hesburgh and others were seeking additional funding to excavate a site of pre-Columbian civilization on one portion of the university's property. As an enjoyable interlude during November, while Shuster was visiting with officials at the Catholic University in Lima and making side-trips to universities in Bogota and Santiago, Chile, his wife and sister were vacationing in South America, and they arranged to spend several days together.[12]

The final report Shuster and his colleagues submitted to the Ford Foundation was complete and detailed. It noted, first of all, the recent progress already made by the university, chiefly as a result of its own thorough self-study: a vice president for administration was appointed, a vice president for academic affairs was approved, five additional professors of engineering had been hired, and alumni gatherings had been better attended and more productive. The report emphasized that the university as a whole needed a tighter organization and a clearer structuring, and also lamented that the needs of the various departments in physical facilities and personnel were quite uneven. In some departments the classrooms were adequate but the teaching poor, and in others the buildings badly deteriorating but the instruction good. The report paid special attention to finances: faculty salaries were far too low, with the result that some professors were lured elsewhere and others were forced to accept second jobs, and the library was clearly inadequate. In making its recommendations the report reviewed each major academic unit separately—general studies, social sciences, education, law, and engineering—and made specific suggestions for their improvement. It noted that several of these units might benefit from collaboration with a sister university in the United States or Europe and suggested Notre Dame as a possibility. The report recommended the upgrading of offices of development and public relations, and the possible application for at least limited state aid. Other universities throughout Latin America were benefitting from public aid without compromising their autonomy, the report noted. At a time of student unrest and real danger of student disruption of university services, the report recommended the establishment of a professional department of student life and, in a sentence undoubtedly written by Shuster, stated that "nothing the United States undertook in Germany better served its purpose than the effort made there to help provide student housing, especially in West Berlin." The report closed on a very optimistic note:

> The Catholic University is rich in the service of good men of far more than average ability. It now seeks to enlarge the potential scope of their action, to knit them together in a working academic community, and to make available to them the tools they need. The true foundation of every distinguished university is human. And for this reason we can truly say that the Catholic University of Peru has a foundation. . . . The stake is great and the risk worth taking. We believe that an investment in the Catholic University is one of the soundest one could make.[13]

The report proved effective. The Ford Foundation notified the university in August that it was granting it an award of more than $560,000 over the next three years. The money from Cardinal Cushing would meet many of the construction needs, and the Ford Foundation money would be used in part to upgrade programs and faculty quality at the university and in part to finance exchange programs and inter-university collaboration with the University of Notre Dame. Father John J. Cavanaugh, C.S.C., former president of Notre Dame, visited the university to recommend possible changes in the administrative structure; Notre Dame's associate provost suggested a restructuring of several academic departments; and Notre Dame's vice president for public relations and development helped to set up a more effective fund-raising arm of the university. The university made excellent progress over the next twenty-five years and could look back to this initial Ford Foundation grant as an important and essential first step.[14]

In late September 1963 President John Kennedy appointed Shuster to a small committee to report on the condition of public higher education in the District of Columbia.[15] The situation was indeed critical. D.C. Teachers' College had recently lost the approval of the National Council for the Accreditation of Teacher Education, it was in danger of losing its accreditation by the Middle States Association of Colleges and Secondary Schools at its next review, and it was also the only public institution of higher education in the District. American University, George Washington University, Georgetown University, Howard University, and Catholic University were all private and quite expensive for many District residents. Because of a commitment to UNESCO, Shuster was forced to miss the first meeting in late October, but he did attend the second, a two-day session on December 3 and 4. At that meeting the committee was informed of the demographic profile of the District of Columbia and the Washington metropolitan area, and also of the racial and socio-economic make-up of the public school system. It heard also from the five local university presidents, and these generally favored the establishment of a two-year college and also additional scholarship assistance to allow local students to attend the college of their choice. It also addressed the need of providing better training for teachers in the local elementary and secondary school system. The committee had begun well, but unfortunately events soon overtook it. The committee had held its December 4 meeting in the White House itself, but this was less than two weeks after President Kennedy's tragic assassination. President Johnson had insisted that the meeting continue on schedule, but he and his advisors were soon totally absorbed in other issues and the committee apparently did not meet again.[16]

Although these various commitments absorbed a great deal of Shuster's time in the 1960s, they were only a small percentage of the public and private boards and committees on which he served. He was a member of the Board of Directors or Board of Trustees of the Broadcasting Foundation of America, the Carnegie Endowment for International Peace, the National Educational Television and Radio Center, the National Conference of Christians and Jews, and the Golden Years Foundation, Inc. He served on the Harbison Award Committee of the Danforth Foundation, the

National Science Foundation's Fellowship Review Panel, the Citizens' Scholarship Foundation of America, Inc., and the Pitney-Bowes Scholarship Board. He was on the Board of Trustees of the American-German Cultural Center and Library in New York and continued as president of the American Council on Germany. He served on boards of visitors to Mundelein College in Chicago, Saint Norbert's College in Wisconsin, and the Chicago Province of the Clerics of St. Viator, and he was a member of the Associate Board of Trustees of Saint John's College in Minnesota. He was also appointed to editorial review boards of both *The Commonweal* and the *National Catholic Reporter*.[17]

Shuster also injected himself into two very public religious controversies during the 1960s, one in at least partial defense of the Vatican and in the other quite critical. The first of these concerned Rolf Hochhuth's controversial play "The Deputy," a fictionalized account of Pope Pius XII's refusal to speak out against Nazi persecution of the Jews in the late 1930s and during World War II. Hochhuth seemed to argue that Pius XII was personally not sympathetic to the Jews; that he saw Nazism as at least one defense against the greater evil of expanding Communism; and that he feared antagonizing Hitler and his regime by a public denunciation might result in violent persecution of German Catholics, who were then somewhat protected by the Concordat of 1933. The pope, as nuncio to Germany, had helped to arrange that concordat. Thus, despite the power and prestige of his office, he said nothing, and six million Jews eventually died.

As criticism of Pius XII mounted throughout the country and across the world, Shuster tried to temper some of the accusations in his review in the *New York Times*:

> It is undoubtedly true that Pius XII was at heart no ruler such as his stalwart predecessor had been. Pius XI had bidden Christians to remember that "spiritually we are all Semites," had canonized Thomas More with some disregard for the normal methods of procedure so that men could see what was expected of them, had locked the doors of St. Peter's cathedral when Hitler came to Rome. He challenged all to follow where he led, and, alas, it was often more than in their weaknesses they could manage.
>
> Pius XII was of a different stamp. He was a genuinely notable theologian, perhaps a mystic and a man of unusual breadth of view, but he decided early that Nazism was one of the major

scourges in man's history and that all anyone could do was to suffer until it passed. For this reason he found it difficult to counsel resistance. He had to reckon with the fact, he thought, that when he did so, the victims would be many.

Hochhuth rightly praises the denunciations which the German Bishop of Muenster, Count von Galen, hurled at the Nazis, and it is true that having denounced he survived. But very many of his priests and layfolk did not. The Muenster diocese lost to Dachau, as a result of its Bishop's heroism, by far the greatest number of priests from any part of Germany, and not a few now lie there in nameless graves. Should the Pope have imitated this Bishop? Surely nothing he could have said would have stopped Hitler from doing what was afoot at Auschwitz or elsewhere. The world was arrayed against the Nazi. He was callously sacrificing armies in Russia, he had madly challenged the power of the United States, and he slew any German he wished to slay, including some of the most illustrious marshals of his army. Nothing would have pleased him more than adding a few more Christians to the list.[18]

In a letter to a priest-friend a few weeks earlier, Shuster had suggested another explanation. "The fact is that we made a distinction, after Pius XI, between our obligation to the Jew in terms of charity and our obligation in terms of justice," he wrote. "That is, we tried to help and rescue as many as we could, but did not demand justice for them. I believe it was probably impossible to do this effectively. But I do not see how we can deny what happened by default."[19]

He returned to the controversy a little later:

I once discussed the program with Pius XII while he was Cardinal Pacelli. He maintained that the only ground the Church had to stand on against Hitler was the ground of the Canon Law. That is, the Church had the right to do whatever it could to protect its own flock and its own faith. I don't believe that the reasoning was unsound, but there is no doubt that today we would all rest easier if the Church's attitude had been more ecumenical. After all 6,000,000 Jews perished in gas chambers and we said nothing. I am as sure as I can be of anything that Pope Pius would, looking back from our point of vantage, be sure, too.[20]

In the events surrounding the resignation of Auxiliary Bishop James Shannon of St. Paul, Shuster was highly critical of the Vatican. In late July 1968 Pope Paul VI had issued his long-awaited encyclical on birth control, *Humanae Vitae*, lamenting the selfishness and dehumanization of the so-called "contraception mentality" and restating the church's traditional ban on artificial contraception, stating that "each and every marriage act must remain open to the transmission of life" and requesting all priests to give "loyal internal and external obedience to these teachings." Bishop Shannon did not agree with either the reasoning or the conclusions of the encyclical, and after wrestling with his dilemma privately for two months, he wrote a heartfelt letter to the pope himself. "In my pastoral experience I have found that this rigid teaching is simply impossible of observance by many faithful and generous spouses," he wrote, "and I cannot believe that God binds men to impossible standards." He then admitted his own inner struggle: "I must now reluctantly admit that I am ashamed of the kind of advice I have given some of these good people, ashamed because it has been bad theology, bad psychology, and because it has not been an honest reflection of my own inner convictions." He reviewed generally accepted norms for dissenting from Vatican teachings and acknowledged openly: "I, therefore, as a faithful and believing member of the church wish to accept these norms and to use them as the basis for my formal statement here and now to Your Holiness that I cannot in conscience give internal assent, hence much less external assent, to the papal teaching which is here in question."[21]

At the annual meeting of the American bishops in Washington that November, Shannon's colleagues officially supported the position of Pope Paul, and shortly thereafter the bishop submitted his resignation as auxiliary bishop of St. Paul and took up residence at St. John's College, Santa Fe, New Mexico. In order to lessen the public controversy, or even public scandal, the Vatican offered the bishop the option of taking up residence outside the United States at Vatican expense but without priestly or episcopal ministerial duties. It was this suggestion of quasi-exile and the earlier lack of public support from fellow bishops for one following the dictates of his own conscience that spurred Shuster and others at Notre Dame into action. "The Bishop Shannon case is such a grave and incredible abuse of ecclesiastical authority that I am earnestly considering making a public statement about it," Shuster confided to Father Hesburgh. "All I want to say at the present time is that if I decide to make such a statement I am quite prepared to sunder my relationship with the University if that seems desirable."[22] No such departure was ever deemed necessary, of course.

What Shuster and six of his colleagues at Notre Dame decided to do was to draft a letter of support for Bishop Shannon and collect as many signatures as possible, chiefly among Catholic educators. The letter, addressed to Cardinal John Dearden of Detroit, chairman of the National Conference of Catholic Bishops, read in part:

> That he [Bishop Shannon] has been a singularly loyal, effective and devoted priest is a simple fact to which many thousands of Christians will testify even as we do now. Had he been removed from our midst by illness or accident, we would have mourned the loss which his passing would have created for the Church and all it represents in the world. Now there is added a sense of profound shock about which we must speak for the sake of our Christian faith.
>
> The manner in which Rome has dealt with him is without precedent in the history of our country. Bishop Shannon ventured, honestly and confidentially, to doubt the wisdom of some of the conclusions reached in *Humanae Vitae*. In so doing he said no more than was said collectively by the bishops of Austria, Belgium, Canada, France, Germany and Holland. Indeed, he did not go as far along the road to dissent as did Pope Paul's own Commission and many leading theologians. Yet who of all these men has been declared a pariah?
>
> We are particularly distressed by the proposals made to Bishop Shannon through the Apostolic Delegate: that he accept an agreed-upon place of exile, where ecclesiastical authority would provide financial support; and that upon arriving there would find himself without pastoral duties or canonical appointment. This is clearly a scandalous and inquisitorial exercise of power. In a day when the Church cries out for strong leaders with vision and integrity, the treatment accorded Bishop Shannon can only intimidate these leaders and silence the very voices which the Christian community needs so badly to hear.[23]

Eventually more than five hundred Catholic academicians from across the country signed the letter. Cardinal Dearden's reply was sympathetic but noncommittal:

I must confess that I have no more information about the matter than has been contained in the press reports. And, as you will admit, these have often been less than clear. As a consequence, I have been inclined to suspend judgment in the matter until I know all the circumstances.

At the same time, I want to assure you that the esteem in which you hold Bishop Shannon is shared by me and by many, many others. I have the greatest respect for the honesty, candor, sincerity and loyalty to the Church of Bishop Shannon. Surely we need him in the service of the Church in the United States.[24]

In the midst of these and other efforts of support, it was revealed that Shannon had married a divorcee in a Protestant ceremony in New York and thus, officially excommunicated by the church, all efforts to restore him to active priestly or episcopal ministry were now in vain.[25] For Shuster and others, it was unquestionably a tragic loss for the church.

Despite his numerous university commitments and frequent board and committee meetings off-campus—and in the midst of public controversies—Shuster, ever the journalist, continued his writing. In 1954 he had authored *Religion Behind the Iron Curtain* and in 1956 a study of Cardinal Joseph Mindszenty of Hungary, *In Silence I Speak*. In 1961 he published a personal memoir of his Hunter College years, *The Ground I Walked On*, and in 1969 he published an enlarged edition. He made a strong plea for American support of UNESCO in the *Saturday Review* in 1962, and twice during the decade paid public tribute to Cardinal Spellman of New York, with whom he was rumored to have had differences during his twenty-one years at Hunter. In the field of Catholic education he published "Schools at the Crossroads" in *The Atlantic Monthly* in 1962; "The School: Not Little and Red Any Longer" in *Ave Maria* in 1963; and "So You Have Chosen the Teaching Profession" in *The Catholic Educator* in 1964. He contributed "The Apostolate of the Laity and International Action" for *Ave Maria* in 1966 and "Honesty in the Church" for *America* in 1967. In 1968–69 he wrote a syndicated weekly column for several diocesan newspapers, discussing topics from birth control to campus unrest and from civil rights in America to the war in Vietnam.[26]

Shuster's most significant publication during these years was probably *Catholic Education in a Changing World*. This was meant to be a summary and companion study to the Notre Dame report on Catholic elementary and secondary education, *Catholic Schools in Action*, but it also gave Shuster an opportunity to reflect on the state of Catholic education in America and to make his own recommendations. He admitted that it was in no sense a scholarly work but simply "a congeries of concerns."[27]

Shuster expressed high praise for Catholic elementary schools. They were acquitting well their twin goals of providing religious formation and schooling in secular subjects, and they were providing this education less expensively than the public schools, chiefly because of the lower salaries and contributed services of the religious sisters. But the system clearly had problems: the schools were probably never going to be able to educate more than 50 percent of the Catholic pupils; class sizes were already too large; teacher-training needed to be upgraded; and ways had to be found to utilize lay teachers more effectively. An important advantage for the Catholic schools, of course, was that they could be much more selective in admissions than could the public schools.[28]

Difficulties were even more apparent at the high school level. Only about 35 percent of the eligible Catholic students were enrolled in Catholic schools, and there was no reason to suppose that this percentage would increase. But Shuster gave the high schools high marks also: their academic programs were generally advanced, in part because a large proportion of their students intended to continue on into college, and they communicated religious values to their students at a time in their lives when their values were being formed. Shuster felt that religious women were particularly successful teachers because they had better teacher-training programs, especially the Sister Formation Movement.[29] Considering the expense and the fact that only one-third of eligible Catholic students were enrolled, some wondered if the high school system should not be closed. Shuster disagreed. For him, four years of high school were still less expensive than eight years of elementary school, and those four years seemed more crucial in religious formation.[30]

Shuster's years at Notre Dame had only increased his appreciation for Catholic higher education. College education was becoming more and more the norm in the United States, and if Catholics were to exert significant influence in national life, as the

Second Vatican Council had encouraged, Catholic higher education was essential. But, in fact, Shuster thought there might be too many colleges already, and probably only those that could make a unique and significant contribution were worth the expense to keep open. Shuster insisted again that Catholic colleges needed to find ways of incorporating lay men and women more and more into teaching and administrative positions, but for fund-raising and other reasons, Shuster conceded that the college president probably needed to remain a priest or a religious brother or sister, at least for the present.[31]

Shuster never intended *Catholic Education in a Changing World* to be his final work. After republishing his memoirs of the Hunter College years in 1969, his appetite was whetted to attempt a complete autobiography. As time permitted in the early 1970s he drafted isolated chapters—his Lancaster, Wisconsin, background, student days at Notre Dame, the experience of World War I, reflections on *The Commonweal*, his ties to Germany and German culture—pecking each chapter out on his upright typewriter at home. Eventually his secretary typed them into more finished drafts, but Shuster apparently never had time to revise them, to fill in so many missing gaps, or to complete the story. It is probably well that they were not completed. His typing and unsteady handwritten corrections confirm that his health was failing. The best passages are those that repeat stories from earlier writings; his recollections and judgments are less sure. The job was simply too large. But Shuster remained a writer to the end. The final chapter that he was able to complete was dated August 7, 1976, less than six months before his death.[32]

As the decade progressed, Shuster had increasing difficulty with his back and legs, and, by the fall of 1976, most annoyingly, his eyes began to fail. Reading, the very lifeline of his thinking, became more difficult. More ominously, his heart began to weaken. Doris's Christmas greetings to close friends that year indicated that things were not well and the medication she mentioned confirmed that the doctors were concerned.[33]

That Christmas was especially gratifying because it confirmed that the family reconciliation was complete. On his release from the Hartford clinic following his arrest in 1949, Bob had sought a variety of jobs, working for a time with William Benton in Chicago and then going into business for himself in New York, supplying customers with business forms. In 1960 he had begun sharing an apartment with a young friend. George and Doris had not approved, and relations between Bob and his parents were strained for several years. Bob eventually left the office-supply business and in 1965 opened an art gallery. George and Doris agreed to supply much of the money for its start and attended many of its openings. Relations gradually improved, and Bob flew to South Bend to visit on occasional holidays. Although not well himself in 1976, Bob returned again at Christmas. He was a much better bridge player even than his father but, in this last contest, George and his partner got better cards and George was pleased to emerge the winner. When they separated, mutual respect and affection had been further restored.[34]

As George's health continued to slip, he and Doris went out less and less, especially in the treacherous snow and ice of northern Indiana. On January 18 they attended a Victory Dinner at a local hotel to celebrate the successful completion of a major fundraising campaign for Stanley Clark school, a private school in South Bend of which George had been a trustee in the past. It was their last outing together. Soon after, George was admitted to Memorial Hospital in South Bend for observation and more intensive care, and there he died on the evening of January 25. He was eighty-two years old.[35]

The Midwest's harshest blizzard of the year struck that weekend, and many were prevented from arriving in time for the funeral services. Doris's relatives from nearby Illinois could not drive through the impassable roads, Bob was bedridden with hepatitis in New York, and a university official had to borrow a four-wheel-drive vehicle from the fire department even to bring Doris to the Funeral Mass. For the viewing and wake service on the evening of January 27, the body was laid out in the grand concourse of the Memorial Library on campus, the building in which George had had his office for more than a decade. It was also closer to the entrance to the campus and easier to reach in the heavy snow than the campus church. The Funeral Mass was celebrated in Sacred Heart Church on campus the following day with Father Hesburgh presiding, more than forty other priests assisting, and Bishop William McManus of the Diocese of Fort

Wayne–South Bend, formerly executive secretary of the Department of Education for the United States Catholic Conference,
pronouncing the final commendation.[36]

Tributes to Shuster poured in to South Bend from across the
country and from Europe and South America; others were published in national journals. Doris lovingly preserved them all.[37]
Dr. Mina Rees, Shuster's close collaborator at Hunter College for
so many years, captured the uniqueness of his life well in a memorial service in New York:

> George Nauman Shuster was a rare human being, a man of
> urbanity and charm whose life, varied as it was, was truly of one
> piece, characterized by a deep devotion to the freedom of the
> human spirit, attached to the humanistic ideals of literature and
> learning, committed to the service of his nation, his church and the
> broad community of human beings everywhere.[38]

Father Hesburgh paid tribute to what Shuster had meant to
Notre Dame, and to others, in his funeral eulogy:

> God only knows how many crises I and others brought to
> him, as to a father confessor, who listened sympathetically and
> always gave wise counsel. Like a good gardener, he brought out the
> best in us, all the beauty and goodness that we did not know we
> had until he discovered and encouraged it in us. While he was a
> quintessential layman in a rather clerical Church, I always saw him
> as a priest, a mediator who stood between ignorance and learning,
> badness and goodness, promise and fulfillment, always bridging
> the gap, always leading upward.
>
> I know a once dreary Catholic university in South America
> that is bright and shining today because he cared enough to go
> there often, with great personal sacrifice, and to show them the
> way. I know of discouraged and defeated scholars who came to life
> because he beckoned the way to do it and gave them a gentle push.
> I know so many students who were losing faith, not only in God,
> but everything else, who found in his staunch and unwavering faith
> the means of recovering their own. As an educator, they are per-
> haps his best monument. I know of frustrated priests who were
> ready to call it quits until he opened to them new and exciting vis-
> tas. I know of many young and old members of this community
> today who instinctively call him Father, and I am one of them. He
> engendered faith and hope and love because he lived to the fullest
> these great virtues that lead us to God. . . .

> Although we are small compared to the cosmic reality of eter-
> nal life, I know I speak for all of you when I say that as long as there
> is a cherished spot called Notre Dame, there will be a cherished
> spirit here called George Shuster. May we grow here in faith and
> hope and love as he did, and may he now rest in peace and eternal
> joy.[39]

The most perceptive tribute of all may have been pronounced fifteen years earlier when Fordham University presented
Shuster with its prestigious Insignis Medal for distinguished service to God and humanity. Fordham president Father Lawrence
McGinley, S.J., remarked on that occasion that at times there
seemed to be two kinds of Catholics in America—George Shuster,
and all the others.[40] The remark was facetious but it contained
more than a particle of truth. Shuster had indeed been different,
and the precise paths he walked throughout his life were often
those less traveled by his fellow Catholics. In several areas his contributions were significant—as educator, as public official, and as
publicist and commentator.

Shuster was, first of all, an educator, both in the classroom
and in the administrative office. As a teacher, he was extraordinarily well read; he could devour most books in a few short hours.
And he lectured from a depth of familiarity with history, literature, philosophy, theology, art, music, comparative cultures, and
international affairs. Ever the humanist, whatever shed light on
the human condition was of interest, and this broad knowledge
and thirst for learning were an inspiration to his students. He
thoroughly enjoyed the company of others, especially enthusiastic
youths; he was at ease in front of a classroom; and with a journalist's command of language he expressed himself well. He had a
playful sense of humor, never took himself too seriously, and his
openness and genuine concern encouraged students to question
and challenge. He continued to teach even as president of Hunter
College, and students there, at Notre Dame, and at St. Joseph's
College for Women commented on his classes decades after their
graduation.

He was perhaps even more successful as an administrator. As
president of Hunter College, he was well respected for both his
scholarly interests and his urbanity. He consistently emphasized
the humanities, the fine arts, vocational inlays, and international

concerns, but he always hoped to direct the college by consensus, bringing others through discussion and persuasion to his point of view. His administration did not please everyone—the physical scientists often felt slighted and other administrators were chagrined that, in his personal administrative style, he occasionally bypassed established channels and procedures—but the college progressed steadily during the twenty years of his presidency and both the students and the faculty seemed contented and proud. "The president is a superior man by any standards," an outside accrediting agency had stated in 1956. "His spirit, intellectual discipline, and cultural breadth are clearly reflected in the program, personnel, and atmosphere of the college."[41] Many had questioned Shuster's selection in 1939, but almost none in 1960.

Shuster's work at Notre Dame was more difficult to evaluate. Funding for scholarly research in the humanities and social sciences dramatically increased, but many of those grants would have been awarded without his assistance. Some of his favorite projects were disappointments—the Maritain Center never attracted large donations, the Institute for Higher Religious Studies was not built, and the Carnegie study of Catholic elementary and secondary education received only mixed reviews—but most contributed significantly to the university's mission: programs in Latin American and African studies, population conferences, studies of poverty and crime, theological inquiries, and various curricula revisions. As the decade progressed, more and more members of the faculty and administration came to rely on his advice.

Shuster was an especially calm voice of experience during the turbulent 1960s. Students across the country were becoming alienated over poverty and prejudice at home and the escalating war in Vietnam, but Shuster's contacts with Notre Dame's student leaders remained good. The major campus publication launched its "Shuster for President" campaign in 1963. There was no question, however, of Shuster's loyalty to Father Hesburgh and other university administrators. He had been at the center of controversy before, he had been a perceptive observer of both higher education and American Catholicism for close to fifty years, his reputation was secure, and he could offer his advice honestly and openly. He defended the administration's handling of student unrest, its increasing emphasis on research, and its steps toward coeducation. On the rare occasions when he could not agree, he simply remained silent in public. He brought wise educational counsel to Notre Dame's Board of Trustees, and Father Hesburgh relied on his prudence and judgment in times of faculty dispute or student unrest. Father Hesburgh remained as Notre Dame's president for thirty-five years, and George Shuster was a valued colleague and support during the difficult decade of the 1960s.

As a public official Shuster also made significant contributions, although within limited spheres. He was a good choice for the Enemy Alien Boards during World War II because of his genuine appreciation of other cultures, his tolerance of diversity, and especially his prudence and common sense. This same appreciation of other cultures and his growing international-mindedness made him an excellent appointment for the General Advisory Committee of the State Department's Division of Cultural Affairs. His service on the War Department's Historical Commission in 1945 was adequate, although others more expert on German military and political affairs during World War II might have conducted even more perceptive interviews. As an educator, journalist, and long-time opponent of censureship, he was an excellent choice for Robert Hutchins's Commission on Freedom of the Press, but, although he agreed with the commission's moderate conclusions and recommendations, his contributions to the deliberations were limited. He was chairman of the National Commission on Segregation in the Nation's Capital in 1947, but all research and writing were done by staff; the chairman was appointed chiefly to give the final report wider publicity and credibility, and any of several other better-known public figures might have done this more successfully. His most important contributions to public service probably came from his eighteen months as land commissioner in Bavaria. His influence on policy was limited, but he proved to be an excellent mediator between American officials and the German people. He was an educator, a Catholic, fluent in German, and deeply appreciative of German culture, and he was probably the most successful of all land commissioners in settling outstanding difficulties and in preventing normal tensions and differences from escalating into major crises. Americans and Germans alike were sorry to see him depart in the winter of 1951. As United States representative to the Executive Board of UNESCO from 1958 to 1962, Shuster's work was similarly commendable. His greatest handicap was State Department hesitancy in cooperating with an international organization often controlled by non-aligned and thus potentially unsupportive nations, but Shuster was highly respected personally and was generally successful in presenting the American position convincingly. Little more could have been expected. Shuster's "public service" for major foundations was significant also, especially his part in directing large grants of Ford Foundation money to both the Catholic University of Peru and the Free University of Berlin. His public appointments were rarely to policy-making positions—policy-making may not have been his forte anyway—but the assignments he was given, occasionally thorny and controversial, he acquitted well.

Finally, and perhaps primarily, Shuster was a publicist, a commentator, a popularizer. Despite his long years in education, he produced few strictly scholarly works—his doctoral dissertation, *The English Ode from Milton to Keats*, was certainly one, and *The Catholic Spirit in Modern English Literature* might be another. For most of his life, however, he was much too active with too many offices and too many commitments to enjoy the solitude that scholarly publication demanded. But he had wide interests— history, literature, political theory, theology, comparative cultures, international relations. He had the rapid and usually fluid style of an experienced journalist, he was convinced that he had much worthwhile to say, and he was eager to say it. His style was so rapid, in fact, that mistaken first names and dates often went uncorrected, and in his published introduction to *The Confessions of Saint Augustine* he confused St. Ambrose with St. Anselm, a mistake of seven hundred years.

In the 1930s he wrote popularly on Germany—its history and culture, its recent political developments, and the evils of National Socialism. He traveled widely in Europe during the decade; observed ominous events firsthand, including the German invasion of Austria in 1938; and sent eyewitness accounts back to American journals. As president of Hunter College he was a champion of broad-based education, combining the liberal and fine arts with vocational courses to prepare students for productive and satisfying careers. He was convinced of the importance of religious formation and was concerned that this could not be provided for in the public schools of the nation, including his own Hunter College. In the postwar world of the 1950s and 1960s Shuster became a publicist for internationalism. With rapid transportation the world was too small, and with atomic armaments the stakes were too high, not to encourage closer and more cooperative relations among nations. His numerous speeches and articles on behalf of UNESCO illustrated his concern.

But of all his interests, he was first and foremost a publicist for modern American Catholicism. There was no question that Shuster was Catholic. He had a firm belief in divine revelation, in the Bible, and in eternal, unchangeable truths handed down for centuries through a church established by Christ. He had a deep moral sense and saw human acts as right or wrong. He was attracted to the liturgy and public worship of the church, was a man of prayer who turned instinctively to God in times of joy or crisis, and strove throughout his life to progress toward an eternity of happiness. He spoke respectfully of church leaders, even when he disagreed with their decisions and procedures, and he often recalled his own father's respect for the unfaithful priest years before in their Lancaster parish. He wrote frequently in support of Catholicism—*The Catholic Spirit in Modern English Literature, The Catholic Spirit in America, Catholic Education in a Changing World*, and articles like "The Catholic Conspiracy Myth" in *Outlook and Independent*, and "A Catholic Defends His Church" in *The New Republic*. By mid-century, Shuster was clearly one of the most widely known Catholic laymen in the United States, undoubtedly an important factor in his appointments to Hunter College, to UNESCO conferences, and to Bavaria.

But his was also an *American* Catholicism. He not only saw Catholicism and Americanism as wholly compatible—and he strove to demonstrate this in numerous articles and editorials during his twelve years at *The Commonweal*—but he considered Catholicism more vibrant and even more effective in its mission precisely because of this American environment. He saw genuine benefits in the separation of church and state; in the mix of ethnic and national cultures that made up American Catholicism; in interaction with a predominantly non-Catholic environment, which led Catholics consistently to review and question their own customs; and even in the distance from Rome, which permitted greater local autonomy. Shuster stood unmistakably in the American Catholic tradition.[42] With Bishops John Carroll and John England and other early leaders he was a serious student of Catholic theology and history, he defended religious faith and Catholic doctrine as wholly reasonable, and he supported his church publicly in an environment that could be at least moderately hostile. Following Orestes Brownson, Isaac Hecker, and others of the American Romantic movement, he went beyond the intellectual content of Catholicism and recognized a place in it for intuition, emotion, and poetry also. He saw a harmonious relationship between the finite and the infinite in the universe, and he was convinced of the perfectibility of the individual and the almost limitless opportunities for the church in this American environment. With Father John A. Ryan and other twentieth-century champions of social justice, he sought to apply his church's principles to everyday life of business and labor affairs, politics, poverty, and discrimination. As a close friend and admirer of Jesuit Father John Courtney Murray, he strongly supported Murray's defense in the Second Vatican Council of religious liberty and separation of church and state.

Shuster's Catholicism, finally, was modern—a Catholicism approved in large part by the Second Vatican Council, although Shuster had been championing it years before. He was always uncomfortable with authoritarianism, either from Rome or the local chancery office, and he preferred greater autonomy and independence for local dioceses, parishes, and individual Catholics. He had long advocated a greater voice for the laity in church affairs. He supported the Second Vatican Council's greater emphasis on liturgy and the social mission of the church rather than on more traditional questions of morality and discipline. He was ecumenical and an active member of the National Conference of Christians and Jews long before this was encouraged by the Council Fathers. He was comfortable and at home amid a diversity of opinions and was not disturbed at all by the breakup of the Thomistic and Neo-Scholastic synthesis and unity resulting at least in part from the Second Vatican Council. Shuster's

Catholicism led him to adapt the eternal truths of revelation to an ever-changing American scene of industry and labor, war and peace, wealth and poverty, pluralism and discrimination. Sometimes he did it well; sometimes not so well. He never considered his occasional dissents from non-infallible teachings of his church—its authoritarian structure, its relations with non-Catholics, its stance on birth control—as in any way disloyal. The church could only grow and progress through a diversity of views.

Shuster was thus often surrounded by controversy and opposition—a layman in a clerically dominated church, a deeply committed Catholic in a world of public education, a defender of German culture in an era of two world wars, a public official championing internationalism as State Department policy became more cautious, and despite his numerous government appointments, always an independent in politics. But the diversity and differences were of little personal concern as long as he remained, in his own heart, "on the side of truth."

ABBREVIATIONS

ACCNY	Archives of the Carnegie Corporation of New York
ATPP-UNDA	Assistant to the President Papers, University of Notre Dame Archives
BHECF	Board of Higher Education Central Files (NY)
CISCU, ACE	Committee on International Studies in Colleges and Universities, American Council on Education
DAM-CUA	Department of Archives and Manuscripts, Catholic University of America
DSC-UC	Department of Special Collections, University of Chicago
FDRL	Franklin D. Roosevelt Library
HAMcCA	Historical Analysis of the McCloy Administration
HCA	Hunter College Archives
HIA	Hoover Institution Archives
HICOG-SC	High Commissioner for Germany, Staff Conference Meetings
HML	Hagley Museum and Library
LCB,CF	Land Commissioner for Bavaria, Central Files
MD-LC	Manuscripts Division, Library of Congress
MD, M-SRC-HU	Manuscript Division, Moorland-Spingard Research Center, Howard University
NA	National Archives
OHRO-CU	Oral History Research Office, Columbia University

SCD-GUL	Special Collections Department, Georgetown University Library
SP-HCA	Shuster Papers, Hunter College Archives
SP-UNDA	Shuster Papers, University of Notre Dame Archives
UNDA	University of Notre Dame Archives
USCC	United States Catholic Conference

NOTES

1. EARLY WISCONSIN YEARS, 1894–1919

1. *New York Times*, September 8, 1940: II-9–2; *Hunter College: Facilities Inventory*, Hunter College Archives; Lewis Mumford, "The Sky Line: Skyscraper School," *The New Yorker* 16 (November 16, 1940), pp. 84–86; and Samuel White Patterson, *Hunter College: Eighty-Five Years of Service* (New York, 1955), pp. 150–152.

2. This and the following quotation are from Mumford, "Skyscraper School," p. 84.

3. George N. Shuster, *The Ground I Walked On*, 2d ed. (Notre Dame, 1969), p. 58. Hereafter, in Shuster's own publications, the author's name will be omitted in the footnote references. The Emerson quotation is from *The Conduct of Life* (Boston, 1860), p. 201.

4. Biographical information on Shuster can be found in *The Ground I Walked On*, noted above; "An Autobiography," in *Leaders in American Education*, Seventieth Yearbook of the National Society for the Study of Education, Part 2 (Chicago, 1971), pp. 277–303; Vincent P. Lannie, "George N. Shuster: A Reflective Evaluation," *Leaders in American Education*, pp. 306–320; "George N. Shuster," *Current Biography Yearbook, 1960* (New York, 1960), pp. 378–380; "George Nauman Shuster," *The National Cyclopaedia of American Biography*, vol. H., (New York, 1952), pp. 89–90; William M. Halsey, *The Survival of American Innocence* (Notre Dame, 1980), pp. 84–98; Barry D. Riccio, "American Catholic Thought in the Nineteen Twenties: Frederick Joseph Kinsman and George Shuster," *An American Church*, ed. David J. Alvarez (Morago, Calif., 1979), pp. 113–123; and Frederike Maria Zweig, *Greatness Revisited*, ed. Harry Zohn (Boston, 1971), pp. 105–126.

5. Henry David Thoreau, *Walden* (Boston, 1897), chapt. 18, "Conclusion."

6. Bismarck's cultural revolution of 1871 for a time had a decidedly anti-Catholic bias: laws restricted Catholic worship and education, the Jesuits were expelled, and many bishops were arrested or forced into

exile. The American Protective Association was a nativist, anti-immigrant organization in the 1890s, and the Ku Klux Klan was revitalized and flourished in the South, Midwest, and Far West between 1915 and the late 1920s. Cf. Lillian Parker Wallace, *The Papacy and European Diplomacy, 1869–1878* (Chapel Hill, 1948); Donald Kinzer, *An Episode in Anti-Catholicism: The American Protective Association* (Seattle, 1964); and David M. Chambers, *Hooded Americanism: The History of the Ku Klux Klan*, 2d ed. (New York, 1965).

7. Shuster discussed Germany and German culture in numerous books and articles, but especially in *The Germans: An Inquiry and an Estimate* (New York, 1932), pp. 1–49. The quotation is from page 20.

8. A good study of Bancroft is in Harvey Wish, *The American Historian* (New York, 1960), pp. 70–87.

9. *Look Away!* (New York, 1939), pp. 56–57.

10. *Look Away!*, pp. 288, 289.

11. "Spiritual Autobiography," in *American Spiritual Autobiographies,* ed. Louis Finkelstein (New York, 1948), pp. 25–37. The quotation is from page 25.

12. This and the following quotation are from "Spiritual Autobiography," pp. 26–27.

13. Henry Adams, *The Education of Henry Adams* (Boston, 1927), p. 294.

14. Information on LaFollette's Wisconsin can be found in George E. Mowry, *The Era of Theodore Roosevelt* (New York, 1958); Robert S. Maxwell, *LaFollette and the Rise of the Progressives in Wisconsin* (Madison, 1956); and Herbert F. Margulies, *The Decline of the Progressive Movement in Wisconsin, 1890–1920* (Madison, 1968).

15. "An Autobiography," p. 279.

16. For Shuster's family background, cf. "An Autobiography," pp. 277–280; Zweig, *Greatness Revisited*, pp. 105–107; "George Nauman Shuster," *The National Cyclopaedia of American Biography*, p. 89; and oral history interview of the author with Shuster's sisters, Catherine and Mary, South Bend, Indiana, August 16, 1980. Cf. also C. M. Foote and J. W. Henion, *Plat Book of Grant County, Wisconsin* (Minneapolis, 1895), pp. 28–29.

17. Interview with Shuster's sisters, August 16, 1980.

18. "The New Schoolboy's Shining Face," *The American Scholar* 25 (Winter, 1955–56), p. 72.

19. Cf. the 1900 and 1910 federal censuses for the State of Wisconsin, Library Division, State Historical Society of Wisconsin. Anton

Schuster's obituary notice in the *Grant County Herald*, June 20, 1935, gives the year of his birth as 1856.

20. Much of this information on Shuster's early life is from the author's interview with Shuster's sisters, August 16, 1980.

21. Marriage Registration, Grant County, 1893–97, Library Division, State Historical Society of Wisconsin; interview with Shuster's sisters, August 16, 1980; "An Autobiography," p. 279; and 1900 and 1910 federal censuses for Wisconsin.

22. "An Autobiography," p. 277. For further information on Lancaster and Grant County, cf. Castello N. Hofford, *History of Grant County, Wisconsin* (Reprinted: Marceline, Mo., 1976), pp. 397–452; Resource Committee of Grant County, *Grant County History, 1900–1976* (Lancaster, Wis., 1976), pp. 17–19, 57–71, and 324–331; and William Francis Raney, *Wisconsin: A Story of Progress* (New York, 1940).

23. Interview with Shuster's sisters, August 16, 1980.

24. "An Autobiography," p. 279; interview with Shuster's sisters, August 16, 1980.

25. Interview with Shuster's sisters, August 16, 1980; "An Autobiography," p. 279.

26. The best history of St. Lawrence college is probably Rev. P. Corbinian, O.M.Cap., *The Laurentianum: Its Origin and Work (1864–1924)* (Mt. Calvary, Wis., 1924), pp. 15–49, 53–59. The monastery was actually founded by two diocesan priests from Switzerland who entered the Capuchin order shortly thereafter. Cf. also *The Rise and Progress of the Province of St. Joseph of the Capuchin Order in the United States, 1857–1907* (by a Member of the Order) (New York, 1907), pp. 32–218; Rev. Celestine N. Bittle, O.M.Cap., *A Romance of Lady Poverty* (Milwaukee, 1933); and *Capuchin Century Book* (Detroit, 1957). (The initials O.M.Cap. for the Capuchin Order were later changed to O.F.M.Cap.)

27. *The Official Catholic Directory*, 1907 and 1911 (Milwaukee, 1907 and 1911), pp. 98, 102. These figures probably include the first two years of college. Seminary education was often divided into two six-year programs, the minor seminary of high school and two years of college, and the major seminary of two years of philosophy and four years of theology.

28. "An Autobiography," p. 280; interview with Shuster's sisters, August 16, 1980; interview with Doris Shuster, George's wife, June 24, 1983.

29. "An Autobiography," p. 280.

30. Letter of Rev. Joseph Diermeier, Academic Dean of St. Lawrence Seminary, to the author, February 2, 1985, and Records of the

Office of the Academic Dean, St. Lawrence Seminary, Mt. Calvary, Wisconsin; *St. Lawrence College, 1908–1909, 1909–1910, 1910–1911* (Mt. Calvary, Wis.), pp. 14–15, 24; pp. 14, 26–27; p. 17.

31. "An Autobiography," p. 280.

32. *The Hill of Happiness* (New York, 1926), p. xi.

33. Interview with Shuster's sisters, August 16, 1980.

34. "Frankly, I chose to go there because it had a football team and therefore sounded less formidably academic than St. Lawrence College. One afternoon of practice convinced me that football was not for me. I was strong and wiry at the time, but no match for the replicas of Hercules who had been recruited" ("An Autobiography", p. 280).

35. For this survey of the University of Notre Dame in the early years of the century, cf. Arthur J. Hope, C.S.C., *Notre Dame: One Hundred Years* (Notre Dame, Ind., 1943); Thomas J. Schlereth, *The University of Notre Dame: A Portrait of Its History and Campus* (Notre Dame, Ind., 1976); Philip S. Moore, C.S.C., *Academic Development: University of Notre Dame* (Notre Dame, Ind., 1960); and *Bulletin of the University of Notre Dame: General Catalogue, 1912–1913*, (Notre Dame, Ind., 1913).

36. Paul R. Messbarger, "The Failed Promise of American Catholic Literature," *U. S. Catholic Historian*, vol. 4, no. 2 (1985), p. 150.

37. *Bulletin of the University of Notre Dame: General Catalogue, 1912–1913* (Notre Dame, Ind., 1913), pp. 30–31.

38. "An Autobiography," p. 280; academic transcripts preserved in the University of Notre Dame Archives.

39. "An Autobiography," p. 281; *Bulletin of the University of Notre Dame: General Catalogue, 1912–1913.*

40. "An Autobiography," p. 281.

41. Interview with Shuster's sisters, August 16, 1980.

42. This account and the quotations are from *The [Notre Dame] Scholastic* 47 (May 30, 1914), pp. 694–695. Cf. also ibid., 47 (March 28, 1914), p. 563; 47 (May 9, 1914), pp. 649–650, and 47 (May 16, 1914), p. 664.

43. *The [Notre Dame] Scholastic* 48 (March 27, 1915), p. 422; 48 (May 1, 1915), p. 485; 48 (May 22, 1915), pp. 531–532; *Bulletin of the University of Notre Dame: General Catalogue, 1914–1915* (Notre Dame, Ind., 1915), p. 265; and ibid., *1915–1916*, p. 274.

44. *The [Notre Dame] Scholastic*, 46 (June 14, 1913), pp. 571–573. Quotations are from page 572.

45. "The Guns of Devotion," *The [Notre Dame] Scholastic* 48 (Easter, 1915), pp. 407–410; "Conventional Musings," ibid., 47 (May 11, 1914), pp. 574–575; "The Hallowed Time," ibid., 48 (Christmas, 1914), pp. 204–205; "F. Marion Crawford," ibid., 47 (February 21,

1914), pp. 465–468; "General Lew Wallace," ibid., 48 (January 23, 1915), pp. 257–260; and "Pindar the Superb," ibid., 48 (May 1, 1915), pp. 473–475.

46. "Spring Song," ibid., 47 (May 11, 1914), p. 576; "The Grave of Allouez," ibid., 48 (February 13, 1915), p. 308; "Washington the Free," ibid., 48 (February 27, 1915), pp. 337–338; "The Winged Years—Class Poem," ibid., 48 (June 26, 1915), p. 586; and "The Value of Poetry," ibid., 47 (June 14, 1914), pp. 717–719.

47. *Bulletin of the University of Notre Dame: General Catalogue, 1915–1916* (Notre Dame, 1916), pp. 273–274.

48. Shuster to Rev. John W. Cavanaugh, C.S.C., January 1, 1925, Box 2, Cavanaugh Personal Papers, University of Notre Dame Archives, hereafter abbreviated UNDA.

49. *The [Notre Dame] Scholastic* 49 (February 19, 1916), p. 339. Cf. also ibid. (October 16, 1915), p. 91, and interview with Shuster's sisters, August 16, 1980.

50. Interview with Shuster's sisters, August 16, 1980; *New York Sun,* October 4, 1939, clipping in Public Relations and Development Files, UNDA; "The Psychological Crux," *The [Notre Dame] Scholastic* 49 (November 6, 1915), pp. 129–134 and (November 13, 1915), pp. 150–152; "Livy the Orator," ibid. (May 29, 1916), pp. 482–483; "The Tragedy of Mark Twain," *The Catholic World* 104 (March, 1917), pp. 731–737; "Our Poets in the Streets," ibid., 105 (July 1917), pp. 433–445; and "The Retreat of the American Novel," ibid., 106 (November 1917), pp. 166–178. The quotations are from pages 435 and 177. Cf. also John J. Burke, C.S.P., to Shuster, February 9, 1917, Box 6, Shuster Papers, UNDA, hereafter abbreviated SP-UNDA.

51. *The [Notre Dame] Scholastic* 49 (February 19, 1916), p. 339.

52. "An Autobiography," p. 283.

53. Transcript of Military Record, April 21, 1950, Box 6, SP-UNDA; Shuster to parents, January 7, 1918 and March 13, 1918, Box 6, SP-UNDA; and Shuster to Carrico, March 2, 1918, *The [Notre Dame] Scholastic* 51 (March 2, 1918), p. 342.

54. "An Autobiography," p. 283. The following quotation is from pp. 284–285. See also letter of Shuster to his parents, December 16, 1918, Box 20, SP-UNDA.

55. "Spiritual Autobiography," p. 32.

56. "An Autobiography," p. 285. See also,"The Final Word," *Orate Fratres* 3 (March 1929), pp. 150–154.

57. "Personal Memoir," a draft begun by Shuster toward the end of his life and never completed, preserved in Box 20, SP-UNDA.

58. Shuster to parents, April 6, 1919, Box 20, SP-UNDA. The letter is apparently mistakenly dated "1918."

59. "An Autobiography," p. 285.

60. *New York Sun*, October 4, 1939, from a clipping in Public Relations and Development Files, UNDA.

2. TEACHER AND HUMANIST, 1919–1924

1. For Father Cavanaugh's presidency, see Arthur J. Hope, C.S.C., *Notre Dame: One Hundred Years* (Notre Dame, 1943), pp. 280–340; Thomas J. Schlereth, *The University of Notre Dame: A Portrait of Its History and Campus* (Notre Dame, 1976), pp. 122–142; Thomas T. McAvoy, C.S.C., *Father O'Hara of Notre Dame: The Cardinal-Archbishop of Philadelphia* (Notre Dame, 1967), pp. 17–60; McAvoy, "Notre Dame 1919–1922: The Burns Revolution," *The Review of Politics* 25 (October 1963), pp. 431–436; David J. Arthur, C.S.C., "The University of Notre Dame, 1919–1933: An Administrative History" (Ph.D. dissertation, University of Michigan, 1973); and Anna Rose Kearney, "James A. Burns, C.S.C.—Educator" (Ph.D. dissertation, University of Notre Dame, 1975).

2. Philip S. Moore, C.S.C., *Academic Development: University of Notre Dame* (Notre Dame, 1960), p. 12.

3. Moore, *Academic Development*, p. 12.

4. The best study of Father Burns is Kearney, "James A. Burns, C.S.C.—Educator," but see also Hope, *Notre Dame: One Hundred Years*, pp. 341–355.

5. Arthur, "The University of Notre Dame, 1919–1933," pp. 84–92, and Kearney, "James A. Burns, C.S.C.—Educator," pp. 110–112.

6. The president of Notre Dame also served as the religious superior of the Congregation's priests and brothers on campus. The new Code of Canon Law, which went into effect in 1918, limited the term of religious superiors to six years. Thus Father Cavanaugh, in office since 1905, needed to be replaced in 1919.

7. Arthur, "The University of Notre Dame, 1919–1933," pp. 205–212; Hope, *Notre Dame: One Hundred Years*, p. 347; and Kearney, "James A. Burns, C.S.C.—Educator," p. 113.

8. Arthur, "The University of Notre Dame, 1919–1933," pp. 112–145; McAvoy, "Notre Dame, 1919–1922," pp. 436–447; Hope, *Notre Dame, One Hundred Years*, pp. 347–352; and Kearney, "James A. Burns, C.S.C.—Educator," pp. 121–139.

9. McAvoy, "Notre Dame, 1919–1922," p. 436.

10. Arthur, "The University of Notre Dame, 1919–1933," pp. 241–247; McAvoy, "Notre Dame, 1919–1922," p. 436; Moore,

"Academic Development," pp. 159–162; and Kearney, "James A. Burns, C.S.C.—Educator," pp. 115–118.

11. Arthur, "The University of Notre Dame, 1919–1933," pp. 209–389; Kearney, "James A. Burns, C.S.C.—Educator," pp. 113–120; and Moore, "Academic Development," 131–136. It may seem surprising that religion was not a requirement earlier, but apparently it was considered unnecessary since all of campus life seemed permeated with religious principles and discipline. Burns may have emphasized the intellectual content of religion more.

12. McAvoy, "Notre Dame, 1919–1922," pp. 431–450.

13. Transcript of Military Record, dated April 21, 1950, Box 6, SP-UNDA; and Shuster, "Memoir of the Father Burns Era," unpublished manuscript in possession of the author.

14. Rev. Charles O'Donnell, C.S.C., to Dr. Thomas Walsh, July 9, 1917, Box 2, O'Donnell Personal Papers, UNDA.

15. "Memoir of the Father Burns Era."

16. *Bulletin of the University of Notre Dame: General Catalogue, 1921–1922; 1922–1923; 1923–1924*; and *Summer Session, 1922; 1923; 1925*, (Notre Dame, Ind.); *The Catholic Spirit in Modern English Literature* (New York, 1922); C. P. Irvine of the Macmillan Company to Shuster, September 30, 1921, and contract between Shuster and Macmillan Company, dated November 8, 1921, both in Box 6, SP-UNDA.

17. "Memoir of the Father Burns Era." C. P. Irvine to Shuster, September 30, 1921, and Shuster's contract with the Macmillan Company, November 8, 1921 (Box 6, SP-UNDA) both suggest Shuster's guarantee to purchase a large number of these as textbooks at Notre Dame.

18. *The Catholic Spirit in Modern English Literature*, p. viii.

19. See, for example, "Joris Karl Huysmans: Egoist and Mystic," *The Catholic World* 113 (July 1921), pp. 452–464; "The American Spirit," *The Catholic World* 114 (October 1921), pp. 1–13; and "The Mood for Peace," *The Catholic World* 115 (May 1922), pp. 184–194.

20. *The Catholic Spirit in Modern English Literature*, pp. 20, 32–97, 99, 215, 224, 229, 244–246, and 227.

21. *The Catholic Spirit in Modern English Literature*, pp. 33–87. The quotations are from pages 33–34 and 56.

22. *The Catholic Spirit in Modern English Literature*, p. 75.

23. *The Catholic Spirit in Modern English Literature*, pp. 73–87. The quotations are from pages 84 and 85–86.

24. See Shuster to Doris Cunningham (his future wife), April 13, 1921, August 8, 1923, November 6, 1923, and April ?, 1924; for the

quotations, Shuster to Doris, December 4, 1922, March 17, 1923, and July 17, 1923, Box 20, SP-UNDA. Some letters are difficult to date since Shuster wrote almost daily and identified most only by the day of the week—not day, month, or year.

25. Sister Josephine to Shuster, July 22, 1922; Sister St. Ursula to Shuster, November 1, 1922 and April 22, 1923; Sister Maura to Shuster, April 30, 1923; Sister Augustine to Shuster, February 19, 1924; Shuster to Doris, August 29, 1923; for the quotations see Sister M. Eleanore to Shuster, nd (probably early 1924), and Shuster to Doris, July 8, 1922, Box 20, SP-UNDA. Since most of these sisters did not put the initials of their religious communities after their names in these private letters, they will generally not be used in this work either.

26. *Bulletin of the University of Notre Dame: General Catalogue, 1920–1921*, pp. 63 and 337–338, and *1921–1922*, pp. 11–17, and *Summer Session, 1925*, p. 57; "Joris Karl Huysmans: Egoist and Mystic," 452–464; Rev. James A. Burns, C.S.C., to Shuster, March 5, 1921, and January 21, 1922, Box 45, Burns Presidential Papers, UNDA; Kearney, "James A. Burns, C.S.C.—Educator," pp. 114–115; and Contract of Employment, July 12, 1921, Box 2, SP-UNDA.

27. Shuster to Doris, December 7, 1923, Box 20, SP-UNDA.

28. Shuster to Doris, November 10, 1923, Box 20, SP-UNDA.

29. "Father Hudson," *The Commonweal* 19 (February 16, 1934), pp. 430–432; and "George N. Shuster," *American Spiritual Autobiographies*, p. 34.

30. Three pertinent studies are Donald A. Romito, "Catholics and Humanists: Aspects of the Debate in Twentieth-Century American Criticism" (Ph.D. dissertation, Emory University, 1976); Michael A. Schuler, "Religious Humanism in Twentieth-Century American Thought" (Ph.D. dissertation, Florida State University, 1982); and Arnold J. Sparr, "The Catholic Literary Revival in America, 1920–1960" (Ph.D. dissertation, University of Wisconsin-Madison, 1985).

31. Shuster contributed an Introduction to the Heritage Press edition of *The Confessions of St. Augustine* in 1963. But see also "The Legacy of Plato," *The Commonweal*, XV (Jan. 13, 1932), pp. 289–291, and *The Germans*, p. 22.

32. Herbert A. Deane, *The Political and Social Ideas of St. Augustine* (New York, 1963), pp. 14–77; Paul Henry, S.J., *Saint Augustine on Personality* (New York, 1960), pp. 6–24; and Alfred Warren Matthews, *The Development of St. Augustine: From Neoplatonism to Christianity, 386–391 A.D.* (Washington, 1980), pp. 87–136 and 207–218.

33. *Acta Sanctae Sedis* 11 (1879), p. 114; and William M. Halsey, *The Survival of American Innocence* (Notre Dame, 1980), p. 139.

34. *Summa Theologica*, I, QQ. 44–49 (Treatise on the Creation); QQ. 75–102 (Treatise on Man); I-II, QQ. 1–48 (Treatise on the Last End); and QQ. 49–89 (Treatise on Habits). See also F. C. Copleston, *Aquinas* (New York, 1955), and *Introduction to Saint Thomas Aquinas*, ed. Anton C. Pegis (New York, 1948).

35. *The Germans*, p. 18. See also F. Melian Stawell and G. Lowes Dickinson, *Goethe and Faust* (New York, 1929), one of Shuster's favorites.

36. *Faust I and II*, ed. and trans. Stuart Atkins (Cambridge, Mass., 1984), lines 11,936–11,937.

37. For Shuster's growing attraction to Emerson, see his "The American Spirit," *The Catholic World* 114 (October 1921), pp. 1–13, and *The Catholic Spirit in America* (New York, 1927), pp. 56–63.

38. *Newman: Prose and Poetry*, edited with an Introduction and Notes by George N. Shuster (Boston, 1925), p. ix.

39. *Newman: Prose and Poetry*, pp. xvi and xvii.

40. Newman, *The Idea of a University*, introduction by George N. Shuster (New York, 1959), especially Discourse V ("Knowledge Its Own End"), Discourse VI ("Knowledge Viewed in Relation to Learning"), and Discourse VII ("Knowledge Viewed in Relation to Professional Skill").

41. *Newman: Prose and Poetry*, p. xxi.

42. *Newman: Prose and Poetry*, p. xxi.

43. P. Franklin Chambers, *Baron von Huegel: Man of God* (London, 1945), pp. 11–41, and *Readings from Friedrich von Huegel*, selected by Algar Thorold (London, 1928), pp. xi-xxvi.

44. Friedrich von Huegel, "Experience and Transcendence," *The Dublin Review* 138 (April 1906), p. 361.

45. *The Germans*, p. 326.

46. Author's interview with Doris Shuster, June 17, 1983, and transcripts of Doris Cunningham, Office of the Registrar, Saint Mary's College, Notre Dame, Indiana.

47. The material on Doris's early years is chiefly from the author's interviews with her, June 17 and 24, 1983. See also her transcripts, Office of the Registrar, Saint Mary's College.

48. Interview with Doris Shuster, June 17, 1983.

49. The best histories of Saint Mary's College are Sister Mary Rita Heffernan, C.S.C., compiler, *A Story of Fifty Years* (Notre Dame, 1956), and Sister Mary Immaculate Creek, C.S.C., *A Panorama: 1844–1977: Saint Mary's College, Notre Dame, Indiana* (Saint Mary's College, 1977).

50. Interview with Doris Shuster, June 17, 1983, and transcripts, Office of the Registrar, Saint Mary's College. See also her tribute to

Sister Eleanore, "Mother Eleanore Has Left Us," *Holy Cross Courier* 13 (February 1940), p. 7, and her contributions to *St. Mary's Chimes*: "English Names for American Authors," 28 (April 1920), p. 146; "The Gift of the Celt," 28 (May 1920), pp. 160–161; "Bob's Bad Luck," 30 (December 1921), p. 68; and "To St. Patrick," 30 (March 1922), 113. For the gold medal, see *St. Mary's Chimes*, 30 (June 1922), 194. Sister M. Madeleva Wolff, C.S.C., *My First Seventy Years* (New York, 1959), pp. 38–46.

51. Interview with Doris Shuster, June 17, 1983, and transcripts of Doris Cunningham, Notre Dame, UNDA.

52. Interview with Doris Shuster, June 17, 1983; Doris to Shuster, March 5 and April 29, 1921, Box 20, SP-UNDA.

53. Shuster to Doris, September 26, 1920, Box 20, SP-UNDA.

54. Shuster to Doris, September 26, 1920; October 20, 1920; January 22, 1921; and Doris to Shuster, February 17 and March 5, 1921, Box 20, SP-UNDA.

55. Shuster to Doris, December 15, 1920, and Doris to Shuster, late January, 1921, Box 20, SP-UNDA.

56. Shuster to Doris, January 27, 1923 (?); October 9, 1921; and December 18, 1922; and Doris to Shuster, November 19, 1921, and June 14, 1922, Box 20, SP-UNDA.

57. Shuster to Doris, August 22, 1923, and Doris to Shuster, June 14, 1922, Box 20, SP-UNDA.

58. Doris to Shuster, June 14, 1922, and Shuster to Doris, January 27, 1923 (?), Box 20, SP-UNDA.

59. Shuster to Doris, January 27, 1923 (?), and probably September 15, 1922, Box 20, SP-UNDA.

60. Doris to Shuster, October 4, 1922, and Shuster to Doris, November ?, 1922; April 10, 1923; January 27, 1923 (?); probably September 15, 1922; August 12, 1923; and August 22, 1923, Box 20, SP-UNDA. The identity of the young woman is uncertain.

61. Shuster to Doris, April 10 and June 3, 1923, Box 20, SP-UNDA.

62. Interview with Doris Shuster, June 17, 1983.

63. Interview with Doris Shuster, June 17, 1983; Shuster to Doris, July 13, 1923, and April 7, 1924, Box 20, SP-UNDA.

64. Shuster to Doris, September 9; July 1; July 10; August 8; July 25; July 30, 1923, and March 6, 1924, Box 20, SP-UNDA.

65. Shuster to Doris, July 4; December 12; October 17; November 13; and December 11, 1923, Box 20, SP-UNDA.

66. Shuster to Doris, July 30; August 27; September 9, 1923, and March 4, 1924, Box 20, SP-UNDA.

67. Doris to Shuster, June, 1924; and Shuster to Doris, May 11 and June 19, 1924, Box 20, SP-UNDA.

68. Interview with Doris Shuster, June 17, 1983; Shuster to Doris, July 24 and August 24, 1923; February 20, March 2, and May ?, 1924; and Sister Eleanore to Doris, June 17, 1924, Box 20, SP-UNDA. A beautiful description of the significance of the Chapel of Loretto is found in *Our Mother House: Centenary Chronicles of the Sisters of the Holy Cross* (Notre Dame, 1941), pp. 84–85.

69. Interview with Doris Shuster, June 17, 1983; Shuster to Doris, October 29 and December 22, 1923 and February 20, 1924, Box 20, SP-UNDA. In early 1923 Shuster was denied permission to study for a Ph.D. degree at Notre Dame because he was head of the department in which the degree would be awarded, but Shuster never alluded to this denial as a reason for his departure (Minutes of the Meetings of the Committee on Graduate Studies, Eighth Meeting [May 1, 1923], UNDA).

70. Doris to Shuster, April 1, 1924, Box 20, SP-UNDA.

71. Shuster to Doris, July 29, November 9, and December 22, 1923, Box 20, SP-UNDA, and interview with Doris Shuster, June 24, 1983.

3. THE COMMONWEAL CATHOLIC, 1925–1937

1. Interview with Doris Shuster, June 24, 1983.

2. Interview with Doris Shuster, June 24, 1983.

3. John J. O'Connor, *Polytechnic Institute of Brooklyn: An Account of the Educational Purposes and Development of the Institute during Its First Century* (Brooklyn, 1956), pp. 3–14.

4. Polytechnic Institute of Brooklyn, *Catalogue of the College of Engineering, 1925–1926*, pp. 7–37, and *Evening Technical Courses, 1925–1926*, p. 13. The Institute bulletins probably reflect the faculty membership of the preceding year since the 1925–1926 catalogues are the only ones in which Shuster is noted. See also, interview with Doris Shuster, June 24, 1983.

5. *Bulletin of the University of Notre Dame: Summer Session, 1925* (Notre Dame, 1925), pp. 53–57.

6. Shuster to Paul [Fenlon], December 8, 1924, and Shuster to Doris, "Monday," "Tuesday," and "Sunday," Box 20, SP–UNDA. Since George and Doris corresponded several times a week that summer, no date was usually given except the day of the week.

7. Shuster to Doris, "Sunday," Box 20, SP-UNDA.

8. Doris to Shuster, July 10 and 27, 1925, and Shuster to Doris, "Tuesday" and "Thursday," Box 20, SP-UNDA. The quotations are

from two letters of Shuster to Doris, both marked "Wednesday," Box 20, SP-UNDA.

9. Shuster to Doris, July 17, 1925, and Doris to Shuster, "Thursday," Box 20, SP-UNDA.

10. See numerous letters of Shuster to Doris, written from Milwaukee, in the summer of 1928, Box 20, SP-UNDA; *The Official Catholic Directory* (New York), 1935, p. 218; 1936, p. 220; 1937, p. 230; and Rev. Michael J. Cantley, S.T.D., *A City with Foundations: A History of the Seminary of the Immaculate Conception, 1930–1980* (n.p. or d.), p. 45.

11. "Fifty Years of SJC: 1916–1966," manuscript of Sister Joan deLourdes, copy in the St. Joseph's College Archives. See also *St. Joseph's College for Women: Catalogue, 1930–1931* (n.p. or d.), pp. 13–14.

12. As will be discussed late, Shuster also served as an editor of *The Commonweal* magazine during this period and also made two trips to Europe.

13. *St. Joseph's College for Women: Catalogue, 1926–1927*, p. 15; *Catalogue, 1934–1935*, pp. 43–44; *Loria* 2 (November 1924), pp. 19–20; 2 (April 1925), p. 51; and 4 (March 1927), pp. 42–43; *Footprints: The Year Book of Saint Joseph's College for Women, 1925*, pp. 127, 198; and Mary McGinnis, "The Gentleman from Indiana," *Loria* 2 (November 1924), pp. 10–13. *Loria* is a literary and news journal published three times during the scholastic year by the students of the college. The yearbook, *Footprints*, is the fourth number each year.

14. *Footprints, 1928*, p. 17; *1930*, p. 91; and *1933*, p. 62; the following quotation is from Mary McDonnell to Shuster, May 18, 1950, Box 6, SP-UNDA.

15. J. E. Cusack to Shuster, October 13, 1922; Cusack to Rev. James Burns, C.S.C., June 13, 1922; Thomas Walsh to Shuster, December 11, 1923; and Kipling to Shuster, February 24, 1925, Box 6; Ina Coolbrith to Shuster, March 23, 1927, Box 5; and Shuster to Doris, June 3, 1923, Box 20, SP-UNDA.

16. Rev. Daniel Hudson, C.S.C., to Shuster, July 12, 1924, February 22, 1925, May 11, 1925, August 23, 1925, and November 14, 1925, Box 20, SP-UNDA. See also Shuster, "The Pearl of Paradise Mountain," beginning in *Ave Maria* 20, New Series (July 5, 1924), pp. 25–29; "The Voice of Catholic Germany, *Ave Maria* 21 (February 28, 1925), pp. 257–261; "Catholic Germany: The Romantic Movement," *Ave Maria* 22 (August 8, 1925), pp. 174–179; "At Jesus' House," *Ave Maria* 20 (July 12, 1924), p. 58; and "The Spiritual Journey of Nathaniel Hawthorne," *Ave Maria* 22 (October 24, 1925), pp. 520–523. These last two were written under the name Paul Crowley, a pseudonym Shuster frequently used at this time.

17. The best short summary of this program is perhaps Thomas T. McAvoy, C.S.C., *A History of the Catholic Church in the United States* (Notre Dame, 1969), pp. 375–377. See also John A. Ryan, *Social Doctrine in Action* (New York, 1941), pp. 143–151; Aaron I. Abell, *American Catholicism and Social Action* (Notre Dame, 1963), pp. 199–203; Jay P. Dolan, *The American Catholic Experience* (New York, 1985), pp. 344–346; James Hennesey, S.J., *American Catholics* (New York, 1981), pp. 228–230; and Joseph M. McShane, S.J., *"Sufficiently Radical"*: *Catholicism, Progressivism, and the Bishops' Program of 1919* (Washington, 1986). The statement is published in full in Raphael Huber, O.F.M.Conv., ed., *Our Bishops Speak* (Milwaukee, 1952), pp. 243–260.

18. Shuster interview with Robert B. Clements, June 9, 1969, in possession of the author, and Shuster, "Fortieth Anniversary Symposium," *The Commonweal* 81 (November 20, 1964), p. 273. There are several excellent studies of the early years of *The Commonweal* and the author has relied heavily upon them: Robert B. Clements, *"The Commonweal*, 1924–1938: The Williams-Shuster Years" (Ph.D. dissertation, University of Notre Dame, 1972); Paul E. Czuchlewski, "The Commonweal Catholic: 1924–1960 (Ph.D. dissertation, Yale University, 1972); Rodger Van Allen, *The Commonweal and American Catholicism* (Philadelphia, 1974); and Martin J. Bredeck, S.J., "The Role of the Catholic Layman in the Church and American Society as Seen in the Editorials of *Commonweal* Magazine" (Ph.D. dissertation, The Catholic University of America, 1977). The author has relied most heavily on Clements's and Van Allen's works and is especially grateful for the valuable interviews Clements has given him: with Shuster on June 9, 1969; with Edward Skillin on August 12, 1969; the interview of Clements and Van Allen with Shuster on June 3, 1970; and Van Allen with Shuster that same day.

19. A good summary of the founding of the N.C.W.C. is McAvoy, *A History of the Catholic Church in the United States*, pp. 363–369 and 379–383. See also Abell, *American Catholicism and Social Action*, pp. 192–224; John Tracy Ellis, *American Catholicism* (New York, 1965), pp. 131–135; Hennesey, *American Catholics*, pp. 225–231; Elizabeth McKeown, "War and Welfare: A Study of American Catholic Leadership" (Ph.D. dissertation, University of Chicago, 1972), pp. 218–263; and McShane, *"Sufficiently Radical,"* pp. 57–88.

20. Besides the excellent works listed above of Clements, pp. 42–51, and Van Allen, pp. 5–8, the best sources for the founding of *The Commonweal* are Michael Williams, *The Present Position of Catholics in the United States* (New York, 1928), pp. 17–23, and "Confidential Report to the Financial Supporters of *The Commonweal*," Accession 473, File 457,

Hagley Museum and Library. (Hereafter, citations will be abbreviated Acc. ___, File ___, HML.) See also Williams to Peter Guilday, Oct. 16, 1922, Box 8, Guilday Papers, Department of Archives and Manuscripts, Catholic University of America. The best work on Williams's early life is his own spiritual autobiography, *The Book of the High Romance* (New York, 1924).

    21. Shuster interview of June 9, 1969, and Dorothy Day, *The Long Loneliness* (New York, 1952), p. 169.

    22. Clements, "*The Commonweal,* 1924–1938," pp. 55–70; Van Allen, *The Commonweal and American Catholicism,* pp. 6–9; and "Confidential Report to the Financial Supporters of *The Commonweal,*" Acc. 473, File 457, HML.

    23. Clements, "*The Commonweal,* 1924–1938," pp. 66–68; Williams, "*The Commonweal* Announces Policy," N.C.W.C. *Editorial Sheet* (Washington, D.C.), November 1, 1924, quoted in Clements, pp. 66–67; and "An Introduction," *The Commonweal* 1 (November 12, 1924), p. 2. The point of *The Commonweal* continuing the independent status lost by the original N.C.W.C. is mentioned in the Shuster interview of June 9, 1969, but he may have been misinformed. McKeown gives evidence that the N.C.W.C. was to be under hierarchical supervision from the beginning, "War and Welfare," pp. 112–113. In order to guarantee orthodoxy in theology, Shuster recommended some official relationship with the Dominican Fathers of New York, but Williams rejected this (Shuster, "Fortieth Anniversary Symposium," p. 263).

    24. Rev. Vincent Donovan, O.P., to Shuster, February 18, 1923, Box 6, SP-UNDA.

    25. Shuster to Hudson, August 23 and October 4, 1924, Hudson Papers, X-4-i, UNDA; and Hudson to Shuster, September 23, 1924, Box 20, SP-UNDA. From 1924 through 1938 Shuster published more than four hundred book reviews in the magazine, over his own name or a pen name, in addition to numerous articles, editorials, and poems.

    26. *The Commonweal* 3 (February 10, 1926), p. 367, and 9 (December 12, 1928), p. 45.

    27. "Memorandum for Mr. Williams," February 20, 1928; Williams to Raskob, February 25, 1928; Raskob to Williams, February 29, 1928; William Griffin to Raskob, March 1, 1928; Williams to Raskob, March 1, 1928; Griffin to Raskob, March 21, 1928; and "Commonweal Guaranty Fund," May 24, 1928, all in Acc. 473, File 457, HML.

    28. Williams to Raskob, April 16, 1928; "Memorandum for Contributors to the Guarantee Fund of the Commonweal," November 15, 1929; William Griffin to Raskob, June 18, 1930 and June 2, 1931, Acc. 473, File 457, HML; Shuster to Ryan, April 20, 1933; Ryan to

Shuster, May 4, 1933, Box 6; and John F. McCormick to Ryan, May 18, 1933, Box 7, John A. Ryan Papers, Department of Archives and Manuscripts, Catholic University of America (hereafter abbreviated RP-DAM-CUA). The quotations are from Williams to Raskob, March 22, 1928, and "Campaign to Date," March 8, 1930, Acc. 473, File 457, HML.

29. See, for example, "George N. Shuster," in Friderike M. Zweig, *Greatness Revisited* (Boston, 1972), p. 118.

30. Two pen names frequently used by Shuster were Paul Crowley and Ambrose Farley.

31. "On Teaching Evolution," *The Commonweal* 1 (April 22, 1925), pp. 647–649, and "Concerning Evolution," *The Commonweal* 2 (June 10, 1925), p. 120. An excellent treatment of this issue is Van Allen, *The Commonweal and American Catholicism*, pp. 21–26.

32. Sir Bertram Windle, "The Case Against Evolution," *The Commonweal* 2 (June 10, 1925), pp. 124–126; Forrest Davis, "Tennessee—State of Brave Men" (July 29, 1925), pp. 283–285; Frank R. Kent, "What Dayton Thinks" (July 29, 1925), pp. 288–289; T. Lawrason Riggs, "Fundamentalism and the Faith" (August 19, 1925), pp. 344–346; "On the Freedom of the Teacher" (June 24, 1925), pp. 169–170; "The Scopes Dilemma" (July 15, 1925), pp. 241–242; "Dayton and Great Britain" (August 5, 1925), pp. 301–303; Michael Williams, "At Dayton, Tennessee" (July 22, 1925), pp. 262–265; Williams, "Sunday in Dayton" (July 29, 1925), pp. 285–288; Williams, "William Jennings Bryan" (August 5, 1925), p. 303; and Williams, "Summing-up at Dayton" (August 5, 1925), pp. 304–305. The quotation is from "Concerning Evolution," p. 121.

33. "Concerning the Scopes Case," *The Commonweal* 2 (June 3, 1925), p. 86.

34. Shuster, *The Catholic Spirit in Modern English Literature* (New York, 1922), pp. 56–72, and "A Disturbing Problem," *The Commonweal* 1 (January 7, 1925), pp. 221–222.

35. Shuster, "Have We Any Scholars?" *America* 33 (August 15, 1925), pp. 418–419. To distinguish them from unsigned articles and editorials, Shuster's own writings in *The Commonweal* will be identified by author in this chapter.

36. Shuster, "Have We Any Scholars?" p. 418. See also the author's "George N. Shuster and American Catholic Intellectual Life," in *Studies in Catholic History*, ed. Nelson Minnich, et al. (Wilmington, 1985), pp. 345–365.

37. Shuster, "Have We Any Scholars?" p. 418. The following quotation is from p. 419.

38. Shuster, "Have We Any Scholars?" p. 419.

39. Shuster, "Insulated Catholics," *The Commonweal* 2 (August 19, 1925), pp. 337–338.

40. The best studies of Father O'Hara's work at Notre Dame are Thomas T. McAvoy, C.S.C., *Father O'Hara of Notre Dame: The Cardinal-Archbishop of Philadelphia* (Notre Dame, 1967), pp. 90–123; and Thomas P. Jones, C.S.C., *The Development of the Office of Prefect of Religion at the University of Notre Dame from 1842 to 1952* (Washington, 1960).

41. Shuster, "Insulated Catholics," p. 337. The following quotation is from p. 338.

42. Shuster, "Insulated Catholics," p. 338.

43. Actually, most editorials were unsigned unless there were strong differences of opinion within the editorial staff. There is no evidence that there was such difference here, although the editors of *America* included a disclaimer at the head of his article in the August 15 issue. For Shuster's explanation, see "Memoir of the Father Burns Era" in possession of the author.

44. *The Hill of Happiness* (New York, 1926).

45. Ralph Adams Cram, "A Challenge to Mr. Chapman," *The Commonweal* 1 (December 3, 1924), p. 88.

46. "The Klan Self-Revealed," *The Commonweal* 1 (January 21, 1925), pp. 277–278. An unusually thorough and convincing discussion of toleration and the 1928 election can be found in Clements, "*The Commonweal*, 1924–1938," pp. 71–120.

47. Interview of George Shuster with Roger Van Allen, June 3, 1970. The precise details of this recollection may be inaccurate—the author has not been able to find that article by Crowley and Pakistan was not in existence before World War II—but the basic story is probably true.

48. "The Things Behind the Words," *The Commonweal* 8 (August 29, 1928), pp. 399–400.

49. "A Catholic President?" *The New Republic* 50 (March 23, 1927), pp. 128–131.

50. "An Open Letter to the Honorable Alfred E. Smith," *The Atlantic Monthly* 139 (April 1927), pp. 540–549.

51. "The New Inquisition," *The Commonweal* 5 (March 30, 1927), pp. 561–562.

52. "Should a Catholic Be President? An Open Letter to Mr. Charles Marshall," *The Commonweal* 5 (April 13, 1927), pp. 623–626.

53. See Henry Whitehead's review of Theodore Schroeder, *Al Smith, the Pope and the Presidency, The Commonweal* 8 (May 16, 1928), p.

48; Patrick Healy's review of Charles Marshall, *The Roman Catholic Church in the Modern State* (August 29, 1928), pp. 414–416; Charles Willis Thompson, "The Campaign Begins" (October 3, 1928), pp. 540–541; "Keeping the Record Straight" (October 10, 1928), pp. 559–560; Thompson, "The Battle-Smoke Clears" (October 24, 1928), pp. 622-623; and Michael Williams "Plain Facts for Americans" (October 31, 1928), pp. 652–655.

54. Clements, "*The Commonweal*, 1924–1938," pp. 97–102; Williams to Raskob, September 19, 1928, Acc. 473, File 457, HML.

55. Clements, "*The Commonweal*, 1924–1938," pp. 103–109.

56. Clements, "*The Commonweal*, 1924–1938," pp. 86–94, 109–110; *New York Times*, July 15, 1928: IX-5-1.

57. Interview of George Shuster, June 9, 1969.

58. Shuster, "The Catholic Here and Now," *The Outlook* 148 (February 29, 1928), pp. 336ff.

59. Shuster, "The Catholic Conspiracy Myth," *Outlook and Independent* 150 (November 7, 1928), pp. 1102ff. *(The Outlook* merged with *The Independent* in October 1928; thus the name change.)

60. Shuster, "The Catholic Conspiracy Myth," p. 1141.

61. Shuster, *The Catholic Spirit in America* (New York, 1927).

62. *The Catholic Spirit in America*, pp. 1–36.

63. *The Catholic Spirit in America*, pp. 37–77.

64. *The Catholic Spirit in America*, pp. 78–120, 163–204.

65. *The Catholic Spirit in America*, p. 279.

66. "Weighing the Big Invisibles," *The Commonweal* 6 (September 14, 1927), p. 428. An excellent discussion of this reaction to the Depression is in Van Allen, *The Commonweal and American Catholicism*, pp. 32–56.

67. "Weighing the Big Invisibles," p. 428, and "The American Goose-Step," *The Commonweal* 10 (October 2, 1929), p. 543.

68. John A. Ryan, "The Senate Looks at Unemployment, I," *The Commonweal* 10 (October 2, 1929), pp. 550–552; "The Senate Looks at Unemployment II" (October 9, 1929), pp. 578–580; "The Experts Look at Unemployment ," (October 16, 1929), pp. 612–613; and "The Experts Look at Unemployment II" (October 23, 1929), pp. 636–638.

69. "Wall Street Impoverished," *The Commonweal* 11 (November 6, 1929), pp. 2–3; "The Call to Order" (November 13, 1929), pp. 29–30; "What Can Mr. Hoover Do?" (November 13, 1929), p. 30; "The Billion-Dollar Gamble" (April 9, 1930), pp. 639–640; "The Jobless Millions" (March 19, 1930), p. 544; "Mr. Hoover Today" (March 12, 1930), pp. 521–522; "Patented Prosperity" (February 19, 1930), pp. 437–438; and "The Slough of Despond" (December 4,

1929), pp. 125–126. For a broader study, see Lawrence B. DeSaulniers, *The Response in American Catholic Periodicals to the Crisis of the Great Depression, 1930–1935* (Lanham, Md., 1984).

70. "Father of the Poor," *The Commonweal* 14 (June 3, 1931), pp. 113–114.

71. Interview with George Shuster, June 9, 1969. See also Clements, "*The Commonweal*, 1924–1938," pp. 122–123.

72. "Saving the Social Order," *The Commonweal* 14 (August 26, 1931), pp. 391–392.

73. See, for example, "Socialism and Catholic Action," *The Commonweal* 16 (September 7, 1932), pp. 437–439.

74. "Mr. Roosevelt's Candidacy," *The Commonweal* 16 (May 4, 1932), p. 3.

75. "The Catholic Duty," *The Commonweal* 16 (October 5, 1932), pp. 517–518.

76. "Religion in Politics," *The Commonweal* 16 (October 12, 1932), pp. 545–546.

77. "Results of the Election," *The Commonweal* 17 (November 16, 1932), pp. 57–58.

78. For an excellent summary of *The Commonweal* and the New Deal, see Clements, "*The Commonweal*, 1924–1938," pp. 151–158.

79. Shuster, "Shall We Ban Child Labor?" *The Commonweal* 19 (April 6, 1934), pp. 623–624.

80. "Dangers of Demagogy," *The Commonweal* 19 (December 8, 1933), p. 144; "The Clergy and Politics" 21 (March 22, 1935), p. 580; and "Father Coughlin's Authority" 22 (May 31, 1935), pp. 113–114.

81. Shuster, "Radio Sky Pilot" *Review of Reviews* 91 (April 1935), p. 24.

82. Shuster, "Radio Sky Pilot," p. 27.

83. Shuster, "Radio Sky Pilot," p. 27.

84. Shuster, "Radio Sky Pilot," p. 72.

85. Shuster, "Radio Sky Pilot," p. 72.

86. Edward Oswell, "The Church and the Negro," *The Commonweal* 9 (November 21, 1928), pp. 66–68; George Chester Morse, "A Negro Answers" (December 26, 1928), pp. 226–227; John T. Gillard, "The Negro Challenges Catholicism," 16 (June 1, 1932), pp. 129–131; John LaFarge, "The Negro Apostolate," 22 (July 5, 1935), pp. 257–259; "Radicals at Scottsboro," 15 (December 2, 1931), p. 116; "The Harlem Outburst," 21 (April 5, 1935), p. 653; "The Negro Problem," 20 (June 1, 1934), pp. 113–114; and "Brothers in Black and Red," 21 (March 1, 1935), pp. 495–496.

87. See, for example, "What Shall the Layman Do?" *The Commonweal* 2 (September 23, 1925), pp. 461–463; and "Dilemmas of the Rank and File," 22 (July 26, 1935), pp. 313–314.

88. "Rome Answers Lambeth," *The Commonweal* 13 (January 14, 1931), p. 283; and "Rome Has Spoken" (January 21, 1931), pp. 309–311.

89. Virgil Michel, "The Layman in the Church," *The Commonweal* 12 (June 4, 1930), pp. 123–125; "Catholic Action Again," 9 (February 13, 1929), pp. 418–419; Paul Marx, O.S.B., *The Life and Work of Virgil Michel* (Washington, 1957), pp. 140, 174; and Shuster's interview with Van Allen, June 3, 1970.

90. "Urbi et Orbi," *The Commonweal* 9 (February 20, 1929), pp. 441–442; and "Mussolini Again," 7 (April 11, 1928), p. 1280.

91. "Russian Recognition," *The Commonweal* 19 (November 3, 1933), pp. 5–6; "Russia and Religion" (November 24, 1933), pp. 85–86; and "The Recognition of Russia" (December 1, 1933), pp. 114–115.

92. For the Spanish Civil War, see Burnett Bolloten, *The Spanish Revolution* (Chapel Hill, N.C., 1979); Raymond Carr, *The Spanish Tragedy* (London, 1977); and Hugh Thomas, *The Spanish Civil War*, revised and enlarged edition (New York, 1977).

93. J. David Valaik, "American Catholic Dissenters and the Spanish Civil War," *The Catholic Historical Review* 53 (January 1968), pp. 537–555, and George Q. Flynn, *Roosevelt and Romanism* (Westport, Conn., 1976), pp. 35–52. See also Robert M. Darrow, "Catholic Political Power: A Study of the Activities of the American Catholic Church on Behalf of Franco during the Spanish Civil War, 1936–1939" (Ph.D. dissertation, Columbia University, 1953).

94. Shuster, "Some Reflections on Spain," *The Commonweal* 25 (April 2, 1937), p. 625.

95. Shuster, "Some Reflections on Spain," p. 626.

96. Shuster, "Some Reflections on Spain," pp. 625–627. See also Van Allen, *The Commonweal and American Catholics*, pp. 60–66.

97. Van Allen, *The Commonweal and American Catholics*, pp. 64–65; and Francis X. Talbot, S.J., "In Answer to Some Reflections on the Spanish Situation," *America* 57 (April 10, 1937), pp. 9–10.

98. Shuster, "Some Further Reflections," *The Commonweal* 25 (April 23, 1937), p. 716.

99. Shuster, "Some Further Reflections," pp. 716–717.

100. Shuster, "Some Further Reflections," p. 717.

101. Clements, "*The Commonweal*, 1924–1938," pp. 184–186; Van Allen, *The Commonweal and American Catholics*, pp. 66–70;

Williams, "Open Letter to Leaders of the American Press, on Spain," *The Commonweal* 26 (May 7, 1937), pp. 33–37; "The Truth About Spain: Open Letter to the Press: No. 2" (May 21, 1937), pp. 85–87; "The Truth About Spain: Open Letter to the Press: No. 3" (May 28, 1937), pp. 113–115; "The Truth About Spain: Open Letter to the Press: No. 4" (June 4, 1937), pp. 151–153; "The Truth About Spain: Open Letter to the Press: No. 5" (June 25, 1937), pp. 231–234; "The Commonweal's Spanish Relief Fund" (May 7, 1937), pp. 29–30; "American Committee for Spanish Relief" (May 14, 1937), pp. 57–58; "American Committee for Spanish Relief" (June 4, 1937), pp. 141–143; and "Mr. Shuster Leaves" (June 11, 1937), p. 172.

102. Carlton J. H. Hayes to Dr. F. P. Keppel, May 6, 1936; Hayes to Robert M. Lester, June 14, 1937; Hayes to Lester, December 8, 1938; Shuster to Lester, January 18, 1943; Shuster to Lester, May 17, 1944; and Lester to Dean George Pegram, March 28, 1945, all in Folder "Columbia U.—Council for Research in the Social Sciences— Prep. of Documented History of the German Centre Party, 1919– 1933," Archives of the Carnegie Corporation of New York.

103. "The Truth About Spain: Open Letter to the Press: No. 3," *The Commonweal* 26 (May 28, 1937), p. 113.

104. Clements, "*The Commonweal, 1924–1938,*" pp. 186–197; Van Allen, *The Commonweal and American Catholics,* pp. 69–74; R. Dana Skinner to Msgr. John A. Ryan, June 18, 1937; Michael Williams to Rev. T. Lawrason Riggs and others, June 23, 1937; Skinner to Williams, June 24, 1937; and Carlton J. H. Hayes to Williams, June 29, 1937, all in Box 15, RP-DAM-CUA.

4. UNDERSTANDING GERMANY, 1930–1939

1. Interview with Doris Shuster, June 24, 1983.

2. *The Catholic Spirit in America* (New York, 1927), pp. 213–224; "The High Lights of Humanism," *The Commonweal* 9 (April 17, 1929), p. 675; "The Several Humanists," *The Commonweal* 11 (April 2, 1930), p. 615; "The Catholic Here and Now," *The Outlook* 148 (February 29, 1928), p. 337.

3. "Captains of the Modern Soul," *The Commonweal* 9 (March 20, 1929), pp. 563–565.

4. For Germany during this period, see Andreas Dorpalen, *Hindenburg and the Weimar Republic* (Princeton, 1964); Ellen Lovell Evans, *The German Center Party, 1870–1933* (Carbondale, 1981); Erich Eyck, *A*

History of the Weimar Republic, 2 vols. (Cambridge, Mass.: 1962–1963); Hajo Holborn, *A History of Modern Germany*, vol. 3 (New York, 1969); Godfrey Scheele, *The Weimar Republic* (London, 1946); and Eliot Barculo Wheaton, *Prelude to Calamity: The Nazi Revolution, 1933–35* (Garden City, N.Y., 1968).

5. Shuster's passport is preserved in Box 11, SP-UNDA. "Bruening Memoir," a memoir of Shuster's relations with Heinrich Bruening, composed by Shuster probably in the early 1970s and preserved in Box 4, SP-UNDA; various articles on Germany in *The Commonweal*, from "Germany at Low Tide," *The Commonweal* 12 (November 19, 1930), pp. 70–71, to "A Talk with Chancellor Bruening," *The Commonweal* 13 (April 15, 1931), pp. 659–661; especially "Europe's Windiest Corner," *The Commonweal* 13 (December 24, 1930), pp. 209–211, and "Geneva Once Again," *The Commonweal* 13 (January 21, 1931), pp. 320–321; "The Church in Germany" and "Problems of the Church in Germany," *The Homiletic and Pastoral Review* 31 (August 1931), pp. 1155–1161, and (September 1931), pp. 1259–1265; and interview with Doris Shuster, August 19, 1983.

6. "Bruening Memoir," Box 4, SP-UNDA, and interview with Doris Shuster, August 19, 1983.

7. "Revenna Interlude," *The Commonweal* 13 (February 18, 1931), pp. 429–431.

8. "Munich: Anno Domini 1931," *The Commonweal* 13 (March 11, 1931), pp. 511–513.

9. "Austria As One Finds It," *The Commonweal* 13 (March 25, 1931), pp. 570–572.

10. "Europe's Windiest Corner," 209–211.

11. "Sunrise in the West," *The Commonweal* 13 (November 26, 1930), p. 98.

12. "Germany at Low Tide," *The Commonweal* 13 (November 19, 1930), p. 70; "Il Duce's Handkerchief," *The Commonweal* 13 (December 3, 1930), p. 131; and "A Talk with Chancellor Bruening," p. 660.

13. "Germany at Low Tide," p. 70; and "A Talk with Chancellor Bruening," pp. 659–661. See also Evans, *The German Center Party, 1870–1933*, pp. 355–374.

14. "Il Duce's Handkerchief," pp. 131–132; "Munich: Anno Domini 1931," p. 513, and "Germany at Low Tide," pp. 70–71.

15. "Il Duce's Handkerchief," pp. 131–132; "Munich: Anno Domini 1931," pp. 511–513; "Germany at Low Tide," pp. 70–71; and "Problems of the Church in Germany," p. 1261. See also "Communism or the Catholic Church," *Forum and Century*, 86 (October 1931), pp. 207–212.

16. "The Church in Germany," pp. 1155–1161; and "Problems of the Church in Germany," pp. 1259–1265.

17. *The Germans: An Inquiry and an Estimate* (New York, 1932), especially chaps. 1, 2, 3, 7.

18. "What Germany Really Wants," *Forum and Century* 87 (May 1931), p. 297.

19. *The Germans*, p. 141.

20. *The Germans*, pp. 270, 276.

21. *The Germans*, pp. 277–279.

22. *The Germans*, pp. 21–22.

23. *The Germans*, p. 22.

24. "Bruening Memoir," Box 4, SP-UNDA.

25. For the rise of Adolf Hitler and National Socialism in Germany, see especially Evans, *The German Center Party, 1870–1933*, pp. 335–396; Holborn, *A History of Modern Germany*, vol. 3, pp. 711–762; Wheaton, *Prelude to Calamity: The Nazi Revolution 1933–35*; and Nora Levin, *The Holocaust Years* (Malabar, Fla., 1990), pp. 3–36.

26. "Bruening Memoir," Box 4; Shuster's passport, Box 11, SP-UNDA, and interview with Doris Shuster, August 19, 1983.

27. "Bruening Memoir," Box 4, SP-UNDA.

28. "Bruening Memoir," Box 4, SP-UNDA.

29. "Bruening Memoir," Box 4, SP-UNDA; *The Ground I Walked On*, 2d ed. (Notre Dame, 1969), pp. 146–147; and "Dr. Bruening's Sejourn [*sic*] in the United States (1935–1945)," in *Staat, Wirtschaft und Politik in der Weimarer Republik*, ed. Ferdinand A. Hermens and Theodor Schieder (Berlin, 1967), pp. 450–451.

30. An accessible study of the Concordat is Wheaton, *Prelude to Calamity: The Nazi Revolution, 1933–35*, pp. 330–343, 353–363. See also Shuster's "Germany under the Concordat," *The Commonweal* 18 (September 1, 1933), pp. 420–422, and John Zeender, "The Genesis of the German Concordat of 1933," in *Studies in Catholic History*, ed. Nelson H. Minnich, et al. (Wilmington, 1985), pp. 617–665.

31. "Bruening Memoir," Box 4, SP-UNDA; *The Ground I Walked On*, pp. 152–155; *Like a Mighty Army: Hitler versus Established Religion* (New York, 1935), pp. 185–191.

32. See Chapter 3 for Shuster's other occupations during these years, and his academic records and transcripts in the Department of English and Comparative Literature at Columbia University.

33. *The English Ode from Milton to Keats* (New York, 1940), pp. v–vi, and interview with Doris Shuster, June 24, 1983.

34. *Strong Man Rules* (New York, 1934), p. v.

35. *Strong Man Rules*, pp. 91–100.

36. *Strong Man Rules*, pp. 25–38.

37. *Strong Man Rules*, pp. 42–51.

38. *Strong Man Rules*, pp. 175–224.

39. *Strong Man Rules*, pp. 121–146, 237.

40. *Strong Man Rules*, pp. 138, 141.

41. *Like a Mighty Army*, pp. v-vii.

42. *Like a Mighty Army*, pp. 10–11.

43. *Like a Mighty Army*, pp. 12–13, 60–61.

44. *Like a Mighty Army*, pp. 11, 76.

45. *Like a Mighty Army*, p. 56.

46. *Like a Mighty Army*, p. 64.

47. *Like a Mighty Army*, pp. 57–67.

48. *Like a Mighty Army*, pp. 85–92.

49. *Like a Mighty Army*, p. 81.

50. *Like a Mighty Army*, pp. 94–107.

51. *Like a Mighty Army*, p. 137.

52. *Like a Mighty Army*, pp. 146–170.

53. *Like a Mighty Army*, pp. 172–176. See also "Catholics in Germany," *The Commonweal* 20 (June 29, 1934), pp. 234–236.

54. *Like a Mighty Army*, pp. 186–190.

55. *Like a Mighty Army*, p. 212.

56. *Like a Mighty Army*, pp. 193–271. The quotation is from p. 271. An interesting reflection on Shuster's three books on Germany is contained in a letter of Shuster to John Meng, June 21, 1950, in Meng Papers, Special Collections Division, Georgetown University Library.

57. "Dr. Bruening's Sejourn [*sic*] in the United States (1935–1945)," pp. 450–451, and *The Ground I Walked On*, p. 147.

58. *The Ground I Walked On*, pp. 146–147; Cantley, *A City with Foundations*, p. 45; "Dr. Bruening's Sejourn [*sic*] in the United States (1935–1945)," pp. 450–452; George Barry Ford, *A Degree of Difference* (New York, 1969), pp. 84–86; and "Bruening Memoir," Box 4, SP-UNDA.

59. "Bruening Memoir: Foreword," Box 4; "Conversations" with Dr. Bruening, Box 2; Bruening to Shuster, July 23 and September 1, 1936, Box 1; Memorandum of Bruening to Shuster, November 16, 1936, Box 2, SP-UNDA; and "Dr. Bruening's Sejourn [*sic*] in the United States (1935–1945)," pp. 455–456. As noted in Chapter 3, Shuster left *The Commonweal* in an atmosphere of crisis in 1937. His interests were clearly changing from understanding the Center Party to exposing the evils of Nazism, and in 1939 he was appointed academic dean and acting president of Hunter College.

60. Bruening to Shuster, September 18 and November 9, 1937; April 18, May 19, and June 2, 1939; February 13, September 13, October 5, and October 19, 1940; and September 16, 1942; Bruening to

Mrs. Shuster, November 23, 1940, and December 13, 1944, all in Box 1, SP-UNDA. "Dr. Bruening's Sejourn [sic] in the United States (1935–1945), pp. 460–473, 465.

61. "Dr. Bruening's Sejourn [sic] in the United States (1935–1945)," pp. 464–466.

62. "Bruening Memoir," Box 4, SP-UNDA.

63. "Captains of the Modern Soul," *The Commonweal* 9 (March 20, 1929), pp. 563–565; and "Days in Beuron," *The Commonweal* 19 (November 10, 1933), pp. 43–45.

64. Shuster to Rev. John Burke, C.S.P., February 2, 1934, United States Catholic Conference Archives, Washington, D.C.

65. Rev. John Burke, C.S.P., to Shuster, February 15, and Shuster to Burke, C.S.P., February 20, 1934, USCC Archives, Washington, D.C.

66. "Gen. Sherrill and the Olympics," *The Commonweal* 23 (November 8, 1935), pp. 40–42. The quotations are from p. 41 and p. 42.

67. Petition to Cardinal Patrick Hayes, April 1936, USCC Archives, Washington, D.C.

68. H. A. Reinhold, *H.A.R.: The Autobiography of Father Reinhold* (New York, 1968), pp. 57–101; and Joel Patrick Garner, "The Vision of a Liturgical Reformer: Hans Ansgar Reinhold, American Catholic Educator" (Ph.D. dissertation, Columbia University, 1972), pp. 20–26. See also Reinhold to "Mr. Mann," May 19, 1936, USCC Archives, Washington, D.C.

69. Rev. J. Francis McIntyre, Secretary of the Council, to Msgr. Gallus Bruder, April 25, 1936, USCC Archives, Washington, D.C.

70. Shuster to Rev. R. A. McGowan, June 4; Archbishop Michael J. Curley to Rev. R. A. MacGowan [sic], June 1; McGowan to Burke, June 11; Burke to Shuster, June 9; Shuster to Burke, June 12, 1936; Memorandum for the Record, July 24; and Gregory Feige to McGowan, July 8, 1936, USCC Archives, Washington, D.C. See also Garner, "The Vision of a Liturgical Reformer," pp. 27–28.

71. Reinhold, *H.A.R.*, pp. 106–109.

72. Reinhold, *H.A.R*, pp. 139–149; Garner, "The Vision of a Liturgical Reformer," pp. 29–31, 247–251; and Shuster to LaFarge, July 23 and August 7, 1956, LaFarge Papers, Special Collections Division, Georgetown University Library.

73. Carlton J. H. Hayes to Dr. F. P. Keppel of the Carnegie Corporation, May 5, 1936, Columbia University File, Archives of the Carnegie Corporation of New York, hereafter abbreviated ACCNY.

74. Hayes to Keppel, May 5; Keppel to Hayes, May 19; Robert T. Crane to Keppel, May 25; Hayes to Keppel, June 6; Keppel to Hayes, June 10; Crane to Keppel, July 30; Hayes to Crane, August 24; Philip

M. Hayden to Keppel, October 20; and Secretary of the Carnegie Corporation to President Nicholas Murray Butler, November 4, 1936, Columbia University File, ACCNY. Mrs. Shuster was also approved as assistant and typist.

75. Hayes to Lester, June 14, 1937 and December 8, 1938, Columbia University File, ACCNY, and interview with Doris Shuster, August 19, 1983.

76. As will be described shortly, many of his notes were lost in Vienna.

77. Notes of interviews with Bernhard Letterhaus, Pater Leiber, Joseph Joos, and Rudolf Hilferding, Box 1; Msgr. E. Foehr, Box 2; Joseph Wirth and Paul Schmitt, Box 3; and Hugo Moennig, Box 4, SP-UNDA.

78. *The Ground I Walked On*, pp. 157–159. The quotation is from p. 159. See also Shuster and Arnold Bergstraesser, *Germany: A Short History* (New York, 1944), especially pp. 184–200.

79. *The Ground I Walked On*, p. 165.

80. *The Ground I Walked On*, pp. 164–165, and interview with Doris Shuster, August 19, 1983.

81. *The Ground I Walked On*, pp. 165–166, and interview with Doris Shuster, August 19, 1983.

82. Holborn, *A History of Modern Germany*, vol. 3, pp. 775–777.

83. Interview with Doris Shuster, August 19, 1983, and "Terror in Vienna," *The Commonweal* 27 (April 15, 1938), pp. 678–680.

84. Interview with Doris Shuster, August 19, 1983.

85. Interview with Doris Shuster, August 19, 1983.

86. Interview with Doris Shuster, August 19, 1983.

87. Interview with Doris Shuster, August 19, 1983; Hayes to Lester, December 8, 1938, Columbia University File, ACCNY.

88. In a discussion of recent German history over Hamburg radio in 1987, Dr. Dirk Bavendamm stated his opinion that Shuster had visited these anti-Nazi leaders in 1937–1938, perhaps as a member of the United States secret service, to help foment resistance to and even the overthrow of Adolf Hitler. It is an intriguing theory but without solid evidence. There is no indication that Shuster had any other intention when he left for Europe in 1937 except to collect information for the book he was commissioned to write, no evidence that he was in the service of the United States government, and no evidence that President Roosevelt was then secretly plotting to overthrow Hitler. Shuster would have been interested in and listened to any such hopes, but apparently was not sent to take part. (Bavendamm's radio transcript, dated February 17, 1987, in possession of the author.)

89. John H. Lord to Shuster, January 6, 1938, and Leland B. Morris to George Messersmith, November 18, 1938, Box 2, SP-UNDA. See also Robert E. Herzstein, *Roosevelt and Hitler: Prelude to War* (New York, 1989).

5. HUNTER COLLEGE AND THE WAR YEARS, 1938–1945

1. "Dr. Bruening's Sejourn [*sic*] in the United States (1935–1945)," in *Staat, Wirtschaft und Politik in der Weimarer Republik,* ed. Ferdinand A. Hermens and Theodor Schieder (Berlin, 1967), pp. 460–464.

2. *Brother Flo: An Imaginative Biography* (New York, 1938).

3. *The Vatican as a World Power* (New York, 1939); *Pope Pius XI and American Public Opinion* (New York, 1939); and *Mein Kampf* (New York: Reynal and Hitchcock, 1939).

4. *Look Away!* (New York, 1939).

5. *The Commonweal* 31 (November 10, 1939), pp. 81–82; *New York Times Review of Books,* November 5, 1939, p. 7; and *Saturday Review of Literature* 21 (December 16, 1939), pp. 18–19.

6. George N. Shuster and Arnold Bergstraesser, *Germany: A Short History* (New York, 1944).

7. See especially Carlton J.H. Hayes to [Robert] Lester [of the Carnegie Corporation], August 10, 1940; Shuster to Lester, January 18, 1943 and May 17, 1944; Lester to Shuster, March 9, 1945; Shuster to Robert Lister [*sic*], March 16, 1945; Lester to Dean George B. Pegram [of the Council for Research in the Social Sciences], March 28, 1945; and Philip Hayden [of Columbia University] to Lester, May 5, 1945, all in Columbia University File, Archives of the Carnegie Corporation of New York.

8. Samuel White Patterson, *Hunter College: Eighty-Five Years of Service* (New York, 1955), pp. 2–23; Mae A. Burns, "An Historical Background and Philosophical Criticism of the Curriculum of Hunter College of the College of the City of New York from 1870 to 1938" (Ph.D. dissertation, Fordham University, 1938), pp. 1–2; and *Commemorating the Diamond Jubilee of Hunter College of the City of New York, 1870–1945* (New York, 1945), [pp. 1–2].

9. Lewis Mumford, "The Sky Line: Skyscraper School," *The New Yorker* 16 (November 16, 1940), p. 84.

10. *Commemorating the Diamond Jubilee,* [p. 3]; Burns, "An Historical Background and Philosophical Criticism," pp. 2–3; and Patterson, *Hunter College,* pp. 37–75.

11. Burns, "An Historical Background and Philosophical Criticism," p. 179.

12. Patterson, *Hunter College*, pp. 75–137, and *Commemorating the Diamond Jubilee*, [p. 4].

13. Patterson, *Hunter College*, pp. 134–137.

14. Burns, "An Historical Background and Philosophical Criticism," pp. 124–173, and Patterson, *Hunter College*, pp. 141–172.

15. *New York Times*, May 17, 1933: 19–1; and Patterson, *Hunter College*, pp. 138–146.

16. Patterson, *Hunter College*, pp. 138–146.

17. "The Reminiscences of Ordway Tead," pp. 200–201; "The Reminiscences of Charles H. Tuttle," p. 38; and "The Reminiscences of Harry James Carman," pp. 12–13, 137; all in Oral History Research Office, Columbia University (hereafter abbreviated OHRO-CU); interviews with Dr. Mina Rees, June 27, 1980; Margaret Rendt, June 21, 1980; and Mrs. Antoinette Jehle (secretary to Dr. Shuster), June 14, 1980; and *New York Post*, February 27, 1940 (from a clipping in Box 76, Shuster Papers, Hunter College Archives—hereafter abbreviated SP-HCA).

18. "The Reminiscences of Harry James Carman," pp. 12–13, OHRO-CU; *New York Post*, February 27, 1940; and Minutes of the Meeting of the Board of Higher Education of the City of New York, June 20, 1939, pp. 745–746. As earlier planned, Colligan submitted his official resignation in November, and it was accepted; Minutes of the Meeting of the Board of Higher Education of the City of New York, November 20, 1939, pp. 938–941.

19. Unknown to Shuster, earlier that June confidential letters of recommendation had been requested of, and received from, John S. Burke (president of B. Altman and Company), Samuel McCrea Cavert (Federal Council of Churches), Everett R. Clinchy (National Conference of Christians and Jews), Carlton J.H. Hayes, Alvin Johnson (New School of Social Research), John A. Ryan, and Roger W. Straus, all preserved in File 13, Hunter 005.000, Folder 1, Board of Higher Education Central Files (hereafter abbreviated BHECF).

20. Orway Tead to Shuster, May 12, 1949, Box 73, SP-HCA; "The Reminiscences of Harry James Carman," p. 80, OHRO-CU; and interview with Doris Shuster, September 2, 1983.

21. Interview with Dr. Mina Rees, June 27, 1980, and "The Reminiscences of Harry James Carman," pp. 9–10, 80–81; "The Reminiscences of Ordway Tead," pp. 13, 52–53; and "The Reminiscences of Charles H. Tuttle," p. 40, all in OHRO-CU.

22. "The Reminiscences of Harry James Carman," p. 88, OHRO-CU.

23. Minutes of the Special Meeting of the Board of Higher Education of the City of New York, July 6, 1939, pp. 780–781.

24. *New York Sun,* July 26, 1939, from a clipping in Box 76, SP-HCA.

25. Minutes of the Meeting of the Board of Higher Education of the City of New York, February 26, 1940, pp. 138–139. In the light of this controversy over the dismissal of Colligan and the appointment of Shuster, it is interesting to note that two years earlier, in May 1937, as Shuster was leaving *The Commonweal,* he was interested in applying for a teaching position in the proposed new college in Queens. The person he sought out for advice and whose support he apparently desired was none other than his fellow Catholic educator, Eugene Colligan, president of Hunter. See Rev. Richard McHugh to Colligan, May 15; president's secretary to McHugh, May 19; and McHugh to Colligan, May 24, 1937, Box 73, SP-HCA.

26. Tead to Shuster, August 11, 1939, and Ruth Shoup (secretary of the Board of Higher Education) to Shuster, December 12, 1939, File 13, Hunter 005.000, Folder 1, BHECF.

27. Interview with Dr. Ethel Berl, June 23, 1980.

28. *Hunter College of the City of New York: Bulletin of Information: Evening and Extension Sessions* (September, 1939), p. 15.

29. *New York Times,* September 3, 1939: II-6–2; and "Annual Report of the President of Hunter College for the Year 1939–1940" (File 13, Hunter 010.000, BHECF), pp. 13–15.

30. Newspaper clippings of these teas, open houses, and other social gatherings are preserved principally in Box 76, SP-HCA.

31. *Hunter Bulletin,* February 19, 1940, Hunter College Archives (hereafter abbreviated HCA).

32. Ruth Shoup to Shuster, October 27, 1939, File 13, Hunter 110.4, BHECF; and *New York Times,* September 22, 1940: II-5–3.

33. "Annual Report . . . 1939–1940," File 13, Hunter 010.000, BHECF.

34. "Annual Report . . . 1939–1940," File 13, Hunter 010.000, BHECF, p. 8.

35. "Annual Report . . . 1939–1940," File 13, Hunter 010.000, BHECF, p. 16

36. "Annual Report . . . 1939–1940," File 13, Hunter 010.000, BHECF, p. 18.

37. Lucia Neare (Office of the Dean) to Shuster, March 29, 1940; Dean George B. Pegram to Shuster, no date; Dean Pegram to Shuster, May 2, 1940; and Charles G. Proffill (Columbia University Press) to

Shuster, June 1, 1940, all in Box 83, SP-HCA. See also Shuster's academic transcript, Records in Department of English and Comparative Literature, Columbia University.

38. In his Foreword Shuster mentions especially Professors Ashley Thorndike, Frank Patterson, Hoxie Neale Fairchild, and Emery Neff; *The English Ode from Milton to Keats* (New York, 1940), p. v.

39. *The English Ode from Milton to Keats*, pp. 296–297.

40. G. F. Whicher, in *New York Herald Tribune Books*, January 19, 1941, p. 14.

41. See John D. Jump, *The Ode* (London, 1974), pp. 3, 22, 64; and Paul H. Fry, *The Poet's Calling in the English Ode* (New Haven, 1980), p. 49.

42. *New York Times*, July 5, 1940: 15–1; and July 6, 1940: 13–6. "Dedication Week: Hunter College of the City of New York" was the title of the official program for the ceremonies, a copy of which is preserved in the Hunter College Archives.

43. "Dedication Week," HCA, and *New York Times*, October 9–10, 1940.

44. The program and addresses are reprinted in the inauguration booklet, *The Inauguration of George N. Shuster* (New York, 1940). The quotation is from p. 16.

45. Shuster's recollection of this incident and two letters from Brooks to Shuster, dated April 23, 1937, and November 17, 1938, are preserved in Box 6, SP-UNDA.

46. *The Inauguration of George N. Shuster*, pp. 20–21.

47. *The Inauguration of George N. Shuster*, pp. 31–38. The quotation is from p. 34.

48. *The Inauguration of George N. Shuster*, pp. 39–47.

49. *New York Times*, October 11, 1940: 23–1; and *The Inauguration of George N. Shuster*, p. 55.

50. Hunter College *Financial Reports*, HCA; *New York Times*, April 13, 1940; and *Hunter Bulletin*, February 19, 1940.

51. *Hunter Bulletin*, February 19, 1940; May 27, 1940; September 17, 1940; September 24, 1940; October 29, 1940; November 6, 1940; December 3, 1940; February 10, 1941; February 25, 1941; and *New York Times*, April 13, 1940, 15–1, and May 16, 1944, 21–1.

52. *New York Times*, September 22, 1940: II-5–3.

53. *Hunter Bulletin*, April 22, 1941, and *New York Times*, April 7, 1941: 19–2; June 28, 1941: 17–2; and September 15, 1941: 15–3. See also Florence Brumbaugh, "A School for Gifted Children," *Childhood*

Education 20 (1943–1944), pp. 325–327; and Gertrude Howell Hildreth, *Educating Gifted Children* (New York, 1952).

54. Catherine Mackensie, "Our Youngest Intellectuals," *New York Times,* October 5, 1941; VII-14.

55. *Hunter Bulletin,* October 20, 1942, and *New York Times,* March 11, 1941; 30–2; October 25, 1942; II-5–5, and February 16, 1943; 13–3.

56. *New York Times,* September 3, 1939; II-6–2; January 14, 1940; II-7–3; January 12, 1941; II-6–2; and May 4, 1941; 56–1.

57. *New York Times,* April 6, 1941; II-7–2; September 28, 1941; II-7–4; January 11, 1942; I-36–3 and II-5–4; February 8, 1942; II-5–5; April 5, 1942; II-5–3; June 9, 1942; 20–1; June 21, 1942; II-6–1; September 6, 1942; II-5–5; September 13, 1942; II-5–6; and December 27, 1942; IV-9–5; and Hunter College, *Thousands of Lives* (New York, 1943), pp. 4–5.

58. *New York Times,* December 13, 1942; 41–1.

59. *New York Times,* January 1, 1943; 18–2; see also December 13, 1942; 41–1.

60. *New York Times,* December 14, 1941; 62–1; December 19, 1941; 33–7; and *Hunter Bulletin,* February 10 and 24, 1942.

61. *Hunter Bulletin,* March 17, 1942; and *New York Times,* March 22, 1942; I-2–2; April 28, 1942; 15–3; and April 9, 1944; 35–4.

62. *Hunter Bulletin,* April 28, 1942; September 15, 1942; October 6, 1942; and November 8, 1944; and *New York Times,* May 19, 1940; 21–4; February 7, 1942; 14–1; February 19, 1942; 16–3; February 24, 1942; 31–2; October 14, 1942; 18–2; May 29, 1943; 9–4; August 20, 1943; 12–3; April 4, 1944; 20–8.

63. *New York Times,* May 3, 1942; 14–1. See also *Hunter Bulletin,* September 29, 1942 and April 13, 1943; and *New York Times,* January 31, 1943; IV-9–4; April 6, 1943; 24–4; April 9, 1943; 16–4; June 15, 1943; 24–8; and April 13, 1945; 14–4; and Hunter College, *Thousands of Lives,* pp. 10–12.

64. *New York Times,* July 3, 1942; 14–5; July 22, 1942; 13–4; July 24, 1942; 12–5; and July 31, 1942; 7–1. See also June A. Willenz, *Women Veterans* (New York, 1983), pp. 18–29.

65. *New York Times,* January 10, 1943; 1–1; January 11, 1943; 1–2; January 13, 1943; 1–2; and April 28, 1943; 16–7. The purchase and use of Roosevelt House will be discussed later in this chapter.

66. "Statement of Contract with Navy Department for Operation of Bronx Campus, Hunter College, February 1, 1943 to June 15, 1944," and "Statement of Funds for War Training Programs, Year Ended June 30, 1945," Financial Reports, HCA; *New York Times,* November 6, 1945; 21–4; and February 1, 1946; 28–3.

67. Roosevelt to Shuster, January 19, 1942, President's Personal File (PPF), 1-H, Special Folder, Franklin D. Roosevelt Library (hereafter abbreviated FDRL).

68. Shuster to Roosevelt, January 15, 1942; Roosevelt to Shuster, January 19, 1942; Henry Monsky to Dr. A. L. Sachar, April 4, 1942; and Roosevelt to Monsky, April 14, 1942, all in PPF, 1-H, Special Folder, FDRL; "Suggested Draft for Publicity Release by President Roosevelt," PPF, 1-H, Box 42, FDRL; Shuster, *The Ground I Walked On* (Notre Dame, 1969), pp. 59–61; *Hunter Bulletin,* September 15, 1942; *New York Times,* June 25, 1942; 1–5; June 26, 1942; 23–5; and October 18, 1942; 44–4; "Minutes of the Meeting of the Board of Higher Education of the City of New York, December 20, 1943," HCA; and "Interview #1 with Dr. Abram L. Sachar by Emily Williams on November 10, 1978, for Franklin D. Roosevelt Library." I am especially grateful to Prof. Roger Daniels for acquainting me with this interview.

69. Roosevelt to Monsky, June 1, 1942, PPF, 1-H, Special Folder, FDRL; Roosevelt to Monsky, May 7, 1942; Roosevelt to Shuster, September 14 and 16, 1942; and Shuster to Roosevelt, June 15, 1944, PPF, 8061, FDRL; *Hunter Bulletin,* October 27, 1942; and Interview with Margaret Rendt, director of Roosevelt House, June 21, 1980.

70. Stephen Early to Richard E. Bishop, November 10, 1942, PPF, 8061, FDRL; and quotation from the *New York Times,* November 23, 1943; 27–22.

71. Letter to Richard E. Bishop, quoted in the *New York Times,* November 15, 1943; 21–4.

72. Quoted in the *New York Times,* November 23, 1943; 27–2.

73. Interview with Margaret Rendt, June 21, 1980; and Margaret Rendt, *Roosevelt House,* and *Sara Delano Roosevelt Memorial House for Hunter College,* both in possession of the author.

74. Interview with Doris Shuster, September 2, 1983.

75. Interviews with Mrs. Antoinette Jehle, June 14, 1980; Doris Shuster, September 2, 1983; Mrs. Jenny Newman, April 12, 1985; and Robert Shuster, July 24, 1986.

76. Interviews with Doris Shuster, June 24, August 19, and September 2, 1983; and Robert Shuster, July 24 and 25, 1986.

77. Interviews with Robert Shuster, July 25, 1986, and Mrs. Jenny Newman, April 12, 1985; the letters of Doris Shuster to Bob in Europe in the 1930s are in Box 13, and to her husband in London in 1938 in Box 21, SP-UNDA.

78. Interviews with Mrs. Jenny Newman, April 12, 1985, and Doris Shuster, June 24, 1983.

79. Interview with Mrs. Jenny Newman, April 12, 1985.

80. *The Ground I Walked On*, pp. 229–231; and *New York Times*, March 13, 1942; 1–2; and June 5, 1942; 19–6.

81. *The Ground I Walked On*, p. 231, and Shuster to James P. Baxter, III, June 17, 1944, Box 14, SP-UNDA.

82. *The Ground I Walked On*, pp. 231–232, and John J. Cully, "The Santa Fe Internment Camp and the Justice Department Program for Enemy Aliens," in *Japanese Americans: From Relocation to Redress*, ed. Roger Daniels, et al. (Salt Lake City, 1986), pp. 57–71.

83. Saul Carson (OWI) to Shuster, January 13, 1944; Louis G. Cowan (OWI) to Shuster, January 20, 1944; Franz Schoenberner (OWI) to Shuster, April 20, 1944; S. H. Silverman (OWI) to Shuster, April 22, 1944; Lawrence G. Blochman (OWI) to Shuster, June 18, 1944; Schoenberner to Shuster, July 7, 1944; Shuster to David S. Epstein (OWI), October 20, 1944; and Hans M. Hoffmann (OWI) to Shuster, November 14, 1944, all in Box 1, SP-UNDA.

84. Haldore Hanson, *The Cultural-Cooperation Program, 1938–1943*, Department of State Publication 2137, (Washington, 1944), p. 3, and Frank A. Ninkovich, *The Diplomacy of Ideas: U.S. Foreign Policy and Cultural Relations, 1938–1950* (New York, 1981), pp. 33–128.

85. Breckinridge Long to American Diplomatic and Consular Officers in the American Republics, October 25, 1940, Department of State Decimal File 111.46, Advisory Committee/75A, Record Group 59, National Archives; Sumner Welles to the President, July 30, 1941, and Welles to Shuster, August 28, 1941, DS 111.46, Adv. Cmte/108, RG59, NA. The remaining members of the committee at that time were Robert G. Caldwell of Massachusetts Institute of Technology, Ben Cherrington of the University of Denver, Stephen Duggan of the Institute of International Education, Carl Milam of the American Library Association, and James Shotwell of the National Committee of the United States of America on International Intellectual Cooperation.

86. Minutes of Meetings and Reports of the General Advisory Committee of the Division of Cultural Relations are preserved in Boxes 7 and 11, SP-UNDA.

87. Minutes of Meetings of the General Advisory Committee of the Division of Cultural Relations of the Department of State, September 17–18, 1941; November 5–6, 1941; June 19–20, 1942; and June 9–10, 1943, Boxes 7 and 11, SP-UNDA; Shuster to Charles A. Thomson, May 20, 1942 (DS 111.46, Adv. Cmte./183 1/2, RG59, NA); Thomson to Shuster, July 11, 1942 (DS 111.46, Adv. Cmte./192C, RG59, NA); and Thomson to Shuster, December 24, 1943 (DS 111.46, Adv. Comte./242A, RG59, NA). Unfortunately, Shuster was apparently not able to be present at an informal meeting on January 7, 1944, when the question of Nazi and Fascist influence in postwar

European education was discussed. Thomson to Shuster, January 19, 1944 (DS 111.46, Adv. Comte./232D, RG59, NA).

88. Minutes of the Meeting of the General Advisory Committee of the Division of Cultural Relations of the Department of State, February 25–26, 1942, Box 11, SP-UNDA.

6. PRESIDENT IN A TIME OF CHANGE, 1945–1960

1. A copy of this speech, untitled and undated, is preserved in the Hunter College Archives (hereafter abbreviated HCA). See also the *Hunter Arrow*, February 8, 1960. *Hunter Arrow* was formerly *Hunter Bulletin*.

2. *New York Times*, January 8, 1939: II-9–3.

3. Mina S. Rees, "Dr. George N. Shuster: An Appreciation and a Salute," *Alumni News* (Hunter College) 64 (May 1959), p. 2; Lorraine Goverman, "Presidential Profile: Dr. George Nauman Shuster," *Echo* (Hunter College) (Winter 1944), pp. 10–14; *New York Times*, May 8, 1948: 12–1; and May 19, 1948: 54–2; *Hunter Arrow*, March 25, 1957; and interviews with Ursula Mahoney, July 8, 1980, and Doris Shuster, September 2, 1983.

4. "The Reminiscences of Harry Gideonse," p. 64, and "The Reminiscences of Pearl Max," pp. 173–176, Oral History Research Office, Columbia University, hereafter abbreviated OHRO-CU; and interviews with Ethel Berl, June 23, 1980; Mina Rees, June 27, 1980; Frederic Stewart, June 17, 1980; and Kathryn Hopwood, June 17, 1980.

5. *New York Times*, April 4, 1941: 23–3; December 6, 1949: 39–7; and November 17, 1953: 44–5; and *Hunter Arrow*, November 23, 1953.

6. A copy is in Folder 4, Box 73, SP-HCA.

7. See Chapter 5 for the removal of Colligan and the appointment of Shuster in 1939.

8. "The Reminiscences of Harry James Carmen," p. 80; "The Reminiscences of Harry Gideonse," pp. 69–75; "The Reminiscences of Pearl Max," pp. 173–185; "The Reminiscences of Ordway Tead," pp. 52–53; "The Reminiscences of Charles H. Tuttle, p. 40, OHRO-CU; and interviews with Dr. Gustave G. Rosenberg, July 2, 1981, and John Theobald, November 27, 1984.

9. *New York News*, October 9, 1940 (from a clipping in Box 76-SP-HCA); *New York Times*, October 29, 1940: 13–2; Frederick Ernst to Ordway Tead, March 29, 1950, File 13, Hunter 360.200, Board of Higher Education Central Files, hereafter abbreviated BHECF; list of Littauer lecturers for 1940–1941 preserved in Box 83, SP-HCA; Shuster

to Mrs. Roosevelt, February 25, 1941, Series 90, Box 1107; Mrs. Roosevelt to Shuster, October 13, 1941, Series 100, Box 1620; Mrs. Roosevelt to Mrs. Shuster, June 12, 1942, Series 100, Box 1662; Shuster to Mrs. Roosevelt, August 18, 1942, Series 90, Box 1132; Mrs. Roosevelt to Mrs. Nathan Axelrod, October 20, 1947, Speaking and Other Engagements, Box 4629; Mae A. Burns to Mrs. Roosevelt, April 9, 1952, General Correspondence, Box 3994; Doris Shuster to Mrs. Roosevelt, May 3, 1953, General Correspondence, Box 4116; Doris Shuster to Mrs. Roosevelt, April 5, 1955, General Correspondence, Box 4203; Doris Shuster to Mrs. Roosevelt, March 20, 1958, General Correspondence, Box 4333; and John Meng to Mrs. Roosevelt, December 28, 1959, General Correspondence, Box 4360, all in Eleanor Roosevelt Papers, FDRL.

10. *The Ground I Walked On*, pp. 25–26.

11. For possible weaknesses in Shuster's administration, see interviews with Mina Rees, June 27, 1980; Frederic Stewart, June 17, 1980; and Ruth Weintraub, June 19, 1980; "The Reminiscences of Harry Gideonse," pp. 70–75, OHRO-CU; and Meng to Dr. Mary Gambrell, December 28, 1948, Folder 13, Box 5, Meng Papers, Special Collections Department, Georgetown University Library (hereafter SCD-GUL).

12. Interview with Ruth Weintraub, June 19, 1980.

13. *New York Times*, February 24, 1946: 1–4.

14. *New York Times*, February 28, 1946: 1–7.

15. Minutes of the Meetings of the Board of Higher Education of the City of New York, March 4; March 18; April 22; May 20; and September 23, 1946, HCA.

16. Male veterans from outside the five boroughs could be admitted if they qualified and if space was available after local applicants were accommodated.

17. *New York Times*, June 29, 1946: 11–4; August 18, 1946: IV-9–4; and October 3, 1946: 56–2.

18. *New York Times*, October 13, 1946; 9–1; October 15, 1946; 27–2; April 30, 1947; 11–1; and March 18, 1948; 22–3; and Ruth G. Weintraub and Ruth E. Salley, "Hunter College Reports on its Veterans," *School and Society* 68 (July 24, 1948), pp. 59–63.

19. *New York Times*, April 23, 1947; 27–4; March 13, 1948; 17–6; March 18, 1948; 22–3; and October 7, 1949; 29–4; and *Hunter Arrow*, November 11, 1948.

20. *New York Times*, November 16, 1950: 35–2; January 23, 1951: 1–4; January 28, 1951: IV-9–1; April 15, 1951: 56–5; April 17, 1951: 39–8; January 24, 1951: 29–5; May 15, 1951: 38–2; October 4, 1951: 35–1; and January 27, 1952: 38–1.

21. The Financial Reports for Hunter College and the Board of Higher Education from 1939 to 1960 are preserved in the Hunter College Archives; *New York Times*, March 13, 1948: 17–6; October 7, 1949: 29–4; April 27, 1952: 85–3; October 19, 1952: 36–1; May 22, 1955: 71–2; November 10, 1955: 37–4; March 6, 1956: 28–3; and September 25, 1957: 17–1; Minutes of the Meeting of the Board of Higher Education, April 21, 1952 (HCA); Shuster to Meng, March 20, 1952, Folder 2, Box 5, Meng Papers, SCD-GUL; and Shuster to Members of the Staff, Hunter College, May 22, 1950, File 13, Hunter 110.300, BHECF.

22. Quoted in "Report of the President of Hunter College for the Years 1941–1942 and 1942–1943," File 13, Hunter 010.000, BHECF.

23. Compare, for example, the *Hunter College Bulletins* of 1939–1940 and 1959–1960, HCA.

24. "To the Freshmen of Hunter College: I," *Education and Moral Wisdom* (New York, 1960), p. 42.

25. "The Administration of a Municipal College," *Education and Moral Wisdom*, pp. 7, 8.

26. *Hunter College Bulletin: Graduate Programs, 1959–1960*, pp. 27–74; Patterson, *Hunter College*, pp. 182–187, 212–213; *New York Times*, September 11, 1946: 9–7; December 3, 1950: 76–2; March 15, 1953: 86–4; and June 7, 1953: 44–3; and "Report of the Evaluation of Hunter College, New York, New York, by the Middle States Association of Colleges and Secondary Schools, Commission on Institutions of Higher Education, March 11–14, 1956," File 13, Hunter 108.000, BHECF.

27. "Report of the Evaluation of Hunter College, 1956," File 13, Hunter 108.000, BHECF; *Hunter College Bulletin: College of Arts and Sciences, 1959–1960*, pp. 47–48; *Hunter Arrow*, December 7, 1959, and May 9, 1960, HCA; *New York Times*, May 10, 1953: 57–1 and December 5, 1954; 52–4; and interview with Dean Marguerite Holmes, July 7, 1980 (by 1980 Hunter College was part of the City University system).

28. Minutes of the Meeting of the Board of Higher Education of the City of New York, April 18, 1955; *Hunter College Bulletin: Graduate Programs, 1959–1960*, pp. 111–112; *New York Times*, April 20, 1955: 35–8; and May 15, 1958; 17–5; *Dedication Addresses: Presented at the Ceremonies Dedicating the New Center for the Hunter College School of Social Work, March 5, 1969*; and interview with Dr. Ruth Weintraub, June 19, 1980.

29. "Hunter College of the City of New York: A Report to the Middle States Association of Colleges and Secondary Schools: Completed June 1, 1966," File 13, BHECF; *Hunter College Bulletin: Graduate Programs, 1959–1960*, p. 5; *New York Times*, September 29, 1951: 19–8;

February 22, 1953: 38–3; April 12, 1953: 46–2; and May 22, 1955: IV-9–3; *The Ground I Walked On*, p. 109; and interview with Dr. Ruth Weintraub, June 19, 1980.

30. *The Ground I Walked On*, pp. 144–189; *Hunter Arrow*, March 17, 1952, *New York Times*, September 20, 1955; 27–2; and list of Littauer Lectures for 1940–41 in Box 83, SP-HCA.

31. *The Ground I Walked On*, pp. 196–197; Minutes of the Meeting of the Board of Higher Education of the City of New York, June 18, 1945, and October 20, 1952; and *New York Times*, January 6, 1946: 41–1; and September 19, 1948: IV-9–4.

32. *The Ground I Walked On*, pp. 189–196; Minutes of the Meeting of the Board of Higher Education of the City of New York, March 16, 1953; and *New York Times*, May 30, 1948: 22–1.

33. *New York News*, October 9, 1940, from a clipping in Box 76, SP-HCA.

34. Leathe Hemachandra to Tead, January 20, 1943, File 13, Hunter 171.000, BHECF.

35. Minutes of the Meeting of the Board of Higher Education of the City of New York, October 23, 1944.

36. Tead to Fire Commissioner John J. McElligott, February 10, 1941, File 13, Hunter 303.000, BHECF.

37. *Hunter Arrow*, February 25, 1949, HCA, and *New York Times*, September 5, 1958: 12–1.

38. William M. Halsey, *The Survival of American Innocence* (Notre Dame, 1980), p. 93.

39. *New York Times*, October 25, 1947: 21–2; and December 20, 1947: 20–1.

40. *New York Times*, February 15, 1944: 19–6.

41. *Hunter Arrow*, April 7, 1949, HCA.

42. *New York Times*, October 2, 1952: 22–8; Minutes of the Meeting of the Board of Higher Education of the City of New York, March 18, 1957; *Hunter Arrow*, November 11, 1948; December 16, 1952; and February 9, 1959, HCA.

43. *New York Times*, May 9, 1952: 21–3; and May 17, 1952: 13–5; and *Hunter Arrow*, May 12, 1952, HCA.

44. The most serious conflict not involving academic freedom concerned one of the college assistant business managers who misappropriated approximately forty thousand dollars in the mid-1950s. See Meng to Shuster, January 25 and 28, 1956, and Shuster to Meng, January 31, 1956, Folder 3, Box 5, Meng Papers, SCD-GUL; and Minutes of the Meeting of the Board of Higher Education of the City of New York, March 21, 1956.

45. *New York Times,* June 19, 1951: 1–6.

46. *New York Times,* June 19, 1951: 1–6.

47. *New York Times,* June 19, 1951: 1–6.

48. *New York Times,* June 19, 1951: 1–6.

49. *New York Times,* June 20, 1951: 29–8.

50. Minutes of the Meeting of the Board of Higher Education of the City of New York, May 19, 1952, and *New York Times,* May 20, 1952; 23–1.

51. *Official Catholic Directory, 1968* and *1975.*

52. Alger Hiss was convicted of perjury in 1950, Fuchs confessed to his espionage about the same time, and Gouzenko's testimony had led to the indictment of Fuchs. See Earl Latham, *The Communist Controversy in Washington* (New York, 1969).

53. 1939 N. Y. Laws 547.

54. 1949 N. Y. Laws 360.

55. New York City Charter, Section 903.

56. Minutes of the Special Meeting of the Board of Higher Education of the City of New York, October 6, 1952; *New York Times,* September 25, 1952; 1–2; October 4, 1952; 1–8; and October 7, 1952; 27–1; and *Hunter Arrow,* October 14, 1952, HCA.

57. Minutes of the Meeting of the Board of Higher Education of the City of New York, November 17, 1952; *New York Times,* October 14, 1952: 1–4; October 29, 1952: 10–3; November 18, 1952: 1–3; *Hunter Arrow,* October 20, November 3 and 24, 1952, HCA.

58. Minutes of the Meetings of the Board of Higher Education of the City of New York, October 6 and November 17, 1952, and *New York Times,* November 18, 1952; 1–3.

59. *Hunter Arrow,* November 3, 1952, HCA.

60. Reprinted in Shuster, *Education and Moral Wisdom* (New York, 1960), pp. 28–30.

61. Minutes of the Meeting of the Board of Higher Education of the City of New York, September 30, 1954; and *New York Times,* October 1, 1954; 1–1. For the Rapp-Coudert investigative committee of the early 1940s, see David R. Holmes, *Stalking the Academic Communist* (Hanover, N.H., 1989), pp. 62–79,

62. Minutes of the Meeting of the Board of Higher Education of the City of New York, September 30, 1954; *New York Times,* April 23, 1954; 17–2; May 5, 1954; 22–2; and June 4, 1954; 20–1. See also Broadus Mitchell, "Witch Hunt at Hunter: Triumph of the Primitives," *The Nation* 179 (November 6, 1954), pp. 401–403.

63. *New York Times,* April 14, 1954: 10–5.

64. *New York Times,* April 14, 1954: 10–5.

65. *New York Times,* October 2, 1954: 6–1.

66. *New York Times,* October 18, 1955: 16–4.

67. Minutes of the Meeting of the Board of Higher Education of the City of New York, October 25, 1954.

68. Minutes of the Meeting of the Board of Higher Education of the City of New York, March 17, 1958; and *New York Times,* November 29, 1957: 19–1; and June 20, 1959: 7–1.

69. *New York Times,* February 2, 1955: 8–3; November 24, 1955: 20–1; and April 29, 1958: 31–1.

70. *New York Times,* August 9, 1956: 1–6.

71. *New York Times,* May 29, 1959: 1–1.

72. Minutes of the Meeting of the Board of Higher Education of the City of New York, March 17, 1958, and July 22, 1959; and *New York Times,* June 25, 1959: 5–5; and July 24, 1959: 7–3.

73. Minutes of the Meeting of the Board of Higher Education of the City of New York, March 17, 1958. Two cases at that time were still pending, including that of Hughes.

74. With few modifications, this speech was reprinted as "Academic Freedom," in *The Commonweal* 58 (April 10, 1953), pp. 11–13.

75. *New York Times,* March 22, 1953: 27–2.

76. *New York Times,* March 22, 1953: 27–2.

77. *New York Times,* March 22, 1953: 27–4.

78. Letter to the editor, *New York Times,* February 24, 1959; 28–5. The most recent study of Senator McCarthy and the universities is Ellen W. Schrecker, *No Ivory Tower* (New York, 1986), but see also Donald F. Crosby, S.J., *God, Church, and Flag: Senator Joseph R. McCarthy and the Catholic Church, 1950–1957* (Chapel Hill, 1978), and Richard M. Fried, *Men Against McCarthy* (New York, 1976).

79. For these honors and awards, see *Current Biography, 1960* (New York, 1960), pp. 378–380; the notification from the American Academy is in Box 73, SP-HCA, as is the letter from President Grayson Kirk of Columbia notifying him of the Butler Medal award, May 29, 1953; Frederick Hochwalt to Shuster, January 29, 1952 (Box 165, SP-HCA), and clippings from the *New York Herald Tribune,* May 7, 1954, and the *New York Journal American,* April 19, 1959, both in Box 73, SP-HCA.

80. Interview with Doris Shuster, September 2, 1983.

81. Minutes of the Meeting of the Board of Higher Education of the City of New York, April 18, 1955; September 28, 1955; and April 22, 1957; *New York Times,* May 19, 1959; 23–4; *Hunter Arrow,* October 5, 1959; and "The Reminiscences of Harry James Carman," pp. 154–161, and "The Reminiscences of Pearl Max," pp. 165–169, OHRO-CU.

82. In addition to the preceding citations, see also "The Reminiscences of Harry James Carman," pp. 193–199, OHRO-CU; and interviews with Doris Shuster, September 2, 1983; John Theobald, November 27, 1984; and Robert Shuster, July 24, 1986.

83. Interview with Robert Shuster, July 24, 1986.

84. Minutes of the Meeting of the Board of Higher Education of the City of New York, February 16, 1959.

85. Minutes of the Meeting of the Board of Higher Education of the City of New York, February 16, 1959, and February 9, 1960. The date for leaving office at this second meeting was changed to February 18, 1960.

86. Ethel G. Berl to Mrs. Pearl Max, April 3, 1959, File 13, Hunter 005.000, BHECF; *Hunter Arrow*, February 8, 1960; and "Foreword," *Education and Moral Wisdom*, pp. v-vii.

87. *New York Times*, October 27, 1959: 39–1, and *Hunter Arrow*, February 18, 1960, HCA.

88. *New York Times*, January 27, 1960; *Hunter Arrow*, February 8, 1960; John Meng to Members of the Administrative Staff, January 6, 1960, File 13, Hunter 005.000, BHECF; Robert I. Gannon, S.J., *The Cardinal Spellman Story* (New York, 1962), pp. 316–318; and interview with Doris Shuster, September 2, 1983.

89. A copy of this speech is preserved in HCA.

90. *New York Times*, January 27, 1960: 23–1.

91. Minutes of the Meeting of the Board of Higher Education of the City of New York, February 16, 1959.

7. THE EMERGING NATIONAL FIGURE

1. "Concerning the University Administration," *The [Notre Dame] Scholastic* 104 (March 1, 1963), p. 7.

2. "College Women and the War," delivered at the Annual Meeting of the Association of American Colleges, Baltimore, Maryland, January 2, 1943. A copy is preserved in the Shuster Papers in the Hunter College Archives (hereafter SP-HCA).

3. "American Education and Its Product Abroad," address to the United Parents Association of New York City, December 12, 1953, SP-HCA.

4. "Recipe for Learning," *Today* 12 (November, 1956), pp. 32–33. The quotation is from page 33.

5. "Recipe for Learning," p. 34.

6. "College Women and the War," SP-HCA.

7. "College Women and the War," SP-HCA.

8. Address to the Ninth Conference on Science, Philosophy and Religion, in *Education and Moral Wisdom* (New York, 1960), pp. 4–5.

9. "College Women and the War," SP-HCA.

10. "Centennial Address," reprinted in *Education and Moral Wisdom*, p. 92.

11. "Centennial Address," pp. 93–94.

12. George Seldes, "Catholics and Fascists," *The New Republic* 97 (November 9, 1938), pp. 6–9.

13. "A Catholic Defends His Church," *The New Republic* 97 (January 4, 1939), pp. 246–248. The quotation is from page 246.

14. "A Catholic Defends His Church," p. 248. See also "Christianity in This Hour," *Survey Graphic* 28 (February 1939), pp. 137ff.

15. "The Conflict Among Catholics," *The American Scholar* 10 (Winter 1940–41), pp. 5–16. For the debate over publishing this controversial article, see *The American Scholar* to Shuster, October 18, 1940, American Scholar Papers, Box 37, Manuscripts Division, Library of Congress.

16. "The Conflict Among Catholics," pp. 8–9.

17. "The Conflict Among Catholics," p. 10.

18. "The Catholic Controversy," *Harper's Magazine* 199 (November 1949), pp. 25–32.

19. "The Catholic Conspiracy Myth," *Outlook and Independent* 150 (November 7, 1928), p. 1141. Shuster received more than five hundred letters in response to the *Harper's* article, "ranging all the way from ice bags to hot bricks," and some are preserved in Box 1, SP-UNDA.

20. "The Catholic Controversy," p. 28.

21. "Catholic Culture in America," *Today* 8 (March 1953), pp. 12–13.

22. "Catholic Culture in America," p. 13.

23. "Catholic Culture in America," p. 13.

24. "The Contemporary Situation: As a Catholic Sees It," *Social Action* 14 (January 15, 1948), p. 16.

25. "The Contemporary Situation," p. 20.

26. "Answer to Senator Nye," *The Commonweal* 34 (October 17, 1941), pp. 609–611. See the following chapter for mention of Loyal Americans of German Descent.

27. "The Yalta Division of Germany," *Vital Speeches of the Day* 11 (April 15, 1945), pp. 403–405. The quotation is from p. 404.

28. "The Yalta Division of Germany," p. 405.

29. "Mr. Roosevelt," *The Commonweal* 42 (April 27, 1945), pp. 38–40.

30. "The Hangings at Nuremberg," *The Commonweal* 45 (November 15, 1946), pp. 110–111.

31. "The Hangings at Nuremberg," p. 111.

32. "The Hangings at Nuremberg," p. 111.

33. "The Hangings at Nuremberg," p. 112.

34. "The Hangings at Nuremberg," pp. 112–113. Despite his strong support of American military efforts in World War II, Shuster was also sympathetic to conscientious objectors who declined to serve; see Letter to the Editor, *The Commonweal* 44 (September 20, 1946), p. 551.

35. Troyer S. Anderson to Shuster, June 9, 1945, Box 1, SP-UNDA. See also Oron Hale, "Report on Historical Interrogations of German Prisoners of War and Detained Persons," Record Group 165, Records of the War Department General and Specific Staffs, War Department Historical Commission, Schuster [*sic*] Files, National Archives; *The Ground I Walked On,* pp. 235–243; and *New York Times* July 26, 1945; 4–7.

36. Walter L. Wright, Jr., to Shuster, June 9, 1945, Box 1, SP-UNDA; and Hale, "Report on Historical Interrogations," R.G. 165, Schuster [*sic*] Files, National Archives.

37. Shuster to Wright, June 19, 1945; Wright to Shuster, June 22 and August 30, 1945; and Col. A. F. Clark, Jr., to Shuster, August 6, 1945; Box 1, SP-UNDA.

38. Shuster to Anderson, June 12, 1945 (telegram); and Wright to Shuster, June 9, 19, and 22, 1945, all in Box 1, SP-UNDA.

39. All of these interviews are preserved in R. G. 165, Schuster [*sic*] Files, National Archives.

40. "Conversation with Franz von Papen," July 23, 1945, R. G. 165, Schuster [*sic*] Files, National Archives; and *The Ground I Walked On,* pp. 238–239. The quotation is from p. 239.

41. "Historical Interrogation Report: Col. Gen. Heinz Guderian," September 7, 1945, R. G. 165, Schuster [*sic*] Files, National Archives.

42. "Postscript to the Goering Report of July 19, 1945, R. G. 165, Schuster [*sic*] Files, National Archives.

43. *The Ground I Walked On,* p. 237.

44. "Conversations with Ribbentrop, July 25, 1945," R. G. 165, Schuster [*sic*] Files, National Archives.

45. "Karl Doenitz: End of War 1945 (July 22, 1945)." R. G. 165, Schuster [*sic*] Files, National Archives. See also A. Russell Buchanan, *The United States and World War II,* vol. 2 (New York, 1964), pp. 458–466; and Dwight Eisenhower, *Crusade in Europe* (Garden City, N.Y., 1952), pp. 467–471.

46. "Religious Opposition to Nazism in Western Germany," R. G. 165, Schuster [*sic*] Files, National Archives.

47. *The Ground I Walked On*, pp. 240–241.

48. *The Ground I Walked On*, pp. 244–246.

49. *The Ground I Walked On*, pp. 247–248.

50. Commission on Freedom of the Press, *A Free and Responsible Press* (Chicago, 1947), p. v.

51. Two excellent studies of the commission are Paul Mark Fackler, "The Hutchins Commissioners and the Crisis in Democratic Theory, 1930–1947" (Ph.D. dissertation, University of Illinois, 1982), pp. 141–305; and Margaret A. Blanchard, "The Hutchins Commission, the Press and the Responsibility Concept," *Journalism Monographs* 49 (May 1977), pp. 1–59. See also Donald L. Smith, *Zechariah Chafee, Jr., Defender of Liberty and Law* (Cambridge, Mass., 1986), pp. 99–115, and Richard Fox, *Reinhold Niebuhr: A Biography* (New York, 1985), p. 221.

52. *A Free and Responsible Press*, pp. v–vi.

53. *A Free and Responsible Press*, p. viii.

54. Luce to Hutchins, November 29, 1946, Robert M. Hutchins Collection, Department of Special Collections, The Joseph Regenstein Library, University of Chicago (hereafter abbreviated DSC-UC).

55. Quoted from "Fortune Letters," *Fortune* 35 (June 1947), p. 24.

56. See, for example, Louis M. Lyons, "The Press and its Critics," *The Atlantic Monthly* 180 (July 1947), pp. 115–116; and *Time* 49 (April 7, 1947), p. 65.

57. *A Free and Responsible Press*, pp. 21–28. The quotations are from the section headings.

58. *A Free and Responsible Press*, p. 68.

59. *A Free and Responsible Press*, pp. 30–68.

60. *A Free and Responsible Press*, pp. 82–102.

61. The minutes of the commission's deliberations are preserved in the records of the Commission on Freedom of the Press, DSC-UC; memo of Harold Lasswell, April 3, 1944, Box 7, Folder 6, and Shuster to Hutchins, October 30, 1946, Box 8, Folder 2, Hutchins Papers, DSC-UC; and Fackler, "The Hutchins Commissioners," p. 334.

62. Shuster Memorandum, March 29, 1945, Document 37A, Folder 7, Box II; and Summary of Discussion and Action, Meeting of September 18–19, 1944, Document 21, Folder 9, Box I, Commission on Freedom of the Press, DSC-UC.

63. "Comments on Document 100, June 19, 1946," Document 100B, Folder 5, Box VII, Commission on Freedom of the Press, DSC-UC.

64. Summary of Discussion and Action, Meeting of January 27–29, 1946, Document 90, Folder 9, Box IV, Commission on Freedom

of the Press, DSC-UC. See also Document 90 (con't), Folder 10, Box IV, Commission on Freedom of the Press, DSC-UC.

65. Summary of Discussion and Action, Meeting of January 27–29, 1946, Document 90, Folder 9, Box IV, Commission on Freedom of the Press, DSC-UC. See also meeting of March 21, 1944, Document 14, Folder 3, Box I, same location.

66. Shuster to Hutchins, February 6, 1946, Robert M. Hutchins Collection, DSC-UC.

67. Shuster Memorandum, March 29, 1945, Document 37A, Folder 7, Box II, Commission on Freedom of the Press, DSC-UC.

68. Shuster Memorandum, March 29, 1945, Document 37A, Folder 7, Box II, Commission on Freedom of the Press, DSC-UC.

69. Summary of Discussion and Action, Meetings of January 27–29, 1946 (con't), Document 90 (con't), Folder 10, Box IV, Commission on Freedom of the Press, DSC-UC. See also Comments and Suggestions on Revised Draft, Document 91, Folder 1, Box V, Commission on Freedom of the Press, DSC-UC.

70. *A Free and Responsible Press* was published by the University of Chicago Press in March 1947, and the report also appeared as a supplement to the April issue of Luce's own *Fortune*. For reviews of the commission's report, see A. J. Liebling, "Some Reflections on the American Press," *The Nation* 144 (April 12, 1947), p. 427; Louis M. Lyons, "The Reader Also Has Rights," *The Atlantic Monthly* 179 (April 1947), pp. 148–152; Kenneth Stewart, "Press Rx: Faith Healing?," *Saturday Review of Literature* 30 (April 5, 1947), pp. 13ff; and reviews in *New Republic* 116 (March 31, 1947), pp. 33–34; *American Political Science Review* 41 (June 1947), pp. 559–561; and *The Political Science Quarterly* 62 (September 1947), pp. 441–443.

71. Joseph Lohman (National Committee on Segregation in the Nation's Capital) to E. Franklin Frazier, January 13, August 29, and September 9, 1947; and Dorothy A. Elvidge to Frazier, January 24, 1947, Frazier Papers, Box 131–38 (F. 15), Manuscript Division, Moorland-Spingard Research Center, Howard University (hereafter abbreviated MD, M-SRC, HU). That Shuster was not too well known in this area may be indicated by the fact that in one letter he is identified as "Dr. George Shuster, President of Hunter College" and then later referred to as "Dr. Hunter."

72. Press release of the Interracial Review News Service (January, 1949), Papers of the NAACP-DC Branch, Box 78–74 (F. 1586), MD, M-SRC, HU.

73. Lohman to Frazier, May 4, September 7, and September 16, 1948; and Frazier to Lohman, September 16, 1948, Frazier Papers, Box

131–38 (F. 15), MD, M-SRC, HU; Channing Tobias to The Honorable Harry S. Truman, November 24, 1946, and memorandum of Philleo Nash to Roberta Barrows, December 6, 1946, Papers of Harry S. Truman, Official File, Harry S. Truman Library. See also Wilfred Parsons, S.J., "Race Discrimination in the Capitol," *Interracial Review* 22 (January 1949), pp. 6–8.

74. For these instances, see *Segregation in Washington: A Report of the National Committee on Segregation in the Nation's Capital* (Chicago, 1948), pp. 12–17, 19, 73, and 75–76.

75. *Segregation in Washington,* pp. 18 and 60.

76. *Segregation in Washington,* pp. 18–19 and 60–63.

77. *Segregation in Washington,* pp. 30 and 39.

78. *Segregation in Washington,* p. 30.

79. *Segregation in Washington,* pp. 30–38 and 85.

80. *Segregation in Washington,* p. 64.

81. *Segregation in Washington,* pp. 40–41, 46–47, and 49–53.

82. *Segregation in Washington,* p. 20.

83. Lohman to Ida Fox, January 11, and Fox to Lohman, January 13, 1949, Papers of the NAACP-DC Branch, Box 78–74 (F. 1856), MD, M-SRC, HU.

84. Press release of the Interracial Review News Service (January 1949), Papers of the NAACP-DC Branch, Box 78–74 (F. 1586), MD, M-SRC, HU.

85. Press release of the Interracial Review News Service (January 1949).

86. *Washington Afro-American,* January 11, 1949.

87. Fox to George K. Hunton, January 11; Fox to Lohman, January 13; and Hunton to Fox, January 14, 1949, Papers of the NAACP-DC Branch, Box 78–74 (F. 1586), MD, M-SRC, HU.

88. *Segregation in Washington,* p. 4.

89. *New York Times,* April 20, 1945: 11–4.

90. *New York Times,* November 16, 1948: 26–2; and December 24, 1950: 21–2.

91. Mrs. Ordway Tead to Shuster, November 28, 1956, and Ordway Tead to Shuster, May 21, 1958, Box 5, SP-UNDA.

92. Shuster to James Picker, November 13, 1956, Box 1; Harvey Picker to Shuster, March 27, and July 5, 1957; Shuster to James Picker, October 8, 1957; Harvey Picker to Shuster, December 4, 1959; and Minutes of the Annual Meeting of the Board of Directors of the James Picker Foundation, Inc., April 20, 1959, all in Box 5, SP-UNDA.

93. George E. Probst, Broadcasting Foundation of America, to Shuster, March 22, 1957; Chloe Fox to Shuster, November 19, 1957;

and *Report* of the Broadcasting Foundation of America, September 15, 1959, all in Box 5, SP-UNDA.

94. Sidney Hyman, *The Lives of William Benton* (Chicago, 1969), pp. 404–411, and Chester Bowles, *Promises to Keep: My Years in Public Life, 1941–1969* (New York, 1971), pp. 270–276.

95. Bowles, *Promises to Keep*, p. 273; interviews with Doris Shuster, September 2, 1983, and Robert Shuster, July 25, 1986.

96. Correspondence between Shuster and Bowles in 1947 and 1948, on a "George" and "Chet" basis and chiefly about local and national political matters, is preserved in the Department of Manuscripts and Archives, Sterling Memorial Library, Yale University.

97. *The Hartford Courant*, November 2, 1949, and Bowles to Shuster, November 17, 1949, Box 1, SP-UNDA.

98. Interview with Robert Shuster, July 25, 1986.

99. Shuster to Robert, April 13, 1949, Box 13, SP-UNDA.

100. Shuster to Robert, July 17, 1948, Box 13, SP-UNDA.

101. Interview with Robert Shuster, July 25, 1986, and Hyman, *The Lives of William Benton*, pp. 409–411.

8. THE RECOVERY OF GERMANY, 1945–1960

1. "Our Relations with Germany," *Foreign Policy Reports* 19 (October 15, 1943), p. 199.

2. "Our Relations with Germany," p. 199

3. "Our Relations with Germany," p. 200.

4. "Our Relations with Germany," pp. 200–201.

5. "The Challenge of the Future World," *Vital Speeches* 9 (July 1, 1943), p. 555.

6. "The Challenge of the Future World," p. 557.

7. "The Challenge of the Future World," pp. 557–558.

8. "The Challenge of the Future World," pp. 558–559.

9. "The Yalta Division of Germany," *Vital Speeches* 11 (April 15, 1945), pp. 403–405.

10. "Should Germany Have a Centralized Government? Yes," *The Sign* 26 (March 1947), p. 30.

11. "Should Germany Have a Centralized Government?," pp. 30, 59.

12. "German Reeducation: Success or Failure," *Proceedings of the Academy of Political Science* 23 (1948–50), pp. 232–233.

13. "German Reeducation," pp. 235–237.

14. "German Reeducation," p. 238.

15. "German Reeducation," pp. 237–238. The quotation is from p. 238.

16. Elmer Davis, Office of War Information to Shuster, February 26, 1945, Box 83, SP-HCA. See also Davis to Ordway Tead that same day, Box 83, SP-HCA.

17. Shuster to Davis, March 9, 1945, and May 15, 1945, Box 83, SP-HCA.

18. A copy of Shuster's testimony has been preserved in Official File, Harry S. Truman Papers, Harry S. Truman Library.

19. *The Ground I Walked On*, p. 75.

20. AGWAR for AC of S G-2, signed Clark, August 2, 1945, Mark Wayne Clark Papers, Citadel Archives, The Citadel. Not surprisingly, the Society for the Prevention of World War III, which first called Shuster to Clark's attention, was the publisher of the pamphlet involved in Victor Ridder's earlier libel suit, and thus the Society's offices were quite familiar with Shuster's testimony; see William Duffy, "McCarthyism in Reverse—II," *The New York Post*, August 16, 1950.

21. AGWAR for Patterson from Clark, n.d., Mark Wayne Clark Papers, Citadel Archives, The Citadel.

22. *New York Times*, May 26, 1950: 15–3. See also "Catholic Bavaria Again Ruled By Hitlerites," *The Converted Catholic Magazine* (October 1950), pp. 228–229.

23. A copy of this poster is preserved in Box 73, SP-HCA.

24. "In New York," N.Y. *Daily Mirror*, May 18, 1950, from a clipping in Box 73, SP-HCA; Shuster to Winchell, May 24 and June 1, 1950, Box 73, SP-HCA.

25. "The Shuster Case," Box 73, SP-HCA.

26. *The Germans*, p. 86.

27. *Like a Mighty Army*, p. 130.

28. *Like a Mighty Army*, p. 11.

29. *Strong Man Rules*, p. 69.

30. Shuster's response to the faculty request of June 12, 1950, Box 73, SP-HCA. See also document entitled: *FOR SIGNATURES ADDED SINCE MAY 29*, Box 73, SP-HCA.

31. See, for example, the two lists of signatures of support, dated May 29 and June 12, each containing more than 150 names, Box 73, SP-HCA. More than two hundred other letters of congratulation on his appointment, some of these from Hunter faculty also, are preserved in Boxes 5 and 6, SP-UNDA.

32. Edward N. Peterson, *The American Occupation of Germany: Retreat to Victory* (Detroit, 1978), p. 214.

33. Peterson, *The American Occupation of Germany*, p. 215. See also John Gimbel, *The American Occupation of Germany: Politics and the*

Military, 1945–1949 (Stanford, Cal., 1968); Robert Wolfe, ed., *Americans as Proconsuls: United States Military Government in Germany and Japan, 1944–1952* (Carbondale, Ill., 1984); Roger H. Wells, "State Government," in *Governing Postwar Germany*, ed. Edward H. Litchfield (Ithaca, N.Y., 1953), pp. 84–116; J.F.J. Gillen, *State and Local Government in West Germany, 1945–1953* (Office of the U.S. High Commissioner for Germany, 1953); and Lucius D. Clay, *Decision in Germany* (Garden City, N.Y., 1950).

34. Peterson, *The American Occupation of Germany*, pp. 215–225; Elmer Plischke, "Denazification in Germany," in Wolfe, *Americans as Proconsuls*, pp. 198–225; Clay, *Decision in Germany*, pp. 51–83; and Ladislas Farago, *Patton: Ordeal and Triumph* (New York, 1963), pp. 754–785.

35. Farago, *Patton*, p. 768.

36. Peterson, *The American Occupation of Germany*, pp. 217–225.

37. Peterson, *The American Occupation of Germany*, pp. 226–244, and Farago, *Patton*, pp. 564–570.

38. Clay, *Decision in Germany*, pp. 51–83; and Peterson, *The American Occupation of Germany*, pp. 54–66. See also John M. Blum, *Roosevelt and Morgenthau* (New York, 1972), pp. 559–599; Harold Zink, *The United States in Germany, 1944–1955* (New York, 1957), pp. 93–94; Thomas Alan Schwartz, *America's Germany: John J. McCloy and the Federal Republic of Germany* (Cambridge, Mass., 1991), pp. 18–21; and Bert Peter Schloss, "The American Occupation of Germany, 1945–1952: An Appraisal" (Ph.D. dissertation, University of Chicago, 1955), pp. 71–79.

39. In addition to Peterson, *The American Occupation of Germany*, pp. 226–244, see Plischke, "Denazification in Germany," pp. 198–225.

40. Peterson, *The American Occupation of Germany*, pp. 244–257, and Wilson D. Miscamble, "Deciding to Divide Germany: American Policymaking in 1949," *Diplomacy and Statecraft* 2 (July 1991), pp. 294–320.

41. Alonzo G. Grace, "Education" in Litchfield, *Governing Postwar Germany*, pp. 439–468; Peterson, *The American Occupation of Germany*, pp. 193–214; and Henry P. Pilgert, *The West German Educational System* (Office of the U.S. High Commissioner for Germany, 1953), pp. 9–72.

42. Shuster to John A. Biggs, May 11, 1950, Box 1, SP-UNDA.

43. For Shuster's earlier friendship with Faulhaber, see Chapter 4 above and *The Ground I Walked On*, pp. 154 and 223–225.

44. Interview with John J. McCloy, June 5, 1985; and *New York Times*, April 18, 1950; 1–2. As far back as 1943 the War Department assembled a pool of qualified persons to serve in occupied areas after the war, and Shuster volunteered for service. See correspondence of Shuster

with Col. Jesse I. Miller and Maj. Gen. Allen W. Gullion of the Office of the Provost Marshal General, March–April, 1943, SP-HCA, and *The Ground I Walked On*, p. 209.

45. Peterson, *The American Occupation of Germany*, pp. 257–258; *The Ground I Walked On*, p. 203; *New York Times*, April 18, 1950, 1–2; and July 11, 1950, 21–4; autographed ship menu preserved in Box 2, SP-UNDA; and cable of Shuster to McCloy, June 30, 1950, Box 73, SP-HCA.

46. Official administrative chart, dated October 26, 1949, preserved in Box 73, SP-HCA. See also Zink, *The United States in Germany, 1944–1955*, pp. 59–62.

47. *The Ground I Walked On*, p. 204.

48. This subject is treated in excellent fashion by Schwartz, *America's Germany*, pp. 124–294. See also Ivone Kirkpatrick, *The Inner Circle* (London, 1959), pp. 238–240.

49. "Office of the U.S. High Commissioner for Germany, APO 757, Staff Announcement No. . . . 115, July 18, 1950." RG 466, Records of the U.S. High Commissioner for Germany, Historical Analysis of the McCloy Administration, 1949–1952, National Archives (hereafter abbreviated RG 466, HAMcCA, 1949–1952, NA), documents D (50) 1755 (July 8, 1950); D (50) 1764 (July 11, 1950); D (50) 1800 (July 18, 1950); and Journal entry for July 12, 1950.

50. Edward F. Kennedy to Shuster, May 16, 1950, Box 6, SP-UNDA.

51. McCloy to Shuster, May 1, 1950, Box 8, SP-UNDA.

52. Edward F. Kennedy to Shuster, May 16, 1950, Box 6, SP-UNDA; *The Ground I Walked On*, pp. 225–227; and interview with Robert Shuster, July 25, 1986.

53. Interview with John J. McCloy, June 5, 1985; and *The Ground I Walked On*, pp. 202–229.

54. This and the following quotations are from a reprint of this address: "Objective: Friendship," in Office of U.S. High Commissioner for Germany, *Information Bulletin* (September 1950), p. 53, a copy of which is preserved in Box 73, SP-HCA.

55. "Objective Friendship," p. 53, and *The Ground I Walked On*, p. 205.

56. Schwartz, *America's Germany*, pp. 269–278; *The Ground I Walked On*, p. 212; and Kirkpatrick, *The Inner Circle*, pp. 244–245.

57. Extracts from HICOG Staff Conference Meetings, 1949–1952, meetings of September 12 and 19, 1950, and July 7, 1951, RG 466, HICOG Staff Conference Meetings, 1949–1952, National Archives (hereafter abbreviated RG 466, HICOG-SC, NA) documents D (50)

2154; D (50) 2187; and D (51) 1152; and Shuster to B. J. Buttenwieser, Deputy U.S. High Commissioner, September 14, 1950, RG 466, Records of the U.S. High Commissioner for Germany, Bavaria Land Commissioner, Office of the Land Commissioner, Central Files, 1948–1952, National Archives (hereafter abbreviated RG 466, LCB, CF 1948–1952, NA), Box 16.

58. Extracts from HICOG Staff Conference Meetings, 1949–1952, meetings of October 31 and December 19, 1950, RG 466, HICOG-SC, NA, documents D (50) 2414 and D (50) 2797.

59. Extracts from HICOG Staff Conference Meetings, 1949–1952, meetings of January 16 and October 23, 1951, RG 466, HICOG-SC, NA, documents D (51) 52 and D (51) 1674; and Shuster to Buergermeister Fritz Strobel, Rehau, January 5, 1951; Shuster to Dr. Hans Ehard, Minister President for Bavaria, March 5, 1951; and Shuster to F. J. Miller, Office of Economic Affairs, HICOG, May 25, 1951, RG 466, LCB, CF 1948–1952, Box 21, NA.

60. Peterson, *The American Occupation of Germany*, pp. 256–257.

61. "The American Occupation and German Education," *Proceedings of the American Philosophical Society* 97 (April 1953), pp. 159–162.

62. "The American Occupation and German Education," p. 161, and Zink, *The United States in Germany, 1944–1955*, pp. 207–208.

63. Alois Hundhammer, quoted in Colman J. Barry, O.S.B., *American Nuncio* (Collegeville, Minn., 1969), p. 129. For this education question, see also Alonzo Grace, "Education," pp. 455–467, and Harold Hurwitz, "Comparing American Reform Efforts in Germany," in Wolfe, *Americans as Proconsuls*, pp. 327–328.

64. Eric G. Gration, Office of the Executive Secretary, HICOG, to Shuster, August 1950, RG 466, LCB, CF 1948–1952, Box 10, NA.

65. Plischke, "Denazification in Germany," in Wolfe, *Americans as Proconsuls*, pp. 198–225; and Zink, *The United States in Germany, 1944–1955*, pp. 150–168.

66. Ehard to Shuster, May 19, 1951, RG 466, LCB, CF 1948–1952, Box 15, NA.

67. Ehard to Shuster, November 24, 1950, RG 466, LCB, CF 1948–1952, Box 21, NA.

68. McCloy to Shuster, November 6, 1951, RG 466, LCB, CF 1948–1952, Box 22, NA.

69. Muench, "Progress in Germany," December 8, 1951, Box 138, Muench Papers, Department of Archives and Manuscripts, Catholic University of America.

70. Extracts from HICOG Staff Conference Meetings, 1949–1952, NA, Meetings of September 19, 1950, March 6, 1951; and

July 24, 1951; RG 466, HICOG-SC, NA, documents D (50) 2187, D (51) 290, and D (51) 1031.

71. Shuster to Ehard, October 16, 1950, RG 466, LCB, CF 1948–1952, Box 7, NA.

72. Shuster to Commander-in-Chief, Headquarters European Command, February 19 and September 7, 1951; Shuster to Commanding General, Twelfth Air Force, September 7, 1951; and numerous similar letters in RG 466, LCB, CF 1948–1952, Box 7, NA.

73. Shuster to Commander-in-Chief, Headquarters European Command, March 16, 1951, RG 466, LCB, CF 1948–1952, Box 7, NA.

74. Muench to J. O. Lipman, Resident Officer, Kemnath, January 23, 1951, Muench Papers, Box 126, DAM-CUA.

75. Shuster to McCloy (n.d.) Muench Papers, Box 126, DAM-CUA.

76. Col. Stephen S. Hamilton to F. L. Roessler, U.S. Resident Officer, Garmisch, n.d., RG 466, LCB, CF 1948–1952, Box 6, NA.

77. F. F. Egger, Resident Officer, Bad Toelz, to Elise Brockmann, August 2, 1951, RG 466, LCB, CF 1948–1952, Box 6, NA.

78. HICOG Staff Conference, July 9, 1951, RG 466, Records of the U.S. High Commissioner for Germany, Classified General Records, 1949–1952, National Archives, document D (51) 919.

79. Muench, "Problems Old and New in Germany," Fall, 1950, Muench Papers, Box 138, DAM-CUA; and Extracts from HICOG Staff Conference Meetings, 1949–1952, Meetings of August 1, 15, and 29, 1950, RG 466, HICOG-SC, NA, documents D (50) 1885, D (50) 1978, and D (50) 2071.

80. See, for example, McCloy to Shuster, n.d., outlining steps in processing non-German immigration into West Germany, RG 466, LCB, CF 1948–1952, Box 3, NA.

81. Minutes of the meeting of representatives from Munich Women's groups, August 30, 1950, RG 466, LCB, CF 1948–1952, Box 29, NA.

82. Minutes of the meeting of representatives from Munich Women's groups, September 20, 1950, RG 466, LCB, CF 1948–1952, Box 29, NA.

83. Minutes of the meeting of representatives from Munich Women's groups, October 4, 1950, RG 466, LCB, CF 1948–1952, Box 29, NA; "Good Neighbors Aid Munich Needy," *Information Bulletin: Monthly Magazine of the Office of US High Commissioner for Germany* (April 1951), Box 73, SP-HCA; and Wolfgang Jaenicke to Mrs. Shuster, October 6 and 12, 1950, Box 5, SP-UNDA.

84. "Good Neighbors Aid Munich Needy," *Information Bulletin* (April 1951); and Office of Land Commissioner for Bavaria, Public Relations Branch, Release 847, Munich, June 12, 1951, Box 5, SP-UNDA.

85. Notices of such meetings are preserved in RG 466, HAMcCA, 1949–1952, Boxes 2 and 3, NA. See also interview with McCloy, June 5, 1985.

86. A good summary of the organization of the office of the land commissioner is in Zink, *The United States in Germany, 1944–1955,* pp. 59–65; reports of *Kreis* offices are contained in RG 466, LCB, CF 1948–1952, NA, Box 2 especially; and Journal entries for June 1951, in RG 466, HAMcCA, 1949–1952, Box 3, NA. Shuster's mother died in Lancaster in July 1951, but he did not attempt to return again for the funeral.

87. Extracts from HICOG Staff Conference Meetings, 1940–1952, Meetings of August 1 and September 19, 1950, RG 466, HICOG-SC, NA, documents D (50) 1885 and D (50) 2187; and Clark and others to Shuster, August 3, 1950, RG 466, LCB, CF 1948–1952, Box 14, NA.

88. Extracts from HICOG Staff Conference Meetings, Meetings of March 6 and April 24, 1951, RG 466, HICOG-SC, NA, documents D (51) 290 and D (51) 531; and Shuster to Ehard, March 13, 1951, RG 466, LCB, CF 1948–1952, Box 26, NA.

89. Shuster to Muench, October 23, 1950, Muench Papers, Box 125, DAM-CUA; Extracts from HICOG Staff Conference Meetings, Meeting of November 21, 1950, RG 466, HICOG-SC, NA, document D (50) 2556; and Shuster to Ehard, September 8, 1950, RG 466, LCB, CF 1948–1952, Box 26, NA.

90. Marriage and adoption requests are preserved in RG 466, LCB, CF 1948–1952, Boxes 3 and 4, NA; and Ehard to Shuster, July 9, 1951, and Shuster to Ehard, August 17, 1951, RG 466, LCB, CF 1948–1952, Box 16, NA.

91. Records are preserved in RG 466, LCB, CF 1948–1952, Box 3, NA.

92. Oron Hale to Shuster, December 13, 1950, and P. M. Purves to Shuster, December 14, 1950, RG 466, LCB, CF 1948–1952, Boxes 10 and 12, NA; and Extracts from HICOG Staff Conference Meetings, Meetings of November 28, December 12 and 19, 1950, and January 9, 1951, RG 466, HICOG-SC, NA, documents D (50) 2608, D (50) 2720, D (50) 2797, and D (51) 15.

93. McCloy to Shuster, March 19, 1951, and Shuster to McCloy, March 21, 1951, RG 466, Classified General Records, 1949–1952, NA,

documents D (51) 372 and D (51) 376; and Peterson, *The American Occupation of Germany*, pp. 257–262.

94. Lord Mayor of Kulmbach to President Truman, October 5, 1951, General File, Papers of Harry S. Truman, Harry S. Truman Library; Muench to Shuster, November 26, 1951, Muench Papers, Box 125, DAM-CUA.

95. Interviews with Oron Hale, March 19, 1985, and John McCloy, June 5, 1985.

96. Zink, *The United States in Germany*, p. 79, and Peterson, *The American Occupation of Germany*, pp. 259 and 258.

97. Quoted in the *New York Times*, November 22, 1951: 9–1.

98. *New York Times*, July 28, 1941: 6–2. See also La Vern J. Rippley, *The German-Americans* (Boston, 1976), p. 210, and *The Ground I Walked On*, pp. 20–21.

99. *New York Times*, September 13, 1941: 2–7; September 23, 1941: 6–4; December 12, 1941: 22–8; December 25, 1941: 29–3; and January 9, 1941: 8–6.

100. Emmet to Shuster, April 5, 1952, Box 98, and "Report on the Activities of the American Council on Germany, October 15, 1953," Box 4, Christopher T. Emmet Papers, Hoover Institution Archives, Stanford, California (hereafter abbreviated: Emmet Papers, HIA).

101. "Report on the Activities of the American Council on Germany, October 15, 1953," Box 4; Emmet to Shuster, April 26 and May 3, 1953; Shuster to Emmet, October 16, 1953; and see letterhead stationery, 1962, Box 98, Emmet Papers, HIA.

102. "Report on the Activities of the American Council on Germany, October 15, 1953," and "Report on Activities: American Council on Germany, Inc., January 1, 1954," Box 4, Emmet Papers, HIA.

103. "Secretary's Annual Report of Activities, 1955," Box 4, Emmet Papers, HIA.

104. George Kennan, *Memoirs, 1950–1963* (Boston, 1972), pp. 229–266; Dean Acheson, "The Illusion of Disengagement," *Foreign Affairs* 36 (April 1958), pp. 371–383; Emmet to Shuster, December 16, 1957 and January 28, 1958, and Shuster to Emmet, December 6, 1957 and February 6, 1958, all in Box 98, Emmet Papers, HIA.

105. Excerpt from Minutes of Staff meeting, May 13, 1952; Bernard L. Gladieux to Oliver May, June 13, 1952, Gen. 52, Roll 1157; Shuster to Robert Hutchins, June 6, 1952; Shuster to Paul G. Hoffman, April 17, 1952; and Shuster to Milton Katz, May 15, 1952, Gen. 52, Roll 1156, General Correspondence Files, Ford Foundation Archives (hereafter "General Correspondence Files" will not be repeated).

106. Shuster to Shepard Stone, May 27, 1955, and Ford Foundation to Shuster, June 6, 1955, PA 55–109; and Shuster to Stone, March 15, 1956, and Ford Foundation to Shuster, April 9, 1956, PA 56–119, Grant Files, Ford Foundation Archives (hereafter "Grant Files" will not be repeated).

107. Shuster to Stone, December 1, 1957, and Ford Foundation to Shuster, January 7, 1958, PA 58–56; Shuster to Stone, November 15, 1957, and Ford Foundation to Shuster, February 25, 1958, PA 58–97; and Shuster to Stone, June 17, 1958, and Ford Foundation to Shuster, July 22, 1958, PA 58–302, Ford Foundation Archives.

108. See Grant Files PA 58–305, PA 61–313, PA 64–94, PA 67–160, and PA 70–54, Ford Foundation Archives.

109. Shuster to Stone, May 26, 1958, and brief report contained in PA 58–305, Ford Foundation Archives. See also *New York Times*, October 3, 1959: 1–6; and October 4, 1959: 1–2.

110. American Council on Germany, "Report on Activities, 1960–1961"; "Report on Activities, 1962–1963"; and "Report on Activities, 1963–1965," Box 4, Emmet Papers, HIA; and Shuster to Howard Swearer, April 22, 1969, PA 70–54, and PA 67–160, Ford Foundation Archives.

111. Grace, "Education," pp. 465–466, and James F. Tent, *Mission on the Rhine* (Chicago, 1982), pp. 288–299.

112. Paul G. Hoffman to Hans Freiherr von Kress, n.d., PA 51–41, Ford Foundation Archives.

113. Stone to Price, September 16, 1955, PA 56–22, Ford Foundation Archives.

114. Correspondence pertinent to this grant and trip is preserved in PA 56–22, Ford Foundation Archives.

115. This "Report on the Free University of Berlin" is in PA 56–22, Ford Foundation Archives.

116. These are contained in pages 50–55 of the "Report on the Free University of Berlin."

117. *New York Times*, June 22, 1958: 7–1.

118. Stone to Shuster, September 19, 1958, PA 58–260, Ford Foundation Archives.

119. *New York Times*, November 5, 1958: 3–3; Stone to Shuster, September 19, 1958; Shuster to Stone, September 26, 1958; and telegram of Stone to Shuster, November 3, 1958, PA 58–260, Ford Foundation Archives.

120. A list of Shuster's various awards is preserved in Box 5, SP-UNDA.

9. UNESCO: CONFLICT AND PROMISE

1. Breckinridge Long to American Diplomatic and Consular Officers in the American Republics, October 25, 1940, Department of State Decimal File 111.46 Advisory Committee/75A, Record Group 59, National Archives (hereafter abbreviated DS 111.46 Adv. Cmte./(doc. No.), RG 59, NA). See also Haldore Hanson, *The Cultural-Cooperation Program, 1938–1943* (Washington, 1944), pp. 59–60; and Department of State, *The Program of the Department of State in Cultural Relations* (Washington, 1941), pp. 4–5.

2. General Advisory Committee of the Division of Cultural Relations of the Department of State, Minutes of Meeting of February 18–19, 1944, Box 11, SP-UNDA.

3. MacLeish to Shuster, April 10, 1945, DS 111.46 Adv. Cmte./ 4–1845, RG 59, NA. For the background of UNESCO, see H. H. Krill de Capello, "The Creation of the United Nations Educational, Scientific and Cultural Organization," *International Organization* 24 (Winter 1970), pp. 1–30; F. R. Cowell, "Planning the Organisation of UNESCO, 1942–1946: A Personal Record," *Cahiers d'Histoire Mondiale* 10 (1966), pp. 210–236; Walter H.C. Laves and Charles A. Thomson, *UNESCO: Purpose, Progress, Prospects* (Bloomington, Ind., 1957), pp. 18–23; and James P. Sewell, *UNESCO and World Politics* (Princeton, N.J., 1975), pp. 33–70. See also Chapter 5 above.

4. Sewell, *UNESCO and World Politics*, pp. 68–70, and Frank Ninkovich, *The Diplomacy of Ideas: U.S. Foreign Policy and Cultural Relations, 1938–1950* (New York, 1981), pp. 61–112. See also MacLeish to the Secretary, August 2, 1945, DS 501, PA/8–245, RG 59, NA.

5. William Benton, Assistant Secretary of State, to George Schuster [*sic*], October 20, 1945, DS 501, PA/10–2045, RG 59, NA. See also Dean Acheson to Secretary, September 15, 1945, DS 501, PA/9–1545, RG 59, NA.

6. Memorandum of Conversation, Walter Kelchner, October 19, 1945, DS 501, PA/10–1945, RG 59, NA.

7. Memorandum of Conversation, Walter Kelchner, October 19, 1945, DS 501, PA/10–1945, RG 59, NA.

8. Summary Minutes of Delegation Meetings (DC), October 26 and 27, 1945, DS 501, PA/1–11-45, RG 59, NA.

9. Walter Kelchner to Mrs. Buford, October 25, 1945, DS 501, PA/10–2545, RG 59, NA.

10. Summary Minutes of Delegation Meeting (London), November 8, 1945, DS 501, PA/1–11-45, RG 59, NA.

11. UNESCO, *Constitution*, IV, A, 1, and VII, 1.

12. UNESCO, *Constitution*, I, 1, and Preamble.

13. Report of William Benton to Secretary of State, December 5, 1945, DS 501, PA/12–545, RG 59, NA; *New York Times*, November 10, 1945; 6–6; and Laves and Thomson, *UNESCO*, pp. 26–27.

14. "United Nations Conference for the Establishment of an Educational and Cultural Organization, London, November 1–16, 1945," pp. 51, 59, 60, 66–67, and 72–73, Archibald MacLeish Papers, Box 56, Manuscripts Division, Library of Congress (hereafter abbreviated MD-LC).

15. *New York Times*, November 8, 1945: 5–5; Laves and Thomson, *UNESCO*, p. 28; and Summary Minutes of Delegation Meeting (DC), October 26, 1945, and Summary of Minutes of Delegation Meetings (London), November 9–15, 1945, DS 501 PA/1–11-45, RG 59, NA.

16. Benton to Secretary of State, December 5, 1945, DS 501, PA/12–545, RG 59, NA. See also Sidney Hyman, *The Lives of William Benton* (Chicago, 1969), pp. 335–339.

17. Shuster to Benton, December 26, 1945, Box 6, SP-UNDA.

18. MacLeish to Shuster, December 11, 1945, MacLeish Papers, Box 20, MD-LC.

19. UNESCO, *Constitution*, VII.

20. James Marshall to Shuster, January 29, March 4, and April 15, 1946, and Shuster to Marshall, February 5 and March 8, 1946, Box 6, SP-UNDA. See also Laves and Thomson, *UNESCO*, pp. 315–326, and Howard E. Wilson, *United States National Commission for UNESCO* (New York, 1948), p. 12.

21. For Shuster's early view, see press release of February 25, 1946, DS 501, PA/2–21-46, RG 59, NA.

22. Shuster to Marshall, March 8, 1946, Box 6, SP-UNDA.

23. Shuster to Sen. James Murray, June 18, 1946, Box 6, SP-UNDA.

24. 60 Stat. 712, 713 (1946); telegram of Benton to Shuster, September 6, 1946, DS 501, PA/9–646; and Benton to Shuster, September 12, 1946, DS 501, PA/9–1246, RG 59, NA. See also Wilson, *U.S. National Commission for UNESCO*, pp. 8–23.

25. Benton to Shuster, September 12, 1946, DS 501, PA/9–1246, RG 59, NA.

26. Benton to Shuster, September 27, and October 15, 1946, and "List of US delegates to UNESCO Conference, Paris, November 19, 1946," all in Box 6, SP-UNDA.

27. Shuster to Benton, October 1, 1946, Box 6, SP-UNDA.

28. These two were the creation of a $3 million revolving fund for UNESCO's use and a limit of approximately 40 percent as the percent-

age of the United States' contribution to the UNESCO budget; report of Benton to Secretary of State James Byrnes, December 23, 1946, DS 501, PA/12–2346, RG 59, NA.

29. Benton to Byrnes, December 23, 1946, DS 501, PA/12–2346, RG 59, NA. See also Shuster to Byrnes, December 27, 1946, and Compton to Byrnes, December 28, 1946, Box 6, SP-UNDA.

30. Archibald MacLeish, quoted in Benton to Byrnes, December 23, 1946, DS 501, PA/12–2346, RG 59, NA.

31. Shuster to Waldo Leland, May 17, 1946, Box 6, SP-UNDA.

32. Benton to Acheson, October 28, 1946, DS 501, PA/10–2846, RG 59, NA; Benton to Shuster, October 30, 1946, Box 6, SP-UNDA; and Hyman, *Lives of William Benton*, pp. 368–369.

33. Benton to Byrnes, December 23, 1946, DS 501, PA/12–2346, RG 59, NA. See also Huxley, *Memories II* (New York, 1973), pp. 13–25.

34. Shuster to Byrnes, December 27, 1946, Box 6, SP-UNDA, and "Comments on UNESCO and the Paris Conference" by Shuster, December 18, 1946, Waldo Leland Papers, Box 110, MD-LC.

35. Benton to Shuster, June 25, and Shuster to Benton, June 26, 1947, Box 6, SP-UNDA.

36. Charles Thomson to Shuster, February 27, 1947; Milton Eisenhower to Shuster, May 7, 1947; Max McCullough to Shuster, November 19, 1948; Waldo Leland to Shuster, April 19, 1949, Box 6, and Thomson to Shuster, October 24, 1949, Box 7, SP-UNDA. For another member's activities with the National Commission, see Milton Eisenhower, *The President Is Calling* (New York, 1974), pp. 180–215.

37. (Huxley) to Shuster, May 7, 1947; John Grierson to Shuster, May 17, 1947; and "Proposed Agenda" for Committee on Nominations, May 26, 1949, Box 6, SP-UNDA.

38. Waldo Leland to John Marshall, February 25 and March 3, 1947; Marshall to Leland, February 26 and March 5, 1947; and Leland to Shuster, March 4, 1947, Leland Papers, Box 113, MD-LC.

39. Leland to Marshall, February 25, and Leland to Shuster, March 4, 1947, Leland Papers, Box 113, MD-LC.

40. Shuster to Leland, March 6, 1947, and "Philosophy and Humanistic Studies," March 26, 1947, Leland Papers, Box 113, MD-LC.

41. Eisenhower to Shuster, April 1947 (n.d.), Box 6, SP-UNDA.

42. Shuster was able to attend approximately every second meeting, attending meetings in Chicago and Boston in 1947 and 1948 but absent from those in Denver and Washington.

43. Shuster summarized his views and remarks in a letter to Esther Caukin Brunauer, October 25, 1948, Box 6, SP-UNDA. See also Brunauer to Shuster, October 19, 1948, Box 6, SP-UNDA.

NOTES PAGES 267 TO 271

44. Robert Stanforth to Schuster [*sic*], April 4, and Leland to Shuster, April 19, 1949, Box 6, SP-UNDA.

45. Shuster to Richard Simon, February 21, 1950, Box 7, SP-UNDA.

46. E. J. Carter to M. Jean Thomas, November 4, 1949, DS 501, PA/11–449, RG 59, NA; and Jaime Torres Bodet to Shuster, August 5, 1949, Box 7, SP-UNDA.

47. Shuster to Richard Simon, February 21 and 27; Simon to Shuster, February 24 and March 8; Ethel Gilbert to Shuster, February 28; and Shuster to Gilbert, March 6, 1950, all in Box 7, SP-UNDA; and U.S. National Commission for UNESCO, Release No. 45 (March 1, 1950), Leland Papers, Box 114, MD-LC.

48. Shuster and Ethel B. Gilbert, "Who's Who and What's What in UNESCO's Reconstruction Program," Box 7, SP-UNDA.

49. Shuster to affiliated organizations, October 5, 1949; Shuster to Dr. George Stoddard, October 19, 1949; Ethel Gilbert to Shuster, October 24, 1949; and Constance Roach to Shuster, February 6, 1950, Box 7, SP-UNDA.

50. U.S. National Commission for UNESCO, Release No. 45 (March 1, 1950), Leland Papers, Box 114, MD-LC; and Shuster and Gilbert, "Who's Who and What's What in UNESCO's Reconstruction Program," Box 7, SP-UNDA.

51. Benton to Byrnes, December 23, 1946, DS 501, PA/12–2346, RG 59, NA.

52. "The Paradox of UNESCO," January 14, 1947, a copy of which is in SP-HCA.

53. Address of February 15, 1947, a copy in SP-HCA.

54. This and the following quotations are from an address of April 8, 1947, a copy in SP-HCA.

55. Shuster to Spellman, April 30, 1947, Box 6, SP-UNDA. See also Shuster to Rev. Robert W. Searle of the Protestant Council of New York, April 30, 1947, Box 6, SP-UNDA.

56. "Can UNESCO Succeed," April 16, 1947, a copy in SP-HCA.

57. "Education's New Responsibility," *Survey Graphic* 36 (November 1947), pp. 569–572.

58. Shuster to Thomson, March 10, 1950, and Edward W. Barrett (Assistant Secretary of State) to Shuster, November 6, 1951, Box 7, SP-UNDA. Interestingly, Shuster was reappointed, not as an educator, but as a state and local government representative since, as president of a city college, he was a city government official.

59. Shuster to Max McCullough, May 9, 1950, Box 7, SP-UNDA.

60. McCullough to Grady, December 22, 1950, and June 27, 1951, Box 7, SP-UNDA.

61. *New York Times*, January 27, 1952: 23–1.

62. *New York Times*, January 19, 1952: 7–1; January 30: 8–3; January 31: 16–2; and February 1: 5–7.

63. McCullough to Shuster, November 9, 1951, and January 23, 1952, Box 7, SP-UNDA.

64. Letters of congratulation from George Stoddard, February 13; Ordway Tead, February 7; and Max McCullough, March 12, 1952, are preserved in Box 7, SP-UNDA. See also Shuster to McCullough, March 17, 1952, Box 7, SP-UNDA.

65. See Chapter 6 for further treatment of these matters.

66. Laves and Thomson, *UNESCO*, pp. 241–243; Shuster, *UNESCO: Assessment and Promise* (New York, 1963), pp. 29–31; Shuster to McCullough, January 25, 1952, and Msgr. Frederick Hochwalt to Shuster, June 5, 1952, Box 7, SP-UNDA.

67. Shuster to McCullough, January 25, 1952, Box 7, SP-UNDA.

68. Paulo E. de Berredo Carneiro to Shuster, March 8, and Shuster to de Berredo Carneiro, March 30, 1952, Box 7, SP-UNDA.

69. Shuster to Jean Larnaud of the International Catholic Coordinating Center for U.N.E.S.C.O., May 27, 1952, Box 7, SP-UNDA.

70. McCullough to Shuster, September 29, 1952, January 16, February 20, and June 1, 1953, and Shuster to McCullough, March 16 and June 10, 1953, Box 7, SP-UNDA.

71. David Apter to Shuster, August 31, 1953, and Shuster to President Eisenhower, March 5, 1953, Box 7, SP-UNDA.

72. Tead and Shuster to Benton, March 25, 1952, Box 7, SP-UNDA.

73. Shuster to Rev. Vincent Flynn, President of St. Thomas Military Academy, September 8, 1953; travel vouchers to and from Minneapolis, September 14 and 18; Mrs. Sara B. Ryder to Shuster, September 21; Edward B. Rooney, S.J., to Shuster, September 30, 1953; and J. M. Nolte to Shuster, October 7, 1953, Box 7, SP-UNDA.

74. Dulles to Shuster, September 10, and Shuster to Hon. Joseph B. Cavallaro, September 11, 1953, Box 7, SP-UNDA.

75. Shuster to Cavallaro, September 11; Cavallaro to Shuster, September 15; Cavallaro to Mrs. Antoinette Jehle (Secretary to Shuster), September 15; and Jehle to Shuster, September 16, 1953, Box 7, SP-UNDA.

76. Shuster to Dr. James Eagan, October 13, 1953, Box 7, SP-UNDA.

77. Shuster to Cavallaro, September 11, 1953, Box 7, SP-UNDA.

78. Shuster to J. L. Morrill, November 4, 1953, Box 7, SP-UNDA.

79. Robinson McIlvaine to Shuster, April 16; Shuster to McIlvaine, April 30; Shuster to Carl McCardle, May 5; McCullough to Shuster, May 14; and Shuster to Milan Egert, June 16, 1954, Box 7, SP-UNDA.

80. McCullough to Shuster, February 9, and Shuster to McCullough, February 24, 1954, Box 7; McCardle to Shuster, April 3; Shuster to McCardle, April 26; Wallace J. Campbell to McCardle, April 19; and Shuster to Lawrence M. Stavig, June 30, 1954, Box 5, SP-UNDA.

81. Shuster to Dulles, May 27, 1954, Box 5, SP-UNDA.

82. Two challenging studies of Secretary Dulles are Michael A. Guhin, *John Foster Dulles: A Statesman and His Times* (New York, 1972), and Townsend Hoopes, *The Devil and John Foster Dulles* (Boston, 1973); Shuster to Morrill, November 4, 1953, Box 7, SP-UNDA.

83. Shuster to Benton, June 10, 1954, Box 5, SP-UNDA.

84. Laves and Thomson, *UNESCO*, pp. 333–336; T. V. Sathyamurthy, *Politics of International Cooperation* (Geneve, 1964), pp. 163–170; and Sewell, *UNESCO and World Politics*, pp. 333–338.

85. Shuster to Benton, June 10, 1954, Box 5, SP-UNDA.

86. *New York Times*, July 3, 1954: 4–8.

87. Evans to Benton, May 19, 1954, Box 5, SP-UNDA.

88. Evans to Benton, August 5, 1954, Box 5, SP-UNDA.

89. Evans to Shuster, February 19; Shuster to Evans, March 8; and Herbert Schneider to Shuster, March 23, 1954, Box 7; and Schneider to Shuster, July 20, 1954, Box 5, SP-UNDA.

90. A copy of this speech, "Cultural Relations between the Old World and the New," is preserved in Box 7, SP-UNDA.

91. Shuster to Frank P. Zeidler (mayor of Milwaukee), July 20; Shuster to Evans, July 9; McCullough to Shuster, July 16; Shuster to Dag Hammarskjold, August 5; and John T. Edsall to McCullough, August 9, 1954, Box 5, SP-UNDA.

92. *New York Times*, October 17, 1954: 1–3.

93. *New York Times*, October 17, 1954: 20–3.

94. Shuster to Lawrence M. Stavig, June 30, 1954, Box 5, SP-UNDA, and *New York Times*, October 17, 1954; 20–3.

95. *New York Times*, May 17, 1958: 40–2; August 19, 1958: 17–5; and August 23, 1958: 4–4. See also Shuster to President Hans Simons of the New School of Social Research, July 28, 1958; and Andrew H. Berding, Assistant Secretary of State, to Shuster, August 4, 1958, Box 7, SP-UNDA.

96. Shuster to John A. Perkins, October 2, 1958, Box 7, SP-UNDA.

97. Shuster to McCullough, July 23, 1958; John W. Hanes, Jr., to Shuster, September 18, 1958; letter of December 10, 1958, Box 7, SP-

UNDA; and *Summary Records of the Executive Board of UNESCO*, 51st and 53rd Sessions, 1958.

98. Letter to Shuster, December 10, 1958, Box 7, SP-UNDA.

99. Shuster's earlier opposition is discussed earlier in this chapter.

100. Kellermann to Shuster, January 26, 1959, Box 7, SP-UNDA; and Sewell, *UNESCO and World Politics*, pp. 187–188.

101. Turner to Carneiro, December 3, 1958; Shuster to Carneiro, January 12, 1959; Carneiro to Shuster, January 21 and 30, 1959; and Kellermann to Shuster, January 26, 1959, Box 7, SP-UNDA.

102. Carneiro to Shuster, January 21, 1959; Andy G. Wilkison to Shuster, February 18, 1959; Kellermann to Shuster, January 23 and February 2, 1959; Kellermann to A. E. Manell, July 27, 1959; and Shuster to Kellermann, February 3, August 4, and November 3, 1959, Box 7, SP-UNDA.

103. Magdalen G.H. Flexner to Ralph Hilton, April 23, 1959, Box 7, SP-UNDA. For additional information on this *History*, see also Laves and Thomson, *UNESCO*, pp. 241–243; Sewell, *UNESCO and World Politics*, pp. 185–188; Shuster, *UNESCO: Assessment and Promise*, pp. 29–31; and "Foreword" by Director-General Rene Maheu, and "Preface" by Paulo E. de Berredo Carneiro in Jacquetta Hawkes and Leonard Woolley, *History of Mankind*, vol. I (New York, 1963), pp. xi–xxiii.

104. K. V. Ostrovityanov of the USSR Academy of Science to Carneiro, September 26, 1959, Box 7, SP-UNDA.

105. Shuster to Kellermann, October 19, 1959, and November 3, 1959, Box 7, SP-UNDA.

106. Shuster to Kellermann, November 3, 1959, and enclosure in Kellermann to Shuster, November 12, 1959, Box 7, SP-UNDA.

107. Glyn Daniel in *The Nation* 197 (July 27, 1963), p. 56.

108. M. I. Finley in *New Statesman* 65 (June 14, 1963), p. 907.

109. William McNeill in the *American Historical Review* 73 (June 1968), p. 1479.

110. *New York Times*, August 19, 1958: 17–5; and August 23, 1958: pp. 4–4.

111. Maxwell M. Rabb to Shuster, December 7, 1958, Box 7, SP-UNDA; and *New York Times*, December 6, 1958; 8–3.

112. Kellermann to Shuster, December 10, 1958; James Simsarian to Shuster, December 29, 1958; and Shuster to McCullough, December 30, 1958, Box 7, SP-UNDA.

113. *Summary Records of the Executive Board of UNESCO*, 54th Session, Paris, June 1–12, 1959, pp. 14, 104–107; "Report on the 54th Session of UNESCO's Executive Board by the United States Member—Paris, France," Box 7, SP-UNDA; and Laves and Thomson, *UNESCO*, pp. 437–439.

114. *Summary Records of the Executive Board of UNESCO*, 54th Session, p. 23; and 55th Session, Paris, November 23-December 5, 1959, pp. 27, 151, and 208.

115. *Summary Records of the Executive Board of UNESCO*, 55th Session, pp. 157–158, and Shuster to Secretary of State Christian Herter, December 15, 1959, Box 5, SP-UNDA.

116. Herter to Shuster, December 31, 1959, and Shuster to Herter, January 13, 1960, Box 5, SP-UNDA.

117. Because of ill health, Veronese resigned after only three years in office, in November 1961. See Veronese to Shuster, September 10, 1959, Box 7, SP-UNDA; and Sathyamurthy, *The Politics of International Cooperation*, p. 132.

118. Shuster to William Dix (chairman of the U.S. National Commission), January 4, 1960, Box 7; and Shuster to Laurence Rockefeller, February 9, 1960, Box 5, SP-UNDA.

119. Shuster to William G. Carr of the National Education Association, October 22, 1959, and Kellermann to Shuster, December 16, 1959, Box 7; and Shuster to Veronese, January 19, 1960, Box 5, SP-UNDA. See also *UNESCO: Assessment and Promise*, pp. 15–16 and 105–107.

120. *Summary Records of the Executive Board of UNESCO*, 56th, 57th, and 58th Sessions. Shuster's remarks on educational assistance to the nations of Africa are from the 57th Session, pp. 32–34. See also *UNESCO: Assessment and Promise*, pp. 53–54, and Shuster to Rev. John J. Considine, M. M., January 23, 1961, Box 2, Assistant to the President's Papers, University of Notre Dame Archives (hereafter abbreviated ATPP-UNDA).

121. Shuster to Dr. Harvie Branscomb, September 30, 1963, Box 10, ATPP-UNDA, and Shuster, "An Autobiography," in *Leaders in American Education*, p. 301.

122. Schlesinger, *A Thousand Days* (New York, 1965), p. 348.

123. Shuster's work at Notre Dame from 1961 to 1977 is the subject of the following chapter.

124. *UNESCO: Assessment and Promise*, pp. 52–54. The quotation is from p. 52.

125. *UNESCO: Assessment and Promise*, pp. 52–54.

126. *Summary Records of the Executive Board of UNESCO*, 59th Session, pp. 15 and 29.

127. *Summary Records of the Executive Board of UNESCO*, 59th Session, p. 164, and "Report on 59th Session of UNESCO Executive Board (May 25-June 16, 1961)," Box 2, ATPP-UNDA.

128. "Report on 59th Session of UNESCO Executive Board," Box 2, ATPP-UNDA.

129. Shuster to Rusk, June 23, 1961, Box 2, ATPP-UNDA.

130. Vernon McKay to Shuster, June 1 and November 17, 1961, Box 2, ATPP-UNDA; and *New York Times*, October 23, 1961; 3–4; and October 27, 1961; 10–1. See also A. E. Manell to Shuster, September 1, 1959, and Shuster to Manell, September 8, 1959, Box 7, SP-UNDA.

131. Shuster to L. A. Minnich, September 26, 1961, Box 2, ATPP-UNDA.

132. Shuster to George C. Mitchell, December 12, 1961, Box 2, ATPP-UNDA. See also *Summary Records of the Executive Board of UNESCO*, 60th Session, Paris, October 25-November 29, 1961; and "Report on the 60th Session of the UNESCO Executive Board, Paris, October 25-November 29, 1961," Box 2, ATPP-UNDA.

133. Shuster to Rusk, June 21, 1962, Box 5, ATPP-UNDA.

134. *Summary Records of the Executive Board of UNESCO*, 61st Session, Paris, May 7–29, 1962; and Shuster to Rusk, June 21, 1962, Box 5, ATPP-UNDA.

135. Rusk to Shuster, July 10, 1962, Box 5, ATPP-UNDA.

136. Shuster to Robert H. B. Wade, March 18, 1963, Box 10, ATPP-UNDA.

137. Shuster to Wade, August 7, 1962; Walter Kotschnig to Shuster, October 2, 1962; Shuster to Kotschnig, October 11, 1962; Shuster to Harlan Cleveland, October 1, 1962; September 25 and October 16, 1962; Shuster to Rusk, October 1, 1962, Box 5, ATPP-UNDA; and *Summary Records of the Executive Board of UNESCO*, 62nd Session, Paris and Istanbul, August 27-September 12, 1962.

138. Shuster to Cleveland, September 25, 1962, and Shuster to Prof. Bedrettin Tuncel, October 5, 1962, Box 5, ATPP-UNDA.

139. Shuster to George V. Allen, February 12, 1962, and Allen to Shuster, January 17, 1962, Box 5, and Allen to Shuster, March 19, 1963, Box 10, ATPP-UNDA.

140. Shuster to Ann Jablonski, October 15, 1962, Box 5, ATPP-UNDA.

141. Shuster to L. A. Minnich, February 1, 1963; May 22, 1963; July 30, 1963; and September 23, 1963, all in Box 10, ATPP-UNDA.

142. Benton to Shuster, April 25, 1963, Box 10, ATPP-UNDA.

143. For an earlier view, see Shuster to James Marshall, February 5, 1946, Box 6, SP-UNDA.

144. Shuster to Minnich, July 31, 1961, Box 2, ATPP-UNDA.

145. *UNESCO: Assessment and Promise*, pp. 98–103 and 109–110.

146. Shuster to M. Jimenez, January 30, 1961, Box 2, ATPP-UNDA.

147. Shuster to Benton, April 30, 1963, Box 10, ATPP-UNDA.

148. Shuster to Rusk, June 21, 1962, Box 5, ATPP-UNDA, and *New York Times*, March 8, 1963: 1–2.

149. Published for the Council on Foreign Relations by Harper and Row, 1963.

150. Shuster to Shepard Stone, October 18, 1961, Box 2, ATPP-UNDA.

151. Philip E. Mosely to Shuster, January 31, 1962, Box 5, ATPP-UNDA.

152. Robert Wade to Shuster, March 15, 1963; Shuster to Wade, March 18, 1963; L. A. Minnich to Shuster, September 12, 1963; and Benton to Shuster, September 26, October 28, and November 11, 1963, Box 10, ATPP-UNDA.

153. *UNESCO: Assessment and Promise*, p. x.

154. *UNESCO: Assessment and Promise*, pp. 3, 18, and 67–75; "The Trials and Triumphs of UNESCO," *Saturday Review* 45 (February 24, 1962), p. 63; and *New York Times*, August 27, 1959; 15–4.

155. *UNESCO: Assessment and Promise*, pp. 10–18.

156. *UNESCO: Assessment and Promise*, pp. 85 and 105–107.

157. *UNESCO: Assessment and Promise*, pp. 18, 26–27, 35, 43–44, 50–51, and 61–62; and "The Trials and Triumphs of UNESCO," *Saturday Review* 45 (February 24, 1962), p. 22.

158. *UNESCO: Assessment and Promise*, p. 114.

10. RETURN TO NOTRE DAME

1. Minutes of the Meeting of the Board of Higher Education of the City of New York, February 16, 1959.

2. Minutes of the Meeting of the Board of Higher Education of the City of New York, February 16, 1959, and February 9, 1960.

3. *The President's Annual Report, 1958–1959*, American Council on Education, Washington, D.C.

4. Harry S. Ashmore, *Unseasonable Truths: The Life of Robert Maynard Hutchins* (Boston, 1989), p. 394; Thomas C. Reeves, *Freedom and the Foundation: The Fund for the Republic in the Era of McCarthyism* (New York, 1969), p. 276; and interview with Doris Shuster, September 2, 1983.

5. Shuster to Doris, April 29; Mrs. Sarah Weinberger to Anton Morgenroth, May 6; and Shuster to Dr. Georg Federer, August 11, 1960, Box 5, SP-UNDA.

6. Robert Moses to Shuster, August 12; and Shuster to Moses, August 15, 1960, Box 15, SP-UNDA.

7. Rev. Theodore Hesburgh, C.S.C., to Doris Shuster, July 25, 1960, Box 15, SP-UNDA; and interview with Doris Shuster, September 2, 1983.

8. Arthur Adams to William Stevenson, January 28, 1959; and Minutes of the Meeting of the Committee on Intercultural Studies in Colleges and Universities, December 7, 1959, Papers of the Committee on Intercultural Studies in Colleges and Universities, American Council on Education, Office of President Adams, 1959, Box 134 (hereafter abbreviated CISCU, ACE, Adams, 1959); Robert Byrnes, *The Non-Western Areas in Undergraduate Education in Indiana* (Bloomington, Ind., 1959).

9. *The President's Annual Report, 1958–1959*, American Council on Education, Washington; Shuster to Harry Carman, July 5, 1960, Box 15, SP-UNDA; Dr. Fred Burke to Shuster, October 4, 1960, Box 6, SP-UNDA; stationery of the committee lists Shuster as Director and Mrs. Shuster as one of two Assistants to the Director, Box 15, Assistant to the President Papers, University of Notre Dame Archives (hereafter abbreviated ATPP-UNDA); Shuster to President Adams, April 3, 1959; "Budget," March 31, 1959; and Minutes of Committee meetings of July 17 and December 7, 1959, all in CISCU, ACE, Adams, 1959, Box 134.

10. Minutes of the Committee's Meeting of March 3, 1961, CISCU, ACE, Adams, 1961, Box 157; and Shuster to Richard Humphrey of ACE, May 3, 1962, Box 3, ATPP-UNDA.

11. *American Council on Education: Annual Report, 1963*, Washington, D.C.

12. Minutes of the Committee's Meeting, March 3, 1961, and draft of Chapters I and II of the report, CISCU, ACE, Adams, 1961, Box 157. For the Great Books Program at the University of Chicago, see Ashmore, *Unseasonable Truths*, 98–107ff.

13. Robert Moses to Shuster, August 12, 1960, Box 15, SP-UNDA.

14. Shuster to Robert Moses, August 15 and October 26, 1960, Box 15, SP-UNDA; and Shuster to Robert Hutchins, September 22, 1960, Robert M. Hutchins Collection—Addenda (Shuster File), Department of Special Collections, The Joseph Regenstein Library, University of Chicago (hereafter abbreviated DSC-UC).

15. "A Proposed Educational Exhibit at the World's Fair," Robert M. Hutchins Collection—Addenda (Shuster File), DSC-UC; and Doris Shuster to Dean Howard Wilson, November 1, 1960, Box 15, SP-UNDA.

16. For a critical view of Moses and the World's Fair, see Robert A. Caro, *The Power Broker: Robert Moses and the Fall of New York* (New York, 1974), pp. 1082–1116.

17. Hutchins was president and then chancellor of the University of Chicago from 1929 to 1951. Shuster's membership on the Freedom of the Press Commission is discussed in Chapter 7, and his work for Encyclopedia Britannica, Inc., will be treated in the following chapter.

18. For the establishment of the Fund for the Republic, see Reeves, *Freedom and the Foundation*, pp. 24–34; Ashmore, *Unseasonable Truths*, pp. 328–332; Dwight Macdonald, *The Ford Foundation: The Men and the Millions* (New York, 1956), pp. 69–80; Ford Foundation Press Release, December 13, 1952, PA 53–37, Ford Foundation Archives; and Board of Directors to Henry T. Heald, December 12, 1961, Box 3, ATPP-UNDA. The quotation is from the latter.

19. Shuster to Paul Hoffman, September 3, 1952, Box 3, Fund for the Republic Papers, Princeton University Archives.

20. Ashmore, *Unseasonable Truths*, p. 374–396; Reeves, *Freedom and the Foundation*, pp. 241–242; Board of Directors to Henry T. Heald, December 12, 1961, Box 3, ATPP-UNDA. Years later, Shuster wrote: "Perhaps my most important service to the Center was putting into Bob Hutchins' head the idea of tossing aside the concept of the Fund (which was primarily a combat organization) and adopting that of a discussion oriented establishment, such as the Center now is" (Shuster to Mary Kersey Harvey, May 24, 1971, Box 48, ATPP-UNDA).

21. Ashmore, *Unseasonable Truths*, pp. 386–396 and 408–427, and Reeves, *Freedom and the Foundation*, p. 276. See also Shuster to Hutchins, June 18, 1959, and February 20 and July 21, 1960, and Hutchins to Shuster, May 22, 1959, Robert M. Hutchins Collection— Addenda (Shuster File), DSC-UC; and Hallock Hoffman to Shuster, September 18, 1959, and Shuster to Hutchins, March 7, 1960, Box 139, Fund for the Republic Papers, Princeton University Archives.

22. Interview with Doris Shuster, September 2, 1983.

23. Interview with Doris Shuster, September 2, 1983.

24. Interview with Doris Shuster, September 2, 1983.

25. Shuster's earlier years on the Notre Dame faculty are discussed in Chapter 2.

26. *New York Times*, March 27, 1960: 33–2 and June 6, 1960: 1–8. The establishment of the Laetare Medal is discussed in Arthur Hope, C.S.C., *Notre Dame: One Hundred Years* (Notre Dame, 1943), pp. 232–234.

27. Interview with Doris Shuster, September 2, 1983, and Speer Strahan to Shuster, April 4, 1960, Box 15, SP-UNDA.

28. Interview with Doris Shuster, September 2, 1983.

29. Saul Alinsky to Shuster, January 13, 1961, Box 1, ATPP-UNDA.

30. Robert P. Schmuhl, *University of Notre Dame: A Contemporary Portrait* (Notre Dame, 1986), p. 14; John Lungren, Jr., *Hesburgh of Notre Dame: Priest, Educator, Public Servant* (Kansas City, 1987), p. 37; *New York Times*, September 25, 1960: 1–1. Hesburgh has written in his recent autobiography: "I envisioned Notre Dame as a great *Catholic* university, the greatest in the world! There were many distinguished universities in our country and in Europe, but not since the Middle Ages had there been a great Catholic university. The road was wide open for Notre Dame, I told myself" (*God, Country, Notre Dame* [New York, 1990], p. 64).

31. "The University of Notre Dame and the Study of Contemporary Society," an ad interim report submitted by Shuster, July 1961, in Box 1, ATPP-UNDA.

32. Shuster to Paul Braisted, July 5; L. L. Matthews to Shuster, March 16; Shuster to Macmillan Company, August 14; and Shuster to Thomas Kellermann, December 24, 1961, Box 2, ATPP-UNDA; and interview with Doris Shuster, September 2, 1983.

33. Such letters of regret are preserved in Box 1, ATPP-UNDA. Shuster noted the difficulty in locating funding in a letter to Frank Kelly of the Fund for the Republic, July 11, 1961, Box 1, ATPP-UNDA.

34. Hesburgh to Shuster, August 22, 1964, Box 12, ATPP-UNDA; and "Final Report to the Trustees of the O'Brien Foundation," January 1975, Center for the Study of Contemporary Society, 40-CE-04, Notre Dame Printed Material, UNDA.

35. Shuster to Walsh, September 26, 1962, Box 5; "A Proposal to the Kellogg Foundation for a Continuing Education Center at the University of Notre Dame" (approximately March 1963), Box 7; Walsh to Dr. Emory Morris, November 21, 1963, Box 7; Shuster to Rev. Edmund Joyce, C.S.C., July 10, 1964, Box 11, ATPP-UNDA.

36. Dr. David Willis of Marquette University was probably the first to propose such a study to the Carnegie Corporation, and corporation president John Gardner discussed the idea with Hesburgh in May 1961; memo of telephone conversation between Gardner and Hesburgh, May 8, 1961, Study of Catholic Elementary and Secondary Education, University of Notre Dame, 1961–1963, Archives of the Carnegie Corporation of New York (hereafter abbreviated ND Education Study, ACCNY). For the Conant study, see James B. Conant, *The American High School Today* (New York, 1959).

37. Shuster to John Gardner, August 14, 1961, Box 16, ATPP-UNDA; and memo of meeting of Gardner and Hesburgh, June 4, 1961, and Shuster to Frederick H. Jackson, October 19, 1961, ND Education Study, 1961–1963, ACCNY.

38. Shuster to Frederick Jackson, May 3, 1962; February 27, 1963; July 25, 1963; April 6, 1964, Box 16; Shuster to James Murphy, June 1, 1964, and James Michael Lee to Shuster, September 14, 1964, Box 14, ATPP-UNDA; memo of Frederick Jackson, October 10, 1961; memo of telephone conversation of Jackson with Shuster, October 27, 1961; memo of Jackson, January 8, 1963; record of interviews, January 30, February 12, and June 26, 1964; and memo of Jackson, July 10, 1964, ND Education Study, 1961–1963 and 1964–1966, ACCNY; and Reginald Neuwien, *Catholic Schools in Action* (Notre Dame, 1966), pp. ix–xii.

39. Edited by Reginald Neuwien and published by the University of Notre Dame Press.

40. A readily accessible summary of the report's findings is in *Newsweek* 67 (September 5, 1966), pp. 59–60.

41. *New York Times*, August 28, 1966: 1–2, and Myron Lieberman, *Harvard Educational Review* 37 (Spring 1967), pp. 328–331. See also the reports of Robert D. Cross of Columbia University (March 6, 1967) and Michael E. Schiltz of the National Opinion Research Center (March 22, 1967), both in ND Education Study, 1967—, ACCNY.

42. Neuwien, *Catholic Schools in Action*, p. x, and Lieberman in the *Harvard Educational Review*, pp. 328–331.

43. Record of interview with Peter Rossi, June 26, 1964; memo of Frederick Jackson, July 10, 1964; report of Robert Cross, March 6, 1967; and report of Michael Schiltz, March 22, 1967, ND Education Study, 1964–1966 and 1967—, ACCNY.

44. Daniel Callahan, *Commentary* 43 (January 1967), pp. 81–83.

45. Ralph E. Weber, *Notre Dame's John Zahm* (Notre Dame, 1961), pp. 20–21.

46. Thomas T. McAvoy, C.S.C., *Father O'Hara of Notre Dame: The Cardinal-Archbishop of Philadelphia* (Notre Dame, 1967), pp. 9–16 and 67–77.

47. Philip S. Moore, C.S.C., *Academic Development, University of Notre Dame: Past, Present and Future* (Notre Dame, 1960), pp. 17–45.

48. Shuster to Benton, March 24, 1961, Box 2, ATPP-UNDA.

49. "Projected Latin American Program" (by Shuster), February 6, 1961, Box 2, ATPP-UNDA.

50. Shuster to Walter Nielsen of the Ford Foundation, May 18, 1961, Box 2, ATPP-UNDA. That same month he asked an opinion of the proposal from Director Allen Dulles of the C.I.A.; see Shuster to Dulles, May 18, 1961, Box 1, ATPP-UNDA.

51. William D'Antonio and Fredrick Pike to A. A. Berle, Jr., February 27, 1962; Shuster to Hesburgh, June 21, 1962; and Shuster to the Rockefeller Foundation, July 2, 1962, Box 4, ATPP-UNDA.

52. "Religion and Social Change in Latin America," program, April 22–24, 1963, Box 8, ATPP-UNDA.

53. The book, edited by William D'Antonio and Fredrick Pike, was published by Frederick A. Praeger in 1964. See reviews by Alfred Stepan in *The Commonweal* 81 (January 22, 1965), pp. 547–549; J. Lloyd Mecham in *The American Historical Review* 70 (July 1965), pp. 1264–1265; and Willard F. Barber in *The American Journal of Sociology* 71 (March 1966), pp. 562–563. See also Simon Hanson to Shuster, April 25, 1963, and Lois Carlisle to Shuster, April 26, 1963, Box 8, ATPP-UNDA.

54. Shuster to Hesburgh, June 27, 1963, Box 7, ATPP-UNDA.

55. Hesburgh to Verne Atwater of the Ford Foundation, March 31, 1964, Box 12; and Shuster to Hesburgh, January 4, 1965, Box 21, ATPP-UNDA.

56. "Short Account of the Triangle Seminar," Santiago, Chile, February 21–26, 1965, Box 21, and "Structure of the International Institute for Latin American Affairs (The Triangle)," Box 26, ATPP-UNDA.

57. *New York Times*, September 25, 1960: 1–1; April 8, 1962: 72–1; December 20, 1963: 34–6; and January 12, 1964: 95–4.

58. Shuster to Dr. Kenneth Thompson (Rockefeller Foundation), December 27, 1963; Shuster to J. George Harrar, May 11, 1964; and Flora M. Rhind to Hesburgh, May 27, 1964, Box 18, ATPP-UNDA.

59. *Kellogg Institute: The First Five Years* (Notre Dame, 1987), pp. 1–4.

60. "Notre Dame's Center for the Study of Man," *Notre Dame* 16 (Winter 1963), p. 3.

61. "The University of Notre Dame and the Study of Contemporary Society," July 1961, Box 1; "A Proposal to the W. K. Kellogg Foundation" (1962), Box 4; and Shuster to Hesburgh and Rev. Chester Soleta, C.S.C., March 27, 1961, Box 1, ATPP-UNDA.

62. Summary of Sessions: Conference on Religion and Education, June 15–17, 1962, and Paul Braisted of the Hazen Foundation to Shuster, January 15, 1962, Box 4; Shuster to John H. Neeson, Jr., October 30, 1961 and to Emily Schossberger, August 11, 1961, and Spellman to Shuster, March 28, 1961, Box 2; "Center Projects to Date" (1965), Box 19; Shuster to Humanities Grant Committee (Notre Dame), September 17, 1965, Box 20; Janet M. Paine of the Rockefeller Foundation to Hesburgh, March 23, 1961; Shuster to James Perkins of the Carnegie Corporation of New York, May 4, 1961; Shuster to Victor Ferkiss, February 7, 1961, Box 1; "Memorandum on the Subject of African Studies," November 17, 1966, Box 24; Shuster to Alexander

Aldrich, June 14, 1963, Box 6; Department of Health, Education, and Welfare, "Statement of Grant Award," May 1, 1964, Box 12; Office of Economic Opportunity, Community Action Program, "Statement of CAP Grant" (1965), Box 25; and Galileo Quatercentenary Congress, 1564–1964," Notre Dame, April 9–11, 1964, Box 12, ATPP-UNDA. See reviews in *Science* 162 (November 1, 1968), pp. 553–554, and *Scientific American* (November 1968), p. 164. The book was edited by Rev. Ernan McMullin and published by Basic Books in 1968.

63. See "Jacques Maritain Center" (Notre Dame), a brief publication available through the Maritain Center.

64. Shuster to Mrs. Henry Luce, January 24, 1961, Box 2; Shuster to Huntingdon Cairns of the National Gallery of Art, February 27, 1961, Box 1; and "The Maritain Center at Notre Dame," drafted by Shuster, Box 2, ATPP-UNDA. See Chapter 3 above for Shuster's years with *The Commonweal*.

65. "The Maritain Center at Notre Dame" (Shuster), and Maritain to Shuster, October 17, 1961, Box 2, ATPP-UNDA. For the decline of Thomism in the 1960s, see Philip Gleason, *Keeping the Faith* (Notre Dame, 1987), pp. 172–177.

66. Shuster to Maritain, October 26, 1961, Box 2, ATPP-UNDA.

67. Shuster to Hesburgh, August 5, 1963, and Shuster to Rev. John Walsh, C.S.C., November 27, 1963, Box 7, ATPP-UNDA.

68. Architectural drawings for the proposed institute are preserved in Box 29, ATPP-UNDA.

69. "By-Laws of the Institute for Advanced Religious Studies" (1967), Box 29, ATPP-UNDA.

70. Paul Hellmuth to Hesburgh, January 17, 1965, Box 19; Shuster to James Kritzeck, February 15, 1965, Box 18; and Philip Faccenda to Hesburgh, October 3, 1968, Box 34, ATPP-UNDA. See also *New York Times*, March 24, 1966: 20–8.

71. Shuster to Kritzeck, February 15, 1965, Box 18, and Hesburgh to Phalin, January 11, 1967, Box 29, ATPP-UNDA.

72. Shuster to Rev. Frank DeGraeve, S.J., September 16, 1967, Box 31; "Minutes of the Officers Meeting" (Notre Dame), October 9, 1968, Box 34; and Shuster to Professor Ernest Eliel, May 1, 1972, Box 49, ATPP-UNDA. Shuster's various fund-raising letters are preserved in Box 19, ATPP-UNDA.

73. Shuster to Canfield, July 24, 1962, Box 5, ATPP-UNDA. Canfield's letter to O'Brien, July 6, 1962, is in the same location.

74. Canfield to O'Brien, July 6, 1962; Canfield to Shuster, August 3, 1962; Frank W. Notestein to Shuster, October 18, 1962; and Shuster to O'Brien, August 16, 1962, Box 5, ATPP-UNDA.

75. List of Participants: Conference on Population Problems, January 11–12, 1963, and "Summary of the Conference on Population Problems" (Donald Barrett, Secretary), Box 9, ATPP-UNDA.

76. Shuster to Canfield, August 10, 1962, Box 5, ATPP-UNDA.

77. Shuster to Oscar Harkavy, June 5, 1963, and Robert Schmid to Hesburgh, August 19, 1963, Box 9, ATPP-UNDA.

78. List of conference participants and copies of papers delivered are in Box 9; see also Shuster to Harkavy, September 16, 1963, Box 8, ATPP-UNDA.

79. There had also been a conference in February 1964; Shuster to James M. Kilker, August 25, 1967, Box 28, ATPP-UNDA.

80. "Statement Prepared at the Third Conference of Population held at the University of Notre Dame, Notre Dame, Indiana, on March 17 to March 21, 1965," Box 20, ATPP-UNDA. This was the third conference sponsored by the Ford Foundation; this does not include the conference of early 1963, sponsored by the Population Council.

81. See, for example, William H. Shannon, *The Lively Debate: Response to Humanae Vitae* (New York, 1970), pp. 151–157.

82. Shuster to Henri do Riedmatten, March 22, 1965; John O'Brien to Cardinal Joseph Ritter, August 3, 1965; letter to Hesburgh, October 2, 1965, Box 20, ATPP-UNDA; and *New York Times* (International Edition), September 28, 1965: 1–3.

83. Night letter from Shuster, September 28, 1965, Box 20, ATPP-UNDA.

84. Shuster to Hesburgh, October 5, 1965, Box 20, ATPP-UNDA.

85. Joseph McDaniel to Hesburgh, July 7, 1965; Shuster to Rev. Felix Cardegna, S.J., October 27, 1965, and to William Liu, October 18, 1965, Box 20; Shuster to Donald Barrett, June 2, 1966, and "Family Conference Welcome," Box 25; and Shuster to Oscar Harkavy, March 10, 1969, Box 40, ATPP-UNDA. *Family and Fertility* was edited by William Liu and published by the University of Notre Dame Press in 1967.

86. Shuster to S. Edward Harwood, June 1, 1964, Box 14, ATPP-UNDA.

87. Elena Yu and William T. Liu, *Fertility and Kinship in the Philippines* (Notre Dame, 1980), pp. xi-xvi. See also Shuster to C. G. Snyder (of A.I.D.), September 3, 1968, and Shuster to Oscar Harkavy, September 18, 1968, Box 34; Shuster to Dr. Raymond B. Allen, December 18, 1969, Box 40; and Shuster to Liu, January 12, 1970, Box 45, ATPP-UNDA.

88. Shuster to John Wilkes (A.I.D.), January 15, 1965, and "University of Notre Dame, Office of Research Administrator: Notice of

Award," Box 18; Shuster to Rusk, October 26, 1967, and Shuster to Donald Barrett, December 11, 1967, Box 29, ATPP-UNDA.

89. Pope Paul VI, *Humanae Vitae,* esp. secs. 7–18.

90. *The Catholic Messenger,* August 29, 1968.

91. Draper to Hesburgh, November 5, 1968, Box 37; and Shuster to Thomas Carney, November 20, 1968, Box 35, ATPP-UNDA.

92. Shuster to Hesburgh, December 23, 1968, Box 34, ATPP-UNDA.

93. "Foundation for the Study of Human Reproduction," approximately December 22, 1968, Box 40, ATPP-UNDA.

94. Hesburgh to Cicognani, February 14, 1969, Box 40, ATPP-UNDA.

95. Shuster to Draper, July 8, 1969, Box 40, ATPP-UNDA.

96. Shuster to Draper, July 8, 1969, and September 12, 1969, Box 40; and Arthur McCormack to Hesburgh, December 17, 1970, Box 47, ATPP-UNDA.

97. Shuster to Rev. R. C. Hartnett, S.J., January 16, 1963, Box 9, ATPP-UNDA.

98. Shuster to Rev. Stanley E. Kutz, C.S.B., August 24, 1964, Box 14, ATPP-UNDA.

99. Shuster to Rev. Richard Teall, C.S.C., August 1, 1968, Box 38, ATPP-UNDA.

100. Shuster to Professor John Saunders, March 12, 1971, Box 48, ATPP-UNDA.

101. Shuster to Hesburgh, December 13, 1966, Box 23, ATPP-UNDA.

102. Shuster to James Michael Lee, October 20, 1966, Box 32, and to Victor Butterfield, October 17, 1966, Box 22, ATPP-UNDA.

103. Shuster to Oscar Harkavy, December 22, 1966, and to Mrs. Bernice L. Bernstein, same day, Box 23, ATPP-UNDA.

104. F. Centore to Shuster, May 25, 1972, and Shuster to Norbert Hruby, May 14, 1976, Box 49, ATPP-UNDA.

105. Shuster to Rev. George Nolan, S.J., October 10, 1968, Box 36; to Frank Altschul, October 24, 1969, Box 41; to John Moffitt, June 15, 1970, Box 44; and to Paul Braisted, March 2, 1970, Box 46, ATPP-UNDA.

106. Shuster to Hesburgh, December 13, 1966, Box 24, ATPP-UNDA. Box 29 contains correspondence over a possible successor in 1967.

107. Shuster to Hesburgh, August 24, 1967, and Hesburgh to Bartell, September 5, 1967, Box 29; Bartell to Shuster, February 21, 1969, and Rev. Ferdinand Brown, C.S.C., to Shuster, December 1,

1969, Box 39, ATPP-UNDA. Bartell resigned in the summer of 1971 in order to accept the position of president of Stonehill College in Massachusetts; Shuster to Oscar Harkavy, July 30, 1971, Box 47, ATPP-UNDA.

108. Hesburgh to Shuster, April 3, 1967, Box 29, ATPP-UNDA.

109. Shuster to Cleon Swayzee, April 5, 1962, Box 3; "Conference on the Condition of Western Man: The Problem of Freedom and Authority" (October 10–13, 1966), Box 32; Shuster to Richard Burke, November 3, 1966, Box 26; Shuster to Rev. John Walsh, C.S.C., December 6, 1966, Box 24; Shuster to Stephen Kertesz, September 13, 1967, Box 28; Shuster to Kenneth Thompson, May 23, 1967, Box 29; Shuster to Frederick DeW. Bolman, Jr., July 12, 1964, Box 12; Shuster to Walsh, December 23, 1965, Box 17; Box 5 contains correspondence with the University of Notre Dame Press; Shuster to Paul Hellmuth, April 15, 1963, Box 6; Shuster to Bernard Kohlbrenner, May 12, 1964, Box 14; "Minutes of the Organizational Meeting for the Establishment of a Local Phi Beta Kappa Chapter" (October 5, 1967), Box 30; "Itinerary for Father Joyce Panel," October, 1967, Box 31, ATPP-UNDA; and Final Report to the Trustees of the O'Brien Foundation, Notre Dame Printed Material, 40-CE-o4, UNDA.

110. *New York Times*, May 4, 1963: 12–2; and Shuster to Cavanaugh, June 3, 1963, Box 6, ATPP-UNDA.

111. The best review of Notre Dame in the 1960s is Hesburgh, *God, Country, Notre Dame*, especially pp. 106–131 and 170–188. See also Joel Connelly and Howard Dooley, *Hesburgh's Notre Dame* (New York, 1972).

112. "The Faculty Affairs Committee of the Board of Trustees: Statement of Purpose" (February 18, 1971), Box 47; see also Shuster to Hesburgh, September 15, 1967, Box 29, ATPP-UNDA.

113. Hesburgh, *God, Country, Notre Dame*, pp. 106–131; Lungren, *Hesburgh of Notre Dame*, pp. 41–47; and Connelly and Dooley, *Hesburgh's Notre Dame*.

114. Shuster to Sydney Hook, May 4, 1965, ATPP-UNDA.

115. "Statement of Policy on Student Life by Board of Trustees, University of Notre Dame," May 15, 1968, Box 35, ATPP-UNDA.

116. Shuster to Hesburgh, November 26, 1968, Box 33, ATPP-UNDA. See also Connelly and Dooley, *Hesburgh's Notre Dame*, and pertinent issues of the student newspaper, *The Observer*.

117. Shuster to James Plonka, March 17, 1965, Box 19; and Shuster to John Chesire, February 3, 1966, Box 24, ATPP-UNDA.

118. Shuster to Joseph Amter, September 8, 1965, Box 20, ATPP-UNDA.

119. Shuster to Rev. Raymond Bosler, July 25, 1966, Box 22, ATPP-UNDA.

120. Shuster to O'Gara, January 3, 1967, Box 28, ATPP-UNDA.

121. Shuster to Rev. Ferdinand Brown, C.S.C., May 21, 1969, Box 39, ATPP-UNDA.

122. Shuster to World University Service, February 18, 1970, Box 46, ATPP-UNDA.

123. "Why Not 'Chancellor' Hesburgh?," *Scholastic* 104 (February 22, 1963), pp. 7–8. The quotation is from p. 7.

124. "Concerning the University Administration," *Scholastic* 104 (March 1, 1963), pp. 7–8.

125. There was also a student movement in 1970 to replace Father Hesburgh as president with Professor Willis Nutting, but Shuster took little part in this short-lived controversy; Shuster to Hesburgh, May 20, 1970, Box 44, ATPP-UNDA.

126. Shuster to Rev. Edmund P. Joyce, C.S.C., February 3, 1967, Box 29, ATPP-UNDA, and *New York Times*, July 14, 1970: 27–5.

127. "Memorandum on the Attitude of the Administration of Notre Dame toward Problems of Student Life Currently under Discussion;" Shuster to Sheedy, March 19, 1968; and Shuster to Hesburgh, April 4, 1968, Box 35, ATPP-UNDA.

128. Information on the coeducational trend in the 1960s can be found in Robert Hassenger, ed., *The Shape of Catholic Higher Education* (Chicago, 1967), and Janet Lever and Pepper Schwartz, *Women at Yale* (Indianapolis, 1971). See also Kathy Ellis, "Through the Years," *Scholastic* 129 (September 17, 1987), pp. 6–9, and Andy Hilger, "Looking Both Ways," *Scholastic* 129 (February 4, 1988), pp. 17–19.

129. Document "To the Two Presidents" (by Sister Mary Grace, C.S.C., and Father Charles Sheedy, C.S.C.), January 22, 1965; Memorandum of Leo Corbaci, November 4, 1965; and Memorandum of Robert Waddick, May, 1966, Box 25, ATPP-UNDA. See also Sister Mary Immaculate Creek, C.S.C., *A Panorama: 1844–1977: Saint Mary's College, Notre Dame, Indiana* (Saint Mary's College, 1977), pp. 149–150; and Hesburgh, *God, Country, Notre Dame*, pp. 178–184.

130. Hesburgh to Shuster, April 29, and Shuster to Hesburgh, May 3, 1966, Box 25; and "A Memorandum Concerning Potential Relationships between St. Mary's College and Notre Dame University," Box 30, ATPP-UNDA.

131. Shuster to William D'Antonio, June 15; Sister Mary Grace, C.S.C., to Shuster, November 9; Shuster to Sister Mary Alma, C.S.C., November 15; and Shuster to D'Antonio, December 2, 1966, Box 25, ATPP-UNDA; a copy of the questionnaire is in File "Co-education,"

1965–1970" in the Public Relations and Information Office, Notre Dame; "Touchy About Merger," *Scholastic* 109 (April 14, 1967), pp. 12–13.

132. Shuster to Hesburgh, December 12, 1966, Box 23; "Notre Dame-St. Mary's Co-Exchange Committee Appointed by the respective Presidents;" F. L. Benton to Schuster [*sic*], October 10, 1966; and Minutes of Joint Co-Ex Committee, October 18, 1966, Box 25, ATPP-UNDA.

133. "Two-Way Street," *Scholastic* 109 (March 10, 1967), p. 23.

134. "A Memorandum Concerning Potential Relationships between St. Mary's College and Notre Dame University," Box 30, ATPP-UNDA.

135. Sister Mary Immaculate Creek, C.S.C., *A Panorama, 1844–1977*, pp. 156–158; National Catholic News Service (domestic) release, November 27, 1967, Box 30; Shuster to Hesburgh, December 12, 1966, Box 23; and Shuster to Msgr. William G. Ryan, December 22, 1967, Box 32, ATPP-UNDA.

136. Sister Mary Immaculate Creek, C.S.C., *A Panorama, 1844–1977*, pp. 164–166 and 198–199; "President's Newsletter," March, 1968, and *Chicago Tribune*, December 24, 1968, both in File "Co-Education, 1965–1970," Public Relations and Information Office, UND; McGrath to Hesburgh, March 4, 1969; Hesburgh to McGrath, March 4, 1969; and "St. Mary's College-University of Notre Dame: Joint Meeting," April 4, 1969, Box 41, ATPP-UNDA.

137. Sister Mary Immaculate Creek, C.S.C., *A Panorama, 1844–1977*, pp. 199–201; "Key Biscayne Statement," April 15, 1970, Box 45; "Minutes of the Board of Trustees: University of Notre Dame," May 14–15, 1971, Box 47, ATPP-UNDA; the Park-Mayhew Report of December 29, 1970, and a response of Fr. James Burtchaell, C.S.C., of February 24, 1971, are contained in File "Co-education, 1965–1970," Public Relations and Information Office, UND; and "Joint Policy Statement on Unification," May 14, 1971, Box 47, ATPP-UNDA.

138. Sister Mary Immaculate Creek, C.S.C., *A Panorama, 1844–1977*, p. 201, and Hesburgh, *God, Country, Notre Dame*, pp. 180–182.

139. Shuster to Edmund Stephan, December 2, 1971, Box 47, ATPP-UNDA. For Mrs. Shuster's tenure on Saint Mary's College Board of Associate Trustees, see Board of Associate Trustees Files, Saint Mary's College Archives.

140. Annual statistics available courtesy of the University of Notre Dame Archives.

11. ELDER STATESMAN

1. See Chapter 9 for Shuster's work for UNESCO, and Chapter 10 for his project for the American Council on Education.

2. Shuster to Mary Kersey Harvey, May 24, 1971, Box 48, ATPP-UNDA.

3. *New York Times*, February 18, 1965: 3–1; February 19, 1965: 3–2; February 20, 1965: 3–1; and February 21, 1965: 4–1; Harry S. Ashmore, *Unseasonable Truths: The Life of Robert Maynard Hutchins* (Boston, 1989), pp. 431–437; Hallock Hoffman to Board of Directors, December 12, 1963, Box 6; "Pacem in Terris" (program), February 18–20, 1965; Shuster to Dr. Leslie Paffrath, March 2, 1965; and Shuster to Hutchins, February 23, 1965, Box 20, ATPP-UNDA.

4. Mrs. Lecomte du Noüy to Shuster, March 21, 1961, Box 2; Shuster to du Noüy, October 29, 1962, Box 4; Shuster to du Noüy, April 22, 1966, and to Ernan McMullin, June 7, 1966, Box 23; du Noüy to Shuster, January 6, 1967, Box 30; Shuster to Ellen Lucey, March 16, 1970, Box 46; du Noüy to Shuster, November 20, 1972, Box 49, ATPP-UNDA; and Shuster and Ralph Thorson, eds., *Evolution in Perspective: Commentaries in Honor of Pierre Lecomte du Noüy* (Notre Dame, 1970).

5. Sidney Hyman, *The Lives of William Benton* (Chicago, 1969), pp. 241–296; and Ashmore, *Unseasonable Truths*, pp. 254–263 and 397–416.

6. Shuster to Hutchins, January 15, 1965, Box 18, ATPP-UNDA.

7. Shuster to Hutchins, September 6, 1966, Box 22, ATPP-UNDA.

8. Warren Preece to Shuster, January 19, 1961, and Warren Everote to Shuster, May 8, 1961, Box 1; Shuster to Preece, May 4, 1964, and Shuster to Mr. H. J. Joy, May 4, 1964, Box 12; Donald G. Hoffman to Shuster, March 8, 1965, and Shuster to Preece, June 1, 1965, Box 17; Preece to Shuster, May 23, 1966, Box 22; Benton to Shuster, April 12, 1967, Box 32; and Benton to Shuster, February 25, 1972, Box 49, ATPP-UNDA.

9. See Chapter 8 for Shuster's study of the Free University of Berlin.

10. Hesburgh to Rev. Laurence J. McGinley, S.J., November 8, 1963, Box 11, ATPP-UNDA; and memo of Verne S. Atwater to James Ivy, September 30, 1964, PA 62–324, Ford Foundation Archives.

11. Peter Fraenkel to Dr. Raul Deves, January 10, 1964, Box 11, ATPP-UNDA.

12. Shuster to MacGregor, February 27, July 23, August 27, October 14, and December 16, 1964; Hesburgh to MacGregor, March 23, 1964; Hesburgh to Dr. S. Dillon Ripley, April 17, 1964; Peter Fraenkel to Shuster, May 26, June 19, and July 27, 1964; Shuster to Fraenkel, July 10, 1964; Shuster to Hesburgh, July 23, 1964; and Shuster to Miss M. Meijer, October 14, 1964, Box 11, and Shuster to Hesburgh, January 31, 1964, Box 12, ATPP-UNDA.

13. A copy of this report is preserved in Box 16, ATPP-UNDA.

14. William H. Nims to MacGregor, August 17, 1965, Box 16; Shuster to Paul Hellmuth, October 11, 1965, Box 19; Shuster to James Frick, March 27, 1969, Box 42; and Shuster to MacGregor, April 1, 1970, Box 44, ATPP-UNDA; and William H. Nims to Hesburgh, August 17, 1965, PA 65–325, Ford Foundation Archives. See also Sam Zuckerman, "Public University in Peru Is Deteriorating, While Private Institution Flourishes Nearby," *The Chronicle of Higher Education* 34 (March 16, 1988), A40. In the summer of 1965 Shuster and two colleagues made a similar report for the Ford Foundation on the Pontifical Catholic University of Chile, and the foundation eventually awarded that university a grant of $49,054; PA 66–447, Ford Foundation Archives.

15. Charles A. Horsky to Shuster, September 28, 1963, Box 9, ATPP-UNDA.

16. Shuster to James Case, October 21, 1963; Case to Shuster, October 28 and November 7, 1963; and Minutes of Meeting of the President's Committee on Public Education in D. C., December 3–4, 1963, Box 9, ATPP-UNDA.

17. Basil Thornton to Shuster, January 3, 1962, Box 3; Shuster to Lee Harris, December 14, 1961, Box 1; Warren A. Kraetzer to Shuster, November 16, 1961, Box 2; Oscar M. Lazarus to Shuster, December 13, 1962, Box 5; Minutes of Meeting of Board of Directors of Golden Years Foundation, Inc., March 9, 1966, Box 23; Shuster to Victor Butterfield, October 1, 1968, Box 36; Leland Haworth to Shuster, May 19, 1967, Box 32; Minutes of Meetings of the Board of Directors of the Citizens' Scholarship Foundation of America, Box 11; M. J. Holahan to Shuster, March 7, 1962, Box 5; Shuster to Sam Reber, March 13, 1961, Box 1; Shuster to Christopher Emmet, February 18, 1963, Box 7; Norbert J. Hruby to Shuster, December 20, 1962, Box 4; Shuster to Rev. D. M. Burke, O.Praem., November 7, 1963, Box 9; Rev. Donald Lund, C.S.V., to Shuster, May 15, 1966, Box 27; Shuster to Rev. Baldwin Dworschak, O.S.B., January 15, 1962, Box 5; Shuster to James O'Gara, June 9, 1967, Box 28; and Robert Hoyt to Shuster, March 16, 1966, Box 26, ATPP-UNDA. Shuster was also on the boards of Science

and Arts Camps, Inc., Szabo Food Services, and Stanley Clark School in South Bend, and attempted to arrange a cooperative program between Notre Dame and the Priests' Association of the Archdiocese of Chicago to study ways of making the priests' pastoral ministry in the archdiocese more effective, but the project never materialized; correspondence is in Box 29, ATPP-UNDA.

18. "Of Gross Evil and a Man's Choice," *New York Times Book Review*, March 1, 1964; VII; p. 1ff.

19. Shuster to Rev. Robert Graham, S.J., November 7, 1963, Box 6, ATPP-UNDA.

20. Shuster to Edwin Clark, April 6, 1964, Box 12, ATPP-UNDA.

21. Pope Paul VI, *Humanae Vitae*, secs. 11, 17, and 28. Bishop Shannon's letter of September 23, 1968, was printed in the *National Catholic Reporter*, June 4, 1969. See also William H. Shannon, *The Lively Debate*: pp. 213–216.

22. The American bishops pastoral letter in support of the papal position that November was entitled *Human Life in Our Day; New York Times*, May 29, 1969: 21–1; and July 1, 1969: 20–4; Shuster to Hesburgh, June 6, 1969, Box 42, ATPP-UNDA.

23. A copy of this letter is preserved in Box 43, ATPP-UNDA.

24. Dearden to Shuster, June 27, 1969; Shuster to Mrs. John H. Mulliner, June 25, 1969; and Memo of Richard Conklin of July 15, 1969, "Additional Dearden letter names," Box 43, ATPP-UNDA.

25. *New York Times*, August 10, 1969: 1–7; August 11, 1969: 29–1; August 20, 1969: 28–1; Shuster to Dearden, July 15, 1969, Box 43, ATPP-UNDA; and "American Catholics Watch Their Hopeful Symbols Fade," *The Catholic Messenger*, September 4, 1969.

26. *Religion Behind the Iron Curtain* was published by Macmillan and *In Silence I Speak* by Farrar, Straus, and Cudahy. The 1961 edition of *The Ground I Walked On* was published by Farrar, Straus and Cudahy, and the 1969 edition by the University of Notre Dame Press; "The Trials and Triumphs of UNESCO," *Saturday Review* 45 (February 24, 1962), pp. 21ff; "The Cardinal Spellman Story," *Ave Maria* 95 (March 3, 1962), pp. 5ff; "Francis Cardinal Spellman," *Ave Maria* 107 (January 6, 1968), pp. 4–5; "Schools at the Crossroads," *The Atlantic Monthly* 210 (August 1962), pp. 95–100; "The School: Not Little and Red Any Longer," *Ave Maria* 97 (February 9, 1963), pp. 9–12; "So You Have Chosen the Teaching Profession," *The Catholic Educator* 34 (January 1964), pp. 451–452; "The Apostolate of the Laity and International Action," *Ave Maria* 103 (March 26, 1966), pp. 21ff; "Honesty in the Church," *America* 116 (April 1, 1967), pp. 498–499. Shuster's syndicated column appeared in the Davenport *Catholic*

Messenger, among others, from August 22, 1968 until December 4, 1969.

27. *Catholic Education in a Changing World* (New York, 1967). The quotation is from p. ix.

28. *Catholic Education in a Changing World,* pp. 55–74 and 88–93.

29. *Catholic Education in a Changing World,* pp. 48–59.

30. *Catholic Education in a Changing World,* pp. 74–87.

31. *Catholic Education in a Changing World,* pp. 59–69 and 168–236.

32. Drafts of this memoir, in Shuster's typing and his secretary's, are preserved in Box 20, SP-UNDA.

33. Elisa Zanetti to Doris, February 5, 1977, and Wilbur Miller to Doris, February 8, 1977, Box 19, SP-UNDA.

34. Interview with Robert Shuster, July 24–25, 1986.

35. *New York Times,* January 26, 1977: II, 6–4; "The Stanley Clark School Idea Campaign," Dinner Program, January 18, 1977; Lillian Corrigan to Doris, February 3, 1977; Elisa Zanetti to Doris, February 5, 1977; Henry Kellermann to Doris, March 14, 1977; and Robert Shuster to Hesburgh, June 3, 1977, Box 19, SP-UNDA.

36. Bernard and Elizabeth Cunningham to Doris, January 30, 1977, and "The Liturgy of Christian Burial in Memory, Thanksgiving and Prayer for Dr. George N. Shuster," January 28, 1977, Box 19, SP-UNDA.

37. *The Commonweal* 104 (February 18, 1977), pp. 100–101, and (March 18, 1977), p. 163; *Süddeutsche Zeitung,* February 7, 1977, p. 13; *Themen zur Zeit,* February 20, 1977, p. 2; Dr. H. C. Goppel, President of the Bavarian Land Federation, to Doris, January 31, 1977; Rev. Richard Teall, C.S.C., to Doris, February 7, 1977; and Father Placidus, O.S.B. (Max Jordan), to Doris, February 25, 1977, Box 19, SP-UNDA.

38. "George N. Shuster: Memorial Service," Church of St. Vincent Ferrer, New York, April 29, 1977, and Doctor Rees' "Eulogy for George Nauman Shuster," Box 19, SP-UNDA.

39. "Eulogy for George Nauman Shuster," January 28, 1977, General Pamphlet Collection, UNDA. Because of the wintry blizzard, no graveside service was held after the Funeral Mass on January 28. Later that spring, on May 14, a second Mass was offered and Father Hesburgh conducted a brief graveside service. Hesburgh to Doris, April 13, 1977, and Msgr. John J. Egan to Doris, April 21, 1977, Box 19, SP-UNDA.

40. *The Ground I Walked On* (Notre Dame, 1969), p. 23.

41. "Report of the Evaluation of Hunter College, New York, New York, by the Middle States Association of Colleges and Secondary Schools, Commission on Institutions of Higher Learning, March 11–14, 1956," File 13, Hunter 108.000, BHECF.

42. Excellent recent studies of the American Catholic tradition are Patrick W. Carey, ed., *American Catholic Religious Thought* (New York, 1987), pp. 3–70; Philip Gleason, *Keeping the Faith* (Notre Dame, 1987); and Margaret Mary Reher, *Catholic Intellectual Life in America* (New York, 1989).

SELECTED BIBLIOGRAPHY

An exhaustive bibliography of the life and work of George Shuster would not be feasible in a book of this size—his own book reviews in *The Commonweal* from 1924 to 1938 numbered more than four hundred. This bibliographical essay, therefore, will include only Shuster's most significant writings, the various archive and manuscript collections consulted, and those secondary works found most pertinent to this particular study.

Shuster's Own Writings

Even a selective listing of Shuster's writings is extraordinary. His most revealing autobiographical publications are his "Spiritual Autobiography," in Louis Finkelstein, editor, *American Spiritual Autobiographies* (New York: Harper and Brothers, 1948), pp. 25–37; *The Ground I Walked On*, second edition (Notre Dame, Ind.: University of Notre Dame Press, 1969); and "An Autobiography," in Robert J. Havighurst, editor, *Leaders in American Education* (Chicago: The National Society for the Study of Education, 1971), pp. 277–303. Shuster discussed his experience in World War I in "The Final Word," *Orate Fratres* 3 (March 1929), pp. 150–154.

Shuster's own academic discipline was English and comparative literature, and many of his earliest writings were in literary criticism: "The Tragedy of Mark Twain," *The Catholic World* 104 (March 1917), pp. 731–737; "Our Poets in the Streets," *The Catholic World* 105 (July 1917), pp. 433–445; "Joris Karl Huysmans: Egoist and Mystic," *The Catholic World* 113 (July 1921), pp. 452–464; "The Surrender of Robert Louis Stevenson," *The Catholic World* 120 (October 1924), pp. 89–95; "Newer Catholic Poets," *The Catholic World* 122 (December 1925), pp. 314–319; "Thomas Hardy" *The Catholic World* 126 (March 1928), pp. 721–729; "Patmore: A Revaluation," *The Commonweal* 24 (October 23, 1936), pp. 604–606; and "Thoughts on Francis Thompson," *The Commonweal* 25 (February 12, 1937), pp. 431–433. Shuster's most scholarly work was his doctoral dissertation, *The English Ode from Milton to Keats* (New York: Columbia University Press, 1940). He also published one full-length novel, *Look Away!* (New York: Macmillan, 1939), and two shorter creative pieces, *The Hill of Happiness* (New York: Appleton, 1926), and *Brother Flo: An Imaginative Biography* (New York: Macmillan, 1938).

Shuster was probably best known as a Catholic publicist. Several of his early works, in addition to numerous unsigned editorials in *The Commonweal*, emphasized the contributions of Catholics to American and world culture: "The Retreat of the American Novel," *The Catholic World* 106 (November 1917), pp. 166–178; "The American Spirit," *The Catholic World* 114 (October 1921), pp. 1–13; *The Catholic Spirit in Modern English Literature* (New York: Macmillan, 1922); *The Catholic Spirit in America* (New York: Dial Press, 1927); and "Captains of the Modern Soul," *The Commonweal* 9 (March 20, 1929), pp. 563–565. "Catholic Culture in America," *Today* 8 (March, 1953), pp. 12–13, echoed the same theme. Other works were written to defend the church from outside attack: "The Catholic Here and Now," *The Outlook* 148 (February 29, 1928), pp. 336ff; "The Catholic Conspiracy Myth," *Outlook and Independent* 150 (November 7, 1928), pp. 1102ff; "A Catholic Defends His Church," *The New Republic* 97 (January 4, 1939), pp. 246–248; "Christianity in This Hour," *Survey Graphic* 28 (February 1939), pp. 137ff; and "The Catholic Controversy," *Harper's Magazine* 199 (November 1949), pp. 25–32. Other articles addressed internal Catholic concerns: "Opportunities for the Educated Layman," *Catholic Action* 14 (June 1932), pp. 5–6; "Catholics and Other People," *The American Scholar* 6 (Summer 1937), pp. 282–293; "The Conflict Among Catholics," *The American Scholar* 10 (Winter 1940–41), pp. 5–16; and "Honesty in the Church," *America* 116 (April 1, 1967), pp. 498–499. Shuster also contributed introductions for new editions of Catholic classics: *Newman: Prose and Poetry* (Boston: Allyn and Bacon, 1925); John Henry Newman, *The Idea of a University* (Garden City, N.Y.: Image Books, 1959); and *The Confessions of St. Augustine* (New York: Heritage Press, 1963).

Shuster's major writings on Catholic education included "Have We Any Scholars?'" *America* 33 (August 15, 1925), pp. 418–419; "Insulated Catholics," *The Commonweal* 2 (August 19, 1925), pp. 337–338; "Schools at the Crossroads," *Atlantic Monthly* 210 (August 1962), pp. 95–100; "The School: Not Little and Red Any Longer," *Ave Maria* 97 (February 9, 1963), pp. 9–12; "So You Have Chosen the Teaching Profession," *The Catholic Educator* 34 (January 1964), pp. 451–452; "Religion and Education," *The Commonweal* 79 (January 31,

1964), pp. 504–507; "Catholic Education Once More," *The Catholic World* 201 (April 1965), pp. 50–54; and *Catholic Education in a Changing World* (New York: Holt, Rinehart and Winston, 1967). His major writings on education in general were "Education and Journalism," *Catholic Educational Review* 31 (February 1933), pp. 65–71; "Education and Religion: The Making of a Rounded Individual," *The Saturday Review of Literature* 27 (September 1944), pp. 26–30; "Education's New Responsibility," *Survey Graphic* 36 (November 1947), pp. 569–572; "Academic Freedom," *The Commonweal* 58 (April 10, 1953), pp. 11–13; "The New Schoolboy's Shining Face," *The American Scholar* 25 (Winter 1955–56), pp. 69–79; "Recipe for Learning," *Today* 12 (November 1956), pp. 32–34; "What Is Education" *Daedalus* 88 (Winter 1959), pp. 25–39; "Of What Use Are Poets," *Ave Maria* 92 (September 10, 1960), pp. 9–11; "Goals of American Education," *Current History* 41 (July 1961), pp. 1–4; and "American Scholarship: Nostalgia and Prediction," *Review of Politics* 31 (October 1969), pp. 436–441. Insights into Shuster's own Christian Humanism can be gotten from "The High Lights of Humanism," *The Commonweal* 9 (April 17, 1929), pp. 674–675; "The Several Humanists," *The Commonweal* 11 (April 2, 1930), pp. 613–615; "The Legacy of Plato," *The Commonweal* 15 (January 13, 1932), pp. 289–291; and "Greek Tradition," *The Commonweal* 38 (September 10, 1943), pp. 509–513. Some of Shuster's best writings and addresses on education were collected in *Education and Moral Wisdom* (New York: Harper and Brothers, 1960).

Shuster wrote widely in the 1930s on the deteriorating political and economic conditions in Europe, the rise of Adolf Hitler, and the evils of Germany's Nazi government. There were three full-length books: *The Germans: An Inquiry and an Estimate* (New York: Dial Press, 1932); *Strong Man Rules* (New York: D. Appleton-Century, 1934); and *Like a Mighty Army: Hitler versus Established Religion* (New York: D. Appleton-Century, 1935). Several articles were the result of personal visits and experiences in Europe: "Germany at Low Tide," *The Commonweal* 13 (November 19, 1930), pp. 70–71; "Il Duce's Handkerchief," *The Commonweal* 13 (December 3, 1930), pp. 131–132; "War Clouds Over Europe," *The Commonweal* 13 (December 10, 1930), pp. 149–150; "Berlin," *The Commonweal* 13 (December 17, 1930), pp. 183–185; "Europe's Windiest Corner," *The Commonweal* 13 (December 24, 1930), pp. 209–211; "Geneva Once Again," *The Commonweal* 13 (January 21, 1931), pp. 320–321; "Munich: Anno Domini 1931," *The Commonweal* 13 (March 11, 1931), pp. 511–513; "Austria As One Finds It," *The Commonweal* 13 (March 25, 1931), pp. 570–572; "Twilight in the Third Reich," *The Commonweal* 27 (February 4, 1938), pp. 397–399;

and "Terror in Vienna," *The Commonweal* 27 (April 15, 1938), pp. 678–680. Shuster discussed the Catholic church in Germany in "The Church in Germany," *The Homiletic and Pastoral Review* 31 (August 1931), pp. 1155–1161; "Problems of the Church in Germany," *The Homiletic and Pastoral Review* 31 (September 1931), pp. 1259–1265; "Germany Under the Concordat," *The Commonweal* 18 (September 1, 1933), pp. 420–422; "Days in Beuron," *The Commonweal* 19 (November 10, 1933), pp. 43–45; and "Catholic Resistance in Nazi Germany," *Thought* 22 (March 1947), pp. 12–15. Heinrich Bruening was the subject of "A Talk with Chancellor Bruening," *The Commonweal* 13 (April 15, 1931), pp. 659–661; "The Man Who Might Have Saved Europe," *The Catholic World* 145 (July 1937), pp. 420–426; and "Dr. Bruening's Sejourn [*sic*] in the United States (1935–1945)," in Ferdinand Hermens and Theodor Schieder, *Staat, Wirtschaft und Politik in der Weimarer Republik* (Berlin: Duncker and Humblot, 1967), pp. 449–466. Two other pertinent works were "The Jew and Two Revolutions," *The Commonweal* 29 (December 30, 1938), pp. 262–264, and, with Arnold Bergstraesser, *Germany: A Short History* (New York: W. W. Norton, 1944). Shuster also contributed notes for an edition of Hitler's *Mein Kampf* (New York: Reynal and Hitchcock, 1939).

Shuster's two major writings on General Franco and the Spanish Civil War were "Some Reflections on Spain," *The Commonweal* 25 (April 2, 1937), pp. 625–627, and "Some Further Reflections," *The Commonweal* 25 (April 23, 1937), pp. 716–717.

Shuster's thoughts on the reconstruction of postwar Germany are contained in "The Challenge of the Future World," *Vital Speeches* 9 (July 1, 1943), pp. 555–559; "Our Relations with Germany," *Foreign Policy Reports* 19 (October 15, 1943), pp. 198–201; "The Yalta Divison of Germany," *Vital Speeches* 11 (April 15, 1945), pp. 403–405; "The Hangings at Nuremberg," *The Commonweal* 45 (November 15, 1946), pp. 110–111; "Should Germany Have a Centralized Government? Yes," *The Sign* 26 (March 1947), pp. 30ff; "German Reeducation: Success or Failure," *Proceedings of the Academy of Political Science* 23 (1948–1950), pp. 232–238; and "Objective: Friendship," *Information Bulletin* (Office of U.S. High Commissioner for Germany, September, 1950), p. 50.

Three of Shuster's writngs on UNESCO were "Implications of UNESCO for the N.C.E.A.," *Bulletin of the National Catholic Educational Association* 44 (August 1947), pp. 242–248; "The Trials and Triumphs of UNESCO," *Saturday Review* 45 (February 24, 1962), pp. 21ff; and *UNESCO: Assessment and Promise* (New York: Harper and Row for the Council on Foreign Relations, 1963).

Other significant writings of Shuster, less easy to categorize, are "The Mood for Peace," *The Catholic World* 115 (May 1922), pp.

184–194; "Shall We Ban Child Labor?," *The Commonweal* 19 (April 6, 1934), pp. 623–624; "Radio Sky Pilot," *Review of Reviews* 91 (April 1935), pp. 23ff; "Gen. Sherrill and the Olympics," *The Commonweal* 23 (November 8, 1935), pp. 40–42; "Answer to Senator Nye," *The Commonweal* 34 (October 17, 1941), pp. 609–611; *Religion Behind the Iron Curtain* (New York: Macmillan, 1954); *In Silence I Speak* (New York: Farrar, Straus, and Cudahy, 1956); and "Notre Dame's Center for the Study of Man," *Notre Dame* 16 (Winter 1963), pp. 3ff.

Archives and Manuscripts

Manuscript sources for a study of Shuster's life and work are abundant. The most important collections are the Shuster Personal Papers and the Assistant to the President Papers in the University of Notre Dame Archives. For Shuster's ancestry and Wisconsin background, the Marriage Registration and Federal Census Records in the Library Divison, State Historical Society of Wisconsin at Madison are helpful.

The most useful collections for Shuster's *Commonweal* years and the history of American Catholicism are: Correspondence in the Archives of the United States Catholic Conference, Washington, D.C.; Peter Guilday Papers, John A. Ryan Papers, and Rectors' Papers in the Department of Archives and Manuscripts of the Catholic University of America, Washington, D.C.; Gallery of Living Catholic Authors Papers, John LaFarge, S.J., Papers, Theodore Maynard Papers, and *America* Papers in the Special Collections Divison of the Georgetown University Library, Washington, D.C.; John J. Raskob Papers in the Hagley Museum and Library, Wilmington, Del.; and Riggs Family Papers in the Manuscript Divison of the Library of Congress. Material on Shuster's years at Notre Dame can be found in Daniel Hudson, C.S.C., Papers, John Talbot Smith Papers, James A. Burns, C.S.C., Personal and Presidential Papers, John W. Cavanaugh, C.S.C., Personal and Presidential Papers, Matthew Walsh, C.S.C., Personal and Presidential Papers, Charles O'Donnell, C.S.C., Personal and Presidential Papers, and Notre Dame Printed Material, all in the University of Notre Dame Archives, and the files of the Public Relations and Information Office of the University of Notre Dame. Information on Doris Shuster is available in the Saint Mary's College Archives.

Important manuscript sources for the study of Shuster's work at Hunter College and in New York are the Shuster Papers and the *Hunter Arrow* and *Hunter Bulletin* in the Hunter College Archives, New York; Central Files in the Board of Higher Education of the City of New York Archives; President's Personal File and Eleanor Roosevelt Papers in the

Franklin D. Roosevelt Library, Hyde Park, New York; Nicholas Murray Butler Papers, Harry J. Carman Papers, Carlton J. H. Hayes Papers, Special and General Manuscript Library of Columbia University, New York; the Office of the Secretary and the Department of English and Comparative Literature of Columbia University; Oral History Reminiscences of Harry James Carman, Harry Gideonse, Pearl Max, Ordway Tead, John Theobald, and Charles H. Tuttle in the Oral History Research Office of Columbia University; and the John Meng Papers in the Special Collections Division of the Georgetown University Library.

Shuster's government work is documented in Record Group 59, Department of State Decimal File; R.G. 165, War Department General and Specific Staffs File; and R.G. 466, Records of the U.S. High Commissioner for Germany, National Archives and Records Service; Waldo Leland Papers, Archibald MacLeish Papers, and Reinhold Niebuhr Papers in the Manuscript Division of the Library of Congress; E. Franklin Frazier Papers and the NAACP-DC Branch Papers in the Moorland-Spingard Research Center of Howard University, Washington, D.C.; Mark Wayne Clark Papers in the Citadel Archives, South Carolina; Chester Bowles Papers in the Sterling Memorial Library of Yale University; Cardinal Aloisius Muench Papers in the Department of Archives and Manuscripts of the Catholic University of America; and Oral History Reminiscences of Chester Bowles, Benjamin J. Buttenwieser, and Luther Evans in the Oral History Research Office of Columbia University. Further involvement in German-American relations is documented in the Christopher Emmet Papers in the Hoover Institution Archives, Stanford, California, and H. A. Reinhold Papers in the Boston College Library.

Sources for the study of Shuster's relations with philanthropic foundations are Columbia University File, Hunter College File, Institution of International Education File, Fund for the Republic File, UNESCO File, and University of Notre Dame File in the Archives of the Carnegie Corporation of New York; Series 200, R.G. 2, United States, and R.G. 1.2, Hunter College in the Rockefeller Archive Center, North Tarrytown, New York; and General Correspondence File and Grant File in the Ford Foundation Archives, New York.

Other worthwhile manuscript sources are the Archives of the American Council on Education (now housed at Stanford University); *American Scholar* Papers in the Manuscript Division of the Library of Congress; Robert M. Hutchins Papers and Commission on Freedom of the Press Collection in the Department of Special Collections of the Joseph Regenstein Library of the University of Chicago; Van Wyck Brooks Papers in the Department of Special Collections of the Van Pelt

Library of the University of Pennsylvania, Philadelphia; Fund for the Republic Papers in the Princeton University Archives, New Jersey; George N. Shuster File at the Federal Bureau of Investigation; Official File, General File, and President's Personal File in the Dwight D. Eisenhower Library, Abilene, Kansas; WHCF Name File, Douglas Cater File, and Office Files of John Macy in the Lyndon B. Johnson Library, Austin, Texas; and Harry S. Truman Official File and General File in the Harry S. Truman Library, Independence, Missouri.

Secondary Sources

There are several brief biographical studies of George Shuster. The two most accessible are "George N. Shuster," *Current Biography Yearbook, 1960* (New York: H. W. Wilson, 1960), pp. 378–380, and "George Nauman Shuster," *The National Cyclopaedia of American Biography*, vol. H, (New York: James T. White, 1952), pp. 89–90. Longer studies are Vincent P. Lannie, "George N. Shuster: A Reflective Evaluation," in *Leaders in American Education* (Chicago: The National Society for the Study of Education, 1971), pp. 306–320, and Frederike Maria Zweig, *Greatness Revisited*, edited by Harry Zohn (Boston: Branden Press, 1971), pp. 105–126. More specialized are Thomas E. Blantz, C.S.C., "George N. Shuster and American Catholic Intellectual Life," in Nelson Minnich et al., editors, *Studies in Catholic History* (Wilmington, Del.: Michael Glazier, 1985), pp. 345–365; Lorraine Goverman, "Presidential Profile: Dr. George Nauman Shuster," *Echo* (Hunter College: Winter, 1944), pp. 10–14; Mary McGinnis, "The Gentleman from Indiana," *Loria* 2 (November 1924), pp. 10–13; and Barry D. Riccio, "American Catholic Thought in the Nineteen Twenties: Frederick Joseph Kinsman and George Shuster," in David J. Alvarez, editor, *An American Church* (Morago, Calif.: Saint Mary's College of California, 1979), pp. 113–123. See also Mina S. Rees, "Dr. George N. Shuster: An Appreciation and a Salute," *Alumni News* (Hunter College) 64 (May 1959), p. 2.

Good studies of Wisconsin during Shuster's early years are Herbert F. Margulies, *The Decline of the Progressive Movement in Wisconsin, 1890–1920* (Madison: State Historical Society of Wisconsin, 1968); Robert S. Maxwell, *LaFollette and the Rise of the Progressives in Wisconsin* (Madison: State Historical Society of Wisconsin, 1956); George E. Mowry, *The Era of Theodore Roosevelt* (New York: Harper and Row, 1958); and William Francis Raney, *Wisconsin: A Story of Progress* (New York: Prentice-Hall, 1940). Grant County is described in C. M. Foote and J. W. Henion, *Plat Book of Grant County, Wisconsin* (Minneapolis:

C. M. Foote and Co., 1895); Castello N. Hofford, *History of Grant County, Wisconsin* (Reprinted: Marceline, Mo.: Walsworth Publishing, 1976), and Resource Committee of Grant County, *Grant County History, 1900–1976* (Lancaster, Wis., 1976). For the Capuchin Order in the United States and St. Lawrence College, see Celestine N. Bittle, O.M.Cap., *A Romance of Lady Poverty* (Milwaukee: Bruce, 1933); P. Corbinian, O.M.Cap., *The Laurentianum: Its Origin and Work (1864–1924)*, (Mt. Calvary, Wis., 1924); and *The Rise and Progress of the Province of St. Joseph of the Capuchin Order in the United States. 1857–1907* (New York: Benziger Brothers, 1907). Worthwhile works on the background of Shuster's Christian Humanism are Herbert A. Deane, *The Political and Social Ideas of St. Augustine* (New York: Columbia University Press, 1963); Paul Henry, S.J., *Saint Augustine on Personality* (New York: Macmillan, 1960); Alfred Warren Matthews, *The Development of St. Augustine: From Neoplatonism to Christianity, 386–391* (Washington: University Press of America, 1980); F. Melian Stawell and G. Lowes Dickinson, *Goethe and Faust* (New York: Dial Press, 1929); P. Franklin Chambers, *Baron von Huegel: Man of God* (London: G. Bles, 1945); Algar Thorold, editor, *Readings from Friedrich von Huegel* (London: J. M. Dent and Sons, 1928); and Friedrich von Huegel, "Experience and Transcendence," *The Dublin Review* 138 (April 1906), pp. 357–379.

Works on twentieth century American Catholicism abound. The best of the more general histories are Jay P. Dolan, *The American Catholic Experience* (Garden City, N.Y.: Doubleday, 1985); John Tracy Ellis, *American Catholicism* (Garden City, N.Y.: Image Books, 1965); Patrick W. Carey, editor, *American Catholic Religious Thought* (New York: Paulist Press, 1987); Philip Gleason, *Keeping the Faith* (Notre Dame, Ind.: University of Notre Dame Press, 1987); James Hennesey, S.J., *American Catholics* (New York: Oxford University Press, 1981); and Thomas T. McAvoy, C.S.C., *A History of the Catholic Church in the United States* (Notre Dame, Ind.: University of Notre Dame Press, 1969). For American Catholicism since World War I, see George Q. Flynn, *American Catholics and the Roosevelt Presidency* (Lexington: University of Kentucky Press, 1968), and *Roosevelt and Romanism* (Westport, Conn.: Greenwood Press, 1976); Robert I. Gannon, S.J., *The Cardinal Spellman Story* (Garden City, N.Y.: Doubleday, 1962); William M. Halsey, *The Survival of American Innocence* (Notre Dame, Ind.: University of Notre Dame Press, 1980); Elizabeth McKeown, "War and Welfare: A Study of American Catholic Leadership" (Ph.D. dissertation, University of Chicago, 1972); Joseph M. McShane, S.J., *"Sufficiently Radical:" Catholicism, Progressivism, and the Bishops' Program of 1919* (Washington: Catholic University of America Press, 1986); and

David J. O'Brien, *The Renewal of American Catholicism* (New York: Paulist Press, 1972). For a negative view of Catholicism in the 1930s, see George Seldes, "Catholics and Fascists," *The New Republic* 97 (November 9, 1938), pp. 6–9. Catholic social teachings are presented well in Aaron I. Abell, *American Catholicism and Social Action* (Notre Dame, Ind.: University of Notre Dame Press, 1963); David J. O'Brien, *American Catholics and Social Reform* (New York: Oxford University Press, 1968); and John A. Ryan, *Social Doctrine in Action* (New York: Harper and Brothers, 1941). Valuable studies of American Catholic intellectual life include Paul R. Messbarger, "The Failed Promise of American Catholic Literature," *U.S. Catholic Historian*, vol. 4, no. 2 (1985), pp. 143–158; Margaret Mary Reher, *Catholic Intellectual Life in America* (New York: Macmillan, 1989); Donald A. Romito, "Catholics and Humanists: Aspects of the Debate in Twentieth Century American Criticism" (Ph.D. dissertation, Emory University, 1976); Michael A. Schuler, "Religious Humanism in Twentieth Century American Thought" (Ph.D. dissertation, Florida State University, 1982); and Arnold J. Sparr, "The Catholic Literary Revivial in America, 1920–1960" (Ph.D. dissertation, University of Wisconsin-Madison, 1985). Other helpful studies include David M. Chambers, *Hooded Americanism: The History of the Ku Klux Klan*, second edition (New York: New Viewpoints, 1965); George Barry Ford, *A Degree of Difference* (New York: Farrar, Straus and Giroux, 1969); Raphael Huber, O.F.M. Conv., editor, *Our Bishops Speak* (Milwaukee: Bruce, 1952); Donald Kinzer, *An Episode in Anti-Catholicism: The American Protective Association* (Seattle: University of Washington Press, 1964); Paul Marx, O.S.B., *The Life and Work of Virgil Michel* (Washington: Catholic University of America Press, 1957); and William H. Shannon, *The Lively Debate: Response to Humanae Vitae* (New York: Sheed and Ward, 1970).

Shuster's years at *Commonweal* are discussed in Martin J. Bredeck, S.J., "The Role of the Catholic Layman in the Church and American Society as Seen in the Editorials of *Commonweal* Magazine" (Ph.D. dissertation, Catholic University of America, 1977); Paul E. Czuchlewski, "The Commonweal Catholic: 1924–1960" (Ph.D. dissertation, Yale University, 1972); Robert B. Clements, "The *Commonweal*, 1924–1938: The Williams-Shuster Years" (Ph.D. dissertation, University of Notre Dame, 1972); Dorothy Day, *The Long Loneliness* (New York: Harper and Row, 1952); Rodger Van Allen, *The Commonweal and American Catholicism* (Philadelphia: Fortress Press, 1974); and Michael Williams, *The Book of the High Romance* (New York: Macmillan, 1924), and *The Present Position of Catholics in the United States* (New York: Calvert Publishing Corporation, 1928). Lawrence B. DeSaulniers, *The Response in American Catholic Periodicals to the Crisis of the Great Depression,*

1930–1935 (Lanham, Md.: University Press of America, 1984), surveys the wider Catholic press during this period, and Michael J. Cantley, *A City with Foundations: A History of the Seminary of the Immaculate Conception, 1930–1980* (No date or publisher), describes the seminary where Shuster taught. For the controversy over the Spanish Civil War, see Burnett Bottoten, *The Spanish Revolution* (Chapel Hill: University of North Carolina Press, 1979); Raymond Carr, *The Spanish Tragedy* (London: Weidenfeld and Nicolson, 1977); Robert M. Darrow, "Catholic Political Power: A Study of the Activities of the American Catholic Church on Behalf of Franco During the Spanish Civil War, 1936–1939" (Ph.D. dissertation, Columbia University, 1953); Francis X. Talbot, S.J., "In Answer to Some Reflections on the Spanish Situation," *America* 57 (April 10, 1937), pp. 9–10; Hugh Thomas, *The Spanish Civil War*, revised and enlarged edition (New York: Harper and Row, 1977); and J. David Valaik, "American Catholic Dissenters and the Spanish Civil War," *The Catholic Historical Review* 53 (January 1968), pp. 537–555.

Informative works on Germany before World War II and German-American relations include Andreas Dorpalen, *Hindenburg and the Weimar Republic* (Princeton, N.J.: Princeton University Press, 1964); Ellen Lovell Evans, *The German Center Party, 1870–1933* (Carbondale: Southern Illinois University Press, 1981); Erich Eyck, *A History of the Weimar Republic*, two vols., translated by Harlan P. Hanson and Robert G.L. Waite, (Cambridge, Mass.: Harvard University Press, 1962–1963); Robert E. Herzstein, *Roosevelt and Hitler: Prelude to War* (New York: Paragon House, 1989); Hajo Holborn, *A History of Modern Germany*, vol. 3 (New York: Knopf, 1969); Nora Levin, *The Holocaust Years* (Malabar, Fla.: Robert E. Krieger, 1990); La Vern J. Rippley, *The German-Americans* (Boston: Twayne, 1976); Godfrey Scheele, *The Weimar Republic* (London: Faber and Faber, 1946); and Eliot Barculo Wheaton, *Prelude to Calamity: The Nazi Revolution, 1933–1935* (Garden City, N.Y.: Doubleday, 1968). Lillian Parker Wallace, *The Papacy and European Diplomacy, 1869–1879* (Chapel Hill: University of North Carolina Press, 1948), and John Zeender, "The Genesis of the German Concordat of 1933," in Nelson Minnich et al., editors, *Studies in Catholic History* (Wilmington, Del.: Michael Glazier, 1985), pp. 617–665, focus on Catholic issues. For Rev. H. A. Reinhold, see Joel Patrick Garner, "The Vision of a Liturgical Reformer: Hans Ansgar Reinhold, American Catholic Educator" (Ph.D. dissertation, Columbia University, 1972), and Reinhold, *H.A.R.: The Autobiography of Father Reinhold* (New York: Herder and Herder, 1968).

Important works on Hunter College include Mae A. Burns, "An Historical Background and Philosophical Criticism of the Curriculum of

Hunter College of the City of New York from 1870 to 1938" (Ph.D. dissertation, Fordham University, 1938); Broadus Mitchell, "Witch Hunt at Hunter: Triumph of the Primitives," *The Nation* 179 (November 6, 1954), pp. 401–403; Lewis Mumford, "The Sky Line: Skyscraper School," *The New Yorker* 16 (November 16, 1940), pp. 84–86; Samuel White Patterson, *Hunter College: Eighty-five Years of Service* (New York: Lantern Press, 1955); *Thousands of Lives* (New York: Hunter College, 1943); Ruth G. Weintraub and Ruth E. Salley, "Hunter College Reports on its Veterans," *School and Society* 68 (July 24, 1948), pp. 59–63: and June A. Willenz, *Women Veterans* (New York: Continuum, 1983). Hunter College elementary school is discussed in Florence Brumbaugh, "A School for Gifted Children," *Childhood Education* 20 (1943–44), pp. 325–327; Gertrude Howell Hildreth, *Educating Gifted Children* (New York: Harper and Row, 1952); and Catherine Mackensie, "Our Youngest Intellectuals," *New York Times*, October 5, 1941: VII-14. The Communist controversy is explored in Donald F. Crosby, S.J., *God, Church, and Flag: Senator Joseph R. McCarthy and the Catholic Church* (Chapel Hill: University of North Carolina Press, 1978); Richard M. Fried, *Men Against McCarthy* (New York: Columbia University Press, 1976); David R. Holmes, *Stalking the Academic Communist* (Hanover, N.H.: University Press of New England for the University of Vermont, 1989); Earl Latham, *The Communist Controversy in Washington* (New York: Atheneum, 1969); and Ellen W. Schrecker, *No Ivory Tower* (New York: Oxford University Press, 1986). John J. O'Connor, *Polytechnic Institute of Brooklyn, An Account of the Educational Purposes and Development of the Institute during its first Century* (Brooklyn, 1956), traces the history of that institution. Shuster's doctoral dissertation is noted by both Paul H. Fry, *The Poet's Calling in the English Ode* (New Haven: Yale University Press, 1980), and John D. Jump, *The Ode* (London: Methuen, 1974).

Writings on post–World War II Germany and the American occupation are most extensive. Some of the most helpful for this study were Dean Acheson, "The Illusion of Disengagement," *Foreign Affairs* 36 (April 1958), pp. 371–383; Colman J. Barry, O.S.B., *American Nuncio* (Collegeville, Minn.: Saint John's University Press, 1969); Lucius D. Clay, *Decision in Germany* (Garden City, N.Y.: Doubleday, 1950); Carolyn Eisenberg, "U. S. Policy in Post-War Germany: The Conservative Restoration," *Science and Society* 46 (Spring 1982), pp. 24–38; Ladislas Farago, *Patton: Ordeal and Triumph* (New York: I. Obolensky, 1963); J.F.J. Gillen, *State and Local Government in West Germany, 1945–1953* (Office of the U.S. High Commissioner for Germany, 1953); John Gimbel, *The American Occupation of Germany: Politics and the*

Military, 1945–1949 (Stanford, Cal.: Stanford University Press, 1968); George Kennan, *Memoirs, 1950–1963* (Boston: Little, Brown, 1972); Ivone Kirkpatrick, *The Inner Circle* (London: Macmillan, 1959); Edward H. Litchfield, *Governing Postwar Germany* (Ithaca, N.Y.: Cornell University Press, 1953); Wilson D. Miscamble, "Deciding to Divide Germany: American Policymaking in 1949, *"Diplomacy and Statecraft* 2 (July 1991), pp. 294–320; Edward N. Peterson, *The American Occupation of Germany: Retreat to Victory* (Detroit: Wayne State University Press, 1978); Henry P. Pilgert, *The West German Educational System* (Office of the U.S. High Commissioner for Germany, 1953); Bert Peter Schloss, "The American Occupation of Germany, 1945–1952: An Appraisal" (Ph.D. dissertation, University of Chicago, 1955); Thomas Alan Schwartz, *America's Germany: John J. McCloy and the Federal Republic of Germany* (Cambridge, Mass.: Harvard University Press, 1991); James F. Tent, *Mission on the Rhine* (Chicago: University of Chicago Press, 1982); Robert Wolfe, editor, *Americans as Proconsuls: United States Military Government in Germany and Japan, 1944–1952* (Carbondale: Southern Illinois University Press, 1984); and Harold Zink, *The United States in Gemany, 1944–1955* (Princeton, N.J.: Van Nostrand, 1957).

The work of UNESCO and the United States National Commission for UNESCO is described in F. R. Cowell, "Planning the Organisation of UNESCO, 1942–1946: A Personal Record," *Cahiers d'Histroire Mondiale* 10 (1966), pp. 210–236; H. H. Krill de Capello, "The Creation of the United Nations Educational, Scientific and Cultural Organization," *International Organization* 24 (Winter 1970), pp. 1–30; Milton Eisenhower, *The President Is Calling* (Garden City, N.Y.: Doubleday, 1974); Michael A. Guhin, *John Foster Dulles: A Statesman and His Times* (New York: Columbia University Press, 1972); Jacquetta Hawkes and Leonard Woolley, *History of Mankind* I (New York: Harper and Row, 1963); Townsend Hoopes, *The Devil and John Foster Dulles* (Boston: Little, Brown, 1973); Julian Huxley, *Memories* II (New York: Harper and Row, 1973); Walter H.C. Laves and Charles A. Thomson, *UNESCO: Purpose, Progress, Prospects* (Bloomington, Ind.: Indiana University Press, 1957); T. V. Sathyamurthy, *Politics of International Cooperation* (Geneve: Droz, 1964); Arthur M. Schlesinger, Jr., *A Thousand Days* (Boston: Houghton Mifflin, 1965); James P. Sewell, *UNESCO and World Politics* (Princeton, N.J.: Princeton University Press, 1975); and Howard E. Wilson, *United States National Commission for UNESCO* (New York: Macmillan, 1948).

Useful background material for Shuster's other public work can be found in John M. Blum, *Roosevelt and Morgenthau* (Boston: Houghton Mifflin, 1970); Chester Bowles, *Promises to Keep: My Years in Public Life,*

1941–1969 (New York: Harper and Row, 1971); A. Russell Buchanan, *The United States and World War II*, two vols., (New York: Harper and Row, 1964); Robert A. Caro, *The Power Broker: Robert Moses and the Fall of New York* (New York: Knopf, 1974); Roger Daniels et al., editors, *Japanese Americans: From Relocation to Redress* (Salt Lake City: University of Utah Press, 1986); Dwight Eisenhower, *Crusade in Europe* (Garden City, N.Y.: Permabooks, 1952); Sidney Hyman, *The Lives of William Benton* (Chicago: University of Chicago Press, 1969); and Sam Zuckerman, "Public University in Peru Is Deteriorating, While Private Institution Flourishes Nearby," *The Chronicle of Higher Education* 34 (March 16, 1988), A40. *Segregation in Washington: A Report of the National Committee on Segregation in the Nation's Capital* (Chicago: No publisher, 1948) presents that committee's findings. For Shuster's work for the Division of Cultural Relations, see Haldore Hanson, *The Cultural-Cooperation Program, 1938–1943* (Washington: U.S. Government Printing Office, 1944); Frank A. Ninkovich, *The Diplomacy of Ideas: U.S. Foreign Policy and Cultural Relations, 1938–1950* (New York: Cambridge University Press, 1981); and *The Program of the Department of State in Cultural Relations* (Washington: Department of State, 1941). The work of the Commission on Freedom of the Press is described in Margaret A. Blanchard, "The Hutchins Commission, the Press and the Responsibility Concept," *Journalism Monographs* 49 (May 1977), pp. 1–59; Commission on Freedom of the Press, *A Free and Responsible Press* (Chicago: University of Chicago Press, 1947); Mark Paul Fackler, "The Hutchins Commissioners and the Crisis in Democratic Theory, 1930–1947" (Ph.D. dissertation, University of Illinois, 1982); Richard Fox, *Reinhold Niebuhr: A Biography* (New York: Pantheon Books, 1985); and Donald L. Smith, *Zechariah Chafee, Jr., Defender of Liberty and Law* (Cambridge, Mass.: Harvard University Press, 1986). For the Ford Foundation and its projects, see Harry S. Ashmore, *Unseasonable Truths: The Life of Robert Maynard Hutchins* (Boston: Little, Brown, 1989); Dwight Macdonald, *The Ford Foundation: The Men and the Millions* (New York: Reynal, 1956); and Thomas C. Reeves, *Freedom and the Foundation: The Fund for the Republic in the Era of McCarthyism* (New York: Knopf, 1969).

Informative writings about Notre Dame abound also. The best general histories are Arthur J. Hope, C.S.C., *Notre Dame: One Hundred Years* (Notre Dame, Ind.: University Press, 1943); Philip S. Moore, C.S.C., *Academic Development: University of Notre Dame* (Notre Dame, Ind.: University of Notre Dame, 1960); Thomas J. Schlereth, *The University of Notre Dame: A Portrait of Its History and Campus* (Notre Dame, Ind.: University of Notre Dame Press, 1976); and Robert P. Schmuhl,

University of Notre Dame: A Contemporary Portrait (Notre Dame, Ind.: University of Notre Dame Press, 1986). For the early decades of the twentieth century, see David J. Arthur, C.S.C., "The University of Notre Dame, 1919–1933: An Administrative History" (Ph.D. dissertation, University of Michigan, 1973); Thomas P. Jones, C.S.C., *The Development of the Office of Prefect of Religion at the University of Notre Dame from 1842 to 1952* (Washington: Catholic University of America Press, 1960); Anna Rose Kearny, "James A. Burns, C.S.C.—Educator" (Ph.D. dissertation, University of Notre Dame, 1975); Thomas T. McAvoy, C.S.C., *Father O'Hara of Notre Dame: The Cardinal-Archbishop of Philadelphia* (Notre Dame, Ind.: University of Notre Dame Press, 1967), and "Notre Dame, 1919–1922: The Burns Revolution," *Review of Politics* 25 (October 1963), pp. 431–450; and Ralph E. Weber, *Notre Dame's John Zahm* (Notre Dame, Ind.: University of Notre Dame Press, 1967). The Hesburgh years are chronicled in Joel Connelly and Howard Dooley, *Hesburgh's Notre Dame* (New York: Hawthorne Books, 1972); Theodore Hesburgh, C.S.C., *God, Country, Notre Dame* (New York: Doubleday, 1990); and John Lungren, Jr., *Hesburgh of Notre Dame: Priest, Educator, Public Servant* (Kansas City, Mo.: Sheed and Ward, 1987). Publications at Notre Dame that Shuster helped sponsor include William D'Antonio and Fredrick Pike, editors, *Religion, Revolution, and Reform: New Forces for Change in Latin America* (New York: Praeger, 1964); William Liu, editor, *Family and Fertility* (Notre Dame, Ind.: University of Notre Dame Press, 1967); Ernan McMullin, editor, *Galileo: Man of Science* (New York: Basic Books, 1968); Reginald Neuwien, *Catholic Schools in Action* (Notre Dame, Ind.: University of Notre Dame Press, 1966); and Elena Yu and William Liu, *Fertility and Kinship in the Philippines* (Notre Dame, Ind.: University of Notre Dame Press, 1980). Additional information can be found in James B. Conant, *The American High School Today* (New York: McGraw-Hill, 1959); Andrew M. Greeley and Peter H. Rossi, *The Education of Catholic Americans* (Chicago: Aldine, 1966); Robert Hassenger, editor, *The Shape of Catholic Higher Education* (Chicago: University of Chicago Press, 1967); and Janet Lever and Pepper Schwartz, *Women at Yale* (Indianapolis: Bobbs-Merrill, 1971).

The story of Saint Mary's College is told in Sister Mary Immaculate Creek, C.S.C., *A Panorama: 1844–1977: Saint Mary's College, Notre Dame, Indiana* (Notre Dame, Ind.: Saint Mary's College, 1977); Sister Mary Rita Heffernan, C.S.C., *A Story of Fifty Years* (Notre Dame, Ind.: Ave Maria Press, 1956); *Our Mother House: Centenary Chronicles of the Sisters of the Holy Cross* (Notre Dame, Ind.: Saint Mary's of the Immaculate Conception, 1941); and Sister M. Madeleva Wolff, C.S.C., *My First Seventy Years* (New York: Macmillan, 1959).

INDEX